MODERN SPORTS LAW

The aim of this book is to provide an account of how the law influences the operation, administration and playing of modern sports. Although the book focuses on legal doctrine it has been written bearing in mind sport's historical, cultural, social and economic context, including the drama and colour of sport's major events and leading personalities. And although it is inevitably very much concerned with elite professional sports it is not dominated by them, and seeks to cover the widest possible range of sports, professional and amateur.

Initially, the book addresses practical issues such as the structures of national and international sport, and examines the evolution of the body of law known as 'sports law'. Thereafter three main themes are identified: regulatory; participatory; and financial aspects of modern sport. The regulatory theme is dealt with in chapters considering the manner in which decisions of sports governing bodies may be challenged in the ordinary courts and the development of alternative dispute resolution mechanisms in sport. The participatory theme includes the legal regulation of doping and violence in sport, as well as the broader topic of tortious liability for sporting injuries. The financial theme, reflecting the enhanced commercialisation of sport at all levels, is developed in chapters concerning issues in applied contract and employment law for players and legal matters surrounding the organisation of major sports events. The conclusion summarises modern sport's experience of EU law, pointing the way to the future direction of sports law more generally.

While the book is aimed primarily at students, and is designed to cover fundamental and topical areas of sports law (sports law in general; sports bodies and the courts; arbitration in sport; corruption; doping; violence; civil liability; discrimination; the commodification of modern sport; and the likely future of sports law), it should also prove of wider interest to practitioners, sports administrators and governing bodies; and though focused primarily on UK law it will also appeal to readers in Australia, Canada, New Zealand and the USA.

Modern Sports Law

A Textbook

Jack Anderson

·HART·
PUBLISHING
OXFORD AND PORTLAND, OREGON
2010

Published in the United Kingdom by Hart Publishing Ltd
16C Worcester Place, Oxford, OX1 2JW
Telephone: +44 (0)1865 517530
Fax: +44 (0)1865 510710
E-mail: mail@hartpub.co.uk
Website: http://www.hartpub.co.uk

Published in North America (US and Canada) by
Hart Publishing
c/o International Specialized Book Services
920 NE 58th Avenue, Suite 300
Portland, OR 97213-3786
USA
Tel: +1 503 287 3093 or toll-free: (1) 800 944 6190
Fax: +1 503 280 8832
E-mail: orders@isbs.com
Website: http://www.isbs.com

British Library Cataloguing in Publication Data
Data Available

ISBN: 978-1-84113-685-1

Typeset by Compuscript Ltd, Shannon
Printed and bound in Great Britain by
TJ International Ltd, Padstow, Cornwall

To Teresa, Daniel and Katherine

It may be that sports are silly; but then so are humans.

Robert Lynd

Nearly everything possible has been done to spoil this game: the heavy financial interests, the absurd transfer and player-selling system, the lack of any birth or residential qualification for the players, the betting and coupon competitions, the absurd publicity given to every feature of it by the Press, the monstrous partisanship of the crowds; but the fact remains that it is not yet spoilt, and it has gone out and conquered the world.

J B Priestley, 1933

Virtually every single one of our international sports were invented or codified by the British. And I say this respectfully to our Chinese hosts, who have excelled so magnificently at Ping-pong. Ping-pong was invented on the dining tables of England in the 19th century, and it was called Wiff-waff! And there, I think, you have the difference between us and the rest of the world. Other nations, the French, looked at a dining table and saw an opportunity to have dinner; we looked at it and saw an opportunity to play Wiff-waff. And I say to the Chinese, and I say to the world, that ping pong is coming home!

Mayor of London, Boris Johnson, at the handover of the Olympic flag in Beijing in 2008

Hopefully I can prove to the other companies going forward that I am a worthy investment; that I can help their company, help their company grow and represent them well.

Tiger Woods, 2010

PREFACE

Although the drama and colour of major sports events, individual sports and their leading personalities is diverting, the emphasis in this book is on the manner in which the operation of modern sport must come to terms with applied aspects of the law, notably, administrative law, contract, torts, criminal and commercial law, as well as facets of EU law. At its narrowest therefore, this text presents a concise doctrinal analysis of the law's impact on sport in England and Wales. This approach prompts three points of note. First, a feature of this text is its careful legal analysis of relevant case law and applicable legislation to sports-related disputes, including the identification of generic principles of sports law. Second, the text is also informed by a socio-legal approach given that the law's application to sport cannot properly be discussed other than against the backdrop of sport's social, cultural, economic and, at times, strongly political context. In short, the 'specificity' of sport—that is, the manner in which sport both as a leisure activity and as an industry seeks inter alia by way of its social utility to minimise its exposure to the general law—is not underestimated by this text. Third, the jurisdictional focus of the text is on England and Wales; nonetheless, frequent reference is made to the nascent sports law jurisprudence of Australia, Canada, Ireland, New Zealand, Scotland and South Africa. More importantly, the established and sophisticated tradition of the teaching, research and practice of sports law within the United States is alluded to, and particularly the manner in which developments there might be indicative of forthcoming trends in Europe.

The book is written primarily for final year law students who have already undertaken the study of core law subjects and now seek to apply that knowledge to sport. This prerequisite is reflected in the text's structure and analytical style. For instance, although presented thematically with reference to the individual professional sports participant—the generic term 'athlete' will be used from now on—the book's eight chapters have also been written in a self-contained manner for ease of dedicated study. Cross-referencing within and between chapters is kept to a minimum with the footnotes generally reserved for a brief review of applicable first principles or a more detailed secondary commentary on the point at hand. In line with these pedagogical objectives, the body of the text frequently gives a comprehensive analysis of seminal case law and principle. Each chapter concludes with suggestions for further reading and, in summary, posits questions as to possible future developments, thus provoking and sustaining debate on the topic at issue. The accessible nature of this presentation means that the book should appeal to practitioners seeking an introduction to this burgeoning area of practice, and it should also appeal to those interested in the deepening academic discourses on sport in fields such as sociology, economics, history and medicine.

The book is divided into eight chapters, which range across the historical development of sports law: issues relating to the operation and administration of sport both nationally and internationally; matters pertaining to the playing of, and participation in, sport; and, finally, the manner in which the commercialisation of sport and the evolution of the professional sports industry has attracted dedicated legal attention.

Chapter one—What is Sports Law?—addresses the eponymous question directly by way of an historical review of the relationship between sport and the law and includes a more contemporary theoretical analysis. In brief, the modern view is that the law (and lawyers) became interested in sport only in the last quarter of the twentieth century owing to the intense commercialisation or 'industrification' of sport during that period.[1] The chapter makes the point however that law and sport have a much longer (and colourful) history. In Ancient Greece and Rome, issues of violence were prevalent, as were more complex issues relating to the socio-political role of sport. Subsequently, in late medieval England, the socio-political role of participation in sports such as archery and fencing, which were seen to prepare men for war, thus facilitating 'the defence of the realm', prompted legislation promoting such activities to the detriment of riotous, folk-based events such as football. Later still, the great writers on the early common law such as Blackstone, East and Foster wrote about the need to regulate fighting-based sports, particularly those associated with secondary criminality such as gambling and alcohol. With typical Victorian earnestness, the mid-nineteenth century heralded the official end of many traditional, agrarian-based sports especially those involving animal cruelty such as cock-fighting, badger, bear and dog fighting and their replacement with socially acceptable pursuits, such as greyhound racing, that could (literally) fit into the emerging urban landscape. Similarly, the codification of many of today's leading sports took place in the public schools of the period where the privileged elite sought to sanitise the ritualistic and sometimes gratuitously violent pursuits of previous eras. Simultaneously, but across the Atlantic, a more commercialised form of sport was emerging with first baseball and later American football, basketball and ice hockey leading to the development of 'major league' sport and complex matters of labour and antitrust law. With this historical background in mind, chapter one concludes by assessing the current status of 'sports law', and the contrasting perspectives as to whether it is a discrete, if still emerging, area of the law; or whether it is simply an applied, if engaging, amalgam of more established areas of the law.

---

[1] See generally the lively introduction by I Hewitt, *Sporting Justice* (Cambridge, SportsBoooks, 2008).

Chapter two—Challenging Decisions of Sports Governing Bodies—picks up on a point made towards the end of the previous chapter. The most salient example of the law's influence on sport is in the reaction of sports bodies which are increasingly forced to defend decisions, particularly those within their disciplinary remit, in the ordinary courts.[2] The chapter is premised on four points. First, the ordinary courts are generally reluctant to interfere with the decision-making competencies of private associations such as sports organisations. For good social policy reasons, it is recognised that sports governing bodies are in a better position than the ordinary courts to determine how their affairs are to be run or, to paraphrase Lord Denning MR in *Enderby Town FC v Football Association*, justice in a domestic sports tribunal can 'often be done better by a good layman than a bad lawyer.'[3] Nevertheless, and as Lord Denning's remarks continued, where, for example, a sports organisation has acted contrary to natural justice, the ordinary courts can, and should, intervene. The second point in chapter two is that intervention by the ordinary courts is usually predicated on a claim for breach of a private or contractual right, given that the relationship between a sports governing body and its members is most likely to be of that nature. The third point is that this private-rights approach appears to preclude judicial review of the competency of sports bodies. Chapter two considers the sustainability of this preclusion of public law and the practical implications of a finding that sports bodies might be considered 'hybrid' public authorities pursuant to section 6 of the Human Rights Act 1998. Finally, chapter two observes that where on the rare occasion a decision of a sports tribunal is subjected to judicial scrutiny, it appears clear that the review will amount to no more than an assessment of whether the disciplinary process ended in what was once neatly referred to as 'a fair result'[4]; thus if it is one that a tribunal properly instructing itself as to the facts and the law could have reasonably reached, it will probably not be set aside by the ordinary courts.

Chapter three—Arbitration and Alternative Dispute Resolution in Sport—compliments the previous chapter in the sense that on the grounds of basic fairness to its members, efficacy of administration and the avoidance of hefty litigation-related costs, national and international sports organisations have sought to enhance their internal disciplinary tribunals. These tribunals often take the form of quasi-independent, arbitral-based mechanisms. Alternative dispute resolution (ADR) in sport is dealt with in two ways. First, and on examining the benefits of ADR over formal litigation, the chapter gives a brief history and assessment of the Court of Arbitration for Sport (CAS), including the reasons

---

[2] The chapter is based on previous research by the author. See J Anderson, 'An Accident of History: Why Decisions of Sports Governing Bodies are not Amenable to Judicial Review' (2006) 35 *Common Law World Review* 173.

[3] *Enderby Town FC v Football Association* [1971] Ch 591, 605. See also *McInnes v Onslow-Fane* [1978] 1 WLR 1520, 1535, Megarry VC.

[4] *Calvin v Carr* [1980] AC 574, 593, Lord Wilberforce.

underpinning its establishment and its present, increasingly influential, role in the governance of international sport. Second, and using an example of an existing arbitral mechanism associated with a national sports body, the typical disputes, the practical functioning and procedural framework in which such a body operates (including the guidelines set by Article 6 ECHR) will be outlined.

Chapter four—The Legal Regulation of Drugs in Sport—makes three fundamental points in its discussion on the use of performance enhancing substances in sport. First, the manner in which sport as a whole has reacted to doping, in terms of governance, is outlined. This includes an examination of the World Anti-Doping Agency. Second, three legal facets of the disciplining of athletes found to have engaged in doping are reviewed: the principle of strict liability; the proportionality of sanctioning; and issues of privacy. The chapter concludes by engaging in a debate, somewhat philosophical in nature, as to why sport seeks to proscribe the use of performance enhancing substances.

Chapter five—Criminal Violence in Sport—asks when, as a matter of policy and legal certainty, and on what basis, criminal liability might attach to a violent incident on the sports field? The chapter suggests that the answer in located in the principle of 'implied sporting consent' and discusses the critical level at which such an implied consent ordinarily ceases to be an answer to a prosecution for inflicting harm during the course of a game. Overall, the chapter reviews the current status of the 'law of sporting assault', mainly in the context of the English Court of Appeal's decision in *R v Barnes*.[5] The analysis is informed by a comparative approach whereby reference is made to the sophisticated approach of the Canadian courts to violence in sport, principally in the context of ice hockey. The chapter ends by reflecting upon the suitability of the ordinary law of violence in addressing unnecessarily aggressive behaviour in sport, and the specific influence it might have on the 'playing culture' of contact sports.[6]

Chapter six—Civil Liability in Sport—begins by considering personal injury liability for injuries inflicted by a participant upon an opponent during a sports pursuit. The sporting emphasis of the chapter is on competitive, body contact games. The legal emphasis is on the tort of negligence. Analogous to the law of criminal assault, breach of 'implied sporting consent' or the *volenti* of the claimant is seen as central in application, as assessed through a number of objective criteria, including the skill level of the injuring party and whether that defendant was acting in 'reckless disregard' of the claimant's safety. The chapter also has a broader focus beyond the litigating of sports injuries. It assesses practical matters relating to vicarious liability, insurance and the measure of damages for 'lost sporting opportunity'. It also refers to the underlying policy-related issue of sport's social utility. Moreover, the chapter demonstrates that sports-related personal injury claims now extend to a consideration of the duties of coaches, referees, sports

---

[5] *R v Barnes* [2004] EWCA Crim 3246, [2005] 1WLR 910.
[6] The chapter is based on previous research by the author. See J Anderson, 'No Licence for Thuggery: Violence, Sport and the Criminal Law' [2008] *Crim LR* 751.

governing bodies and schools. These duties are discussed in depth and with particular respect to the safety and welfare of minors and children. Finally, chapter six is set against the backdrop of an apparently spiralling 'compensation culture' and the threat that this 'blame culture' poses for the future promotion, operation and administration of sport.[7]

Chapter seven—Sports-related Contracts of Employment—seeks to locate professional sports contracts, and particularly those involving elite professional footballers, in the context of the abridged, precarious but lucrative nature of a professional career in sport. The chapter has two overlapping parts. First, and with principal reference to professional football, standard contractual issues relating to capacity, formation, standard terms and performance are outlined. This part of the chapter reflects on individual matters such as remuneration and image rights and also addresses briefly the role of player agents, and the manner in which the power of player agents, again in football, has led to attempts to regulate this aspect of the modern professional sports industry. A second aspect of the chapter equates professional sports persons to 'workers' and their right to avail of, and operate within, the norms of employment, labour and anti-discrimination law both domestically and at an EU level. This apparently straightforward premise will be seen as somewhat controversial when examined in the context of the premature and unilateral termination of a player's contract, which of itself forms part of a wider discourse involving the desire of football's various authorities to preserve some element of contractual stability and an EU law-driven demand for reasonable employee mobility within any professional services industry.

The concluding chapter speculates upon the future of sports law. The chapter observes that in the longer term the legal and regulatory structure of sport will, most likely, be shaped by the outcome of the debate on whether the special character or 'specificity' of sport should mean that a special legal status should attach to sport under EU law. On the one hand, many practices of the professional sports industry have economic implications and accordingly such activities must be subject to and reconciled with, for example, the various fundamental freedoms of the internal market. On the other hand, sport has characteristics that are not found in other sectors of the economy and thus sports organisations seek to exempt their practices from the full force of EU law. The concluding chapter, which seeks to serve as a conclusion to this text as whole, goes on to discuss matters of fundamental concern, including whether EU law has the capacity to go beyond an examination of sports-related rules that have an 'economic effect' and scrutinise rules of a 'purely sporting nature'. Given that a central aim of this book is to demonstrate that 'Law's Empire' stretches 'beyond the touchline' and that there is no blanket immunity for sport from the law, this book ends with an attempt to provide an intellectually durable

---

[7] The chapter is based on previous research by the author. See J Anderson, 'Personal Injury Liability in Sport: Emerging Trends' [2008] 16 *Tort Law Review* 95.

rationale as to when and why the practices and governance of sport should or should not be deemed compatible with (EU) law.[8] In this, the book as a whole is partly guided by what can be called the Weatherill maxim: 'Sport *is* special but not *that* special'[9]; but also by a paraphrasing of that maxim—the European sports model is special but not *that* special. The latter refers to the fact that as the landscape of sports law in Europe emerges incrementally on a case by case basis, the picture that is emerging is very recognisable to US sports lawyers and thus the future of sports law may take us in a westward direction towards Boston rather than eastwards towards Brussels.

The layout and structure of the book apart, four further points need to be made as to its contents and substance in terms of accompanying and complimentary literature; its pedagogical and theoretical nature; the 'American' influence; and the use of the term 'sport'. On the first point, and as stated previously, the emphasis in this text is on doctrinal legal analysis within the England and Wales jurisdiction. It is admitted that without context, doctrinal analysis, particularly of a popular activity such as sport, would only partially explain the deepening relationship between sport and the law. When necessary, the book alludes to broader issues relating to sport's societal and cultural role, as well as its unique regulatory and economic framework, and including references to developments in other common law jurisdictions and the European Union. However, those who wish to delve deeper into socio-legal aspects of sports law;[10] law and the business of sport;[11] the practice of sports law;[12] sports law in jurisdictions such as Australia,[13] Canada,[14] Ireland,[15] New Zealand,[16] Scotland,[17] South Africa,[18] the United States,[19] including

---

[8] Note recently and generally R Parrish and S Miettinen, *The Sporting Exception in European Union Law* (The Hague, TMC Asser, 2008).

[9] See generally S Weatherill, *European Sports Law: Collected Papers* (The Hague, TMC Asser Press, 2007).

[10] S Gardiner *et al*, *Sports Law*, 3rd edn (London, Cavendish, 2006) and S Greenfield and G Osborn (eds), *Law and Sport in Contemporary Society* (London, Frank Cass, 2000).

[11] D Griffith Jones, *Law and the Business of Sport* (London, Butterworths, 1997) and R Verow, C Lawrence and P McCormick, *Sports Business: Law, Practice and Precedents*, 2nd edn (Bristol, Jordans, 2005).

[12] A Lewis and J Taylor (eds), *Sport: Law and Practice*, 2nd edn (London, Tottel Publishing, 2008).

[13] D Thorpe *et al*, *Sports Law* (Melbourne, Oxford University Press, 2009) and D Healey, *Sport and the Law*, 4th edn (Sydney, UNSW Press, 2009).

[14] J Barnes, *Sport and the Law in Canada*, 3rd edn (Toronto, Butterworths, 1993).

[15] N Cox and A Schuster, *Sport and the Law* (Dublin, FirstLaw, 2004).

[16] E Toomey (ed), *Keeping the Score: Essays in Law and Sports* (Christchurch, University of Canterbury Press, 2005).

[17] W Stewart, *Sport and the Law—A Scots Perspective* (Edinburgh, Tottel Publishing, 2003).

[18] R Cloete and S Cornelius (eds), *Introduction to Sports Law in South Africa* (Durban, LexisNexis Butterworths, 2005).

[19] For instance, M Cozzillo *et al* (eds), *Sports Law: Cases and Materials*, 2nd edn (Durham NC, Carolina Academic Press, 2007); M Mitten *et al* (eds), *Sports Law and Regulation: Cases, Materials and Problems*, 2nd edn (New York, Aspen, 2009); J Spengler *et al*, *Introduction to Sport Law* (Champaign; Ill, Human Kinetics, 2009); P Weiler and G Roberts, *Sports and the Law: Text, Cases and Problems*, 3rd edn (Westport Conn, Thomson West, 2004); and G Wong, *Essentials of Sports Law*, 4th edn (Westport Conn, Praeger, 2009).

the EU[20] and at an international level;[21] or those who simply wish to obtain a broader perspective on contemporary issues in sport and the law[22]—should consult the expanding body of literature that critiques an area of law that has recently attracted the rather grand title of *lex sportiva*.[23]

Second, the reluctance to broaden the debate beyond strict legal analysis might be said to reflect a certain defensiveness with respect to engaging more fully with sports-related issues and popular culture more generally. Admittedly, the study of sports law remains at an early stage in its development and still tends to be deemed, even dismissed as, a rather niche or esoteric area of interest. Often its popularity among students as an elective part of their studies—and sports law is a popular choice—is seen as being in some way detrimental to more worthy or serious areas of special interest.[24] More importantly however, it is argued that sports law as a corpus of law is fundamentally weakened by not being underpinned with a unifying theoretical coherency. This debate is dealt with more fully in chapter one; for now, it suffices to state that this book attempts to highlight that the application of established areas of the law—commercial, contract, employment etc—to sport can not only teach us something about those discrete legal areas but it might also, *in time*, lead to a distinct area of the law befitting the term 'sports law'. In sum, it is argued that the evolution of sports law is continuing at a satisfactory pace, as reflected, it is hoped, in the complexity and sophistication of the issues highlighted in this book and others, to the point that there is no real need to attach any hyperbole to the existence of sports law.

In this regard, this book is influenced by an article published a decade ago by Lawrence Lessig in the *Harvard Law Review*.[25] Lessig's commentary is a critique of the practice and study of the law of cyberspace. The analysis had an unusual

---

[20] R Blanpain, M Colucci, F Hendrickx (eds), *The Future of Sports Law in the European Union* (London, Kluwer, 2008); B Bogusz, A Cygan and E Szyszczak (eds), *The Regulation of Sport in the European Union* (London, Edward Elgar, 2007); A Caiger and S Gardiner (eds), *Professional Sport in the EU: Regulation and Re-regulation* (The Hague, TMC Asser, 2005); S Gardiner, R Parrish and R Siekmann (eds), *EU, Sport, Law and Policy: Regulation, Re-regulation and Representation* (The Hague, TMC Asser, 2009); R Parrish, *Sports Law and Policy in the European Union* (Manchester, Manchester University Press, 2003); and R Siekmann and J Soek, *The European Union and Sport: Legal and Policy Developments* (The Hague, TMC Asser, 2005).

[21] J Nafziger, *International Sports Law*, 2nd edn (New York, Transnational Publishers, 2004).

[22] M Beloff, T Kerr and M Demetriou, *Sports Law* (Oxford, Hart Publishing, 1999); E Grayson *Sport and the Law*, 3rd edn (London, Butterworths, 2000); and H Hartley, *Sport, Physical Recreation and the Law*, New ed (London, Routledge, 2009). Leading periodicals include: *Entertainment and Sports Law Journal*; *International Sports Law Journal*; *International Sports Law Review*; *Journal of Legal Aspects of Sport*; *Marquette Sports Law Review*; *Seton Hall Journal of Sports and Entertainment Law*; *Villanova Sport and Entertainment Law Journal*; and *Sport and the Law Journal*.

[23] See M Beloff, 'Is There a Lex Sportiva?' [2005] *International Sports Law Review* 49.

[24] For an interesting American perspective on this point see generally J Standen, *Taking Sports Seriously: Law and Sports in Contemporary American Culture* (Durham NC, Carolina Academic Press, 2008). For a lighter English perspective on sport and society see S Barnes, *The Meaning of Sport* (London, Short Books, 2007) and E Smith, *What Sport Tells us about Life* (London, Penguin, 2009).

[25] L Lessig, 'The Law of the Horse: What Cyberlaw Might Teach' (1999) 113 *Harvard Law Review* 501.

premise—an American federal court judge's disparaging quip that there was no more a 'law of cyberspace' than there was a 'law of the horse'. More fully, the judge in question remarked that the best way to learn the law applicable to specialised endeavours was to study general rules and principles. Numerous cases, the judge observed, dealt with sales of horses; others dealt with people kicked by horses; still more dealt with the licensing and racing of horses; but any effort to collect those strands into a course entitled 'The Law of the Horse' was doomed to be shallow and to miss unifying principles.[26] Lessig countered that the distillation of tort in cyberspace, contract in cyberspace, property law issues in cyberspace etc into a 'law of cyberspace' would not lead to the cross-*sterilisation* of topics and issues because, by illustrating the regulatory and geographical limits of traditional legal principles, cyberspace law 'illuminated the entire law'. In sum, Lessig went on to suggest reasons to study cyberspace law for reasons beyond the particulars of cyberspace. This book proceeds on similar lines: providing a justification for the study of sports law beyond the peculiarities of sport as a social phenomenon with a view towards demonstrating that in analysing the legal regulation of sport we might learn something about the general law that other more established areas of the law might not reveal.

The third point, which follows from the above, is a comment on the American influence on sports law. Although the birth of modern sport is often traced to the public schools and Victorian social values of mid-nineteenth century Britain, thereafter the commercial heart of modern sport was transplanted to the United States where, football apart, it remains. Europeans often, and sometimes rightly, accuse Americans of an insular appreciation of sport, as limited to American football, baseball and basketball.[27] That insularity is however often reciprocated by Europeans' ignorance of the fact that the structure of major league sport, the commodification of sport and the study and practice of sports law is at its most sophisticated and advanced in the United States to the point that lawyers have long had a central role in the operation of contemporary sport in America as administrators, agents or in pursuing employment and antitrust-related lawsuits that have changed fundamentally the structure of major leagues. The national sport of baseball is a case in point, with the legal status of that sport's commercial framework coming to the attention of the US Supreme Court as early as the 1920s.[28]

---

[26] See F Easterbrook, 'Cyberspace and the Law of the Horse' (1996) *University of Chicago Legal Forum* 207, 207.

[27] See M Dyreson and J Mangan (eds), *Sport and American Society: Exceptionalism, Insularity and Imperialism* (London, Routledge, 2007) where the contributors outline the story of American sport as premised historically on a symbolic rejection of British rule and British sports.

[28] *Federal Baseball Club of Baltimore, Inc v National League of Professional Baseball Clubs* (1922) 259 US 200 (US Supreme Court upholding professional baseball's immunity from federal antitrust laws). For an introduction to some of the legal and commercial complexities surrounding Major League Baseball, see M Nagel *et al*, 'Major League Baseball Anti-Trust Immunity: Examining the Legal and Financial Implications of Relocation Rules' (2006) 4 *Entertainment and Sports Law Journal* available online at www2.warwick.ac.uk/fac/soc/law/elj/eslj/issues/volume4/number3/nagel.

In short, and as the concluding chapter of this book argues, there is much to learn from the United States, and in particular the manner in which the law, principally in the form of labour law, assists in maintaining the 'competitive balance' that is the hallmark of major league sport in the United States.[29] In the major league sports of North America—Major League Baseball, the NBA in basketball, the NFL in American Football, and the NHL in ice hockey—a highly regulated system, which includes team franchising, player drafts, salary caps and collective bargaining agreements between key stakeholders in the sport, strives to ensure some element of equality of opportunity for all members of the league. The underlying idea is that if a select number of clubs through private investment, or other advantage, gain a monopoly on winning, the league in question will slowly lose its competitiveness and attractiveness to the commercial detriment of all. At first glance, this approach appears to work and is demonstrated by comparing the winners of the Super Bowl (American football) against the Premier League (English football) since the inception of the latter in 1992/1993:

Season Ending	Super Bowl	Premier League
2010	New Orleans Saints	Chelsea
2009	Pittsburgh Steelers	Manchester United
2008	New York Giants	Manchester United
2007	Indianapolis Colts	Manchester United
2006	Pittsburgh Steelers	Chelsea
2005	New England Patriots	Chelsea
2004	New England Patriots	Arsenal
2003	Tampa Bay Buccaneers	Manchester United
2002	New England Patriots	Arsenal
2001	Baltimore Ravens	Manchester United
2000	St Louis Rams	Manchester United
1999	Denver Broncos	Manchester United
1998	Denver Broncos	Arsenal
1997	Green Bay Packers	Manchester United
1996	Dallas Cowboys	Manchester United
1995	San Francisco 49ers	Blackburn Rovers
1994	Dallas Cowboys	Manchester United
1993	Dallas Cowboys	Manchester United
18 seasons	*12 clubs*	*4 clubs*

---

[29] See the though-provoking review by P Weiler, *Leveling the Playing Field: How the Law Can Make Sports Better for Fans* (Cambridge; Mass, Harvard University Press, 2000).

This competitive balance notwithstanding, it must be reiterated that the governance of sport in Europe and the United Kingdom differs appreciably, in terms of history and structure, from the 'American Sports Model'.[30] For example, the American model is very much closed to new entrants and thus the system of promotion/relegation, which is fundamental to the English and European understanding of league sport, is unknown. It follows that, given the historical and domestic allegiances of English and European football clubs including their commercial freedom to attract outside investment and hire playing staff, any proposals to develop the current UEFA Champions' League in football into, say, a 32-club franchised model such as the NFL, would be unlikely to succeed. In any event, such a tightly regulated system would probably encounter legal difficulties in reconciling itself with the fundamental freedoms underpinning the European Union's internal market. Nevertheless, the American experience of the economic and legal regulation of sport is a useful resource because trends established there may be indicative of that which will be experienced here in the near future. Consequently, where relevant, and with due caution, some specific analogies are made to the situation pertaining in the United States.

The fourth point that needs to be made is that there is a tendency in the United Kingdom to equate sport generally with male pursuits and specifically with professional football.[31] It is hoped that where possible this inclination can be avoided to draw on as broad a range of sports as possible, and to discuss sport in all its guises—male, female, amateur, professional, recreational and elite; and thus, where appropriate, the word 'athlete' is used as a gender neutral reference for all sportspersons. That being said, elite professional football often best illustrates individual topics within the umbrella of sports law. Moreover, professional football also demonstrates the more general evolution and emerging sophistication of sports law. For instance, it can be argued that standing outside a Premiership football ground is now every much an experience of law in action, as it is sport at play.

The ticket the spectator holds is a licence to enter the ground and is quasi-contractual in nature. The merchandising and advertising that the spectator encounters on entering the stadium is subject to significant legal protections such as trademark, copyright legislation and the tort of passing-off. The spectator will sit (and be monitored by CCTV) in an all-seater stadium designed and operating within the raft of health and safety and public order legislation that followed the Hillsborough stadium disaster of 1989. The players on the

---

[30] See the account by S Weatherill, 'Resisting the Pressures of "Americanization": The Influence of European Community Law on the "European Sport Model"' in S Greenfield and G Osborn (eds), *Law and Sport in Contemporary Society* (London, Frank Cass, 2000).

[31] The participation of women in sport, and the surrounding legal issues, is complex in nature. If discussed properly, the topic of women in sport would need to be located in its broader context of gender studies, cultural theory and economic development, similar to the approach taken by J Williams, *A Game for Rough Girls? A History of Women's Football in Britain* (London, Routledge, 2003).

pitch are as much commercial entities as they are athletes. Their contracts are complicated documents including provision for insurance and image rights, and reflecting the precarious and abridged nature of any professional career in sport. Elite players will now more likely be employed not by football clubs but by a public limited company quoted and traded daily on the stock exchange. If players commit playing offences, their hearings and appeals will be heard by sophisticated arbitral tribunals that seek to adhere to the principles of natural justice and even the European Convention on Human Rights. If the injury inflicted is sufficiently serious and is outside that which is ordinary and incidental to the game of football, the culprit might be sued in negligence by the injured player or even face criminal liability. On completion of the game, a number of players will be chosen randomly for routine tests for performance enhancing drugs—tests that flirt with the very boundaries of personal privacy. When the spectator returns home, they will in all likelihood look at the highlights of the other Premiership matches of the day. The contest for these broadcasting rights will have been every bit as (anti-)competitive as the game itself and they will also have, in large part, funded events on the field, thus are in need of advanced legal protections.

In this light, when faced with an industry, such as professional football, which is becoming ever more complex and diverse, and in a society that has become more litigious and risk averse, the involvement of the law and lawyers in sport is likely to become ever more prevalent. This involvement does not necessarily always have to be seen in a negative, opportunistic or adversarial light. It is hoped that immutable principles of the law such as certainty and fairness, and more general attributes associated with the law such as deterring violence, eliminating corruption, ensuring equality of opportunity and promoting inclusivity, will compliment and ultimately benefit sport as a whole. Admittedly, this perspective may be somewhat idealistic; at best the expectation is that the law might operate in a manner similar to a good referee. It should be firm but unobtrusive. It should, where possible, fade into the background and not unduly influence matters on the pitch or in the arena. In sum, it should act primarily to enhance the enjoyment of games, and to facilitate participation in, rather than the litigation of, sport.

Finally, and as with most academic projects, the finishing of this book has been accompanied with some regret. Certain matters have had to be dealt with briefly or not at all. This occasional abruptness is not because of an overly demanding editor (all at Hart Publishing have been more than accommodating). It has more to do with my attempt not to be overly self-indulgent and let my enthusiasm for this subject divert me from analysis to punditry and thus into what Umberto Eco once disparagingly referred to as sport's endless and empty 'chatter'. My principal regrets (which hopefully and without being overly presumptuous, might feature in future editions of this text) are threefold. First, I would have liked to dedicate more to the (corporate) social responsibility of sports clubs, national associations and international federations as conduits for policies promoting anti-racism, anti-discrimination and social inclusion.[32] Second, I would like in the future to address the emerging issue of financial crime in sport, including the manner in which certain sports-related activities appear vulnerable to money laundering and the link between corruption in sport (such as match-fixing) and online betting scams.[33] Third, and as a legacy of the London Olympics of 2012, it is hoped in the future to give more attention to the hosting of major sports events ranging from issues of safety and security for spectators within and outside the sports arena[34] to the various complex commercial dealings, especially those involving proprietary rights, that now surround the holding of such events.[35]

But enough for now. For good or bad the central thrust of this book is the increasingly zealous manner in which the law impacts on the rights, interests and conduct of individual athletes, and not, directly at least, on how it affects spectators, clubs, sports governing bodies and sports event organisers. Even in this abridged format, it will, to paraphrase Beloff, be seen that sports law is, at times, as infuriating as a magpie: you never quite know what it is going to pick up next. It follows that the best that I can say about this book is that its somewhat eclectic contents reflect the assorted nature of the subject matter. In any event, I have learnt a huge amount about this topic in writing this book. On reading it, I hope you learn something too. I have endeavoured to state the law as of 30 April 2010.

---

[32] On sport's potential in this regard see generally s 2 of the European Commission's White Paper on Sport, 11 July 2007, COM(2007) 391 final.

[33] On the former see the report by the Financial Action Task Force (FAFT), an inter-governmental body whose purpose is to monitor money laundering and terrorist financing at a global level, *Money Laundering through the Football Sector* (FAFT, Paris, July 2009) 26–29 available to download through www.fatf-gafi.org. On the latter, a number of organisations in world sport, led by the Denmark-based NGO, Play the Game, have been pushing for the creation of a World Anti-corruption Agency (WACA) for sport as a sister organisation for the World Anti-doping Agency (WADA). In October 2009, the organisation wrote an open letter to the President of the International Olympic Committee calling on him to instigate measures to combat corruption in sport. The letter and accompanying petition is available online at www.playthegame.org. For an introduction to the 'why' and 'how' of match-fixing see R Caruso, 'The Basic Economics of Match Fixing in Sports Tournaments' (2009) 39 *Economic Analysis and Policy* 355.

[34] The painful lessons learned in the UK from the various stadium disasters and the policing of football-inspired hooliganism in the 1980s has resulted in much legislation dedicated to both enhancing spectator safety and combating crowd disorder at sports events, including, in chronological order: Safety of Sports Ground Act 1975; Sporting Events (Control of Alcohol) Act 1985; Part IV (Exclusion Orders) of the Public Order Act 1986; Fire Safety and Safety of Places of Sport Act 1987; Football Spectators Act 1989; Football (Offences) Act 1991; Football (Offences and Disorder) Act 1999; Football (Disorder) Act 2000; ss 52 and 53 of the Violent Crime Reduction Act 2006. For an introductory history and application of the stated provisions see M James, *Sports Law* (Basingstoke, Palgrave, 2010) chs 8–10. For a broader theoretical approach see R Giulianotti and F Klauser, 'Security Governance and Sport Mega-Events: Towards an Interdisciplinary Research Agenda' (2010) 34 *Journal of Sport and Social Issues* 49.

[35] Note, for example, the London Olympic and Paralympics Games Act 2006 the thrust of which is to assure the IOC that all reasonable measures are being taken to prevent unauthorised commercial use of Olympic-related symbols, trade makes and merchandising in the build up to the 2012 Games. See generally the discussion by I Blackshaw, 'Protecting Major Sporting Events with Particular Reference to the 2012 London Olympic Games' (2009) 7 *Entertainment and Sports Law Journal* available online at www2.warwick.ac.uk/fac/soc/law/elj/eslj/issues/volume7/number2/blackshaw.

ACKNOWLEDGEMENTS

In writing this book, I am deeply grateful for the support given to me by a number of colleagues at the School of Law at Queen's University Belfast, particularly by the Head of School, Professor Colin Harvey and Professor Sally Wheeler. Of especial note are my good friends at the Law School, Dr Gordon Anthony and Dr Dimitrios Doukas, who were endlessly encouraging and full of advice, some of which was even useful!

I am also hugely obliged to all at Hart Publishing. Richard Hart has always treated me with great respect, courtesy and patience (probably more than I deserved at times!) and I thank him and all on his team most sincerely for their professionalism and this opportunity.

I would also like to thank my family and notably my parents for giving me their love and instilling in me an enduring set of values that have served me well in life. They also passed on a passion for sport and more importantly an interest in sport that is driven not by marketing or merchandising but by real community involvement and participation.

I have huge appreciation for and thanks to give to my wife Teresa, who has now, mainly due to a sudden addiction to BBC Radio 5 Live, begun to fancy herself as quite the sports expert. Finally, when the contract for this book was signed, Daniel (now aged 2½) and Katherine (aged ½) were not yet with us. As I write this sentence on the laptop at the kitchen table, I have one eye on Daniel's latest attempt to use his sister as a tackle-bag, and so just have time to say that this book is dedicated to them.

Jack Anderson, April 2010

TABLE OF CONTENTS

3. Arbitration and Alternative Dispute Resolution in Sport

4. The Legal Regulation of Drugs in Sport

8. Conclusion: Brussels or Boston? The Future of Sports Law

TABLE OF CASES

References are to paragraph numbers

UNITED KINGDOM

Northern Ireland

Scotland

COMMONWEALTH AND OTHER JURISDICTIONS

Australia

Canada

Ireland

New Zealand

South Africa

United States

EUROPEAN COURT OF JUSTICE

EUROPEAN COURT OF HUMAN RIGHTS

TABLE OF STATUTES

References are to paragraph numbers

UNITED KINGDOM

(Pre-1800 by regenal year, chronological)

(Post-1800 by short title, alphabetical)

COMMONWEALTH AND OTHER JURISDICTIONS

Australia

Canada

Ireland

New Zealand

United States

TABLE OF INTERNATIONAL TREATIES

References are to paragraph numbers

TABLE OF COURT OF ARBITRATION
FOR SPORT AWARDS

1

What is Sports Law?

Introduction

[**1.01**]   In a four part series entitled '21st Century Sport' published by *The Observer* at the end of 2007, the newspaper reflected on the relentless commercialisation of sport both nationally and globally, and speculated on future trends.[1] The report noted that the largest sports—Formula 1 racing; the four major league sports in America and the Premier League in England—were becoming global brands with new 'post-TV' technologies, such as worldwide internet and mobile phone access, making it easier for them to reach audiences and new customers, and particularly in the emerging markets of China and India. The origins of the relationship between sport and the law are usually located in this relatively recent phenomenon whereby the corporate owners of the mass media seek cooperation with the corporate owners of sport to attract millions of so-called 'post-fans'— that is, fans who consume sport rather than witness it first hand—to brand names such as the New York Yankees and Manchester United or to global events such as the Olympic Games and the FIFA World Cup.[2]

[**1.02**]   Put simply, there is no doubt that the economic dimension of sport is now significant, and the pace of change has accelerated exponentially from the birth of modern sport in nineteenth century Britain to its enhanced corporatisation in the late twentieth century. Some of the statistics are astounding. For example, in 2006 the total revenue attributed to the National Football League in the US was £3.35 billion, making it the largest sports league in the world, while in the same year a report estimated that the macro-economic impact of sport in the European Union (EU) accounted for 3.7 per cent of EU GDP, providing employment for 15 million people or 5.4 per cent of the labour force and, in a

---

[1]   B Oliver and R Gillis, '21st Century Sport, Part One, Games without Frontiers' *Observer* (London 28 October 2007) Sport 11; J Robinson, '21st Century Sport, Part Two, Screen Grab' *Observer* (London 4 November 2007) Sport 11; B Oliver, R Gillis and N Briggs, '21st Century Sport, Part Three, The Gulf' *Observer* (London 11 November 2007) Sport 11; and B Oliver, '21st Century Sport, Part Four, New World Order' *Observer* (London 18 November 2007) Sport 11.

[2]   In 2008, a poll of 9,000 adults from 16 countries in Europe, America, Asia and Australasia suggested that, although double the international average—40%—of Britons class themselves as sports fans who watch games in pubs and bars, only half actually participate in any physical activity. See A Simpson, 'Britain Wins First Gold for Pessimistic Supporters' *Daily Telegraph* (London 7 August 2008) News 4.

broader sense, generating value-added €407 billion to the EU economy as a whole.[3] Moreover, according to a recent report, and typical of the hyperbole of sport, the opening ceremony at the 2008 Olympic Games was 'the most watched live event in human history, outstripping the moon landings, the funeral of Princess Diana and Barack Obama's inauguration'.[4] The report showed that on average at least 593 million people worldwide, including 5 million in Britain, watched the ceremony in its entirety, while 984 million tuned in for part of it. The commodification of sport, that is, the attempt to exploit the financial potential of all aspects of sport—from the organisation and broadcasting of major events to the contractual arrangements of individual players, and including issues of commercial law interest such as the protection of official sponsorships and intellectual property—has led, inevitably, to the involvement of the legal profession. In turn, this has led to litigation of such a specific sports-related nature that collectively it is now referred to as 'sports law'.

[**1.03**]   The increasingly prevalent role of law and lawyers in sport, and particularly in the business of sport, can be explained because, although the playing rules of football, rugby, boxing, horse racing, cricket etc have remained more or less the same for well over a century, the legal, commercial and contractual framework that surrounds them has changed utterly. This chapter seeks to discuss four matters of concern related to the 'juridification' of sport.[5] First, the chapter makes the point that the relationship between sport and the law stretches back to antiquity, and the organisation of sport in Ancient Greece and Rome. Later, the experience of the early common law with sporting activities of an unusually violent even seditious nature heralded the emergence of more socially acceptable leisure pursuits, which, by the mid-nineteenth century, had led in Britain to the codification of many sports.[6] Second, this historical review traces the evolution of sport from its beginnings, through a 'civilising process', and on into the twentieth century, by which time elite sport had taken on a sophisticated, heavily commercialised aspect to its promotion and structure. The third part of this chapter reviews the contemporary debate as to the existence or not of a discrete body of law known as sports law. On one side of the debate is the argument that there is an identifiable, if still developing, branch of law that genuinely deserves the autonomy of the term sports law. Unsurprisingly, this view is supported by leading academics in the area who, nonetheless, struggle to identify a unifying theoretical coherence underpinning the claimed existence of the topic.[7] On the other hand, there is the

---

[3] Figures taken from D Dimitrov *et al*, *Die Makroökonomischen Effekte des Sports in Europa* (Vienna, Studie im Auftrag des Bundeskanzleramts, Sketion Sport, 2006).

[4] N Harris, 'Beijing Sets World TV Record' *Sunday Times* (London 10 May 2009) Sport 11.

[5] For an introduction to this debate see S Gardiner, 'Birth of a Legal Arena: Sport and the Law or Sports Law?' (1997) 5 *Sport and the Law Journal* 10. For an American perspective see T Davis, 'What is Sports Law?' (2001) 11 *Marquette Sports Law Review* 211.

[6] For a personal history of the emerging relationship between sport and the law see E Grayson, 'The Historical Development of Sport and Law' in S Greenfield and G Osborn (eds), *Law and Sport in Contemporary Society* (London, Frank Cass, 2000).

[7] Note the summary of the various efforts at conceptualising the term 'sports law' by K Foster, 'Is There a Global Sports Law?' (2003) 2 *Entertainment Law* 1 and R Parrish, 'The Birth of European Union Sports Law' (2003) 2 *Entertainment Law* 20.

practitioner-led contention that sports law is merely the application of established areas of the law within a sporting environment.[8]

[**1.04**] Finally, and in an attempt to move beyond the semantics of the 'sport and the law or sports law' debate, it is suggested that it might be better to ask what the law contributes to the operation of modern sport. It is argued that the clearest manifestation of sports law lies in the fact that lawyers, general principles of the law and legal proceedings are now often central to modern sports' seemingly continuous struggle to address inter alia the corrosive impact of corruption, discrimination, doping and violence, as well as overarching problems relating to the state of labour relations in professional sport.[9]

Sport and The Law: A History

[**1.05**] Regrettably, even the briefest history of sport and the most abridged account of the many theories on why humans are attracted to sport and games is beyond the scope of this book.[10] Nevertheless, the framework provided by leading sports historians such as Guttmann;[11] the insight of sociologists such as Huizinga;[12] and Dunning's interpretation of Elias's idea of sport reflecting a general societal 'civilising process', enlightens our understanding of sports law.[13] Briefly, sports historians tend to identify five significant periods in the history of sport. First, and in antiquity, the period from the fourth century BC to the third century AD when Greek athletic contests based on the festival at Olympia spread throughout much of Europe and later merged with Roman-inspired gladiatorial events and 'games'. The influence of this era in terms of the architecture

---

[8] See the comments in the prefaces to D Griffith Jones, *Law and the Business of Sport* (London, Butterworths, 1997) *vii* and A Lewis and J Taylor, *Sport: Law and Practice* (London, Butterworths, 2003) *vii*.

[9] This objective is a (more pragmatic) advance on Edward Grayson's hope that the rule of law might return sport to Corinthian values of fair play and respect as outlined in the preface to his seminal text, *Sport and the Law*, 3rd edn (London, Butterworths, 2000) *xxvii*.

[10] For a different perspective on the meaning of sport see the reproduction of Roland Barthes's little known essay (translated by R Howard), *What is Sport?* (New Haven, Yale University Press, 2007).

[11] See, eg, A Guttmann, *From Ritual to Record: The Nature of Modern Sports* (New York, Columbia University Press, 1978); *Sports Spectators* (New York, Columbia University Press, 1986); *A Whole New Ball Game: An Interpretation of American Sports* (London, University of North Carolina Press, 1988); *Women's Sports: A History* (New York, Columbia University Press, 1991); *Games and Empires: Modern Sports and Cultural Imperialism* (New York, Columbia University Press, 1996); *The Olympics: A History of the Modern Games*, 2nd edn (Urbana, University of Illinois Press, 2002); and *Sports: The First Five Millennia* (Amherst, University of Massachusetts Press, 2004).

[12] J Huizinga, *Homo Ludens: A Study of the Play-element in Culture* (London, Routledge and Kegan Paul, 1949).

[13] See, eg, N Elias and E Dunning, *Quest for Excitement: Sport and Leisure in the Civilizing Process* (Oxford, Blackwell, 1986); E Dunning and C Rojek (eds), *Sport and Leisure in the Civilizing Process: Critique and Counter-critique* (Toronto, University of Toronto Press, 1992); E Dunning, J Maguire and R Pearton (eds), *The Sports Process: A Comparative and Developmental Approach* (Leeds, Human Kinetics, 1993); E Dunning, *Sport Matters: Sociological Studies in Sport, Violence and Civilisation* (London, Routledge, 1999); and E Dunning, D Malcolm and I Waddington, *Sport Histories: Figurational Studies of the Development of Modern Sports* (London, Routledge, 2003).

of the modern sports arena, and the promotion of competitive sport as mass entertainment, remains profound.[14] The second period coincides with the fall of the Roman Empire and lasts through the Middle Ages. It is characterised by a marked decline in organised sport, due principally to socio-economic factors. Life during the period in question was, to paraphrase Hobbes, 'nasty, brutish and short' with an atmosphere not conducive to pastimes of a sporting nature, or any nature. Additionally, leading scholars in Christianity, such as Saint Augustine and Saint Jerome, viewed the customary rites celebrated at the Coliseum as powerful symbols of pagan decadence and, according to Scanlon and Cleveland, 'in the process tarred all sports with the same brush'.[15] The third period—broadly the feudal era—sees the gradual revival of folk-based leisure activities usually held on religious pattern days and the promotion of pursuits deemed useful in preparing men for war, such as archery, jousts and tournaments.[16] The fourth period, which runs parallel to the industrial revolution in Britain, witnesses the birth of modern sport, leading both to the codification of many of today's leading team sports and the demise of agrarian-based sports based on the baiting of animals, and the adaptation of this sporting process elsewhere, particularly in the US.[17] The fifth and final period is taken to begin in the latter half of the twentieth century with the intensive corporatisation and commodification of sport.[18]

There are numerous themes linking these periods in sports history and five are of importance to our understanding of modern sports law—a definition of the term 'sport'; the societal nature of sport; sport's correlation with technological and economic advances; socio-political aspects of sport; and the law's instrumental role in 'civilising' sport.

What is Sport?

[1.06]   It is clear from history that 'sport' is not homogeneous in nature. The term can refer to localised, non-competitive, quasi-physical leisure pursuits of a custom-based nature; or, in a more contemporary sense, codified, competitive and highly regulated physical activities that have global appeal. This text is concerned with the latter though ironically it is in the context of the former—the informal recreations of the local village green—that the term 'lawful sports and games'

---

[14] For an introduction see N Crowther, *Sport in Ancient Times* (London, Praeger, 2007) and D Kyle, *Sport and Spectacle in the Ancient World* (Malden, Blackwell, 2007).

[15] J Scanlan and G Cleveland, 'The Past as a Prelude: The Early Origins of Modern American Sports Law' (1981) 8 *Ohio Northern University Law Review* 433, 440.

[16] See generally T Henricks, *Disputed Pleasures: Sport and Society in Preindustrial England* (London, Greenwood Press, 1991).

[17] See generally N Tranter, *Sport, Economy and Society in Britain, 1750–1914* (Cambridge, Cambridge University Press, 1998); E Gorn and W Goldstein, *A Brief History of American Sports* (Illinois, University of Illinois Press, 2004) chs 1–3; and B Rader, *American Sports: From the Age of Folk Games to the Age of Televised Sports*, 5th edn (NJ, Prentice Hall, 2004) chs 1–2.

[18] For a lively, accessible account of the business of sport see T Harris, *Sport: Almost Everything You Ever Wanted to Know* (London, Yellow Jersey Press, 2007) 587–688.

has been most frequently considered by the House of Lords. In cases such as *R v Oxfordshire County Council (Ex p Sunningwell Parish Council)*,[19] *R (Beresford) v Sunderland City Council*[20] and *Oxfordshire CC v Oxford City Council*,[21] the House of Lords had to address the issue of the registration of village greens wherein proof of the playing of lawful sports, games and informal recreations was often integral to attempts by claimants to establish (or deny) user rights to the land in question.[22] Unfortunately, the definition of 'sport' in the stated litigation was necessarily broad, and in the context of this text, not especially useful.[23] The challenge is to arrive at an objective workable definition of an activity that now appears to encompass everything from chess to combat sports; from darts to synchronised diving. In this regard, a definition of sport is important for two reasons: on account of specific advantages that might accrue from such a status and, more generally, with regard to the certainty it might provide as a starting point for the study of sports law.

[**1.07**]   On the first and more specific point, a declaration that an activity is a legally recognised sport or game entails a number of benefits. These include the capacity to attract a favourable tax assessment for an individual participant or to obtain charitable status for that sporting association.[24] Similarly, a lawful sport or game may avail of exemptions from applications of fundamental legal principles that might otherwise severely restrict the enjoyment of that sport. The most immediate example is the qualified immunity that lawful games and sports receive from the application of the ordinary threshold of consent to assault in the criminal law, which will be discussed in chapter five of this text. In this context—consent and the criminal law—the Law Commission of England and Wales, in consultation with bodies such as the Central Council of Physical Recreation, suggested a 'recognition scheme' as to whether an activity might equate to a lawful game or sport.[25] The criteria are useful, though they are principally concerned with safety and controlling the risk of avoidable injury in contact sports such as boxing and martial arts.[26]

— *Physical Skills*: Does the activity involve physical skills? Are physical skills important for successful participation? Can they be developed or are they inherent in the individual?

---

[19] *R v Oxfordshire County Council (Ex p Sunningwell Parish Council)* [1999] UKHL 28; [2000] 1 AC 335.

[20] *R (Beresford) v Sunderland City Council* [2003] UKHL 60; [2004] 1 AC 889.

[21] *Oxfordshire CC v Oxford City Council* [2006] UKHL 25; [2006] 2 AC 674.

[22] Principally under ss 13 and 22 of the Commons Registration Act 1965, as amended by s 98 of the Countryside and Rights of Way Act 2000 and s 15 of the Commons Act 2006.

[23] See, eg, *R v Oxfordshire County Council (Ex p Sunningwell Parish Council)* [2000] 1 AC 335, 347, Lord Hoffman: 'Local people use the glebe for such outdoor pursuits as walking their dogs, playing family and children's games, flying kites, picking blackberries, fishing in the stream and tobogganing down the slope when snow falls.'

[24] Note s 2(3)(d) of the Charities Acts 2006 which defines sport to include 'sports or games which promote health by involving physical or mental skill or exertion.'

[25] Law Commission of England and Wales, 'Criminal Law: Consent in the Criminal Law' (Law Com, CP 139, 1995) [13.10].

[26] Ibid [12.32]–[12.50].

— *Physical Effort*: Does the activity involve physical effort? Is it important for successful participation? How important are any mechanical or other aides in comparison to skills and physical effort?
— *Accessibility*: Is participation available to all sections of the community and not overly restricted for reasons of cost, gender or any other grounds?
— *Rules and Organisation*: Is there an established structure to the activity with rules, and where appropriate, organised competitions nationally and/or internationally?
— *Strategy and Tactics*: Are there strategy and tactics within the framework of the rules? Is developing and employing an awareness of them important for successful participation?
— *Essential Purpose*: What is the essential purpose of the activity? Is it some form of physical recreation or is physical recreation a means to another, more basic purpose?
— *Physical Challenge*: Does the activity present a physical and/or mental challenge to the participant whether against himself/herself, others or the environment?
— *Risk*: Does the activity involve any degree of risk? Is this level acceptable? What safeguards are employed by those taking part to minimise any risk?
— *Uniqueness*: Is this a unique activity or is it a variation of another more similar activity that is already recognised?
— *Other Considerations*: Are there any other political, moral or other ethical considerations which might prohibit [a national sports council] from recognising the activity?

[1.08]   Returning to the second and broader point, it is also argued that a legal definition of sport is necessary because without it the coherency of sports law more generally is undermined.[27] Griffith Jones, for example, links his circumspection towards the idea that a discrete area of law exists to which can aptly be attached the label sports law to the fact that 'the very concept of "sport" embraces many different activities with no discernible common denominator and no obvious definable boundaries.'[28] Unfortunately, many attempts within the sporting world at defining sport are linked either to issues of governance or funding, thus are of limited appeal. For instance, the International Olympic Committee's (IOC) perspective on the term 'sport' is largely dependent on whether the governing organisation of that sport is affiliated to, and abides by, the Olympic Charter. At a national level, many domestic sports councils define sport narrowly with respect to their funding remit and resources.[29] It follows that an underlying

---

[27] See generally S Gardiner, 'Sport: A Need for a Legal Definition' (1996) 4 *Sport and the Law Journal* 31.
[28] Griffith Jones, (n 8) *vii*.
[29] Recognition of darts as a sport by the various sports councils of the UK proved somewhat controversial and problematic. The British Darts Organisation (BDO) finally achieved recognition for the sport in 2005. See I Herbert, 'Darts Steps Up to the Oche to Stake Claim for Olympics' *Independent* (London 2 October 2006) News/Home 4.

theme in the recognition of a lawful sport or game is often whether the sport's governing body can be entrusted with (a) the various health and safety issues surrounding its participants, spectators, equipment and facilities; and (b) any government funding directed towards it.[30] In the UK, the principal criterion used by the various sports councils—UK Sport; Sport Scotland, Sports Council Wales; and Sport Northern Ireland—in recognising a sporting activity is whether that activity meets the definition of sport found in article 2.1 of the Council of Europe's *European Sports Charter* (1992). That definition, which is adhered to by this text, states:

> Sport means all forms of physical activity, which through casual or organised participation, aims at expressing or improving physical fitness and mental well-being, forming social relationships or obtaining results in competition at all levels.[31]

Sport as a Diversion

[**1.09**] The second theme that can be drawn from the history of sport is Huizinga's idea that the history of sport reveals that its value to, and role in, society lies in its capacity to distract from the demands of everyday life with the value-added benefit of promoting physical well-being. This attractive pleasurable element to sport notwithstanding, many societies, from the Ancient Greeks to the England of the Early Middle Ages and onto mid-nineteenth century Britain, also viewed a physically fit and disciplined society as vital to national security and military preparedness.[32] For instance, in Plato's *Dialogues on Laws*, the Athenian Stranger urged the 'legislator' to:

> … ordain that soldiers shall perform lesser exercises without arms every day … fighting with boxing gloves and hurling javelins … in order that the sport may not be altogether without fear, but may have terrors and to a certain degree show the man who has and who has not courage … considering that if a few men should die, then the citizens will never find a test … which is a far greater evil to the state than the loss of a few.[33]

Later, the medieval English peasantry practised war-related sports, notably archery and wrestling,[34] while the aristocracy also saw sport, in the form of jousts

---

[30] See further the comments by N Cox and A Schuster, *Sport and the Law* (Dublin, Firstlaw, 2004) 6–9.

[31] The European Sports Charter and access to the Council of Europe's related policies on sport are available online at www.coe.int/t/dg4/sport/SportinEurope.

[32] J Sugden, *Boxing and Society: An International Analysis* (Manchester, Manchester University Press, 1996) 10, observing that this aspect of the popularity of sport was unsurprising in an era when 'physical prowess was directly related to self and community survival and when, behind sword and shield, the body was the most important military resource.'

[33] Citation taken from B Jowett (trans), *The Dialogues of Plato* (Oxford, Oxford University Press, 1892), Vol V, Laws, Book VII, s 839, 211–12.

[34] Note J Carter, *Medieval Games: Sports and Recreations in Feudal Society* (London, Greenwood Press, 1992) and W Hone (ed), *Strutt's Sports and Pastimes of the People of England* (London, Kessinger, 2007).

and tournaments, as an enjoyable means of preparation for war.[35] Later still, and fortified by their reading of the classics, those who promoted sports in the public schools of Victorian Britain understood that 'through sport boys acquire virtues which no books can give them; not merely daring and endurance but better still, temper, self-restraint, fairness, honour, unenvious approbation of another's success and all that "give and take" of life which stands a man in good stead when he goes forth into the world.'[36] In contemporary terms, the benefits of participation in sport are seen in broader terms, and the 'societal role of sport' now encapsulates sport's capacity to enhance public health through physical activity; to facilitate educational initiatives; to promote volunteering; to increase civic participation; and to assist initiatives in social inclusion.[37]

[1.10]   From a legal perspective, the public-interest benefits accruing from sport are seen in terms of sport's 'social utility'. Sport's social utility was alluded to frequently in the preparatory and consultative process leading to the Compensation Act 2006.[38] The Act was drafted against the backdrop of an apparently spiralling compensation culture in Britain.[39] As explained in chapter six of this text, section 1 of the Compensation Act's account for 'desirable activities', *viz* the setting of the required standard of care in negligence, can be seen as an attempt to protect sporting activities, particularly those entailing enhanced risk and physicality, from the perceived excesses of Britain's 'blame culture'. Chapter six also demonstrates that this underlying policy approach, related to sport's social utility, can be seen through an analysis of occupiers liability cases such as the decision of the House of Lords in *Tomlinson v Congleton Borough Council*.[40] In addition, social utility is vital to an understanding of the manner in which contact sports in particular have been granted exemption from the ordinary law of personal violence, referred to in chapters five and six. The historical roots of this exemption can be located in ancient A Greek law where a homicide during the course of a recognised sporting event was deemed 'involuntary'[41] and in Roman law where in the *Digest of Justinian*, Book 9.2.7, the *lex Aquilia*, an account of causes of actions relating to compensation for unjustly inflicted damage, specifically provided:

> If a man kills another in the colluctatio [wrestling] or in the pancratium [a hybrid form of wrestling and boxing] or in a (public) boxing match, the lex Aquilia does not apply

---

[35] See generally D Crouch, *Tournament* (London, Hambledon, 2005).

[36] R Holt, *Sport and the British: A Modern History* (Oxford, Clarendon, 1989) 93.

[37] See typically s 2 of the EC Commission's, 'White Paper on Sport' (COM(2007) 391, Brussels, 11 July 2007) final.

[38] See the documents archived online at www.dca.gov.uk/legist/compensation.htm.

[39] See especially A Morris, 'Spiralling or Stabilising? The Compensation Culture and our Propensity to Claim Damages for Personal Injury' (2007) 70 *MLR* 349.

[40] *Tomlinson v Congleton Borough Council* [2003] UKHL 47; [2004] 1 AC 46. See also *Tedstone v Bourne Leisure Ltd* [2008] EWCA Civ 654.

[41] *The Dialogues of Plato* (n 33) 212: 'If anyone dies in these mimic contests, the homicide is involuntary, and will make the slayer when he has been putrefied according to the law [when he has paid compensation to the victim's family], to be pure of blood.'

because the damage is seen to have been done in the course of glory and valour and not for the sake of inflicting unlawful harm.[42]

[**1.11**]   Today, actions on the football or rugby field, to which civil or even criminal liability might otherwise attach, continue to attract an exemption from the ordinary law of assault on the grounds that such conduct takes place consensually and under the conditions of a legally recognised, socially beneficial sport. Finally, sport's social utility is also an understated factor in the interface between sport and EU law described in the concluding chapter of this text. In this, a number of leading sports organisations, such as UEFA, European football's governing authority, argue that football's unique structures and contribution to society means that it should be excused from the full impact of the fundamental freedoms underpinning the EU's internal market.

Technology, Media and the Development of Sport

[**1.12**]   The third premise that can be identified from the history of sport is self-evident: there is a correlation between the sophistication of organised sports and the technological and economic maturity of a country or society. The most obvious example is that of the birth of modern sport in nineteenth century Britain at a time when the country was the world's leading industrial power. Dedicated leisure time and increased disposable income, allied to developments in communications and transport meant that not only were all sections of society able to read about sports events more or less as they happened, but some could also travel to and attend those events relatively easily and cheaply. This rise in the popularity and accessibility of sport meant that some sports could sustain a professional code, augmenting basic revenue from 'gate receipts' by either attracting commercial sponsors or by other means of exploiting their 'product'. The role that the railways, the telegraph wire, and the early sporting press had in the advancement of sport is well documented.[43] The relationship between sport, media and technology has now evolved into one of dependency, to the point that many major sports leagues and events are underwritten financially by the selling of TV, multimedia and sponsorship-related rights.[44] The most celebrated example of this can be seen in the bidding for the American television rights to the Olympics with the

---

[42] Citation taken from A Watson (trans), *The Digest of Justinian* (Philadelphia, University of Pennsylvania Press, 1998).

[43] For an accessible introduction see generally M Wuggins, *The Victorians and Sport* (London, Hambledon & London, 2004) and N Wigglesworth, *The Story of Sport in England* (New York, Routledge, 2007) chs 2–3.

[44] See the review by G Whannel, 'Television and the Transformation of Sport' (2009) 625 (1) *The Annals of the American Academy of Political and Social Science* 205. Note also the concern of the governing authorities of English rugby, football and cricket, to the request by the communications regulator, Ofcom, that BSkyB should cut the price it charges rival cable, terrestrial and internet broadcasters to show its premium sports channels. See A Mostrous, 'Premier League to take action over Ofcom's Sky Price Ruling' *The Times* (London 5 April 2010) Business 35.

broadcasting rights for the 2008 Summer Games in Beijing costing NBC almost US$900 million. Domestically, the relationship between sport and the modern media is illustrated by BSkyB's deal with the Premier League, which in 2009 resulted in their paying £1.6 billion for a three-year deal to broadcast 115 games a season.[45]

[1.13] The correlation between the modern media and sport has a number of further points of interest. First, for many, the relationship manifests itself in the manner in which the scheduling of sport events, such as the demise of the three o'clock Saturday kick-off for Premier League matches, is determined frequently by the whims of broadcasters. This re-scheduling pales in comparison to the Olympics where the Games are carefully calibrated so that the most appealing TV events for American viewers—swimming and gymnastics—are frontloaded to attract and 'hook' viewers. Moreover, in their negotiations with the IOC for the Beijing 2008 games, NBC ensured that these events took place in the morning in China so that they could be broadcast live in prime time for American Eastern and Central time zones.[46] The second aspect of this relationship is that media corporations such as NBC and BSkyB are evidently profit-orientated thus their interest in sport is driven by altogether larger financial concerns. The reason that Premier League football is central to BSkyB's overall programming output is that football, as a sports product, was seen as the 'battering ram' that allowed the Rupert Murdoch owned group to muscle into and maintain a position within the highly competitive British TV, satellite and broadcasting industry. In short, the four successive rights auctions won by BSkyB since the inception of the Premier League in 1992 not only resulted in millions of pounds being poured into football, they also attracted millions of subscribers for BSkyB.[47] In a similar vein, Jeffrey Immelt, the chairman of General Electric, the owners of NBC, on explaining that the corporation stood to enjoy a range of 'ancillary benefits' based on its sponsorship of the Summer Games of 2008, summarised their strategy in simple terms: 'We have a huge footprint in China, where we do more than US$4 billion worth of business, with a lot of employees there.'[48] Given the extent of these investments, and their returns, it is

---

[45] Recent figures suggest that TV money (domestic and overseas broadcasting rights) is responsible for insulating the finances of the Premier League from the general global economic downturn. See the summary of Deloitte's Annual Review of Football Finance for the 2007/2008 season by B Wilson, 'Premier League Defies Downturn' *BBC News Online* 3 June 2009 available at http://news.bbc.co.uk/go/pf/fr/-/1/hi/business/8078533.stm.

[46] NBC's strategy appeared to pay off. Benefitting from the eight gold medals secured for the US by swimmer Michael Phelps, it was estimated that approximately 86% of all US television households watched the first 16 days of the Beijing Games, equating to 211 million viewers. For further insight see B Carter, 'On TV, Timing is Everything at the Olympics' *New York Times* (New York 25 August 2008) New York Edition C1.

[47] Accordingly, and despite the fact that a global economic downturn was in full swing, BSkyB bucked market trends, paying £300million more for its three-year Premier League TV packages in 2009 (£1.6 billion) than in did in 2006 (£1.3billion). See the background in D Milmo, 'Investors Count the Cost of BSkyB's Premiership Deal' *Guardian* (London 9 May 2006) Financial 26 and P Kelso, 'BSkyB strengthen grip on Premier League football' *The Daily Telegraph* (London 8 February 2009).

[48] B Carter and R Sandomir, 'A Surprise Winner at the Olympic Games in Beijing: NBC' *New York Times* (New York 18 August 2008) Business/Financial Pages C1.

unsurprising that corporations such as NBC and BSkyB and sports organisations such as the IOC and the Premier League would seek to protect them aggressively.[49] This regulation spans a spectrum of concerns from concerted 'ambush' marketing by rival, non-official sponsoring companies at the Olympics,[50] to recent efforts by the Premier League and BSkyB to stop rival suppliers from offering alternatives to Sky's coverage of football.[51] Finally, the relationship between the media and sport, which a century ago amounted to crowds gathering around the nearest telegraph station, is now, owing to the digital revolution and the emergence of new multimedia platforms such as mobile phone and internet rights, set to become ever more immediate and ever more lucrative. Consequently, the legal framework surrounding this exploitation of sport will have to keep apace, thus adding another facet to the study and practice of sports law.

Socio-Political Aspects of Sport

[1.14]   The fourth theme of interest that can be gleaned from the history of sport is that sport's value as a diversion has long been manipulated by authorities for socio-political reasons. Traditionally, this was done with a view to distracting the masses from further civic engagement thus maintaining the ruling elite's privileges. This rather complex analysis is neatly encapsulated in the Roman maxim of *panem et circenses* (bread and circuses). In this, there is little doubt that the sporting festivals of Imperial Rome were, at root, sophisticated methods of social control and political manipulation whereby in times of instability or insecurity, the mob could be appeased and distracted by events at the Coliseum.[52] Later, in eighteenth century Britain, wealthy landowners sought to secure their political power by establishing a rapport with the peasantry through the promotion of sports such as cricket and prize fighting thus 'allowing gentlemen to at once mingle with the multitude, cementing the loyalty of their social inferiors, but simultaneously to distance themselves through displays of wealth and largesse.'[53] Subsequently, sport was seen as an important cathartic outlet for the

---

[49] Outside of the Chinese market, which boosted TV viewing figures for the Beijing Olympics, the statistics reveal that the 'market' for TV sport remains robust. In the US, over 150 million viewed some part of Super Bowl 2008; while in Europe over 200 million saw some of the action in that year's Champions League final between Manchester United and Chelsea. In the UK alone, over 12 million (or 20% of the population) watched the match in its entirety. An annual catalogue of the most popular TV sporting events is prepared by *Futures Sport + Entertainment* available online atwww.futuressport.com.

[50] For an introduction see N Burton and S Chadwick, 'Ambush Marketing in Sport: An Assessment of Implications and Management Strategies' (2008) 3 *Coventry University Centre for the International Business of Sport Working Paper Series* available online through www.coventry.ac.uk/researchnet/d/755.

[51] *FA Premier League Ltd & Ors v QC Leisure & Ors* [2008] EWHC 1411 (Ch); [2008] FSR 32 and also *Murphy v Media Protection Services Ltd* [2008] EWHC 1666 (Admin); [2008] FSR 33.

[52] A Futrell, *Blood in the Arena: The Spectacle of Roman Power* (Austin, University of Texas Press, 1997) 212–13.

[53] E Gorn, *The Manly Art: Bare Knuckle Prize Fighting in America* (Ithaca, Cornell University Press, 1989) 27.

industrialised and urbanised masses of nineteenth century Britain.[54] Accordingly, the proletarianism and professionalisation of sport, otherwise at odds with the more Corinthian values of the public schools, was partly indulged.[55] The political manipulation of sport continued in the twentieth century. For instance, the Berlin Olympic Games of 1936 were used for propaganda purposes by the Nazis, while success at major sporting events served a similar purpose for the Soviet Union and its satellite states throughout that century.[56] In sum, although issues of class, power and politics in sport are not generally or expressly reflected in sports law, they do explain much about the origins of modern sport, and may also, in terms of the impact of globalisation, explain a little about the future of sport as a global social movement.[57]

[1.15]   More specifically, social policy has expressly informed the legal regulation of sporting activities in terms of not only *what* type of sports we play but *how* we play them. Arguably, the English passion for sport, and one shared by its Celtic neighbours, has always had a violent tenor. Apart from its paramilitary nature and a propensity for riotous violence, medieval sport in England, for instance, was also characterised by the consumption of alcohol and its association with gambling.[58] Football has a particularly long history in this regard with Magoun noting that one of the earliest official references to the sport occurred in the report of an accidental stabbing of a player during a game played at Newcastle in 1280.[59] At this time, football frequently came to the attention of authorities and was regularly denounced and proscribed by statute. As early as 1314, the Lord Mayor of London had to issue a proclamation prohibiting football as a public nuisance. Admittedly, the authorities had good reason to prohibit football because 'matches' were gratuitously violent affairs played between indeterminate group of youths and often leading to urban riots and damage to property and person.[60] Later during

---

[54] See generally J Hargreaves, *Sport, Power and Culture: A Social and Historical Analysis of Popular Sports in Britain* (Oxford, Polity Press, 1986).

[55] See also W Vamplew, *Pay Up and Play the Game: Professional Sport in Britain, 1875–1914* (Cambridge, Cambridge University Press, 1988) and the account of the specific example of rugby league by T Collins, *Rugby's Great Split: Class, Culture and the Origins of Rugby League Football* (London, Routledge, 2006).

[56] For an introduction see P Arnaud and J Riordan (eds), *Sport and International Politics: The Impact of Fascism and Communism on Sport* (London, E & FN Spon, 1998) and S Jackson and S Haigh (eds), *Sport and Foreign Policy in a Globalizing World* (London, Routledge, 2009).

[57] See the work of D Birley, *Sport and the Making of Britain* (Manchester, Manchester University Press, 1993) and *Land of Sport and Glory: Sport and British Society, 1887–1910* (Manchester, Manchester University Press, 1995). See also S Redhead, *Unpopular Cultures: The Birth of Law and Popular Culture* (Manchester, Manchester University Press, 1995) and, most recently, J Harvey, J Horne and P Safai, 'Alterglobalisation, Global Social Movements, and the Possibility of Political Transformation Through Sport' (2009) 26 *Sociology of Sport Journal* 383.

[58] For the long established links between sport, gambling and alcohol see D Miers, *Regulating Commercial Gambling: Past, Present and Future* (Oxford, Oxford University Press, 2004) and T Collins and W Vamplew, *Mud, Sweat and Beers: A Cultural History of Sport and Alcohol* (Oxford, Berg, 2002).

[59] F Magoun, 'Football in Medieval England and in Middle English Literature' (1929) 35 *American Historical Review* 33, 35.

[60] J Walvin, *The People's Game—A Social History of British Football* (London, Allen Lane, 1975) 12.

the reign of Edward III, football's popularity, described in a proclamation dated 12 June 1365 as 'vain, dishonest, unthrifty and idle' was seen to interfere with the practice of the 'noble and simple' sport of archery.[61] Subsequently, monarchs from Richard II in 1388[62] to Edward IV in 1477[63] had to restate the proclamation and seek the proscription of certain ball and dice games.[64] All sports benefited from Henry VIII's ascent to the throne. In 1541, the monarch relaxed the existing legislative prohibitions on games of skill (such as ball games) but not games of chance (such as dice games)—the latter remaining restricted because of their association with gambling.[65] Henry VIII's favourable opinion of sport reflected not only a personal interest but three other facets of contemporary English society. First, the approving view of sport reflected the increased confidence and security of the English realm at the time. The practice and promotion of archery lost its strategic value as the bow and arrow was replaced by gunpowder technology and, overall, the realm felt sufficiently secure in its authority to permit the revival of previously worrisome leisure pursuits, save on the politically unstable island of Ireland where traditional sports remained banned.[66] The promotion of sports also had the added bonus, from the monarch's personal perspective, of discommoding the Church because the sports events of the time were usually held on, and disrupted, Catholic feast days.[67] The third point is of most significant interest. The relaxation of the various restrictions on sport reflected the fact that the games involved were slowly and incrementally changing in character. This 'civilising process' would intensify in later centuries to become the most important underlying feature in the emergence of the modern form of many of our leading sports and games.

Sport, Law and the Civilising Process

[**1.16**]   In an influential body of work, Norbert Elias argued that from a sociological perspective the history of modern European society for the past five centuries can be characterised around a civilising process.[68] At its simplest, Elias contended that our 'threshold of repugnancy' for public acts of violence has been falling for quite some time and this trend can be illustrated by reference to the parallel

---

[61] 39 Edw 3 (1365).

[62] 12 Ric 2 c6 (1388).

[63] 17 Edw 4 c3 (1477).

[64] For a detailed review of the attempts to ban 'football' during the period in question and related legal proceedings see E Dunning and K Sheard, *Barbarians, Gentlemen, and Players: A Sociological Study of the Development of Rugby Football* (Oxford, Robertson, 1979) ch 1.

[65] 33 Hen 8 c9, Unlawful Games (1541), finally repealed by the Betting and Gaming Act 1960.

[66] The original ban can be traced to 40 Edw 3, Statute of Kilkenny (1366).

[67] See the account in *Barbarians, Gentlemen, and Players* (n 64) 23–24.

[68] N Elias, *The Civilising Process* (Oxford, Blackwell, 1978). Elias's work was originally published as two separate volumes (*History of Manners*; *State Formation and Civilisation*) under the title *Uber den Prozess der Zivilisation* (Basel, Haus zum Falker, 1939). The 1978 volume was translated by Edmund Jephcott.

evolution or sanitisation of sport during the period. An account of the theoretical merits and practical manifestations of Elias's process is beyond the scope of this book, though three brief points provide some insight. First, Elias observed that since the early medieval era there has been a pattern of civilising the more uncouth and aggressive aspects of human behaviour, including the propensity for personal violence. Second, Elias noted that in parallel to that pattern the state acquired a monopoly on the use and regulation of violence through, for example, the establishment of the criminal justice system and thus violence by individual citizens decreased. Third, the backdrop to both of these developments was the demise of the feudal, agrarian, kin-based society and the beginnings of the industrialisation and urbanisation of western societies, allied to centralised government. In short, as western societies became more advanced in terms of political and economic structure, Elias and Dunning interpreted this to mean that such societies also became less coarse in terms of personal, social *and* sporting relationships. Before elaborating on the application of the civilising process to sport, it is well to note that this perspective has been subject to criticism mainly on the grounds that Elias and Dunning placed too much emphasis on the elimination of violence in the development of modern sport—not all traditional folk sports involved physical contact or resulted in violence—and that in any event Elias's process is clearly not linear in its evolution; for instance, many of today's newer sports, such as 'ultimate' fighting, continue to betray a violent underbelly to our sporting passions.[69] Nevertheless, there are a number of enduring aspects to Elias's approach, which have some residual importance to the evolution of sports law.

[1.17]　　Those who adhere to the idea of a civilising process locate the origins of modern sport in the gradual stabilisation of English political and social life from the seventeenth century onwards. Elias and Dunning claim that from that period the 'parliamentarisation' of the ruling landed classes of England went hand in hand with the 'sportisation' of their pastimes, that is to say 'the ruling groups who devised means for conducting political struggles non-violently also worked out means for reducing the violence of their pastimes'.[70] Put simply, at this time, a greater sensitivity to, and consciousness of, violence generally was reflected in the changing social habits of the gentrified aristocracy and this included their sporting pastimes. Consequently, the modern, more restrained and regulated forms of fox-hunting, boxing, cricket and horseracing (sports that the ruling elite sponsored and frequently participated in) began to emerge.[71] The pace of evolution

---

[69] For some criticism of Elias see A Hunt, 'The Role of Law in the Civilizing Process and the Reform of Popular Culture' (1995) 10 *Canadian Journal of Law and Society* 5 and the debate summarised by K Green *et al*, 'Violence, Competition and the Emergence and Development of Modern Sports: Reflections on the Stokvis-Malcolm Debate' (2005) 40 *International Review for the Sociology of Sport* 119.

[70] *Quest for Excitement* (n 13) 21–22.

[71] See, for instance, D Malcolm, 'Cricket and the Civilizing Process' (2002) 37 *International Review for the Sociology of Sport* 37; K Sheard, 'Aspects of Boxing in the Western Civilizing Process' (1997) 32 *International Review for the Sociology of Sport* 31 and W Vamplew, *The Turf: A Social and Economic History of Horse Racing* (London, Allen Lane, 1976).

and sophistication of sport increased in Britain as the industrial age occurred. During the nineteenth century, a bourgeois model of sport developed whereby in order to fit in with the emerging 'respectable' middle class and Christian values of the time, popular sports of the pre-industrial era either had to submit to codification and rid themselves of their association with gambling, violence, animal cruelty and the inobservance of the Sabbath; or face proscription.[72] During this period, football, rugby, tennis, hockey, athletics and water sports such as rowing and swimming began to take on their modern form.[73] For the first time, the rules of these sports were written down. These rules were orientated on the ethos of fair play and were implemented by dedicated officials or umpires. Regulations were thus standardised nationally and later internationally and were administered by centralised governing bodies or associations.[74]

[**1.18**]   The general law and the courts played an understated instrumental role in this civilising process of promoting 'rational', socially acceptable recreations and sports.[75] McArdle notes that, although they were enacted ostensibly to prevent poaching and illegal gaming, the enclosure laws of the eighteenth century onwards significantly curtailed customary leisure pursuits on commons land or forests.[76] Pointing to cases such as *Fitch v Rawling*,[77] McArdle argues authoritatively that 'judgments on the legality of leisure interests that the enclosure movement engendered may be properly regarded as one of the earliest cogent bodies of "sports law"'.[78] Later, as England became increasingly urbanised, the loss of public spaces for sporting amenities was seen as detrimental to public health and beneficial only to the 'debasing pleasures' of the local pub or gambling den.[79] A series of statutes, commencing with the Inclosure Act 1845, sought to prohibit any further enclosure of green spaces and promote the creation of public walks and parks for 'the purposes of exercise and recreation for inhabitants of the

---

[72] See generally J Mangan (ed), *Reformers, Sport, Modernizers: Middle-class Revolutionaries* (London, Frank Cass, 2002) and J Mangan (ed), *A Sport-loving Society: Victorian and Edwardian Middle England at Play* (London, Routledge, 2006).

[73] Note the establishment of the Football Association in 1863; the Rugby Football Union (1871); the Amateur Athletics Association (1880); the Amateur Rowing Association (1882); the Amateur Swimming Association (1886); the Hockey Association (1886); the Lawn Tennis Association (1888); and the Northern Rugby (League) Football Union (1895). See generally J Norridge, *Can We Have Our Balls Back, Please? How the British Invented Sport* (London, Allen Lane, 2008).

[74] See generally W Vamplew, 'Playing with the Rules: Influences on the Development of Regulation in Sport' (2007) 24 *International Journal of the History of Sport* 843.

[75] See generally P Bailey, *Leisure and Class in Victorian England: Rational Recreation and the Contest for Control* (London, Routledge and Kegan Paul, 1978).

[76] D McArdle, 'A Ruling Class Conspiracy: Law, Enclosure and the Politics of Leisure' (1999) 8 *Nottingham Law Journal* 69.

[77] 126 ER 614; (1795) 2 H Bl 393 (KB). The case was based on a customary right to play cricket on the plaintiff's close.

[78] D McArdle, *From Boot Money to Bosman: Football, Society and the Law* (London, Cavendish, 2000) 10–11, where he also notes that by extension the roots of sports law can also be seen in the myriad of hunting and gaming laws enacted since Norman times.

[79] Note generally the observations by the House of Commons' Select Committee on Public Walks, Report and Minutes of Evidence (Sessional Papers xv (1833), no 448).

neighbourhood'.[80] Subsequent, rigorous judicial interpretation of this legislation ensured that these recreational green belts were preserved.[81] Similarly, the Highways Act 1835 proved useful in eliminating traditional forms of football, and later shaping the development of modern football. Section 72 of that Act deemed it a criminal offence to play 'Football or any other game on any part of said [public] Highways, to the Annoyance of any Passenger or Passengers'.[82] In combination with more effective and formalised policing, and torts such as public nuisance, this led to the demise of riotous street football involving large crowds of opposing local youths.[83] Concomitantly, it meant that football in its various forms could only be held in large private grounds, which is one of the reasons why football continued to flourish in the public schools of the era and whose influence would lead to the subsequent codification of the rules of modern football, and the establishment of the Football Association in 1863.[84]

[1.19]   The success of section 72 of the Highway Act 1835 in restricting the sometimes centuries-old traditions of folk football, and the rapid acceptance of the modern form of the game, is evidenced by the fact that a little over half a century after its enactment, the provision was repealed as no longer necessary.[85] The 1830s also saw the proscription of numerous blood sports involving the baiting and fighting of animals pursuant to the Cruelty to Animals Act 1835.[86] In addition, that decade witnessed an increase in a series of 'pugilistic prosecutions' whereby the criminal law in various actions—assault, affray, riot and illegal assembly—was used to eradicate the practice of bare fisted prize fighting.[87] Overall, the Victorian policy on sport was underpinned by concerns regarding public morality (sport's association with gambling and alcohol), social instability (the potential for sporting events to attract large, mob-like assemblies) and the regulation of public spaces (related to the town planning demands of a rapidly

---

[80] Section 30 of the Inclosure Act 1845 empowered a newly established Inclosure Commission to appropriate land for recreational allotment. Note also the provisions permitting local authorities to, effectively, 'zone' land for recreational purposes in the Commons Act 1876; the Metropolitan Commons Act 1876; the Commons Act 1899; the Public Health Acts 1875–1890; and the Open Spaces Act 1906. See generally B Harris and G Ryan, *An Outline of the Law Relating to Common Land and Public Access to the Countryside* (London, Sweet & Maxwell, 1967).

[81] See, eg, *A-G v Mayor of Southampton* (1859) 1 LT 155; 63 ER 957 and *Attorney-General v Corporation of Sunderland* [1876] 2 Ch D 634.

[82] Note the conviction in *Woolley v Corbishley* (1860) 24 JP 773.

[83] See, eg, the powers contained in s 54(17) of the Metropolitan Police Act 1839, which declared it an offence to 'play at any game to the annoyance of the inhabitants or passengers' and authorising a constable to take any person committing such an offence into custody without warrant.

[84] See T Mason, *Association Football and English Society, 1863–1915* (Brighton, Harverster Press, 1980) 9–20. For a revisionist perspective see A Harvey, *Football: The First Hundred Years, The Untold Story* (London, Routledge, 2005).

[85] Statute Law Revision (No 2) Act 1888.

[86] Replaced by the Cruelty to Animals Act 1849, as expanded by the Cruelty to Animals Act 1876. For background see M Radford, *Animal Welfare Law in Britain: Regulation and Responsibility* (New York, Oxford University Press, 2001) chs 2–4.

[87] See the review of the case law in J Anderson, 'The Legal Response to Prize Fighting in Nineteenth Century England and America' (2006) 57 *Northern Ireland Legal Quarterly* 265.

urbanising and increasingly sedentary society). Numerous legislative provisions of the period reflected these concerns, and were subsequently interpreted by the courts so as to support 'rational recreations' more attuned to the changing moral and physical landscape of the day.[88] In sum, the Victorian policy on sport sought to promote activities that were as regulated, and controllable, as the factory whistle. Arguably, the most symbolic manifestation of this policy lies in the link between the various Factory Acts of the era—which eventually led to the stoppage of work at 2 pm on Saturdays—and the tradition of holding football matches one hour later.[89] It must also be noted that these social reforms were a unique experience in nineteenth century Europe—the five and a half day week was referred to as *la semaine anglaise*—and go to explain Britain's influence in the development of new forms of sport and recreation.[90]

[1.20] This brief historical review highlights that the law, as a reflection of a generalised civilising process, had an instrumental effect on the birth of modern sport. It also begs the question as to whether this civilising process continues to have an influence upon the functioning of contemporary sports law. It is submitted that traces of the civilising process can be indentified in the attitude of the criminal courts to violence in sport; in the legislative response of the British government to hooliganism in the 1980s and 1990s; and in the more recent attempt at regulating fox-hunting. On the first point, and as discussed generally in chapter five, the English Court of Appeal has consistently commended trial courts for their intolerance of 'unacceptable' levels of violence on the playing field. This approach was seen clearly and recently in *R v Garfield*[91] where, despite a strong plea in mitigation of sentence, the Court of Appeal upheld a sentence of 15 months' imprisonment for unlawful wounding imposed on a rugby player who, during the course of a game, had stamped on the head of a defenceless opponent. Second, it is suggested that many of the underlying policy aspects of the legal response to the 'English disease' of hooliganism in the 1980s (which included legislation concerning stadium safety, public order generally and specific football banning orders) resonates with the concerns in the Victorian era regarding public morality, illegal assembly, urban planning, associated alcohol-related criminality and class.[92] Third, the debates and discussions surrounding the Hunting Act 2004 had as their source the animal cruelty debates of the early Victorian period, where, once more, traditional rural-based ('blood') sports, in this instance fox-hunting and hare-coursing, struggled to reconcile themselves with the changing moral

---

[88] See generally R Vorspan, 'Rational Recreation and the Law: The Transformation of Popular Urban Leisure in Victorian England' (2000) 45 *McGill Law Journal* 891.

[89] Note the consolidation of these provisions in the Factory and Workshop Act 1878 and again in 1910.

[90] See J Lowerson and J Myerscough, *Time to Spare in Victorian England* (Sussex, Harverster Press, 1977) 30.

[91] *R v Garfield* [2008] 2 Cr App R (S) 62; [2008] EWCA Crim 130.

[92] See generally C Stott and G Pearson, *Football Hooliganism, Policing and the War on the English Disease* (London, Pennant Books, 2007).

compass of contemporary society. In fact, in *R (on the application of Countryside Alliance & Ors) v Attorney General & Anor,*[93] which is one of the few sports-related cases ever to be heard by the House of Lords, Lord Bingham encapsulated the matter neatly by observing:

> Fox-hunting in this country is an emotive and divisive subject. For some it is an activity deeply embedded in the tradition, life and culture of the countryside, richly portrayed in art and literature, a highly cherished, skilful, healthy and useful form of communal outdoor exercise. Others find the pursuit of a small animal across the countryside until it is caught and destroyed by hounds to be abhorrent.[94]

Furthermore, in going on to dismiss that part of the appeal that claimed that the prohibitions imposed by the Hunting Act 2004 were inconsistent with Articles 28 and 49 of the EC Treaty, Lord Bingham justified his approach by remarking expressly that the 2004 Act addressed a subject long rooted in public morality and policy, and was the latest link in a long chain of statutes devoted to what could only be seen as 'social reform' falling within the constitutional responsibility of the legislature.[95]

[1.21]   It is hoped that the origins of sports law, as part of overarching civilising process of social reform and public policy, have been made clear. The civilising process has one final (and crucial) part to play in an understanding of modern sports law. As illustrated, by the late nineteenth century a number of sports, sometimes on pain of criminalisation, underwent a process of transformation whereby they agreed to submit to codification and rationalisation in order to be reconciled within the moral and spatial landscape of modern industrialised Britain. Many 'reconstituted' sports then went on to flourish in an era when all members of society were benefitting from more disposable income and increased leisure time. Football was quite obviously a success in this regard, but so also were sports as diverse as boxing and dog-racing. For example, although the effect of the Queensberry Rules written in 1865 was not immediate, the gradual move by the prize-fighting fraternity away from the bare-fisted bout held at a secluded makeshift venue and towards the gloved match at the local hall or gentleman's club, not only sanitised the sport; it saved it.[96] Similarly, many dog-racing sports, some of which were pushed to the margins by the various anti-cruelty to animals provisions of the era, survived by evolving from irregular events held in the open countryside involving live targets; into the modern, circuit-based version of greyhound racing. The logistics of a greyhound stadium, often a track laid around a football field, were easily accommodated in the

---

[93] *R (on the application of Countryside Alliance & Ors) v Attorney General & Anor* [2007] UKHL 52; [2008] 1 AC 719 (dismissal of appeals as to whether to the prohibition of fox hunting and other sporting activities, imposed by the Hunting Act 2004, was incompatible with the European Convention on Human Rights or inconsistent with the EC Treaty).

[94] Ibid [2007] UKHL 52 [1].

[95] Ibid [36]–[37]. See also Lord Hope at [85].

[96] See generally J Anderson, 'The Business of Hurting People: A Historical, Social and Legal Analysis of Professional Boxing' (2007) 7 *Oxford University Commonwealth Law Journal* 35.

developing urban landscape and that, combined with the fact that local meetings provided an affordable night out with the opportunity to gamble, meant that by the inter-war period Britain could truly be said 'to have gone to the dogs'.[97]

[1.22] From a more law-oriented perspective, it is clear that the newly emerging sports governing bodies of the mid to late nineteenth century had received a reward for submitting to the civilising process: the withdrawal of the threat of further legal intervention and the largely unrestricted liberty to self-regulate. This regulatory autonomy has been cherished and fiercely protected ever since by sporting organisations with many arguing the 'good (corporate) governance'—the latest buzzword in sports administration—rather than more of Denning's 'bad lawyers' or worse again, meddling politicians, will enable sport to deal adequately with future challenges.[98] Similarly, it is argued that the sharp and defensive reaction of many sporting organisations to the creeping juridification of their remit (a theme that runs throughout this book) is located in sports bodies' historical experience of having *earned* the right to self-regulation, as underwritten by the fact that many of these private sports organisations feel that they are doing a good and efficient job administering a socially beneficial activity that would otherwise have to be supported directly by government agencies.[99] For instance, more than a century subsequent to the establishment of the Football Association, traces of the general law's respect for the self-regulatory authority and expertise of that sports organisation can be identified clearly in all three judgments in *Enderby Town Football Club v the FA*,[100] where the Court of Appeal held that a rule made by the FA (prohibiting legal representation at its domestic tribunal) was not necessarily contrary to the rules of natural justice. Aspects of Cairns LJ's brief judgment go beyond the point at issue and reflect a respect for the autonomy of sport and circumspection about the role of law in sport that many contemporary sports administrators still adhere to:

> It is in the interest of justice and not only of administrative convenience that a decision should be arrived at quickly and cheaply. Where the tribunal is composed of intelligent laymen who have a great knowledge of the sport or business concerned, I think that the employment of lawyers is likely to lengthen proceedings and certainly greatly to increase the expense of them without any certainty of bringing about a fairer decision.[101]

---

[97] *Sport and the British* (n 36) 86. See also N Baker, 'Going to the Dogs—Hostility to Greyhound Racing in Britain; Puritanism, Socialism and Pragmatism' (1996) 23 *Journal of Sport History* 97.

[98] See generally M Taylor and N O'Sullivan, 'How should National Governing Bodies of Sport be governed in the UK? An Exploratory Study of Board Structure' (2009) 17 *Corporate Governance* 681. The issue of better governance in football, in the guise of giving supporters the opportunity to buy a stake in their club, was even mentioned in Labour's Westminster election manifesto of 2010.

[99] In a broader context, it should be noted that in the 1990s a number of questions were raised about the efficacy of self-regulation more generally. In that decade, Britain, which was traditionally seen as a haven for self-regulation, witnessed the growth of a greater degree of government-led regulatory formalisation. See R Baldwin, 'The Punitive Regulation' (2004) 67 *MLR* 351 and A Ogus, 'Rethinking Self-regulation' (1995) 15 *OJLS* 97.

[100] [1971] Ch 591.

[101] Ibid 609.

[1.23]   Nevertheless, the stated case also demonstrates that during the latter half of the twentieth century (and much earlier in the US) governing bodies, such as the FA, were, due to the deepening professionalization of sport, increasingly involved in disputes of a contractual, employment and commercial law nature thus bringing sports organisations back into more frequent contact with the ordinary courts and the general law. The point is well made by Beloff (who along with Edward Grayson may be called a 'founding father' of sports law), and it is worth citing at length:

> More lawyers and more law in sport does not necessarily mean more justice in sport, but it may do, and should do. The growth of legalism in sport is borne of a desire for higher standards of justice, demanded by the sporting community as a consequence of the rise of professionalism and the increase in earnings potential within sport. If one wishes to make a cogent case against increased involvement of lawyers in sport, one must make a corresponding case against the increased power of sportsmen and women to dictate terms to sports administrators. For it is this increase in power within sport, less often criticised within the sporting community than legal intrusion into its sphere of influence, that leads the sporting community more frequently than in the past to seek advice and representation from lawyers.[102]

In sum, it is this fault line—the interface of sport's historical regulatory and administrative freedom and sport's various 'economic effects'—that is crucial to an understanding of the theoretical and practical expression of modern sports law.

Sport and the Law or Sports Law?

[1.24]   This text is about the actuality of the interface between sport and the law. In this, the term 'sports law' is used to describe inter alia the collective applications of (a) traditional areas of law, such as contract, tort, criminal, administrative and EU law, to the general circumstances of, and various stakeholders within, modern sport; (b) the particular impact that a range of statutory provisions might have on sport; for example, legislation governing discriminatory and unsafe practices in a workplace or monopolistic or fraudulent behaviour in an industry; (c) issues of public and social policy otherwise influencing the legislature and the courts, from the allocation of resources to the allocation of risk; and (d) *lex sportiva*, where that term is taken to portray the co-existence of the various internal administrative regulations and dispute-resolving mechanisms of sport with domestic,

---

[102] M Beloff, T Kerr and M Demetriou, *Sports Law* (Oxford, Hart Publishing, 1999) 6. *Cf* Grayson, *Sport and the Law* (n 9) who had the more idealistic view that law and lawyers could, almost in a fiduciary manner, assist sport in returning to its traditional Corinthian values of fair play and integrity. Whether sport was ever truly Corinthian in nature, and whether the (adversarial nature) of the law is the most suitable mechanism in fulfilling Grayson's laudable objective, is doubtful; nevertheless, it must be acknowledged that Grayson's work in highlighting the role of law in sport should be appreciated as seminal in nature.

supra-national and international law. It must be noted that a number of leading commentators contend that the relationship between sport and the law is now more than the occasional and casual tryst and that it should, more properly, be regarded as a discrete, stand-alone and substantive union worthy of dedicated legal analysis ('sports law'). This quibbling over semantics can be somewhat distracting in the sense that irrespective of the label that attaches—from this chapter onwards the terms are used interchangeably—it is hoped that the empirical evidence contained in this book and others, demonstrates that examples of the intertwining of principles of law and practices of sport are increasing in frequency and deepening in sophistication. Nevertheless, for the sake of completeness the 'sport and the law vs. sports law' debate is addressed briefly in three ways: a slight preference for the former 'applied' approach to sport and the law; an acknowledgement that the indications are that the latter, that is, the use of the term 'sports law', might soon be warranted; but that in the immediate, a rationale that might assist in predicting the *substance* of the law's influence on matters 'beyond the touchline', rather than the *form* by which that influence is described, is of much greater importance for the future good governance of sport. This last factor not only forms the conclusion to this chapter as a whole, it also is a theme that is returned to, in a slightly different setting (EU law), in the final chapter of this book.

[**1.25**]   The process by which an area of the law evolves to the point that it is viewed as a discrete part of the general law is one that is very much dependent on the vagaries of history, economic developments and political preferences.[103] There is no equivalent of the IOC within the common law whereby an area of law can lobby for official recognition or even associated status, though it of interest to note that 'sport' is not one of the 150 or so sub-headings within *Halsbury's Laws of England*, which includes well-thumbed sections on the law relating to 'Library and Other Scientific and Cultural Institutions' and the law on 'Weights and Measures'. Although issues of sport and the law do appear sporadically throughout *Halsbury's Laws*, the absence of a dedicated sports law section appears to reaffirm the argument made by Gardiner and Beloff, amongst others, that until sports law is recognised as a discrete, mature, intellectually rigorous and theoretically coherent legal discipline, it will remain at the margins as an esoteric area of law providing the occasional snapshot of other more substantial areas of the law.[104] The sincerity of this argument notwithstanding, it is countered that the contention that there is now an autonomous corpus of law called sports law is not yet entirely convincing, and is undermined by three reasons all related to the premature use of the term. In short, although the indications are that sports law is evolving rapidly, it might be more pragmatic at this point to recognise that the subject is still at a very nascent stage in its development.

---

[103] See, eg, the account of the sometimes inconsistent and illogical nature of the evolution of the law of torts, contract law and unjust enrichment by D Ibbetson, *A Historical Introduction to the Law of Obligations* (Oxford, Oxford University Press, 1999).

[104] See generally Beloff *et al* (n 102) ch 1 and S Gardiner *et al*, *Sports Law*, 3rd edn (London, Cavendish, 2006) 39–40 and 88–93.

[1.26]   On the first point, there is merit in Cox and Schuster's argument that this debate is an 'abstraction' because in reality, 'the totality of the law can simply be divided into public and private law and so-called branches of law may be viewed simply as applications of each.'[105] It follows that the preference for the term 'sport and the law' or 'sports law' is really one of emphasis. For instance, although there is little doubt that an analysis of the House of Lords decision in *Bolton v Stone*[106] would be incomplete without reference to its sporting context, that context of itself hardly merits the case being labelled as one concerning sports law.[107] The better approach might be to understand that the interface of sport and the law is premised on the application of established legal principles to the circumstances of disputes involving sport participants, clubs and governing bodies while at the same time recognising, as a former Lord Chief Justice has recognised, that the application of those principles to the circumstances of sport do on occasion result in *legal difficulties discrete to sport.*[108]

[1.27]   On the second point, and as Beloff has acknowledged, the mere labelling of this area as 'sports law' does little to address the fact that sports law remains 'a field which has yet to be subject to thorough treatment from a theoretical perspective.'[109] Thus far, Parrish has probably made the most sophisticated and successful attempt at providing a conceptual framework for the study of sports law, albeit one written within the context of EU law and policy.[110] This text does not attempt to address the 'under-theorisation' of sports law except to state that it might still be somewhat premature to establish a model of theoretical coherency and certainty for this emerging branch of the law, in the sense that it might be better to permit the subject to develop a little of its own accord, as others have done. For example, company law took a number of decades to emerge before any meaningful, functional theory of corporatisation was attempted and even then predicating the legal rights and duties surrounding the 'legal personality' of a company on its relationship with key stakeholders was seen of more practical importance than attempting to explain the development of corporate law through a single unifying theoretical analysis.[111] In this regard, it is also of interest to note the recent attempt by Stevens to posit a reductionist account of the law of torts when he argued that a rights-based approach can be identified as the primary

---

[105] Cox and Schuster (n 30) 6.

[106] *Bolton v Stone* [1951] AC 850 (an injury resulting from a cricket ball struck onto an adjacent public road could not sustain a claim of negligence for want of reasonable foreseeability).

[107] See generally M Lunney, 'Six and Out? Bolton v Stone After 50 Years' (2003) 24 *Journal of Legal History* 1.

[108] Foreword to Lewis and Taylor (n 8) *v*, Lord Wolf LCJ.

[109] Beloff *et al* (n 102) 15.

[110] R Parrish, *Sports Law and Policy in the European Union* (Manchester, Manchester University Press, 2003) ch 2.

[111] See generally E Fruend, *The Legal Nature of Corporations* (Chicago, Chicago University Press, 1897); W Geldart, *Legal Personality* (1911) 27 LQR 90; A Machen, *Corporate Personality* (1911) 24 *Harvard Law Review* 253 and 347; and J Dewey, *The Historic Background of Corporate Legal Personality* (1926) 35 *Yale Law Journal* 655.

norm, goal, principle or 'reductionist' feature underpinning the disparate and sometimes haphazard causes of action that comprise the law of torts.[112] In criticism of that approach, Murphy highlights a point that has analogy to the debate on the (under) theorisation of sports law:

> … sight must not be lost of the fact that the virtues of such reductionist theories seem never to be unaccompanied by a number of salient problems that sooner or later call into question the overall value of the theory as a whole. Accordingly, it seems wise to approach [reductionist approaches to law] with the aphoristic advice of Alfred North Whitehead in mind: that we should both 'seek simplicity, and distrust it'.[113]

[1.28]   The third point regarding the supposed autonomy of sports law is more a clarification than a criticism, and it concerns the Latin nomenclature *lex sportiva*. There is no doubt that both in its play element and in its administrative element, sport is an extremely rule-bound activity, and combined with sport's long standing freedom to self-regulate, this means that the governance of professional sport in particular is characterised by a highly sophisticated system of internal regulation. For instance, in football, FIFA's international reach from its headquarters in Switzerland to the local soccer pitch in England is based not only on the 140 pages of the Laws of the Game of Football (2009/2010 season); the 88 pages of FIFA's Statutes and Regulations (August 2009 edition); the 76 pages of its Disciplinary Code (2009 edition); the 52 pages of its Regulations on the Status and Transfer of Players (October 2009); but it also stretches through a series of supranational (UEFA), national (the FA) and regional or local associations, all with their own internal regulatory regimes and relationships.[114] Moreover, this pyramid of governance must also take into account football's adherence to external bodies such as the World Anti-Doping Agency (WADA) and the remit of the International Court of Arbitration for Sport (CAS). In short, the density of regulation within the organisation of a sport such as football is remarkable and unsurprisingly it often appears quasi-legal in substance and even overtly legalistic in interpretation.

[1.29]   The jurisprudence of CAS acting *qua* the 'Supreme Court of Sport' is now especially influential, particularly in the manner in which its accompanying jurisprudence is facilitating a process of harmonisation thus benefitting the more efficient and equitable resolution of disputes throughout the sporting world. The impact and import of this jurisprudence is such that it is often labelled *lex sportiva*.[115] In this respect, there is however a note of caution. Although CAS has a wide jurisdictional remit with respect to the type of sports-related disputes it can hear; although its decisions are binding and enforceable upon the immediate

---

[112] R Stevens, *Torts and Rights* (Oxford University Press, Oxford, 2007).

[113] J Murphy, 'Rights Reductionism and Tort Law' (2008) 28 *QJLS* 393, 407.

[114] All FIFA-related documents are available through the 'official documents' section of www.fifa.com.

[115] The use of the term *lex sportiva* can probably be first attributed to the Secretary General of CAS, Matthieu Reeb. See, eg, M Reeb, 'The Role of the Court of Arbitration for Sport' in W Heere (ed), *International Law and The Hague's 750th Anniversary* (The Hague, TMC Asser Press, 1999).

parties; although its jurisprudence is incrementally forming a body of precedent useful in resolving sports disputes more generally; this *lex sportiva* is not law as ordinarily understood. It is an arbitral expression only of the internal regulation of sport, and outside of this limited meaning; the phrase *lex sportiva* should be avoided. To reiterate, this book is devoted primarily to situations where 'ordinary' law (domestic, EU and international), as administered through the civil and criminal justice systems (of England and Wales, etc), interacts with disputes of a sporting nature. It follows that the *lex sportiva* of CAS, though subject to a dedicated review in chapter three of the text, is generally of secondary concern to this book's study of sports *law*.

[**1.30**]　　In summary, although this book uses the descriptive term sports law, it does not follow that sports law is, as of yet, worthy of being depicted as a discrete, autonomous branch of law. It may be a relatively conservative approach to take but it is argued that a purely sports law discourse will not be established until such time as the courts or the legislature adjust accepted legal principles because what is at issue is sporting in nature.[116] Nevertheless, the *indications* are that sports law is moving rapidly in that direction. Three signals are particularly evident.[117] First, and picking up a point made in the preface of this text, sports law is, similar to emerging disciplines (such as cyberspacelaw) an engaging (and enjoyable!) means of teaching the geographical limitations of traditional law and the necessarily global jurisdiction within which 'law' must now operate. So, for example, some have noted that the nature of global administrative law can be explained through the relationship between powerful non-state private regulatory actors operating with their own sophisticated arbitral regimes of dispute resolution (such as the IOC/CAS) and national public law.[118] Similarly, topics such as the personal inter-dependent nature of contracts of employment (chapter seven); and even the free movement of workers and provision of services within the EU (chapter eight), can all be explained clearly and innovatively with reference to sports law. It follows that an appreciation of the 'specificity' of sports law might relate to whether one considers unusual applications of existing legal doctrine and public policy to be sufficient *of themselves* to serve as the foundation for the recognition of a discrete branch of law.[119]

---

[116] It appears that in the US sports law had long since crossed this threshold of recognition. See further D Lazaroff, 'The Influence of Sports Law on American Jurisprudence' (2001) 1 *Virginia Sports and Entertainment Law Journal* 1.

[117] Sports law is not the only putative branch of law that is suffering this debate. See also the internal discussion within environmental law as introduced by T Aagaard, 'Environmental Law as a Legal Field: An Inquiry in Legal Taxonomy' (2010) 95 *Cornell Law Review* 221 and J Wexler, 'The (Non)Uniqueness of Environmental Law' (2006) 74 *George Washington Law Review* 260.

[118] Note, eg, the discussion of sports law in the context of global administrative law by A Van Vaerenbergh, 'Institute for International Law and Justice Working Paper 2005/11: Regulatory Features and Administrative Law Dimensions of the Olympic Movement's Anti-doping Regime' (Global Administrative Law Series, New York University School of Law, 2005).

[119] See the analogy to cyberspacelaw by J Sommer, 'Against Cyberlaw' (2000) 15 *Berkeley Technology Law Journal* 1145, 1149: '… applying our old law to cyberspace … can be an excellent lens for seeing other things. It is not, however, a particularly useful focal plane of legal analysis.'

[1.31] The second signal relates to the fact that sports law is much more than an example of so-called 'soft law'—regulatory instruments of governance produced by a multiplicity of public and private actors, which, while indicating a normative commitment, do not rely on a regime of formal binding sanctions.[120] In fact, the indication is that sports law as a discrete field of law is 'hardening' around the premise that it addresses the legal treatment of a distinct set of relations. The analogy here is with family law and a point made by succinctly by Elhauge:

> Consider family law, which addresses the legal framework of relations between family members. Here, ordinary rules of contracts, torts, and property are often varied in ways that subordinate them to understandings of what best advances the interests of familial relations. And although one could try to separately address each of these areas, there does seem to be some value added by thinking through how common issues regarding the family affect each of the legal doctrines that bear on familial relations.[121]

Elhauge applies his 'value added' approach to the coherency of 'health law', but it is an approach that also lends itself to a straightforward definition of sports law—sports law addresses a unique set of relations among persons and undertakings involved in the playing and organisation of sport.

[1.32] The third signal as to the robustness of sports law is an altogether more practical one. A number of leading practitioners in the area argue that the debate on the discreteness of sports law is an abstraction and of academic concern only.[122] Their approach is premised on the fact that irrespective of whether the legal principles applied to problems of a sporting nature are now sufficiently homogeneous to warrant their identification as a separate branch of law, these problems are arising with greater frequency and complexity thus clients (sports participants, clubs and associations) are demanding tailored legal advice. At its narrowest therefore, a practitioner can argue that there is no such thing as sports law, merely the business of sport and the manner in which the legal profession services that industry. There is some merit in this analysis, nevertheless, the inherent logic of offering quality legal advice pertaining to sports-related problems (and also, presumably, the capacity to produce quality academic commentary) implies a specialised knowledge of the relationship between sport and the law with respect not only to the narrow commercial realities of elite modern sport but also to its long-standing, self-regulatory structures and its broader societal role as a popular, recreational activity. In simple terms, and with due regard to the aforementioned commercial, regulatory and societal aspect of sport, it is difficult to deny the fact the sports law 'has arrived' in light of the reality that it is being

---

[120] See generally A Robilant, 'Genealogies of Soft Law' (2006) 54 *American Journal of Comparative Law* 499.

[121] E Elhague, 'Can Health Law Become a Coherent Field of Law? (2006) 41 *Wake Forest Law Review* 365, 369.

[122] Note, eg, Griffith Jones, (n 8) *vii*.

taught in law schools, written about by academics and practitioners, practised by dedicated units in law firms and, as demonstrated sharply by the next chapter, litigated in the courts.

Conclusion

[1.33]   This chapter has argued that, although the historical origins of modern sports law can be traced through the paradigm of the civilising process, the contemporary nature of sports law is now largely, though not exclusively, determined by the continuing commercialisation and commodification of sport. The chapter has also outlined that this book's preferred analysis of sports law is empirical rather than outwardly theoretical in nature. Accordingly, the underlying idea of this book is not to seek a unitary reductionist theory of sports law but to elaborate upon the multiple functions that the various branches of law (contract, tort, administrative law, etc) serve in relation to sport, and the implications that this interaction has for the playing and administration of modern sport. In this, the reply to the question what is sports law, might be framed best by way of analogy to family law: the legal regulation of the unique set of relations and specifically the various grievances that arise from time to time in sport including inter alia problems relating to unacceptable levels of violence, inequality or unfairness. Arguably however, the more important question is what role does, and should, the law have in sport? In a general sense, the response to this question is located in a standard threefold critique of the instrumental role of law: law's role is adjudicatory and/or supervisory and/or ameliorative. The adjudicatory role of law is where the law's function is to resolve conflicts that arise in the given setting; the supervisory role is where the law's task is to provide a stable framework for human and corporate interaction in the given setting; and the ameliorative role accounts for the law's responsibility to promote social justice and equality.[123] It is not difficult to isolate instances in which the law fulfils these roles in relation to sport, and a myriad of examples are given throughout this book. In contrast, it is much more difficult to identify the boundary as to when the law's (multi-functional) role in sport should end. For instance, is there a 'purely' sporting sphere of rule and regulation or are all aspects of sport, particularly those to which an economic effect may attach, subject to the 'Law's Empire'? This debate is currently played out in the context of EU law, and is returned to in the concluding chapter of this text.[124] At this point, it suffices to express the wish that the threshold to the law's role in sport might adhere to Braithwaite's test of 'responsive regulation':

---

[123] See generally S Smith, 'Reductionism in Legal Thought' (1991) 91 *Columbia Law Review* 68.
[124] See, eg, Case C-519/04 P *Meca Medina and Majcen v Commission* [2006] ECR I-6991, discussed in context by S Weatherill, 'Anti-doping Revisited: The Demise of "Purely Sporting" Interest' (2006) 27 *European Competition Law Review* 645.

Governments should be responsive to the conduct of those they seek to regulate in deciding whether a more or less interventionist response is needed. In particular, law enforcers should be more responsive to how effectively citizens or corporations are regulating themselves before deciding whether to escalate interventions.[125]

It might not always be possible to reconcile the law's 'responsiveness' with the 'internal' regulatory structures of sport nor, of course, might it be proper to deny an aggrieved party 'external' access to the ordinary courts, nevertheless (and as the next chapter illustrates) in the event that an ostensibly sporting matter does become the subject of formal litigation, it is hoped that in exercising its role, the judiciary might display a light and restrained touch. After all, sport is principally about playing, not litigating.

Further Points of Interest and Discussion

1. Is chess a sport?
2. How do you think the 'civilising process' might be reconciled with so-called 'ultimate' and 'cage' fighting contests?
3. What do you think of Beloff's contention that the growth of legalism in sport is borne of a desire for higher standards of justice?
4. If the law of torts is the law of civil wrongs, might the most succinct definition of sports law be that it concerns the law of sporting wrongs?
5. On reading *Tomlinson v Congleton Borough Council* [2004] 1 AC 46, do you consider it one of the rare instances when the House of Lords had to consider a matter of 'sports law'? Why do you think that matters pertaining to sports law have so rarely been considered by the House of Lords?

---

[125] J Braithwaite, *Restorative Justice and Responsive Regulation* (Oxford, Oxford University Press, 2002) 29.

2

Challenging Decisions of Sports Governing Bodies

Introduction

[2.01] This chapter considers the various ways in which decisions within the disciplinary remit of sports governing bodies might be challenged in the courts. The emphasis is on challenges by individual athletes and the chapter's narrative is presented around litigation taken by three individuals: an athlete, Diane Modahl; one of the leading horse racing owners in Britain, the Aga Khan; and a jockey, Graham Bradley. It will be seen that common to all three challenges is a frustration arising from the belief that the relevant internal disciplinary procedures had been applied unfairly by the governing sports body and/or had resulted in an irrational, disproportionate sanction. Until recently, legal challenges of this nature were relatively infrequent and, on the odd occasion when they did eventuate, were almost exclusively characterised by their private law (contractual) basis. The chapter subjects this orthodoxy to further examination and raises five points of interest; all of which are discussed against the reality that the increasingly commercial nature of sport, encompassing a professional athlete's right to earn a livelihood, has witnessed an end to the previous reticence towards such litigation.

[2.02] The first point of interest, and one that is evident from the Diane Modahl litigation, is that the principal means of challenging a decision of a sports body's disciplinary mechanism is by way of an allegation of procedural unfairness such that the implication of a contractual duty to act fairly has been breached. In *Modahl*, the main allegation centred on a specific claim of bias against members of the disciplining tribunal but 'procedural unfairness' can also encompass allegations that the disciplining body in question either did not have the jurisdiction to hear the case; or did not properly instruct itself to the facts; or denied the participant the right to make representations during the course of the disciplinary hearing; or had, in sanction, acted disproportionately or irrationally.[1] All of these

---

[1] For an interesting general application of these principles note the Tribunal de Grand Instance de Paris's decision to quash the lifetime ban imposed on the former Renault Formula 1 boss Falvio Briatore by F1's governing body, the FIA. Briatore was banned by the FIA for his part in Nelson Piquet Junior's deliberate crash at the 2008 Singapore Grand Prix. See generally the report by D Tremayne, 'Briatore in Clear as Court Overturns Crashgate Ban' *The Independent* (London 6 January 2010) Sport 58.

allegations of procedural irregularity in breach of the principles of natural justice are discussed in light of the standard expected by the courts of domestic sporting tribunals, namely, that the process as a whole ends in a 'fair result'. The second point that arises, again from *Modahl*, is a brief consideration of the nature and depth of the contractual relationship between an individual participant in a sport, his or her club and the relevant national and international governing bodies. This legal nexus is crucial, both in a procedural and substantive sense, because whatever other remedies the claimant might have, in the absence of contract, there can be no claim for damages.

[**2.03**]   Third, outside of a challenge seeking to enforce a contractual obligation to act fairly, a number of sports participants have argued that decisions of sports bodies might be amenable to judicial review on the basis that they are sufficiently within the 'public interest'. The susceptibility of sports bodies to public law review is examined through a review of the litigation taken by the Aga Khan against the Jockey Club in the 1990s. The approach of the Court of Appeal in that instance, which has since been applied on a number of occasions by the High Court, is that it appears to wholly preclude public law review. The fourth point of concern is that this is not, for three reasons, an entirely accurate portrayal of the courts' potential to question the decision-making competency of private sports bodies. For instance, a claimant's inability to pursue 'formal' judicial review notwithstanding, it might remain open to the aggrieved participant to appeal to the inherent supervisory jurisdiction of the courts over domestic tribunals. Moreover, it is suggested that in the near future this debate will move on to consider the repercussions of a finding that a sports body is, pursuant to section 6 of the Human Rights Act 1998, a 'hybrid' public authority. In any event, where a claimant is 'confined' to private law proceedings, proceedings such as those involving the jockey, Graham Bradley clearly demonstrate that the standard of review undertaken by the courts is now similar, in language and in substance, to judicial review proceedings. The fifth section of this chapter moves away somewhat from the procedural issues relating to the private/public law divide and considers the fundamental, substantive premise of the majority of these proceedings: unreasonable restraint of the claimant's 'right to work'.

Diane Modahl

[**2.04**]   As Lewis and Taylor note succinctly, it is 'a well-established proposition' that the rules of a sports governing body constitute a contract between the members of the sports governing body, and between each member and the sports governing body itself such that perceived breaches of those rules can therefore 'be the subject of legal action in the normal way'.[2] Issues such as the nature of

---

[2] A Lewis and J Taylor, *Sport: Law and Practice*, 2nd edn (London, Tottel Publishing, 2008) 225.

the contract (express or implied); the parties who might be privy to its scope (the international governing body; the national governing body; a club; and a member); and the extent of the review that will be carried out by a court for breach of such a contract were discussed in detail during the course of the *Modahl* litigation. The background to these lengthy proceedings originates in the testing of a then leading British athlete, Diane Modahl, after an athletics meeting in Portugal in the summer of 1994.[3] The test appeared to reveal levels of testosterone in breach of the International Amateur Athletic Federation's (IAAF) code on doping. This initiated a disciplinary process administered initially by the British Athletics Federation (BAF), the then national governing body for athletics in Britain, which acted as the representative affiliated member for the UK at the IAAF.[4]

[**2.05**]   In August 1994, Diane Modahl, a world class middle distance runner, and defending 800 metres Commonwealth champion, was in Canada undertaking the final stages of her preparations for that month's Commonwealth Games. Modahl would not however get to compete in Victoria, after being informed that a urine sample she had given after a relatively low key event at the Lisbon University Stadium in June 1994 had recorded a testosterone level well above that permissible by the then anti-doping provisions of the sport. Modahl returned to England and by early September it was confirmed that her 'B' sample had recorded a similar analytical result to her 'A' sample. Modahl was suspended pending a hearing of a BAF Disciplinary Committee in December 1994. The BAF Disciplinary Committee unanimously found that a doping offence had been committed. Modhal appealed to the BAF's Independent Appeal Panel (IAP). That appeal, which was heard in July 1995, was upheld unanimously and Modahl was reinstated from 26 July 1995. In early 1996, Modahl issued civil proceedings against the BAF claiming that she had suffered loss and expense as a result of her disqualification. This element of the claim is noteworthy because it highlights an underlying element that underpins many of these cases. The career of an elite professional athlete is quite short and precarious; rarely will an athlete remain competitive at the lucrative elite level for two or more Olympic cycles ie, eight years. It follows that the nine-month suspension was, in relative terms, quite a lengthy and potentially financially debilitating one for Modahl. In a technical sense, Modahl's grounds of complaint were twofold. First, that the laboratory which carried out the analysis of her urine samples was not properly accredited to do so under the applicable doping regulations and therefore did not permit the BAF to institute disciplinary proceedings. In this light, Modhal argued forcefully

---

[3] See similarly the litigation that ensued when the then world record holder at 400 metres, Harry 'Butch' Reynolds, tested positive for steroids in 1990, culminating in a federal court of appeals judgment denying that the IAAF was amendable to suit in Reynolds' home state of Ohio, *Reynolds v International Amateur Athletic Federation* 23 F 3d 1110, United States Court of Appeal for the Sixth Circuit (1994) cert. denied 115 S Ct 423 (1994).

[4] For an insight into attitudes amongst elite athletes to doping at that time see further D McArdle, '"Say it ain't so Mo" International Performers' Perceptions of Drug Use and the Diane Modhal Affair' in J O'Leary (ed), *Drugs and Doping in Sport: Socio-Legal Perspectives* (London, Cavendish, 2000).

that the BAF's regulations (in this instance, the BAF's procedures surrounding anti-doping violations) formed a contract between her and the BAF and that the BAF was in breach of that contract by not, as its regulations expressly required, processing the urine sample at an accredited laboratory. Second, Modahl alleged bias against certain members of the BAF Disciplinary Committee. Under this part of the claim, Modahl contended that it was an implied term of the BAF's regulations (specifically, the BAF's rules governing its disciplinary mechanisms) that a party to those disciplinary proceedings would act neither with bias nor with the appearance of bias; but that this had not been the case.

The Popplewell Principle

[**2.06**] In counterclaim, the BAF argued that as Modahl was ultimately exonerated by its disciplinary process, her action should be dismissed for disclosing no reasonable cause of action. In *Modahl v British Athletic Federation Limited*,[5] Popplewell J rejected the application to strike out and, with specific reference to the two central aspects of Modahl's claim, analysed succinctly the approach a court should take in cases of challenges to the decision-making authority of a domestic [non-statutory] sporting tribunal.[6] First, on reviewing the approach of three previous Vice-Chancellors,[7] Popplewell J held that generally a court should be slow to interfere with the findings of fact of 'an independent tribunal [which has] the experience of matters. But it does have the right to interfere where a point of law is involved, or where there is alleged to be a breach of natural justice'.[8] Consequently, although the concepts of natural justice and the duty to be fair should not be permitted to 'discredit themselves by making unreasonable requirements and imposing undue burden'[9] on sporting bodies who seek to promote a socially beneficial activity through better regulation, neither should, according to Popplewell J, a sports body through its rules, or through an ultra vires misinterpretation of its rules, be permitted to 'contract out' of the principles of fairness and consistency, particularly where the resulting detriment might deprive a person of their livelihood.[10] This general principle prompted Popplewell J to

---

[5] *Modahl v British Athletic Federation Limited* Unreported, Queen's Bench Division 28 June 1996, Popplewell J.

[6] It should be reiterated that the authority of the 'Popplewell' principle must be seen in context of the case at hand, which was merely a decision that Modahl's claim should not be struck out, since it was capable of succeeding. It was not a decision that Modahl's claim should in fact succeed.

[7] *McInnes v Onslow-Fane* [1978] 1 WLR 1520, Megarry VC; *Cowley v Heatley*, *The Times* 24 July 1986, Brown-Wilkinson J; *Gasser v Stinson*, Unreported, Queen's Bench Division 15 June 1988, Scott J.

[8] *Modahl* Unreported, Queen's Bench Division 28 June 1996, Popplewell J, 8 (official transcript). See also *Enderby Town FC v Football Association* [1971] Ch 591, 605, Lord Denning MR.

[9] See similarly *McInnes v Onslow-Fane* [1978] 1 WLR 1520, 1535, Megarry VC.

[10] Citing with approval from *Lee v The Showmen's Guild of Great Britain* [1952] 2 QB 329, 342, Denning LJ. The basic principle appears to be that where, in circumstances in which a person's livelihood might depend upon membership of a voluntary association, a decision of a domestic tribunal expelling that person from membership was made without good faith or dishonestly, the Court should

surmise that the initial part of Modahl's claim (founded on the use by the athletics authorities of an unaccredited laboratory) could not be said to be a frivolous one. More importantly, and as will be shown throughout this chapter, the sound public policy reasons underpinning the Popplewell principle (that a sports body cannot contract out of the duty to act fairly and with intra vires consistency to the applicable rules) also remains good law on the supervisory approach of the ordinary courts to domestic tribunals of a sporting nature.

[**2.07**]   Popplewell J's consideration of the second allegation, the allegation of bias, also confronted a contention that is raised frequently in the review of decisions of sporting tribunals. The matter was not so much with the test that might apply to ascertaining actual or perceived bias;[11] it was with the well-established principle in law that a defect in procedure can be cured by a subsequent independent de novo appeal ie, that where there is a full appeal by way of a rehearing of the case on its merits, that will normally cure procedural errors in the tribunal appealed from.[12] Thus, in the stated case, the BAF argued that by having a full, impartial, de novo hearing before the IAP, any question of alleged bias by individual members of the BAF Disciplinary Committee should be taken to have gone. Popplewell J, who did not have to comment on the substantive nature of this allegation, did however make an important accompanying point, observing that it seemed to him that 'though it may be that the actual decision has been cured in one sense by the subsequent hearing, the *consequences* of it are not necessarily cured'.[13] This point went to the heart of Modahl's argument: the *consequence* of the alleged procedural defects in the initial hearing was (notwithstanding her ultimate exoneration on appeal) that she remained suspended from her profession for a nine-month period in 1995, suffering loss and expense as a result.

The De Novo Cure

[**2.08**]   Popplewell J with the agreement of both parties gave leave to appeal his dismissal of the BAF's striking out application, which was heard by the Court of Appeal in July 1997.[14] In his judgment, Lord Woolf MR quickly came to the point

---

intervene. See here *Cater v NSW Netball Association* [2004] NSWSC 737 [100]-[109], Palmer J, where it was held, quite rightly, that the consequence of a mala fides decision of a domestic tribunal can also affect the claimant's livelihood in a number of indirect ways by, eg, damaging their reputation in the community and their self-esteem. In the stated case, the claimant was a coach who was, in effect, accused of child abuse by a sports disciplinary committee. The claimant successfully sought a declaration that the decision was invalid and of no effect.

[11] For that test see *Flaherty v National Greyhound Racing Club Limited* [2005] EWCA Civ 1117 [26]-[28], Scott-Baker LJ.

[12] See *Calder and the Visitors of the Inns of Court* [1994] QB 1, 58, Stuart-Smith LJ.

[13] *Modahl* Unreported, Queen's Bench Division 28 June 1996, Popplewell J, 14–15 (official transcript).

[14] *Modahl v British Athletic Federation Limited* [1997] EWCA Civ 2209, Lord Woolf MR, Morritt and Pill LJJ.

of the matter at hand—that as a result of breaches of the contract that existed between the parties (based on the BAF's and IAAF's disciplinary and anti-doping regulations) the claimant was alleging the she was put to expense in connection with two disciplinary hearings and that but for the stated breaches of contract (the accreditation issue and the allegation of bias) Modahl would have earned the sum of £230,708 during the period of suspension. Lord Woolf MR, applying Denning LJ's 'true construction' test to the applicable anti-doping provisions, held that it was not unreasonable to hold that the analysis of a sample by an accredited laboratory was not a condition precedent to BAF's power to suspend.[15] Moreover, the then Master of the Rolls went on to observe that the BAF had not deliberately chosen an unaccredited laboratory and that, consistent with the general scheme of the BAF's and the IAAF's anti-doping scheme, the procedural departure in question was not such that it cast doubt on the substantive reliability of the analysis of the sample. Lord Woolf MR (Morritt and Pill LLJ concurring) moved to strike out the pleaded accreditation cause of action. This was appealed to the House of Lords.[16] Lord Hoffmann, delivering the judgment of the House, noted that, although there was no doubt that the IAAF's anti-doping policy was 'draconian' in nature and carried the risk of 'grave injustice' to an athlete if a laboratory test was wrong, in the stated case, the lack of accreditation objection was of little merit within the overall procedural context of the BAF's and IAAF's anti-doping scheme.

[**2.09**]   In sum, Modahl's contention to the House of Lords was that by not giving the IAAF notice that it had moved premises to a new site, the laboratory should have been taken to have lost its accreditation status, thus no disciplinary jurisdiction could follow. Echoing the Court of Appeal's view that it was not as if the laboratory had moved to 'a potting shed' (it being uncontested that the laboratory had retained all of its capacities and services at the new site) and that in any event the BAF had initiated its disciplinary proceedings in good faith, Lord Hoffmann dismissed Modahl's appeal. The frivolity of this part of Modahl's claim aside, there is an important underlying aspect to Lord Hoffmann's judgment, which is applicable to the general theme of this chapter: although it is always advisable that such errors should be avoided, minor technical departures from procedural guidelines, which have no material bearing on the substantive outcome of the matter, should not be permitted to found 'capricious' legal challenges to the decisions of sports tribunals.

[**2.10**]   Returning to the Court of Appeal, all three judges of the Court of Appeal decided not to strike out the pleaded allegation of bias. In referring to the

---

[15] *Lee v Showmen's Guild of GB* [1952] 2 QB 329, 344, Denning LJ, a court 'cannot permit a domestic tribunal to deprive a member of his livelihood or to injure him in it, unless the contract, on its true construction gives the tribunal power to do so … and … I desire to emphasise that the true construction of a contract is to be decided by the courts and no one else.'

[16] *Modahl v British Athletic Federation Limited* [1999] UKHL 37. The Modahl proceedings therefore join the very limited number of 'sports law' cases heard by the House of Lords.

BAF's contention that the perfectly proper de novo hearing before the IAP cured any (bias) defect in the proceedings from the Disciplinary Committee, Lord Woolf MR, using the established principle of public law, noted that normally defects will be cured by the right of full appeal and that many private regulatory schemes (including the BAF rules) anticipate that such a situation might arise by giving power to remit for a new hearing.[17] In this, the then Master of the Rolls referred to the Privy Council's decision in *Calvin v Carr*.[18] In that case, the claimant (the part-owner of a racehorse that had been disqualified by the stewards of the Australian Jockey Club for breach of the applicable rules of racing) had exercised his right of appeal to the Committee of the Australian Jockey Club. The key issue was whether, by conducting a hearing de novo, the Committee had cured the alleged procedural defects of the stewards' inquiry. In delivering the judgment of the Privy Council, Lord Wilberforce established the parameters around which the duty of a private sports body to act fairly within the reasonable construction of its disciplinary rules may be viewed. Lord Wilberforce recognised that the decision of the stewards, resulting in disqualification, had serious economic and reputational consequences for the claimant and that there were cases where the defect is so flagrant and the consequence so severe, that the most perfect of appeals or rehearing will not be sufficient to produce a just result. Equally his Lordship warned that 'it is undesirable in many cases of domestic disputes, particularly in which an inquiry and appeal process has been established, to introduce too great a measure of formal judicialisation. While flagrant cases of injustice, including corruption or bias, must always be firmly dealt with by the courts, the tendency in their Lordships' opinion in matter of domestic disputes should be to leave these to be settled by the agreed methods without requiring the formalities of judicial processes to be introduced'.[19] Crucially, Lord Wilberforce was of the opinion that 'the conclusion to be reached on the rules and on the contractual context, is that those who have joined an organisation, or contract, should be taken to have agreed to accept *what in the end is a fair decision*, notwithstanding some initial defect'.[20]

A Fair Decision

[**2.11**]   Applying the fair decision principle to the case at hand, Lord Wilberforce (Morritt and Pill LJJ concurring) noted that Modahl was evidently not seeking to set aside the ultimate decision of the IAP, which found in her favour, but that she was seeking compensation for the *consequences* of a defect (bias) at the initial stage in the disciplinary process, which the overall procedure could not have avoided. In short, the alleged bias at the Disciplinary Committee stage might well have cured the original bias but of more concern to Modahl was that in the intervening seven

---

[17] *Modahl* [1997] EWCA Civ 2209, citing *Lloyd v McMahon* [1987] 1 AC 625.
[18] *Calvin v Carr* [1980] AC 574.
[19] Ibid 593.
[20] Ibid, italics inserted.

to nine-month wait for exoneration, she had not been permitted to compete at, or earn from, her profession. On this ground, the Court of Appeal agreed that a full trial of the bias issue could proceed. That trial took place in December 2000.[21] The High Court, affirmed on appeal by the Court of Appeal,[22] held that an implied element of the contractual nature of the applicable BAF rules was a 'duty to act fairly' and that ultimately, and thanks to the decision of the IAP, that duty had been discharged. Both the High Court and the Court of Appeal noted that the IAP had reversed the decision of the Disciplinary Committee because, and only because, consistent with its de novo status, the IAP had permitted, and was convinced by, evidence that Modahl's sample might have suffered some sort of bacterial contamination. The Court of Appeal also held that, although a member of the Disciplinary Committee might have been somewhat prejudiced in his approach, this did not, in an overall sense, affect or infect the integrity of the Committee's decision as based on the facts presented to them.[23] In sum, the Court of Appeal was satisfied that the BAF's disciplinary process had eventually concluded in 'a fair result'.[24]

[**2.12**]   Overall, it is suggested that the 'what in the end is a fair decision' principle, as construed against the relevant regulatory background of the body in question, is a good and workable guideline to take in assessing the merits of a private law challenge to the decision of sports disciplinary tribunal. Put another way, the approach can be divided into two parts: (a) that in exercising their decision-making and disciplinary remit, sports bodies are, on pain of judicial scrutiny, under a duty to act fairly in accordance with the principles of natural justice; and (b) that the participant facing such authority has the legitimate expectation that the disciplinary mechanism in question will avoid arbitrary or capricious decision-making at odds with the substantive regulatory and procedural ambit of its rules.[25] The 'fair decision' approach has been seen to good effect in the Court of Appeal's decision in *Flaherty v National Greyhound Racing Club Limited*.[26] In that case, a greyhound trainer challenged a decision by the National Greyhound Racing Club's (NGRC) stewards to reprimand and fine him £400 on a charge of administering a prohibited performance enhancing substance to a dog in his charge contrary to the racing rules of the NGRC, the governing body for the sport of greyhound racing in Britain. Flaherty instigated legal proceedings arguing that the stewards' findings were invalid, ultra vires and otherwise unlawful on the grounds that the disciplinary proceedings against him had been conducted contrary to the principles of natural justice, thus in breach of an implied obligation

---

[21] *Modahl v British Athletic Federation Limited (No 2)* Unreported, Queen's Bench Division 14 December 2000, Douglas Brown J.

[22] *Modahl v British Athletic Federation Limited (No 2)* [2001] EWCA Civ 1447.

[23] Ibid [68] Latham LJ.

[24] Ibid [61] Latham LJ. *Calvin v Carr* applied.

[25] See similarly the approach in *McInnes v Onslow-Fane* [1978] 3 All ER 211; [1978] 1 WLR 1520,1528–30, Megarry VC.

[26] *Flaherty v National Greyhound Racing Club Limited* [2005] EWCA Civ 1117.

of fairness under the contract (namely the NGRC rules) to which Flaherty and the NGRC were parties.[27] The factual background to the case was, after performing well in a preliminary heat, the dog in question had become a favourite for the English Greyhound Derby, one of the most prestigious and richest races of the season. The dog performed poorly in the next heat and thereafter tested positive for a substance called hexamine. A sub-plot to the case was the suggestion that 'persons unknown', and most likely motivated by a gambling scam, had contaminated the dog's foodstuff in order to stop it from performing well.

[**2.13**]   In December 2004, the High Court declared that the stewards' decision had, principally by reason of apparent bias, been reached in breach of the NGRC's implied obligation of fairness under the contract between the parties and thus should be set aside.[28] The NGRC appealed successfully to the Court of Appeal, where in delivering the judgment of the Court, Scott Baker LJ held that, although the High Court stated the law of apparent bias correctly, Evans-Lombe J had applied it erroneously to the facts.[29] The specific issue of bias aside, there are three other aspects of the Scott Baker LJ's judgment which are of interest. First, an underlying element of the judgment is a sensitivity and understanding of the sporting circumstances at hand, which sports bodies, who often reflexively criticise what they perceive to be the increasing legalisation of the administration of sport, would do well to recognise. In this case, as in other racing-related cases, both the Court of Appeal and the High Court had a particular appreciation that the substantive nature of the complaint was not with the relatively minor nature of the sanction but more with the damage to the trainer's reputation (eg, would other dog owners trust in the care of their animals in the future?) and associated commercial losses relating to the fact that if the dog had gone on to win the Derby his stud value would have been greatly enhanced.[30] Second, Scott Baker LJ's judgment demonstrates a forceful appreciation of the fair decision approach of Lord Wilberforce in *Calvin v Carr*, as applied in the *Modahl* litigation.[31] This appreciation is neatly summarised in the penultimate paragraph of Scott Baker LJ's judgment: 'The judge [Evans-Lombe J of the High Court] never confronted the ultimate question of whether the procedural defects that he found had occurred affected the *overall result*.[32] The third noteworthy aspect of the Court of Appeal's decision relates to the patent irritability throughout Scott Baker LJ's judgment

---

[27] *Flaherty v National Greyhound Racing Club Limited* [2004] EWHC 2838 (Ch) Evans-Lombe J.

[28] Ibid [42] where other concerns relating to procedural unfairness were noted, including the allegation that the stewards had come to their conclusion as a result of assumptions not fully disclosed to the claimant in the course of the hearing; that the claimant had not been given an opportunity to have the urine sample independently tested; or to raise matters relating to security video evidence.

[29] *Flaherty v NGRC* [2005] EWCA Civ 1117 [55], Scott Baker LJ.

[30] These factors were also of critical underlying importance in, eg, cases such as *R v Disciplinary Committee of the Jockey Club, ex parte Aga Khan* [1993] 1 WLR 909 and *R (Mullins) v Appeal Board of the Jockey Club* [2005] EWHC 2197 (Admin).

[31] Note the references to the stated cases in *Flaherty v NGRC* [2005] EWCA Civ 1117 [29] and [77]–[79], Scott Baker LJ.

[32] Ibid [80] italics inserted.

that the matter had ever been granted a court hearing. This irritability had two sources, one of which was fact-specific; and one of which, again, reiterates the importance that in cases involving domestic tribunals the courts' supervisory jurisdiction should be de minimis in nature.

[**2.14**] The fact-specific source of Scott-Baker LJ's irritability related to, what even the claimant admitted was, the 'highly improbable' explanation of the positive drug test—that unknown third parties had administered the drug to the dog.[33] The policy-led source of Scott Baker LJ's irritability related to that fact that, although there was no doubt that it was within the courts' inherent jurisdiction to control illegality and make sure that domestic tribunals do not act outside their powers, 'it is not in the interest of sport or anybody else for the courts to seek to double guess regulating bodies in charge of domestic arrangements. Sports regulating bodies ordinarily have unrivalled and practical knowledge of the particular sport that they are required to regulate. They cannot be expected to act in every detail as if they are a court of law. Provided they act lawfully and within the ambit of their powers, *the courts should allow them to get on with the job they are required to do*'.[34] The clarity of the Scott Baker LJ's judgment in *Flaherty* is welcome. It is hoped that in such circumstances the courts will continue to be guided by its fair decision approach, asking, in a positive sense, whether the internal disciplinary proceedings at issue produced a fair result or whether, in a slightly more negative vein, the procedural defects, which are claimed to have infected the process, led ultimately to an unfair result.[35]

[**2.15**] In terms of the contractual obligations of a sports body to ensure that its disciplinary rules are correctly and fairly applied, the fair decision approach also has an inherent logic. As Scott J stated in *Singer v The Jockey Club* 'no judge would ever guarantee that he had reached the right result' therefore, logically, the limits of the contractual bind on a sports body can only extend to the holding of a fair and proper disciplinary inquiry taking all reasonable steps to ensure that the applicable rules are applied.[36] In addition, the inherent flexibility of the fair decision approach means that it is also adequately sophisticated to accommodate the fundamental competing interests that are characteristic of legal challenges to the decisions of sports bodies, and to do so in a manner that will ultimately benefit sport as a whole. The technical, legal arguments of *Modahl* and *Flaherty* aside, an important underlying feature of the proceedings was the courts' recognition that a balance must be struck between the serious consequences that might follow immediately

---

[33] Ibid [52]–[55]. It turned out that the drug is question was not one that could be used with any great effect in any attempt to 'stop' a dog and was, in all likelihood, used for the rather more prosaic purposes of treating a urinary infection. The dog had, apparently, developed a tendency to wet his bedding.

[34] Ibid [20]–[21] italics inserted.

[35] To paraphrase Lord Radcliffe in *Edwards v Bairstow* [1956] AC 14, 36 where the decision is one that a domestic tribunal properly instructing itself to the facts, law and regulatory context could have reasonably reached then it is unlikely to be set aside by any subsequent judicial scrutiny.

[36] *Singer v The Jockey Club* Unreported, Chancery Division 28 June 1990, Scott J, 18E-19A (official transcript).

for the (wrongly) disqualified participant versus the sports body's desire to protect the long term integrity of the sport from the insidious practice of doping and ill-discipline. With the long term health of the sport (and participants) in mind, the argument is that in anti-doping hearings (for example) it might not always be easy for a sports body to act with the necessary 'detached impartiality' when dealing with a participant whose sample has tested adversely for a performance enhancing substance. In contrast, a participant, frustrated by a perception of unfairness, disproportionality, irrationality or delay on the part of the disciplining sports body, might be moved to adopt a somewhat opportunistic approach in challenging the disputed decision or sanction. As Lord Woolf MR noted in the Court of Appeal's in *Modahl*, the courts have to strike a careful balance in such instances, taking cognisance of the attendant problems that will inevitably 'arise if athletes are able to come to the courts instead of availing themselves of the intended domestic appeal procedure ... allegations of [procedural unfairness] are easy to make and difficult to refute. If more than a process which as a whole is fair is required the courts will have to take care not readily to interfere by injunction as otherwise the whole war against drugs in sport could be undermined'.[37] It follows perforce that if the courts are seen as being amenable to interlocutory applications for injunctive relief on some alleged breach of contract at an early stage of a sports disciplinary process, the whole disciplinary and regulatory scheme of a sport might be undermined.

'Ambush' Injunctions

[**2.16**]   Generally, the courts are sensitive to the dangers of readily granting interim injunctive relief in the circumstances of a sports dispute so as not to overly interfere with the regulatory authority of a sports body. A prime example and application of many of the issues at hand is provided by the Irish High Court's decision in *Jacob v Irish Amateur Rowing Union Ltd*.[38] In that case, the applicant-rower claimed that the defendants, contrary to natural justice and in the face of previous assurances, failed to select the applicant for a crucial qualifying regatta for the Beijing Olympics. In the week prior to the regatta the applicant sought an injunction requiring the defendant to take all necessary steps to ensure the claimant's participation in the regatta. The Irish High Court, notwithstanding its admiration for the claimant's dedicated pursuit of Olympian status, refused the order on two grounds. First and generally, Laffoy J observed that in the absence of proof of bad faith or some obvious egregious injustice to the applicant, a court should be reluctant to intervene in the decision of a sports governing body. Second and specific to the circumstances at hand, Laffoy J accepted that the defendant had made the decision with genuine regret and, more importantly, within its discretion and area of expertise as to the applicant's inability to perform at the

---

[37] *Modahl* [1997] EWCA Civ 2209, Lord Woolf MR.
[38] *Jacob v Irish Amateur Rowing Union Ltd* [2008] IEHC 196.

required level of performance and fitness. From this case, and others, two general principles can be drawn. First, in refusing to grant interim relief a court may be persuaded inter alia by the margin of appreciation that should be extended to sports bodies in the proper exercise of their administrative functions; their inherent expertise in the matters at hand; the repercussions that such relief might have on the smooth timely running of a sports league or tournament; and the effect such disruption might have on the interests of other individuals or clubs.[39]

[**2.17**]   Equally however there is no doubt that just because the circumstances are sporting in nature, it does not follow from that consideration that the court should refrain from assessing whether on the balance of convenience there is an 'arguable' breach or implication of the general duty of the sports body to act fairly.[40] Nevertheless, and as hinted at by Lord Woolf MR in *Modahl*,[41] this low threshold might be exploited by an aggrieved sports-claimant to facilitate what can be called

---

[39] See, eg, *Badrick v British Judo Association* [2004] EWHC 1891 (applicant refused relief in attempt to challenge the refusal to hold an arbitral hearing for non-selection on a British representative team on the grounds that the applicant had not participated in an important pre-qualifying tournament); *Hearn v Rugby Football Union* [2003] EWHC 2690 (Ch) (applicants refused relief in attempt to have governing body sanction a club for fielding an ineligible player to the detriment of the applicants' prospects of promotion on grounds that the consequent disruption to the league structure would be undesirable); *Moloney v Bolger and Leinster Branch of the IRFU* [2000] IEHC 63 (applicants refused relief in attempt to challenge their relegation to a lower division because of points docked for failing to fulfil a fixture on grounds that the inconvenience to the other clubs in the league transcended 'by a very large factor' the inconvenience to the applicants); *Phoenix Finance Ltd v FIA and others* [2002] EWHC 1028 (Ch) (applicants refused relief in attempt to participate on an interim basis, and as a replacement for, a defunct competitor in Formula 1 on grounds that it might be unfair to existing participants); *Stevenage Borough FC v Football League Ltd*, *The Times* 1 August 1996, Carnwath J; (1997) 9 Admin LR 109 (CA) (applicant refused relief in attempt to challenge the refusal to promote the club, inter alia on the grounds of delay); *West Harbour Rugby Football Club Ltd v New South Wales Rugby Union Ltd* [2001] NSWSC 757 (applicants refused relief in attempt to challenge their loss of a playoff place because of points docked for selecting an ineligible overseas player on grounds their case lacked clarity and its effect on a number of other clubs involved in the playoff stages of the league); *Wilander and Novacek v Tobin and Jude* Unreported, Chancery Division 19 March 1996, Lightman J; affirmed by Court of Appeal, *The Times* 8 April 1996 (applicants refused relief in attempt to challenge their suspension for violations of the defendants anti-doping code for tennis on grounds that the alleged procedural defects were insufficient to underpin an arguable case).

[40] *Williams v Pugh and others* [1997] CLY 86 (litigation by two rugby clubs challenging the requirement by the Welsh Rugby Union that the clubs commit from a 10-year period to the Union). In that case, Popplewell J held that an interim injunction for a limited period of one playing season with the commitment to a speedy full trial was, in the sporting circumstances, the most appropriate means of implementing the order sought. See also the successful applications in *Conteh v Onslow-Fane*, *The Times* 6 June 1975, Walton J; affirmed by the Court of Appeal, *The Times* 26 June 1975 (applicant boxer restraining the British Boxing Board of Control from proceeding with disciplinary action pending litigation involving the applicant, his manager and a fight promoter); *Jones v Welsh Rugby Union*, *The Times* 6 March 1997, Ebsworth J; affirmed [1997] EWCA Civ 3066 (applicant rugby player lifting 30 days' suspension by the Welsh Rugby Union for indiscipline pending full trial on allegations of procedural defects in the course of the disciplinary hearing); *Newport v Football Association of Wales* [1995] 2 All ER 87 (applicant club seeking declaration that actions of the defendants in preventing the applicant from playing in an English league were unlawful and in restraint of trade); and *Tyrrell Racing Organisation Ltd v RAC Motor Sports Association Ltd & Another*, Unreported, Queen's Bench Division 20 July 1984, Hirst J (applicants seeking order to compel the defendants to permit them to compete in a race pending a hearing into the fairness of a suspension imposed on them by the governing body).

[41] *Modahl* [1997] EWCA Civ 2209, Lord Woolf MR.

an 'ambush' injunction. At its most opportunistic this litigation tactic can arise where a participant, on pain of a decision by a domestic sports tribunal of first instance rendering them ineligible for a major forthcoming event, seeks an interlocutory injunction to stay or lift the sanction. Fully aware that they need only make an arguable case (usually one based loosely on an allegation of procedural unfairness), the claimant argues at this summary stage that on the balance of convenience they should be given an opportunity to participate in the imminent competition and that the suspension should be set aside until the merits of the case are debated at full trial. On a technical level, in such scenarios the application for injunctive relief becomes, in effect, one dealing with the major subject matter of the suit for all practical purposes (if not for legal purposes). In such circumstances, and taking into account the discretionary element of any injunctive relief, it is, doubtless, open to a court to 'look a little deeper'[42] into the applicant's case and to seek a 'higher degree of assurance' that the claimant will be able to establish a breach of his rights at trial.[43] On a human level, the above principles notwithstanding, and given the pressures of time involved, it can be difficult for a court to refuse interim relief where, for example, the background is such that the sports-applicant, if unsuccessful, will be denied the opportunity to play in an important event to which they may have dedicated a large part of their career. While, in the short term, this is of benefit to applicants, in the longer term it can potentially, to reiterate Lord Woolf's observation, undermine the authority of a sport body's disciplinary process to the detriment of the sport as a whole.[44]

[**2.18**]   To be fair, the courts are cognisant of the above issues as exemplified by Mackay J's approach in *Chambers v British Olympic Association*.[45] The stated

---

[42] *West Harbour Rugby Football Club Ltd v New South Wales Rugby Union Ltd* [2001] NSWSC 757 [13] Young CJ. See also the approach of the Irish High Court in *Jacob v Irish Amateur Rowing Union Ltd* [2008] IEHC 196 and *Moloney v Bolger and Leinster Branch of the IRFU* [2000] IEHC 63.

[43] On the law in relation to interlocutory injunctions see generally the 'serious issue to be tried' test of *American Cyanamid Co v Ethicon Ltd* [1975] AC 396. Where the grant or refusal of an interlocutory injunction would dispose of an action finally in favour of whichever party was successful in the action (ie, the relief sought is mandatory in nature) the approach taken appears to be twofold: (a) consideration can be given to the degree of likelihood that the claimant would have succeeded in establishing his right to an injunction if the action had gone to trial; and (b) whether, in light of (a), the applicant's case on the evidence is so strong that to refuse an injunction would constitute an injustice. See further *NWL Limited v Woods* [1979] 3 All ER 614, 626, Lord Diplock; *Cayne v Global Natural Resources plc* [1984] 1 All ER 225, 238, May LJ; *Zockoll Group Ltd v Mercury Communications Ltd* [1998] FSR 354, 366 Phillips LJ; and the brief review of the authorities at *Shilmore Enterprises Corpn v Phoenix Aviation Ltd* [2008] EWHC 169 (QB) [5]–[7], Coulson J. This is particularly the case where the interlocutory application seeks the granting of a mandatory injunction. Note the refusal to grant such an interlocutory, mandatory application by Gray J in *Rubython v FIA* [2003] All ER (D) 182 (May) (applicant challenging the denial of press accreditation by the governing body of Formula 1).

[44] Note the comments in the Irish High Court in *JRM Sports Ltd (t/a Limerick FC) v Football Association of Ireland* [2007] IEHC 67 where, in dismissing an application by a club seeking to overturn the defendant's decision to refuse them a licence to compete in the domestic football league, Clarke J observed: 'If every time a party was able to pass the relatively low threshold of suggesting that it had a legal case against a sporting body and was able to interfere with the way in which that sporting body carried out the management of the sport on that basis it is likely that the administration of major sports would grind to a halt'.

[45] *Chambers v British Olympic Association* [2008] EWHC 2028 (QB). See generally N da Silva, 'Too Slow Off the Blocks?' (2008) 158 *New Law Journal* 1127.

case concerned Dwain Chambers who, after much success in the earlier part of
the decade, tested positive for a banned substance in 2003 receiving a mandatory two-year ban from UK Athletics. On serving his ban, Chambers returned
to competitive action and on 12 July 2008, he won the pre-Beijing Olympics
Final Trial staged by UK Athletics but nevertheless remained ineligible for
selection to the British Olympic Team (Team GB) due to a byelaw within the
British Olympic Association's (BOA) eligibility criteria, which regarded it as
inappropriate to select any athlete who has 'at any point committed a serious doping offence involving fault or negligence and without any mitigating
factors'.[46] Although Chambers had an internal right of appeal, given that the
Beijing Olympics were set to begin within weeks (and Team GB was due to
be announced within days), he decided to instigate legal proceedings at what
Mackay J called 'the eleventh hour'.[47] Chambers sought what was in effect an
interlocutory mandatory order designed to compel the BOA to select him for
Team GB in advance of a final ruling on, and full consideration of, the enforceability of the byelaw. At the hearing Chambers conceded that the application
for interim relief would dispose of the core issue (the claimant's entitlement to
run at the Olympics) in its entirety.[48] Given the circumstances and the nature of
the relief sought, Mackay J held that he would require 'a high degree of assurance' that the claimant would succeed in demonstrating the unlawfulness of the
byelaw at trial.[49]

[**2.19**]   Chambers' argument was that he had served his ban for doping violations in full and that he should be entitled not only to his rehabilitation as a
'clean' athlete but also to pursue his livelihood to its fullest by availing himself of
the opportunities that might flow from being an Olympian. In brief, Chambers
contented that the effect of the byelaw in question was excessive and disproportionate and that the BOA had gone beyond what was reasonably necessary for
the proper conduct of its sport. The application for relief failed on three grounds.
The first ground was that of delay, and the impact the tardy and untidy nature
of the proceedings were having on other athletes and the proper administration by the BOA of the organisation of the British Olympic effort for Beijing.[50]

---

[46] The byelaw, the right of appeal thereunder and its underlying justifications are set out by Mackay J
in *Chambers v BOA* [2008] EWHC 2028 (QB) [5]–[8] and [21]–[22], Mackay J.

[47] Ibid [9]–[10].

[48] Ibid [15]. Mackay J agreed with the BOA that if Chambers did not succeed in the immediate he
would surely not take his claim to trail for a final ruling as he would (on his own evidence) be too old
to be a serious candidate for the London Olympics 2012.

[49] Ibid [14] and [16]. Mackay J held therefore that he should give more consideration to the merits
of Chambers' claim than is stipulated in the *American Cyanamid* test and he would be guided by the
'risk of injustice' approach in *Zockoll Group Ltd v Mercury Communications Ltd* [1998] FSR 354, 366
Phillips LJ.

[50] Ibid [56]–[65] citing *Stevenage Borough FC v Football League Ltd*, *The Times* 1 August 1996,
Carnwarth J; (1997) 9 *Admin LR* 109 (CA). Note that there were two other athletes (a shot putter
and a cyclist) in the same position as Chambers who, Mackay J noted, might be tempted to apply
for relief if Chambers was successful thus further aggravating the delay in the final selection of
Team GB.

Second, Mackay J doubted whether, in any event, a reviewable 'right to work' claim (which may more properly be referred to as a claim based on the common law doctrine of restraint of trade) existed given that even if Chambers won an Olympic medal (and his times and form suggested that this was unlikely) there would be no direct financial gain and little other than 'speculative' indirect gain.[51] Third, although Chambers demonstrated that the bar on eligibility did not appear to be one replicated in the criteria used by other countries, Mackay J held that he was, given the context and objectives surrounding the bar, still not sufficiently assured as to the claimant's ultimate prospects of proving that the byelaw was not proportionate.[52]

[**2.20**]   The merits of the Mackay J's approach notwithstanding, and returning to the point at hand, although the decision in Chambers was advantageous to the BOA, it also highlights the lurking dangers of so-called 'ambush' injunctions for all sports bodies. In the penultimate paragraph of his judgment Mackay J noted perceptively that, even if Chambers had obtained injunctive relief this would not, as a matter of law, have amounted to a declaration that the byelaw was unlawful; nevertheless, 'many people inside and outside the sport, would see it and describe it as such, understandably, having little interest in the niceties of the legal issues'.[53] It follows that if an applicant succeeds in giving the necessary 'assurance' to the Court, the actuality of the resulting interim relief may have significant long term effects for the sports body. The lessons that ambush injunctions present for sports bodies are neatly encapsulated in the Irish example of *Kinane v Turf Club*.[54] In that case, a leading Irish jockey was banned for two days by the stewards at a Dublin racecourse after a minor race held there on 18 July 2001. The two-day ban was to apply to 27 and 28 July 2001, thus rendering Kinane unavailable to ride the favourite, Galileo, for one of the most prestigious events on the flat racing calendar—the King George VI and Queen Elizabeth Diamond Stakes at Ascot. Kinane appealed the suspension to the Irish Turf Club

---

[51] Ibid [41]–[47]. See also *Currie v Barton* Unreported, Court of Appeal 11 February 1988, *The Times* 12 February 1988. The claimant-tennis player was, as a result of ill discipline, banned for three years from playing for his county team by a committee of the county tennis association. The ban meant, no more and no less, that the claimant would not be selected for the county. The Court of Appeal (O'Connor LJ; Nicholls LJ; and Lloyd LJ) acting unanimously dismissed the claim (based on an alleged breach of natural justice by the disciplinary committee) noting that not only did selection for the county team not attract any remuneration but also, given the limited scope of the ban, the claimant's capacity to pursue his livelihood as a professional coach and tournament-player was otherwise completely unaffected.

[52] Ibid [48]–[54]. See especially point (iv) of the BOA's argument outlined by Mackay J at [53], which reveals that an important underlying aspect of this application was the issue as to whether Chambers' presence in Beijing might upset the overall 'harmony' of Team GB at the Games. Compare the treatment by the BOA of Chambers to its dealings with Christine Ohuruogu, the subsequent winner of the 400 metres at the Beijing Games in *BOA Appeals Panel: Christine Ohuruogu v BOA* (2003) 3 *International Sports Law Review* SLR-113.

[53] Ibid [66].

[54] *Kinane v Turf Club* Unreported, Irish High Court 27 July 2001, McCracken J. See B O'Connor 'Kinane Back on Galileo' *The Irish Times* (Dublin 28 July 2001) Sport 30.

Appeals and Referral Committee, which sat on the morning of 27 July, but was unsuccessful. That afternoon, Kinane's legal representatives went to High Court in Dublin seeking an interim order freeing him to ride in the King George on the following afternoon. The High Court was satisfied that Kinane's case, based on a breach of his constitutional right to fair procedure, was a statable one given the applicant's evidence that he had not been given any opportunity to make representations in mitigation of sentence prior to the decision to uphold the ban. McCracken J also held that the Court was satisfied that the balance of convenience lay in granting Mr Kinane the interim order taking into account the significant detriment, economic and reputational, to the jockey if the ban stood. In contrast, McCracken J stated that the Irish Turf Club had 'no financial interest in the matter' and would not suffer any great detriment if the matter was postponed.[55] The extent of the economic interests at play were revealed the following day when it was reported that Galileo's victory had seen his potential stud value increase to $100 million.[56]

[**2.21**]   At the subsequent (full) hearing one month later, the matter was resolved when the Irish Turf Club admitted to the Irish High Court that its Appeals and Referral Committee had breached their duty of fairness towards Kinane.[57] Ultimately, a freshly constituted Appeals and Referral Committee imposed a two-day ban on Kinane, which he served. The ban did not coincide with any major race. Responding to this litigation, and in recognition that challenges of this kind would be likely only to intensify in frequency and sophistication, the Irish Turf Club considered a series of rule changes.[58] In 2006, these reforms culminated in the appointment of a retired Chief Justice of the Irish Supreme Court and a former Irish Attorney-General as the independent chair and vice-chair of a reconstituted disciplinary mechanism.[59] Ambush injunctions were also the catalyst for the establishment of an independent arbitral tribunal by Ireland's largest sports organisation, the Gaelic Athletic Association (GAA), in 2005.[60] In debating the matter the GAA realised that it had a choice: either it had enough faith in its existing disciplinary scheme to contest interlocutory

---

[55] M Carolan, 'Jockey Gets Turf Club Ban Lifted' *The Irish Times* (Dublin 28 July 2001) Home News 4.

[56] See further 'Reaching for the Stars' *BBC News Online* 28 July 2001 available at http://news.bbc.co.uk/sport1/hi/other_sports/1462086.stm.

[57] See B O'Connor, 'New Appeal for Kinane' *The Irish Times* (Dublin 23 August 2001) Sport 23.

[58] In the immediate aftermath of the *Kinane* litigation the Turf Club considered amending its rules so that a minor ban would not rule a jockey out of a major 'Group 1' race. See B O'Connor, 'Kinane Issue is Resolved' *The Irish Times* (Dublin 28 August 2001) Sport 18. Also, see previously *Bolger v Osborn and others* [2000] 1 ILRM 250 necessitating that the Irish Turf club amend it rules relating to the vicarious liability of trainers for the actions of a jockey under their instruction during a race.

[59] B O'Connor, 'Keane to Chair New Appeals Body' *The Irish Times* (Dublin 1 February 2006) Sport 27.

[60] See generally J Anderson, 'Rushing to Judgment: Lessons from the Judicial Scrutiny of Sports Governing Bodies in Ireland' (2006) 4 *Entertainment and Sports Law Journal* published online at www2.warwick.ac.uk/fac/soc/law/elj/eslj/issues/volume4/number3/Anderson.

injunctions into full trial, seeking argument of the substantive issues and, if successful, costs based on the undertakings given by the claimant; or it could take a more preventative approach by way of enhancing its internal disciplinary mechanisms. The latter option was chosen on the grounds that it would provide the better long term solution. It was felt that contesting litigation taken by members, and seeking costs against them would, ultimately, prove unpopular and self-defeating. Neither would it address the genuine frustration (evidenced by the legal costs that aggrieved participants were willing to bear personally) that members had with the procedural and dilatory nature of the GAA's then extant disciplinary structures.[61]

A Fair Go

[2.22]   The reaction of the above Irish sports organisations resonates with what the English courts appear to have been advocating for quite some time, namely, that sports bodies should be encouraged to continue to develop sophisticated, arbitral-based means of dispute resolution. Accordingly, where a decision by a sports body's disciplinary or decision-making mechanism is made in the context of: a relatively transparent process, which is underpinned by a sensible, speedy, quasi-independent appeals outlet; is broadly attuned to the principles of natural justice; has properly instructed itself to the facts and the law; is designed in structure to produce a fair result; and has ultimately produced such a result; then the courts should rarely be moved to entertain a challenge to that decision.[62] Although there is no doubt that the courts do, of course, retain the right to intervene where there has been some obvious egregious injustice or illegality, it can be said with some predictability that the final decision of a sports tribunal, that has abided by the above principles, will not be set aside in a court of law.[63] As compared to judicial proceedings, the benefits to aggrieved participants and sports bodies of the less costly, less adversarial, private and expertise-led forum that is a well-run domestic tribunal (many of which are elaborated upon in chapter three of the text) are clear.[64] The benefits of alternative dispute resolution

---

[61] For more information of the GAA's Dispute Resolution Authority, which operates under the Irish Arbitration Acts 1954–1998, see www.sportsdra.ie.

[62] These principles clearly underlie the decision of Simon J in *Sankofa v Football Association Ltd* [2007] EWHC 78 (Comm) (applicant refused interim relief in attempt to challenge a one game suspension imposed by the defendants, inter alia on the grounds of effect on third parties and failure to exhaust all available internal remedies).

[63] Note here the brief but succinct comments of Thorpe LJ in *Jones v Welsh Rugby Union* [1997] EWCA Civ 3066 where his Lordship acknowledged that the courts should be slow to intervene but that in the instant case this could not be avoided because the defendant's disciplinary procedures had become antiquated and were ripe for challenge.

[64] It is also clear that the courts would prefer not to have to adjudicate on such matters. Note the frustration that spices Scott Baker LJ's judgment in *Flaherty v NGRC* [2005] EWCA Civ 1117 [19]: 'It seems to me inherently unsatisfactory that a hearing before a sporting tribunal lasting between 1 and 2 hours should be followed by a High Court hearing lasting 10 days and an appeal taking up a further day and a half'.

were placed in stark context by the *Modahl* litigation which, ultimately, came at great financial cost to the claimant and, indeed, to the BAF, which, largely as a result of the associated legal costs, went into administration.[65] In overall summary of all the issues raised thus far by the *Modahl* litigation, it can be said that in a private law-based challenge to the decision of sports tribunal (such as breach of the implied contractual duty to act fairly towards the claimant) the courts will, at first glance, be anxious to ascertain whether, to borrow the Australian colloquialism, the claimant received a 'fair go'. If that is the case, it then appears difficult to countenance how further court involvement could be warranted.

The Presence of a Contract: Fact or Fiction?

[**2.23**] By 2000 and following strike-out proceedings which reached the House of Lords, only one of Diane Modhal's allegations against the BAF remained—bias breaching the BAF's implied obligation that all its disciplinary proceedings would be fairly conducted. An interesting aspect of the substantive hearing in *Modahl*, was (even before *Modahl* could seek to establish fault and causation relative to the BAF's duty to act fairly) the BAF's argument that a contract did not exist between Modahl and the BAF so that whatever other remedies Modahl might have in reliance on the court's inherent supervisory jurisdiction to review the operation of domestic tribunals (such as a declaration) in the absence of contract she clearly had no claim for damages.[66] The BAF's (somewhat disingenuous) contention was that, although Modahl was a member of a club affiliated to the BAF, she was not a member of the BAF. Moreover, the BAF noted that at no point had Modahl either entered into a contract with the BAF by competing at the Lisbon meeting (which was organised by the European Athletics Association) or by submitting to the (IAAF-mandated) dope testing procedure in Lisbon. At trial, Douglas Brown J agreed with the BAF as to the 'unreality' of the contractual relationship and citing extensively from Lord Denning's judgment in *Nagle v Feilden*[67] (on the undesirability of 'investing in fictitious contracts') held that no contract existed. Subsequently, the Court of Appeal led by Latham LJ took a different view holding that the fundamental principles of a contract (intention to create legal relations; offer; acceptance; and consideration) could be implied when one considered all the surrounding circumstances.[68] Relying on the High Court's decision in *Korda*

---

[65] T Knight, 'Modahl Faces Financial Ruin as Appeal Fails' *The Daily Telegraph* (London 13 October 2001) News 8.

[66] *Modahl (No 2)* Unreported, Queen's Bench Division 14 December 2000, Douglas Brown J; on appeal [2001] EWCA Civ 1447; [2002] 1 WLR 1192.

[67] [1966] 2 QB 633, 644–46, Lord Denning MR and 652, Salmon LJ. See also Lord Denning's comments in *Enderby Town FC v Football Association* [1971] Ch 591, 606.

[68] *Modahl (No 2)* [2001] EWCA Civ 1447 [25] –[52], Latham LJ. Mance LJ concurred but Jonathan Parker LJ dissented citing at [83] from *Blackpool and Fylde Aero Club Ltd v Blackpool Borough Council* [1990] 1 WLR 1195, 1202, Bingham LJ, 'contracts are not lightly to be implied'.

v International Tennis Federation Limited,[69] Latham LJ was of the opinion that, taking Modahl's career as a whole, her regular participation in, and compliance with, events under the regulatory auspices of the BAF and IAAF indicated a clear offer of submission to that regulatory authority, which had, in turn, been accepted by the BAF and IAAF to the mutual benefit or consideration of the parties. This implied contractual framework could, Latham LJ argued, be extended to the meeting and events in Lisbon.[70] The Court of Appeal then went on to hold that the BAF had ultimately adhered to the ambit of its obligations to act fairly towards the claimant.[71]

[**2.24**] Arguably, the debate in *Modahl* on the existence of a contractual relationship is very much a product of its time. In the 1990s, the demands placed on national and international sports governing bodies by the need to develop comprehensive anti-doping programmes, allied to the increase in full-time professional athletes determined to exploit their commercial potential to its fullest, revealed that the loose and informal administrative frameworks of many leading sports (such as athletics, swimming and rugby union) which had largely remained unchanged for decades, were now badly outdated and even amateurish in nature.[72] In *Modhal (No 2)*, the best that the Court of Appeal could do was to describe the binds that held together the then pyramidal model of British/European/International athletics as being loosely based on an application of the principle of agency; whereby Modahl's club was the agency by which she was contractually bound to the BAF; the BAF was the agency by which athletics clubs in Britain were contractually bound to the IAAF; and the IAAF, as the international governing body, was the agency which contractually bound all of athletics.[73] Since the stated proceedings most of the leading sports organisations in Europe have moved to a situation where recognition of their regulatory authority is now expressly incorporated

---

[69] *Korda v International Tennis Federation Limited The Times* 4 February 1999, Lightman J. The claimant was a professional tennis player who signed an application form to participate at Wimbledon in 1998. The form contained a clause requiring Korda to undergo drug testing administered by the defendants. Korda tested positive and was given a mandatory one-year suspension, which he appealed successfully to the ITF independent appeals body. The ITF sought to challenge that leniency in the Court of Arbitration for Sport. Korda countered by seeking a declaration that the ITF was not entitled to appeal for lack of a contractual relationship. Lightman J held that a contractual relationship between the parties could plainly be inferred from the fact that Korda had expressly submitted to the anti-doping programme in place for that Wimbledon championship.

[70] *Modahl (No 2)* [2001] EWCA Civ 1447 [52].

[71] Ibid [68], Latham LJ.

[72] Ibid [91], Mance LJ, arguing that this lack of factual and regulatory clarity was the root of the 'contract' problem in *Modahl (No 2)*. See also *Korda v ITF* [1999] EWCA Civ 1098 where Auld LJ observed that the problem at issue lay in the 'bad fit' between the ITF's anti-doping programme and the authority of the Court of Arbitration for Sport.

[73] Note also, in order to prove the existence of a contractual obligation, the rather convoluted 'umbrella contract' arguments that had to be made by the appellants in *Aberavon and Port Talbot RFC v Welsh Rugby Union Ltd* [2003] EWCA Civ 584 [19]–[26], May LJ (unsuccessful claim by a club for breach of a 'contractual' right to promotion). See also the discussion in *Bradley v Jockey Club* [2004] EWHC 2164 [48]–[54], Richards J, as to whether a contractual relationship arose out of a claimant's licence as a jockey.

into the rules of the national body, thus providing a clear contractual link between 'grassroots' members of sports clubs affiliated to a national body and the overarching authority of the international sports governing body.[74] It follows that the true lingering importance of the 'existence of a contract' issue in *Modahl (No 2)*, lies in the available remedy or, more negatively, that monetary compensation is unavailable in the absence of a contract. In a broader sense, the usefulness of *Modahl* lies in the fact that the litigation touches on virtually all procedural and substantive aspects of the proceedings that might surround a private law challenge to the decision of a sports body. In contrast, a number of litigants have sought to argue that the decisions of sports bodies should be subject to public law review and it is to the procedural and substantive differences of such claims that we now turn.

The Aga Khan

[**2.25**] In a series of cases in the 1990s, principally involving the Football Association (FA) and the Jockey Club, the English courts held that challenges to the actions of sports governing bodies should be brought in private law proceedings and not by way of judicial review. In these cases, the courts stressed that because the relationship between a sports governing body and its members is generally private and contractual in nature, it gives rise to private rights on which effective actions for damages, a declaration or an injunction might be based without resort to judicial review. The seminal case on the domestic or private nature of the acts of sports bodies is probably that of *R v Disciplinary Committee of the Jockey Club, ex parte Aga Khan*.[75] Utilising that specific decision, what follows is a brief discussion of its precedent that appears to preclude the judicial review of the decisions of sports governing bodies in England and Wales. The discussion of this 'public law preclusion' is threefold in nature. First, there is an attempt to show that the courts decline to intervene by way of judicial review on the grounds that the required level of 'governmental' involvement and/or linkage to a scheme of statutory regulation cannot be identified within the domestic sports tribunal. Second, consideration is given to whether, in line with recent developments in public law, the decisions of sports bodies should, on occasion, now be exposed to judicial review on the basis that it is sufficiently within the 'public interest' that they are held accountable in this fashion. Finally, there is some examination of the

---

[74] See, eg, Rule A of the Rules of the Football Association available through www.thefa.com/TheFA/RulesandRegulations.aspx and section 2.1 of the 'General Administrative' Rules and Regulation of the Rugby Football Union available through www.rfu.com/TheGame/Regulations.

[75] *Aga Khan* [1993] 1 WLR 909. His Highness the Aga Khan is the honorific, hereditary title of the Imam of the Nizari Muslims, the largest branch of the Ismaili followers of the Islamic Shia faith. The incumbent, Prince Karim al Hussaini, became Aga Khan IV in 1957. HH Aga Khan has owned four winners of the Epsom Derby, of which the most celebrated was the ill-fated Shergar in 1981.

probability that in the near future leading sports regulatory bodies will be treated as 'hybrid' public bodies under the Human Rights Act 1998.

The Aliysa Affair

[**2.26**]   On 10 June 1991, Aliysa won the Epsom Oaks, the most prestigious event on the horse racing calendar for fillies. Subsequently, the horse's urine sample revealed the presence of a prohibited substance and, pursuant to the Jockey Club's Rules of Racing, the filly was disqualified by the Club's Disciplinary Committee. The owner of the horse, the Aga Khan, sought to challenge the lawfulness of that decision by way of judicial review proceedings. Leave for appeal was granted on the proviso that a determination on whether the decision of the Disciplinary Committee of the Jockey Club was susceptible to judicial review would be con-cluded as a preliminary matter. Ultimately, the Court of Appeal held, as the High Court did before it, that, although the Jockey Club exercised dominant control over racing activities in the UK, its powers and duties were in no sense govern-mental but derived from the contractual relationship between the Jockey Club and those agreeing to be bound by the Rules of Racing, and that that contractual relationship gave rise to private rights enforceable by private action in which effec-tive relief by way of declaration, injunction and damages was available. Although at first glance the precedent set by, and the ratio of, the case appears firm, the question of the amenability of the decision of sports bodies to judicial review has distracted the courts (and academic commentators) on a number of occasions since that ill-fated June day on the Epsom Downs.[76] One of the more interesting and recent cases is that of *R (Mullins) v Appeal Board of the Jockey Club*.[77]

Be My Royal

[**2.27**]   The Hennessy Gold Cup at Newbury is an important race in the early part of the National Hunt season in England. In the November 2002 edition of the race, Irish jockey David Casey rode the Willie Mullins trained Be My Royal to victory at odds of 33/1. Subsequently, a urine sample taken from the horse was found to contain morphine. The Disciplinary Committee of the Jockey Club acknowledged that morphine might be found in a horse entirely innocently and that in this case its presence had probably resulted from contaminated foodstuff. Nevertheless, and applying a strict liability construction, the Disciplinary Committee of the Jockey

---

[76] Michael Beloff QC has written extensively on the topic: M Beloff, T Kerr and M Demetriou, *Sports Law* (Oxford, Hart Publishing, 1999) 224–34; and, more recently, M Beloff, 'Who—Whom? Unresolved Issues in Judicial Review: Inaugural Lecture at the University of Buckingham 29 May 2007' (2008) 20 *Denning Law Journal* 35.

[77] *Mullins* [2005] EWHC 2197 (Admin); decision on costs at [2005] EWHC 2517 (Admin). See generally the discussion in J Anderson, 'An Accident of History: Why Decisions of Sports Governing Bodies are not Amenable to Judicial Review' (2006) 35 *Common Law World Review* 173.

Club found that there had been a breach of Rule 53 of the Orders and Rules of Racing and disqualified the horse. Mr Mullins appealed to the Appeal Board of the Jockey Club, which upheld the decision of the Disciplinary Committee. In the stated proceedings, Mullins sought judicial review of the decision of the Appeal Board, eventually confining his claim to a declaration that the disqualification of Be My Royal was unlawful. The decision before Stanley Burton J was principally a procedural one: whether the decision of the Appeal Board of the Jockey Club was amenable to judicial review under Part 54 of the Civil Procedure Rules 1998 (CPR). The Administrative Court answered in the negative, holding that the decision of the Court of Appeal in *Aga Khan* was binding and determinative of the inapplicability of the judicial review jurisdiction of the Administrative Court.

[**2.28**]   As applied by the Court of Appeal in the *Aga Khan* litigation, and later followed by the Administrative Court in *Mullins*,[78] the resolve to treat decisions of sports bodies as matters of private not public law can be sourced in the authority of *Law v National Greyhound Racing Club*.[79] In *Law v NGRC*, the claimant was a trainer whose licence had been suspended because he had charge of a greyhound, which had been found on examination to have taken prohibited performance enhancing substances. The claimant issued an originating summons seeking a declaration (and an injunction and damages) that the stewards' decision was void and ultra vires and reached in breach of natural justice. The NGRC moved to strike out the action on the ground that he should have sought judicial review under section 31 of the Supreme Court Act 1981. That contention was rejected at first instance and by the Court of Appeal where Lawton LJ noted simply that 'in the past the courts have always refused to use the orders of certiorari to review the decisions of domestic tribunals'.[80] Lawton LJ went on to hold that, although consequences affecting the public generally can flow from decision of domestic sports tribunals (such as the benefit to the public of the stamping out of malpractices in a sport) there was no public element to the tribunal at issue as it concerned 'only those who voluntarily submitted themselves to the stewards' jurisdiction'.[81]

[**2.29**]   Thereafter, and upon this authority, the English courts refused similar applications for the judicial review of decisions of sports disciplinary tribunals.[82] The manner in which the *Law* judgment forms the basis of the test applied in the *Aga Khan*, and followed in *Mullins*, will be further examined shortly. More

---

[78]   [2005] EWHC 2197 (Admin) [21]–[25], Stanley Burton J.

[79]   *Law v National Greyhound Racing Club* [1983] 1 WLR 1302.

[80]   Ibid 1307 citing *R v Criminal Injuries Compensation Board, ex parte Lain* [1967] 2 QB 864, 882, Lord Parker CJ. Note the concurring judgments in *Law* of Fox LJ, 1309 and Slade LJ, 1311–12. See also *R v BBC ex p Lavelle* [1983] 1 All ER 241.

[81]   Ibid.

[82]   See, eg, *R v Disciplinary Committee of the Jockey Club, ex parte Massingberd-Mundy* [1993] 2 All ER 207; *R v Eastern Counties Rugby Union, ex parte Basildon Rugby Club* Unreported, Queen's Bench Division 10 September 1987, Macpherson J; *R v Football Association, ex parte Football League Ltd.* [1993] 2 All ER 833; *R v Football Association of Wales, ex parte Flint Town* Unreported, Queen's Bench Division 11 July 1990 Farquharson LJ; and *R v Jockey Club, ex parte RAM Racecourses Ltd.* [1993] 2 All ER 225.

immediately, dicta from *Law* raise an interesting and sometimes overlooked aspect of the amenability of decisions of sports governing bodies to judicial review. In the stated case, it was the sports governing body, the NGRC, that sought to argue that the claim against it should more properly have proceeded by way of judicial review. Acknowledging the importance to the general public of the activities which the NGRC performed (in relation to the integrity of the sport and the interests of the race going public that the sport was free of doping scandals) Slade LJ understood why the NGRC might prefer that any person seeking to challenge the exercise of its disciplinary structures should be compelled to do so, if at all, by way of an application for judicial review.[83] This was because, as Slade LJ observed, the safeguards imposed by public law on judicial review proceedings (such as the need to seek leave, limitation periods, the non-availability of damages, the discretions as to relief, disclosure, cross-examination and interim relief) means that the validity of decisions of 'public' authorities could and would be protected against groundless, unmeritorious or tardy attacks.[84] Moreover, and with respect to more recent and general principles of judicial review, it is also possible that sports bodies could now benefit from the 'margin of discretion' doctrine whereby in instances where a decision-maker is attempting to balance an individual's rights against those of wider society, the judiciary may defer to the 'considered opinion' of the decision-maker.[85] Therefore the irony of what follows in the following sections of the text is that in their struggle to preclude their decisions from judicial review, it might be that sports organisations have missed an opportunity to redirect challenges to their authority into the more controlled environment of judicial review proceedings.[86]

[**2.30**]   In effect, the *ratio* in *Law v NGRC* was refined by the Court of Appeal in *Aga Khan* into a single question: whether the domestic tribunal in question was sufficiently 'governmental' in operation and nature to be amenable to judicial review.[87] In *Aga Khan*, the Court of Appeal acknowledged that the Jockey Club regulated a significant national activity; that it exercised powers that affected the public; that it exercised powers in the *interest* of the public; nonetheless, the Court of Appeal held that neither in its framework nor its rules nor its function did the Jockey Club fulfil a governmental role.[88] As Hoffmann LJ noted succinctly, 'the fact the certain functions of the Jockey Club could be exercised by a statutory body and that they are so exercised in some other countries does not make them governmental functions in England. The attitude of the English legislator

---

[83]   *Law v NGRC* [1983] 1 WLR 1302, 1311–12.

[84]   Citing *O'Reilly v Mackman* [1983] 2 AC 237, 282, Lord Diplock.

[85]   *R v DPP ex parte Kebeline* [2000] 2 AC 326, 381, Lord Hope and *Tweed v Parades Commission for Northern Ireland* [2007] 1 AC 650, 673, Lord Brown. See also the parallel use of the proportionality principles of review outlined with respect to the Human Rights Act in *R v Home Secretary ex parte Daly* [2001] UKHL 26; [2001] 2 AC 532 and cited approvingly in *Bradley v Jockey Club* [2004] EWHC 2164 (QB) [45], Richards J.

[86]   See also the comments by Lewis and Taylor (n 2) 164–65.

[87]   *Aga Khan* [1993] 1 WLR 909, 923–24, Lord Bingham MR.

[88]   Ibid 930, Farquharson LJ.

to racing is much more akin to his attitude to religion: it is something to be encouraged but not the business of government'.[89]

Hoffmann LJ went on to reconcile this approach with the fact that the Jockey Club had considerable economic powers, which purported to apply to the public at large, by observing that 'the mere fact of power, even over a substantial area of economic activity is not enough. In a mixed economy, power may be private as well as public. Private power may affect the public interest and the livelihoods of many individuals. But that does not subject it to the rules of public law'. Lord Hoffmann concluded that if controls for curbing the excesses of private power were needed they could be found elsewhere in, for example, 'the law of contract, the doctrine of the restraint of trade, the Restrictive Trade Practices Act 1976 [and] articles 85 and 86 of the E.E.C. Treaty'.[90]

[**2.31**]   In *Mullins*, Stanley Burton J added to this by noting that the purported exercise under the Rules of Racing by the Jockey Club of jurisdiction over the public must be seen in light of the fact that none of the rules of the Jockey Club had any statutory force and could only be enforced by contractual means or through the exercise of the Club's property rights. It followed that 'a body which would otherwise exercise only private functions cannot assume public functions by its own action alone. Some governmental intervention is required. There has been none'.[91] In further reinforcing this point, Stanley Burton J approved of the colourful analogy made by counsel for the Jockey Club: that Tesco plc may wield immense economic power; nonetheless, it remains a body exercising private functions. Accordingly, Stanley Burton J concluded that, although monopolistic bodies exercising power over the livelihoods of considerable number of people might warrant greater regulation and public review by the courts, the English courts have held firm to their belief that the desirability of such regulation and review cannot convert a private function into a public function.[92]

[**2.32**]   The judgments of Lord Hoffmann in *Aga Khan* and Stanley Burton J in *Mullins* also betray a frustration with the academic criticism that accompanies the reluctance to view the decisions of sports bodies as amenable to judicial review. Typical of that criticism is Beloff's view that if there is an 'organic link' between decisions of public bodies and those of domestic, private tribunals, the justification for separate procedural treatment by the courts 'appears to vanish'.[93] The riposte by the courts is that that analysis is undermined by its 'all or nothing' assumption that if judicial review proceedings are unavailable to challenge a disciplinary decision of a body such as the Jockey Club, an aggrieved claimant has no remedy. As Farquharson LJ stated in *Aga Kahn*, there could no hardship to the applicant

---

[89] Ibid 932 citing *Heatley v Tasmanian Racing and Gaming Commission* [1977] HCA 39; [1977] 137 CLR 487 and *R v Chief Rabbi of the United Hebrew Congregations of Great Britain and the Commonwealth, ex parte Wachmann* [1992] 1 WLR 1036.

[90] Ibid 932–33.

[91] *Mullins* [2005] EWHC Admin 2197 [30].

[92] Ibid [31].

[93] Beloff *et al* (n 76) 231.

in his being denied judicial review because if his complaint that the disciplinary committee had acted unfairly was well-founded, he could have proceeded by writ seeking a declaration and an injunction; a tactic, which Farquharson LJ observed 'may be a more convenient process'.[94] However, despite this comprehensive dismissal of judicial review in *Aga Khan*, applications for judicial review have persisted and claimants continue to be attracted to the contention that the *Aga Khan* decision might be vulnerable given its inflexible preclusion of public law towards the regulation of sport. An assessment of the arguments upon which these challenges to the authority of *Aga Khan* have been based now follows.[95]

An Unnecessary Preclusion of Public Law?

[**2.33**]   There are three principal elements to the argument that the decisions of sports governing bodies should be susceptible to judicial review. First and in a general sense, sport now occupies a more substantial place in our society. Specifically, this means that the decisions of the Jockey Club, for instance, are now of greater socio-economic importance than at the time of the decision in *Aga Khan*. Second and in a persuasive sense, it appears that the English view is at odds with the trend in other common law jurisdictions. Third and substantively, that the parameters of judicial review, as laid down by the English Court of Appeal in cases such as *R v Panel on Take-Overs and Mergers, ex parte Datafin*,[96] should consistently extend to some, if not all, the decisions of sports governing bodies.[97]

Sport and Society

[**2.34**]   The contention here is that, although in a cultural, economic and health policy sense, sport plays an increasingly prominent role in national life and consciousness, nevertheless, until recently, the organisation of sport in the UK was characterised by the lack of direct governmental involvement. In *Mullins*, the claimant suggested that the Court of Appeal in *Aga Khan* had overlooked a relevant factor namely that despite its long standing history of self-regulation, the Jockey Club receives substantial sums from the Government derived from the betting levy, and that this went towards demonstrating that the Jockey Club

---

[94] *Aga Khan* [1993] 1 WLR 909, 930. See also *Mullins* [2005] EWHC Admin 2197 [32], Stanley Burton J.

[95] This specific debate on sports bodies takes place within the context of a much wider and deeper debate on the public law/private law distinction generally, including its impact on judicial review proceedings and the Human Rights Act 1998. For an introduction see P Leyland and G Anthony, *Textbook on Administrative Law*, 6th edn (Oxford, Oxford University Press, 2009) 222–33.

[96] *R v Panel on Take-Overs and Mergers, ex parte Datafin* [1987] QB 815.

[97] What follows is largely informed by Anderson (n 77) 178–96. For a broader perspective on the issue of the exercise of public power and amenability to judicial review see the excellent assessment by C Campbell, 'Monopoly Power as Public Power for the Purposes of Judicial Review' (2009) 125 *LQR* 491 and C Campbell, 'The Nature of Power as Public in English Judicial Review' (2009) 68 *CLJ* 90.

occupies a more substantial, and necessarily 'public', place in society than its ostensibly private nature suggested.[98] Stanley Burton J doubted the factual veracity of this contention, further remarking that 'in any event state funding is a weak indication that a body or its functions are public. Many indisputably private bodies, such as many bodies whose activities are cultural, and many charities, receive state funding; this does not make them governmental in nature'.[99]

[**2.35**]   It is respectfully submitted that the stated view of the Administrative Court somewhat evaded the issue at hand. The Jockey Club, and its modern manifestation, The British Horseracing Authority, are not 'indisputably' private bodies. They regulate in a largely unfettered and monopolistic fashion an important aspect of national life and were it not for their existence it would be necessary for Parliament to create a public body (and only a public body would suffice) to perform their functions.[100] Moreover, the Jockey Club does in fact receive significant funding via the betting levy. The Horserace Betting Levy Board (HBLB), a statutory body established by the Betting Levy Act 1961, and operating in accordance with the provisions of the Betting, Gaming and Lotteries Act 1963, administers that levy.[101] The HBLB's role is to assess and collect monetary contributions from bookmakers, which it then distributes for the improvement of horseracing. For the financial year 2008/2009, the levy raised approximately £102 million. Approximately 60 per cent of this levy was distributed as prize money for British racing, while nearly one-third of the levy was directed towards covering the costs of the so-called 'integrity services' provided by the British Horseracing Authority. Ironically (in the context of the *Mullins* litigation) the key integrity service underwritten by the levy is that provided by the Horseracing Forensic Laboratory with respect to drug testing and research. Overall, public or governmental support of racing in Britain is significant and transparent. It cannot be dismissed lightly; nevertheless it must be admitted that such financial and governmental linkage does not of itself demand that the decisions of the racing authorities should be held amenable to judicial review. At best, it is a factor that can be taken into account along with the persuasive authority emerging from other jurisdictions, which holds that, as sports bodies on occasion attract significant public funding, so they should also on occasion attract public law review.

Comparable Jurisdictions

[**2.36**]   The question as to whether decisions of private sports bodies might be amenable to judicial review has been answered in the positive in Australia,

---

[98] *Mullins* [2005] EWHC Admin 2197 [35].
[99] Ibid.
[100] On the historical nature of the Jockey Club's regulatory remit see generally W Vamplew, 'Reduced Horse Power: The Jockey Club and the Regulation of British Horseracing' (2003) 2(3) *Entertainment Law* 94.
[101] For further details see www.hblb.org.uk.

New Zealand, Scotland and South Africa.[102] In *Forbes v NSW Trotting Club Ltd*,[103] the High Court of Australia held amenable to review a decision of the defendant that had resulted in the disqualification of the claimant (a successful, if notorious, professional gambler) from entering its racecourses. Although the High Court acknowledged that the defendant was not strictly a public body, its decision was held to be judicially reviewable on the basis that its function was to control 'public activity'.[104] In New Zealand, the combined effect of section 3 of the Judicature Amendment Act 1972, which provides an artificially extended definition of what constitutes both a 'statutory power' and a 'statutory power of decision', and the celebrated judgments surrounding the *Finnigan v New Zealand Rugby Football Union*[105] litigation, has meant that sports bodies there are much more susceptible to review than those in England and Wales.[106] In sum, the position in New Zealand is representative of the approach taken throughout the common law world: judicial review of the decision-making competencies of domestic (sports) tribunals, though permitted, is not an excuse for excessive judicial interference in the operation of appropriately established domestic tribunals who have arrived, ultimately, at a 'fair result'.[107]

[**2.37**]   In Scotland, it is well established that the decisions of sports governing bodies,[108] even individual clubs,[109] are judicially reviewable in the

---

[102] For the South African authority see *Jockey Club of South Africa v Forbes* (1993) (1) SA 649. Note also the applicability of s 33 of the Constitution of the Republic of South Africa (1996) concerning 'just administrative action'. See generally R Cloete and S Cornelius (eds), *Introduction to Sports Law in South Africa* (Durban, LexisNexis Butterworths, 2005) ch 2.

[103] *Forbes v NSW Trotting Club Ltd* (1979) HCA 27 (1979) 143 CLR 242.

[104] Ibid [4]. On the influence of Australian administrative law principles on sports disciplinary proceedings more generally see J Griffiths, 'Procedural Fairness and the Regulation of Sport: Lessons from the Common Law' (2009) 9 *International Sports Law Review* 69 and D Thorpe *et al*, *Sports Law* (Melbourne, Oxford University Press, 2009) ch 3.

[105] *Finnigan v New Zealand Rugby Football Union* [1985] 2 NZLR 159; (No 2) [1985] 2 NZLR 181; (No 3) [1985] 2 NZLR 190. In the first case, the NZ Court of Appeal held that the claimants had locus standi to challenge NZRFU's decision to permit the All Blacks to tour apartheid South Africa, notwithstanding the lack of contractual relationship between the claimant and the respondent organisation.

[106] See, eg, *Stininato v Auckland Boxing Association (No 1)* [1978] 1 NZLR 1 and *(No 2)* [1978] 1 NZLR 609; *Stewart v Judicial Committee of Auckland Racing Club* [1992] 3 NZLR 693; and *Naden v Judicial Committee of Auckland Racing Club* [1995] 1 NZLR 307. See generally J Caldwell, 'Judicial Review of Sports Bodies in New Zealand' in E Toomey (ed), *Keeping the Score: Essays in Law and Sport* (University of Canterbury: Christchurch, 2005) and, more recently, the observations in *Stratford Racing Club Inc & Anor v Adlam* [2008] NZCA 92 [53]–[56], Chambers J.

[107] This appears to have been the approach taken by the courts in the unsuccessful challenges to the length of the suspensions imposed on the claimants resulting from their ill-discipline on the field of play in *Loe v New Zealand Rugby Football Union* Unreported, High Court (CP/209/93 Wellington) 10 August 1993 and *Le Roux v New Zealand Rugby Football Union* Unreported, High Court (CP/346/94 Wellington) 14 March 1995. For the background to these proceedings see M Haggie, 'The Judicial Disciplinary Procedures of the New Zealand Rugby Football Union' [1999] 29 *Victoria University of Wellington Law Review* 317.

[108] See, eg, *St Johnstone FC v Scottish Football Association* [1965] SLT 171; *Gunstone v Scottish Women's Amateur Athletic Association* [1987] SLT 611; and *Dundee United FC v Scottish Football Association* [1998] SLT 1244.

[109] See, eg, *Irvine v Royal Burgess Golfing Society of Edinburgh* [2004] ScotCS 49; *Crocket v Tantallon Golf Club* [2005] ScotCS CSOH 37; *Wiles v Bothwell Castle Golf Club* [2005] ScotCS CSOH 108; and *Smith v Nairn Golf Club* [2007] ScotCS CSOH 136.

public interest.[110] Again, where the Scottish courts are moved to scrutinise the decision of a sports body, they will seek to ascertain whether, having regard to the course of the entire disciplinary proceedings, the tribunal in question reached a 'fair result'.[111] Of especial interest is the decision in *Lennox v British Show Jumping Association, Scottish Branch*,[112] wherein the applicant had been removed from an administrative post. The action was held incompetent because it was brought against the 'Scottish Branch', which was found not to have a separate existence as an association.[113] It was confirmed that the action could have been brought against the British Show Jumping Association prompting comment that the case might serve incidentally as a reminder that British or UK-wide bodies might be susceptible to review in Scotland thus 'in disputes where there are no obviously Scottish connections, there may be potential for something akin to forum shopping, at least when general rules or policies are under challenge'.[114]

[**2.38**] In this regard, 'forum shoppers' within the UK might turn their attention to the Northern Ireland, where the courts have held that the decisions of private societies (although not as of yet one of a direct sports governing nature) might be susceptible to judicial review when the decision at issue has characteristics that import an element of public law.[115] The ambiguity of the applicable test may prove attractive in the future for sports litigants.[116] The test also prompts deeper consideration of the quasi-public/private nature and function of leading sports bodies. According to Kerr J, 'an issue is one of public law where it involves a matter of public interest in the sense that it has an impact on the public generally and not merely on an individual or group … [but] … that is not to say that an issue becomes one of public law simply because it generates interest or concern in the minds of the public. It must affect the public rather than merely engage its interest to qualify as a public law issue. It seems to me to be equally clear that a matter may be one of public law while having a specific impact on an individual in his personal capacity'.[117]

---

[110] The grounds for judicial review in Scotland are similar to those in England and Wales—illegality, irrationality and procedural impropriety; per *West v Secretary of State for Scotland* [1992] SLT 636.

[111] *Fotheringham, Re Application for Judicial Review* [2008] ScotCS CSOH 170 [27], Lord Pentland.

[112] *Lennox v British Show Jumping Association, Scottish Branch* [1996] SLT 353.

[113] Ibid 355.

[114] C Munro, 'Comment: Sports in the Courts' [2005] *Public Law* 681, 683 noting that a plea of *forum non conveniens* might, however, be entered.

[115] See generally *Re Phillips Application* [1995] NI 322, 334, Carswell LCJ and, eg, *Re Alan Kirkpatrick's Application* [2004] NIJB 15 [26], Kerr J, where the decision of a privately owned Co-operative Society, which had historical and exclusive rights to grant commercial licences for eel fishing, was held amenable to judicial review for refusal to grant the applicant a licence to fish.

[116] On the 'vague and value laden' nature of this test see G Anthony, *Judicial Review in Northern Ireland* (Oxford, Hart Publishing, 2008) [2.14]–[2.17].

[117] *Re McBride's Application* [1999] NI 299, 310, Kerr J; subsequently approved by the NI Court of Appeal in *Re McBride's Application (No 2)* [2003] NI 319, 336, Carswell LCJ.

Datafin Parameters

[**2.39**]   Admittedly, the persuasive authority mentioned above must be seen in the context that a number of the stated jurisdictions (for instance, Scotland and South Africa) do not recognise the public/private divide to the formal extent present in England and Wales. Nevertheless, the uniformity of this trend cannot be denied, particularly when it is taken in conjunction with the fact that for 35 years, sports governing bodies have been treated as 'emanations of the state' for the purposes of EU law,[118] and, more relevantly still, such bodies might in some aspects be considered public authorities pursuant to section 6(3)(b) of the Human Rights Act 1998.[119] Therefore for a number of distinguished commentators, the English perspective (on the amenability of sports bodies to judicial review) is very much a pyrrhic victory of form and procedure over substance and function.[120] What follows is a critical examination of this 'English perspective'.

[**2.40**]   The traditional approach in assessing whether the decision-making authority of a body might be amenable to judicial review is to hold that the source of power of decision is usually decisive and thus if the source of power is statutory in nature such that the body is established to perform a public duty, then that body is amenable to judicial review; if the source is solely contractual in nature such that it arises from the agreement of the parties, then the body is not subject to public law.[121] It follows that where, as is the case in a number of the countries previously mentioned, a sports body has a statutory footing, it must, on pain of judicial review, act intra vires its legislative framework,[122] and may in fact, pursuant to the establishing legislative scheme, have obligations of fairness imposed upon them.[123] Given the long history of self-regulation in sport in the UK, few sports bodies are however fully or expressly statutory in nature and most remain of a private, self-regulatory nature. Nevertheless, the position

---

[118]   *Walrave and Koch v Association Union Cycliste Internationale* [1974] ECR 1405 [12]–[25].

[119]   See below [2.54]–[2.55].

[120]   See Beloff *et al* (n 76) and also D McArdle, 'Judicial Review, "Public Authorities" and Disciplinary Powers of Sports Organisations' (1999) 30 *Cambrian Law Review* 31; P Morris and N Little, 'Challenging Sports Bodies Determinations' (1998) 17 *Civil Justice Quarterly* 128; and D Pannick, 'Judicial Review of Sports Governing Bodies' [1997] *Judicial Review* 150.

[121]   See the review in *R v Criminal Injuries Compensation Board, ex parte Lain* [1967] 2 QB 864, 882, Lord Parker CJ.

[122]   In Australia, Ireland and New Zealand, eg, it is usual that sports bodies associated with dog and horse racing in their various forms operate on a statutory basis. For Australia, see *Heatley v Tasmanian Racing and Gaming Commission* [1977] 137 CLR 487; [1977] HCA 39. For New Zealand, see *New Zealand Trotting Conference v Ryan* [1990] 1 NZLR 143; *New Zealand Harness Racing v Kotzikas* [2005] NZAR 268; *Cropp v Mathie Welch & Ors* [2006] NZHC 1368; *Carter v Judicial Control Authority (New Zealand Thoroughbred Racing Inc)* [2006] NZHC 1526; and *Clotworthy v Judicial Control Authority (New Zealand Thoroughbred Racing Inc)* [2008] NZHC 204. For Ireland, compare the three contrasting approaches of *BLE v Quirke* [1988] IR 83; *Murphy v Turf Club* [1989] IR 171; and *Moran & Ors v Sullivan & Ors* [2003] IEHC 35.

[123]   An analogy here would be to a trade union member's 'right not to be unjustifiably disciplined' per ss 64–65 of the Trade Union and Labour Relations (Consolidation) Act 1992 and s 16 of the Trade Union Reform and Employment Rights Act 1993.

is complicated by the fact that the traditional 'either/or' approach is difficult to reconcile with the modern administrative demands of state and government, which has resulted in an increasing number of 'public' decisions being taken by non-statutory, self-regulating private bodies performing 'contracted out' government functions.[124] *Datafin* itself presented such a problem for the Court of Appeal. Central to the stated proceedings was a Takeover Panel, which was a non-statutory, self-regulating association, established by persons who had a common interest in devising and operating a code of conduct regulating take-overs and mergers of public companies. The association had government backing and was exercising duties in the public interest in the sense that the Department of Trade and Industry relied on the Takeover Panel to enforce the City Code on Take-overs and Mergers. The Court of Appeal held that if a body has a public function and is clearly performing public duties so that it follows logically that its decisions produce public law consequences, then, in principle, it is within the public law jurisdiction of the courts to intervene.[125] Applying that approach, the Court of Appeal held that it could intervene, subjecting the Takeover Panel in question to the control of public law but that since, on the facts, there were no grounds for interfering with the Takeover Panel's decision, the Court declined to do so.

[**2.41**]   More precisely, the *Datafin* test held that in assessing the amenability of a body to judicial review, the source of that entity's power (statutory or contractual) is usually, but not always, decisive. On occasion, the Court of Appeal indicated, a court can peer between these 'extremes' of power in order to look at the nature of that power; thus if the body in question is exercising public law functions, or if the exercise of its functions have public law consequences, then that may be sufficient to bring the body within the reach of judicial review.[126] Accordingly, in *Datafin*, although the birth and constitution of the Takeover Panel owed little to any exercise of governmental power, the Court of Appeal held that the position had evolved so that the Panel could now be considered sufficiently woven into the fabric of public regulation (in the field of take-over and mergers) to be held amenable to judicial review. In contrast, in *Aga Khan*, a unanimous Court of Appeal held that the Jockey Club was not sufficiently woven into the fabric of public regulation as to be susceptible to judicial review.[127]

[**2.42**]   As stated, the *Aga Khan* decision has attracted academic criticism and, writing in 1995, Lord Woolf argued that the preclusion of sports bodies

---

[124] Note the general discussion and approach of the House of Lords in *YL v Birmingham City Council* [2008] 1 AC 95; [2007] 3 All ER 957; [2007] UKHL 27 (in the context of s 6 of the Human Rights Act 1998).

[125] *Datafin* [1987] QB 815, 838–39, Sir John Donaldson MR; 846–47, Lloyd LJ; 850–51, Nicholls LJ.

[126] Ibid 847, Lloyd LJ.

[127] *Aga Khan* [1993] 2 All ER 853; [1993] 1 WLR 909, 921–23, Sir Thomas Bingham MR citing extensively from *R v Football Association Ltd, ex parte Football League Ltd* [1993] 2 All ER 833, 848–49, Rose J.

from public law review was 'questionable'.[128] Lord Woolf contended that, where activities of a public nature are being performed, the body performing those duties should be required to conform to the standards that public law requires in the performance of those duties and that this was of especial importance whether the body in question was in a monopolistic position of power (as is the case with a number of leading sports organisations). When applied retrospectively to *Aga Khan*, Lord Woolf's comments prompt four points of interest.[129] First, there is an inherent contradiction within the *Aga Khan* approach to the Jockey Club's status: on the one hand the Jockey Club was said not to have been 'woven into any system of governmental control of horse racing'; yet, on the other hand, it is admitted that in the absence of the Jockey Club, the government would 'probably be driven to create a public body' to control the horse racing industry in Britain.[130] Second, to state, as Farquharson LJ did in *Aga Khan* that, where available, contract-based private law remedies offer the 'more convenient process'[131] is not entirely accurate. The writ procedure with pleadings, discovery, and oral evidence, is arguably more elaborate, time-consuming and expensive than judicial review.[132] Third, the Court of Appeal in *Aga Khan* did not address in an entirely satisfactory manner the fact that the Jockey Club (now in the guise of the British Horseracing Authority) was the principal and sole regulatory agent for horse racing in Britain and whose monopolistic authority operated on a 'take it or leave it' basis[133] so that consequently 'no serious racecourse management, owner, trainer or jockey can survive without the recognition or licence of the Jockey Club'.[134] In this, the warning in the dissenting judgment of Lord Denning in *Breen v Amalgamated Engineering Union*,[135] against the 'unfettered discretion' of entities such as the Stock Exchange, the Jockey Club and the Football Association (FA), continues to resonate.[136]

[2.43]   The fourth point of concern with the *Aga Khan* case is the reliance placed by the Court of Appeal upon a number of cases involving challenges to decisions made by the FA. In *Aga Khan*, the Court of Appeal was much taken with the decision of Rose J in *R v Football Association, ex parte Football League Ltd*. The stated case centred on the FA's decision in 1991 to form a Premier League. In order to facilitate the breaking away of top division clubs from the Football League, the

---

[128] Lord Woolf, 'Droit Public—English Style' [1995] *Public Law* 57, 63–64.

[129] Discussed fully by Anderson (n 77) 182–85.

[130] Note the concluding remarks of Sir Thomas Bingham MR in *Aga Khan* [1993] 1 WLR 909, 923.

[131] Ibid 930 and 933, Hoffmann LJ.

[132] See the comments in *Law v NGRC* [1983] 1 WLR 1302, 1311–12, Slade LJ.

[133] *Aga Khan* [1993] 1 WLR 909, 929–30, Farquharson LJ.

[134] Ibid 915, Sir Thomas Bingham MR: 'There is in effect no alternative market in which those not accepted by the Jockey Club can find a place or to which racegoers may resort. Thus by means of the rules and its market domination the Jockey Club can effectively control not only those who agree to abide by it rules but also those ... who do not'.

[135] *Breen v Amalgamated Engineering Union* [1971] 2 QB 175.

[136] Ibid 190.

FA amended its regulations to provide that any rule by which the Football League purported to require a club to give longer notice of membership termination than that required by the FA's regulations was to be void. The Football League brought proceedings for judicial review of the FA's decision. Rose J held that given the contractual relationship between the parties, the FA was not amenable to judicial review at the instance of the Football League. Rose J then went on to state that, irrespective of the contractual relationship, the FA was not a public body underpinned by statute because there was nothing to suggest that the government would step in if the FA did not exist: 'On the contrary a far more likely intervener to run football would be a television or similar company rooted in the entertainment business or a commercial company seeking advertising benefits'.[137]

[**2.44**]   The elite Premiership level aside—which is effectively subsidised by a TV company's sponsorship and dictated to by them—Rose J appeared to misconstrue the overall objective of the FA, which is to promote the sport at all levels throughout England. It is suggested that only a statutory body would have the administrative competency and depth of resourcing to realise the stated objective, and that it is merely an accident of history that the FA, and similar sporting bodies, remain 'private' in nature.[138] Moreover, it appears much more satisfactory and transparent to admit as Neill LJ and Simon Brown J did respectively, albeit obiter, in *R v Disciplinary Committee of the Jockey, ex parte Massingberd-Mundy* and *R v Jockey Club, ex parte RAM Racecourses Limited*, that in some decisions at any rate the Jockey Club is capable of being judicially reviewed. In *Massingberd-Mundy*, the High Court held that the decision of the Jockey Club (upheld by its disciplinary committee) to remove the applicant from the list of stewards approved to act as chairman of stewards at race meetings, was not a decision within the sphere of public law because the Jockey Club's competency in this matter was domestic in nature and empowered by a consensual submission to that private jurisdiction. Nevertheless, the High Court observed that 'an examination of the charter and the powers conferred upon the Jockey Club strongly suggest that in some aspects of its work it operates in the public domain and that its functions are at least in part public or quasi-public functions'.[139] In *RAM Racecourses Limited*, the Jockey Club accepted a report stating that additional race fixtures needed to be allocated to existing and new racecourses. The Jockey Club refused to commit to allocating race fixtures to the applicant's new racecourse. The applicant sought judicial review of this decision, which was refused on the grounds that the report was not accompanied by a legitimate expectation (of fixture allocation) in favour of the application, who, in any event, was not in the class of persons entitled to rely on the report. That rejection notwithstanding, the High Court did go on to observe that, although the Jockey Club for the most part takes decisions which

---

[137] *R v FA* [1993] 2 All ER 833, 848–49.
[138] This point is well made by M Beloff and T Kerr, 'Why Aga Khan is wrong' [1996] *Judicial Review* 30.
[139] *Massingberd-Mundy* [1993] 2 All ER 207, 219, Neill LJ.

affect only—or at least essentially—those voluntarily and willingly subscribing to their rules and procedures, just occasionally (the example used was in exercising quasi-licensing powers) the public interest in, and public nature of, the decision-making authority of the Jockey Club might demand that it is subjected to judicial review.[140]

[**2.45**]   In sum, despite the merits of these observations, the High Court in *Massingberd-Mundy* and in *RAM Racecourses Limited* felt bound by the decision in *Law v NGRC* and dismissed the applications for judicial review. The Court of Appeal in *Aga Khan* held similarly in precluding the stated decision of the Jockey Club from public law review, and when the purported weaknesses and inconsistencies in that decision were raised by the applicant in *Mullins,* they were again thoroughly rejected by Stanley Burton J.[141] In short, the assertion that the *Datafin* parameters should be extended so that the decisions of sports bodies might come within the orbit of judicial review has not been made out to the temptation of the courts. The courts have reiterated on a number of occasions that the functions of sports bodies such as the Jockey Club and the FA are distinguishable from the functions of the Takeover Panel in *Datafin*. The Takeover Panel exercised regulatory control in a public sphere where governmental regulatory control was absent and, although leading sports bodies carry out functions that would probably otherwise have to be provided by a statutory body, disputes involving their decision-making competency remain, so far as the High Court and Court of Appeal are concerned, matters confined to the working out of private contractual arrangements.[142] The frustration with this approach is that, although it is, doubtless, in the public's interest that sports industries such as horse racing remain free of doping and associated malpractice (particularly where the gambling public is dependent on each race and animal being run on its merits); it appears, nevertheless, that even with respect to decision-making of this gravity, which goes to the heart of the horse racing industry's integrity, the English courts remain firm in their view that this is not sufficiently public in nature as to be amenable to judicial review.

[**2.46**]   Finally, it must be pointed out that the full consequences of the preclusion of sports bodies from public law review are allayed in at least three ways. First, where, upon the existence of a contractual relationship, the aggrieved sports participant is 'forced' to proceed by private law means, it is clear that, in any event, the principles and standard of review are now of a similar nature to that in public law review. Second, even in the absence of a contractual relationship, it remains

---

[140] *RAM Racecourse Ltd* [1993] 2 All ER 225, 248, Simon Brown LJ.

[141] Note the comments of Stanley Burton J in the subsequent hearing on costs in *Mullins* [2005] EWHC 2197 (Admin) [4]–[7].

[142] See similarly the approach taken to attempts to judicially review disciplinary-related decisions of the Director of the National Crime Squad in *R (on the application of Tucker) v Director General of the National Crime Squad* [2003] EWCA Civ 2 [12]–[38] Scott Baker LJ and of a conduct committee of Lloyd's of London in *R (on the application of West) v Lloyd's of London* [2005] EWCA Civ 506 [27]–[32] Brooke LJ.

the case that a sports claimant might be able to appeal to the inherent supervisory jurisdiction of the High Court over a domestic tribunal (where again a quasi-public law standard of review will take place). Third, there may soon be yet another claims procedure for the aggrieved sports participant, which can be located in recent authority suggesting that sports governing bodies might possibly be considered 'quasi-public authorities' pursuant to section 6 of the Human Rights Act 1998. All of these matters are discussed in the context of yet another challenge to the authority of the Jockey Club; in this instance, a decision that resulted in a lengthy suspension being imposed on a leading jockey.[143]

Graham Bradley

[**2.47**]   Ever since his victory in the 1983 Cheltenham Gold Cup, Graham Bradley had always been considered one of the most naturally gifted National Hunt jockeys in Britain. In the 1990s though he became a central figure in a long-running investigation into race-fixing and corruption in the sport, which, in 1999, led him to be questioned by both the London Metropolitan Police's Serious Crime Squad and the Jockey's Club Licensing Committee.[144] After these inconclusive investigations, Bradley retired and became a bloodstock agent sourcing racehorses for a number of high profile clients such as Robbie Fowler and Steve McManaman. The investigations in 1999 had centred on Bradley's friendship with a fellow jockey called Barrie Wright and a professional gambler, Brian Brendan Wright.[145] In 2001, Barrie Wright was charged with involvement in a conspiracy to import cocaine and part of the prosecution's case against him was that he had received cash payments from Brian Brendan Wright (who by then appears to have fled to North Cyprus) in connection with a drugs operation. Barrie Wright's (successful) defence was that his involvement with Brian Brendan Wright had related not to drugs but to the provision of information about racehorses for the purposes of a gambling organisation led by Brian Brendan Wright.[146] Bradley was called to give evidence in support of

---

[143] *Bradley v Jockey Club* [2004] EWHC 2164; [2005] EWCA Civ 1056.

[144] The background to this story is related to the fact that the Jockey Club's Head of Security during the 1990s was an ex-army officer Roger Buffham who, on being made redundant in 2001, became a 'whistleblower' culminating in a celebrated BBC Panorama investigation into the extent of corruption in horse racing. The Panorama programme was eventually broadcast in the autumn of 2002 despite the objections of a leading bookmaker (*Chandler v Buffham* [2002] EWHC 1426 (QB)) and the Jockey Club itself (*Jockey Club v Buffham* [2003] QB 462) as to breaches of confidence.

[145] For a partial account of these investigations see Bradley's autobiography (with S Taylor), *The Wayward Lad* (Exeter, Greenwater, 2000).

[146] In 2007, after one of the most wide-ranging drugs investigations in British policing history, Brian Brendan Wright was eventually extradited from Spain and sentenced to 30 years' imprisonment on various drugs trafficking charges. Horse racing had provided Mr Wright with the opportunity to launder his drug smuggling profits. See generally B Roche, 'No More Deliveries' *The Irish Times* (Dublin 7 April 2007) News Features 5.

the defence and admitted under cross-examination that for over a decade he had 'for reward' and to the benefit of Brian Brendan Wright's gambling operation, regularly passed on sensitive, privileged and confidential information.[147]

[**2.48**]   On the back of that evidence, Bradley was, in 2002, charged by the Jockey Club with a number of breaches of the Rules of Racing during his time as a licensed jockey. The Jockey Club's Disciplinary Committee found certain of the charges proved and imposed a disqualification order against Bradley banning him for a period of eight years. The Jockey Club's Appeal Board dismissed an appeal by Bradley as to liability but reduced the sanction to five years. The sanction or disqualification was, in effect, of a 'warning off' nature excluding Bradley from any premise owned, controlled or licensed by the Jockey Club. As the High Court noted subsequently, the nature of the penalty was such that if implemented it would 'almost certainly bring the claimant's current [bloodstock agent] business to an end and have an extremely serious effect on his livelihood and his family'.[148] In the stated proceedings, Bradley sought an injunction and damages for breach of contract against the Jockey Club. The challenge was not on liability but on the ground that the imposition of sanction (which was suspended pending the outcome of the legal proceedings) was disproportionate.[149]

[**2.49**]   Richards J in the High Court wholly endorsed the Appeal Board's decision, holding that the five-year period of disqualification was proportionate and lawful.[150] Although the claimant attempted to highlight the lengthy nature of the penalty in comparison to previous sanctions handed down by the Jockey Club,[151] Richards J found that the Appeal Board had struck the correct balance between the principles underlying their sanctioning powers (punishment, deterrence and prevention) and the correct legal test on proportionality outlined in *De Freitas v Permanent Secretary*[152] and modified in *Colgan v Kennel Club*.[153] In short, Richards J was satisfied that the Appeal Board had carefully, and within the 'margin of discretion' that should be granted to a tribunal with expertise in the area, calibrated the sanction to reflect, on the one hand, that the impact on Bradley of disqualification for such a period would seriously jeopardise his bloodstock

---

[147] On the 'sensitivity' of the information in question and the nature of the 'presents' given to Bradley see *Bradley* [2004] EWHC 2164 [6], Richards J.

[148] Ibid [1] and [21], Richards J.

[149] Ibid [1], [19] and [25]. Although the decision was not challenged, Bradley did take issue with certain aspects of the Jockey Club's findings insofar as they touched on the sanction. Bradley was of the opinion that a proportionate penalty would have been measured in weeks or months not years.

[150] Ibid [117]: 'I do not think that I would have decided on any lesser period of disqualification as the proportionate penalty had I been standing in the shoes of the [Appeal] Board'.

[151] Ibid [95]–[105].

[152] [1998] UKPC 30; [1999] 1 AC 69 [25]–[26], Lord Clyde. See also the principles outlined in *R (Daly) v Secretary of State for the Home Department* [2001] UKHL 26; [2001] 2 AC 532 [27]–[28], Lord Steyn, noting that in law 'context is everything'.

[153] [2001] All ER (D) 403 (Oct) [42] Cooke J. 'As amended the proportionality (of sanction) test is threefold: the objectives of the disciplinary procedures are sufficiently important to justify limiting a fundamental right; the measures designed to meet the objectives are rationally connected to it; the means used to impair the right or freedom are no more than is necessary to accomplish the objective'.

business and that outside of his 'Wright connection' Bradley appeared to be of good character and good standing within the racing community; against, on the other hand, the fact that Bradley had been supplying confidential information for a considerable period of time to a professional gambler and had thus seriously compromised the integrity of the horse racing industry as a whole.[154] Moreover, given the 'totality of the evidence', Richards J held that the Jockey Club's Appeal Board was right to reject Bradley's contention that he had deliberately exaggerated his evidence in the Wright trial in order to protect his friend.[155] In addition, Richards J dismissed the claimant's argument that he was a 'scapegoat' and was being singled out unfairly by the Jockey Club in its attempts to eliminate a practice that, according to Bradley, most jockeys engaged in.[156] In sum, Richards J held that given the seriousness of Bradley's actions—the provision of insider information distorting the betting market on specific races to the corruption of the sport's integrity as a whole—the Appeal Board's decision on sanction was proportionate. In a subsequent, unsuccessful appeal to the Court of Appeal, Richards J's approach to the proportionality of sanction issue was commended in its entirety.[157]

Quasi-Public Law Approach in Private Law Claims

[**2.50**]   In *Bradley*, both parties accepted as a premise to their arguments that the decision of the Jockey Club's Appeal Board was not subject to judicial review.[158] Bradley based his claim principally on the contention that there had been a breach of an implied term of his contractual relations with the Jockey Club to submit to its Rules of Racing: namely, that the Jockey Club would carry out its disciplinary functions in accordance with the Rules of Racing reasonably and fairly and only impose a sentence proportionate to the facts proven or admitted.[159] The basis of the contractual relationship between the parties was an exchange of correspondence in the aftermath of Bradley's evidence at Wright's trial, whereby Bradley consented to be treated at all material times to be bound by the Rules of Racing.[160] On holding that a contractual relationship existed, Richards J went on to hold that the role of the court in such a contractual context should be 'supervisory and that

---

[154] *Bradley* [2004] EWHC 2164 [106]-[116], Richards J. *Colgan v Kennel Club* [2001] All ER (D) 403 (Oct), distinguished.

[155] Ibid [76]–[80]. Bradley contended that he had exaggerated the frequency with which he passed on confidential information and that, in reality, the information that he did pass on was confined principally to one horse owned by Brian Brendan Wright.

[156] Ibid [81]–[94]. Bradley claimed that most jockeys had their own 'punter' to whom they would give tips in return for reward.

[157] *Bradley* [2005] EWCA Civ 1056 [19]–[27], Lord Phillips MR.

[158] *Bradley* [2004] EWHC 2164 [33], Richards J.

[159] *Bradley* [2005] EWCA Civ 1056 [13], Lord Phillips MR.

[160] For the effect of that exchange of correspondence see *Bradley* [2004] EWHC 2164 [55]–[56], Richards J. There was some debate as to whether Bradley's former status as a licensed jockey might have given rise to a continuing contractual relationship between the parties. Richards J, [51]–[54] citing *Aga Khan*, hinted that it might, but that, in any event, neither party had proceeded on that basis.

the approach of the court should be similar to that adopted when considering the lawfulness of a like decision of a public body in proceedings for judicial review'.[161] Accordingly, Richards J, citing from Lord Woolf's judgments in *Modahl*[162] and *Wilander v Tobin*,[163] observed that, while in some situations public and private law principles can differ, there is no reason why (as in the present case) there should be any difference as to what constitutes 'unfairness', or why the standard of fairness required by an implied contractual term should differ from that required by a similar tribunal under public law.[164]

Inherent Supervisory Jurisdiction

[**2.51**] Interestingly, Richards J held that, consistent with the Court of Appeal's decision in *Modahl (No 2)*, the implied contractual obligations on the Jockey Club did not extend beyond ensuring that the disciplinary process as a whole, including a sensible appellate process, was made available to the claimant, an obligation with which the Jockey Club 'plainly complied'.[165] It is of some importance that Richards J went on to say that there was no basis for implying a general term the effect of which would hold the Jockey Club responsible, and potentially liable, in damages for any error made by the (independently constituted) Appeal Board and neither would it be sensible to imply a term whereby specifically the Jockey Club would undertake that any penalty decided on by the Appeal Board should be proportionate. In this non-contractual context, Richards J held that the decision of the Appeal Board was more properly subject to the supervisory jurisdiction of the Court in accordance with the principles stated in *Nagle v Feilden*.[166] That case concerned the rejection of an application by a woman for a trainer's licence from the Jockey Club. The claim, which was struck out at first instance for lack of contractual relation, was based on the allegation that the Jockey Club's refusal was based on a policy of gender discrimination. An appeal to the Court of Appeal was allowed unanimously, where it was held that, even in the absence of any contractual relationship, where a person's right to work was at issue, a decision of a domestic body affecting that right could be the subject of a claim for a declaration of invalidity and an injunction requiring the body to rectify their error.[167] Richards J, noting that Bradley's challenge in this respect was, effectively, one of a 'right to work' basis ie, that the imposition of the

---

[161] Ibid [66].

[162] Ibid [41]–[42], citing *Modahl* [1997] EWCA Civ 2209, Lord Woolf MR.

[163] Ibid [39]–[40], citing *Wilander v Tobin* [1997] 2 Lloyd's Rep 293, 299–300, Lord Woolf.

[164] See also *Lee v Showmen's Guild of GB* [1952] 2 QB 329, 346.

[165] *Bradley* [2004] EWHC 2164 [50] and [56]–[70], Richards J, citing from all three principal judgments in *Modahl (No 2)* [2001] EWCA Civ 1447; *Singer v The Jockey Club* Unreported, Chancery Division 28 June 1990, Scott J, 18E–19A (official transcript) and *Colgan v Kennel Club* [2001] All ER (D) 403 (Oct) [42] Cooke J.

[166] [1966] 2 QB 633, Lord Denning MR. See also *Breen v Amalgamated Engineering Union* [1971] 2 QB 175, 190–91 Lord Denning MR.

[167] Ibid [1966] 2 QB 633, 646, Lord Denning MR.

disproportionate disqualification would operate in unreasonable restraint of trade, then went on to consider the nature of the court's supervisory jurisdiction in such instances.[168] Approving the observations of Lord Denning MR in *Enderby Town FC v Football Association;*[169] Megarry VC in *McInnes v Onslow-Fane;*[170] Millett LJ in *Stevenage Borough FC v Football League Ltd;*[171] and Latham LJ in *Modahl (No 2);*[172] Richards J held that the role of the court was essentially *supervisory* in nature. By this Richards J meant that the function of the court is not to take the primary decision but to ensure that the primary decision-maker has operated within lawful limits and that in this light the Court's review function would be 'very similar to that of the court of judicial review' to the point that it would be 'surprising and unsatisfactory if a private law claim in relation to the decision of a domestic body required the court to adopt a materially different approach from a judicial review claim in relation to the decision of a public body'.[173]

[**2.52**]   Applying this approach to the case at hand, Richards J held that an analysis of the lawfulness of the decision by the Jockey Club's Appeal Board required a review of when in exercising their (expert-led) judgment, the Appeal Board had acted within the discretionary limits open to them as the decision-maker to the point that their decision to impose a five-year disqualification was within their discretionary area of judgment such that it could be considered proportionate.[174] As noted previously Richards J held that the sanction was proportionate, as, subsequently, did the Court of Appeal. A factor in the permission to appeal, granted by the (then) Vice Chancellor, Clarke LJ, appears to have been that Richards J erred in his approach to the Court's jurisdiction and function in respect of reviewing domestic tribunals, but that contention was subsequently abandoned on appeal.[175] Overall, Richards J's approach to the supervisory jurisdiction of the courts over domestic tribunals in non-contractual contexts appears to be good and sensible law.[176] There may be one caveat: its applicability extends, arguably, only to situations where the claimant's right to work or trade is the fundamental, underlying issue of the disciplinary proceedings at issue.[177] This is debatable and,

---

[168]   *Bradley* [2004] EWHC 2164 [37]–[42], Richards J.

[169]   [1971] Ch 591, 606.

[170]   [1978] 1 WLR 1520, 1535.

[171]   (1997) 9 *Admin LR* 109.

[172]   *Modahl (No 2)* [2001] EWCA Civ 1447 [44]–[47].

[173]   *Bradley* [2004] EWHC 2164 [37].

[174]   Ibid [45]–[47] where Richards J cited that his approach was analogous to the proportionality principles of review outlined with respect to the Human Rights Act 1998 in *R v Home Secretary, ex parte Daly* [2001] UKHL 26; [2001] 2 AC 532.

[175]   *Bradley* [2005] EWCA Civ 1056 [18], Lord Phillips MR.

[176]   Note its application in *Chambers v British Olympic Association* [2008] EWHC 2028 (QB) [31]–[38] Mackay J.

[177]   *Bradley* [2005] EWCA Civ 1056 [30]–[31], Buxton LJ reminding the Court of Appeal that in strict terms '*Nagle v Fielden* went no further than to say that the court could intervene when there was a general and discriminatory rule preventing a certain category of people practising a professional irrespective of their behaviour, their competence, or their disciplinary record … but it says little or nothing in respect of how professions should conduct their disciplinary functions'.

in any event, the *Mullins* proceedings provide a limited alternative. In *Mullins*, the claimant sought neither damages for breach of contract nor injunctive relief but sought, ultimately and simply, a declaration. The applicant took the proceedings as a claim for judicial review under CPR Part 54.1 but, as discussed, the Administrative Court held that the Court of Appeal's decision in *Aga Khan* was applicable thus the decisions of the Jockey Club's Appeal Board could not be consider amenable to judicial review.[178] Nevertheless, given that declaratory relief only was sought, Stanley Burton J agreed, pursuant to CPR Part 54.20, to transfer the application to the Queen's Bench Division.[179] In this, Stanley Burton agreed with the claimant's contention that a similar jurisdiction to that exercised by the Administrative Court under CPR Part 54 was available under private law in the Queen's Bench Division pursuant, in the circumstances of *Mullins*, to CPR Part 8.[180] In *Mullins v McFarlane*,[181] the claimant availed of this opportunity to argue that the decision to disqualify his horse for a positive drugs test was based on a scientific threshold implemented in an arbitrary and capricious manner. The defendants argued that if the courts had a supervisory jurisdiction in such instances it should be limited, as in *Bradley*, to 'right to work' cases.[182] Stanley Burton J was not of that opinion holding more generally that private associations have long been under a duty to act lawfully, in accordance with the general principles of fairness, avoiding arbitrary or capricious decision-making at odds with the regulatory ambit and consistency of their rules.[183] Nevertheless, despite some concerns about the 'retrospective effect' of the Jockey Club's anti-doping regime,[184] the allegation that it was implemented arbitrarily and capriciously was ultimately not made out to the satisfaction of Stanley Burton J.

Bradley: A Summary

[**2.53**]   In *Bradley*, the fundamental question for the Court, in its supervisory role, was whether the Jockey Club's Appeal Board had reached a lawful decision, in particular whether the Appeal Board's decision on penalty fell within the limits of its discretionary area of judgment and thus could be said to be proportionate.[185] It is clear from the language, case law and analytical approach used by Richards J in his consideration of this question that the non-availability of judicial review in challenges to domestic sports bodies is now of little practical import. This is because *Bradley* illustrates that even in ostensibly private law challenges,

---

[178] *Mullins* [2005] EWHC 2197 (Admin) [45]–[46], Stanley Burton J.
[179] Ibid [47]–[49].
[180] Ibid [7].
[181] *Mullins v McFarlane* [2006] EWHC 986 (QB).
[182] Ibid [38].
[183] Ibid [37] and [39].
[184] Ibid [50]–[52].
[185] Ibid [75].

the standard of review will be analogous to that of public law proceedings.[186] In short, it appears that sports governing bodies in England and Wales owe broadly the same obligations as a matter of private law as, for example, do their Scottish counterparts whose decisions are susceptible to judicial review to the point that, damages apart, it is now unlikely that a claimant would be deprived of relief (injunctive or declaratory) in a private law proceeding that he or she would otherwise be able to obtain in public law review.[187] Accordingly, although, at first instance, English law appears quite isolated in its reluctance to extend the boundaries of judicial review to the decisions of sports bodies, in actuality there is little to distinguish the English approach from the more 'amenable' jurisdictions outlined previously.[188] In sum, though it loses some of its precision in its brevity, it can now be argued that the approach of the courts can be condensed as follows: in scrutinising the disciplinary mechanisms of private sports bodies, the courts consider, as they do for bodies subject to public law review, whether, and with due respect to its inherent expertise, that sports disciplinary mechanism acted as a 'rational decision maker' should.[189] Finally, the *Bradley* proceedings prompt two further points of interest. First, Bradley's challenge relied in part on the doctrine of restraint of trade. The manner in which this doctrine has been considered in the disciplinary control of members by sports governing bodies is discussed shortly. Second, a feature of *Bradley* is the occasional references to Article 6 of the European Convention on Human Rights (Article 6ECHR) and specifically some initial claims by Bradley (subsequently dropped) that the Appeal Board's conduct breached Article 6's requirements on impartiality and lack of bias.[190] Taken as a whole this chapter should illustrate that the best way to protect the decision-making authority of a sports governing body from legal challenge is for that body to ensure that its disciplinary mechanism could withstand an 'audit' of its workings pursuant to the demands of Article 6 ECHR. Chapter three provides guidance on just such an audit but, to borrow from the language of human rights, the

---

[186] Ibid [37] and [66]. See similarly the approach of the Supreme Court of British Colombia in *Street v BC School Sports* [2005] BCSC 958 and in *Wang v British Columbia Medical Association* [2008] BCSC 1559.

[187] See how Lord Pentland's view of 'the role of the court in relation to disciplinary decisions by sports bodies' in *Fotheringham, Re Application for Judicial Review* [2008] ScotCS CSOH 170 [24]–[27] is entirely similar in application to the 'quasi-public' standard of review taken by both the English High Court and the Court of Appeal in *Flaherty v National Greyhound Racing Limited* [2004] EWHC 2838 (Ch); [2005] EWCA Civ 1117.

[188] Even in 'amenable' jurisdictions such as Australia, influential cases such as *Australian Football League v Carlton Football Club and Williams* [1998] 2 VR 546 suggest that sports litigants appear satisfied that an enhanced private law understanding of procedural fairness will adequately protect their interests. In that case, the second defendant sought unsuccessfully to challenge a nine-week suspension as a result of physical interference with an umpire. The proceedings were founded on alleged ultra vires breaches by the AFL of the Standard Playing Contract to which the player, his club and the AFL were parties. The proceedings were purely in the nature of a civil action, nothing in the nature of judicial review was considered; and the relief sought was limited to a declaration and an injunction.

[189] See *Huang v Secretary of State for the Home Department* 2007] UKHL 11; [2007] 2 AC 167 [16], Lord Bingham.

[190] *Bradley* [2004] EWHC 2164 [11]; [18]; [36]; [59] and [2005] EWCA Civ 1056 [11].

'horizontal' application of Article 6 to sports disciplinary mechanisms might become even more immediate or 'vertical' if the functional and decision-making competencies of sports organisations is taken to be encapsulated by section 6(3)(b) of the Human Rights Act's definition of a 'public body'.

Quasi-Public Sporting Authorities

[**2.54**]   Under section 6 of the Human Rights Act 1998, public authorities must, on pain of a claimant being entitled to any relief or remedy that the court may grant subject to section 8 of the Act, act in accordance with the ECHR.[191] The fundamental issue for sports authorities is whether they fall within section 6's definition of a public body.[192] At first instance, it must be noted that section 6(3)(a) of the Human Rights Act 1998 provides that it is unlawful for a public body, including any court or tribunal in which legal proceedings may be brought, to act in a way that is incompatible with a Convention right. This is of interest to sports bodies because, arguably, the provision creates a 'horizontal' effect mandating courts and tribunals to ensure that Convention rights are not violated in situations such as internal disciplinary sports hearings. This contention, and the extent of the obligations and rights most likely to be at issue, remain at a nascent stage.[193] In the immediate context, the most regular matter for consideration by the courts or tribunals will, undoubtedly, be the horizontal effect of Article 6 ECHR—the right to a fair and public hearing within a reasonable time by an independent and impartial tribunal established by law.

[**2.55**]   The question as to whether, in a vertical sense, section 6(3)(b) of the Human Rights Act 1998's definition of a 'mixed function' or 'hybrid' public body—any person certain of whose function are functions of a public nature—might extend directly to a sports disciplinary tribunal, has been viewed restrictively.[194] In *Mullins*, for instance, Stanley Burton J, as part of his analysis as to why, for lack of a sufficiently governmental function, the Jockey Club was not amenable to judicial review under CPR Part 54, held that the administration of the anti-doping scheme

---

[191]   Remedies include damages, which is of relevance for those claimants who have no contractual cause of action. For the influence that the Human Rights Act 1998 might have on sports disciplinary mechanisms see R Anderson, J Mulchay and A Reindorf, '"Independent and impartial?" The Potential Impact of the Human Rights Act 1998 on Sports Tribunals' (2000) 4 *International Sports Law Review* 65.

[192]   See the admission by the New Zealand Thoroughbred Racing Inc that is was a public body in terms of s 3(b) of the New Zealand Bill of Rights 1990 in *Cropp v Judicial Committee (New Zealand Thoroughbred Racing Inc)* [2008] NZSC 46 [5] Blanchard J.

[193]   See generally S Boyes, 'The Regulation of Sport and the Impact of the Human Rights Act 1998' (2000) 6(4) *European Public Law* 517 and S Boyes, 'Regulating Sport after the Human Rights Act 1998' (2001) 151 *New Law Journal* 444.

[194]   See *Rubython v FIA* [2003] All ER (D) 182 (May) where the applicant, a journalist, sought to rely on Art 10 ECHR to challenge the decision by the Paris-based governing body of Formula 1 denying him access to a Grand Prix event in Australia. The unlikely extra-territorial effect of the Human Rights Act 1998 notwithstanding, Gray J held that 'there is a formidable argument available to the FIA that the granting of press accreditation cannot be said to be a public authority function'.

in question was, similarly, not in the exercise of a public function for the purposes of section 6 of the Human Rights Act 1998.[195] This narrow view of the applicability of section 6(3)(b) to 'mixed function' or 'hybrid' bodies ie, private bodies that, on occasion, carry out or have contracted-out to them public functions,[196] is consistent with the outcome of the most recent House of Lords decision on the matter in *YL v Birmingham City Council*.[197] If section 6(3)(b) is to extend in the future to sports disciplinary tribunals then it is suggested that it will do so along the lines noted obiter by Lord Nicholls in *Aston Cantlow and Wilcote with Billesley Parochial Church Council v Wallbank*.[198] In that case, Lord Nicholls, adopting a broad function-based approach, suggested that a 'hybrid' authority will be embraced by section 6(3)(b) if it fulfils certain criteria such as whether it is publicly funded or is exercising statutory powers or is taking the place of central government/local authority or is providing a public service.[199] It is submitted that not only is Lord Nicholls's view consistent with the broad reading of the Human Rights Act 1998 intended by the legislature,[200] but that on any reasonable review of the Jockey Club's regulatory and operational remit, it fulfils the Nicholls criteria, or, as Gray J noted succinctly, if again obiter, in *Jockey Club v Buffham*, the Jockey Club is 'a public authority in every sense of that term'.[201] Moreover, it is it noteworthy that the Jockey Club itself was of the view that its authority would be encompassed by section 6(3)(b), as premised on remarks made by the then Home Secretary Jack Straw during the committee stage of the Human Rights Bill: 'There will be occasions—it is the nature of British society—on which various institutions that are private in terms of their legal personality carry our public functions … I would suggest that it … includes the Jockey Club … The Jockey Club is a curious body: it is entirely private in nature, but exercises public functions in some respects, and to those extents, but to no other, it would be regarded as falling within [this classification of a quasi-public body]'.[202] As a consequence of those remarks, the Jockey

---

[195] *Mullins* [2005] EWHC 2197 (Admin) [35]–[44]. See also *R (on the application of West) v Lloyd's of London* [2005] EWCA Civ 506 where it was held that a Lloyd's conduct committee was neither embraced by s 6(3)(b) nor amenable to judicial review.

[196] Pursuant to s 6(5) of the Human Rights Act 1998, mixed function or hybrid authorities have to give effect to Convention rights only when performing 'public' functions.

[197] *YL v Birmingham City Council* [2007] UKHL 27; [2008] 1 AC 95. In that case, the House of Lords held that a privately owned care home, when providing care to a resident pursuant to agreements made with a local authority under the National Assistance Act 1948, was not performing functions of a public nature, at least, not for the purposes of s 6(3)(b) of the Human Rights Act 1998. See also the Joint Committee on Human Rights Report, *The Meaning of Public Authority under the Human Rights Act* (Ninth Report of Session 2006–2007, HL 77/HC 410).

[198] *Aston Cantlow and Wilcote with Billesley Parochial Church Council v Wallbank* [2003] UKHL 37; [2004] 1 AC 546 where the House of Lords held that, although the Church of England, as the established church, has its special links with central government and performed certain public functions, it was not acting as a hybrid public authority in the context of a property dispute.

[199] Ibid [12].

[200] See generally N Bamforth, 'The Application of the Human Rights Act 1998 to Public Authorities and Private Bodies' (1999) 58 *CLJ* 159.

[201] [2003] QB 462, 479.

[202] Hansard HC vol 312 col 1020 (20 May 1998).

Club carried out a 'human rights audit' of its disciplinary procedures, resulting, in 2001, in the creation of an independent appeals body, which (and with neat symmetry) was the respondent disciplinary body in *Mullins*.[203]

Restraint of Trade

[**2.56**]   In *Bradley*, as in many of the cases mentioned in this chapter, the claimant's case was, in part at least, founded on the common law doctrine of restraint of trade.[204] The principles and case law surrounding the 'sporting' application of the doctrine of restraint of trade are dealt with shortly (and briefly).[205] There are five points of note at the outset. First, the usual application of the doctrine is to instances where there is an alleged restraint imposed by contract in a business relationship and thus in sport the typical scenario is where the claimant (as a professional athlete) attempts to argue that a specific contractual clause in their relations with their club and/or sports governing body should be deemed unenforceable and void on the ground that it is restraining, without reasonable justification, their right to work or trade.[206] The doctrine is not however confined to a contractual nexus.[207] This brief analysis focuses on the doctrine's wider (equitable) scope and the manner in which it can be availed of by a participant who may not be in contractual relations with a sports body but who argues that as a consequence of an application of that sports body's rules and/or a decision of that body's disciplinary authority, their 'right to work' has been adversely and unreasonably affected and thus seek a declaration that the rule or decision is void or enforceable.[208] Second, as a consequence of the preliminary or interim nature of many of the cases at issue (with either the sports body seeking to strike out a claim

---

[203] See R Evans, 'Club Acts on Rights' *The Daily Telegraph* (London 20 February 2001) Sport 43. The FA had previously carried out a similar review as noted by M Gerrard, 'Life is Sweet at the FA' *Legal Week* (London 2 November 2000) News 29.

[204] For a typically thorough account and analysis of the accompanying case law see Lewis and Taylor (n 2) 237–54.

[205] The case law focuses on the England and Wales jurisdiction. An interesting case study on the use of the doctrine of restraint of trade in sport is provided by a number of rugby league-related cases in Australia and New Zealand. See, eg, and in chronological order: *Blackler v New Zealand Rugby Football League* [1968] NZLR 547; *Buckley v Tutty* (1971) 125 CLR 353, [1971] HCA 71; *Kemp v New Zealand Rugby Football League* [1989] 3 NZLR 463; *Adamson v NSW Rugby League* (1991) 27 FCR 535, rev'd (1991) 31 FCR 242; and the review by A Edwards, 'Restraint of Trade in Sport: In a League of its Own?' (2009) 1 *Sports Law Administration & Practice* 13. For a summary of the case law wherein the doctrine has been used against other Australian sports bodies see Thorpe *et al* (n104) 286–99.

[206] See, eg, *Leeds Rugby Ltd v Harris* [2005] EWHC 1591 (QB).

[207] See *Pharmaceutical Society of Great Britain v Dickson* [1970] AC 403, 440, Lord Wilberforce.

[208] The cause of action is not, of course, limited to individuals and has been availed by clubs as in, eg, *Newport v Football Association of Wales* ('FAW') Unreported, Queen's Bench Division 15 April 1995, Blackburne J. The stated case concerned rules of the FAW designed to promote a Welsh Football League by restricting the right of clubs who were members of the English league to play their games from grounds within Wales. Blackburne J held that there was an unreasonable and unjustified restraint of trade because the rules in question went beyond that which was reasonably necessary to protect the FAW's legitimate interests.

against it for want of cause of action or the claimant applying for an interlocutory order) a necessarily cursory (and often dictum) analysis only of the application of the doctrine within a sporting context has often sufficed the courts.[209] Third, this fleeting treatment notwithstanding, sports claimants appear to have had infrequent success with the doctrine and arguably this is due to what the Court of Appeal in *Bradley* called the 'paradoxical' nature of such claims, namely, how can 'someone who has broken the rules of his profession then seek to claim that he has nonetheless a right in uncontrolled terms to practise it'.[210]

[**2.57**]   Fourth, there is a doubt as to whether the doctrine will remain a distinct basis of challenge for much longer.[211] The contention is that the 'mischief' or restriction which the doctrine seeks to address is now better dealt with in at least two other ways: either (a) that the question of whether the doctrine provides a 'jurisprudentially distinct' basis for supervision by a court of the decisions of domestic (sports) tribunals is obviated by the creep of public-law values such as proportionality;[212] or (b) that this common law cause of action should now more properly be framed in, and cede to, an action for breach of competition law.[213] Fifth, and following on from the previous point, it is suggested that in sports law related cases the use of the phrase 'restraint of trade' or related phrases should be viewed more as a 'term of art' or mechanism by which the nature of the claimant's grievance with the defending body can be more broadly and properly understood.[214] It follows that restraint of trade should not be permitted to overly distract from the issues that are fundamental and common to the case law: namely,

---

[209] See, eg, Carnwarth J's analysis of the restraint of trade issue in *Stevenage Borough FC v Football League Ltd, The Times* 1 August 1996. Although Carnwarth J's analysis of whether the entry/promotion criteria into the Football League were an unreasonable restraint of trade (and he was minded that they were) is most useful, accurate and succinct, ultimately, the claimant's application for interim relief was rejected, in the court's discretion, on the grounds of delay and prejudice to third parties. Moreover, the Court of Appeal's subsequent affirmation, (1997) 9 *Admin LR* 109 (CA), is again concerned principally with the question of delay and not restraint of trade.

[210] *Bradley* [2005] EWCA Civ 1056 [29], Buxton LJ. See, eg, *Gasser v Stinson*, Unreported, Queen's Bench Division 15 June 1988, Scott J. In that case, Scott J agreed with the claimant, a Swiss athlete of international standard, that the strict liability nature of the anti-doping rules of the IAAF, and the accompanying mandatory suspensions for violation of those rules, were a restraint of trade but that, in the context of the 'war against doping in sport', the rules in question were reasonable, justified and in the interest of athletes and the public at large. See also the rejection of the 'unarguable' restraint of trade claim in *Wilander and Novacek v Tobin and Jude* Unreported, Chancery Division 19 March 1996, Lightman J; affirmed by Court of Appeal, *The Times* 8 April 1996.

[211] See generally Lewis and Taylor (n 2) 253–54.

[212] Note the approach of Richards J in *Bradley* [2004] EWHC 2164 [35].

[213] See *Days Medical Aids Ltd v Pihsiang Machinery Manufacturing Co Ltd* [2004] EWHC 44 (Comm) [2004]; UKCLR 384 [254]–[266], Langely J and more generally the review by M Catherine Lucey, 'EC Competition Policy: Emasculating the Common Law Doctrine of Restraint of Trade' (2007) 15 *European Review of Private Law* 419. This means that the approach of this common law doctrine should be fully reconcilable in outcome with the domestic and EU legislative provisions on competition law; an outcome that seems to have been understood previously by the courts in a number of sports-related cases, eg, *Hendry v World Professional Billiards and Snooker Association Ltd* [2002] UKCLR 5 [100]–[118], Lloyd J.

[214] Arguable, this is, for example, the best way to approach the decision in *Nagle v Feilden* [1966] 2 QB 633.

although private sports bodies have a wide margin of appreciation in carrying out their regulatory remit, they are not immune from supervision by the courts, but that that supervision is itself restrained, abiding generally to the immutable principles of fairness, reasonableness and proportionality.[215]

[**2.58**]   The principles and policies underpinning the doctrine of restraint of trade can be drawn from three House of Lords decisions.[216] Summarising *Nordendfelt v Maxim Nordenelft Guns and Ammunition Co Ltd*,[217] *Herbert Morris v Saxelby*[218] and *Esso Petroleum v Harper's Garage Ltd*,[219] the doctrine holds as its basic premise that every member of the community is entitled to carry on any trade or business that they choose and in such a manner as they think most desirable in their own interests so long as they do nothing that is unlawful. Consequently, any contract or agreement or obligation that interferes with the free exercise of an individual's trade or business by, for example, restraining them in the work they may pursue for themselves or restricting them in the commercial arrangements they may make with others, is unenforceable and void. This general approach to the doctrine, what Lord Denning MR once called simply the 'right to work'[220] is applied flexibly to reflect the commercial reality that it is often to an individual's benefit to enter into what appears to be a restrictive obligation for example, by agreeing to operate by the licensing regime of a professional body in order to gain entry and credibility within that profession. Put simply, once the individual agrees to be bound by the rules of, for example, a professional body, they have, in effect, agreed that their 'right' to pursue a living as they see fit is no longer an absolute one.[221] Nevertheless, the restraints of the individual's right to work must be reasonable. They must be justifiable as being reasonable in the interests of the parties concerned. They must not otherwise be injurious to the interest of public. They must be in pursuit of legitimate objectives and the means of achieving those objectives must be proportionate and not go beyond what is reasonably necessary to realise them.[222] The accompanying test used by the courts is twofold in nature. First, can the claimant prove that a restraint of trade exists; for instance, is there

---

[215] Not the pragmatic approach taken by Mackay J to the claimant's various heads of challenge in *Chambers v British Olympic Association* [2008] EWHC 2028 (QB) [28]–[30].

[216] See also the exhaustive review (and application) of the doctrine by Jonathan Parker LJ in *Panayiotou & Ors v Sony Music* [1994] EMLR 229.

[217] *Nordendfelt v Maxim Nordenelft Guns and Ammunition Co Ltd* [1894] AC 535.

[218] *Herbert Morris v Saxelby* [1916] 1 AC 688.

[219] *Esso Petroleum v Harper's Garage Ltd* [1968] AC 269.

[220] *Nagle v Feilden* [1966] 2 QB 633, 644 and 646.

[221] This explains the background to Buxton LJ's somewhat jaundiced view of 'sporting' restraint of trade claims in *Bradley* [2005] EWCA Civ 1056 [29].

[222] An interesting case in this regard is *McInnes v Onslow-Fane* [1978] 1 WLR 1520 where the claimant was unsuccessful in seeking a declaration that the British Boxing Board of Control had unfairly denied him a licence to operate as a boxing manager. Megarry VC felt that Lord Denning MR's use of the phrase 'right to work' (*Nagle v Feilden* [1966] 2 QB 633, 644 and 646) lacked legal precision. He preferred Salmon LJ's succinct phrase (*Nagle v Feilden* [1966] 2 QB 633, 653) that an unreasonable restraint of trade equates to the violation of a man's 'right not to be capriciously and unreasonably prevented from earning his living as he wills'.

evidence that a rule or decision of the sports body is restricting their liberty to trade? If so, and second, can the sports body demonstrate that the restraint is reasonable within the context and organisation of the sport as a whole by, for example, seeking to maintain a competitive balance within the sport?

[**2.59**]   Although, to reiterate, the importance of the doctrine of restraint of trade as a means of challenge is now fading, it has been associated with some of the more celebrated cases in the brief history of sports law. Two cases are note-worthy and what follows is a brief summary of each and the manner in which the 'sporting' interpretation and application of doctrine has evolved over the years. In *Eastham v Newcastle United FC Ltd & Ors*;[223] the claimant challenged the extant 'retain and transfer' system in professional football whereby the rules of the Football League permitted a club to retain a player's registration at the end of each season or to otherwise seek a transfer fee for that player from another club. Implicitly applying the approach of Lord Macnaghten in *Nordendfelt v Maxim Nordenelft Guns and Ammunition Co Ltd*,[224] Wilberforce J (as he then was) sum-marised the principal issue in the case succinctly: does the retain and transfer system unreasonably interfere with the liberty of professional players, after their employment with a particular club has ceased, to use their skill in some other employment and, if so, are the restraints within that system no more than such as are reasonably necessary for the protection of the defendants, the Football League and its members?[225]

[**2.60**]   On reviewing the system as a whole, Wilberforce J held that certainly in respect of the retention part of the system, the system operated substantially in restraint of trade because, even though a player was no longer an employee of the retaining club, that player effectively remained at the mercy of that club: if that player was put on the end of season retention list they could not be transferred elsewhere, and may even face a reduced wage; if that player succeeded in convinc-ing the retaining club to place him on the transfer list, he could be transferred but only when another club satisfied the retaining club's transfer or compensation fee for the player's registration.[226] Could then, Wilberforce J asked, the system be justified as affording no more than adequate protection to the parties (the club-employers, the Football Association and the various club-members of the Football League) in whose favour the restraint has been imposed? Although, at first instance, it might be difficult in the presented circumstances to ascertain any interference for which protection could legitimately be claimed, Wilberforce J reminded the court that pursuant to the leading cases on restraint of trade, it would be wrong 'to pass straight to the conclusion' that no such justifiable interest

---

[223] *Eastham v Newcastle United FC Ltd & Ors* [1964] Ch 413.
[224] [1894] AC 535, 565, Lord Macnaghten. Wilberforce J also relied on the dictum of Lord Finlay in another House of Lords case on restraint of trade, *McEllistrim v Ballymacelligot Co-operative Agricultural and Dairy Society* [1919] AC 548, 571.
[225] *Eastham* [1964] Ch 413, 427.
[226] Ibid 428–31, Wilberforce J observing that the restraint inherent in the transfer system was miti-gated slightly by the player's right of appeal to the Football League.

existed and that 'regard must be had to the special character of the area in which the restraints operate—different from that of industrial employment—and to the special interests of those concerned with the regulation of professional football'.[227] Advancing arguments that would echo down the decades, the defendants sought to justify the then transfer system, arguing inter alia: that freedom of mobility would destabilise the game as a whole by resulting in leading players being attracted to the limited number of top clubs; that without it smaller clubs would be denied a lucrative and steady source of income; and that its removal would discourage investment in youth football.[228] Hinting that a modified retention system or a transfer system divorced entirely from retention (which is what was subsequently implemented, in England and Wales at least, and lasted until the European Court of Justice's ruling in *Bosman*) might be justified, Wilberforce J concluded that the system at issue was not justified to the point that that not only did the defendants not discharge the onus resting on them to show that the restraints were no more than reasonable to protect their interests but also that they were of such a nature that the could be deemed ultra vires the objectives of the defendant-entities.[229]

[**2.61**]   In 1977, the *Nordenfelt* test, and its interpretation in *Eastham*, was used successfully by the claimants in *Grieg v Insole*.[230] The background to these proceedings was that in the mid-1970s, the International Cricket Council (ICC), which for decades had controlled the promotion of first-class international cricket, faced a challenge from a rival organisation—World Series Cricket— promoted by an Australian media mogul, Kerry Packer.[231] The effect of the ICC's constitution was that it had full control and responsibility for the status of official test or international matches and for the eligibility of players participating in such matches. In the UK, similar powers regarding eligibility to play test and county representative cricket lay with the Test and County Cricket Board (TCCB). In May 1977, Packer's plans, which saw him begin a worldwide and secretive recruitment drive of leading players to play in a series of games in Australia beginning in the autumn of 1977, became public. In July 1977, the ICC met and passed a series of resolutions changing its rules relating to qualification for test matches, the effect being that any player who made himself available for WSC matches would face disqualification from international test cricket. The ICC recommended the each of its member countries ensure a similar sanction in their domestic cricket activities. The TCCB proposed to hold a meeting in early August 1977, the result of which would have been that WSC-contracted players would also have been rendered ineligible for all first-class domestic cricket. In the days before the TCCB

---

[227] Ibid 432.

[228] Ibid 432–37.

[229] Note the subsequent application of the *Eastham* approach to the rules of the Football Association of Ireland (Dublin) in *Cooke v Football Association* [1972] CLY 516 and the Irish Football Association (Belfast) in *Johnston v Cliftonville Football and Athletic Club* [1984] NI 9.

[230] *Grieg v Insole* [1978] 1 WLR 302.

[231] For background to the two-year long WSC/ICC rivalry see G Haigh, *The Cricket War* (Melbourne, Melbourne University Press, 2007).

meeting, the claimants, three WSC-contract players who faced the full effect of the proposed ICC/TCCB sanctions, sought a declaration that the changes of rules by both cricket bodies were ultra vires and in unlawful restraint of trade.[232] Slade J held that, although both the ICC and TCCB had legitimate interests, relating to the proper administration of the sport, which they were entitled to protect by appropriate restraints, the restraints in question were, in the stated circumstances, neither reasonable nor justifiable, thus were unenforceable and ultra vires.[233]

Conclusion

[**2.62**]   Unless a claimant can convince the House of Lords otherwise, the authority of the Court of Appeal's decision in *Aga Khan* holds that a sports participant, aggrieved at a disciplinary decision made against them by a sports body based in England and Wales, should not instigate judicial review proceedings pursuant to CPR Part 54. Moreover, the interpretation given to the *Aga Kahn* in *Mullins* suggests that neither should the aggrieved sports participant premise a challenge on the argument that the sports body might be encapsulated by the broad definition of a 'public body' in section 6 of the Human Rights Act 1998. In any event, the proceedings in *Modahl*, *Bradley* and *Flaherty* clearly show that in a private law-based challenge, be it one founded on contract or in appeal to the supervisory jurisdiction of the courts over domestic tribunals, the standard of review will, in language and in substance, be virtually indistinguishable from that applied in public law proceedings. More broadly, *Modahl* suggests that where a court agrees to scrutinise the procedural fairness of a decision made by a sports tribunal, the guiding principle of intervention is whether the decision ultimately arrived at by that tribunal was 'fair'. In short, were the internal proceedings designed to produce, and did they in fact produce, a 'fair result'? It is argued that this 'fair go' principle is a good and sound guideline for the courts because challenges of this nature often present them with an awkward set of technical and emotive circumstances. They are frequently made by way of interim relief with the applicant pleading to the court to be given the opportunity to participate in an imminent event around which, it is often claimed, much of their career has been built and most of their future earnings even livelihood depends.

---

[232] In parallel proceedings, the WSC were successful in their claim that they were entitled to a declaration that the proposed changes were an unlawful inducement to the players contracted to the WSC to break those contracts.

[233] In sum, Slade J held that the restraining rules in question were 'unreasonable' for three reasons: the all encompassing nature of the bans; the fact that the bans would have deprived the cricket-going public of the pleasure of watching such players for the duration of the ban, thus likely to result in a diminution of gate receipts from 'official' test matches; and, although the WSE matches presented an immediate threat to Australian cricket, they presented no serious immediate threat to other test-playing countries.

[**2.63**]   Overall then, when it comes to the review of the decisions of largely voluntary and socially beneficial organisations (and the majority of sports bodies remain of this nature) it is clear that the judiciary should exercise, and generally do exercise, a light, restrained touch. Nevertheless, as individual sports participants become more aware of their commercial interests, it is inevitable that challenges to the disciplinary-making competency of sports bodies will increase in frequency and deepen in sophistication. This chapter has attempted to illustrate the basis on which an aggrieved participant might attempt to protect their interests. The next chapter seeks to advise sports bodies as to the preventative measures they might implement and in this guidance is taken from the direction taken by leading sports organisations such as the Jockey Club/British Horseracing Authority and the FA, whose regulatory ambit encompasses issues of material, national sporting importance and whose decisions can have significant economic and proprietary impact upon the reputation and livelihoods of individual members. In preparation for the coming into effect of the Human Rights Act 1998, both of these organisations submitted their then extant disciplinary mechanisms and procedures to an audit predicated on the principles surrounding Article 6 ECHR; and it is to the standards of that provision, and to the demands it places on sports disciplinary bodies, that we now turn.

Further Points of Interest and Discussion

1. Are there any other means of challenging decisions of sports bodies outside those outlined in this chapter?
2. Consider the possibility of a challenge based on the *law of torts*, for example: a defamation suit against a sports governing body for the malicious taking of disciplinary charges; or a negligence-based, personal injury actions against sports governing bodies; or the use of the economic torts of inducing breach of contract or unlawful interference with contractual relations.
3. Consider the possibility of a challenge based on *competition law* as in, for example, *Attheraces Ltd v British Horseracing Board Ltd* [2007] EWCA Civ 38; *Bookmakers' Afternoon Greyhound Services & Ors v Amalgamated Racing Ltd & Ors* [2009] EWCA Civ 750; and *Racecourse Association & Ors v Office of Fair Trading* [2005] CAT 29. In all three stated cases, recourse was made to competition law in an attempt to affect the distribution of economic resources within the business of horseracing.
4. Consider the possibility of a challenge based on a domestic court's application of EU *free movement* rules as in, for example, *Edwards v BAF and IAAF* [1998] 2 CMLR 363 and *Wilander v Tobin* [1997] 2 CMLR 346.

3

Arbitration and Alternative Dispute Resolution In Sport

Introduction

[**3.01**]   The previous chapter demonstrated the courts' reluctance to review disciplinary decisions of a sports body save in instances of egregious breaches of the principles of fairness and proportionality. The English courts have long acknowledged that in general sports-related disputes are better dealt with 'in-house', and preferably by way of the utilisation of quasi-independent, arbitral-based, disciplinary mechanisms. Indeed, sport provides a good example of the benefits of alternative dispute resolution (ADR) over judicial proceedings. The advantages of ADR (arbitration, mediation and conciliation) over litigation include its consensual basis, whereby the parties voluntarily agree to enter into the ADR process and be bound by the decision of the independent, third-party adjudicator of their choice; privacy; speed and flexibility of procedure; the ability to use adjudicators who are experts in the field of dispute; and cost effectiveness.[1] For many, the first thing that will come to mind when one speaks of ADR in sport is probably the Court of Arbitration for Sport (CAS) based in Lausanne.[2] CAS's jurisdiction, its evolving authority and credibility, its jurisprudence, and its place at the apex of a now complex pyramid of national

---

[1]   This chapter concentrates on the adversarial concept of arbitration rather than the more conciliatory-based concept of mediation. For a thorough review of mediation in sport see I Blackshaw, *Mediating Sports Disputes: National and International Perspectives* (The Hague, TMC Asser Press, 2002). Moreover, the focus is on the UK and European experience, although, as ever, there is much to learn from the US. For an introduction see the seven articles in the special issue entitled 'Alternative Dispute Resolution in (US) Sports' (2005) 16 *Marquette Sports Law Review* 1–155 and the seven articles in the similarly themed issue of (2009) 10 *Pepperdine Dispute Resolution Law Journal* 1–182.

[2]   CAS's website, www.tas-cas.org, is now an excellent resource with information on its code of operation, its history, membership and jurisprudence. This continues the work of CAS Secretary-General, Matthieu Reeb, who previously edited three digests of CAS jurisprudence: M Reeb (ed), *Digest of CAS Awards, 1986–1998* (Berne, Editions Staempfli SA, 1998) '1 Digest of CAS Awards'; M Reeb (ed), *Digest of CAS Awards II, 1998–2000* (The Hague, Kluwer Law International, 2002) '2 Digest of CAS Awards'; and M Reeb (ed), *Digest of CAS Awards III, 2001-2003* (The Hague, Kluwer Law International, 2004) '3 Digest of CAS Awards'.

and international arbitral bodies has been well-documented elsewhere.[3] Consequently, the topic is dealt with briefly and CAS's specific role with respect to appeals from decisions regarding violations of anti-doping rules pursuant to Article 13 of the World Anti-Doping Code (2009) is examined in the next chapter of this text. This chapter does however give a brief history of the CAS from its relatively low-key beginnings in the mid-1980s as a 'creature' of the International Olympic Committee (IOC) to its highly influential role in contemporary sport whereby the regulations of virtually every leading sports body provide reference to its competency.[4] Thereafter, the concentration is on one, technical, if multifaceted, aspect of CAS—the manner in which the recognition and enforcement of CAS awards domestically and internationally is said to be establishing a growing body of private international sports law (sometimes referred to as *lex sportiva*) which some claim might soon be seen to override national law.[5]

[3.02]   Having analysed CAS, and suggested some reforms to its existing structure, the chapter moves to consider arbitration domestically as it operates in its legal framework under the Arbitration Act 1996 and, in a sports-related framework, in entities such as Sport Resolutions UK, an independent dispute resolution service for sport in the UK. Finally, this chapter attempts to give some practical advice to national sports bodies on the legal issues that might need to be addressed (and the legal gaps that might need to be closed) in the various steps of a disciplinary process namely the investigatory, charging, hearing, sanctioning, and appeals stages. The idea here is that based on weaknesses identified by the types of legal challenges outlined in chapter two, national sports bodies will by the end of this chapter have a 'checklist' against which they can measure the contents of, and procedures surrounding, their disciplinary scheme.[6] This should equate to a sports governing body subjecting its disciplinary process to what might be called 'an Article 6 ECHR audit' wherein the guiding principle can be paraphrased as follows: in the determination of their sporting rights, an individual has the entitlement to a fair hearing within a reasonable time by an independent and impartial tribunal established by law.

---

[3] Again, a good place to start is with the work of Ian Blackshaw, 'The Court of Arbitration for Sport: An International Forum for Settling Disputes Effectively "Within the Family of Sport"' (2003) 2 *Entertainment and Law* 61 and I Blackshaw, *Sport, Mediation and Arbitration* (The Hague, TMC Asser Press, 2009).

[4] See, eg, arts 62–64 of the FIFA Statutes (August 2009) available through the 'official documents' section of www.fifa.com, and art 15 of the IAAF Constitution (November 2009) available through the 'publications' section of www.iaaf.org.

[5] The most recent analysis of this debate is carried out by M Mitten, 'Judicial Review of Olympic and International Sports Arbitration Awards: Trends and Observations' (2009) 9 *Pepperdine Dispute Resolution Journal* 51.

[6] For a similar approach to the practical management of disciplinary issues see generally M Beloff, T Kerr and M Demetriou, *Sports Law* (Oxford, Hart Publishing, 1999) 211–17.

Court of Arbitration for Sport

[**3.03**] The former President of the IOC, Juan Antonio Samaranch, is generally credited with the creation of what is now CAS.[7] In 1983, the CAS Statutes were officially ratified by the IOC at its 86th Session held in New Dehli.[8] The Statutes came into effect in 1984, though it was not until 1986 that CAS processed a request for arbitration to its final award stage.[9] Over the first decade of its existence, the average number of requests for arbitration filed with CAS was less than nine.[10] The reason for such inactivity had much to do with sports governing bodies' reticence in having 'in-house' disputes adjudicated upon by an external entity of novel jurisdiction.[11] International sports federations were slow therefore to submit to the voluntary jurisdiction of CAS and it was not until 1991 that a leading sports organisation, the International Equestrian Federation (FEI), became the first major body to integrate an arbitration clause referring to CAS into its constitution.[12] Moreover, claimant-athletes appeared equally reluctant to avail themselves of CAS because of the perception of bias: as initially conceived, CAS appeared less an independent tribunal and more a 'creature' of the IOC.[13] Under its enabling 1983 Statutes, CAS was not only created, it was also fully funded, by the IOC.[14] Moreover, its Statutes could be amended only by a proposal of the IOC's Executive Board and a two-thirds

---

[7] In typical understatement, Samaranch labelled his idea as 'a kind of Hague Court [International Court of Justice] in the sports world.' See 'Speech delivered by Mr Juan Antonio Samaranch IOC President' (1982) 176 *Olympic Review* 314, 317.

[8] The following sections concentrate on CAS's arbitration procedure though it should be noted that CAS also offers a mediation procedure and an advisory opinion service. The opinion service is a consultation procedure which permits certain organisations to request an opinion from CAS on the legal issues surrounding a sport-related issue. For a comprehensive review of all aspects of the first 20 years of CAS see I Blackshaw, R Siekmann and J Soek (eds), *The Court of Arbitration for Sport, 1984–2004* (The Hague, TMC Asser Press, 2006). The collection reproduces a number of newly and previously published pieces on CAS including the very useful D Kane, 'Twenty Years On: An Evaluation of the Court of Arbitration for Sport' (2003) 4 *Melbourne Journal of International Law* 611. See also D Yi, 'Turning Medals into Metal: Evaluating the Court of Arbitration for Sport as an International Tribunal' (2006) 6 *Asper Review of International Business and Trade Law* 289.

[9] The first case was a relatively mundane affair with the CAS Tribunal rejecting an appeal by an ice hockey coach against a disciplinary sanction imposed by the Swiss Ice Hockey League, CAS 86/1 *HC X v Ligue Suisse de Hockey sur Glace.*

[10] The average number of requests for arbitration leading to an award was less than four. See further the information compiled at www.tas-cas.org/statistics.

[11] See R McLaren, 'A New World Order: Athlete's Rights and the Court of Arbitration at the Olympic Games' (1998) 7 *Olympika: The International Journal of Olympic Studies* 1, 5.

[12] It remains the case that, although an arbitration agreement incorporating CAS's jurisdiction can occur on a one-off contractual basis, the vast majority of cases are triggered by an arbitration clause in the statutes or regulations of the governing sports organisation. Standard CAS arbitration clauses are provided at www.tas-cas.org/clause-templates. For a review of such clauses and the issues of choice of law and applicable law clauses see A Bell, 'Dispute Resolution and Applicable Law Clauses in International Sports Arbitration' (2010) 84 *Australian Law Journal* 116.

[13] See S Kaufman, 'Issues in International Sports Arbitration' (1995) 13 *Boston University International Law Journal* 527, 533–34 noting that the close CAS/IOC relationship was epitomised by the fact that initially CAS's physical location was at IOC headquarters in Lausanne.

[14] CAS Statutes 1983, art 6.

majority voted by the IOC in full session.[15] The link between CAS and the IOC was seen clearly in its membership: the Executive President of CAS had to be an IOC member; of the 60 CAS members, half of them were either IOC members or appointed directly by the President of the IOC.[16] The remaining 30 members were nominated by the Associations of the National Olympic Committees (NOC) and the Summer and Winter Olympic International Federations (Summer/Winter IFs) thus, because there was no one to represent and protect athletes' interests, it was no surprise that the number of applications for CAS arbitration remained low.

The *Gundel* Effect

[**3.04**]   In 1993, CAS's perceived lack of independence was the basis of a judicial challenge at the First Civil Division of the Swiss Federal Tribunal (SFT, effectively, the Supreme Court of Switzerland) in *Gundel v International Equestrian Federation (FEI)*.[17] The background to the case involved a CAS hearing wherein a German equestrian competitor appealed against a decision of the FEI's Judicial Commission to suspend and fine him after his horse tested positive for a prohibited substance. CAS upheld the merits of the sanction though it reduced the fine (marginally) and the suspension (from three months to one).[18] Gundel remained unhappy and challenged the CAS award at the SFT principally on the grounds that CAS did not offer sufficient guarantees of independence and impartiality to rule in his appeal such that CAS awards could not be deemed recognisable and enforceable international arbitral awards.[19] The SFT, whose competency to hear a public law appeal against CAS rested in an application of articles 190 and 191 of the Swiss Federal Statute on Private International Law (LDIP), held that on balance CAS satisfied the essentials of a 'true' arbitral tribunal thus the SFT dismissed Gundel's appeal. The longer term importance of *Gundel* lay in its underpinning of CAS's competency as an arbitral body and the recognition and enforceability of its awards pursuant to the UN Convention on the Recognition and Enforcement of Foreign Arbitral Awards (1958).[20] In the more immediate term, what was of

---

[15]   Ibid, art 75.

[16]   Ibid, art 7.

[17]   An excerpt from the judgment of 15 March 1993 can be found at (1993) 1 Digest of CAS Awards 561.

[18]   CAS 92/63 *Gundel v Fédération Equestre Internationale.*

[19]   It remains the case that CAS awards can be appealed to the SFT only on the five limited grounds of art 190(2) LDIP, namely that the arbitral tribunal was not properly constituted; the tribunal's jurisdiction was incorrectly drawn; the tribunal's decision went beyond the claim submitted to it or did not deal with all parts of the stated claim; breach of one the parties' rights to equal treatment and a fair hearing; and incompatibility with public policy. See generally the thorough review by A Rigozzi, 'Challenging Awards of the Court of Arbitration for Sport' (2010) 1 *Journal of International Dispute Settlement* 217.

[20]   The New York Convention is the foundation instrument of international arbitration and requires courts of contracting States (a) to give effect to an agreement to arbitrate when considering an action in a matter covered by an arbitration agreement and (b) to recognise and enforce awards made in other contracting States, subject to specific limited exceptions. As of 2009, 144 countries were party to the Convention.

interest in *Gundel* was dicta suggesting that a greater effort needed to be made in order to sever the 'organic and economic ties' then existing between CAS and the IOC.[21] To be fair, the IOC and CAS recognised that reform was needed with a view to guaranteeing CAS's absolute independence; to clarifying its remit; and to ensuring the protection of the rights of parties before CAS.[22]

[**3.05**]   In the so-called Paris Agreement of 1994 approval was given to the creation of an International Council of Arbitration for Sport (ICAS), which was to act as CAS's independent executive council.[23] Crucially, the parties to the Paris Agreement—the IOC, the NOCs and the Summer/Winter IFs—agreed that the activities of CAS would no longer be financed solely by the IOC.[24] These reforms on CAS's independence were given further expression with the implementation of a *Code of Sports-related Arbitration* (CAS Code), which came into force on 22 November 1994.[25] The CAS Code clarified CAS's remit by reorganising it into two divisions, the Ordinary Arbitration Division (OAD) and the Appeals Arbitration Division (AAD), which reflect broadly the type of disputes now heard by CAS.[26] The OAD acting as a court of 'sole instance' hears disputes of a contractual or commercial law nature such as those relating to employment issues between players, clubs and agents; or general commercial issues surrounding the staging of major sports events such as sponsorship and broadcasting rights.[27] The second category of disputes are mainly related to disciplinary cases, such as doping violations, initially dealt with by the competent governing sports body, but subsequently becoming the subject of an appeal to the AAD acting as a court of 'last instance'.[28] It follows that it is a prerequisite of the AAD procedure that a claimant has exhausted all their internal avenues of appeal. Arbitration proceedings submitted to CAS are assigned by the central CAS secretariat to the appropriate division according to their nature.[29] Both divisions are administered by a President who also handles the initial stages of the ordinary or appeals procedure. This task can be no more than the appointment of one of the three arbitrators that

---

[21] *Gundel* (1993) 1 Digest of CAS Awards 561, 569–70, Swiss Federal Tribunal.

[22] See the comments of the then CAS Secretary General Gilbert Schwaar in 'Court of Arbitration for Sport' (1993) 309 *Olympic Review* 305, 305–06.

[23] The Paris Agreement is reproduced under its formal title 'Agreement related to the Constitution of the International Council of Arbitration for Sport' at 2 Digest of CAS Awards 883.

[24] Ibid, art 3 of the Paris Agreement.

[25] The CAS Code was revised in 2004 and again in 2009. The current edition, in force since 1 January 2010, is available under its formal title 'Statutes of the Bodies Working for the Settlement of Sports-related Disputes' at www.tas-cas.org/statutes. References to the CAS Code from herein are to the 2010 edition.

[26] CAS Code, S20–22.

[27] The procedures surrounding an OAD arbitration, from request to award, are set out in CAS Code, R38–46.

[28] The procedures surrounding an AAD arbitration, from commencement to award, are set out in CAS Code, R47–59.

[29] See further CAS Code, S20–22, which holds that, under certain conditions, it will be possible to transfer an arbitration procedure from the Ordinary Division to the Appeals Division and vice versa. Such reassignment will not affect the constitution of the Panel or the validity of the proceedings that have taken place prior to such reassignment.

typically sit on a CAS arbitral panel (one is appointed by the claimants; one by the respondents), though a divisional President can be asked on occasion to decide upon any interim, provisional and conservatory measures.[30] Moreover, in an AAD procedure it is common for the appellant to make an application to stay the execution of the decision appealed against (together with reasons) as part of their submission to CAS of a statement of appeal.[31] Pursuant to CAS Code R52, the President of the AAD should decide 'promptly' on an application for a stay or for interim measures, and inform all affected parties accordingly.[32]

[**3.06**]   Finally, and with respect to the protection of parties before CAS (and mainly with regard to greater athlete representation), although the majority of ICAS members are still nominated by the IOC, NOCs and Summer/Winter IFs, four of the twenty appointed members of ICAS must be proposed 'with a view to safeguarding the interest of athletes' and four must be chosen from 'among personalities independent of the bodies designating the other members of the ICAS'.[33] Similarly, one-fifth of CAS's arbitrators must be selected with 'a view to protecting athletes' rights' and another 20 per cent from among 'indepen-dent personalities'.[34] Arguably, of more practical importance were the changes made to the manner in which arbitrators are selected for a CAS hearing. Prior to 1994, parties could only select or nominate an arbitrator from an official list of CAS arbitrators. The list was relatively short and closed. The 1994 reforms, though retaining an official list of arbitrators, aimed to give parties a much wider choice of arbitrators from within that list by holding that the CAS list must consist of *at least* 150 names.[35] In fact, CAS currently has 279 arbitrators on its lists coming from more than 80 countries, working languages and sports. In sum, although it can be argued that the *Gundel*-inspired reforms of 1994 could have gone a little further, especially in terms of the residual influence of the IOC in the selection of ICAS/CAS members, there is no doubt that the previously overt nature of the IOC's shadow over CAS has faded. Moreover, since the mid-1990s, CAS has manifestly gained the confidence not only of the sports world generally but in itself. Three examples—administrative, legal and

[30] CAS Code, R37 'Provisional and Conservatory Measures'. See further I Blackshaw, 'Provisional and Conservatory Measures—an Under-Utilised Resource in the Court of Arbitration for Sport' (2006) 4 *Entertainment and Sports Law Journal* available online at www2.warwick.ac.uk/fac/soc/law/elj/eslj/issues/volume4/number2/blackshaw.

[31] CAS Code, R48.

[32] A well-publicised example of this process occurred in late 2009 when on 22 October 2009, Chelsea FC and Gael Kakuta filed appeals at CAS against a decision issued by FIFA's Dispute Resolution Chamber (DRC) on 27 August 2009. The DRC imposed inter alia a restriction of four months' ineligibility on Kakuta, and Chelsea FC was banned from registering any new players for the next two consecutive transfer windows. In their October petition, both Chelsea FC and Kakuta requested that the DRC decision be stayed pending the outcome of the CAS arbitration. On 6 November 2009, CAS announced that it had granted the request for a stay.

[33] CAS Code, S4. S5 holds that ICAS members are appointed for a renewable period of four years.

[34] CAS Code, s14. S13 holds that CAS members are appointed for a renewable period of four years.

[35] CAS Code, s13.

practical—underpin this positive analysis that CAS is no longer 'the vassal' of the IOC.[36]

Administrative Independence

[**3.07**] In 1996, ICAS (conscious of the fact that CAS's physical location at Lausanne was also that of the IOC) decentralised its court offices with one in Sydney and one in the US (initially in Denver but later relocated to New York in 1999). In the same year, ICAS sanctioned the first CAS ad hoc division for the Atlanta Olympics. The basic idea of the ad hoc division is that CAS arbitrators are, for the duration of an Olympic Games, on call to settle quickly (preferably within a 24-hour period) any disputes arising during the Games.[37] The first ad hoc CAS dispute had, as it transpired, a number of characteristics that were to become fairly typical of ad hoc panels.[38] The case concerned an objection by US Swimming to a decision by FINA, the world swimming authority, permitting an Irish swimmer, Michelle Smith, to modify her entry forms thus allowing her to compete in the 400-metre freestyle event at the Atlanta Games. The appeal was dismissed and, at first glance, a contemporary reading of the panel's decision appears to reveal that it did little more than apply the *contra preferendum* rule to its reading of the relevant FINA regulations.[39] Nevertheless, the background was that the case had to be decided, within its limited timeframe, under significant pressure and in the face of intense media coverage. This was because Smith, an unexpected winner of swimming gold at the Atlanta Olympics, was surrounded by the suspicion of doping, and there appeared to be a concerted effort by a number of swimming federations to use technical procedures to disqualify the Irish swimmer from further participation at the Games.[40] Although similarly pressurised circumstances have not surrounded every decision taken by ad hoc CAS panels, it is unsurprising that ICAS tends to nominate only its most experienced arbitrators to its ad hoc divisions.[41]

[**3.08**]   For a time, there was a concern that given the pressures involved CAS ad hoc panels might—in a subconscious effort to avoid controversy at, and disruption to, the Games—tend to side with the IOC and/or international

---

[36] A phrase used by the SFT in *Danilova and Lazuntina v IOC and FIS* (2003) 3 Digest of CAS Awards 649, 688.

[37] See generally R McLaren, 'Introducing the Court of Arbitration for Sport: The Ad Hoc Division at the Olympic Games' (2001) 12 *Marquette Sports Law Review* 515 and R McLaren, 'The CAS Ad Hoc Division at the Athens Olympic Games' (2004) 15 *Marquette Sports Law Review* 175.

[38] In order, mainly, to promote accessibility and speed of delivery, ad hoc panels operate under a modified, abridged version of the CAS Code available at www.tas-cas.org/adhoc-rules.

[39] CAS ad hoc Division (OG Atlanta) 96/001 *US Swimming v FINA*.

[40] Smith did not test positive during the Atlanta Games. In 1998 (as Michelle de Bruin) she was banned for four years for tampering with a urine sample. A subsequent appeal against the ban was dismissed in CAS 98/211 *B v FINA*.

[41] In *US Swimming v FINA*, the CAS panel was chaired by Mr Jan Paulsson (a world renowned international arbitration lawyer and currently President of the London Court of International Arbitration). Also on the panel was Hugh Fraser, a former international athlete, Canadian judge and member of the Dubin Commission Inquiry established in Canada in the aftermath of the Ben Johnson doping scandal at the 1988 Olympics.

federations over and above individual applicants. At the Sydney Games, much controversy surrounded a decision by CAS upholding the IOC's order that the Romanian gymnast Andreea Raducan return the gold medal awarded to her for her first place in the Gymnastics (Artistic) Women's Individual All-round competition.[42] A doping control sample taken from Raducan revealed traces of a prohibited substance though it became clear that its source was a headache tablet taken by the gymnast under the instruction of her personal doctor. The evidence also illustrated that not only was the gymnast not 'at fault' in her breach of the applicable anti-doping criteria but that the Nurofen tablet did not give her any appreciable performance-enhancing advantage. Despite much public and media sympathy for the slight, young gymnast, the CAS panel, abiding by the principle of strict liability, held that in balancing 'the interests of Miss Raducan with the commitment of the Olympic Movement to drug-free sport, the Anti-Doping Code must be enforced without compromise'.[43] The *Raducan* award though strict appears fair and overall it is clear that on any objective analysis of the decisions of CAS ad hoc panels, this division of CAS has matured quickly to the point that it is now an accepted part of the organisation of many international sport events.[44] Indeed, not only have ad hoc divisions been a feature of every Summer and Winter Olympics since 1996, they have also been a facet of every Commonwealth Games since 1998 and every European Football Championships since 2000. In 2010, it is envisaged that CAS will provide ad hoc facilities at the Olympic Winter Games in Vancouver, the Commonwealth Games in New Delhi and the FIFA World Cup in South Africa.

Legal Recognition

[**3.09**]   In May 2003, CAS's reconstituted administrative basis was the subject of a judicial challenge at the SFT in *Danilova and Lazuntina v IOC and FIS*.[45] The background to the case involved a CAS hearing wherein the claimants, two Russian cross-country skiing international competitors, appealed decisions to disqualify them consequent to positive tests for blood doping at the Winter Olympic Games of 2002 in Salt Lake City.[46] CAS dismissed the appeals and the skiers took

---

[42] CAS ad hoc Division (OG Sydney) 2000/011 *Raducan v IOC*.

[43] *Raducan v IOC* (2000) 2 Digest of CAS Awards 665, 673. Subsequently, Raducan attempted to appeal the CAS decision to the SFT but she was unsuccessful. Those legal proceedings are recounted by G Kaufmann-Kohler, *Arbitration at the Olympics: Issues of Fast-Track Dispute Resolution and Sports Law* (The Hague, Kluwer, 2001) 80–94.

[44] For a short but succinct review of CAS ad hoc decisions at the Olympic Games see the following reviews by M Beloff: 'The CAS Ad Hoc Division at the Sydney Olympic Games' (2001) 1 *International Sports Law Review* 105; 'The CAS Ad Hoc Division at the Games of the XXVIII Olympiad at Athens in 2004' (2005) 1 *International Sports Law Review* 4; and 'The Court of Arbitration for Sport at the Beijing Olympics' (2009) 1 *International Sports Law Review* 3.

[45] An excerpt from the judgment of 27 May 2003 can be found at (2003) 3 Digest of CAS Awards 649.

[46] See CAS 2002/A/370 *L v IOC*, CAS 2002/A/397 *L v FIS*; and CAS 2002/A/371 *D v IOC*, CAS 2002/A/397 *D v FIS*.

a public law appeal pursuant to article 190 LDIP. The appellants argued, largely along *Gundel* lines, that CAS's links, particularly its financial links, with the IOC were such that CAS could not offer sufficient guarantees of impartiality and independence. They also sought to distinguish their case from *Gundel* on the ground that unlike *Gundel* their situation was exacerbated by the fact that the IOC was a party to the stated proceedings. In an extremely thorough judgment the SFT held that, although some improvements could be made in terms of transparency in the appointment of arbitrators,[47] on the whole the 1994 reforms were such that CAS had the necessary independence to pass judgment in a case involving the IOC without any fear of partiality or prejudice towards the claimants. The SFT's response to the claimants' argument on the close financial links between the IOC and CAS is useful in that it has application to many other quasi-independent, arbitral bodies in sport:

> … it should be added that there is not necessarily any relationship of cause and effect between the way a judicial body is financed and its level of independence. This is illustrated, for example, by the fact that State courts in countries governed by the rule of law are often required to rule on disputes involving the State itself, without their judges' independence being questioned on the ground that they are financially linked to the State. Similarly, the CAS arbitrators should be presumed capable of treating the IOC on an equal footing with any other party, regardless of the fact that it partly finances the Court of which they are members and which pays their fees.[48]

[**3.10**]   In the present case, the claimants also challenged the independence of the appointed arbitrators (danger of bias) and their conduct (breach of natural justice) during the hearings. The allegations concerning misconduct, which related to the calling of witnesses, were dismissed by the SFT, which held that, minor procedural errors apart, fundamentally the equality of the parties and their right to a fair hearing was respected throughout the proceedings. The claim as to lack of impartiality was also rejected but, again, in its dismissal, the SFT laid down some important guidelines for arbitration in sport more generally. The essence of the claimants' argument was that at least one of the arbitrators in the stated proceedings had worked with the IOC's principal lawyer in previous CAS hearings and that more generally the relatively small number of CAS arbitrators (and international sports lawyers) meant that 'they forge such close personal and professional relationships with one another that their independence is affected when, at a later time and in different roles, they are involved in cases submitted

---

[47] *Danilova and Lazuntina v IOC and FIS* (2003) 3 Digest of CAS Awards 649, 686, Swiss Federal Tribunal where it was argued that it would be preferable if the published list of CAS arbitrators indicated clearly by whom they were nominated so that the parties 'would then be able to appoint their arbitrator with full knowledge of the facts. For example, it would prevent a party in dispute with the IOC, in the belief that he was choosing an arbitrator completely unconnected to the latter, from actually appointing a person who was proposed by that organisation.' As of May 2009, the list of arbitrators on CAS's website, available at www.tas-cas.org/arbitrators-genlist, still does not indicate who proposed individual panellists.

[48]   Ibid 688.

to the CAS'.[49] On this point, the SFT took a pragmatic approach noting that in the small world of international sports arbitration, and as is frequent in private arbitration, relations between arbitrators and lawyers are, because of professional necessities, much more frequent than judicial proceedings but that that of itself should not be considered a ground for challenge. Proof of prejudice should, according to the SFT, go beyond 'purely subjective reactions' and be evaluated on a case-by-case basis with reference to the existence of any 'objective facts which are likely, for the rational observer, to arouse suspicion concerning the arbitrator's independence'.[50] Otherwise, the SFT held, one should assume that experienced arbitrators 'are capable of rising above the eventualities linked to their appointment when they are required to render concrete decisions in discharge of their duties'.[51]

[**3.11**]　　The approach of the SFT is a good one. Sports communities tend to be relatively small and provided that certain precautions are taken, subjectively based suspensions as to bias, prejudice and conflicts of interest, should not be permitted to overly hinder the work of sports arbitral tribunals. In this, it is of interest to note that following the stated case the CAS Code was revised somewhat in 2004 in order to address this issue. The precautions taken in the revised code could be usefully adapted for any sports arbitral body. The revised 2004 CAS Code reiterates that ICAS and CAS members must, upon their appointment, exercise their functions personally with total objectivity and independence and in conformity with the operating CAS Code.[52] Members of ICAS can neither appear on the list of CAS arbitrators nor can they 'act as counsel to one of the parties in proceedings before the CAS'.[53] The President of either of CAS's divisions must 'spontaneously disqualify himself if, in arbitration proceedings assigned to his Division, one of the parties is a sports-related body to which he belongs, or if a member of the law firm to which he belongs is acting as arbitrator or counsel'.[54] On 29 September 2009, ICAS announced, at its annual meeting, that it was to amend the CAS Code in order to prohibit CAS arbitrators and mediators from acting as counsel before CAS. The accompanying media release stated that, 'This prohibition of the double-hat arbitrator/counsel role was decided in order to limit the risk of conflicts of interest and to reduce the number of petitions for challenge during arbitrators.' CAS Code S18 now includes the following, 'CAS arbitrators and mediators may not act as counsel for a party before CAS.' Finally, the CAS Code expressly states that, on pain of a 'legitimate doubt' challenge to their independence, 'every arbitrator shall be and remain independent of the parties and shall

[49]　Ibid 689.
[50]　Ibid 691.
[51]　Ibid 692.
[52]　CAS Code, S5 and S18.
[53]　Ibid S5.
[54]　CAS Code, s21.

immediately disclose any circumstances likely to affect his independence with respect to any of the parties'.[55]

Practical Acceptance

[**3.12**]   In *Danilova and Lazuntina v IOC and FIS* the Swiss Supreme Court was satisfied that CAS was no longer 'the vassal of the IOC'.[56] The SFT highlighted evidence supplied by the Secretary General of CAS that of the 12 cases submitted between 1996 and 2003 in which the IOC was the respondent, the IOC had won eight but lost four.[57] Although as the SFT observed, this statistic had 'indicative value' only, it did provide concrete evidence of CAS's independence and authority. Put simply, by the turn of the century interested parties appeared to have more confidence in CAS, a confidence that was reflected in the statistics on CAS applications and in a number of developments that expanded CAS's 'reach' into the world of sports disputes. With regard to the statistics, the average number of annual requests for arbitration filed at CAS increased tenfold, from nine in its first decade of existence, to 99 during the period 1996–2006.[58] In respect of 'reach', not only were the years 2002 and 2003 important for CAS in terms of the validation it received from the SFT, it was also the period during which FIFA finally recognised CAS's jurisdiction (in 2002) and the World Anti-Doping Agency designated CAS as the tribunal of 'last instance' in disputes relating to breaches of the then World Anti-Doping Code (in 2003).[59]

The Future of CAS

[**3.13**]   In 2003, the Swiss Supreme Court commended CAS for having 'gradually built up the trust of the sporting world' such that it has earned its status as one of the 'principal mainstays' of the administration of international sport.[60] The qualified exception of major league sport in the US notwithstanding, it is difficult

---

[55] CAS Code, R33. The challenge must be brought to ICAS (R34) and can result in the removal (R35) and/or replacement (R36) of the arbitrator. See also CAS Code, S19. ICAS may remove, temporarily or permanently, an arbitrator from the list of CAS members if they breach their duty of confidentiality regarding the disclosure to any third party of any facts or other information relating to proceedings conducted before CAS.

[56] *Danilova and Lazuntina v IOC and FIS* (2003) 3 Digest of CAS Awards 649, 688, Swiss Federal Tribunal.

[57] Ibid. In addition, the three arbitrators in the stated proceedings had all been part of CAS Panels that had ruled against the IOC.

[58] The average number of requests for arbitration leading to an award increased seventeen fold from four (1986–1995) to 69 (1996–2006). See further www.tas-cas.org/statistics. In 2008 alone, the number of requests for arbitration reached a record total of 311.

[59] The subsequent integration of CAS into the administration of world football can be illustrated by the establishment of an ad hoc CAS division for the FIFA World Cup in Germany in 2006. The importance of football and the FIFA-link can also be seen in the fact that there is a dedicated list of 'football-related' CAS arbitrators. See www.tas-cas.org/arbitrators-footlist.

[60] *Danilova and Lazuntina v IOC and FIS* (2003) 3 Digest of CAS Awards 649, 688–89, Swiss Federal Tribunal.

to disagree with that commendation to the point that it appears clear that CAS's influence on the administration of sport globally looks set to widen and deepen. There are at least two reasons for this outlook on CAS's continuing influence: the scope of CAS's jurisdiction including the finality of its authority on key specific issues in modern sport such as doping; and the consistency of its approach to general principles of law and policy common to all sports-related disputes, which might, in time, be worthy of the label *lex sportiva*.

CAS's Jurisdiction

[**3.14**]   A somewhat underestimated aspect of the debate on CAS is the scope of its jurisdiction. CAS's jurisdiction is extremely broad and effectively any dispute directly or indirectly related to sport may be submitted to it. Admittedly, and as is elemental to private arbitration, that jurisdiction extends 'only insofar as the statutes or regulations of the said sports-related bodies or a specific agreement so provide'.[61] Moreover, under its appeal arbitration procedure, it must also be noted that an appeal against the decision of a federation, association or sports-related body may be filed with CAS only 'insofar as the statutes or regulations of the said body so provide'.[62] In this, the appellant must have exhausted all the internal 'legal' remedies available to him prior to the appeal in accordance with the statutes or regulations of said sports-related body.[63] Nevertheless, where such formalities are fulfilled, CAS decisions indicate that it will rarely declare itself to lack jurisdiction on the ground that a dispute is not 'sports-related'.[64] Recent decisions—ranging from whether the biomechanical and metabolic effects of a prosthetic device are such as to give a disabled athlete a competitive advantage[65] to appeals by athletes who, because of 'off-field' misconduct, have been sanctioned for bring their chosen sport 'into disrepute'[66]—reflect that broad jurisdiction (and also the factual diversity and medico-legal complexity of cases now presented to CAS). In addition

---

[61] CAS Code, R1.

[62] Ibid, R47. In short, the statutes or regulations of the sport-related body from whose decision the appeal is being made must expressly recognise CAS as an arbitral body of appeal in order for CAS to have jurisdiction to hear an appeal. See the discussion in CAS 2004/A/676 *Ismailia Sporting Club v Confédération Africaine de Fooball*; CAS 2005/A/952 *Ashley Cole v Football Association Premier League*; and CAS 2008/A/1503 *Flamengo FC & Ors v Conmebol.*

[63] At its simplest this means that an appeal can only be made once the said sports body has reached a 'final decision' on the matter. See the discussion in CAS 2005/A/899 *FC Aris Thessaloniki v FIFA and* CAS 2007/A/1251 *Aris FC v FIFA.*

[64] Note, eg, the approach in CAS 92/81 *L v Y SA* (an employment contract dispute between an architect and a sports body arising out of the exclusive design of catamarans and yachts).

[65] CAS 2008/A/1480 *Pistorius v IAAF* (eligibility dispute concerning a double leg amputee athlete who sought, with the aid of prosthetic legs, to compete in IAAF-sanctioned events alongside able-bodied athletes).

[66] See, eg, CAS 2008/A/1574 *D'Arcy v Australian Olympic Committee* and CAS 2008/A/1605 *Jongewaard v Australian Olympic Committee* (athletes unsuccessfully appealing sanctions imposed by the AOC for disreputable behaviour). See also CAS 2008/A/1647 *NOC of Sweden and Ara Abrahamian v IOC* (Swedish Greco-Roman wrestler appealed a decision by the IOC to strip him of his bronze medal won at the Beijing Olympics on the ground that his behaviour at the medal ceremony was inappropriate).

and on the specific issue of doping, CAS, which in the early 1990s took the lead on the interpretation of the strict liability principle,[67] has had a significant influence on the harmonisation of anti-doping policy worldwide.[68] Since 2003, that role has been formalised with the designation of CAS by the World Anti-Doping Agency as the tribunal of last instance for disputes resulting from breaches of the World Anti-Doping Code. Consequently, CAS will not only, in a general sense, be the final decision-maker with respect to interpretations of the various provisions of the World Anti-Doping Code but CAS will also be the final adjudicator on the various 'creative' ways by which banned athletes have sought, and presumably will continue to seek, to challenge doping-related suspensions. This element of CAS's jurisdiction in dealt with in the next chapter of the text.

Lex Sportiva *or Ludicrous Latin?*

[**3.15**]   CAS's broad jurisdiction and its influential role in doping appeals apart, CAS's future will be determined by the manner in which it continues to address the relatively small number of core principles of law and policy that appear time and time again in sports-related disputes. Disciplinary panels at all levels of sport from those established by national sports bodies to the sophisticated dispute resolution 'chambers' of leading international federations, all now look to CAS in order to seek guidance and consistency with regard to the interpretation of issues such as: breaches of natural justice; abuse of discretion; the proportionality of sanctioning; the appropriate standard of proof in sports disciplinary cases; the application of the doctrine of legitimate expectation; specific technical issues such as the scope and effect of de novo appeal hearings; and broader issues such as guidelines on the characteristics of unreasonable, arbitrary or capricious decision-making in sport.[69] It follows that CAS's most important contribution to modern sport is that it facilitates the collation of a corpus of sports jurisprudence that, by way of precedent, can be availed of to resolve sports-related disputes without the need for a formal determination by CAS on the point at hand.

[**3.16**]   It is suggested that, for two overlapping reasons, the usefulness of this corpus of sports-related jurisprudence has not yet been fully realised. The first reason is of more theoretical or academic concern. The second reason is structural and practical in outcome. On the first point, and as a number of leading

---

[67]   See, eg (and in chronological order), the comments of CAS Panels in CAS 94/129 *USA Shooting & Q v UIT*; CAS 95/150 *V v FINA*; and CAS 96/149 *AC v FINA*.

[68]   See generally T Kavanagh, 'The Doping Cases and the need for the International Court of Arbitration for Sport (CAS)' (1999) 22 *University of New South Wales Law Journal* 721 and F Oschutz, 'Harmonization of the Anti-Doping Code through Arbitration: the Case Law of the Court of Arbitration for Sport' (2002) 12 *Marquette Sports Law Review* 675.

[69]   See generally the influence of CAS decisions on the approach taken by FIFA's Dispute Resolution Chamber (DRC) outlined by F de Weger, *The Jurisprudence of the FIFA Dispute Resolution Chamber* (The Hague, TMC Asser Press, 2008). DRC decisions are available through the 'official documents' section of www.fifa.com. See also www.fifa.com/aboutfifa/federation/administration/disputeresolution.html.

commentators in the field of sports law such as Beloff[70] and Nafziger[71] highlight, one must be careful to avoid the tendency to view the jurisprudence emerging from CAS as unequivocal evidence of sports law's elevation into a discrete branch of general law that can be known internationally as *lex sportiva*. Whether CAS-inspired jurisprudence is deserving of, or even requires, such a label is open to debate as are the very contents of the 'lex' upon which the label is said to attach. To clarify, and as Erbsen observes, the term *lex sportiva* is accompanied by a false sense of gravitas because its proponents never make it clear just what exactly the term is supposed to encapsulate.[72] For example, apart from CAS precedent (*lex arbitrii*) should the term also include the regime of private law, regulation and convention that arises from the tangle of agreements that bind individual athletes with their national and international sporting bodies (equivalent to a *lex mercatoria*)? Does it include the application to sports disputes of the general equitable principles, rules and customs common to all major legal systems (*lex ludica*)? In short, and as Erbsen argues convincingly, there is little to be achieved in distilling this medley of positive law and internal institutional regulation and then attempting to bottle it into some sort of *lex speciali* and, moreover, the 'descriptive and normative scholarship about CAS would benefit from a more subtle account of how CAS has tailored general legal principles to the circumstances of disputes involving athletes and sports officials'.[73]

[**3.17**]   Erbsen's point is that while the initial use of the phrase *lex sportiva* may have been useful in the sense that by evoking 'an ascendant new form of sports regulation' it helped CAS gain recognition and respect, it is now little more than an 'oversimplified motto' and a slightly misleading one at that.[74] Other commentators such as Foster go even further and argue that the concept of *lex sportiva* is used by leading sports bodies (such as the IOC) as a 'cloak for continued self-regulation' and avoidance of 'intervention' by sovereign actors.[75] An interesting manifestation of Foster's concerns arose in the months preceding the Turin Winter Olympics of 2006 law dispute between the IOC and the Italian government on the regulation of doping at the Games.[76] Under Italian state law, where tests or investigations carried out by Italy's anti-doping commission revealed the use of prohibited substances by an athlete, that athlete could face criminal sanction, including up to three years' imprisonment. The IOC, apparently worried about the impact

---

[70] See, eg, M Beloff, 'Is there a Lex Sportiva?' (2005) 5 *International Sports Law Review* 49 and Beloff *et al* (n 6) 1–15.

[71] See, eg, J Nafziger, 'The Future of International Sports Law?' (2006) 42 *Williamette Law Review* 861 and J Nafziger, *International Sports Law*, 2nd edn (New York, Transnational Publishers, 2004) 48–61.

[72] See A Erbsen, 'The Substance and Illusion of *Lex Sportiva*' in I Blackshaw, R Siekmann and J Soek (eds), *The Court of Arbitration for Sport, 1984–2004* (The Hague, TMC Asser Press, 2006).

[73] Ibid 441.

[74] Ibid.

[75] See K Foster, 'Is there a Global Sports Law? (2003) 2 *Entertainment Law* 1, 2.

[76] For background see N Vinton, 'IOC Stops Fighting Doping Laws in Turin' *The New York Times* (New York 29 October 2005) Sport (Olympics) 5 and J Macur, 'Looking for Doping Evidence, Italian Police Raid Austrians' *The New York Times* (New York 19 February 2006) Sport (Olympics) 1.

that overzealous police raids might have on competitors, wanted the Italian government to impose a moratorium on these statutory provisions for the duration of the Games and instead permit the IOC to process doping offences according to WADA guidelines, including sports-related sanctions only. Ultimately, a successful compromise was reached as was evidenced when, acting on an IOC tip-off, a raid by Italian police revealed an extensive blood-doping conspiracy within the Austrian cross-country skiing team.[77] Returning to the point on the status or concept of *lex sportiva*, the Turin affair is of interest because it was not, as some have suggested, a victory for (IOC-inspired) *lex sportiva* over (Italian) state or public law—it was a compromise; but, equally, it gives a hint as to the theoretical pathway along which sports law might travel in future years.[78]

[**3.18**]   The Turin affair underpins Erbsen and Foster's contention that, for the moment at least, the concept of *lex sportiva* remains a nebulous one, and, certainly, one that should not be used to grant the institutional and regulatory mechanisms of international sport an autonomous legal character that is in some way elevated from state and public law. Nevertheless, as Foster admits, in the longer term, a coherent theoretical framework will have to be found through which international sports law and national public law can interact.[79] Erbsen puts it neatly when he observes that the 'customs and practices of the sports world are not an immovable object, and general legal norms are not an unstoppable force. Each must accommodate the other and when they collide in litigation there will always be a question of which should yield and to what extent'.[80] Erbsen goes on to reiterate that developing a theory that can help facilitate such an 'accommodation' between sport and law is a prerequisite to any normative assessment of so-called *lex sportiva*.[81] Without getting overly distracted by this debate, it is suggested that the Turin compromise—between *lex olympica* and Italian state law—might answer Erbsen's call because it illustrates that the future of *lex sportiva* lies not in a conflict between national (public) law and

---

[77] The fallout from the raid led both to lifetime Olympic bans for a number of skiers and to the passing of a comprehensive anti-doping provision by the Austrian parliament. For a review both of the Turin affair and a typically comprehensive CAS award, note CAS 2008/A/1513 *Hoch v FIS and IOC* (successful appeal by the coach of the Austrian cross-country ski team in reducing his lifetime ban to one of 15 years).

[78] See T Schultz, 'The *Lex Sportiva* Turns Up at the Turin Olympics: Supremacy of Non-State Law and Strange Loops' *JusLetter* 20 February 2006, available through http://jusletter.weblaw.ch, who, in an otherwise interesting analysis of *lex sportiva*'s interaction with public legal systems, appears to suggest that the Turin affair was an example of the 'pre-eminence' of the former over the latter. If anything Italian state law prevailed, and it is of interest that one year later the IOC/WADA were urging the UK government to follow Italy's lead and implement more stringent public law provisions in order to combat doping during the London Olympics. See, eg, O Slot, 'Coe urged to make Criminals of Drug Users at 2012 Games' *The Times* (London 24 July 2007) Sport, 56.

[79] See, for instance, K Foster, '*Lex Sportiva* and *Lex Ludica*: the Court of Arbitration for Sport's Jurisprudence' (2005) 3 *Entertainment and Sports Law Journal* published online at www2.warwick. ac.uk/fac/soc/law/elj/eslj/issues/volume3/number2/foster.

[80] Erbsen (n 72) 453.

[81] Ibid. For an interesting analogy see the debate on the future status of 'global commercial law' analysed by R Michaels, 'The True *Lex Mercatoria*: Law Beyond the State' (2007) 14 *Indiana Journal of Global Legal Studies* 447.

*a*national (global sports) law but in a combination of both so that what emerges, in time, is a corpus of law that is identifiably *trans*national in nature and thus truly deserving of its Latin nomenclature. This seems to be the thrust of what was said by a CAS Panel in 2007 in *FIFA and WADA v CBF, STJD and Dodo* where the claimants sought to appeal the acquittal, on doping charges, of a Brazilian footballer by the statute-based sports tribunal of Brazil (STJD).[82] The player challenged CAS's appellate jurisdiction on the grounds that under applicable Brazilian law the only right of appeal from the STJD was through the ordinary court system of Brazil. The Panel held that, on their interpretation of the STJD's enabling legislation, there was in fact a right of appeal to CAS and, in so holding, the Panel noted obiter that this integration of international sports law (*lex sportiva*) did not undermine Brazilian law but (as was intended) enhanced it by ensuring that Brazilian athletes competing on the international stage would receive equal treatment in the application and interpretation of anti-doping regulations. In short, it was not a choice between either Brazilian law or *lex sportiva* but a case of 'and/both'.

A Permanent CAS?

[**3.19**]   Whatever long term theoretical premise is settled upon for sports law/*lex sportiva*, there is no doubt the CAS jurisprudence will play an important role therein and it follows that in the short to medium term the concentration should be on how, as a matter of practice, that jurisprudence (and how the expertise and experience of the arbitrators who create it) can be used to better process and resolve the sporting disputes of the future. Although a full evaluation would be beyond the scope of this brief text, there is some space to highlight a possible structural defect that might be hindering the optimal impact of CAS jurisprudence. The nature of private arbitration is that, as compared to litigation, it is based not only on the consent of the parties but also their involvement in the process—such that they can, as in CAS-mandated arbitration, directly appoint one of the arbitrators. It follows that in a private arbitration the focus for both parties (and the arbitrators themselves) is very narrow and wholly dispute specific. The question as to whether the arbitration will add to the general body of jurisprudence in the area by, for instance, laying down general guidelines as to what parties might reasonably expect, or how parties might reasonably behave in a particular set of circumstances, is very much of secondary concern. To borrow from social contract theory, private arbitration can be characterised by its contractarian nature, as opposed to adhering to a boarder contractualism premise.[83] That of itself is not problematical—legal and quasi-legal systems of dispute resolution are well used to parties acting in a manifestly self-interested

---

[82]   CAS 2007/A/1370 &1376 *FIFA and WADA v CBF, STJD and Dodo.*

[83]   See generally S Darwall (ed), *Contractarianism/Contractualism* (London, Wiley-Blackwell, 2002).

way but combined to the fact that there is a large and diverse body of arbitrators from which to choose in CAS arbitrations (270 or so), it can inevitably lead to an inconsistency in the way CAS adjudicates upon matters, or, similarly, difficulties in identifying a consistent pattern in CAS awards. In short, when, to use the vernacular of the common law, almost every CAS award can be distinguished on (and to) its facts, the value of precedent that can be drawn from such awards is adversely affected such that in the long term this unpredictability might even end up deterring parties from availing themselves of CAS.

[**3.20**]   Commenting specifically on how CAS has approached issues of doping violations, Straubel has argued that the accusatory, penal and quasi-criminal nature of doping-related appeals are such that every effort should be made by CAS to ensure the harmonisation of the principles that apply to athletes 'accused' of doping infractions.[84] Straubel's fundamental point is that the inconsistency of CAS doping awards—their sheer 'arbitrariness'—is unfair on athletes and puts the future legitimacy of CAS in doubt. Straubel contends that the fair and equitable treatment of those accused of doping infractions will be achieved only if CAS doping hearings surround themselves with the procedural safeguards of criminal trials and are heard in a separate CAS chamber dedicated to doping cases with an accompanying discrete list of arbitrators.[85] There is some merit to this, though it must be pointed out that, in effect, the sport of football already has a separate CAS chamber—there is a dedicated list of 'football' arbitrators from which relevant CAS Panels may be drawn—and this has not always resulted in a consistency of approach. An excellent illustration of this is the contrast between two recent CAS decisions (the so-called *Webster*[86] and *Matuzalem*[87]appeals) relating to the matter of compensation on the premature ending of a professional footballer's contract (and assessed in chapter seven of the text). Although there is little doubt that inconsistencies and differences of opinion are necessary characteristics of the jurisprudential evolution of any system of dispute resolution; nevertheless, the current arbitrariness and unpredictability of CAS awards is such that it might be limiting their usefulness as precedent in resolving sports disputes more generally. The question is therefore, how does one adhere to an underlying principle of certainty of approach without CAS arbitration becoming (as the early common law became) bound rigidly by precedent?

---

[84]   M Straubel, 'Enhancing the Performance of the Doping Court: How the Court of Arbitration for Sport can do its Job Better' (2005) 36 *Loyola University Chicago Law Journal* 1203. The basic thrust of Straubel's piece is that CAS as originally conceived was a mechanism for dealing with disputes of a contractual and commercial nature and though it continues to do a good job in that regard, the principles of private commercial arbitration are ill-suited to doping disputes.

[85]   A possible analogy to Straubel's criticism of CAS's current inconsistency of approach is that CAS might be flouting the principles of legitimate expectation, legal certainty and proportionality inherent in Art 7 ECHR.

[86]   CAS 2007/A/1298, 1299 & 1300 *Wigan Athletic FC v Heart of Midlothian; Heart of Midlothian v Webster & Wigan Athletic FC; and Webster v Heart of Midlothian.*

[87]   CAS 2008/A/1519-1520 *FC Shakhtar Donetsk (Ukraine) v Matuzalem Fancelion da Silva (Brazil) and Real Zaragoza SAD (Spain) v FC Shakhtar Donetsk (Ukraine) & FIFA.*

[**3.21**]　Straubel suggests that 'a single supervisory panel' should be created within CAS to reconcile conflicting precedent. Straubel bases the competency of this panel on a qualified use of CAS's existing advisory opinion procedure which, although not changing the result of an award, could, on the direction of, or on petition to, CAS's Secretary General be asked to reconcile the conflicting issue of law and policy.[88] Again there is much of merit in Straubel's approach, though it is most likely that this supervisory panel would in time have to be recognised formally as CAS's 'Grand Chamber', adding another layer of appeal to the dispute-resolution structure of international sport and, arguably, taking away from the efficacy of the system as a whole. In contrast, a much more modest proposal in ensuring greater consistency in CAS awards is by promoting and facilitating the greater use, reliance and citation of previous CAS jurisprudence in contemporary CAS awards. This could be done through the provision of a comprehensive narrative statement of CAS jurisprudence, drawn from previous CAS awards, developing this resource into an encyclopaedic reference for CAS arbitrators, potential applicants and the wider public. In brief, CAS's secretariat might consider the creation of a Halsbury-like treatise on CAS jurisprudence and CAS practice directions, which could be updated, supplemented and fully indexed as appropriate, and ideally be made available online.

[**3.22**]　More radically, and in summary, if CAS is to live up to Samaranch's vision of it as a 'supreme court of world sport', then CAS's future probably lies in aping the structures and approach of the International Court of Justice.[89] For instance, given the complexity and frequency of disputes now being heard by CAS, and given the financial stakes involved for many applicants, should CAS and world sport now consider the establishement of a permanently sitting International Court of Justice for Sport (ICJS)? Although, again, this proposition has to be dealt with in framework only, this so-called ICJS could, for sake of argument, have the following four features, all of which would be designed to enhance the current working of CAS. First, the ICJS could not only build on existing CAS facilities such as its advisory and ad hoc procedures but it could also, for example, add to them by way of a summary procedure for the speedy dispatch of proceedings. Second, the ICJS, which would, it is submitted, have around 15–20 permanent members selected carefully to represent all interested parties and relevant areas of expertise, could, at first instance, be divided into separate chambers dedicated to, for example, doping; football; administrative appeals, for example eligibility/selection disputes; commercial rights; and contractual breaches (employment disputes). Third, where a case stated is deemed by the ICJS Secretariat to be of such importance to sport generally (a *Webster/Matuzalem* scenario for example), it could be heard directly by the ICJS Grand Chamber, that is, the ICJS sitting in full quorum. Fourth, and most importantly however, it is argued (admittedly with little elaboration) that

---

[88]　Straubel (n 84) 1257–60.
[89]　Judge Kéba Mbaye, the inaugural President of CAS, was a former Vice-President of the International Court of Justice.

such an ICJS, would, given the uniformity of its structure and purpose, address the extant problems with regard to the alleged arbitrariness and precedential value of CAS awards and would in time delineate the boundaries of a discrete and credible corpus of law that can truly merit its branding as *lex sportiva*.[90]

A UK Sports Tribunal?

[**3.23**]   In the early part of this decade, and after a number of leading Irish sports organisations had faced legal challenges seeking to quash or stay disciplinary sanctions, an Irish barrister called for the creation of an Irish Court of Arbitration for Sport.[91] The proposal itself was not particularly radical: it suggested simply that the existing procedures and services provided by CAS be integrated into an Irish legal environment by the Irish Sports Council, the statutory agency responsible for the promotion and administrative coordination of sport in Ireland, and that this be done in consultation with leading stakeholders in Irish sport, such as the Olympic Committee of Ireland.[92] There are however two brief points of interest arising from the proposal. First, the Irish barrister in question was Michelle de Bruin; the former Irish swimmer who won three gold and one bronze medals at the Atlanta Olympics and who subsequently had a four-year doping ban for purported irregularities in an out-of competition test upheld by CAS.[93] Despite her lack of success at CAS, de Bruin's firsthand experience appeared to convince her of the merits of CAS-related arbitration. In explaining the motivation behind her initiative she contended that it would ensure that in the increasingly complex 'fight against doping' sports bodies would not use disciplinary procedures in an overly repressive and reactionary manner against athletes because, she concluded, 'people involved in running sport should think about service rather than control'.[94] Although it easy to be cynical about de Bruin's call, it should not be dismissed in its entirety and it should be reiterated that credible independent arbitral bodies in sport do provide an important 'check and balance' between the sometimes sharply competing interests of a sports body's desire, through its disciplinary remit, to preserve the integrity of the sport as a whole and the rights of individual competitors.[95]

---

[90]   This ICJS proposal might also address the broadly similar concerns that the leading international sports law jurist James Nafziger has had with CAS and the evolution of *lex sportiva*. See especially J Nafziger, 'Lex Sportiva' (2004) 1–2 *International Sports Law Journal* 3.

[91]   M de Bruin, 'An Irish Court of Arbitration for Sport' (2005) 3–4 *International Sports Law Journal* 28.

[92]   See also J Anderson, 'Sports and the Courts: Time for a Sports Disputes Tribunal of Ireland' (2005) 23 *Irish Law Times* 149.

[93]   CAS 98/211 *B v FINA*.

[94]   De Bruin (n 91) 30.

[95]   See also the concerns outlined by J O'Leary, 'Doping Solutions and the Problem with "Problems"' in J O'Leary (ed), *Drugs and Doping in Sport: Socio-Legal Perspectives* (London, Cavendish, 2001).

Sport Resolutions UK

[**3.24**]   The second point of interest is that for various political and economic reasons the Irish Sports Council did not answer de Bruin's call, preferring instead that such a facility be (self) regulated (and funded) by national sports bodies. In 2007, an independent dispute resolution facility for Irish sports was launched by the Federation of Irish Sports, an independent, representative body for over 60 national sports organisation in Ireland.[96] This body, Just Sport Ireland, is very much modelled on its UK equivalent—Sport Resolutions UK.[97] Sport Resolutions UK (founded as the UK Sports Dispute Resolution Panel in 1997) is an independent and private dispute resolution mechanism, which offers arbitration, mediation and advisory opinion services for sports bodies in the UK. The consensual jurisdiction and governing rules or code surrounding its arbitration service are similar to those of CAS though they are, ultimately governed by the Arbitration Act 1996. It is however its 'tribunal appointment' service that has proved the most popular—of the 250 or so disputes referred to Sport Resolutions UK thus far nearly 60 per cent have been referrals of this nature. This service is one whereby professional or community sports bodies request that a member of one of Sport Resolutions UK's specialised list of arbitrations be designated to chair and resolve an internal dispute. The usefulness of this procedure for sports bodies, and particularly amateur/community based entities, is that instead of having to create and maintain their own quasi-independent appeals committee, they can, on an ad hoc basis, draw upon the pre-vetted expertise of Sport Resolutions UK panellists, who offer a broad level of experience and specialisation across the range of sports dispute-related areas including discipline; anti-doping; section; eligibility; child welfare; personal injury; intellectual property; commercial and employment law; and professional negligence.[98] This tribunal appointment procedure also ties in with the twin objectives of Sport Resolutions UK which are to make available to all sports in the UK both (a) independent, expert, timely and cost effective resolution of all disputes but also (b) preventative measures in the guise of information, education and training seeking to minimise the risk of disputes arising. Of crucial importance here, and discussed in detail in the concluding section of this chapter, is a 'Dispute Guidance' service, which is, in effect, a series of guidelines on how a sports body's grievance/disciplinary process may be made less vulnerable to legal challenge.

[**3.25**]   Of the 250 referrals that have been made by over 50 different types of sports bodies to Sport Resolutions UK, approximately half of the referrals

---

[96] See further www.justsport.ie.

[97] See further www.sportresolutions.co.uk. The background and statistical information contained in [3.24] and [3.25] has been taken from this site.

[98] According to its website, Sports Resolution UK has at present 65 members on its panel of arbitrators and 25 members on its panel of mediators, all of whom subscribe to a Panel Members Code of Conduct.

have involved issues relating to discipline (typically appeals against the length of bans arising from ill-discipline on the field of play). Approximately one-quarter of referrals have related to eligibility and selection disputes, while the remainder have concerned general commercial and employment issues. The wide range of sports bodies and sports-related disputes reflect Sport Resolutions UK's growing importance to the modern administration and regulation of sport in the UK. This is enhanced by the fact that Sport Resolutions UK panellists are now used by leading sports organisations, as part of their sophisticated dispute resolution mechanisms.[99] Arguably however, the clearest indication of Sports Resolution UK's increasing authority and competency is the fact that it is the provider of the National Anti-Doping Panel (NADP),[100] which is the independent body established to determine anti-doping disputes in the UK.[101] In sum, Sport Resolutions UK now appears to be fulfilling the role of a national CAS for the UK.[102] The importance of this role cannot be underestimated to the point that it is argued that not only should greater use be made of Sport Resolutions UK by national sports bodies but, it should probably receive more formal governmental recognition of its role.

Time to Get STUK?

[**3.26**]   Three related points follow from this contention that Sport Resolutions UK deserves greater acknowledgement as a decentralised, domestic CAS. First, it is contended that such a body would over time develop a body of decisions and awards that would be of useful precedential value in the resolution of sports disputes, ensuring the equal treatment of similarly situated, aggrieved sports parties. Second, it is projected that sports disputes are going to become ever more complex in content and legalistic in form and thus ever more difficult to deal with for sports bodies under their internal structures and within their own resources. Appeals relating to the alleged violation of athletes' due process rights in doping and disciplinary-related hearings are a case in point but so also are those relating to commercial issues. Two examples suffice both of which refer to

---

[99] The success and robustness of Sport Resolutions UK is reflected in its annual report of 2008–2009 published on 30 October 2009 in the 'news' section of www.sportresolutions.co.uk.

[100] Further information on the operation of NADP, including transcripts of recent decisions, is available on the 'national anti-doping panel' of www.sportresolutions.co.uk.

[101] The UK Sport Anti-Doping Rules (2009) facilitate the incorporation of the World Anti-Doping Code into the regulatory framework of UK sport. On the recommendation of UK Sport, the Department for Culture, Media and Sport has recently (December 2009) created a new stand alone national anti-doping agency called UK Anti-doping (UKAD), which is the national body responsible for the implementation and management of the UK's anti-doping policy. Under this regulatory scheme, the NAPD will hear all related anti-doping charges and appeals. See generally the information available at www.ukad.org.uk.

[102] In terms of doping-related disputes this is recognised expressly by the fact that, pursuant to article 13 of the UK Sport Anti-Doping Rules (2009), an appeal arising from a NADP decision can be taken to CAS. The rules and other policies are available at www.ukad.org.uk/publications.

professional football. The first of these is where the FA and the Football League authorities have lately had to deal with the regulatory fallout from clubs going into administration. It is of interest that in the postscript to its award on the arbitration pursued (unsuccessfully) by Leeds United FC (seeking a declaration that the imposition of a 15-point deduction by the Football League of the 2007–2008 season was unlawful and void) the Independent Arbitration Panel (IAP) noted that the extant Football League's (Insolvency) Policy, should integrate an appeal to an independent tribunal.[103] The reason for this was that under the FA's then Insolvency Policy an appeal could be made only to representative members of the Football League and this, according to the IAP, was 'unsatisfactory' given that 'some clubs in the same league may not readily agree to reduce a points sanction in the understandable self-interest of their clubs'.[104]

[**3.27**]   Another illustration of why a statutory Sports Tribunal UK (which might (or might not!) be known by the acronym STUK) should be considered is, again, to be found in professional football, and namely the relatively troublesome and elongated manner in which the contractual arrangements surrounding the ownership of Argentinean footballer Carlos Tevez were dealt with by the FA Premier League (FAPL) authorities in England.[105] Tevez and his international team mate, Javier Mascherano, joined West Ham United on loan from the Brazilian club, Corinthians, in late August 2006. When the latter moved to Liverpool in January 2007, it was revealed that two offshore companies owned the players' registration and their accompanying economic and commercial rights. This arrangement was in breach of FAPL rules relating to 'third party' ownership of players, which are designed to minimise the influence that outside entities might have on the operation of the Premier League. Although Liverpool was permitted to sign Mascherano on a revised contractual basis, the FAPL set up an independent disciplinary tribunal to investigate the continuing Tevez/West Ham arrangement. At that tribunal, held in April 2007, West Ham pleaded guilty to the charges of having breached FAPL rules and was fined a substantial sum of £5.5 million. Crucially however, having pointed out to the tribunal that West Ham had changed ownership since the signing of Tevez, and further agreeing to end the contractual arrangements with the third party owners, the club was not docked any league points. This was significant because the hearing took place against the backdrop of West Ham's then relegation battle to remain in the Premier League whereupon a points deduction would probably have seen them demoted to the Championship, losing up to £30 million in TV-related revenue.[106] As it transpired, Tevez contributed enormously to West Ham's victories in the final three

---

[103] *Leeds United 2007 Ltd and Rotherham United FC Ltd v Football League Ltd* [2008] BCC 701, Arbitration.

[104] Ibid 712.

[105] A succinct review of this saga is provided by P Kelso, 'The Mysterious Case of Who Owns Carlos Tevez' *The Daily Telegraph* (London 15 May 2009) Sport (Soccer) 4.

[106] See D Bond, 'No Justice if Tevez Keeps West Ham Up' *The Daily Telegraph* (London 28 April 2007) Sport (Soccer) 2.

games of the season and thus helped them to an unlikely escape from relegation. Sheffield United were however relegated and, arguing that West Ham's breach of FA Premier League rules had been the effective cause, pursued the matter (unsuccessfully) to independent arbitration[107] and in court.[108]

[**3.28**]   Subsequently, Sheffield United sought compensation of up to £45 million from West Ham for breach of contract said to consist of breaches of the rules of the FAPL and causing their relegation from the Premier League. Another independent arbitration panel, established in the summer of 2008 under Rule K of the rules of the FA, agreed that Sheffield United were entitled to compensation, noting the West Ham had not, as they had promised to do, fully clarified Tevez's contractual arrangements.[109] Despite this success, Sheffield United had to take a final court action restraining West Ham from appealing to CAS.[110] In March 2009, it was announced that the parties had reached an out of court settlement whereby West Ham agreed to pay an estimated £20 million to Sheffield United in compensation.[111] The conclusion to the Tevez dispute brings to mind two points of reflection. First, the dispute was, in effect, based on a simple and single premise (well known to all those who play park league football)—an attempt by a club to avoid having points docked for playing a 'ringer'. Nevertheless, it resulted in a complex array of disciplinary, arbitral and court hearings, which may not yet be complete.[112] Given the stakes involved, it was probably inevitable that, the best efforts of the various eminent arbitrators used by the FA notwithstanding, the parties would seek to explore every avenue of redress from the Commercial Court

---

[107] *Sheffield United FC Ltd v West Ham United FC Plc* Unreported Arbitration 3 July 2007 and [2007] (3) *International Sports Law Review* SLR-77. The Panel held that, although it would, if it sat at first instance, probably have decided differently, it was not possible to condemn the FAPL's decision not to terminate Tevez's registration, and not to permit further investigation by way of a Disciplinary Commission, as unreasonable in the sense of the decisions being perverse or capricious.

[108] It appears (the High Court challenge was heard in private) that leave was sought to appeal the arbitral award on a point of law pursuant to s 69 of the Arbitration Act 1996 (appeal on point of law). See further J Ley, 'Interpol Pursue the Man who Brought Tevez to Premiership as Sheffield United Lose Court Fight' *The Daily Telegraph* (London 14 July 2007) Sport 2.

[109] *Sheffield United FC Ltd v West Ham United FC Plc* Unreported Arbitration 18 July 2008 and [2009] (1) *International Sports Law Review* SLR-25.

[110] *Sheffield United FC Ltd v West Ham United FC Plc* [2008] EWHC 2855 (Comm). Sheffield United's application was based on the contention that CAS had no jurisdiction to entertain an appeal because on a reading of Rule K of the FA rule, the award of the arbitral tribunal was final and binding and only challengeable by way of an application in the domestic courts under the Arbitration Act 1996.

[111] P Kelso, 'West Ham to pay £20m over Tevez Claim' *The Daily Telegraph* (London 17 March 2009) Sport (Soccer) 6.

[112] As of March 2009, a number of employees of Sheffield United at the time of its relegation, including the manager, were claiming that they were considering suing West Ham for loss of earnings while clubs such as Wigan and Fulham, who were not relegated but were ranked below West Ham at the end of the 2006/2007 season, were considering suing for loss of prize money based on their league placement. In addition, the FA and the Premier League were considering opening another inquiry into West Ham's failure to fully comply with the initial disciplinary commission's requests regarding Tevez's contractual status. See further G Jacob, 'Sheffield United Players Want to Sue West Ham in Tevez Affair' *The Times* (London 17 March 2009) Sport 77 and P Kelso and J Ley, 'West Ham to Resist Compensation Claims' *The Daily Telegraph* (London 18 March 2009) Sport (Soccer) 7.

to CAS. Although the question as to whether the early involvement of a STUK-like body might have helped in bringing the dispute to a quicker conclusion is open to debate, it is however clear from the Tevez affair, that if such disputes are a precursor of what is to come, then it is only a statutory Sports Tribunal UK that would have the capacity and competency to deal with them and in doing so STUK would be simultaneously assisting sports bodies in resolving disputes that are sometimes framed in complex legal argument without overly burdening the ordinary courts with proceedings that remain, at core, sport-specific in substance. In this regard, a body such as STUK would be adhering to the fundamental principle of ADR.

[**3.29**]   To reiterate, it is evident that a body such as the Sport Resolutions UK model would have the necessary expertise (and independence) to handle such disputes effectively thus removing the financial and administrative burden of such cases for the football authorities, eliminating any possible conflict of interests and gradually improving the quality and consistency of decision making in similar cases.[113] This leads to a third and final point, which is, given that Sport Resolutions UK is de facto acting as national CAS, is it not time for UK Sport and the Department for Culture, Media and Sport to go further and give de jure recognition to Sport Resolutions UK's competency and authority? This could be promoted by way of a 'carrot and stick' approach with the stick being that it is made a condition precedent of any application for public funding to the various sports councils in the UK that a sports body agrees expressly to vest the final, independent and appellate stage of its internal dispute resolution scheme to Sport Resolutions/CAS (UK). The 'carrot' would be that instead of having to resource and call upon independent arbitration panels to resolve internal disputes, UK sports bodies could avail themselves of Sport Resolutions/CAS (UK) to deal with the matter. It would follow that the burden of any litigation that might surround such arbitration (under the Arbitration Act 1996) would be carried by Sport Resolutions/CAS (UK). In fact when one stands back and looks at the current structure of sports arbitration in the UK—with less well resourced sports bodies seeking to avail of body such as Sport Resolutions UK; the better resourced, such as the FA and the Jockey Club, utilising their own quasi-independent arbitral mechanisms; others selecting arbitrators on an ad hoc basis; and all loosely bound by adherence to private codes of conduct and the Arbitration Act 1996[114]—it could be argued that for the sake of clarity, efficacy and consistency, the proposal

---

[113] It is of interest to note that during the course of their award in the Leeds United-led arbitration, the IAP noted that as of April 2009, they had been informed of 40 or more current and anticipated football club insolvencies.

[114] See, eg, the broad and complex remit of the FA's Disciplinary Procedures—encompassing players and clubs in the Premier League, Football League, and Football Conference National Division. Although it is difficult to be succinct about the accompanying disciplinary mechanisms, the basic structure is that, at first instance, charges are prosecuted in front of a Regulatory Commission from which there is a right of appeal to an Independent Appeals Board (IAP) and a further and final layer of arbitral appeal provided by Rule K of the FA's Rules and Regulations. The FA has a service level agreement with Sport Resolutions UK to provide chairpersons for regulatory commissions, independent appeals panels and Rule K arbitrations.

for a Sport Resolutions/CAS UK should be elevated to that of a call for it to be placed on a statutory basis similar to that of Sport Dispute Resolution Centre of Canada (SDRCC)[115] or the Sports Tribunal of New Zealand (STNZ).[116]

An Audit under Article 6 ECHR

[**3.30**]   In many ways the debate as to a whether a statutory body such as STUK should be created is one for the future. Of more immediate concern for sports bodies in the UK is how, at first instance, they can ensure, through imbuing their disciplinary procedures and mechanisms with sufficient fairness, efficiency and transparency, that the risk of subsequent appeal and/or legal challenge is lowered appreciably. To reiterate, and as illustrated by chapter two, for a myriad of reasons—costs, adverse publicity, delay and disruption to competitions—sports bodies are anxious to minimise the risk of legal challenge. Equally however it must be noted that individual participants or clubs are also affected by the costs of legal proceedings: in fact, it could be argued that the risks are aggravated for participants or clubs because they might struggle to gather the resources necessary to sustain a claim to full hearing. Accordingly, and as many of the claims outlined in chapter two (*Modahl*; *Mullins*; *Bradley* and *Chambers*) illustrate, sports claimants are often reluctant claimants, seeking recourse to the ordinary courts only when they perceive that the respondent sports body has engaged in egregious procedural impropriety; unfairness; delay; bias; or heavy-handedness. It is evident that where a national sports governing body's internal disciplinary process attracts the confidence of, and is trusted by, individuals and clubs, those parties will rarely be moved to litigation. In addition, and again returning to chapter two, where the ordinary courts see that a disciplinary process is designed both to give parties 'a fair go' and reach 'a fair result', then the courts will rarely be moved to intervene. The remainder of this chapter gives examples of how a national sports governing body's disciplinary mechanisms might be underpinned by the principle of fairness, as guided by the interpretation of that concept in the jurisprudence surrounding Article 6 ECHR.

---

[115] Physical Activity and Sport Act SC 2003 c 2 s 9. The SDRCC's mandate was mentioned favourably recently in *Barrie Tornado Lacrosse v SDRCC* (2008) CanLII 15766 (Ontario SC) [28]–[30], Lederer J. The SDRCC's comprehensive website has reports of recent decisions, SDRCC services and accompanying procedures and codes available at www.crdsc-sdrcc.ca. For a review of the workings of the SDRCC see further H Findlay, 'Scope of Review, Standard of Review and Authority to Grant a Remedy: An Analysis of Three Policy-Based Rules in a Sport-Specific Arbitration Process' (2006) 4 *Entertainment and Sports Law Journal* published online at www2.warwick.ac.uk/fac/soc/law/elj/eslj/issues/volume4/number1/findlay. See also A Jodouin, 'The Sport Dispute Resolution Centre of Canada: An Innovative Development in Canadian Amateur Sport' (2005) 15 *Journal of the Legal Aspects of Sport* 295.

[116] Sport and Recreation New Zealand Act 2002 s 8(i) and Sports Anti-Doping New Zealand Act 2006 s 29. STNZ's comprehensive website has reports of recent decisions, STNZ's services and accompanying procedures and codes available at www.sportstribunal.org.nz.

Fairness and Article 6 ECHR: General Legal Principles

[**3.31**]   To reiterate, the issue here is not whether sports bodies as hybrid public authorities *must*, pursuant to section 6 of the Human Rights Act, give effect to the rights and freedoms guaranteed under the ECHR, but to suggest ways in which a sports body's disciplinary processes *might*, as a matter of best practice, be safely reconciled with Article 6 ECHR's requirement that determinations about an individual's civil rights are made at a fair hearing within a reasonable time and by an independent and impartial tribunal established by law. In short, the underlying idea of this brief section is to assist sports bodies in ensuring that their grievance procedures are Convention-compliant, not because the law tells them that they should be so, but because that is what a properly run sports body should want them to be.[117] In this light, it must be noted that the procedural guarantees of Article 6 ECHR are fundamental to the work-ings of the ECHR as a whole and it follows, unsurprisingly, that the jurisprudence on the protections that the provision affords to individuals is substantial.[118] A recent case of interest, which gives a succinct account of Article 6 ECHR's core concept—that of fairness—is provided by the House of Lords decision of *Secretary of State for the Home Department v AF & Anor*.[119] In the stated case, the appellants were made the subject of control orders involving significant restriction of their liberty, pursuant to section 2 of the Prevention of Terrorism Act 2005, on the ground that the respondent had reasonable grounds for suspecting that the appellants were, or had been, involved in terrorism-related activity. Under section 3 of the Act, the Secretary of State must (and did so in this case) justify the imposition of the orders at an in camera court hearing. The issue raised successfully by the appellants was that at the stated hearings there was a violation of their right to a fair hearing guaranteed by Article 6 ECHR because the judge relied upon material the nature of which was not disclosed to the appellants. In short, the appellants' contention was that a fair hearing requires that a party must be informed of the case against him so that he can respond to it. Although self-evidently, the matters involved in a sports disciplinary hearing are in no way as grave or weighty as those at issue in terrorism-related control orders (effectively the com-peting interests of the right to be informed of the case against one and the public interest in national security), the manner in which the House of Lords outlined the parameters of the necessary 'fairness' of a fair hearing is useful.[120]

---

[117] Put simply, the principles inherent in Art 6 ECHR are the optimal standard expected of a sports body's disciplinary procedures; while a system that sustains arbitrary and capricious decision-making is the least desirable and most vulnerable to legal challenge.

[118] The concluding sections of this chapter are generally informed by A Lester, D Pannick and J Herberg (eds), *Human Rights Law and Practice*, 3rd edn (London, Lexis-Nexis Butterworths, 2009) ch 4.

[119] *Secretary of State for the Home Department v AF & Anor* [2009] UKHL 28.

[120] The appeals were upheld principally on the grounds that the Grand Chamber of the European Court of Human Rights in *A & Ors v United Kingdom* [2009] ECHR 301 had made it clear that, for the purpose of Strasbourg jurisprudence and Art 6(1) ECHR, a judicial process the purpose of which was to impose, or to confirm the imposition of, onerous obligations on individuals on grounds and evidence of which they were not and could not be informed does not constitute a fair hearing.

[**3.32**]   Utilising the approach of the House of Lords in *Secretary of State for the Home Department v AF & Anor,* it appears that Article 6 ECHR's view of the requisite fairness of a fair hearing is based around three criteria: the context-specific nature of fairness; that the person charged has the fullest information of both the allegations that are made against him and the evidence relied upon in support of those allegations; and that that party is given the opportunity to explain or contradict those allegations and evidence.[121] On the first criterion, the fundamental point was made succinctly by Lord Phillips: 'The requirements of a fair trial depend, to some extent, on what is at stake in the trial'.[122] In the context of sports disciplinary hearings this means that the graver the charges against, hence consequences for, a party; the more serious the commitment must be to the fundamentals of a fair hearing. It follows that hearings regarding minor disciplinary infractions do not really have to be treated with the solemnity of a case involving abuse of a person's human rights though, in contrast, doping allegations against an elite athlete, for instance, should have due regard to the serious economic and reputational repercussions that a finding of guilty might have for the party involved.

[**3.33**]   On the second of the three 'fairness' criteria, and again citing Lord Phillips, there are 'strong policy considerations that support a rule that a trial procedure can never be considered fair if a party to it is kept in ignorance of the case against him'.[123] The reason that the person affected must be told what is alleged against him, and the material upon which those allegations are based, is that an essential requirement of a fair hearing is that a party against whom relevant allegations are made must be given the opportunity to rebut the allegations.[124] In this, the applicable standard can be taken as one which gives the party sufficient information to enable him, or his representative, the opportunity 'effectively to challenge' the case brought against him.[125] The third criterion overlaps with the previous one and is encapsulated in the Latin maxim of *audi alteram partem* (hear the other side). This rule of natural justice means that not only should a directly affected party be given an opportunity to know and answer the other side's case but they should also be given a fair opportunity to state their own case beyond a simple denial of the charges. The full disclosure and discussion of the evidence is

---

[121]   Although the stated case was discussed in terms of Art 6 ECHR, Lord Scott observed that neither would the process at issue have met the common law's view of the essential requirements of a fair hearing, see *Secretary of State for the Home Department v AF & Anor* [2009] UKHL 28 [96].

[122]   Ibid [57]. See also *A & Ors v United Kingdom* [2009] ECHR 301 [203] noting that the analogous requirement of fairness under Art 5(4) ECHR does not impose a uniform, unvarying standard to be applied irrespective of the context, facts and circumstances.

[123]   Ibid *Secretary of State for the Home Department v AF & Anor* [63]. See also [83] Lord Hope stating that the 'principle that the accused has a right to know what is being alleged against him has a long pedigree' and outlining some of the domestic, European and American authorities on which the principle rests.

[124]   Ibid [96] Lord Scott.

[125]   Ibid [81], Lord Hope who called this standard the 'core irreducible minimum'. The phrase 'effectively to challenge' was used by Lord Bingham in *Secretary of State for the Home Department v MB and AF* [2007] UKHL 46 [34] and adopted by the Grand Chamber in *A and others v United Kingdom* [2009] ECHR 301 [218].

important even in the most obvious and apparently irrefutable of cases because as Megarry J's judgment in *John v Rees* put it (eloquently): '... the path of the law is strewn with examples of open and shut cases which, somehow, were not; of unanswerable charges which, in the event, were completely answered; of inexplicable conduct which was fully explained; of fixed and unalterable determinations that, by discussion, suffered a change'.[126]

[**3.34**]   In sum, the thrust of the rule on hearing both sides is twofold. First, by ensuring that a tribunal properly and fully instructs itself in all the facets of the case, it improves the chances of that tribunal's reaching a fair decision. Second, it also avoids the subjective sense of injustice, which an accused may feel if he knows that the tribunal relied upon material of which he was not informed.[127] The latter point is of particular note for sports bodies because this sense of injustice might transpire to be the catalyst and motivation for a claimant losing confidence in and respect for the internal disciplinary structures of that body and opting instead to litigate. Accordingly, sports bodies would do well to take note of Sedley LJ's dictum in the Court of Appeal in *Secretary of State for the Home Department v AF & Ors* warning about the 'fallibility of judgment' based on partial evidence and how the common law and all systems governed by the European Convention on Human Rights (and many others beside) ensure and 'insist, not that everything must be known before judgment is given, but that everyone affected must have had a proper chance (which they may of course forfeit) to advance as much material as may help the tribunal in reaching a judicious conclusion'.[128]

The Ten 'Commitments' of a Fair Sports Disciplinary Process

[**3.35**]   While the abstract principled adherence to the concept of fairness is admirable in any sports disciplinary process, it should also be complemented by a concrete procedural commitment to natural justice and due process. It is suggested that in realising an objective of being fair in procedure and fair in outcome, a sports disciplinary process should guided by 10 'commitments' or general guidelines reflecting the various stages in the overall process.[129] These 10 commitments of a 'responsible sports discipline' are informed generally by

---

[126] *John v Rees* [1970] Ch 345, 402 and cited by Lord Phillips in *Secretary of State for the Home Department v AF & Ors* [2009] UKHL 28 [61]. See also *Secretary of State for the Home Department v AF & Ors* [2008] EWCA Civ 1148 [113] Sedley LJ.

[127] Ibid *Secretary of State for the Home Department v AF & Anor* [72], Lord Hoffmann.

[128] *Secretary of State for the Home Department v AF (FC) and others* [2008] EWCA Civ 1148 [114] Sedley LJ. Referred to approvingly by Lord Hope in *Secretary of State for the Home Department v AF (FC) and others* [2009] UKHL 28 [84].

[129] For a very useful summary of the basic framework of a sports disciplinary process for a national sports governing body see the 'Dispute Guidance' service available at www.sportresolutions.co.uk. See also the practical considerations and checklists provided in A Lewis and J Taylor (eds), *Sport: Law and Practice,* 2nd edn (London, Tottel Publishing, 2008) 77–98.

an analysis of best practice identified in the case law on professional misconduct hearings.[130]

1. The first commitment is to clarity in the manner in which applicable rules and regulations are written and transparency in the manner in which these rules and regulations are made available to and understood by all parties.[131] The point of departure for many sports related disputes is ambiguously-phrased rules, which may be open to various interpretations. 'Plain language' regulation should be promoted and unnecessarily technical legal language avoided. Plain language should apply not only to the expression of disciplinary procedures but also to playing rules and codes of conduct and documents such as lists of prohibited substances; all of which should be reviewed and updated regularly in line with the constitutional procedures of the sports body in question.[132] In sum, the underlying thrust of any sports disciplinary process and its surrounding procedures, can be encapsulated in a single phrase—the prohibition of acts contrary to good sportsmanship.[133]

2. Depending on the type of sports body involved, a disciplinary process can be a complex one operating at many different levels from the initial investigatory stage to final arbitral appeal. Accordingly, and with a view to coordinating the scheme as a whole, sports organisations frequently appoint a dedicated disciplinary officer and/or establish a compliance unit within their regulatory structure. This officer or unit not only ensures that, when violated, the rules and regulations of that sports body are enforced and disciplinary proceedings instigated but also can be used in a preventative manner by seeking to educate, consult and advise individual and clubs on disciplinary-related matters.[134]

3. In a number of leading sports bodies, disciplinary officers or the compliance unit act, in effect, as the sports body's prosecution service, investigating the substance of and evidence surrounding allegations of disciplinary breach made against an individual, official or club. Moreover, they are often, on the back of a thorough inquisitorial investigation, given the power to recommend both that a charge is brought and the type and length of sanction that might follow. Typically, the charged party is then placed on interim suspension and given the

---

[130] See, eg, the case law reviewed by A Lidbetter, 'Professional Discipline and Regulation: Top Cases of 2008–2009' [2009] *Judicial Review* 291.

[131] See generally the comments in CAS 94/129 *USA Shooting & Q v UIT*, Law [34]: 'Regulations that may affect the careers of dedicated athletes must be predictable. They must emanate from duly authorised bodies. They must be adopted in constitutionally proper ways. Athletes and officials should not be confronted with a thicket of mutually qualifying or even contradictory rules that can only be understood on the basis of de facto practice over the course of many years by a small number of insiders.'

[132] Note that in *Mullins v McFarlane* [2006] EWHC 986 (QB), the High Court held that internal email correspondence did not equate to proper and adequate amendment of the applicable Rules of Racing regarding adverse doping thresholds in horses.

[133] See the guidance provided by R MacDonald, 'Legal Language as a Trauma of Law and the Road to Rehabilitation' (2006) 4 *Journal of Commonwealth Law and Legal Education* 5.

[134] See, for instance, the 'Discipline Department' established by the Rugby Football Union outlined at www.rfu.com/TheGame/Discipline.

option to either accept the sanction and thus ensuring that the matter is dealt with expeditiously or to avail of a full, personal hearing in front of a specially convened disciplinary tribunal.

4. In convening the tribunal, the rules of natural justice encapsulated in the Latin maxims *audi alteram partem* (hear the other side) and *nemo judex in causa sua* (no man may be a judge in his own cause) should apply; otherwise the hearing may be unfair. The first rule of natural justice means that not only should a directly affected party be given due notice of the specific charges and evidence against them but they should also be given a fair opportunity to answer the charges and state their own case beyond a simple denial. The second rule concerns bias and the legitimate expectation of the charged party that their case will be heard by an impartial tribunal, whose members have not prejudged the issue at hand. Guidance on the applicable test was given by the Court of Appeal in *Flaherty v National Greyhound Racing Club Limited*.[135] Three points may be taken from that guidance. First, bias is context-specific and the fact that the proceedings at issue are tribunal not judicial proceedings should be taken into account. It follows that the issue of bias (actual or apparent) should be approached with a 'measure of realism and good sense',[136] reflecting that in sport, the relevant community is often a small one with the personalities involved having to interact frequently with and being well known to each other. Second, as a matter of caution, and as will often (and should) be required by a disciplinary tribunal's code of conduct, tribunal members should disclose any circumstances likely to affect their independence with respect to the matter or parties at hand, and then it will be for the parties to decide whether to proceed with the stated member(s). Third and in sum, the key test and one that the Court of Appeal in *Flaherty* has said meets the demands of Article 6 ECHR is 'whether the fair minded and informed observer, having considered the facts, would conclude that there was a real possibility that the tribunal was biased'.[137]

5. Although it is somewhat ironical in the context of this chapter—the promotion of ADR and avoidance of litigation—the involvement of lawyers in tribunal hearings either as tribunal panellists or party representatives has some advantages. This is because sports tribunal hearings in the UK and most common law countries tend to be adversarial in nature utilising a standard of proof based on the balance of probabilities. It follows that it is of the utmost importance in sports tribunal hearings that the parties receive equality of

---

[135] *Flaherty v National Greyhound Racing Club Limited* [2005] EWCA Civ 1117 [23]–[29] Scott-Baker LJ.

[136] *Modahl v British Athletic Federation Limited (No 2)* [2001] EWCA Civ 1447 [128], Mance LJ.

[137] *Flaherty v NGRC* [2005] EWCA Civ 1117 [26] Scott-Baker LJ citing *Porter v Magill* [2002] 2 AC 357, 494, Lord Hope. In general law terms see also the observations of A Olowofoyeku, 'Bias and the Informed Obseerver: A Call for a Return to Gough' (2009) 69 *CLJ* 388. In sports-specific circumstances, note also the view of the SFT on conflicts of interest at CAS noted at [3.10]–[3.11].

treatment or what chapter two deemed 'a fair go'.[138] Although it is, again, very much context-specific and related to the seriousness of the case at hand, surrounding a tribunal process with procedural directions such as statements of claim; disclosure requirements; preparation of bundles; time limits; and provisions for the cross-examination of witnesses is the best way of ensuring that the requisite equality is achieved.[139] Arguably, those with legal training will not only have the experience of operating under such directions but also should have the capacity to move the process along more expeditiously than a lay person. In addition, permitting an individual to have legal representation is advised if only because it might avoid the subjective sense of injustice that an accused may feel if he or she thinks that they were not equally or adequately represented at the tribunal hearing.[140]

6. The basic duty of the tribunal panel is to reach 'what in the end is a fair decision'.[141] This can be best achieved by the tribunal properly instructing itself with and acting reasonably upon the facts, law and regulatory context of the matter at hand.

7. It appears best practice that any award made by a tribunal panel should be supported by a reasoned written decision attested by the panellists and made available to the parties.[142] Traditionally and in terms of administrative law, the common law did not impose on domestic tribunals a general duty to give reasons, principally because of the burden that this might place on decision-makers. Equally however, the benefit of giving reasons is that it leads to both greater transparency and enhanced public confidence in an administrative/disciplinary process.[143] The advice now with respect to the jurisprudence surrounding Article 6 ECHR is that it is better to furnish reasons of 'adequate and intelligible' quality to enable the individual to understand the 'essence of the decision' taken against them and thus enabling them, if they so chose, to challenge that decision. In the circumstances of a typical sports disciplinary

---

[138] See the discussion in the text at [2.22].

[139] For a useful summary of these procedural directions see the approach taken in the arbitration rules suggested by Sport Resolutions UK and available under the 'services' section of www.sportresolutions.co.uk.

[140] For an interesting review of this topic, albeit not in a sports setting, see *Kulkarni v Milton Keynes Hospital NHS Trust* [2009] EWCA Civ 789; [2009] IRLR 829.

[141] *Calvin v Carr* [1980] AC 574, 593, Lord Wilberforce and see the discussion in the text at [2.11]–[2.15].

[142] Increasingly, and presumably because of the benefits of so doing from the perspective of transparency and precedential value, reports on the findings of disciplinary tribunals and arbitral panels are being published. This should only be done with the prior consent of both sides though it can be kept in mind that if one of the parties is reluctant to permit the publication of an award for, say, reasons of commercial confidentiality, it might still be possible to publish the award subject to redaction of the commercially sensitive information.

[143] For an eloquent review of the benefits/burdens of giving reasons for a decision see *R v Higher Education Authority, ex parte Institute of Dental Surgery* [1994] 1 WLR 242, 256-257, Sedley LJ. See also *R (on the application of the Asha Foundation) v Millennium Commission* [2003] EWCA Civ 88.

decision, it appears safe to suggest that 'the extent and substance of the reasons need not be elaborate or lengthy. But they should be such as to tell the parties in broad terms why the decision was reached. In many cases (and in the context of Article 6 ECHR) a very few sentences should suffice to give such explanation as is appropriate to the particular situation'.[144]

8. With respect to the imposition of sanctions, there should be strict compliance with the relevant regulations such that a sports disciplinary tribunal or panel should impose only those penalties specifically provided for in the regulations. Where a panel is satisfied that based on the evidence, and where the rules allow it, a sanction below that which is normal should be imposed (due, for example, to mitigating circumstances) or a sanction above that which is normal should be imposed (due to aggravating circumstances) the reasons for the exercise of that discretion should be explained. In this, the fundamental issue in sanctioning is not whether a penalty is 'soft' or strict but whether it can be reconciled with the 'margin of appreciation' extended to all administrative decision-makers under the principle of proportionality such that it can be said that a tribunal's decision on sanction was within that tribunal's reasonable range of responses. Guidance in the application of the test of proportionality was given by the Court of Appeal in *Bradley v the Jockey Club*.[145] The thrust of that guidance is where, as it is required to do, a sports tribunal directs itself correctly as to its authority to impose sanction, and where that tribunal gives proper consideration to all the relevant facts and evidence, the tribunal should carry out a careful balancing act looking at (a) the fundamental purpose served by, and objective of, the rules (such as punishment, deterrence or the maintenance of standards of fair play and safety in sport); (b) the seriousness of the breach of the rules in question; and (c) any mitigating factors such as the impact that the disqualification might have on the economic and reputational interests of the culprit. Finally and similarly, where disciplinary rules include provisions for costs, the usual principle is that 'costs follow the event' thus the party deemed by the tribunal to have been successful in the tribunal proceedings is, on application, entitled to their reasonable costs. Any departure from the norm should be explained clearly in the accompanying written award.

9. It is best practice that a sports disciplinary process has an appeals procedure. Carefully calibrated grounds of appeal and time limits should ensure that an appeals procedure strikes the right balance between meeting the demands of those claimants who seek to pursue 'justiciable' flaws in the

---

[144] *Stefan v General Medical Council* [1999] UKPC 10; [1999] 1 WLR 1293 [32], Lord Clyde. See also *English v Emery Reimbold & Stick Ltd* [2002] EWCA Civ 605; [2002] 1 WLR 2409 [16], Lord Phillips MR: 'justice will not be done if it is not apparent to the parties why one has won and the other has lost.'

[145] *Bradley v Jockey Club* [2005] EWCA Civ 1056 [17]–[27], Lord Phillips MR endorsing the approach of Richards J in *Bradley v Jockey Club* [2004] EWHC 2164. See the discussion in the text at [2.47]–[2.53].

original hearings (which may highlight areas of improvement for the sport's disciplinary process as a whole) and, in contrast, quietening the demands of 'vexatious' claimants (whose frivolous and unmeritorious appeals do little more than waste time and resources). Although it will depend on the needs and resources of the sports body in question, it is suggested that a typical disciplinary scheme for a national sports body could consist of four levels: the initial investigatory stage consisting of an assessment of the accusation by the sport body's disciplinary office or compliance unit including the recommendation of an acquittal or sanction; beyond that an accused should still have the right to request a full hearing at the sports body's principal disciplinary tribunal; third, the opportunity either to appeal the decision to the sports body's appeals disciplinary tribunal on limited review or, in exceptional circumstances, to convince the appeals tribunal that a de novo hearing of the matter is necessary; and fourth, the possibility of recourse to an independent arbitration panel acting in accordance with the Arbitration Act 1996.[146] On the fourth step, it could be provided that such an 'appeal'—or, more properly, the resolution of the dispute by mandatory arbitration—is to be by way of limited 'judicial review' only, that is, a challenge on the grounds of an ultra vires error of law; irrationality; or procedural unfairness with the independent arbitration panel exercising a supervisory jurisdiction only. This limited review by way of arbitration is the approach taken in Rule K1(d) of the Rules of the Football Association. In *Stretford v the FA*,[147] the claimant challenged the operability of Rule K arguing that its binding nature could not be reconciled with the protections of Article 6 ECHR and especially his right to a public hearing. The Court of Appeal rejected his argument on the ground that the claimant had, through his players' agent's licence, entered into contractual relations with the FA under which he had agreed both to be subject to the voluntary nature of Rule K and waive his rights to a hearing before the courts (except in accordance with the 1996 Act). In addition, the Court of Appeal noted that the sophistication of the arbitral mechanism established by the FA, and the supervisory provisions of the 1996 Act, were such that, in any event, a very few of the substantial procedural safeguards on natural justice contained in Article 6 ECHR were constrained. And finally, in a manner which endorses succinctly the use of ADR in sport, the Court of Appeal concluded that not only were there no relevant public interest considerations to stand in the way of the arbitral process provide by Rule K but also that 'it seems to us that the public interest encourages arbitration in cases of this kind'.[148]

---

[146] A national sports body might wish to 'rationalise' the proposed disciplinary scheme by either merging steps three and four of the process or simply assigning them to the competency of a body such as Sport Resolutions UK.

[147] *Stretford v The FA* [2007] EWCA Civ 238.

[148] Ibid [66], Sir Anthony Clarke MR.

10. Finally, the nature of justice in the common law tradition is that of the adversarial resolution of disputes. This approach has filtered down into alternative means of resolving disputes. For instance, many of the more sophisticated arbitral-based sports tribunals have become as procedurally driven and rigid as judicial proceedings. Irrespective of whether it occurs in a committee or court room, the adversarial means of resolving disputes can sometimes aggravate disputes particular those where the surrounding community, such as in sport, is a small one well known to, and largely interdependent, upon each other. It is argued that conciliation, mediation and advisory opinion mechanisms should play a greater preventative role in the alternative resolution of sports-related disputes.

Conclusion

[**3.36**]   The basic premise of this chapter has been to promote the benefits of alternative dispute resolution in sport. The advantages of ADR in sport—in terms of cost, privacy, and efficacy—are well established and arbitral-based tribunals now frequently sit at the apex of sports bodies' disciplinary schemes. Sports bodies should however remember that irrespective of how sophisticated their dispute resolution scheme might appear that process must still earn the confidence of the parties—individual participants, officials and clubs—who are to avail themselves of its services, and must do so on a continuous basis. These parties (and the wider public who have an interest in the manner in which a sports body conducts its business) must *see* that fairness is an integral part of how a sports body's disciplinary process operates, rather than taking it on trust that claims or appeals will be dealt with fairly. It is sometimes forgotten by sports bodies that, although they are private organisations against whose competency the ordinary courts are reluctant to intervene and especially so if the claimant has not exhausted all internal avenues of appeal; the constitutional right of access to the courts is not obviated by membership of a sports body. In this light, this chapter has sought to suggest ways in which a sports body might inculcate greater levels of fairness, consistency and clarity into their dispute resolution mechanisms so that the frustrations of individuals with sports disciplinary proceedings will not result in litigation of the type outlined in the previous chapter. This chapter has taken a 'top-down' approach to its objective, beginning with ways in which CAS acting qua the supreme court of sport might now need to evolve into a permanent International Court of Justice for Sport through which the precedential value of its awards can be better used from the benefit of sports dispute resolution worldwide. In a domestic setting, this chapter has promoted the services provided by Sport Resolutions UK and suggested that it might have to be elevated onto a statutory platform, given the increasing complexity and gravity of sports disputes. In conclusion, this chapter has provided some general guidelines around which a national sports body might 'stress-test' its own disciplinary structures and procedures, as against the standards of fairness and equity recognised by Article 6 ECHR, thus avoiding arbitrary, capricious and challengeable decision-making. It must be noted, and in line with all suggestions made in this chapter, that the underlying idea is not the slightly negative one of how sports bodies might be alerted to ways of minimising or evading the external recourse to litigation, more on how to convince individual athletes, officials or clubs that any fears or reluctance they might have in availing themselves of the internal means of dispute resolution can be assuaged by the inherent fairness and independence of that process. As a postscript, it is argued that the one type of sports dispute that will, with alacrity, reveal the inherent flaws in any sports dispute resolution system—be it at its investigatory, hearing or appeal stage—is that of a doping-related dispute where the matter might have serious economic and reputational repercussions both for the individual athlete and for the integrity of sport as a whole. And it is to the legal aspects of doping in sport that we now turn.

Further Points of Interest and Discussion

1. Having analysed at least six CAS awards, do you think that CAS Panels do a good job in tailoring both the practices of sport to the principles of law and legal doctrine to sporting values?
2. The decision of the independent arbitration panel in *Sheffield United FC Ltd v West Ham United FC plc* (18 July 2008) has been criticised for opening a 'Pandora's box' of potential litigation from former employees of Sheffield United and other affected clubs and parties. On the other hand, it has been argued that the problems surrounding the ownership of Carlos Tevez began with the failure of the April 2007 disciplinary tribunal to impose a point deduction penalty on West Ham, and that that tribunal was overly sympathetic to West Ham's relegation plight. Applying the principles of procedural fairness and proportionality in sanctioning, do you think that the Tevez affair was well handled by the football authorities in England?
3. Having analysed the workings of the *either* the Sport Dispute Resolution Centre of Canada *or* Sports Tribunal of New Zealand, including its history, code of operation and recent decisions, do you think that the UK should follow suit and place a national sports dispute resolution body on a statutory footing?
4. An amateur sports body, which governs the playing of X-fieldsport in the UK, has recently received a letter from a member/player arguing that a decision by his club to suspend him for 10 years from the club premises was taken in breach of his right to natural justice and was irrational and disproportionate. The decision arose out of an incident that occurred during a coaching session

when the member/player in question is alleged to have verbally abused a coach in front of a number of children. In the letter, the player/member requests a personal hearing in front of 'the executive board' of X-fieldsport UK, seeking to have the decision overturned. X-fieldsport UK is worried not only because the member in question is a barrister by profession but also because its disciplinary appeals mechanism is very much an ad hoc affair, which has not been used for quite some time. They write to you for assistance. What advice would you give them?

4

The Legal Regulation of
Drugs in Sport

Introduction

[**4.01**]   In broad terms, this chapter concentrates on three aspects of the so-called fight against doping in sport. Given that the regulatory and legal framework through which international sports federations organise their anti-doping programmes is now harmonized by the World Anti-doping Agency (WADA), this chapter is dedicated in part to a descriptive outline of WADA's history, powers and functions as expressed primarily through the operation of the World Anti-doping Code (WADC). The second concern of this chapter, and one that it interwoven in the discussion on WADA, considers specific legal issues that might arise in a disciplinary hearing involving an athlete accused of doping. This discussion includes an examination of a principle that is fundamental to current anti-doping policy, that of strict liability, which holds that any athlete who tests positively or adversely for a banned substance is solely responsible for the substance being found in their body, irrespective of whether they unintentionally or negligently consumed the prohibited substance.[1]

[**4.02**]   All of these matters must first however be placed in context. There are three aspects to the regulatory context surrounding the establishment of WADA (and the legal and administrative repercussions of its remit). First, the context includes a long history of doping in sport stretching from the use of herbal remedies by athletes in ancient Greece to the modern day exploitation of gene transfer bio-technology.[2] Second, the background to the core ethical premise of current anti-doping policy is contemporary in origin and according to Houlihan, the leading commentator in the area, can be located in the

---

[1] In many ways this chapter attempts to update, though hardly improve upon, the issues raised by the various contributors in J O'Leary (ed), *Drugs and Doping in Sport: Socio-Legal Perspectives* (London, Cavendish, 2001). For an American perspective, see the various contributions to the special issue on 'Doping in Sports: Legal and Ethical Issues' in (2008) 19 *Marquette Sports Law Review* 1–344.

[2] This analysis of the history of doping in sport is necessarily brief. See further D Rosen, *Dope: A History of Performance Enhancement in Sport from the Nineteenth Century to Today* (London, Praeger, 2008).

late 1960s.[3] The ethical premise is one of a benevolent, paternalistic concern for the health of athletes and the 'spirit' of sport.[4] In 1990, this concern was encapsulated eloquently by the Dubin report, a commission of inquiry into the use of performance-enhancing drugs (PEDs) in sport initiated by the Canadian government in the wake of sprinter Ben Johnson's infamous positive test at the Seoul Olympics of 1988: 'The use of banned performance-enhancing drugs is cheating, which is the antithesis of sport. The widespread use of such drugs has threatened the essential integrity of sport and is destructive of its very objectives. It also erodes the ethical and moral values of athletes who use them, endangering their mental and physical welfare while demoralising the entire sport community'.[5]

[**4.03**]　　The third context-specific element to the debate on PEDs relates to the various legal and administrative controversies that surround the attempts to ban athletes who have tested positively for PEDs. The paternalistic nature of current anti-doping policy has mandated a rigorous response by international sports authorities, however, as noted by Flint, 'too unyielding an approach—for example, adopting a strict liability approach to doping charges, with a tariff of substantial fixed or minimum sanctions, including suspensions from the sport for lengthy periods, without any ability to take account of relative culpability of the individual athletes—risks compromising basic fairness and respect for participants' individual rights … [and may leave anti-doping programmes vulnerable to] … forceful challenge' in the guise of arbitral and/or legal proceedings.[6] The manner in which this three-part context informs this chapter is implicit, at least until the chapter's third and concluding part. There, the chapter ends by presenting a provocative analysis of the current approach to the 'war' on drugs in sport, and one that can be distilled into a single, inflammatory hypothesis: the problematical administrative and legal repercussions arising from the current strict proscription of doping in sport could be resolved by permitting the controlled use of PEDs.

The World Anti-Doping Agency

[**4.04**]　　The administrative and legal repercussions that have followed from the establishment of WADA prior to the Sydney Olympics of 2000 are summarised

---

[3] See, eg, B Houlihan, 'Anti-doping Policy in Sport: The Politics of International Policy Coordination' (1999) 77 *Public Administration* 311 and B Houlihan, *Dying to Win: Doping in Sport and the Development of Anti-Doping Policy*, 2nd edn (Strasbourg, Council of Europe, 2002).

[4] This analysis of the ethical dimensions to doping in sport is necessarily brief. See further A Schneider and F Hong (eds), *Doping in Sport: Global Ethical Issues* (London, Routledge, 2007).

[5] C L Dubin, Commissioner, *Commission of Inquiry into the Use of Drugs and Banned Practices Intended to Increase Athletic Performance* (Ottawa, Ministry of Supply and Services, Canada, 1990) *xxii*.

[6] C Flint, 'Drug Use in Sport: the Regulatory Framework' in A Lewis and J Taylor (eds) *Sport: Law and Practice*, 2nd edn (London, Tottel Publishing, 2008) 835–36.

here in two parts. The first part has three elements to it: it begins with the historical context surrounding WADA's birth; it is followed by an outline of how its hybrid public/private law global agenda is influencing national and global anti-doping sports policy; and then the core element of WADA's agenda is discussed by way of an overview of WADC and the accompanying list of prohibited substances. The second part of this discussion on WADA centres on an assessment of the various ways by which athletes have attempted to exploit perceived administrative and legal loopholes within WADC and the prohibited list.

WADA: A History

[**4.05**]   The men's marathon at the 1904 Olympic Games in St Louis was a gloriously corrupt affair. It was eventually won by Thomas Hicks with the aid of a cocktail of strychnine, egg whites and brandy.[7] In the early part of the twentieth century, sports science was at a nascent stage and this combined with fairly rudimentary training regimes, particularly for endurance events, meant that the use of stimulants such as caffeine, cocaine and alcohol was fairly commonplace, so much so that in 1928 the International Amateur Athletics Federation (IAAF) become the first international sports federation to formulate anti-doping regulations. Developments in the production and sophistication of amphetamines, arising out of their use by, and on, soldiers in World War II, soon trickled into sport. The autopsy following the death of Danish cyclist, Knud Enemark Jensen, during the Rome Olympics of 1960 revealed traces of amphetamines,[8] and amphetamine abuse was also understood to have contributed to the death of England's Tommy Simpson during a stage of the 1967 Tour de France.[9] The Simpson fatality prompted the International Olympic Committee (IOC) to act and it established a dedicated Medical Commission with an accompanying list of prohibited substances.

[**4.06**]   The IOC of the late 1960s was a very different creature from that of today. That era pre-dated the multi-million dollar TV and corporate sponsorships that have now made the IOC a wealthy and influential entity. Moreover, apart from lacking the resources to underwrite a testing regime for prohibited substances, the IOC, bluntly, lacked the political will to do so. In the 1970s and into the 1980s, the IOC was well aware that the Olympic Games were a pawn in the Cold War between West and East—political disturbances, terrorism and boycotts marred the Games of the era and doping slipped down the list of priorities. Furthermore, the IOC tended to leave the substantive part of doping

---

[7] See G Matthews, *America's First Olympics* (Columbia, University of Missouri Press, 2005) 137–44.

[8] See D Maraniss, *Rome 1960: The Olympics that Changed the World* (London, Simon & Schuster, 2008) ch 5.

[9] See generally W Fotheringham, *Put me Back on my Bike: In Search of Tommy Simpson* (London, Yellow Jersey Press, 2003).

policy to individual international sports federations but they were subject to similar pressures and constraints and thus were equally lax in their attitude to blatant steroid abuse by athletes, particularly in strength and power-related events.[10] The situation was exacerbated by the fact that one side in the Cold War had instigated comprehensive state-sponsored doping programmes, using any subsequent sporting success for propaganda purposes. To borrow a phrase once used to characterise the attitude of major league baseball to steroid abuse, the 1970s and 1980s was a 'loosey goosey' era in the regulation of doping in sport. Arguably, illustrations of the 'loosey goosey' nature of the era are still in evidence today in the following examples of world records that remain comfortably out of reach of contemporary participants: women's 100 metres (10.49 secs) set by Florence Griffith-Joyner (US) in 1988; women's 100 metres hurdles (12.21secs) set by Yordanka Donkova (Bulgaria) in 1988; women's 200 metres (21.34) set by Florence Griffith-Joyner (US) in 1988; women's 400 metres (47.60 seconds) set by Marita Koch (East Germany) in 1985; women's 800 metres (1:53:28 minutes) set by Jarmila Kratochvilova (Czechoslovakia) in 1983; women's 4 × 100 metres relay (41.37 seconds) set by East Germany in 1985; women's 4 × 400 metres relay (3:15:17 minutes) set by USSR in 1988; women's shot putt (22.63 meters) set by Natalya Lisovskaya (USSR) in 1987; and women's discus throw (76.80 meters) set by Gabriele Reinsch (East Germany).[11]

[4.07]   It is of interest to note that the cut-off for many of these longstanding records is the 1988 Seoul Olympics during which the winner of the men's 100 metres, Ben Johnson, tested positive for a prohibited substance. By 1988, the IOC was, thanks mainly to massive American TV revenues, a well-resourced organisation. The then President of the IOC, Jan Antonio Samaranch, had also ensured that the IOC was firmly positioned at the apex of the pyramid of global governance of sport. Moreover, as the Cold War ended, political tensions became less of a problem for the IOC and it could (and had to) devote more time to placating the worries that its sponsors were having on being associated with 'unclean', drug-fuelled events. Nevertheless, it was not until a decade later when one of the most iconic events of the annual sporting calendar, the Tour de France, became enveloped in the so-called Festina scandal that the IOC decided to dedicate time and resources into formulating a detailed response to *la crise du dopage*.[12] In 1999, the IOC convened the World Conference on Doping in Sport in Lausanne, which adopted the so-called Lausanne Declaration. Part 4 of that Declaration called for an independent international anti-doping agency. WADA was duly established on 10

---

[10] See B Houlihan, 'Anti-doping Policy in Sport' (n 3) 321–24 who notes that at this time, and to their credit, the Council of Europe attempted to initiate debate and formulate policy on the area. The Council continues to do so mainly through its 1990 Anti-Doping Convention (1990). See further the 'doping' section of www.coe.int/T/dg4/Sport.

[11] These records, which can be compared to today's times, are available through www.iaaf.org/statistics/inex.html.

[12] The Festina team 'pharmacist' subsequently recounted the story in depressing detail in W Voet, *Breaking the Chain: Drugs and Cycling, the True Story* (London, Yellow Jersey, 2001).

November 1999. The mandate set out for the agency in the Lausanne Declaration remains integral to the operation and understanding of WADA, 'consideration should be given in particular to expanding out-of-competition testing, coordinating research, promoting preventative and educational actions and harmonizing scientific and technical standards and procedure for analysis and equipment'.[13]

[**4.08**]   In 1999, WADA was established as a foundation or private entity in Swiss law with its initial seat in Lausanne.[14] For the first two years of its existence it was not only located near the headquarters of the IOC but was also wholly funded by the IOC. Learning from the experience of the Court of Arbitration for Sport, and fearing that WADA might be seen as a 'creature' of the IOC, from 2001 onwards its funding base has been provided for equally by the Olympic Movement and various world governments, and its headquarters moved to Montreal. These 2002 developments were also related to WADA's determination that if it were to pursue its key objective—of harmonising anti-doping policy in all sports and in all countries—with any authority, it had to be seen as a truly global and independent entity. Even though it is hardly a decade old, WADA can now be said to be the principal actor in sport's global anti-doping agenda and there is no doubt that it has managed to engender a greater degree of cooperation than previously existed between intergovernmental organisations, governments, sports federations, public authorities and other private bodies with an interest in anti-doping policy.

WADA: An Example of Global Administrative/Criminal Law?

[**4.09**]   The most practical legal manifestation of WADA's success in aligning governmental responses with its agenda lies in the International Convention against Doping in Sport, which was adopted unanimously by the 33rd UNESCO General Conference in 2005, and which came into force on 1 February 2007. The Convention, which has been ratified by 130 countries, is designed to support WADA-led initiatives by underpinning them with the force of international law.[15] UNESCO's recognition of, and support for, WADA's competency and administrative reach in the field of global anti-doping policy, has led to an interesting debate within the discourse of the emerging area of global administrative law as to WADA's hybrid public/private law status.[16] In a more practical sense, the Convention (primarily through articles 8 and 13) supports a key and sometimes overlooked priority of WADA, namely cooperation with global law enforcements

---

[13] The Lausanne Declaration can be read in full at (1999) 26 (25) *Olympic Review* 17–18.

[14] For further details on WADA's history, functions and policies see www.wada-ama.org.

[15] For access to the Convention and a summary of UNESCO's anti-doping policy see further www.unesco.org/en/antidoping. See also article 22 WADC on the 'involvement of governments'.

[16] See, for instance, A Van Vaerenbergh, 'IILJ Working Paper 2005/11—Global Administrative Law Series: Regulatory Features and Administrative Law Dimensions of the Olympic Movement's Anti-Doping Regime' (New York, NYU Institute for International Law and Justice, 2005) available at www.iilj.org/publications/documents/2005.11Vaerenbergh.pdf.

agencies, national sports anti-doping authorities and individual governments in efforts to investigate and combat the trafficking of substances that are then abused for sports doping purposes; for example, human growth hormone.[17] The underlying idea is that, unlike WADA and various national anti-doping agencies, law enforcement and government agencies have the investigatory powers and jurisdiction to investigate the sources and supply of such products.[18] The (underestimated) importance of such an initiative is put into context when one considers that currently only three out of the eight listed anti-doping rule violations set out in article 2 WADC can be detected solely through the testing process (presence of a prohibited substance or method; refusing or failing to give a sample; and 'whereabouts' violations).[19]

[**4.10**]   In this light, WADA announced in 2008 that it had entered into a 'Memorandum of Understanding' with Interpol, the global international police cooperation authority, in order to provide a formal framework for cooperation between the two organisations in tackling doping, in particular in the areas of evidence-gathering and information-sharing.[20] At a national level, WADA promotes the so-called 'Australian model' whereby the legislation that established the Australian Sports Anti-Doping Authority (ASADA) in 2006 permits it to exchange sensitive information with Australian custom officials.[21] The idea is that, although a PED might be prohibited in sport by WADA regulations, formal legal proceedings against suppliers or importers of such products might be constrained because that PED might not be illegal under domestic laws. However, the Australian legislation permits customs officials to share information gained in the course of investigations with ASADA where such information is within ASADA's remit.[22] It is envisaged that this integrated approach will be fundamental to the

---

[17] For more on this issue see the so-called 'Donati Report on Trafficking' available at www.wada-ama.org/rtecontent/document/Donati_Report_Trafficking_2007-03_06.pdf.

[18] The obvious example is the close links that the US Anti-Doping Agency (USADA) has built with the US Drug Enforcement Agency (DEA), which lead to the DEA uncovering the BALCO scandal. BALCO was a sport nutritionist centre based in California and run by Victor Conte which supplied designer steroids, including THG, to a host of leading American sports stars and British sprinter, Dwain Chambers. For the background see M Fainaru-Wada and L Williams, *Game of Shadows* (New York, Penguin, 2006).

[19] The trafficking or attempted trafficking of PEDs is a violation of art 2.7 WADC. The seriousness with which WADA takes trafficking is reflected in the fact that pursuant to art 10.3.2 WADC, a violation of art 2.7 WADC can attract a minimum of four years to a lifetime ban from sport. The usual ban for a doping violation under WADC is two years. Further, art 10.3.2 WADC states that 'significant violations' of art 2.7 WADC, 'shall be reported to the competent administrative, professional and judicial authorities.'

[20] See also R Noble (Secretary-General Interpol), 'Interpol: Committed to the Anti-Doping Fight' (2007) (1) *Play True: An Official Publication of WADA* 12.

[21] Australian Sports Anti-Doping Authority Act (Cth) 2006 and Australian Sports Anti-Doping Authority Act (Consequential and Transitional Provisions) Act (Cth) 2006. See further www.asada.gov.au and the report by E Parham, 'Australia and the World Anti-doping Code, 1998-2008' available online at www.wada-ama.org/rtecontent/document/Australia_and_the_World_Anti_Doping_Code_1999_2008.pdf.

[22] Australian Sports Anti-Doping Authority Act (Cth) 2006 ss 67–73.

operation of UK Anti-doping (UKAD), the recently established national body responsible for the implementation and management of the UK's anti-doping policy. It is envisaged that UKAD will work closely with the Serious Organised Crime Agency, the UK Borders Agencies, the Advisory Council on the Misuse of Drugs and the Medicines and Healthcare Products Regulatory Authority, through a formal information-sharing gateway based on amendments to the existing legislation governing these agencies.[23]

[**4.11**]   In announcing plans to create UKAD, it is interesting to note that the UK Sports Minister reiterated comments made by his predecessor to a House of Commons' Committee, in which he stopped short of advocating the criminalisation of doping in sport.[24] The approach of the current UK government appears to be that the criminalisation of doping—through, for example, an amendment of the Misuse of Drugs Act 1971—would not only encounter practical difficulties (misuse of a drug in terms of sports performance is very context specific), it would also, because of the custodial sentences that might result, be a disproportionate response.[25] It is suggested that the integrated approach favouring statutory 'gateways' of cooperation between sports bodies and drug/law enforcement agencies is a better way to proceed than one of full criminalisation. Although at first instance criminalisation would appear, as many of it advocates in the sports world suggest, to carry a significant deterrent effect, the reality of the criminal law and the criminal justice system is that it is a rather blunt instrument to use in combating what is, after all, a relatively narrowly defined social 'evil'. Criminalisation could ultimately lead only to the 'scapegoating' of small number of athletes for what really is a problem for sport as a whole. Moreover, an unintended side effect for WADA and sports authorities might be that if individual jurisdictions proceed and criminalise doping in sport they will, presumably and understandably, do so in a manner specific to their criminal code and criminal justice system. This may lead to specific problems for sports federations seeking to hold major events across jurisdictions and may also lead more generally to both a lack of harmonisation of anti-doping laws globally and further legal uncertainty for athletes.[26] Nevertheless, the lessons to be learned from countries

---

[23] See further the information at www.ukad.org.uk.

[24] Science and Technology Committee, 'Human Enhancement Technologies in Sport' HC (2006–2007) 67, 35–36.

[25] Ibid, meaning that, as compared to custodial sentences, sports-specific sanctions may be more appropriate, effective and flexible in nature and in consequence.

[26] In January 2010, the Canada Border Services Agency announced that it had agreed to give the IOC the names of athletes and support personnel caught bringing PEDs into the country. The agreement covers substances listed under both Canada's controlled drug and substances laws and WADC. The agreement followed two years of protracted negotiations, mainly in attempting to reconcile the agreement with Canada's privacy laws. Under the terms of the agreement, the CSBA will only disclose information it collects between 25 January 2010 and 25 March 2010 ie, the three-month period surrounding the hosting of the Vancouver Winter Olympics. See J Lee, 'Border Agents to Disclose Names of Doping Athletes' *Vancouver Sun* (Vancouver 16 January 2010) WC News 16.

such as Italy, France, Sweden, Denmark and, most recently, Austria (where sports doping is, in certain aspects, a matter of criminal law), is that if the scale of the problem is such that the criminalisation of doping has to be considered, it should be done so only in a very targeted manner, for example, criminalising *the supply* of PEDs.[27]

WADA: Codification and Prohibition

[**4.12**]   There are three essential aspects to WADA's programme: its anti-doping code (the WADC); the prohibited list; and so-called 'models of best practice' and guidelines.[28] In a broad administrative sense, WADA seeks to provide harmony in doping control rules through the principles outlined in the WADC and principally with regard to the detection, deterrence and prevention of doping. WADC, described as the fundamental and universal document upon which WADA's anti-doping programme is based, first emerged from the second World Conference on Doping in Sport in Copenhagen in 2003. That original code came into effect on 1 January 2004.[29] At the third World Conference on Doping in Sport in Madrid in 2007, a revised WADC was endorsed. This revised Code came into effect on 1 January 2009.[30] According to the transitional provisions of article 25 WADC, in a situation where an anti-doping rule violation case is brought after January 2009 but is based on an anti-doping rule violation which occurred in 2008, the case should be governed by the substantive anti-doping rules in effect at the time of the alleged violation, unless the panel hearing the case determines that the principle of *lex mitior* should apply.[31] With regard to the second part of WADA's programme, WADA releases an annual list of the various substance and methods, the use of which is proscribed.[32] In the third part of its programme, WADA provides

---

[27] In late 2009 the Conservative peer and chairman of the British Olympic Association, Lord Moynihan, announced his intention to introduce a Bill into the House of Lords for just such purposes. The Bill apparently contains another controversial measure entitling the police, on obtaining a 'doping warrant', to search London 2012 athletes' rooms where they have a reasonable belief that doping is taking place. See O Gibson, 'Athletes to Face Anti-Doping Raids on Rooms at London 2012' *Guardian* (London 16 October 2009) Sport 1.

[28] For a detailed list of WADA's roles and responsibilities see the eight subsections to art 20.7 WADC.

[29] The original code was accompanied by a political document, the Copenhagen Declaration on Anti-Doping in Sport, through which governments can signal their intention to enforce and implement WADC. To date, nearly 200 governments have signed the Copenhagen Declaration.

[30] See generally P David, *A Guide to the World Anti-Doping Code: A Fight for the Spirit of Sport* (Cambridge, Cambridge University Press, 2008).

[31] For an example of the application of the doctrine of *lex mitior* (which permits a criminal court to apply current sanctions to the case before it, if such sanctions are less severe than those which existed at the time of the offence) to doping-related disciplinary proceedings, see the award of the CAS panel in CAS 96/149 *AC v FINA*.

[32] For the regulations surrounding the maintenance and publication of the prohibited list, including the criteria for inclusion of a substance or method, see generally art 4 WADC.

a series of documents or 'models of best practice' to assist organisations with the adoption of the WADC.[33]

[**4.13**]   The first and second elements of WADA's anti-doping programme are mandatory for any sports organisation that seeks to be fully compliant with WADC. Full compliance with WADC means not only that a sports organisation amends its rules and policies to include the mandatory articles of WADC but also that those articles are enforced in accordance with WADC's principles. The implementation of, and compliance with, WADC is monitored by WADA.[34] At the time of writing, more than 570 sports organisations have accepted the WADC and the accompanying prohibited list, mainly comprising of all the international federations of Olympic sports.[35] The core of WADA's programme, and the link between the first and second mandatory elements of that programme, can be found in the annotation to article 4.3.2 WADC, which states that a substance or method shall be considered for inclusion on the prohibited list if the substance/method either has or masks two of the following three criteria: (1) it has the potential to enhance or enhances sport performance; (2) it represents a potential or actual health risk; or (3) it is contrary to the spirit of sport. Read as a whole, it will be shown shortly that the ethical premise of the current paternalistic approach to the use of PEDs in sport revolves around these criteria. For now it suffices to note that while criteria (1) and (2) are largely a matter of scientific opinion, criterion (3) goes to the heart of WADA's agenda and, indeed, is described in the preamble as WADC's 'fundamental rationale'. Consequently, it is worth citing at length because it informs and explains much of the debate that follows on the administrative and legal difficulties surrounding the implementation of WADA's anti-doping agenda:

> Anti-doping programs seek to preserve what is intrinsically valuable about sport. This intrinsic value is often referred to as 'the spirit of sport', it is the essence of Olympism; it is how we play true. The spirit of sport is the celebration of the human spirit, body and mind, and is characterized by the following values:

> Ethics, fair play and honesty
> Health
> Excellence in performance
> Character and education
> Fun and joy
> Teamwork

---

[33] For reasons of space, little attention can given to the manner in which, under this element of its programme, WADA facilitates global research to identify doping substances; accredits anti-doping laboratories; promotes prevention and educational strategies amongst athletes; funds capacity building and training programmes for regional anti-doping agencies; and liaises with pharmaceutical companies and other interested stakeholders. See generally art 18 WADC (for education programmes) and art 19 WADC (for the coordination of research initiatives).

[34] See generally art 23 WADC.

[35] The roles and responsibilities of such signatories are set out in art 20 WADC.

Dedication and commitment
Respect for rules and laws
Respect for self and other participants
Courage
Community and solidarity.

Administrative and Legal Aspects of Doping Infractions

[**4.14**]   The underlying idea of this section is to give an overview of WADC and to identify key aspects of the code, particularly those which have been subject to (internal) administrative and (external) legal challenge. It is hoped that all of the major issues that might arise in a disciplinary hearing involving an athlete accused of a doping infraction will be touched upon. There are four principal points of concern: a definition of doping and anti-doping rule violations; the policy of strict liability; defending an athlete on a doping charge; and privacy and data protection concerns surrounding certain aspects of the code.[36]

Definition of Doping

[**4.15**]   The first point of note is that doping is defined under article 1 WADC as the occurrence of at least one of the eight anti-doping violations set out in article 2 WADC. The eight anti-doping violations in that provision are:[37] article 2.1. Presence of a prohibited substance or method; 2.2. Use or attempted use of a prohibited substance/methods; 3. Refusing or failing to give a sample collection; 4. Whereabouts violations; 5. Tampering or attempting to tamper with any part of the doping control process; 6. Possession of prohibited substances/methods; 7. Trafficking or attempted trafficking or prohibited substances/methods; 8. Administration or attempted administration of a prohibited substance.[38] Articles 1 and 2 WADC (as with all of the code's provisions) must be read in light of both the preamble and article 21.1.1 WADC. The Preamble holds that anti-doping rules equate, in a quasi-contractual manner, to sports competition rules governing the

---

[36] Unless stated otherwise, all references to WADC in the following sections are to the revised 2009 code. For a similar overview based on the original version of WADC, see R McLaren, 'CAS Doping Jurisprudence: What can we learn?' (2006) 1 *International Sports Law Review* 4.

[37] These are the general headings only. The eight sections in art 2 WADC are also broken down into subsections and accompanied in the code by detailed annotations. Pursuant to art 24.2 WADC, these annotations, which accompany virtually all of the articles in the code, are to be used as interpretative aids.

[38] From this point on when a reference is made to an anti-doping infraction the presumption should be, unless specifically mentioned otherwise, that it is to art 2.1 WADC and the presence of a prohibited substance.

conditions under which the stated sport is played and that athletes are taken to accept and be bound by these rules 'as a condition of participation'. Further, and pursuant to article 21.1.1 WADC, athletes are taken to have constructive notice of their roles and responsibilities and 'to be knowledgeable of and comply with all applicable anti-doping policies and rules adopted pursuant to the Code'.[39]

Strict Liability

[**4.16**]   Concentrating on the most straightforward doping infraction, that of article 2.1 WADC, where urine or blood samples collected from an athlete have produced a positive test for the presence of a prohibited substance, the WADC adopts the rule of strict liability.[40] That doctrine holds that an athlete is strictly liable for the prohibited substance found in, and revealed by, the testing of their bodily specimen and that an anti-doping violation occurs whether or not the athlete intentionally or unintentionally used a prohibited substance or was negligent or otherwise at fault.[41] Arguably, the underlying thrust of this policy is best summarised by article 21.1.3 WADC, which holds that athletes must 'take responsibility, in the context of anti-doping, for what they ingest and use.' The use of the doctrine is justified on two grounds. First, the strict approach is said to operate to the benefit of all 'clean' athletes or as the annotation to article 9 WADC states simply, 'when an athlete wins a gold medal with a prohibited substance in his or her system, that is unfair to the other athletes in that competition regardless of whether the gold medallist was at fault in any way. Only a "clean" athlete should be allowed to benefit from his or her competitive results.' Second, the strict approach is, it is argued, counterbalanced by the fact that an athlete has the opportunity to avoid or reduce the applicable sanction if they can demonstrate that, pursuant to article 10 WADC, the substance in question was not taken with the intention to enhance performance or was ingested negligently or through no fault or no significant fault of that athlete. In sum, while the determination of whether an anti-doping violation has occurred is based on strict liability, the imposition of sanction—typically, a fixed period of ineligibility—is not automatic.

[**4.17**]   The strict liability approach has been consistently upheld in arbitral awards delivered by CAS and in a number of instances by the High Court in England. Arguably, the seminal CAS award is that of CAS 94/129 *USA Shooting &*

---

[39] Art 21.2.1 WADC makes similar demands of so-called 'athlete support personnel', who are defined in appendix 1 of the code as 'Any coach, trainer, manager, agent, team staff, official, medical, paramedical personnel, parent or any other person working with, treating or assisting an athlete participating in or preparing for a sports competition.' For a strange, and ultimately unsuccessful, attempt to implicate a coach for the doping-related misconduct of an athlete see CAS 2008/A/1585 and 1586 *Kop v IAAF & TAF.*

[40] For a wide-ranging review of the various issues surrounding strict laiblity and doping see generally J Soek, *The Strict Liability Principle and the Human Rights of Athletes in Doping Cases* (The Hague, TMC Asser Press, 2006).

[41] See further the annotation to art 2.1.1 WADC.

Quigley v UIT (*Quigley*), which reveals four points of note on the doctrine of strict liability: the policy reasons underpinning the promotion of the collective interest of athletes above the 'just' treatment of the individual; the manner in which the purely absolutist nature of the strict liability approach lacks a principled and proportionate basis of liability and thus as a policy can be seen as draconian and legally questionable; the emergence of the current modified version of strict liability; and the manner in which the amended policy still shapes the possible defences available to an athlete on a doping charge.

Individual Unfairness versus the Collective Interest

[**4.18**]   In *Quigley*, the CAS Panel acknowledged that a strict liability test was likely to result in unfairness in individual cases (in the stated case, Quigley had taken the medication containing a banned substance as the result of poor labelling on a cough bottle and faulty advice given to him by a doctor) but that nevertheless it remained a 'laudable policy objective not to repair an accidental unfairness to an individual by creating an intentional unfairness to the whole body of other competitors'.[42] According to the Panel, this is what would happen if banned PEDs were tolerated when absorbed inadvertently and moreover, 'it is likely that even intentional abuse would in many cases escape sanction for lack of proof of guilty intent. And it is certain that a requirement of intent would invite costly litigation that may well cripple federations—particularly those run on modest budgets—in their fight against doping'.[43] For these reasons, the CAS Panel in *Quigley* held as a matter of principle that the strict liability test should be applied and remained unconvinced by objections that it might be either contrary to natural justice (because it did not permit the accused to establish moral innocence) or an unreasonable restraint of trade. In sum, the Panel in *Quigley* considered that 'in principle the high objectives and practical necessities of the fight against doping amply justify the application of a strict liability standard'.[44] The *Quigley* approach has since been cited with approval in a number of CAS awards[45] and, indeed, is at one with the approach of the English courts in cases such as *Gasser v Stinson* and *Wilander and Novacek v Tobin and Jude*.[46]

---

[42]   CAS 94/129 *USA Shooting & Quigley v UIT* [15].

[43]   Ibid.

[44]   Ibid [16].

[45]   See, for example, CAS 95/122 *National Wheelchair Basketball Association v International Paralympic Committee*; CAS 95/141 *C v Fina*; CAS 95/150 *V v Fina*; CAS 2000/A/281 *H v FIM*; CAS 2000/A/310 *L v IOC*; CAS 2002/A/385 *T v FIG*; CAS 2002/A/399 *P v Fina*; CAS 2002/A/432 *D v Fina*; and CAS 2004/A/690 *H v ATP*.

[46]   In *Gasser v Stinson*, Unreported, Queen's Bench Division 15 June 1988, Scott J agreed with the claimant, a Swiss athlete of international standard, that the strict liability nature of the anti-doping rules of the IAAF, and the accompanying mandatory suspensions for violation of those rules, were a restraint of trade but that, in the context of the 'war against doping in sport', the rules in question were reasonable, justified and in the interest of athletes and the public at large. See also the rejection of the 'unarguable' restraint of trade claim in *Wilander and Novacek v Tobin and Jude* Unreported, Chancery Division 19 March 1996, Lightman J; affirmed by Court of Appeal, The Times 8 April 1996.

Absolute (and overly) Strict Liability?

[**4.19**]   The *Quigley* award flagged some of the difficulties a number of commentators had in the early 1990s with the application of strict liability.[47] The difficulties were twofold. The first was that the approach was unnecessarily and unreasonably dogmatic, both in the manner in which it did not allow for the absence of any real moral fault on the part of the athlete. The second difficulty lay in the justification offered for the strict liability approach—that without it the floodgates would open, overwhelming sports organisations by forcing them in all cases to prove the necessary subjective elements (intention or negligence) of the stated offence. On the first point, the inherent injustice of the strict liability approach—and *Quigley* itself was an alleged example of this—was that at its most absolutist, the approach did not allow for any number of circumstances that might have resulted in a positive test but might not have entailed 'fault' on the part of the athlete, for instance: a prescription error by a medical adviser; a dispensing error by a pharmacist; an honest and reasonable belief that the substance was not prohibited; or, even, the malicious act of a third party who might have 'spiked' the drink or food or an opponent. The failure to allow for moral innocence should also, opponents of absolute strict liability claimed, have been placed in the context of the consequences for an athlete of a doping ban namely the reputational, financial and psychological costs of being rendered a cheat, and bearing in mind that in an abridged, precarious career such as professional sport, the typical two-year ban for doping equates to a significant sanction.[48] It follows that, given the dedication, effort and sacrifice that it takes for a professional athlete to reach and remain at the highest level, it appeared unconscionable even uncivilised to promote a system that could lead to the lengthy disqualification of an athlete in the absence of any moral fault. Apart from *Quigley*, examples of the harshness of the absolute strict liability approach in this regard include the disciplinary case taken by the IOC during the Sydney Olympics against a 16-year-old Romanian gymnast, Andrea Raducan, who had to forfeit her gold medal as a result of following her doctor's orders to take a headache tablet that unfortunately contained a prohibited substance[49] and the case taken against the British skier Alain Baxter, who had to forfeit a bronze medal after purchasing a US version of a Vick's inhaler, which, unlike the UK version, contained traces of a prohibited substance.[50]

---

[47] See, eg, A Wise, 'Strict Liability Drug Rules of Sports Governing Bodies' [1996] 146 *New Law Journal* 1161.

[48] For an interesting legal perspective on the reputational damage that might be suffered by an athlete who is surrounded by doping allegations see J Cooke, 'Doping and Free Speech' (2007) 5 (2) *Entertainment and Sports Law Journal* published online at ww2.warwick.ac.uk/fac/soc/law/elj/eslj/ issues/volume5/number2/cooke. The article reviews the libel action brought by leading US cyclist and multiple Tour de France winner, Lance Armstrong against the *Sunday Times*.

[49] CAS ad hoc Division (OG Sydney) 2000/011 *Raducan v IOC*. See further [3.08] above.

[50] CAS 2002/A/376 *Baxter v IOC*.

[**4.20**]   On the second aspect of the difficulties relating to absolute or pure strict liability, in the late 1980s/early1990s international sports bodies, various CAS Panels and, on two occasions, the English High Court stated consistently that, while there may be instances where an individual's plight may provoke much sympathy, the reality of elite competitive sport was that a defence of 'moral innocence' was all too likely to be abused by athletes and would likely prove all too difficult for the sports body or anti-doping agency to rebut. The contrary argument, and one that eventually found favour, was that the above absolutist adherence to strict liability was based somewhat falsely on the view that the only alternative to strict liability was to require sports bodies to prove intent when in fact there were other, fairer means of dealing with doping infractions without necessarily having to accept the risk of sanctioning an athlete who was not guilty of an offence or whose level of guilty might not justify the full extent of the sanction. Specifically, the modified approach that eventually emerged retained a principle of presumed fault on the part of the athlete but gave the athlete the right to rebut that presumption by adducing evidence that the presence of the prohibited substance in their body was not due to any intent or negligence on their part and thus merited no sanction or a reduced sanction.[51]

Modified Strict Liability

[**4.21**]   The origins of the 'modified' approach to strict liability lie in the *Quigley* award when the CAS Panel—and the award is best known for this—held that if a strict liability standard is to be applied, it must be clearly articulated and, although the fight against doping is 'arduous' and requires strict rules, it should be the case that:

> [R]ule-makers and the rule-appliers must begin by being strict with themselves. Regulations that may affect the careers of dedicated athletes must be predictable. They must emanate from duly authorised bodies. They must be adopted in constitutionally proper ways. They should not be the product of an obscure process of accretion. Athletes and officials should not be confronted with a thicket of mutually qualifying or even contradictory rules that can be understood only on the basis of the de facto practice over the course of many years of a small group of insiders.[52]

---

[51] See generally the discussion in this text at [4.34]–[4.38]. For a typical example of what was to emerge see CAS 2001/A/317 *A v FILA* where the athlete sought to exculpate himself by simply stating that the container of the nutritional supplements taken by him did not specify that it contained a prohibited substance. The CAS Panel applied the principle of strict liability but partly reduced the sentence for lack of intent. See in particular paragraph 34 of the award, where the Panel noted that anti-doping agencies were really only in a position to establish the presence of a prohibited substance. In contrast, the manner in which that substance came to be in the athlete's body would, save in exceptional circumstances, be extremely difficult to prove and particularly because neither the agency nor CAS have the investigatory powers available to, for instance, a public prosecutor in criminal proceedings. See also CAS 96/156 *F v FINA*.
[52] CAS 94/129 *USA Shooting & Quigley v UIT* [34].

[**4.22**]   In broad terms, the (eventual) answer to the call in *Quigley* for a transparent and consistent process of accretion of anti-doping regulation was the establishment of WADA and in many ways, the CAS Panel in *Quigley* wrote WADA's mission statement. More specifically, and in application to the stated facts, the CAS Panel held that Quigley *was* confronted with a 'thicket of mutually qualifying, contradictory rules' and upheld his appeal on the grounds that the respondent international sports body's anti-doping regulations lacked the clarity and certainty that an athlete should legitimately expect such a strict regime to have. A more recent example occurred during the 2004 Athens Olympics when a urine sample taken from the bronze medallist in the women's point race for track-cycling revealed traces of a stimulant. Although the stimulant in question was not on the official list of prohibited substances, the IOC asserted, as was their right under the applicable anti-doping regulations, that the substance had 'a similar chemical structure or similar pharmacological effect' to substances on the list and thus the IOC moved to disqualify the cyclist. The cyclist appealed to CAS and her appeal was upheld on the grounds that it was not sufficient for the IOC (or WADA or an anti-doping agency) simply to assert (as the IOC had attempted to do) that a stimulant, broadly defined, has similar characteristics to prohibited substances without specifying the particular prohibited substance with which the similarity is supposed to exist. In this, the Panel noted that the logic of the IOC's argument—according to which 'every stimulant' would be prohibited no matter whether it was expressly listed because even if not listed it would by definition be similar to prohibited listed substances—would be that those who drafted the WADC could have simply distilled many of its rules into a single 'stimulants are prohibited' regulation. This, the Panel observed, would evidently 'not pass the test of clarity and predictability'.[53]

[**4.23**]   Since *Quigley*, and with the introduction of WADC in 2003, the pure absolutism of the original stance on strict liability has been diluted in at least four ways: a shifting burden of proof; an onerous standard of proof; a hybrid presumed fault/flexibility of sanction approach; and a respect for the principle of proportionality.[54]

Burden of Proof

[**4.24**]   The first of these four points alludes to the fact that, although the principle of strict liability renders obsolete proof of guilt on the part of the offending

---

[53] CAS 2004/A/726 *Maria Luisa Calle Williams v IOC* [25].

[54] The introduction of the original WADC in 2003 did not assuage all critics of the then approach to anti-doping regulation. Compare A Rigozzi, G Kaufmann-Kohler and G Malinverni, 'Doping and Fundamental Rights of Athletes: Comments in the Wake of the Adoption of the World Anti-Doping Code 2003' (2003) 3 *International Sports Law Review* 39 and O Niggli and J Sieveking, 'Selected Case Law Rendered under the World Anti-doping Code' *JusLetter* 20 February 2006, available through http://jusletter.weblaw.ch with N Hooper, 'The WADA Code is Fundamentally Flawed. Discuss' (2006) 14 (3) *Sport and the Law Journal* 21 and C Auget, The World Anti-doping Code: An Athlete's Perspective' *JusLetter* 20 February 2006, available through http://jusletter.weblaw.ch.

athlete, it does not exempt the charging sports or anti-doping organisation from proving the existence of the doping offence, that is, it does not eliminate the need to establish both the wrongful act itself and the causal link between that wrongful act and its consequence as an anti-doping infraction. It follows that a presumption of innocence operates in the athlete's favour until that sports body or anti-doping agency discharges that burden. The various evidential methods of establishing facts and presumptions that may be used in discharging this burden are noted in article 3.2 WADC and include, most straightforwardly, proof based on an adverse analytical finding of an athlete's bodily sample by a WADA-accredited laboratory in adherence with the 'results management' process outlined in article 7 WADC, that is, a positive test.

Standard of Proof

[**4.25**]   It must be noted that the standard of proof required of the sports body or anti-doping agency is high and according to article 3.1 WADC is 'whether the [sports body or anti-doping agency] has established an anti-doping rule violation to the *comfortable satisfaction* of the hearing panel bearing in mind the serious-ness of the allegation which is made. This standard of proof is in all cases greater than a mere balance of probabilities but less than proof of beyond a reasonable doubt'.[55] In a broad sense, a useful analogy to this standard might be found in the English Court of Appeal's approach in *Gough v Chief Constable of Derbyshire Constabulary*.[56] That case concerned football banning orders and specifically section 14(b) of the Football Spectators Acts 1989. Football banning orders, the Court of Appeal decided, were in the nature of civil proceedings, nevertheless, the Court held that given the serious restraints of freedom orders might impose on a citizen, an exacting standard of proof should be applied which might on occa-sion become hard to distinguish from the criminal standard.[57] More specifically, in CAS 2004/O/645 *USADA v Montgomery* the contention that on occasion there might be little to distinguish the criminal standard of proof from that which might 'comfortably satisfy' a disciplinary panel as to proof of a doping infrac-tion was supported on the ground that in general the more serious the allegation the less likely it is that the alleged event occurred and, hence, the stronger the evidence required before the occurrence of the event is demonstrated to be more probable than not.[58]

---

[55] The wording used in this article comes from CAS ad hoc Division (OG Atlanta) 96/003-004 *K and G v IOC* and CAS 98/208 *N, J, Y, W, v FINA*. The award of the CAS Panel in the latter was subse-quently challenged before the SFT but that appeal was dismissed and the approach of the CAS in this (strict liability towards doping) regard upheld. For a summary of the judgment see (1999) 2 Digest of CAS Awards 775.

[56] *Gough v Chief Constable of Derbyshire Constabulary* [2002] QB 1213.

[57] Ibid 1242–43, Lord Phillips MR.

[58] The stated case is one of a number of CAS awards that arose out of the BALCO doping con-spiracy of 2003 (details at n 18). Montgomery was a former world 100 metres record holder and as a result of the CAS award he was banned for two years, leading to his retirement from the sport.

Presumed Fault/Flexibility of Sanction

[**4.26**]   Third, proponents of the strict liability approach acknowledge that the combination of the mandatory sanctioning provisions of article 9 WADC (automatic disqualification of individual results)[59]; article 7.5 WADC (provisional suspension based on A-sample adverse analytical finding);[60] and article 10.2 WADC (two-year period of ineligibility on confirmation, A and B sample, of adverse analytical finding);[61] the overall strict liability 'package' appears draconian.[62] Nevertheless, it is countered that when the WADC's provisions are examined in depth, it becomes clear that its core principle is less one of strict liability and more one of presumed fault as accompanied by significant flexibility on sanction. More specifically, apart from the automatic disqualifying nature of article 9 WADC, subsequent sanctions, including the two-year ban, can be reduced or even avoided if the athlete can establish to the satisfaction of the anti-doping tribunal that they bear no fault or negligence or that the prohibited substance was not intended to enhance or mask the enhancement of their performance. The details surrounding the workings of this presumed fault/flexibility on sanction approach, mainly contained in article 10 WADC, will be elaborated upon shortly.[63]

---

[59] An anti-doping violation in connection with an in-competition test by an individual athlete automatically leads to the disqualification of the individual result obtained in that competition and the forfeiture of any medals, points and prizes. See also art 10.1 WADC which can extend the disqualification to all results in a stated competition or tournament and art 10.12 on the possibility of imposing financial sanctions.

[60] Art 7.5 WADC provides for expedited appeals against such suspensions. It also provides, in conjunction with art 10.9.3 WADC, that athletes will receive credit for a provisional suspension against the period of ineligibility, if any, imposed against them.

[61] The period of ineligibility imposed for a violation of arts 2.1, 2.2 or 2.6 WADC is, on first violation, two years. See further art 10.10 WADC on the various accompanying restrictions, such as the withdrawal of any financial support, imposed on an athlete during the two-year period of ineligibility. Note also that pursuant to art 10.11 WADC a condition of regaining eligibility is that a suspended athlete must at all time make themselves available for 'reinstatement' testing. Finally, multiple anti-doping violations can, per art 10.7 WADC, result in lifetime bans see CAS 2008/A/1572/1632/1659 *Gusmao v FINA*.

[62] In addition, note the mutual recognition of sanctions provision in art 15.4 WADC, which holds that sanctions imposed by one signatory of the WADC should be recognised and respected by all other signatories ie, a two-year ban imposed on an athlete now, in effect, restrains them from competing in any other elite sport for the stated period.

[63] See the text at [4.34]–[4.38]. The discussion therein will focus on sanctions against individual athletes. See further art 11 WADC on the consequence for team sports, especially art 11.2 WADC, which holds that if two or more members of a team are found to have committed an anti-doping rule violation, an appropriate team sanction (disqualification, loss of points, etc) can be imposed. See CAS 2004/1/593 *Football Association of Wales v UEFA*, where the FAW sought to have Russia excluded from Euro 2004 on the grounds that one of Russia's players, who played in Russia's Euro 2004 play-off defeat of Wales, subsequently tested positive for a prohibited substance. The appeal was unsuccessful on the ground that, although the anti-doping rule in question did impose strict liability on the player, it did not provided for the vicarious liability of the player's club or national football federation. A further interesting application of 'team' sanctions is the practice whereby a medal winning relay team (such as the US women's sprint team at the Sydney Olympics) is asked by the IOC to return their medals on the ground that one of their members (Marion Jones) has subsequently found to have been doping. See further the evolving case of CAS 2009/A/1545 *Anderson et al v IOC*.

Principle of Proportionality

[**4.27**]   Finally, a key underlying feature of any discussion on the aforementioned article 10 WADC is that not only can such a provision (and particularly subsection 5 thereof) be used appropriately to blunt the sharper edge of strict liability to the benefit of the deserving athlete but it can also be reconciled with the general legal principle of proportionality. In this, it must be acknowledged that WADA *has* taken on board the criticisms made a decade or so ago regarding the unduly absolutist nature of strict liability.[64] Further, in the annotation to article 10.5 WADC, WADA states that the presumed fault/flexibility of sanction approach in the revised code 'is consistent with basic principles of human rights and provides a balance between those Anti-Doping Organisations that argue for a much narrower exception, or none at all, and those that would reduce that two-year suspension based on a range of other facts even when the athlete was admittedly at fault.' In sum, the revised WADA/WADC approach, although in a policy sense clearly tilted towards the 'collective good', in a legal sense appears to achieve a satisfactory balance between: on the one hand, WADA's attempts to make the fight against doping more effective by harmonising the surrounding regulatory and sanctioning framework; and, on the other hand, athletes' legitimate expectation of both fairness in the conduct of that regulatory process and, where relevant, proportionality in its outcome.[65]

Defending an Athlete on a Doping Charge

[**4.28**]   The modified version of strict liability outlined above, and its underlying principle of presumed fault means that, in effect, there are three broad defences available to the athlete who tests positive for a prohibited substance: the therapeutic use exemption process; 'direct' chain of custody challenges; and 'indirect' pleas for mitigation of sanction.[66] The first of the three possible defences is what might loosely be translated as an attempt by the athlete to strike out the proceedings against them for lack of a cause of action on the ground that the athlete has an exemption based on the necessary therapeutic use of the stated substance. These second and third defences are more substantive and concern direct challenges (questioning the integrity of the testing, analysis or 'results management'

---

[64] See the comments in CAS 2006/A/1133 *WADA v Stauber & Swiss Olympic Committee* [44]–[48].

[65] See the support for this 'tilted scales of justice' approach in the following CAS awards: CAS 2004/A/690 *H v ATP* [48]-[55]; CAS 2006/A/1025 *Puerta v ITF* [11.7.22]; and CAS 2007/A/1290 *Diethart v IOC* [80]. See also the comments made by CAS in the advisory opinion sought by FIFA & WADA, CAS 2005/976 & 986.

[66] What follows is very much a 'broad brush' approach concentrating on violations of art 2.1 WADC. For a more extensive review see Flint (n 6) 903–1006. See, eg, at 1005, where he mentions that a 'resourceful defence counsel' should consider the exceptions in art 10.9 WADC that permit the backdating of the commencement date of a doping-related period of suspension.

process surrounding the adverse analytical finding against the athlete); and/or a mitigating defence seeking the elimination or reduction of sanction pursuant to the provisions available under article 10 WADC. Before reviewing the scope of these defences, it must also be noted more generally that the WADC does, in four regards, expressly provide for certain due process rights of athletes, and breach of any of these provisions may also provide a useful means of challenge for the athlete charged with an anti-doping rule violation. These natural justice-related rights include aspects of article 14 WADC (confidentiality and reporting); article 8 WADC (right to a fair hearing); article 13 (appeals); and article 17 WADC (statute of limitations).

General Issues of Due Process

[**4.29**]   Under article 14.1.1 and 14.1.3 WADC, an athlete whose bodily sample tests positive for a prohibited substance has the right to be given due notice of the adverse analytical result reported by the laboratory and the asserted anti-doping rule violation.[67] It is only after that notification to the athlete that the anti-doping agency in question may, pursuant to article 14.2.1 WADC, publicly disclose the identity of that athlete. Manifestly, there is a 'name and shame' element to this provision but the code (article 14.2.5 WADC) is also careful to note that where an athlete seeks a hearing on a finding against them, no official of that anti-doping agency or the laboratory should publicly comment on the specific facts of a pending case, save general descriptions of the scientific process. Inexplicably, the understandably cautious 'sub judice' thrust of this approach appears somewhat undone by the fact that article 14.2.5 WADC goes on to permit responses 'to public comments attributed to' the athlete or their representatives. Although it is understandable, in a situation where an athlete might make outlandish claims regarding conspiracies or vendettas against them by a named official that from a human perspective that official might be tempted to respond; there is, it is suggested, little to be gained by engaging in any 'tit-for tat' media comment on a pending hearing. The accompanying disciplinary process as whole should be permitted to take its course without prejudice and the sporting public can make up their own minds as to the final outcome by reading the reasoned decision of the hearing panel. Finally, article 14.1.4 WADC holds that at all stages throughout the process the athlete should be regularly updated in writing on the status and findings of any review or proceedings conducted against them pursuant to the procedures laid down in article 8 WADC (right to a fair hearing) and article 13 WADC (appeals).

[**4.30**]   Article 8 WADC is, in effect, the sporting equivalent of article 6 ECHR. It succinctly outlines the fundamentals of any doping infraction-related hearing (and, indeed, the natural justice fundamentals of sports disciplinary

---

[67] Other interested 'need to know' parties such as the athlete's relevant club or sports federation are also entitled to notification per art 14.1.2 and 14.1.5 WADC.

hearings more generally).[68] Pursuant to article 8.1 WADC, a hearing process on a doping-related charge should, at a minimum, respect the following eight principles: a timely hearing; a fair and impartial hearing panel; the right to be represented by counsel at the athlete's own expense; the right to be informed in a fair and timely manner of the asserted anti-doping rule violation; the right to respond to the asserted anti-doping violation and resulting consequences; the right of each party to present evidence, including the right to call and question witnesses; the athlete's right to an interpreter at the hearing; and a timely, written, reasoned decision, specifically including an explanation of the reasons for any period of ineligibility.[69] Article 8 WADC is accompanied by article 13 WADC, which provides for a detailed (right of) appeals process. In sum, pursuant to article 13 WADC, the ultimate avenue of appeal (for athletes or sports bodies or national anti-doping agencies or WADA) is to CAS. In this light, CAS both provides the final, definitive and quasi-judicial interpretation of the code's various provisions and is developing a body of precedence or *lex sportiva* with regard to doping offences, which it is hoped will in time bring greater certainty and harmonisation to anti-doping policy at all levels of the sporting world.[70] Finally, any discussion of the right to a fair hearing and avenues of appeal may be obviated by reference to article 17 WADC, which provides that no action may be commenced against an athlete for an anti-doping violation contained in the WADC unless such action is commenced within eight years from the date the violation is asserted to have occurred. This is why, for example, WADA was time-barred from taking any direct action against tennis player Andre Agassi, who wrote in his 2009 autobiography that he took a banned substance with a former assistant and then lied to the sport's governing body that his drink had been accidently spiked.[71]

Therapeutic Use Exemption

[**4.31**]   Under article 4.4 WADC, international sports federations are obliged to put in place a process whereby athletes with documented medical conditions, which in treatment may require the use of prohibited substances, may request a therapeutic use exemption. Under article 4.4 WADC, WADA is mandated to

---

[68] With due regard to the gravity of an doping charge/hearing, art 8 WADC complements the 10 'commitments' of a sports disciplinary process outlined previously at [3.35] of the text.

[69] See also art 8.2, which holds that a doping hearing can be expedited on an ad hoc basis in circumstances where the resolution of the anti-doping infraction is necessary to determine an athlete's eligibility to compete in a major, imminent event or in circumstances where the resolution of the case might effect that athlete's continued participation in that event.

[70] See generally T Kavanagh, 'The Doping Cases and the need for the International Court of Arbitration for Sport (CAS)' (1999) 22 *University of New South Wales Law Journal* 721 and F Oschutz, 'Harmonization of the Anti-Doping Code through Arbitration: the Case Law of the Court of Arbitration for Sport' (2002) 12 *Marquette Sports Law Review* 675.

[71] See further N Harman, 'Andre Agassi Sparks Cries of Cover Up' *The Times* (London, 29 October 2009) Sport, 116. The issue of a time barring and retrospective sanctioning is also playing a part in the ongoing arbitration of CAS 2009/A/1545 *Anderson et al v IOC*.

harmonise the international standards and criteria that surround the granting of therapeutic use exemptions (TUE) and also reserves the right to review at any time the granting of therapeutic use exemptions.[72] The underlying idea of the process is to accommodate athletes who would otherwise experience serious health problems without using the prohibited substance. The classic example of this process is where an athlete suffering from asthma uses medication containing salbutamol, a prohibited substance.[73] There has always been a suspicion that the TUE process is being abused by athletes in the sense that it has been suggested that a substance such as salbutamol can be used not only by asthmatic athletes to prevent exercise-induced asthma but also by non-asthmatic athletes as a potential performance enhancing agent. WADA has monitored this closely and now appears satisfied that inhaled salbutamol even in high doses does not have a significant performance-enhancing effect.[74] Recently, in announcing its approved list of prohibited substances for 2010 WADA's Executive Committee noted that the use of salbutamol by inhalation will no longer require a therapeutic use exemption but rather a simplified 'declaration of use'. The suspicion has now returned to a substance called pseudoephedrine found in, for example, nasal decongestion products, which WADA has reintroduced onto the prohibited list as a specified stimulant.[75] These wider issues aside, the basic element of the TUE process is that evidence of the athlete's medical condition and the need for an accompanying exemption is registered with the relevant national anti-doping organisation. It follows that upon receipt of an A-sample adverse analytical finding, the relevant anti-doping organisation is obliged to conduct a review to determine whether an applicable therapeutic use exemption has been granted and if it has the investigation then ends to the benefit of the exempted athlete.[76]

Chain of Custody

[**4.32**]   The second means of challenging the consequences of a positive dope test by the athlete in question is to query any one or all of the following: whether

---

[72] For a review of the process and an interesting application see CAS 2008/1452 *Kazuki Ganaha v Japan Professional Football League*.

[73] For pre-WADA examples see CAS 95/142 *I v FINA* and CAS 96/149 *AC v FINA*.

[74] See, eg, the findings by B Sporer *et al*, 'Dose Responses of Inhaled Salbutamol on Exercise Performance and Urine Concentrations' (2008) 40 *Medicine & Science in Sports Exercise* 149.

[75] Note the nine-month ban given to Paddy Kenny of Sheffield United FC after the goalkeeper tested positive for traces of ephedrine. Kenny knowingly ingested an over-the-counter medicine above the prescribed dosage without reading the accompanying package or leaflet and without reference to the club doctor or other medical staff. Kenny appealed on the grounds that the suspension was excessive and disproportionate in light of the fact that there had been no intention to enhance sporting performance. The FA's Appeal Board acknowledged this but dismissed the appeal on the grounds that his actions still 'fell significantly short of what is expected of a professional sportsman in his position.' See P Lansley, 'Kenny gets Nine-Month Ban for Doping' *The Times* (London 8 September 2009), Sport 81 and 'Kenny Appeal Fails' *The Times* (London 21 October 2009) Sport 80. The written awards both at first instance and on appeal are available through www.thefa.com/TheFA/Disciplinary/NewsAndFeatures.

[76] Art 7.1 and 7.2 WADC.

their bodily sample was taken properly by the testers in question;[77] whether there was a complete chain of custody of the sample on its way to the laboratory;[78] and whether the analysis of the sample, as carried out by a WADA-accredited laboratory,[79] was state of the art.[80] In challenges of this nature, the athlete is effectively arguing that there has been a departure from the regulations surrounding WADA-mandated standards for the proper laboratory analysis of samples and that this departure could have reasonably caused the adverse analytical finding.[81] The burden of proof (to the standard of the balance of probabilities) is on the athlete to establish such a departure and if that burden is discharged it then shifts to the anti-doping agency to prove to the comfortable satisfaction of the disciplinary panel that the departure did not cause the adverse analytical finding.[82] It has been noted that this 'burden-shifting' rule provides the necessary balance between, on the one hand, the needs of accredited laboratories to implement new, reliable testing methods as quickly as possible and, on the other hand, the interest of athletes and the sporting community in ensuring trustworthy test results.[83]

[**4.33**]   Challenges of this nature, which are often quite technical and scientific in basis, have the potential to be quite disruptive and distracting for sports authorities, and frequently necessitate the attention of CAS.[84] Since its inception the challenge for WADA has been to ensure that the regulatory framework that accompanies anti-doping rules strikes the requisite balance between the competing interests of sports bodies (attempting to maintain the integrity of their sport in the face of vexatious appeals by drug cheats) and individual athletes (who have a legitimate expectation that all objective elements of a doping infraction are demonstrated to a standard that reflects the grievous nature and consequences of such a charge). To be fair, WADA has worked assiduously both

---

[77] See, eg, the unsuccessful attempt by the Irish international swimmer, Michelle De Bruin, to question the conduct of the testers in CAS 98/211 *B v FINA* and, more recently, the successful appeal by two Italian footballers against a ban relating to their alleged failure to submit to a drugs test in CAS 2008/1551 *WADA v CONI, FIGC and Cherubin* and CAS 2008/1557 (No 2) *WADA v CONI, FIGC, Daniele Mannini and Davide Possanini.*

[78] See, eg, the third pleaded ground in CAS 94/129 *USA Shooting & Quigley v UIT* [39]–[52].

[79] See, eg, the discussion on this point by Lord Hoffmann in *Modahl v British Athletic Federation Limited* [1999] UKHL 37.

[80] What is meant by 'state of the art' refers inter alia to claims made by athletes that the tests used by the laboratory in question were, eg, not sensitive or sophisticated enough to pick up on the fact that a prohibited substance might be produced endogenously ie, naturally, by the body. In the late 1990s, a significant cluster of nandrolone positives resulted in much debate on this issue, though it appears that contaminated nutritional supplements were ultimately to blame. See T Kerr, 'Doped or Duped? The Nandrolone Jurisprudence' [2001] *International Sports Law Review* 97. See similarly the cluster of cases surrounding the sensitivity of the testing for synthetic EPO eg, CAS 2003/A/452 *IAAF v MAR and B* and also the exhaustive and unsuccessful effort of the claimant to challenge the adequacy of the laboratory testing in CAS 2005/A/884 *Hamilton v USADA and UCI.*

[81] See further art 3.2.1 WADC.

[82] See further art 3.2.2 WADC.

[83] CAS 2003/A/452 *IAAF v MAR and B* [56].

[84] See, for instance, the CAS jurisprudence noted by Flint (n 6) 937–66.

through amendments to WADC and by constantly reviewing its guidelines and international standards on testing, in order to maintain this balance.[85] Although successful CAS appeals based on the procedural impropriety of a drugs test still arise on occasion,[86] and although some doubts remains as to the scientific sensitivity and accuracy of the WADA-accredited testing process,[87] it does appear that the success rate of such 'direct' challenges to positive dope tests is on the decline.[88]

Article 10 WADC

[**4.34**]   The most frequent argument to appear before anti-doping disciplinary panels, including CAS, is the contention by the athlete that they can avail themselves of one or other of the 'elimination or reduction of the [usual two-year] period of ineligibility' provisions contained in article 10 WADC.[89] The two provisions of note are article 10.4 WADC (elimination or reduction of sanction in specific circumstances) and article 10.5 WADC (elimination or reduction of sanction based on exceptional circumstances). It must be stressed that the code envisages that these provisions are meant to have an impact in circumstances which are 'truly exceptional' in nature and thus, for instance, the annotations to both provisions stress that for the purposes of assessing the athlete's 'fault' the evidence must be specific and relevant to the justify any departure from the expected strict duty of care upon athletes to take responsibility for the substances they use and ingest. The fact therefore that an athlete might, on receiving a standard two-year ban for doping, lose the opportunity to earn large sums of money in prizes and endorsements during the period of ineligibility or the fact that the athlete has only a short time left in their career or the fact that the timing of the ban means that the athlete will miss out on

---

[85] See generally art 5 WADC (testing); art 6 WADC (analysis of samples); and art 7 WADC (results management). Note specifically the duties on anti-doping agencies to investigate 'atypical' analytical sample findings eg, prohibited substances which may also be produced endogenously, contained in art 7.3 WADC.

[86] See, eg, CAS 2008/A/1607 *Varius v IBU*. In that case, despite finding EPO in both the 'A' and 'B' samples of a Finnish biathlete, CAS cancelled the sanction imposed by the International Biathlon Union on the ground that the IBU had not been sufficiently reasonable in attempting to accommodate the athlete's right to be represented at the opening and analysis of her B sample—a right to which she was entitled under the IBU's anti-doping regulations.

[87] See, eg, the observations on the possibility of 'false' positives by D Berry, 'The Science of Doping' (2008) 454 *Nature* 692.

[88] See recently the sanctions resulting from CAS 2007/A/1370 and 1376 *FIFA and WADA v Dodo*; CAS 2007/A/1394 *Floyd Landis v USADA*; CAS 2008/A/1564 *WADA v IIHF & Busch*; CAS 2008/A/1569 *Kurten v FEI*; CAS 2008/A/1608 *IAAF v Athletic Federation of Slovenia and Helena Javornik*; CAS 2008/A/1718–1724 *IAAF v All Russia Athletic Federation & Ors*; CAS 2009/A/1805–1847 *IAAF v RFEA & Josephine Onyia*; CAS 2009/A/1768 *Hansen v FEI*.

[89] Note, in contrast to the emphasis on mitigation herein, that art 10 WADC also provides for aggravating circumstances which may increase the period of ineligibility up to a maximum of four years (art 10.6 WADC). Aggravating circumstances can include, eg, being part of a larger doping conspiracy and/or having used multiple prohibited substances or a prohibited substance on multiple occasions.

a rare event in the sporting calendar, for example, the Olympics, should not be relevant factors in reducing or eliminating the period of ineligibility under article 10.4 and 10.5.[90]

Article 10.4 WADC

[**4.35**]   Article 10.4 WADC holds that where an athlete can establish how a 'specified' substance entered their body and that such a substance was not intended to enhance their sports performance, the two-year period of ineligibility can be eliminated in its entirety or otherwise reduced. To justify any elimination or reduction, the athlete must, on the balance of probabilities, show both that the substance in question is a 'specified' substance and establish how that substance entered their body.[91] Arguably, the crucial aspect of the provision is, however, that the athlete must produce corroborating evidence, additional to their word, which establishes to the comfortable satisfaction of the disciplinary panel the absence of intent to enhance sports performance. One of the more creative, if unsuccessful, attempts to use this provision was undertaken by the American sprinter Justin Gatlin who appealed a doping suspension on three inter-related grounds: that the substances used by him (amphetamines), which had resulted in the positive test, were 'specified' in nature; that they were also a necessary part of his treatment for 'attention deficit disorder'; and that any attaching suspension might violate his rights under the Americans with Disabilities Act 1990.[92] Finally, even if an athlete succeeds in their article 10.4 claim, the article provides that that the athlete's 'degree' of fault should correlate with the assessment of the reduction, if any, in the period of ineligibility. It appears therefore that only in the most exceptional of cases will the two-year period of ineligibility be eliminated in its entirety.[93]

Article 10.5 WADC

[**4.36**]   Article 10.5 WADC has five subsections and what follows is a brief summary.[94] Under article 10.5.1 WADC, if an athlete establishes in an individual case that he or she bears 'no fault or negligence', the otherwise applicable period of ineligibility is eliminated. In order to avail him or herself of this absolute 'defence', the athlete would, on the balance of probabilities, have to provide proof establishing

---

[90]   This approach appears to end what WADA viewed as the (overly) sympathetic approach taken in awards such CAS 2007/A/1252 *FINA v Mellouli* [32]–[41].

[91]   WADA's prohibited list distinguishes between strictly prohibited substances (eg, classes of anabolic agents and hormones) and substances which are specified only (ie, substances which, because of their general availability in medicinal products, there is a greater likelihood that their use is open to a credible non-doping explanation).

[92]   CAS 2008/A/1461 and 1462 *Gatlin v USADA and IAAF v Gatlin and USATF*.

[93]   For an example of how the scheme of this provision might come to the aid of an athlete see CAS 2006/A/1175 *D v International Dance-Sport Federation* and note also the comments of the Panel in CAS 2008/A/1488 *P v ITF* [22]–[23].

[94]   The subsections are heavily and usefully annotated with examples of art 10.5 WADC's various applications. For an interesting CAS application, leading to a partial reduction of a two-year suspension, see CAS 2005/A/847 *Knauss v FIS*.

how, notwithstanding their utmost caution, the prohibited substance entered their system through no fault or negligence on their part. An example given in the code is where the athlete proves that, despite all due care, he or she was 'sabotaged' by a competitor, that is, their drink or food was spiked by a rival.[95] Article 10.5.1 WADC is an extremely difficult defence to make out and has only been applied in the most exceptional of circumstances.[96]

[**4.37**]   Under article 10.5.2 WADC if an athlete establishes in an individual case that they bear 'no significant fault or negligence', the otherwise applicable period of ineligibility may be reduced, but the reduced period of ineligibility may not be less than half of the period otherwise applicable. In order to avail him or herself of this partial 'defence', the athlete would, on the balance of probabilities, have to provide proof establishing how the substance entered their system through no significant fault or negligence on their part. An example given in the code is where the athlete proves that, despite taking all due care and exercising the utmost of caution, their positive test can be shown to be attributable to contamination in a vitamin or nutritional supplement purchased from an official, open source. Article 10.5.2 WADC is, again, a difficult defence to make out and has, despite some 'creative' pleas on the part of athletes, only rarely been satisfied.[97] One of the more interesting CAS awards relates to the finding of no significant fault or negligence on the part of an Argentinean tennis player who was found to have inadvertently ingested a prohibited substance after drinking water in which his wife had left traces of her PMT medication.[98] More recently, the French tennis player, Richard Gasquet, was exonerated from any significant fault or negligence when a CAS Panel agreed that the amount of cocaine metabolite (which led to Gasquet testing positively for a prohibited substance) was so minute that it must have reflected incidental exposure. In the stated case, the CAS Panel concluded that it was more likely than not that the player's 'contamination' resulted, as Gasquet has always asserted, from kissing a woman in a nightclub in Miami on the day before the anti-doping.[99]

[**4.38**]   Article 10.5.3 WADC holds that where an athlete provides substantial assistance in discovering or establishing anti-doping infractions against

---

[95]   The annotation to art 10.5.1 WADC goes on to note that any claim of 'sabotage' by a spouse, coach or other person within the athlete's circle of associates will not suffice for the purposes of the provision because athletes are strictly responsible for what they ingest and for the conduct of those persons to whom the entrust access to their food and drink. This is to cater for a situation where an associate of a doping athlete, such as a coach or parent, might agree cynically to 'take the hit' for 'their' athlete by claiming to have spiked the athlete's food or drink. See further the comments in CAS 2002/A/432 *D v FINA* [44].

[96]   See, eg, the extreme circumstances in CAS 2005/A/990 *P v IIHF* (the prohibited substance resulted from emergency treatment given by a doctor in an attempt to deal with the cardiac arrest suffered by P after a serious injury sustained on the ice rink).

[97]   See, for instance, its rejection in CAS 2003/A/484 *V v USADA*; CAS 2003/A/493 *V v FINA*; CAS 2006/A/1067 *IRB v Keyter*; and CAS 2007/A/1364 *WADA v FAW and James*.

[98]   CAS 2006/A/1025 *Puerta v ITF*. See similarly CAS 2005/A/830 *Squizzatto v FINA*; CAS 2005/A/921 *FINA v Kreuzmann*; and CAS ad hoc Division (OG Turin) 2006/001 *WADA v Lund & USADA*.

[99]   CAS 2009/A/1926 and 1930 *ITF v Gasquet* and *WADA v ITF and Gasquet*.

others a disciplinary panel can, in certain circumstances, reduce the usual period of ineligibility. In this instance, no more the three-quarters of the otherwise applicable period of ineligibility may be suspended.[100] Article 10.5.4 WADC holds that where an athlete voluntarily admits the commission of an anti-doping rule violation a disciplinary panel can in certain circumstances reduce the usual period of ineligibility.[101] No more than one-half of the otherwise applicable period of ineligibility may be suspended. Article 10.5.5 WADC is technical in nature and applies to a scenario where an athlete establishes an entitlement to a reduction in sanction under more than one subsection of article 10.5 WADC.

Whereabouts and Privacy

[**4.39**]   The era when athletes took a substance in the immediate moments before a race or event ('in competition'), in the hope that that substance would give them a speed or endurance advantage over their opponents, has now largely disappeared. Blood-doping methods and the more sophisticated 'designer' drugs are now used by athletes in the off-season ('out of competition') to enable them to train more intensely and recover more quickly. As Victor Conte, the 'mastermind' behind the BALCO doping conspiracy once remarked, in competition testing is the equivalent of an IQ test—where only the stupid, incautious or desperate athlete gets caught.[102] In contrast, out of competition testing is now seen as vital to the integrity and effectiveness of WADA's programme as a whole. The original WADC did provide (in article 2.4) for the 'unannounced', out of competition testing of athletes and, moreover, placed the onus on athletes to be responsible for providing and updating information on their 'whereabouts' so that they could be located for what was called 'no advance notice out of competition testing'. In reality, this whereabouts rule was the reverse of the Theodore Roosevelt maxim and though it spoke loudly; it carried a small stick.

[**4.40**]   The primary reason for this was that the applicable requirements surrounding the implementation of the whereabouts rule were left to the various international federation and national anti-doping agencies, 'in order to allow some flexibility based upon the varying circumstances encountered in different sports and countries'.[103] The failure by WADA to push for the harmonisation and standardisation of the regulations surrounding the whereabouts rule resulted in inconsistencies in both the manner in which various sports jurisdictions defined

---

[100] The American sprinter Kelli White obtained a reduced period of ineligibility after giving evidence against fellow athletes involved in the so-called BALCO scandal (details at n 18) and leading to the suspensions outlined in CAS 2004/O/645 *USADA v Montgomery* and CAS 2004/O/649 *USADA v Gaines*.

[101] See similarly art 8.3 WADC and the possible repercussions where an athlete waives their right to a hearing on an anti-doping violation.

[102] See R Broadbent, 'What Victor Conte Destroyed He Must Now be Asked to Mend' *The Times* (London 12 October 2007) Sport 88.

[103] Annotation to art 2.4 WADC (2003).

and mutually recognised the exact criteria for a whereabouts infraction, and the length of any accompanying sanction. Accordingly, while a number of sports federations took the whereabouts rule seriously and vigorously pursued athletes on its account;[104] other sports federation were not so enthusiastic.[105] This lack of administrative uniformity and political will undermined not only the credibility of the rule but also brought into question the true efficacy (in terms of deterrence) of WADA's various anti-doping programmes. Unsurprisingly, the effectiveness of the whereabouts rule was a key element in the debates surrounding the revision of the WADC, and the 2009 version of article 2.4 WADC is now representative of a much more harmonised and focused whereabouts regime.

[**4.41**]   At its most basic the whereabouts regime demands that international elite athletes should file whereabouts information with their national anti-doping agency or relevant sports federation, outlining where they will be residing and training for the forthcoming three-month period. The athlete is permitted to identify in this whereabouts documentation one specific location where for a set 60-minute period they know that they will be available for out of competition testing. Failure to file the stated information and/or failure to present for an out of competition test on three occasions within an 18-month period can result in a violation of article 2.4.1 WADC and can, pursuant to article 10.3.3 WADC, lead to a maximum two-year ban for that athlete or minimum one-year period of ineligibility, depending on the athlete's degree of fault. The question has arisen as to whether the whereabouts rule is overly intrusive with regard to the demands it places on athletes.[106] In 2009, it was reported that a group of Belgian professionals had instigated legal proceedings seeking to challenge the whereabouts policy principally on the ground that it violated Article 8 ECHR but also on for possible breaches of EU privacy and data protection law, including the consideration of whether the policy constitutes a breach of EU 'working time' regulations.[107] In this light, the whereabouts rule and in particular the manner in which WADA collates

---

[104] One of the more famous athletes to fall foul of the whereabouts rule was Britain's Christine Ohuruogu who unsuccessfully appealed a 12-month ban—CAS 2006/A/1165 *Ohuruogu v UK Athletics and IAAF*. On her return to athletics, Ohuruogu went on to win gold in the 400 metres at the Beijing Olympics.

[105] In an interview with *The Times* in 2009 (n 102), Victor Conte noted that out of competition testing, as originally conceived, was easily evaded by athletes, who could either disappear during the winter to remote training camps for a number of weeks or simply ensure that their mobile phones or email inboxes were overloaded with messages thus rendering them 'uncontactable'. See also [4.65]–[4.66] of this text.

[106] See generally J Halt, 'Where is the Privacy in WADA's Whereabouts Rule?' (2009) 20 *Marquette Sports Law Review* 267 and A Pendlebury and J McGarry, 'Location, Location, Location: The Right to Privacy and WADA's Whereabouts Rule' (2009) 40 *Cambrian Law Review* 63.

[107] See further O Gibson, 'WADA Head Tells Athletes to Stop Moaning at Whereabouts Clauses' *Guardian* (London, 18 February 2009) News and Features 8; S Hart, 'Key Doping Rule to be Challenged in Court' *Daily Telegraph* (London 23 January 2009) Sport 18; M Slater, 'Legal Threat to Anti-Doping' *BBC News Online* 22 January 2009 available at http://news.bbc.co.uk/sport1/hi/front_page/7844918. stm and M Slater, 'Anger Grows over Anti-doping Code' *BBC News Online* 4 February 2009 available at http://news.bbc.co.uk/sport1/hi/front_page/7870729.stm.

all relevant information in its so-called ADAMS database,[108] has also attracted the concern of the European Commission.[109]

The Controlled Use of Drugs in Sport: A Philosophical Digression

[**4.42**] It is now time to step back from the minutiae of EU Directives and WADC regulations, and consider the broader picture in the so-called 'war' on drugs in sport. In this light, the remainder of the chapter will attempt to discuss this topic from the competing jurisprudential perspectives of liberalism and paternalism and with reference to any analogies that can be drawn from the wider societal debate on the criminalisation of 'soft' drugs such as cannabis. Put simply, the remainder of this chapter asks why we bother banning PEDs in sport or, in a slightly more sophisticated manner, it presents a provocative analysis of the current approach to the 'war' on drugs in sport, and one that can be distilled into a single, inflammatory hypothesis: the problematical administrative and legal repercussions arising from the current strict proscription of doping in sport would be eliminated by permitting the controlled use of PEDs. Finally, this brief examination of the ethical and philosophical rationale of the current proscriptive policy on PEDs in sport also serves as a synopsis of the various issues that surround the regulation of drug use in sport today and in the future, including the bewilderingly fast technological advances in the exploitation of potentially undetectable doping techniques.

Liberalism

[**4.43**] The current policy on the use of PEDs in sport is clearly paternalistic in nature and is underpinned by both an outwardly benevolent desire to protect athletes' health and the long term integrity or 'spirit' of sport. In narrow administrative terms, the policy is manifested in the WADC and the prohibited list. In technical legal terms, the policy is supported by the principle of strict liability. In a broader sense, it might be argued that by denying athletes the 'right to choose'

---

[108] The Anti-Doping Administration and Management System is a web-based information clearing house system that permits athletes to file their relevant whereabouts information online. It also is used by WADA and other anti-doping agencies (on a secure server basis) as a doping control planning mechanism on which athlete biological 'passport' information recorded from individual sample testing can be stored and compared. See further www.wada-ama.org/en/ADAMS.

[109] There is an ongoing 'dialogue' between WADA and the European Commission on these matters. Note, for instance, the conclusions from the EU Conference on Anti-Doping organised by the Commission on 13-15 May 2009 in Athens available at www.ec.europa.eu/sport/news/doc/athens_conf_conclusions_final_version_en.pdf.

PEDs, the prohibitory proscription-based nature of current anti-doping policy violates a central tenet of liberalism—that of personal autonomy.[110] For the liberal, personal autonomy is an essential component of life and living; nevertheless, since individual choice is integral to an autonomous life there is never any guarantee that the individual will in fact lead an autonomous life, that is something for the individual to decide for him or herself. In other words, the price to be paid for respecting individual autonomy and personal liberty is the danger that the ostensibly autonomous individual might voluntarily decide to trade their liberty or risk their bodily integrity for some other value, possibly economic. In the classic liberal tradition of Mill[111]—refined by writers such as Feinberg[112]—the only caveat to this respect for the sanctity of personal autonomy is whether in exercising that autonomy there is a likelihood that harm will be inflicted upon others.[113]

[**4.44**]   In sum, the radical libertarian propounds that the individual should be free to act on their own decisions even if those decisions will probably end up hurting them but provided that those decisions do not involve the hurting or harming of others. In application to the taking and abuse of PEDs in sport, if an athlete wishes to, for example, blood dope to the extent that they know the scientific evidence is such that it will almost certainly shorten their life expectancy, then the liberal must accept that choice because (a) there is no justification in telling an autonomous adult exercising a free and informed choice that he may not do what he wants to do now on the sole grounds that 'he will be sorry later';[114] and (b) blood doping by the stated athlete will not directly or passively harm the physical well-being of any competing athlete. Therefore, at its most extreme or radical, liberalism can provide some justification for the unregulated approach to the use of PEDs in sport. This philosophical approach is accompanied by three further practical repercussions, all of which resonate with the policy debate in wider society as to the (de)criminalisation of 'soft' drugs—inefficient use of resources; a blurred ethical line; and a questionable moral basis.

Resource Implications

[**4.45**]   The thrust of this point can be encapsulated in the oft quoted remark by the German playwright Berthold Brecht, 'competitive sport begins where healthy

---

[110]   Much of what follows in this section on the jurisprudential, moral and legal framework surrounding doping in sport is adapted from the author's work on the legality of boxing in J Anderson, *The Legality of Boxing: A Punch Drunk Love?* (London, Birkbeck, 2007) 142–65 and repeated at [5.38]ff of this text. See also the excellent analysis given by M Mehlman, E Banger and M Wright, 'Doping in Sports and the Use of State Power' (2005) 50 *St Louis University Law Journal* 15.

[111]   J S Mill, *On Liberty* (Harmonsworth, Penguin Classics, 1974) ch I [9].

[112]   J Feinberg, *The Moral Limits of the Common Law*, 4 vols (Oxford, Oxford University Press, 1984–1988).

[113]   For a succinct introduction to the debate on the 'harm principle' see W Wilson, *Central Issues in Criminal Theory* (Oxford, Hart Publishing, 2002) ch 1.

[114]   Feinberg (n 112) vol 3, 77.

sport ends'.[115] In this light, libertarians argue that doping in sport is mainly confined to the elite professional level where the financial rewards (and associated fame) are such that athletes are willing to endanger their health for the sake of that additional element of speed or endurance that might make them successful. Attempting to monitor such highly motivated athletes is, it is argued, a costly and ultimately futile pursuit because such athletes will always find ways to evade and stay ahead of testing criteria and regimes, principally by availing themselves of more sophisticated, undetectable, 'designer' drugs. It follows that the scarce resources currently spent on complicated testing and appeals processes—and one recent estimate is that the annual bill for fighting drugs in sport is now £300 million—might be better directed elsewhere to the benefit of the wider development of sport.[116]

[**4.46**]   This cost-benefit contention is further supported by the view that with sports such as professional road cycling and athletics a tipping point has been reached because such is the general public's suspicion of these sports that even where they successfully reveal and sanction major doping conspiracies, the net effect is merely to add (in a 'this is only the tip of the iceberg' way) to the public's level of cynicism. For instance, despite the protestations of the organisers of the Tour de France and the world governing body of cycling (UCI); many remain unconvinced that, after a decade of doping-related scandals, the sport or *Le Tour* is an entirely 'clean' event.[117] Similarly, the repercussions of the so-called BALCO scandal—where a federal investigation revealed systematic abuses of then undetectable designer PEDs by American athletes and culminated in the jailing of American sprinter Marion Jones—dealt a severe blow to the credibility of track and field in the US because, as it turned out, the incredible achievements of Jones at the Sydney Olympics, where she won three gold and two bronze medals, were exactly that—beyond belief.[118] In short, the 'tipping point' contention is that there is now a diminishing return from whatever (sporadic) successes that sports organisations might have against drug cheats such that the 'deregulation' of PEDs is becoming a more attractive and pragmatic option.

---

[115] Cited by T Harris, *Sport: Almost Everything You Ever Wanted to Know* (London, Yellow Jersey Press, 2007) 396 who then goes on to give an entertaining and light-hearted review of the various ways in which athletes have doped over the centuries.

[116] O Slot, 'Cost hits £300m to stop cheats prospering; the anti-doping fight has become a global growth industry' *The Times* (London 18 March 2009) Sport 72.

[117] The many scandals associated with recent tours which are too numerous to mention but the most infamous is probably the Team Festina scandal of 1998, which was the catalyst for the creation of WADA. The Festina team 'pharmacist' subsequently recounted the story in depressing detail in Voet (n 12). For a more recent view of the disheartening state of professional road cycling see J Whittle, *Bad Blood: The Secret Life of the Tour de France* (London, Yellow Jersey, 2009).

[118] Marion Jones was jailed for six months in 2008, principally for lying to US federal investigators as to her use of steroids during her career: see L Zinser, 'Six-Month Sentence for Jones Meant to be a Message' *The New York Times* (New York 12 January 2008) Section D, Sport 3.

Blurred Ethical Line

[**4.47**]   The second and related point in favour of deregulation is that not only is the monitoring of drug cheats a costly task, it is also, given medico-techno-logical advances, quickly becoming Sisyphean in nature in the sense that the line between what can and should be prohibited will soon be impossible to maintain.[119] The most obvious example is with so-called 'gene-doping' or genetic manipulation, which, it appears, will lead to doping methods undetectable by blood or urine analysis. A full debate on gene transfer technology is beyond the scope of this text though it is of note that given recent research indicating that in many athletic events humans are reaching the limits of their physiological capaci-ties, it is likely that during the twenty first century more reliance will be placed on such technologies in order to improve upon world records.[120] The current ambiguity with which this particular matter is dealt with—in the annotation to article 4.3.2 WADC it is stated that the use of genetic transfer technology to dramatically enhance sport performance should be prohibited as contrary to the spirit of sport *even if it is not harmful*—indicates how problematical this topic might become.[121] Moreover, to what extent has WADA dealt with the ethical and physiological repercussions from the practice whereby athletes, injected with their own blood—in a process called platelet rich plasma therapy (PRPT)—can speed recovery from a whole range of injuries?[122] Is it realistic to think that one can determine definitively when such an infusion is a surgical procedure designed simply to increase the rate of repair of damaged tissue or tendons and one which effectively seeks to regenerate same to the point that it 'unfairly' enhances the athlete's athletic capacity?[123]

[**4.48**]   Taking a step back from the types of PEDs that might be used in the future; it is also argued that at present the 'ethical' line between that which is

---

[119] The analogy here is with the attempts by sports organisations to regulate the use of technol-ogy in sports equipment and apparel. See generally T Magdalinski, *Sport, Technology and the Body* (London, Routledge, 2009). Note also FINA's ban from 1 January 2010 on polyurethane swimsuits after 40 of the 43 world records set at World Swimming Championships in Rome in 2009 were achieved by swimmers using the enhanced suits.

[120] See G Berthelot *et al*, 'The Citius End: World Record Progression Announces the Completion of a Brief Ultra-Physiological Quest' (2008) 3 *PloS One* e1552 and F Desgorces, 'From Oxford to Hawaii: Ecophysiological Barriers Limit Human Progression in Ten Sport Monuments' (2008) 3 *PloS One* e3653.

[121] See, eg, E Gatzidou *et al*, 'Genetically Transformed World Records: A Reality or in the Sphere of Fantasy?' (2009) 15 *Medical Science Monitor* RA41–47.

[122] See M Chittenden, 'Blood Jab puts Sports Stars on Fast Track to Beating Injury' *The Times* (London 22 February 2009) News 11 and M Sanchez *et al*, 'Platelet-rich Therapies in the Treatment of Orthopaedic Sport Injuries' (2009) 39 *Sports Medicine* 345. In 2010, PRPT came to the fore when Tiger Woods admitted that he had used this blood-spinning therapy to recover from knee surgery, as well as to repair a torn Achilles.

[123] According to current anti-doping policy, it appears that the former is therapeutic and there-fore permitted; but the latter is prohibited. See S 8 of WADA's Prohibited List (2009) available at www.wada-ama.org/en/World-Anti-Doping-Program/Sports-and-Anti-Doping-Organizations/International-Standards/Prohibited-List.

allowed (for example, hypoxic air machines that simulate altitude training giving the athlete an EPO-like but 'legal' blood boost) [124] and that which is proscribed (minute traces of banned PEDs in otherwise over the counter medications) is now so blurred that it is difficult to recognise and defend.[125] In addition, the rationale underpinning the therapeutic use exemption process—that sick athletes may use substances otherwise proscribed for healthy athletes—can also be criticised on this basis. As Kayser notes, not only is the boundary between the therapeutic and ergogenic use of certain drugs quite blurred but also the rules accompanying the policy lead to 'complicated and costly administrative and medical follow up'.[126]

[**4.49**]   This latter point appears to be supported by a recent CAS decision involving inter alia a successful claim by the US Anti-Doping Agency to overturn a decision by an independent arbitration panel partially reducing the sentence of a table tennis international who tested positive for cannabinoid use.[127] On testing adversely, the athlete responded by admitting that he used marijuana but did so only for medicinal purposes relating to an existing, stress-induced, medical condition. He further argued that, although he had not engaged with WADA's TUE process, his use of marijuana was medically supervised in the sense that it had been prescribed to him by his personal doctor in California, who was permitted to do so under the Compassionate Use Act 1995, a Californian statute that allows the use of medicinal cannabinoids when prescribed by a licensed physician. In this light, and pursuant to article 10.5.2 WADC, an independent appeals panel reduced the standard two-year suspension period to one of 15 months, on the ground that no significant negligence or fault attached to the athlete's actions. CAS reinstated the two-year suspension period noting that the issue of the legality (or, indeed, the illegality) of cannabinoid use under Californian or any state law was irrelevant to the jurisdictional basis of the dispute at hand, which concerned the integrity of and engagement with WADA's therapeutic use exemption process. Although there is little to doubt as to the technical correctness of the CAS Panel's award in this instance; overall, it seems a very costly and elongated process in which to pursue what in effect amounted to a supplementary 12-week penalty, particularly when throughout that process it was uncontested that no performance enhancing advantage had been obtained by the athlete.

---

[124] See M Spriggs, 'Hypoxic Air Machines: Performance Enhancement Through Effective Training— or Cheating?' (2005) 31 *Journal of Medical Ethics* 112.

[125] See the points raised by S Loland, 'The Ethics of Performance-Enhancing Technology in Sport' (2009) 36 *Journal of the Philosophy of Sport* 152; W Morgan, 'Athletic Perfection, Performance-Enhancing Drugs and the Treatment-Enhancement Distinction' (2009) 36 *Journal of the Philosophy of Sport* 162; and A Schneider and J Rupert, 'Constructing Winners: The Science and Ethics of Genetically Manipulating Athletes' (2009) 36 *Journal of the Philosophy of Sport* 182.

[126] B Kayser, A Mauron, A Miah, 'Current Anti-Doping Policy: A Critical Appraisal' (2007) 8 *BMC Medical Ethics* 2 published online at www.biomedcentral.com/1472-6939/8/2.

[127] CAS 2008/A/1577 *USADA v R*. In-competition, cannaboid use is prohibited by S 8 of WADA's Prohibited List (2009).

Questionable Moral Basis

[**4.50**] Given that it appears that the line between what may or may not be performance enhancing is now drawn so arbitrarily (and ultimately might be based on whether WADA considers the substance or method to be contrary to the 'spirit' of sport), the libertarian argues that fundamentally WADA's policy equates to that of a moral value judgement. In turn, given this moralistic basis, libertarians are unsurprised when, on occasion, the 'war' on drugs in sport degenerates into an emotive, shrill and institutionalised crusade by sports organisations against individual athletes.[128] This libertarian perspective leads to three further points: drugs in sport as a 'moral panic'; the 'transactional deviance' of doping infractions; and the strict legal moralism of current anti-doping policy. First, it would be interesting to analyse both the moral panic that surrounds PED abuse in sport and the manner in which PED-taking athletes are seen as a 'deviant' subgroup through an understanding of Stanley Cohen's criminological study of the, at times, lazy vilification by the media and public of deviant subgroups in society—society's so-called 'folk devils'.[129] It is beyond the brief of this book to do this other than to note that Cohen's work appears to support the libertarian view, especially his observation that, while the deviant label is easy to attach to any subgroup that threatens predominant norms; it is not that easy to stop the subsequent exaggerated amplification of the threat posed and the inevitable reactionary policies that follow.[130]

[**4.51**] Moreover, and this is the second point on its dubious moral basis, the current anti-doping policy is characterised by what can be described as the high minded assumption about the 'spirit' of sport and the 'solidarity' of sport participants or, more specifically, that the essential norms and values of sport are underwritten by the presumption that all athletes wish to uphold them through a communal, communtarian respect for the universal sporting virtue that is 'fair play'. As Kayser points out not only is this a dubious analysis of modern sport and the modern sports participant, it also imposes a ridiculously high standard of policing on modern sports administrators and one that is inevitably and regularly breached thus further corroding the long term integrity of sport.[131] Accordingly, libertarians can argue that the current strict approach to PEDs has seen modern

---

[128] Historically, it has been argued that was not until the end of the 1950s that a framework of ethics surrounded the use of PEDs in sport but that more recently the debate is characterised by over-zealousness to the detriment of constructive deliberation and consistent policy making. See generally P Dimeo, *A History of Drug Use in Sport, 1876-1976* (London, Routledge, 2007).

[129] See generally S Cohen, *Folk Devils and Moral Panic: The Creation of Mods and Rockers* (London, MacGibbon and Kee, 1972).

[130] In the third edition of Cohen's book (London, Routledge, 2002) the author tracks (in ways and through examples that, arguably, resonate with PED debate in sport) moral panics over the previous 30 years such as the demonisation of young offenders and asylum seekers.

[131] In contrast, Kayser *et al* (n 126) argue that normative systems designed to police society at large, such as the criminal justice system, do not make high minded assumptions about universal virtues and 'are therefore, more resilient as regards the continued existence of transgressions.'

sport hoisted by, and isolated upon, its own (overly moralistic) petard. The face-saving solution, for libertarians at least, is attractively straightforward—permit the use of all PEDs or as Savulescu puts it: 'Drugs are against the rules. But we define the rules of sport. If we made drugs legal and freely available, there would be no cheating'.[132] It is suggested that the work of sociologists/criminologists such as Becker support this libertarian perspective and that the hollowness that exists within the current approach is there because that approach is a classic example of transactional or created deviance.[133] Translated into a sports-specific context, the transactional approach to deviance would point out that sports organisations have created PED-deviance by making the rules whose infraction leads to 'offenders' being labelled sports deviants or drug cheats. It follows that if the efficacy and consequences of those rules are open to question (and liberals suggest that they are in terms of the exorbitant costs associated with their implementation as set against the public's cynicism as to the 'real' level of PED abuse in sport) then it is reasonable to ask the question: why do these rules exist at all?

[4.52]   The third contention is that the current policy on drugs in sport equates to one of strict legal moralism—that it can be morally legitimate to prohibit conduct on the sole ground that it is inherently immoral or 'evil' notwithstanding both the informed consent of the party involved and the fact that the party's conduct does not harm other actors.[134] Vague moral repugnancy, which Dworkin has dismissesed as often amounting to no more than groundless prejudice, is never enough, libertarians suggest, to form the premise of a punitive policy.[135] This is principally because proponents of the prohibitory approach often encounter difficulties in avoiding sliding down a slippery slope 'to interferences with relatively harmless self-regarding behaviour for trivial reasons',[136] which in the case of PEDs in sport may extend to moral value judgements on the private 'recreational' lives of athletes. For some commentators, this slide down the moral slope is evidenced by the WADA's in-competition prohibition of cannabinoid use (hashish, marijuana). This view can be traced back to one of the more celebrated 'cannibas cases' in sport when at the 1998 Winter Olympics the IOC attempted to rescind the gold medal awarded to Ross Rebagliati as winner of the snowboard giant slalom competition on the ground that traces of marijuana were found in his urine. An appeal to CAS was successful: the applicable IOC rules treated the use of marijuana as doping only if there was an agreement between the IOC and the relevant sports

---

[132] J Savulescu, B Foddy and M Clayton, 'Why we should Allow Performance Enhancing Drugs in Sport' (2004) 38 *British Journal of Sports Medicine* 666.

[133] See especially H Becker, *Outsiders: Studies in Sociological Deviance* (New York, Free State Press, 1963) 1–18.

[134] Feinberg (n 112) vol 4, 27. Legal moralism as a theoretical approach to an understanding of the law is usually discussed in light of the celebrated Hart-Devlin debate on the enforcement of morals. For an introduction see P Cane, 'Taking Law Seriously: Starting Points of the Hart/Devlin Debate' (2006) 10 *Journal of Ethics* 21.

[135] See, eg, R Dworkin, *Taking Rights Seriously* (London, Duckworth, 1977) 257–58.

[136] N Dixon, 'Boxing, Paternalism and Legal Moralism' (2001) 27 *Social Theory and Practice* 323, 340.

federation to that effect and in fact there was none in this instance.[137] The Panel did however note that 'we do not suggest for a moment that the use of marijuana should be condoned, nor do we suggest that sports authorities are not entitled to exclude athletes found to have used cannabis' because, the Panel claimed, 'from an ethical and medical perspective, cannabis consumption is a matter of serious social concern'.[138] Nevertheless, and as Kayser highlights, given that cannabinoid use has few performance enhancing or ergogenic attributes, its subsequent express inclusion on WADA's 'Prohibited List' appears to be based solely on the vaguely moral premise that as role models athletes should not be using such substances.[139] In sum, the libertarian argues, and with broader reference to current anti-doping policy as a whole, not only is the idea about the role model status of athletes (and particularly snowboarders!) problematical in itself, it is also argued that 'the intrusive monitoring of athletes might actually undermine this status as role models, since it stigmatizes athletes as people who, without surveillance, will behave improperly'.[140]

Paternalism

[**4.53**]   The current attitude to PEDs in sport is uncompromisingly paternalistic even moralistic in nature. In broad jurisprudential terms, paternalists argue that the unregulated approach of radical libertarians to PED use in sport is undermined by its adherence to 'the grand myth' of liberal fundamentalism, which holds that 'the interest of all lies in the maximum liberty of all'.[141] However, as McGlynn and Ward have recently observed, in reality 'the liberty of some always shapes the subjection of others' thus sometimes it is in the interests of all that choices have to be proscribed.[142] These prohibitory strategies must of course be justified as reasonable and rational. The paternalist defends the rationale underpinning the context-specific nature of the proscription of PED use in two ways: first, that radical libertarians have a dangerously *laissez-faire* attitude to the well-being of athletes ('the health argument'); and second, that the uncontrolled use of PEDs would corrode the elemental ethical and moral 'spirit' of sport which is based on fairness ('the cheating argument'). As noted previously, these arguments appear in the preamble to the WADC which holds that one of the core purposes of the Code and WADA's anti-doping programme more generally is to 'protect athletes' fundamental right to participate in doping-free sport and thus promote health, fairness and equality for athletes worldwide.'

---

[137] CAS ad hoc Division (OG Nagano) 1998/002, *R v IOC*.

[138] Ibid [26].

[139] Kayser *et al* (n 126) citing the findings in D Campos, 'Marijuana as Doping in Sports' (2003) 33 *Sports Medicine* 395.

[140] Ibid Kayser *et al* (n 126). See generally R Welch, 'A Snort and a Puff: Recreational Drugs and Discipline in Professional Sport' in J O'Leary (ed) (n 1).

[141] C McGlynn and I Ward, 'Pornography, Pragmatism, and Proscription' (2009) 36 *Journal of Law and Society* 327, 341.

[142] Ibid.

Health and the Well-being of Athletes

[**4.54**]   In general terms, paternalism holds that the prohibition of an activity or conduct can be justified where it is necessary to prevent harm (physical, psychological or economic) to the parties who participate in that activity.[143] Consequently, the legal paternalist advocates what the liberal denies: the state may be justified in using coercive powers (such as the criminal law) to force a person to act against his will in order to protect that person's welfare and well-being or, simply, to protect them from themselves. In application to drugs in sport, the paternalist argues that given the health risks that might flow from the unregulated use of PEDs, the current strict liability approach is justified on the ground of, simply, protecting athletes from themselves. In this light, proponents of the extant regime regularly refer to Goldman's infamous 1982 survey in which nearly 200 elite athletes were asked if they would take an undetectable PED that would guarantee them success in their sport but would result in their death within five years.[144] Fifty two per cent of athletes answered in the affirmative and in a decade long series of biannual surveys thereafter, that figure remained consistent with half of the athletes stating that they would accept this Faustian bargain.[145]

[**4.55**]   Those who support the current regime on PEDs in sport argue that the liberal view—that in respect of personal autonomy athletes should be free to take dangerous PEDs if that is their voluntary, informed choice—is not only overly detached but also that its key principles (such as informed consent) are undermined by the results of the Goldman survey. In short, in practical terms, the paternalist argues that athletes must be protected from themselves because in comparison to the general population and non-elite sports participants—who would, presumably, reject Goldman's bargain—the norms and values of elite athletes are so perversely competitive in outlook that, if left to their own devices, they would assume the risk of premature death for fleeting sporting success.[146] In abstract jurisprudential terms, this means that paternalistic PED controls can be justified because the decision-making abilities of the controlled individuals have, it is argued, been 'temporarily diminished'.[147] The paternalistic approach appears difficult to refute when one reads about the sad deaths of cyclists such as Tommy Simpson;[148] and the death of Italy's Marco Pantani—winner of the Tour de France in 1998 but who

---

[143] Feinberg (n 112) vol 1, 26.

[144] B Goldman, P Bush and R Klatz, *Death in the Locker Room* (London, Century, 1984) 32.

[145] See generally B Goldman and R Klatz, *Death in the Locker Room* 2nd edn, (Chicago, Elite Sports Medicine Publications).

[146] The essence of this phenomenon is captured in Houlihan's evocative phrase 'dying to win' (n 3).

[147] See generally A Fuchs, 'Autonomy, Slavery and Mill's Critique of Paternalism' (2001) 4 *Ethical Theory and Moral Practice* 239. See also C Ten, 'Paternalism and Morality' (1971) 13 *Ratio* 55.

[148] See W Fotheringham (n 9), where the author notes that Simpson was a 'man of contradictions' who, despite admitting that he used banned substances, inspired huge affection from cycling fans for his obsessive will to win, which was to cost him his life ultimately. Simpson remains a divisive figure in the sport, viewed either as a victim or perpetrator of a doping culture in cycling.

failed a blood test for abuse of EPO (a banned form of endurance-boosting, blood doping) the following year and who within five years was found dead in tragic circumstances;[149] and on reviewing the statistics on the cluster of premature fatalities in professional cycling allegedly relating to the abuse of EPO in the late 1990s and mid-2000s.[150] On a more practical, empirical level, some corroboration of the paternalistic approach can be found by the most recent research on the issue—a 2009 Australian survey that counterbalanced the Goldman dilemma for the general public and reported that only two out of 250 members of the Australian public would agree to the Faustian bargain on offer.[151]

[**4.56**]   In reflecting on their findings, the authors of this post-Goldman research (Connor and Mazanov) make two points of interest which appear to underpin the present paternalistic approach to PEDs in sport. First, they argue that the marked difference between the personal health decision-making of elite athletes and the wider population might be explained by the peculiarly 'obsessive' and self-absorbed world of elite athletes (particularly those in individual sports such as athletics, cycling and swimming) which has its origins in the fact that 'athletes, to reach the elite level must display a singular focus (usually from early childhood) and desire often to the exclusion of other life-affirming activity.' The skewed social world of the athlete, where, as the authors suggest, 'winning is given precedence over survival' is 'not one that necessarily reflects or supports public discourses that drug use to improve sporting performance is against the spirit of sport'.[152] Moreover, and this is the second point hinted at by Connor and Mazonov, elite athletes tend to have what might be called a 'real-time' relationship with their body that is they are primarily concerned with what they can push their body to do now (at their physical peak, say, in their twenties) rather than thinking about how it might cope in the future. As a result, many elite athletes, who do not have an adequate amount of objective self-awareness to understand the consequence of their actions alone, effectively assign their long term health, and become heavily dependent upon, their support staff—be they personal coaches or physicians or the support supplied by their national sports federation or government.[153]

---

[149] See M Rendell, *The Death of Marco Pantani* (London, Weidenfeld & Nicolson, 2006) where the author though sympathetic to Pantani notes that his career was in many respects 'a pharmaceutical creation'.

[150] See M Cazzola, 'A Global Strategy for Prevention and Detection of Blood Doping with EPO and Related Drugs' (2000) 85 *Haematologica* 561 and W Fotheringham, 'Inquiry in Belgium Cyclist's Death Raises New Fears over EPO' *The Guardian* (London 16 February 2004) Sport 25.

[151] J Connor and J Mazanov, 'Would you Dope? A General Population Test of the Goldman Dilemma?' (2009) 43 *British Journal of Sports Medicine* 871.

[152] Ibid 872. The article cites some of the 'growing literature' explaining the willingness to use PEDs by way of reference to the peculiar social circumstances of the elite athlete. See also I Waddington and A Smith (eds), *An Introduction to Drugs in Sport: Addicted to Winning?* (London, Routledge, 2009).

[153] Ibid. For an interesting review of a sports physician's role and responsibility in this regard see the report by the British Medical Association, *Drugs in Sport: The Pressure to Perform* (London, BMJ Books, 2002).

[**4.57**]   The paternalist points out that the history of sports shows painfully that the ethical norms of support staff can also become corrupted by the potential for drug-fuelled sporting success. The role of the athletics coach Trevor Graham in the aforementioned BALCO affair is a recent example[154] but most infamously there was the policy of the communist government of the former East Germany which used sporting success for political propaganda purposes and which systematically forced elite athletes to take dangerous quantities of steroids resulting in catastrophic and chronic health problems for athletes.[155] The decade-long (1976–1986) dominance of East Germany's female competitors on the track and in the pool (East Germany won 11 of the 13 gold medals available to female swimmers at the Montreal Olympics of 1976) appeared to be the nadir of international sport's attitude towards drugs in sport, at least until the East German method was repeated (with the help of former GDR coaches) by the Chinese in the 1990s, who at the 1994 World Swimming Championships in Rome won 12 out of the 16 gold medals available to female swimmers.[156] There is little doubt that the strictness of the eventual response, manifested in the creation of WADA, is rooted in the lingering embarrassment felt by the IOC, the IAAF and FINA at their omission to act during this period.[157]

Cheating and the Integrity of Sport

[**4.58**]   To recap, paternalism demands that a strict anti-doping policy can be justified not only in protecting athletes from themselves but also from those within their inner circle who might be tempted to sacrifice the athlete's long-term health for short-term glory. The second policy aspect of the current, paternalistic approach to PEDs in sport is straightforward—the reason that PEDs are

---

[154] Graham coached a number of the leading American sprinters caught in the BALCO investigation (details at n 18) but eventually turned whistleblower when sending an anonymous package to the US authorities enclosing a syringe containing BALCO's premier doping product—the previously undetectable steroid THG. See D Walsh, 'The Whisteblower' *The Sunday Times* (London, 11 May 2008) Sport 13. In May 2008, Graham was convicted of lying to federal investigators when denying that he knew a sports steroids dealer. In October 2008, Graham was sentenced to one year of home confinement thus becoming, at that time, the tenth BALCO figure convicted since the probe began in 2003. See C Pogash and M Schmidt, 'Graham Sentence to Year's House Arrest in Balco Case' *The New York Times* (New York, 22 October 2008) Section B, Sport 17.

[155] See G Spitzer, 'Sport and the Systematic Infliction of Pain: A Case Study of State-sponsored Mandatory Doping in East Germany' in S Loland, B Skirstad and I Waddington (eds), *Pain and Injury in Sport: Social and Ethical Analysis* (London, Routledge, 2006) and G Spitzer (ed), *Doping and Doping Control in Europe* (Aachen, Meyer & Meyer, 2007). The barbarity of the East German system is epitomised by the story of Heidi (now Andreas) Kreiger who won the European shot put championship in 1986 but needed a sex change operation such were the effect of the drugs given to her. See M Syed, 'The Little Girl that Communism Turned into a Man for Sport' *The Times* (London 5 July 2008) Sport 110.

[156] See further D Galluzi, 'The Doping Crisis in International Athletic Competition: Lessons from the Chinese Doping Scandal in Women's Swimming' (2000) 10 *Seton Hall Journal of Sport Law* 65.

[157] Arguably, it is in this historical light that the sweeping conspiracy-related offence of art 2.8 WADC may be read with its reference to 'assisting, encouraging, aiding, abetting, covering up or any other type of complicity involving an anti-doping violation or any *attempted* anti-doping violation.'

prohibited is that they give an unfair advantage and this equates to cheating. In this, proponents of the current regime on PEDs usually support their approach on four grounds.[158] First, and in somewhat informal terms, it is argued that the regulated approach to PEDs is about equality of opportunity in the sense that it is an attempt to ensure, as far as is practicable, that the athlete of best ability, rather than the athlete with the best pharmacist, wins. Second, and more broadly, that sports administrators owe a duty of care not only to those who now participate and enjoy sport but also in securing sport's future, bearing in mind that neither sponsors nor parents like their money[159] or children[160] to be associated with a 'dirty' sport. On the latter point, 'clean' athletes, it is claimed make better role models for children thus not only encouraging them to take up the sport but also discouraging them from taking PEDs at a vulnerable age.[161]

[**4.59**]   The third and fourth planks of the paternalistic view of PEDs in sport are direct attacks on the liberalist perspective. The third one is the attempt to refute a fundamental premise of the liberal approach to PEDs in sport—that personal autonomy should include the right to take PEDs even dangerous PEDs because it does not result in harm to others and thus is 'victimless'. The paternalist's contention is that harm *is* inflicted on others by the taking, and tolerance, of PEDs. At the elite professional level that harm may be economic in nature that is, suffering consistent defeats by drugged athletes affects a clean athlete's prize winnings and sponsorship endorsements. Outside of that, 'perceptions of drug use amongst rivals can only increase the already huge pressures on sportsmen and women preparing for competition'.[162] In other words, not only does the perception of drug abuse have a demoralising affect on all clean athletes it might also tempt some of them to take the PED option and thus contribute to a corrosive spiral of PED abuse. Similarly, those who advocate the current approach note that the 'harm to others' principle should include a recognition that the acceptance of drugs at the elite level in sport might have a 'trickledown' effect on drug abuse at amateur or school sports levels and thus have general public health implications.[163]

[**4.60**]   Fourth and finally, the paternalist is unashamedly and unapologetically moralistic in approach arguing, for instance, that in light of the tragedies surrounding the many athletes who were either coerced into taking PEDs (as

---

[158] See, for instance, the arguments made by Dick Pound, former Vice-President of the IOC and the first President of WADA, in *Inside Dope* (London, Wiley & Sons, 2006).

[159] See, eg, 'German TV Boycotts Tour de France' *The Times* (London, 17 October 2008) Sport 85.

[160] See Select Committee on Culture, Media and Sport, 'Drugs and Role Models in Sport: Making and Setting Examples' HC (2003-04) 499-I, 3.

[161] A Miah, 'Doping and the Child: An Ethical Policy for the Vulnerable' (2005) 366 *The Lancet* 874.

[162] Ibid. In a combat sport such as boxing, fighting a drugged opponent can enhance the already high risks of harm inherent in the sport. See M Costello and N Hassan, 'Boxing's Dirty Secret: Victor Conte Slams Professional Boxing's Drug Testing' BBC News Online 28 January 2010 available online at http://news.bbc.co.uk/sport1/hi/boxing/8485892.stm.

[163] See generally Select Committee on Culture, Media and Sport, 'Drugs and Role Models in Sport' (n 160) 42–50.

in East Germany) or who, despite the associated dangers, could not resist the transient glory promised by them (for example, Tommy Simpson, Marco Pantani), PED abuse in sport should stir 'a real feeling of reprobation' in the hearts and minds of those who have the integrity and long-term future of sport in mind. This view rejects the unregulated approach as being one of appeasement laced with defeatism—where one might as well replace the Olympic Charter with a Cheater's Charter—and reiterates that the libertarian's view of the consequences of the unregulated use of PEDs is at best naive; at worst, callous.[164] In this, the moral paternalist presumes that if, for instance, all elite athletes were to be given the choice of either taking PEDs or not, the competitive nature of sport would mean that in order to have any chance of success *all* such elite athletes would have to take PEDs. Consequently, the paternalist holds that libertarian arguments about respecting an athlete's autonomy in voluntarily assuming or consenting to the risks that go with PED-taking are vitiated by the circumstances of competitive sport, resulting eventually in virtually all participating athletes being coerced into taking PEDs. At a jurisprudential level therefore the paternalist argues convincingly that the liberal fundamentalist approach to PEDs in sport would subject participants to what might be described as a culture of 'sporting sadism',[165] and would, in sports terms, result in many sports degenerating into the grotesque, pharmaceutical circus that is professional bodybuilding.[166] From a practical legal perspective, it might also be argued that the liberal approach would, in terms of professional sport in Europe, expose worker-athletes to levels of danger that might be difficult to reconcile with the demands of EU-driven health and safety law in the workplace.[167]

[**4.61**]   In sum, while liberals feel that the war on drugs is unwinnable, paternalists argue the fight is far from lost and that the gap between cheating athletes using undetectable, designer drugs and the sophistication of WADA-led anti-doping testing regimes is closing.[168] Indeed, some argue—pointing to the recent successes against CERA (an advanced form of EPO)—that new WADA-led

---

[164] See similarly and generally how this (naive/callous) flaw in liberalism's approach to the moral limits of the criminal law has been identified by, amongst other, P McCutcheon, 'Morality and the Criminal Law: Reflections on Hart-Devlin' (2002) 47 *Criminal Law Quarterly* 15.

[165] This paraphrases the phrase 'cultural sadism' used by Susan Easton and others to describe libertarian-based arguments against the regulation of pornography. See McGlynn and Ward (n 141) 341 citing S Easton, *The Problem of Pornography: Regulation and the Right to Free Speech* (London, Routledge, 1994) 25–27.

[166] Note Paul Solotaroff's classic essay from 1991 on bodybuilding in the US entitled, 'The Power and the Gory' and reproduced in D Halberstam (ed), *The Best American Sports Writing of the Century* (New York, Houghton Mifflin, 1999) 574–92. Note also that in 2009 the organisers of the Belgian Bodybuilding Championships had to call off that year's event after all 20 contestants fled when three drug testers arrived at the weigh-in. None of the entrants was said to be prepared to give a urine sample. See 'Drug Testers Show Muscle' *The Times* (London, 20 May 2009) News 36.

[167] See paragraph 18 of A Vermeersch, 'The European Union and the Fight against Doping in Sport: On the Field or on the Sidelines? (2006) 4 *Entertainment and Sports Law Journal* published online at www2.warwick.ac.uk/fac/soc/law/elj/eslj/issues/volume4/number1/vermeersch.

[168] See generally D Catlin, K Fitch and A Ljungqvist, 'Medicine and Science in the Fight Against Doping in Sport' (2008) 264 *Journal of Internal Medicine* 99.

initiatives such as biological passports, blood profiling and the retrospective testing of blood samples means that the gap might soon be closed completely.[169] Furthermore, the paternalist argues that whatever the immediate and exorbitant costs of funding anti-doping programmes may be; however stubbornly low the rates of adverse, positive findings may remain; and however deflating the revelations from scandals such as the BALCO affair are for sport; this is the price that must be paid to secure the long-term integrity and future of sport. It follows that although the BALCO affair was a low point for international sport, and markedly so for baseball, given the alleged involvement of Barry Bonds (who holds that sport's most sacrosanct of statistics, the all time home run record) it did result in some significant anti-doping developments.[170] In sum, paternalists argue that as the Ben Johnson affair of the late 1980s resulted in the influential Dubin report; so the Festina affair of the late 1990s led (eventually) to the creation of WADA; and so BALCO has led to significant reform in baseball[171] and American sport more generally.[172]

Soft Paternalism: Replacing *Strict* Liability with *Safety* Liability

[**4.62**]   The (extreme) liberal, unregulated approach to PEDs in sport is not on the agenda of any leading international sports organisation. Paternalistic concerns underpin the current administration of PEDs in sport, and once those concerns are acknowledged, the workings of the regulatory structure that surrounds anti-doping, namely WADA, and many of the legal issues that accompany anti-doping schemes in sport can be understood more readily. Overall, the paternalistic approach favoured by contemporary sports administrators is largely convincing and markedly so when placed against any policy that might promote the unregulated use of PEDS is sport.[173] Nevertheless, it is argued that the softer, benevolent

---

[169] See P Kelso, 'Tour de France Offers Glimpse of Hope in the Fight against Drugs' *The Daily Telegraph* (London, 29 July 2009) Sport 9.

[170] Bonds is currently awaiting trial on perjury-related charges for lying to US federal investigators as to his use of steroids during his career see N Vinton, 'Is this the end of BALCO?' *The Daily News* (New York 1 March 2009) Sports 72.

[171] In major league baseball, testing for steroids did not begin in earnest until the early part of the 2000s and tests from then continue to surprise the sport as to the depth of steroid abuse among star players. They have also led to a number of Congressional hearings and reports on the matter. The weightiest report is probably US Senator George Mitchell's 400 page independent review of illegal PED use in baseball, published in December 2007 and available at http://files.mlb.com/mitchrpt.pdf. The most recent revelation concerns the St Louis Cardinals' Mark McGwire who admitted to using steroids when he broke major league baseball's single season home run record in 1998. See T Dart, 'McGwire Finally Confesses' *The Times* (London 12 January 2010) Sport, 65.

[172] In January 2008, the US Olympic Committee, the US Anti-Doping Agency, Major League Baseball and the NFL announced the establishment of the Partnership for Clean Competition through which they will combine their resources and expertise to support anti-doping research projects. See further www.cleancompetition.org.

[173] See generally E Carolan, 'The New WADA Code and the Search for a Policy Justification for Anti-Doping Rules' (2006) 16 *Seton Hall Journal of Sports and Entertainment Law* 1 and N Cox,

154 The Legal Regulation of Drugs in Sport

side of this approach should be given more emphasis because 'hard' or strict paternalism has a fundamental flaw, which is that sometimes when the implications and consequences of a hard paternalistic-based approach become apparent, the policy becomes much less attractive (and much more difficult to administer in practice). Previous sections in this chapter have illustrated this flaw with respect to, for instance, the controversy that has surrounded the imposition of the somewhat draconian limitations on the general freedoms (the whereabouts rule) of individual athletes and the legal repercussions of the strict liability approach to doping infractions. For now two broader aspects of the weaknesses in the strictly paternalistic approach are identified. The first is a suggestion that there is a slight taint of disingenuousness to the current approach to PEDs in sport. The second aspect is blunter: that the current approach is inherently inefficient to the point that for many sports it can be seen as regressive in nature.

[**4.63**]   Modern elite sport is not just about athletes competing in races or events organised by officials and administrators. High level professional sport is also part of the 'entertainment industry' whereby the sporting public, sponsors and TV companies all play a role in the underwriting of sports events. All three parties enjoy competitive elite sport but they (we) enjoy it even more when it is accompanied by world record times in the pool or on the track or unprecedented acts of endurance by cyclists over mountain stages. Athletes are vulnerable to these (our) demands (and, of course, the financial rewards that accompany success in them) thus the temptation to dope, whether it is to gain that extra hundredth of a second or simply to help pedal another hairpin twist on a mountain road, must be and, as reflected in those willing to risk being caught, *is* intense. It follows that there is an unsettling paradox within the current approach and the manner in which we ask athletes to push their bodies to the limit for our enjoyment but simultaneously threaten them with severe sanction for availing themselves of any pharmaceutical assistance.[174] The demands placed on cyclists were summed up pithily by two of the sports legendary figures, Jacques Anquetil, who won the Tour de France five times and Fausto Coppi, who won it twice. Anquetil was once quoted as saying, 'Only a fool would imagine it possible to win the Tour de France on mineral water.' Similarly, when Coppi was asked if he ever used PEDs, he replied, 'Only when necessary'. And when was it necessary? 'Almost all of the time.' In this light, and on a point elaborated upon shortly, it is suggested that it might be time to amend the current policy of *strict* liability to that of *safety* liability whereby athletes should be permitted to use certain

'Victory with Honour or Victory at all Costs? Towards a Principled Justification for Anti-Doping Rules in Sport' (2000) 22 *Dublin University Law Journal* 19.

[174] Note also the interesting argument made by Sullivan who, with ironical reference to the level of drug dependency in western societies generally, observes that that we impose a level of 'pharmaceutical purity' on sports persons that we would never dream of imposing on ourselves. See A Sullivan, 'In a Drugged-up National, the Steroid Sports Star is King' *The Sunday Times* (London, 12 December 2004) News 15.

PEDs, hitherto prohibited, in a controlled manner and up to medically defined safe limits.[175]

[**4.64**]   The second weakness in the paternalist's argument is that for all the resources devoted to anti-doping schemes; despite the increased frequency and enhanced sophistication of dope testing; and despite the expanding scope and power give to drug testers; the perception remains that it is only 'the unlucky or pharmacologically unsophisticated' that get caught.[176] In this, Connor and Mazanov, for instance, contend that the incidence of PED use in sport, typically reported at less than 2 per cent of athletes by global anti-doping agencies, appears low.[177] Although the authors admit that there is an absence of a reliable epidemiology of estimates of PED usage in sport, such that the incidence of use remains an educated guess, Connor and Mazanov argue that the anecdotal evidence indicates a much higher use rate.[178] Accordingly, they suggest that current anti-doping testing regimes 'are either flawed in administration (athletes can avoid tests or manage their drug use) or accuracy (laboratories cannot detect substances or the limits are too high)'.[179]

[**4.65**]   In a similar vein, Connor and Mazanov highlight the fact that the most high profile victim of the BALCO scandal, the American sprinter Marion Jones, had tested negative for banned substances at the Sydney Olympics of 2000 and that it was the subsequent federal investigation in the US, not testing, that caught her out. The authors could also have cited the recent pronouncements of the man at the heart of the BALCO affair, Victor Conte. Although Conte, the founder of the BALCO organisation, can easily be discredited and dismissed—he served a four-month, BALCO-related jail sentence in California for conspiracy to distribute drugs and money laundering in 2005—his subsequent pronouncements on how easily the demands of the current anti-doping regime can be, and are, evaded by a significant percentage of elite athletes makes for provocative reading.[180] Conte has claimed that there are no effective tests for the manner in which athletes exploit and 'micro-boost' on insulin, thyroid medication, blood-doping

---

[175] See also the point made by Savulescu *et al* (n 132) 666 where they note that 'in many ways the athletic ideal of modern athletes is inspired by the myth of the marathon. [Feidipides death from exhaustion on delivering the message to Athens that the Persian army had been defeated.] Their ideal is superhuman performance, at any cost.'

[176] Connor and Mazanov (n 151) 872. In series of clinical interviews conducted with elite athletes in the early 1990s the general feeling was that most Olympians were using PEDs. See V Rabinowicz, 'Athletes and Drugs: A Separate Pace' (1992) 25 *Psychology Today* 52.

[177] Ibid 871 citing D Mottram, 'Prevalence of Drug Misuse in Sport' in D Mottram (ed), *Drugs in Sport* 4th edn (London, Routledge, 2005).

[178] Ibid Connor and Mazanov, noting that the rate of temptation among athletes indicated by the Goldman survey suggests that 'if any non-trivial proportion (say, 10%) succumbs, the incidence of PED use in sport may be well above that reported by anti-doping agencies around the world.'

[179] Ibid. See further the interesting anecdote recounted by Savulescu *et al* (n 132) 667 and the observation by Italy's Olympic anti-doping director that in 2003 the amount of EPO sold in Italy outweighed the amount needed for controlled medicinal purposes by a factor of six.

[180] See R Broadbent, 'A Guide to Cheating: Dossier Reveals that Chambers was Fuelled by Drugs Cocktail' *The Times* (London 16 May 2008) Sport 78.

and growth hormone for performance enhancing purposes.[181] He has flagged that not only can athletes easily avoid in-competition testing by properly tapering and clearing their bodies in the weeks beforehand but also that the infrequent nature of out-of-competition testing renders it ineffective.[182]

[**4.66**] Anecdotal support for Conte's claims can be found in a recent autobiography of one of his more enthusiastic clients, the British sprinter Dwain Chambers.[183] In 2006, Chambers completed a two-year suspension after testing positive for the designer steroid THG. His autobiography reflects on that suspension and, although there is a self-serving element to many of his largely unsubstantiated claims on the propensity to dope amongst elite athletes, Chambers does at least appear to give a searingly honest account of why he used PEDs:[184] both the pressure literally to keep up with rivals who were engaging widely in undetected and undetectable doping[185] and to maintain his lucrative sponsorship contracts (Chambers claimed that in 2002 and 2003 he had a £200,000 contract with adidas that had a clause in it which reduced his salary by half if he was no longer ranked in the world top three in his main sprint events). His comments also put in stark contrast the challenges facing the current regime because as Chambers reveals, despite having taken more than 300 cocktails of various PEDs in his first year under Conte's regime, he had tested negatively on 10 separate occasions in 2002. Further, he outlines how easy it was to avoid out-of-competition testers over the winter season and it appears that he was caught in 2003 only because, unbeknown to him, the BALCO scandal had helped sports authorities develop a test for THG. It can be implied from this that if Chambers had known that the risk of being caught had increased he would have altered his behaviour and moved to another 'undetectable drug' as, presumably, other athletes have, given that Chambers remains the only elite athlete to have tested positive for THG. Moreover, even though he was eventually caught, the length of ban served (the then mandatory two-year ban) still gave Chambers ample

---

[181] For an interesting review of the issues surrounding the use of growth hormone doping in sport see the various contributions to the special issue on 'The Abuse of Growth Hormone in Sport and its Detection: A Medical, Legal and Social Framework' in (2009) 14 *Growth Hormone and IGF Research* 283–412.

[182] See B Gallagher, 'Deadly Cocktail used by Dwain Chambers' *The Daily Telegraph* (London 16 May 2008) Sport 10.

[183] D Chambers, *Race Against Me: My Story* (Valencia, Libros International, 2009). The Conte/Chambers relationship had a small but fundamental part to play in the BALCO scandal (details at n 18) in that it has been alleged that Chambers' increasingly regular and THG-inspired victories over American sprinters (who were availing themselves only of EPO) led to coach Trevor Graham's anonymous tip-off to the US authorities. See R Broadbent, 'Jealousy of Chambers lead to Balco Trial, Claims Conte' *The Times* (London, 15 April 2008) Sport 66.

[184] The genuineness of Chambers account was however later called into question when he admitted that his successful 'comeback' to athletics, culminating in his selection for Britain at the World Athletic Championships in 2009, was due in part to the support give to him by Conte. See R Broadbent, 'Chambers Already Damned by his own Actions' *The Times* (London, 16 March 2009) News 63.

[185] See Galluzi (n 156) 100 who refers to this perception as the 'defacto glass ceiling for drug-free athletes.'

time to resume his career as a professional athlete.[186] Reflecting on the actions and comments of both Conte and Chambers, it is clear that, the risk of grievous long-term bodily harm notwithstanding, the motivation to dope among elite athletes remains high, as do the odds that they will be caught out by the present system of anti-doping administration.[187] The Conte and Chambers revelations reiterate and identify a number of flaws in the current system and prompt the consideration of a radical solution based, not on strict *zero* tolerance of PEDs but *some* tolerance of PEDs as restrained by a pragmatic principle of participant safety.

Flaws in the Strict Approach to PEDs in Sport

[**4.67**] In addition to the Conte/Chambers revelations, three further criticisms can be made of the current, strict approach to the regulation of PEDs in sport: the cost inefficiency of the current system of anti-doping regulation; the diminishing returns from that system in terms of the general public's confidence in it; and the analogies that can be drawn with both the Prohibition era in the US in the 1920s and contemporary policy on the criminalisation of soft drugs.

Cost/Benefit Analysis

[**4.68**] The first flaw in current anti-doping policy is that when the high costs and the exhaustive efforts that must be put into catching drug cheats are set again the low rates of positive tests and the relatively short length of available sanctions, it becomes clear that the strict approach is of such inefficiency that it is unsustainable in the long to medium term. This inefficiency is aggravated by an even simpler equation namely the temptation for athletes to write off the risk of getting caught (low) against the potential rewards (high). Haugen's logical conclusion from these equations is, as he points out in his game theory model of analysis of the issue, that the inherent deficiencies in the current anti-doping system are such that they present athletes with a prisoner's dilemma: although athletes would clearly be better off in a dope free world, the advantages of taking PEDs so outweigh the likelihood of getting caught that the system works to ensure that athletes continue to engage in a 'cheating game'.[188] Moreover, the two most obvious means of redressing the balance—increasing both the chances of getting caught through improved testing mechanisms and the severity of sanction—are hindered by the fact that (a) even the most sensitive of testing is unlikely ever to

---

[186] Under the regulations of the British Olympic Association, Chambers was, despite serving his ban in full, deemed ineligible to represent Britain at the Beijing Olympics in 2008. For background, including the related legal proceedings of *Chambers v British Olympic Committee* [2008] EWHC 2028 (QB), see [2.18]–[2.19].

[187] R Broadbent, 'The Victor Conte Interview: A Lot of Liars are Kicking Dwain and Speaking of Zero Tolerance' *The Times* (London 15 February 2008) Sport 86.

[188] K Haugen, 'The Performance-Enhancing Drug Game' (2004) 5 *Journal of Sports Economics* 67.

be able to stay ahead of advances in genetic enhancement and (b) truly deterrent penalties would have to be as severe as sanctions for grievous crimes, a policy that would be vulnerable to legal challenge and highly questionable in terms of social ethics. This leads Haugen to conclude that in the absence of the consideration of alternative regulatory policies, the current situation is likely to get worse because logically the nearer to zero the chances of getting caught are; then the nearer we get to a situation where *all* athletes will be tempted to cheat.[189]

Diminishing Returns

[**4.69**]   Second, the level of public weariness and cynicism with the issue of drugs in sport is such that even where the drug testers achieve some success it is often met with, at best, a shrug of indifference, or worse, with the feeling that the athlete in question is simply being made a scapegoat for the sins of the sport as a whole.[190] For athletes, the flip side of this weariness and cynicism is that it is now so ingrained in the public's perception that almost every new, extraordinary feat of endurance or speed is met with a level of incredulity founded on an assumption of cheating. Accordingly, athletes encounter a situation where any generalised notion of innocent until proven otherwise is replaced by one of guilt by rumour or association. The most pertinent example of this in world sport is probably that of Lance Armstrong, the seven-time winner of the Tour de France and self-labelled 'most tested athlete in sport', who admitted during his comeback Tour of 2009 that he may never be able to kill off the suspicion that he used PEDs.[191] Similarly, rumour has long surrounded the winner of the 2009 Tour, Spain's Alberto Condator.[192] Contador's 2009 victory was tainted by accusations from a former three-time winner of the Tour, Greg LeMond, who argued that the pace with which the Spaniard claimed the later mountainous part of that Tour's 15th stage required a level of oxygen transportation (the body's ability to absorb and use oxygen) exceeding that of 'any athlete who had ever lived'.[193] According to LeMond, it was up to the Spaniard to prove that his aerobic ability was not supported by PEDs—over and above the considerable demands of the extant doping system in cycling (with which Contador was, and remains, fully compliant).[194]

---

[189] See also Savulescu *et al* (n 132) 666.

[190] See L Donegan, 'In the Court of Public Opinion No One Cares About Dope Cheats' *The Guardian* (London 6 August 2009) Sport 8.

[191] O Slot, 'Climate of Suspicion over Drug Use Proving Hard to Shrug' *The Times* (London 24 July 2009) Sport 76.

[192] Contador was initially caught up in, but ultimately exonerated by, Operation Puerto, an investigation by the Spanish civil authorities into doping in sport. The history of the investigation is outlined in exhaustive detail by *Cyclingnews* at http://autobus.cyclingnews.com/news.php?id=news/puerto_complete.

[193] G LeMond, 'Prove to me that we can believe in you' *Le Monde* (Paris 23 July 2009).

[194] Rumour also surrounded the surprise fourth place finish in the 2009 Tour by Britain's Bradley Wiggins leading him to release the findings of all his blood tests since 2007. See D McCrae, 'Interview with Bradley Wiggins' *The Guardian* (London, 4 August 2009) Sport 6.

Sport's Prohibition Era

[**4.70**]   The third flaw resonates with the debates in criminal law and criminology as to when an activity may or may not be criminalised by way of punitive paternalistic-based legislation. The general thrust of this argument is that prohibitory, criminal legislation is not justified if it will lead to more harm than good. Although all criminal legislation carries with it some undesirable side effects (such as the increased surveillance of certain groups or even the conviction of some innocent people), where the side effects of proposed legislation can be adjudged to be so serious and/or extensive that they more than offset any good the new statute might produce, then criminalisation of the activity cannot be justified.[195] Translating this into the debate on drugs in sport, the question is whether the current policy of proscription is producing a state of affairs preferable to that which existed before? For many the answer to that question is a qualified no in the sense that, although the current system is said to be underpinned by paternalistic concerns for the health and safety of participants, the system's inefficiencies are such that it is directing a significant number of athletes to seek out underground means of sourcing PEDs where the medical controls are negligible or non-existent. There are two significant problems associated with that secretive environment. First, because is it unregulated it can lead to athletes administering PEDs 'in doses that are commensurate with the amount of performance gain they wish to attain, rather than the doses that can be considered "safe"'.[196] Second, when a doping method or substance becomes detectable, the pattern is such that athletes shift the margins to the very extreme and often seek out substances or methods that are at such an early experimental stage that they have even higher potential health risks. Accordingly, it is argued that the current approach to PEDs in sport portrays paternalism at its coercive worst because, in reality, one of its principal consequences is that some athletes are placing themselves at a much higher risk of sustaining grievous harm or even death.[197]

[**4.71**]   In light of the above, it is argued that future sports historians might well look back at the current era of the prohibition of PEDs in sport in the same way as legal historians view the prohibition of alcohol era in the US.[198] By the

---

[195] Law Commission of England and Wales, 'Criminal Law—Consent in the Criminal Law' (Law Com, CP 139, 1995) 277.

[196] Savulescu *et al* (n 132) 669.

[197] Moreover, as the BALCO scandal demonstrates (details at n 18), by sourcing dope in such a manner, these athletes are also liable to become involved in secondary criminality such as money laundering.

[198] In 1920, the Eighteenth Amendment to the US Constitution sought to prohibit the manufacture and sale of intoxicating liquor. It was widely ignored; inspired a robust underground trade in alcohol; and was associated with much secondary criminality, leading to its inevitable repeal in 1933. It has been long used as an example of the flaw in paternalistic/moralistic driven legalisation. See further K Murchison, *Federal Criminal Law Doctrines: The Forgotten Influence of National Prohibitions* (Durham, NC, Duke University Press, 1994).

1930s, it was quickly realised by the authorities in the US that prohibition actually aggravated the problem (alcohol abuse) it sought to eradicate because the policy carried its own intrinsic public health harms. Crucially, by prohibiting a substance that was already in high demand, prohibition merely promoted a 'black' market in alcohol, which famously was associated with much secondary criminality but also, because the quality of alcohol was unregulated, meant that the incidence of death from alcohol poisoning actually rose.[199] As has been illustrated in the preceding sections, similar concerns may attach to the prohibition of PEDs in sport thus condemning the policy to criticism that it is a wrongheaded, unsustainable, cosmetic exercise based on a misguided and misapplied sense of sporting moralism that ignores the reality of the motivations of, and pressures upon, contemporary, competitive sports participants.

[**4.72**]   In a more contemporary sense, criticism of the current approach to PEDs reflects much of the criticism that surrounds the continuing policy on the criminalisation of so-called 'soft' drugs in the UK and Europe.[200] Here, a number of commentators such as O'Mahony have highlighted the 'seductive folly' that is proscription, which, they claim, has failed to stem the rising demand for, and supply of, recreational drugs and has thus facilitated organised crime.[201] O'Mahony argues for a limited and balanced abandonment of the current policy, which relies almost exclusively on the criminal law and interdiction, in favour of a pragmatic 'harm reductionist' policy based on public health concerns.[202] This policy appears to be twofold in nature combining a medical rationale and an educational rationale. The first rationale highlights that the current situation, whereby many deaths result from the use of drugs of unknown purity, could be transformed by the introduction of strict and ubiquitous quality control of drugs. The second rationale holds that the current disbelief and openly scornful response to prohibitionist propaganda among the younger population in particular could be countered by education and prevention based on a factual, consistent and less condemnatory approach.[203] In this, O'Mahony concludes that the 'abolition of drugs prohibition promises to create a more civilised society and a generally more informed and responsible attitude towards mood-altering substances'.[204] Although it is unlikely to replace the current approach to the 'war on drugs' in western societies, the approach of O'Mahony and others

---

[199] See T Coffey, *The Long Thirst: Prohibition in America, 1920-1933* (New York, Norton, 1975) 196–98.

[200] For a genealogy of the governance of the 'drugs problem' over the past two centuries see generally T Seddon, *A History of Drugs: Drugs and Freedom in the Liberal Age* (London, Routledge-Cavendish, 2009).

[201] P O'Mahony, *The Irish War on Drugs: The Seductive Folly of Prohibition* (Manchester, Manchester University Press, 2008).

[202] O'Mahony's approach is summarised succinctly and favourably in a review by T Murphy (2009) 49 *British Journal of Criminology* 425.

[203] O'Mahony (n 201) 228.

[204] Ibid 230.

like him has recently found favour in influential sectors of the current UK and US administrations.[205]

Implementing *Safety* Liability not *Strict* Liability

[**4.73**]   Could a harm reductionist approach work in the context-specific area of PED abuse in sport? This sub-section considers just such a proposal made separately by a number of commentators who suggest that, rather than striving repressively for the eradication of doping in elite sport, which appears to be an unattainable goal, sports authorities should implement a 'harm reductionist' policy predicated ultimately on participant safety. Five elements of the proposal are reviewed: its jurisprudential basis; its ethical and moral premise; how it might work; whether it might be contemplated by sports authorities in the immediate; and how it might shape future debates on the issue.

Harm Reduction

[**4.74**]   On the first point, the harm-reductionist proposal is a clear illustration of what has been described as soft paternalism, which can, in terms of the criminal law, be defined as the right of the state to prevent self-regarding harmful conduct when but only when that conduct is either a result of a coerced, substantially non-voluntary choice or is clearly an uniformed, irrational choice, and including any temporary intervention necessary to establish whether the conduct might be voluntary or rational.[206] Put simply, and with due deference to the brief of this text, strict or hard paternalism would, for example, advocate the total prohibition of smoking because of the dangers and harms arising from active and passive smoking. Soft paternalism holds that it is better to avoid such a coercive approach, which may in any event be impossible to implement, and to seek to steer or coax people away from smoking through initiatives such as warnings on cigarette packs; punitive taxation; public health/education campaigns, controlled spaces; and by making available various non-judgemental, government sponsored resources such as counselling services.

[**4.75**]   As can be seen from the above example, soft paternalism advocates both an attempt to understand why individuals are addicted to an ostensibly dangerous practice and, taking account of that understanding, provides people with the opportunity to avail themselves of welfare-promoting initiatives without eliminating their freedom of choice. Soft paternalists argue that such an alternative approach eventually provides a more lasting solution to the 'short-termism' of a coercive, repressive policy, which merely attends to the *consequences* of such

[205]   See G Fields, 'White House Czar Calls for 'End to War on Drugs" *The Wall Street Journal* (New York, 14 May 2009) Section A, 3 and the report by the UK Drug Policy Commission, *Refocusing Drug Related Law Enforcement to Address Harms* (London, UKDPC, 2009) available to download at www.ukdpc.org.uk/reports.shtml.
[206]   Paraphrasing Feinberg (n 112) vol 3, 12.

harmful activity.[207] In this, soft paternalism not only blunts the shaper edges of hard paternalistic solutions, it also appeals to the pragmatic or humanist side of liberalism. When it comes to the issue of PED-abuse in sport, the challenge for the soft paternalist is to design an alternative approach that seeks to reconcile the harshness of proscription and the callousness of deregulation. Adapting an approach that has been spoken about elsewhere, this reconciliation should, it is suggested, be driven primarily by a desire to lay down a clear, sports-specific morality on PED-taking that is both ethical in its conception and pragmatic in its application.[208]

Changing the Moral and Ethical Framework of the Debate on PEDs

[**4.76**]   An understanding of soft paternalism—in approach and desired out-come—provides an understanding of the position taken by Savulescu, Kayser and others who advocate the controlled use of PEDs in sport.[209] Savulescu and Kayser reiterate many of the points made previously as to the inherent flaws in current anti-doping policy namely that it performs badly on a cost/benefit analy-sis; that it is rigidly based on a platform of moral fundamentalism; and that it might in consequence be endangering the health and lives of athletes.[210] Without over-interpreting their analysis, Savulescu and Kayser argue that these flaws have corroded the credibility of existing anti-policy to the point that the agenda in the 'war' against drugs in sport is actually being set by doping athletes and their coaches to the detriment of all athletes and sport.[211] Put simply, Savulescu and Kayser contend that the pursuit of doping athletes, as currently constituted, is a race that sports administrators cannot win and that not only should they stop try-ing to 'chase the cheaters' but they should also radically change the conditions of the race itself from one premised on strict liability to one based on the principle of participant safety.

[**4.77**]   Both commentators also highlight a point that has not been alluded to thus far namely that a key ethical presumption in the fight against drugs in sport—that a sporting achievement should in the spirit of fair play reflect the participant's natural athletic capacity—is vulnerable to rebuttal. In arguing the sporting success is very much 'a genetic lottery', Savulescu opines that 'sport discriminates against the genetically unfit. Sport is the province of the genetic

---

[207] Liberals from Mill to Feinberg have long recognised the occasional need for soft paternalistic initiatives. For examples see C Sunstein and R Thaler, 'Libertarian Paternalism in not an Oxymoron' (2003) 70 *University of Chicago Law Review* 1159.

[208] McGlynn and Ward (n 141) 338.

[209] Kayser *et al* (n 126); Savulescu *et al* (n 132).

[210] Ibid Kayser *et al* (n 126) who cite research suggesting that the 'black market' in PEDs has seen dangerous practices emerge such as the sharing of needles, a point corroborated recently by an Australian study. See B Larance *et al*, 'Injecting Risk Behaviour and Related Harm Among Men Who Use Performance and Image Enhancing Drugs' (2008) 27 *Drug Alcohol Review* 679.

[211] See also S Barnes, 'Time to Kick the Habit of Drug Obsession' *The Times* (London, 9 March 2009) Sport 67.

elite (or freak)'.[212] In this, Savulescu highlights the story of the Finnish skier, and multiple Olympian gold medallist in the 1960s, Eero Maentyranta, whose success was in part attributable to the fact that he had a 'natural' genetic mutation that meant that his blood delivered 40–50 per cent more oxygen to the muscles than the average. More modern examples would include that of Spanish cyclist Miguel Indurain who won the Tour de France on five occasions in the 1990s and who, it is claimed, had a lung capacity of eight litres compared to an average of six and, of course, Lance Armstrong, who won the Tour seven times with a heart that is thought to be 30 per cent larger than average.[213] Accordingly, Savlescu questions the 'fairness' of having to compete, for instance, with the legendary Australian swimmer Ian Thorpe, the winner of five Olympic gold medals, and who was reputed to have size 17 feet, giving him an advantage available to no other swimmer, no matter how intensely they trained.[214]

[**4.78**] In a similar vein, Kayser holds that the 'anchoring of today's anti-doping regulations in the notion of fair-play is misguided' because it fails to allow for the reality of widespread biological inequality.[215] Moreover, Kayser observes that, in addition to genetics, 'several other contingent facts about athletes' circumstances fail to be reflected adequately in the current ethical framework of anti-doping'; for instance, environmental inequality. By this, Kayser means that depending on the nationality and sports speciality of an athlete there may be gross inequality in their 'access to care, supervision and high quality medical and technological supervision.' Consequently, Kayser suggests that 'from the perspective of equality, supervised doping practice is likely to provide the greater prospect of ensuring equality of competition,' rather than the undeserved inequalities of the extant policy which is based on genetic capacity. But how might this supervised, controlled scheme work?

How Might the Softly/Safety Liability Approach Work?

[**4.79**] Savulescu suggests that, 'If a drug does not expose an athlete to excessive risk, we should allow it even if it enhances performance'.[216] In this, commentators such as Savulescu and Kayser want us to consider a situation where the sole limit on the use of PEDs in sport is one of safety to the extent that future anti-doping policy should exclude athletes only on the basis of whether they are healthy enough to compete. The practical repercussions of this approach would be that current prohibitions on the use of certain drugs would be abolished

[212] Savulescu *et al* (n 132) 667.

[213] See J Elliot, 'What makes a Great Tour Rider?' *BBC News Online* 6 July 2007 available at http://news.bbc.co.uk/1/hi/health/6273202.stm.

[214] J Savulescu and B Foddy, 'Good Sport, Bad Sport' *The Age* (Melbourne 3 August 2004) A3, 4. Similar claims surround the physiology of swimmer Michael Phelps. See P McMullen, 'Measure of a Swimmer' *The Baltimore Sun* (Baltimore 9 March 2004) available at www.baltimoresun.com/sports/olympics/bal-sp.phelps09mar09,0,7665681.story?coll=bal-sports-olympics.

[215] Citations in this paragraph are taken from Kayser *et al* (n 126).

[216] Savulescu *et al* (n 132) 670.

entirely though others, for example certain forms of anabolic steroids, would remain proscribed given the well-established dangers involved. For a number of other doping methods—Savulescu uses the example of EPO—the system would be designed around permitting medically supervised 'doping' up to a prescribed 'safe' level.[217] Without reiterating the points made previously, it is claimed that this safety-driven approach has five significant advantages over the current anti-doping scheme relating to: greater equity among participants; the ethical position of sports physicians; an athlete's informed consent in taking a PED; the easing of current administrative burdens and legal vulnerabilities; and greater flexibility in dealing with future administrative burdens and legal vulnerabilities.

[**4.80**]   First, the Savulescu-Kayser model seeks to addresses the inequities and deficiencies of the current system that exist in terms of genetics and environment and which can also result in honest and less well-resourced athletes having to miss out on the advantages that 'cheaters enjoy'.[218] Second, given the physical demands and psychological pressures of elite sport and given the dangers inherent in the unsupervised secretive taking of unregulated PEDs by individual athletes, the controlled use of PEDs, it is argued, can be reconciled with (even demanded by) the fundamental medico-ethical principles on intervention that apply to all health professionals. Third, although it is admitted that this change in policy would be likely to result in an increase in the use of PEDs, there would be a number of associated benefits principally that the transparent nature of controlled, medically supervised doping would ensure that an athlete's consent to taking PEDs would be better informed and he or she could not, as in the past, be vulnerable to exploitation by overly demanding coaches or state-mandated doping programmes. In a secondary sense, the idea here is that current policy promotes a cheating game between the testers and athletes that ratchets up the level of dangers faced by athletes as they move increasingly towards the margins of undetectable doping. Medically supervised doping would, it is claimed, not only stop this spiral but could lead to a clearer epidemiology of what is dangerous and what is not. Fourth, it would ease significantly the administrative and legal burdens associated with anti-doping schemes on sports bodies by, for example, undermining the problems resulting currently from false positives and the rigidity of the policy of strict liability. On the latter, Savulescu explains succinctly how its associated problems might be circumvented: 'when we exclude athletes only on the basis of whether they are healthy enough to compete, the question of responsibility and liability becomes irrelevant. Accidental or unwitting consumption of a risky drug is still risky; the issue of good faith is irrelevant'.[219] The fifth advantage is that the safety driven approach might have the flexibility to deal with the challenges that will be presented by the application of genetic technologies; the argument being that so long as they are proven to be safe, sport

---

[217] Ibid 668.
[218] Ibid.
[219] Ibid 670.

should not be afraid to embrace these progressive technologies and the biological manipulation they entail.[220]

Might the Softly/Safety Approach Work Ever be Contemplated?

[**4.81**]   To put it bluntly, it would take a Kuhnian paradigm shift in current thinking on PEDs in sport, if the Savulescu-Kayser proposal was even to be considered.[221] Apart from the established paternalistic concerns regarding the health of athletes and the spirit of sport, the Savulescu-Kayser proposal can be opposed on five grounds. First, proponents of the current approach argue that the value of certain human achievements is intrinsic to the means by which they are attained and that sporting achievements fall into this category.[222] This means that society generally values a sporting endeavour as a task that tests the combination of a participant's innate athletic capacity and skills allied to hard work and rewards the successful application of both. Thus, while the use of robotic equipment to perform surgery more efficiently or safely is clearly to be welcomed, the unrestricted use of technological enhancement in sport would mean that our future enjoyment of elite sport would become, in effect, robotic in nature. This, truly, is not in the 'spirit' of sport, nor is it really 'sport' at all. Equally, the argument goes that if the unrestricted use of gene transfer technology were permitted, the sporting public would hardly derive much satisfaction or enjoyment from watching 'bionic' or 'designer' men and women competing on the track or in the pool. Biegler puts it well when he observes, 'By allowing athletes to use performance-enhancing drugs we are not just altering the means, *but what it means*, to reach the top in sport. What does that mean for sports fan? Staying away'.[223]

[**4.82**]   The second reason to oppose any consideration of the Savulescu-Kayser proposal is that while many contact sports, such as boxing and rugby, contain physical-harm risks, those risks are qualitatively difference from doping risks because the former are intrinsic to, and a necessary part of, competing in such sports. In other words, the assumption of the risks associated with doping is an unnecessary one and thus can be opposed. The third point of opposition to Savulescu-Kayser attacks a central part of that proposal—its ethical premise. In seeking to eliminate the unfairness of the so-called genetic

---

[220]   See generally T Tannsjo, 'Medical Enhancement and the Ethos of Elite Sport' in J Savulescu and N Bostrom (eds), *Human Enhancement* (Oxford, Oxford University Press, 2009).

[221]   In November 2009, the General Assembly of the International Equestrian Federation's voted to introduce a so-called 'progressive' list of substances, which, in effect, permitted the controlled use of certain named drugs (mainly non-steroidal anti-inflammatories). The reaction, especially in Europe, was hugely negative. See, eg, P Cuckson, 'Aachen Organisers set for Showdown with FEI over Vote to Allow Drugs' *Daily Telegraph* (London 26 November 2009) Sport 17 and J MacArthur, 'Badminton Director Joins Row over New Drug Rules' *The Times* (London 1 December 2009) Sport 70. The FEI has since delayed the implementation of this 'progressive list'. See P Cuckson, 'FEI in Climbdown' *Daily Telegraph* (London 7 December 2009) Sport 27.

[222]   See P Biegler, 'Drugs do Enhance Performance—but it's just not Sport' *The Age* (Melbourne 5 August 2004) News, Letters 14.

[223]   Ibid, italics inserted.

and environmental 'lottery' that is contemporary sport, the Savulescu-Kayser proposal fails however to engage with two counterpoints. By permitting the use, controlled or otherwise, of PEDs and genetic or biological enhancements, the Savulescu-Kayser proposal would probably result in a glaring inequality in that athletes from richer countries, backed by sophisticated government-funded sports programmes, would be able to avail themselves of such drugs and technologies more easily than those from developing countries. Is this not an aggravated unfair advantage? On a slightly different note, if all contemporary elite athletes were to take PEDs then, presumably, exactly the same differences in athletic performance would remain but 'just at a slightly difference position on the bell curve' of sporting performance.[224] Logically, it follows that if the Savulescu-Kayser proposal were to realise its objective it would have to implement a policy that would promote PEDs for the weakest and deny them to the strongest. Not only would this handicapping system, to use a horseracing analogy, be impractical to implement but this type of 'flat' equality sits uncomfortably with the nature of human sport, which is one that thrives on the drama associated with the multi-dimensional differences between the physical and psychological capacities of competitors.[225]

[**4.83**]   The fourth concern about the Savulescu-Kayser proposition highlights that the proposal underplays certain crucial parts of the workings of current anti-doping policy and would over-cater for a minority number of athletes. In this, critics of the current approach tend to both over-emphasise the harsh, rigid and fundamentally moralistic basis of the current approach (as manifested in the principle of strict liability) and underplay the current system's flexibilities (notably the discretions in sanctioning provided by article 10 WADC). In fact, proponents of the current approach might well wish that anti-doping policy were as rigid as its critics make out, given that the above provisions are now the most recurrent form of claims made to the CAS by those contesting anti-doping suspensions. Not only can it be said that critics of the current anti-doping scheme underplay its workings, they also can be said to overly generalise in their analysis of the values and motivations of elite athletes who are subject to that scheme. For instance, advocates of the controlled use of PEDs fail to address the following probable consequence of such as policy: although a number of athletes might initially at least, still choose not to avail themselves of PEDs; in time, the majority would probably have to in order to remain competitive. As stated already, this choice is not really a free or voluntary one and is, in effect, coercive in nature. In this light, the

---

[224] Ibid.
[225] See further Carolan (n 173) 7–9. See also L Morgan, 'Enhancing Performance in Sport: What is Morally Permissible' in J Boxill (ed) *Sport Ethics: An Anthology* (London, Blackwell, 2002). There are two other pieces in the Boxill collection that also conclude that banning PED use in sport is justified: R Simon, 'Good Competition and Drug Enhanced Performance' and M Lavin, 'Sport and Drugs: Are the Current Bans Justified?'.

Savulescu-Kayser model underestimates the value that modern athletes put in current anti-doping policy's adherence to maintaining fair play and the spirit of sport such that whatever the constraints of the current system are, in terms of personal autonomy, they are clearly offset by a policy that might, effectively, coerce them into taking PEDs.[226] In sum, the Savulescu-Kayser proposal underestimates both modern athletes' commitment to fair play as sport's universal, immutable virtue and their genuine attempts to abide by the rules that seek to give expression to that virtue not only because it is in their mutual interest to do so, but also for the very simple reason that 'them's the rules'. What is meant by this final point is that, outside of doping regulation, all athletes operate in an intensively rule bound environment and although athletes regularly bend, break and even ignore individual rules, the 'probity' of the system as a whole is bound together by athletes' recognition of the mutual benefits of adhering to a generalised notion of 'systematic restraint'. [227]

[**4.84**]   Fifth, the Savulescu-Kayser proposal proclaims to be a response to the 'climate of cheating' that surrounds and corrodes current anti-doping policy such that its controlled use approach can be seen as a pragmatic attempt 'to draft sporting rules to which athletes are willing to adhere'.[228] The previous section noted that the idea that athletes are unwilling to adhere to the current approach is debatable. In addition, there is no guarantee that even if the current policy of zero tolerance is amended to one of a safety-based tolerance for PEDs, all athletes will abide by the amended regulations. Whether the standard is set as near to zero as is therapeutically possible or is extended to a health and safety-based standard, it is clear that some athletes will continues to exploit any administrative, medical or legal loopholes that might surround that standard. For many, the most damning indictment of the Savulescu-Kayser proposal is that even though a safety based model is used in professional cycling—by establishing a safe EPO-related percentage of the blood that may comprise of oxygen rich red blood cells—the sport continues to be bedevilled by doping-related scandals.[229] In this light, the fundamental criticism of the Savulescu-Kayser proposal is that it both panders to the minority of athletes who, under current anti-doping policy are clearly cheating, and might be the thin edge of the wedge that eventually transforms elite sport into a pharmaceutical-infused charade. In sum, the danger is that by embracing a PED ethos, even to a controlled extent, sport as we know and enjoy it will eventually be overwhelmed by that 'ethos'.[230]

---

[226] See further N Eber, 'The Performance-Enhancing Drug Game Reconsidered: A Fair Play Approach' (2008) *Journal of Sports Economics* 318 and, more generally, R Simon, *Fair Play and the Ethics of Sport*, 2nd edn (Oxford, Westview Press, 2004) ch 4.

[227] See Carolan (n 173) 43.

[228] Savulescu *et al* (n 132) 669.

[229] See, for instance, J Macur, 'Italian Cyclist is Suspended after Testing Positive for Blood Booster at Giro' *The New York Times* (New York 23 July 2009) Section B, Sport 15.

[230] See also Houlihan, *Dying to Win* (n 3) 137, 'the low ethical standards of others provides no justification for lowering one's own.'

The Savulescu-Kayser Model: the Way Forward?

[**4.85**]   Finally, and from the luxury of an academic's perspective, the Savulescu-Kayser proposal is of residual interest if only because it provokes a debate on the ethical premise of current anti-doping policy.[231] This is to be welcomed because, as Houlihan has highlighted, the discourse on doping in sport has largely ignored this aspect of the debate and has concentrated principally on the ways in which the *consequences* of doping might be deterred through the harmonisation of the administrative response to doping.[232] In short, the conversation on the ethical parameters of current anti-doping policy initiated by Savulescu, Kayser and others is one that international sports organisations have only partially engaged with. Given the challenges presented by gene transfer and other biomedical technologies, it is a conversation that really should continue and deepen. Moreover, from a general jurisprudential viewpoint, the safety based approach appeals for two reasons. First, while the occasional overzealousness of the current 'war' of PEDs in sport is understandable it is also, at times, self-defeating. Its absolutism and its moral rigidity means that like many other institutional crusades it is bound to encounter (and sets itself up for) frequent disappointment, which leads only to further demoralisation and even cynicism. The Savulescu-Kayser proposal might be said to lower the ethical standards expected of athletes but it does so in a pragmatic way that seeks to transfers the disappointment of being found to have used unsafe PEDs or risky levels of PEDs onto the athlete and not the sport. Second, by disentangling anti-doping regulations from their burdensome association with the 'spirit' of sport and by focussing on a paramount concern for the health and well-being of athletes, the Savulescu-Kayser proposal renders the administration of these regulations less vulnerable to legal challenge based, for instance, on claims that they dogmatically and/or disproportionally punitive in nature.

[**4.86**]   In final summary of this debate, while the radical pragmatism of the Savulescu-Kayser proposal is in many respects appealing to this author, some reticence in embracing it remains. These reservations relate to the fact that in at least three of its aspects the principles underpinning the proposal lack maturity.[233] First, it must be remembered that the debate on doping in sport operates in an empirical vacuum wherein the true epidemiology of doping in sport is unknown. This means that outside of anecdotal evidence, both the percentage of athletes that are using prohibited PEDs and their motivations for doing

---

[231] See the support for this call for debate in B Kayser and A Smith, 'Globalisation of Anti-Doping Policy: The Reverse Side of the Medal' (2008) 337 *British Medical Journal* a584.

[232] See generally Houlihan, 'Anti-doping Policy in Sport' (n 3).

[233] These reservations also apply to other 'radical' approaches such as that of G Rapp, 'Blue Sky Steroid' (2009) 99 *Journal of Criminal Law and Criminology* 599 who suggests, at 602, 'Rather than ban certain substances and test for them (or their masking agents) sports leagues should simply call for all players to disclose all "non-food" substances put into their bodies. Penalties would exist not for using drugs per se, but only for failing to disclose accurately those substances used.'

so, remain a matter of contention.[234] It may very well be that when this difficult research is carried out the underlying pragmatism of Savulescu-Kayser will be vindicated (and then considered) but at present judgement on the proposal must be reserved until definitive research exists on the true incidence of doping in sport. The second reservation relates to the fact that, while the Savulescu-Kayser proposal doubtless prompts a much needed debate, it does little more than sketch the mechanics of how this alternative might actually work. Would, for instance, some sort of drug licensing regime have to be introduced to regulate safe levels of PED use? Could the current therapeutic use exemption process be replaced by a safety use exemption process that could be known, delightfully, as the SUE process? How would the safety of participants be monitored? Could it be that athletes might still be required to maintain biological passports? And what role, if any, would WADA have in this?

[4.87]   On the last point, it appears reasonable to suggest that the Savulescu-Kayser proposal could transform WADA into, in effect, a global sports-focussed drugs and healthcare regulatory agency whose primary responsible would be to protect athletes by assuring the safety, efficacy and security of PEDs and biological methods and to advance athletes' health by helping them obtain the accurate, science-based information they need to use such drugs and methods in order to improve their performance in a controlled and safe environment.[235] This might be an interesting approach to take with WADA but it needs further consideration as does the confidence that underpins Savulescu-Kayser view that their alternative can rest flexibly on the controlled use of safe levels of PEDs. Unfortunately, the experiment with such an approach in professional road cycling illustrates that not only is the definition of a 'safe level of use' a malleable and contentious issue in sports medicine, it is also one that appears to lend itself to just as many administrative and legal loopholes as the present approach. Again, the problem here with the Savulescu-Kayser proposal (and the manner of its implementation in cycling) is not with its general thrust and objectives, rather that is needs to surround its safety-led approach with a more holistic regulatory framework including education and sanction-led initiatives. In short, the Savulescu-Kayser proposal would need to further integrate a sophisticated range of education programmes tailored separately at youth, amateur and elite sports participants. Concentrating on elite athletes (as the debate on doping in sport largely does) carries a twofold danger of not only overcompensating for those few athletes who reach that level, it also fails to recognise that it may be too late at that point to address the inculcated ethos

---

[234] Some recent research has begun this process. See A Petroczi and E Aidman, 'Psychological Drivers in Doping: the Life-cycle Model of Performance Enhancement' (2008) 3 *Substance Abuse Treatment, Prevention and Policy* published online at www.substanceabusepolicy.com/content/3/1/7 and A Petroczi, E Aidman and T Nepusz, 'Capturing Doping Attitudes by Self-Report Declarations and Implicit Assessment: A Methodolgy Study' (2008) 3 *Substance Abuse Treatment, Prevention and Policy* published online at www.substanceabusepolicy.com/content/3/1/9.

[235]   The sentence paraphrases the mission statement of the US Food and Drug Administration available online through www.fda.gov.

of drug abuse in any meaningful way. In addition, any proposal on the controlled use of PEDs in sport would need to consider greater cooperation with state and regulatory authorities regarding the supply of risky or unsafe products to sport participants by those pharmaceutical companies who 'appear to be indifferent to the misuse of their products by athletes for non-medical purposes'.[236]

[**4.88**]   In both of these regards, a useful analogy is to be found in the nuanced manner in which the Portuguese authorities have, since 2001, effected a policy that decriminalises all drugs, including cocaine and heroin.[237] The introduction of the policy was objected to forcefully by opponents who claimed that it would have an adverse effect on drug usage rates in Portugal. Almost a decade later, these fears have not been realised—drug usage rates remain at roughly the same pre-2001 level—and a political consensus in Portugal now protects the 2001 provision. The provision decriminalises but does not legalise drug use and seeks to treat infractions for drug possession and usage as administrative violations only leading to mandatory treatment programmes with no attaching criminal sanction. The legislation is underpinned by a 'soft' paternalistic concern for the health and welfare of Portuguese citizens, as supported by provisions that continue to permit the prosecution of drug trafficking as a criminal offence. Although, as stated, drug usage rates remain roughly the same as they were pre-2001, proponents highlight that drug related pathologies—such as sexually transmitted diseases and deaths due to drug use—have apparently decreased dramatically.[238] In many ways, the objectives of the Portuguese initiative are similar to those pursued by the Savulescu, Kayser and others. At this point, one can only speculate whether a Savulescu-Kayser type proposal might work in the context-specific arena that is sport however it is interesting to note that if PED abuse in sport is as virulent as the proponents of current anti-doping policy claim; then they might also remember that the best vaccines often contain elements of the virus they seek to defeat. Similarly, *controlled use* might ultimately prove to be the best way of restricting the *ongoing abuse* of PEDs in sport.

Conclusion

[**4.89**]   According to its website, WADA is working 'towards a vision of the world that values and fosters doping free sport'.[239] The vision is a laudable one and it would be nice to think that at some point in the future doping in sport might be

---

[236]   See T Noakes, 'Should we Allow Performance-Enhancing Drugs in Sport? A Rebuttal to the Article by Savulescu and Colleagues' (2006) 1 *International Journal of Sports Science & Coaching* 289, 289.

[237]   This paragraph is informed by the report by G Greenwald, *Drug Decriminalisation in Portugal: Lessons for Creating Fair and Successful Drug Policies* (Washington DC, Cato Institute, 2009) and 'Treating not Punishing; Portugal's Drug Policy' *The Economist* (London, 29 August 2009) UK Edition, 29.

[238]   The approach received a cautious welcome in the *UN World Drug Report 2009* (Vienna, UNODC, 2009) 168.

[239]   See www.wada-ama.org/en/About-WADA.

regulated by something like the collegial enforcement system or 'code of honour' that apparently governs golf, even at the highest level.[240] Nevertheless, how realistic is it that WADA's vision will ever be realised; especially when it is not unreasonable to argue that the only thing that is really fostered by and valued at the elite level of most sports is a 'win at all costs' mentality? That mentality often results in athletes resorting to proscribed and dangerous substance or methods in order to achieve success. When in the 1990s, in the face of this reality and mentality, the leading sports federations and the IOC finally decided, after decades of equivocation, to engage fully in the 'war' against drugs in sport, their policy was premised on a strict liability approach. Initially, that approach was overly rigid and absolutist in nature. To be fair, WADA has subsequently modified it and the contemporary policy of presumed fault/flexibility of sanction—one that it key to an understanding of how the WADC operates its disciplinary remit—is on any objective assessment a fair, reasonable and legally robust policy.

[**4.90**]   In this, and as noted earlier, concerns that the human rights of athletes were being breached were the catalyst for the modifications to the original strict approach.[241] A close (and final) legal analogy for the revised WADC's presumed fault/ flexibility of sanction approach is with that of the strict liability element to certain UK criminal law statutes governing traffic offences and the question as to whether, since the enactment of the Human Rights Act 1998, these offences might violate Article 6(2) ECHR.[242] Similar to the WADC's approach to doping infractions, these types of provisions—for example, section 5 of the Road Traffic Act 1988—qualify the presumption of innocence by reversing the onus of proof so as to impose a legal or persuasive burden onto the defendant to prove certain stated matters in order to be exonerated from liability. The English courts[243] and the Strasbourg court[244] have now confirmed that Article 6(2) ECHR is restricted to providing procedural protection and does not render the imposition of strict liability incompatible with Article 6(2) ECHR provided the policy of reverse onus of proof is imposed in pursuance of a legitimate (social or economic) aim and is proportionate to the achievement of that aim. Is the prevention of doping in sport a legitimate aim? The key stakeholders in sport clearly think that it is. Is that aim pursued in a proportionate manner? The provisions contained in revised article 10 WADC suggest that it is.[245]

---

[240] See generally E Bird and G Wagner, 'Sport as a Common Property Resource: A Solution to the Dilemmas of Doping' (1997) 41 *Journal of Conflict Resolution* 749.

[241] See [4.21]–[4.27] of this text on the evolving 'modification' of the strict liability approach to anti-doping infractions.

[242] See generally D Ormerod, *Smith and Hogan on Criminal Law: Cases and Materials* 10th edn (Oxford, Oxford University Press, 2009) ch 6. Article 6(2) ECHR reads: 'Everyone charged with a criminal offence shall be presumed innocent until proved guilty according to law.'

[243] See, eg, *Attorney-General's Reference (No 4 of 2002); Sheldrake v Director of Public Prosecutions* [2004] UKHL 43; [2005] 1 AC 264.

[244] See, eg, *Salibiaku v France* (1988) 13 EHRR 379.

[245] It is further suggested that the current WADC approach to anti-doping in sport meets all of the six factors relevant to the justifiability of strict liability provisions noted by I Dennis, 'Reverse Onuses and the Presumption of Innocence' [2005] *Criminal Law Review* 901.

[**4.91**]   Finally, there is little doubt that the 'benevolent paternalism' underpinning the so-called World Anti-Doping Programme will face difficult challenges in the years ahead in the shape of gene manipulation technology, micro-boosting techniques and designer or third generation versions of existing PEDs. Already this has seen a ratcheting of WADA's monitoring and detection mechanisms and the implementation of schemes surrounding the enforcement of the whereabouts rule; the introduction of biological passports for athletes and the retrospective testing of athletes' samples.[246] All of these schemes are likely to encounter legal challenge.[247] The narrow legal surrounds of a doping infraction aside, this chapter has also attempted to demonstrate, as predicated on the paternalism/liberalism dichotomy, that it is also worthwhile to have, on occasion, a debate about the broader ethical dimensions of this topic with a view to assessing the durability and sustainability of the current approach to PEDs in sport.

Further Points of Interest and Discussion

1. The fundamental rationale underpinning the World Anti-doping Code is the protection of the 'spirit of sport'. Given the competitive realities of modern professional sport, do you think that WADC's definition of that 'spirit', and WADA's reliance upon it, is somewhat naïve?
2. The policy of strict liability is more trouble than it's worth for sports authorities in their 'fight' against drugs in sport. Discuss.
3. In the debate on drugs on sport, the 'hard' paternalist says we should ban them; the 'soft' paternalist says we should permit their use but in a regulated fashion; and the liberal says we should neither ban them nor regulate them but simply allow them. Which viewpoint do you support? Give reasons for your answer.
4. Have a class debate on the issue of players being suspended by their clubs for using recreational drugs in their 'private' lives. In your debate, keep in mind the following: that such drugs are not taken for sports performance enhancing purposes; that players are seen as sporting and societal role models; and any legal issues that might arise in initiating or challenging such suspensions. See, for example, the scenarios noted by P Horvarth, 'Anti-Doping and Human Rights in Sport: The Case of the AFL and the WADA Code' (2006) 32 *Monash University Law Review* 357 and S Farrow, 'Drug Testing Under Club Employment Contracts' (2009) 7(8) *World Sports Law Report* 8.

---

[246] See A O'Connor, 'Testers catch out Olympic Champion with Stored Sample' *The Times* (London, 30 April 2009) Sport, 80.

[247] The issue of blood profiling (in effect, the screening of athlete's blood for indications of the use of PEDs), has already reached CAS. See CAS 2009/A/1912 and 1913 *Pechstein v ISU and DESG v ISU* and CAS 2009/A/1931 *Iourieva & Akhatiova v IBU*. Although both appeals by the athletes is question were dismissed, it seems that for now blood profiling of athletes cannot be used as evidence of a doping violation but only in support of a decision to 'target test' an athlete.

5

Criminal Violence In Sport

Introduction

[**5.01**]   To a very large part, the history of contact sports can be written in terms of the regulation of societal violence. The underlying idea of the ancient Olympic Games of Greece was to promote peace and harmony between the various city states. The gladiatorial spectacles of Imperial Rome were a complex mix of fighting contests, manipulation of the mob and political opportunism. Medieval sports law sought to eliminate folk-based, gratuitously violent and alcohol-laden pursuits, such as the early precursor to football, in favour of archery and games useful in 'defence of the realm'. Later, the political frustrations of the emerging urbanised working class of mid-nineteenth century Britain would need to be controlled and channelled elsewhere and thus the half-day on Saturdays promoted by the Factories Acts led not only to the tradition of the 3pm kick-off for football matches, it also served an important societal function that can be located in the etymological root of the word 'sport'—that of a 'diversion'.[1] Historically then, the social utility of sport, and contact sports in particular, can, to some extent, be seen as cathartic in nature. In sociological terms, the evolution of contact sports from riotous, expressive forms of violence to the 'rational recreations' of today is seen as an illustration of a general 'civilising process'—described previously in chapter one of this text—wherein the rawness of medieval attitudes to personal aggression can be contrasted to the (apparently) more sophisticated norms of modernity.[2] Finally, and in term of sports psychology, an important part of the backdrop—but only a backdrop—to this chapter is an acknowledgement that what athletes perceive as the nature and boundary of 'legitimate' physical aggression in their

---

[1] For an introduction to this thematic approach to the history of sport see generally D Brailsford, *Sport and Society: Elizabeth to Anne* (London, Routledge & Keegan Paul, 1969); J Carter, *Medieval Games: Sports and Recreations in Feudal Society* (New York, Greenwood Press, 1992); R Holt, *Sport and the British: A Modern History* (Oxford, Clarendon Press, 1989); M Poliakoff, *Combat Sports in the Ancient World: Competition, Violence and Culture* (New Haven, Yale University Press, 1987); and R Malcolmson, *Popular Recreations in English Society, 1700–1850* (Cambridge, Cambridge University Press, 1979).

[2] See the text at section [1.16] and more generally N Elias, *The Civilizing Process* (Oxford, Blackwell, 1994) and N Elias and E Dunning, *The Quest for Excitement: Sport and Leisure in the Civilizing Process* (Oxford, Blackwell, 1986).

sport, and their motivation for perpetrating aggressive acts on the sports field, is not always easy to deduce.[3] In fact, the case law demonstrates that the demarcation line between 'sanctioned aggression' and 'unsanctioned aggression' in a sport—including acts of 'heat of the moment/red mist/white line fever' anger; acts attributable to a 'win at all costs mentality' within a team, club or sport; or premeditated 'targeted' intimation of opponents (often prompted by coaches); or provocation (by an opponent); or retaliation (to an earlier off-the-ball incident) — is often a malleable one even for the criminal law.[4] In short, this chapter tries to demonstrate that the spontaneity of many contact sports, and their accompanying conventions, ethos or spirit is not always easily translated *from* playing field *to* courtroom.[5]

[**5.02**]   To reiterate, this chapter does not dwell so much on the wider issue as to why athletes commit egregious acts of aggression on the sports field but more on the fact that the ordinary criminal law of assault nods to the above historical and sociological perspectives on violence in sport, including perceptions as to the purported 'playing culture' of an individual contact sport. For instance, and crucially in the context of this chapter, the exemption that contact sports have from the normal threshold of consent—referred to in this chapter as 'implied sporting consent'—in criminal law is rationalised on the basis that such sports have a long established history of self-governance and have a social utility located in their promotion of healthy, community-based activities. An assessment of the above 'exemption' (in the context of contact sports such as rugby, ice hockey and football) is the primary focus of this chapter, and this includes a review of the jurisprudential origins of implied sporting consent, its evolution as a principle and its influence on the current state of the 'law of sports-related assault'. The chapter is generally informed by a comparative approach wherein the experiences of jurisdictions such as England and Wales, Scotland, Ireland, New Zealand

---

[3] See generally J Kerr, *Rethinking Aggression and Violence in Sport* (London, Routledge, 2005) and G Russell, *Aggression in the Sports World: A Social Psychological Perspective* (New York, Oxford University Press, 2008).

[4] Recent scientific research also suggests that, although the literature on the psychological analysis of violence in sport is extensive, there is a lack of empirical data on the incidence of sport-related violence, which works to the detriment of effective sports-related preventative interventions. See S Fields, C Collins and R Cornstock, 'Violence in Youth Sports: Hazing, Brawling and Foul Play' (2010) 44 *British Journal of Sports Medicine* 32. The most interesting empirical study to date was carried out by the National Crime Observatory (OND) in France, which, drawing on data from the French Football Federation, noted that there were 12,000 local and regional weekend matches out of 700,000 where there were incidents of serious physical or verbal abuse in the 2007–2008 playing season. Players were responsible for 90 per cent of the violence, which routinely involved kicking, punching and brawling among opposing groups. Full details of this study are available as Factsheet 33 of the OND's Annual Report of 2008, which is available to download through www.inhesj.fr.

[5] Issues such as the 'moral' acceptance of violence within the general sporting culture and sports-related violence as a broad example of interpersonal violence are beyond the brief of this text but see generally B Bredemier, 'Moral Reasoning and the Perceived Legitimacy of Intentionally Injurious Sports Act' (1985) 7 *Journal of Sport Psychology* 110; S Guilbert, 'Sport and Violence: A Typological Analysis' (2004) 39 *International Review for the Sociology of Sport* 45; and M Smith, *Violence in Sport* (Toronto, Butterworths, 1983).

and those of the US, Australia and Canada are noted. The conclusion gives some consideration as to whether the criminal law is the most suitable means by which to address inter-participant violence in sport. Finally, given that many of the debates that arise in this chapter—consent, assumption of risk, deliberate infliction of harm, intention and the physical exploitation of participants—are at their most intense when assessing the dynamics of the sport of boxing, the legality of that sport is examined as a postscript.

Criminal Liability for On-Field Violence

[**5.03**]   An established pattern is identifiable in the attitude of the major common law jurisdictions towards violence in sport: so long as the internal disciplinary mechanisms of the sport in question are satisfactorily drawn, the police, prosecution services and the criminal courts are reluctant to intervene.[6] That reticence is at its most discernible in the US where the various state authorities have demonstrated a marked reluctance to pursue or prosecute violent events on the field of play.[7] A peculiarly American explanation for this might be that in most states District Attorneys are quasi-elected officials and thus well attuned to the fact that

---

[6] Much of this chapter is informed by the author's previous work on the topic: see J Anderson, 'Citius, Altius, Fortius: A Study of Criminal Violence in Sport' (2000) 11 *Marquette Sports Law Journal* 87; J Anderson, 'Policing the Sports Field: The Role of the Criminal Law' (2005) 5 (2) *International Sports Law Review* 25; and J Anderson, 'No Licence for Thuggery: Violence, Sport and the Criminal Law' [2008] *Crim LR* 751.

[7] For a review of the US perspective on this topic see generally R Horrow, *Sports Violence: The Interaction between Private Law-making and the Criminal Law* (Westport, Conn, Greenwood Pub, 1980). See also, and including mention of the limited number of prosecutions taken for violent play during a sports event, P Anderson, 'When Violence Is Not Part of the Game: Regulating Sports Violence in Professional Team Sports' (1998) 3 *Contemporary Issues in Law* 240; C Clarke, 'Law and Order on the Courts: The Application of Criminal Liability for Intentional Fouls During Sporting Events' (2000) 32 *Arizona State Law Journal* 1149; K Fritz, 'Going to the Bullpen: Using Uncle Same to Strike-Out Professional Sports Violence' (2002) 20 *Cardozo Arts & Entertainment Law Journal* 189; L Hanson and C Dernis, 'Revisiting Excessive Violence in the Professional Sports Arena: Changes in the Past Twenty Years' (1996) 6 *Seton Hall Journal of Sports Law* 127; C Harary, 'Aggressive Play or Criminal Assault? An In-depth Look at Sports Violence and Criminal Liability' (2002) 25 *Columbia Journal of Law & Arts* 197; J Katz, 'From the Penalty Box to the Penitentiary: The People Versus Jesse Boulerice' (2000) 31 *Rutgers Law Journal* 833; C Lassiter, '*Lex Sportiva*: Thoughts Towards a Criminal law of Competitive Contact Sport' (2007) 22 *St John's Journal of Legal Commentary* 35; B Nielsen, Controlling Sports Violence: Too Late for the Carrot; Bring on the Big Stick' (1989) 74 *Iowa Law Review* 681; C Samson, 'No Time like the Present: Why Recent Events Should Spur Congress to Enact a Sports Violence Act' (2005) 37 *Arizona State Law Journal* 949; C Schoenfelder, 'Timeout! Prosecuting Juveniles for Sports-Related Violence and the Effect on Youth Contact Sports' (2001) 22 *Journal of Juvenile Law* 139; J Schuette, 'Adolescent Sports Violence: When Prosecutors Play Referee, Making Criminals out of Child Athletes but are they the Real Culprits?' (2001) 21 *Northern Illinois University Law Review* 514; J Standen, 'The Manly Sports: The Problematic Use of Criminal Law to Regulate Sports Violence' (2009) 99 *Journal of Criminal Law & Criminology* 619; J Yates and W Gillespie, 'The Problem of Sports Violence and the Criminal Prosecution Solution' (2002) 12 *Cornell Journal of Law & Public Policy* 145.

the prosecution of a local sports star might become both 'an unnecessary circus' and not be perceived by the public as the most efficient use of taxpayers' money.[8] In a more general sense, state courts in the US are of the opinion that a convicted player might be seen as a 'scapegoat' for the ill discipline of the sport as a whole. In fact, ever since the high-profile prosecution of professional hockey player, David Forbes, failed in 1975 because of a hung jury,[9] it has proved difficult to convince American juries that the criminal law has a place on the sportsfield.[10]

[5.04]   Similar reasons—an authoritative disciplinary mechanism and a general reticence by prosecution services to view the sportsfield as being within their remit—might explain why in New Zealand prosecutions resulting from violence on the rugby field have, in proportion to the popularity and intensity of the sport in that jurisdiction, been an extremely rare occurrence.[11] One of the few recorded prosecutions is *R v Tevaga*,[12] which concerned a fight during an under-21 rugby union football match involving a number of players from both sides. The defendant stated in evidence that he had reacted to the fact that a team mate was on the ground and being 'attacked' by a member of the opposition. He then ran 25 metres and struck the assailant from the rear with a single blow breaking the opponent's jaw. An assault charge was laid under section 196 of the New Zealand Crimes Act 1961. The defendant's defence of 'defence of another' was rejected, the jury finding him guilty. The defendant was sentenced to four months' periodic detention. Although subsequently he successfully appealed the severity of the sentence—reduced to 100 hours' community service—the New Zealand Court of Appeal stated forcefully that so-called 'off the ball' incidents must be considered 'worse than some assaults committed in the heat of a rugby melee or maul by players fighting. The defendant deliberately ran in and delivered a blow directed in a way which was likely to, and did, cause quite serious injury'.[13]

[5.05]   In Australia, the consensus is that there has been a 'marked reluctance in Australia to invoke the law of criminal assault in relation to sport violence. Most disciplinary action is brought by way of the relevant governing bodies

---

[8] See also the reaction of the Scottish Football Association to conviction of two Glasgow Rangers players on charges of conducting themselves in a disorderly manner and in breach of the peace as a result of a fracas during a game against local rivals Celtic in 1988; J Goodbody, 'Alarm as Rangers Players are Fined' *The Times* (London 16 April 1988).

[9] *State v Forbes*, No 63280 (Minn Dist Ct, 1975). See generally R Binder, 'The Consent Defence: Sports, Violence and the Criminal Law' (1975–6) 13 *American Criminal Law Review* 235.

[10] In contrast, note the results of a nationwide survey of trial judges in the US, which found that three-quarters of them were of the opinion that incidents of 'excessive sports violence' should be handled in the criminal courts; M Barry, R Fox and C Jones, 'Judicial Opinion on the Criminality of Sports Violence in the United States' (2005) 15 *Seton Hall Journal of Sports and Entertainment Law* 1.

[11] See generally P Farugia, 'The Consent Defence: Sports Violence, Sadomasochism and the Criminal Law' (1997) 8 *Auckland University Law Review* 472. See also F Aitkin, 'Defences to Violence in Sports: Why New Zealand's Defences Appear Stronger than the Rest' (2009) 77 *ANZLA Commentator* 22, who asserts that the attitude to prosecuting violence in sport in that country 'is traditionally guided by national pride and an implicit consensus to keep sport out of the courts.'

[12] [1991] 1 NZLR 296.

[13] Ibid 297, Cooke P.

of the sport concerned'.[14] By implication, it is clear that the combination of an established pattern of unacceptably violent behaviour in a sport and an 'indecisive' governing body should attract the attention of the criminal authorities.[15] In the 1990s in the state of Victoria, a number of mass brawls in the sport of Australian Rules football culminated in the conviction of a leading player, Leigh Mathews, for assault occasioning bodily harm, after breaking an opponent's jaw in a game.[16] Dangerous tackles said to be beyond that which are ordinarily incidental in a game of rugby league—head high swinging arms, for instance—have also led to convictions and even custodial sentences.[17] Again though, relative to the popularity of, and participation rates in, sport in Australia the case law on sports violence is of a limited nature.[18] There are two reasons for this. First, several state criminal courts have been careful to reiterate that the criminal law should not confuse the 'risk of injury from hard play ... with the risk of injury from criminal assault'[19] and second the small number of cases 'reflects the fact that disciplinary tribunals [through handing down severe punishments for violent play] are doing a good job in providing internal policing of sport'.[20]

[**5.06**]   Ireland is another jurisdiction where prosecutions of this nature are rare, at least until quite recently.[21] In those limited and sporadic number of prosecutions that have been initiated, and particularly those involving Ireland's most popular sports of Gaelic football and hurling (GAA), the level of cooperation from those within the sport has not always been what it might have been. This seems to be attributable either to a misguided machismo based on the maxim 'what happens on the field, stays on the field' or what might be called an ethos

---

[14] S Bronitt and B McSherry, *Principles of Criminal Law* 2nd edn (Sydney, LBC, 2005) 532.

[15] D Healy, *Sport and the Law* 3rd edn (Sydney, UNSW Press, 2005) 138.

[16] *R v Matthews* Unreported, Victoria Magistrates' Court 13 August 1985, Brian Clothier SM. Matthews was fined Aus$1,000 and bound over to keep the peace for two years; see D Ogden, 'Hawk Fury at Conviction of Matthews' *Courier-Mail* (Brisbane 14 August 1985). Having served less than a year of his good behaviour bond, Matthews' conviction was overturned on appeal; see generally R Connolly, 'Case of Trial and Error—15 June 1985—The Moment that Changed the Game' *Sunday Age* (Melbourne 1 June 1995) Sportsweek, 7. See also *Abbott v The Queen* (1996) 16 WAR 313, 81 A Crim R 55 (Western Australia); *McAveney v Quigley* (1992) 58 A Crim R 457 (South Australia); *Watherson v Woolven* (1988) 139 LSJS 366 (South Australia); and generally H Opie, 'Aussie Rules Player Jailed for Behind-Play Assault' (1996) 6(2) *ANZSLA Newsletter* 3.

[17] See, for instance, *R v Carr* Unreported, New South Wales Criminal Court of Appeal 17 October 1990 and *R v Stanley* Unreported, New South Wales Criminal Court of Appeal 7 April 1995. See generally, D Brown and R Hogg, 'Violence, Masculinity and Sport: Governance and the "Swinging Arm"' (1997) 3 *University of Technology Sydney Review* 129 and D Garnsey, 'Rugby League Player Jailed for On-Field Assault' (1995) 5(2) *ANZSLA Newsletter* 7.

[18] See generally D Thorpe *et al*, *Sports Law* (Melbourne, Oxford University Press, 2009) ch 4.

[19] Australian National Committee on Violence, *Violence: Directions for Australia* (Canberra, Australian Institute of Criminology, 1990) 163–64. See also I Warren, 'Violence, Sport and the Law: A Critical Discussion' in D Hemphill (ed), *All Part of the Game: Violence and Australian Sport* (Melbourne, Walla Walla Press, 1998).

[20] C Davies, 'Criminal Law and Assaults in Sport: An Australian and Canadian Perspective' (2006) 30 *Criminal Law Journal* 151, 155.

[21] See P McCutcheon, 'Sports Violence, Consent and the Criminal Law' (1994) 45 *NILQ* 267, 271–72.

of 'sporting omertà' whereby members of individual sports communities appear reluctant to give evidence in criminal investigations (save as character witnesses for the accused!).[22] Manifestations of sporting omertà are not confined to Irish sport. For instance in its Annual Report of 1987 the (then) Criminal Injuries Compensation Board (CICB), although noting that applications from blameless victims of 'sporting' crimes had increased in Britain, also reported that a feature of such applications was that in many cases, and as required by the terms of this state compensation scheme, no accompanying report had been made to the police, to the detriment of the application.[23] Admittedly, although there is no formal evidence to underpin such a claim, might such 'reticence' be evidence of 'sporting omertà'?[24] More recently, in 2005, when the Crown Prosecution Service organised a conference with leading police officers, barristers and judges regarding the 'criminality' of on-field violence, a Premiership referee was refused permission to speak at the conference, prompting a CPS spokesperson to compare the decision by football's governing bodies not to send speakers to the silence within Asian communities over 'honour' crimes.[25]

[5.07]   The dynamics underpinning this omertà phenomenon are still to be assessed in any detail and for now they remain an underlying element in the debate about the general appropriateness of the law of criminal assault to matters of sporting violence and the 'playing culture' of the sport in question. Returning to the GAA, in 2004 the publicity given to the prosecution of a well-known Gaelic footballer, who it was claimed broke an opponent's jaw during the course of a game, appeared to signal a change in attitude. The player in question was found guilty of assault causing harm contrary to section 3 of the Non-Fatal Offences against the Person Act 1997. In a wide-ranging judgment Early J not only commended the victim's considerable courage in taking the case, but also concluded forcefully by stating: 'To strike someone without legal justification is a crime whether it takes place in the street, in the family home, or the football pitch, or

---

[22]   Reviewed generally in J Anderson, 'Violence, Sport and the Law: An Application to Gaelic Games' (1999) 7(2) *Sport and the Law Journal* 51.

[23]   Criminal Injuries Compensation Board, 'Twenty-third Annual Report' (Cm 265, 1987) [37]. It remains the case that the now Criminal Injuries Compensation Authority can refuse or reduce a reward for failure to cooperate with the police. For full details of the scheme, including its possible applicability to those injured as a result of sports-related violence, see www.cica.gov.uk.

[24]   The attitude of players to the role, if any, that the criminal law might have in policing violence in sport is not one that has been subject to significant empirical research save the small field-work project on the attitudes of rugby union players in A Pendlebury, 'Perceptions of Playing Culture in Sport: The Problem of Diverse Opinion in the Light of *Barnes*' (2006) 4 (2) *Entertainment and Sports Law Journal* published online at www2.warwick.ac.uk/fac/soc/law/elj/eslj/issues/volume4/number2/pendlebury.

[25]   See A O'Connor, 'Referee "Gagged" over Violence', *The Times* (London 4 June 2005) Sport 100 citing Nazir Afzal, CPS Director for London West, as stating, 'The CPS works with many communities that refuse to recognise crimes that occur within them. It would appear that the football community is behaving like any one of them.' For a review of the papers presented at the conference see S Barker, 'Is there a Case for more Criminal Justice Involvement in Sporting Incidents?' (2005) 13(2) *Sport and the Law Journal* 13.

elsewhere'.[26] That judgment was followed by two further noteworthy convictions: in 2005, a Gaelic footballer was given an 11-month suspended jail sentence after pleading guilty on an assault charge resulting from an incident during which he kicked a prostrate opponent on the head during the course of a club game; in 2008, a three-month custodial sentence was imposed on a GAA player who assaulted his opponent with such force that the injuries sustained required reconstructive plastic surgery. These judgments notwithstanding, problems of on-field violence in the GAA remain an embarrassment for that organisation and learning from the experience of their Australian counterparts in rugby and rules football, there has been a recognition that if rules changes and disciplinary mechanisms are not adjusted accordingly, prosecutions and accompanying civil litigation may increase in the years ahead.[27] The issue of how sports organisations might act (and have acted) to avert the actuality of having members labelled as criminals or involved in costly litigation is one that is returned to in the conclusion to this chapter. For now, and in a doctrinal application, it is instructive to review generally the manner in which the criminal law of assault might be reconciled with sports violence. Two case studies are presented on criminal prosecutions taken as a result of violence on the rugby pitch (England and Wales) and in ice hockey (Canada).

Implied Sporting Consent

[**5.08**] By definition, contact sports carry the risk of physically invasive collisions. Player to player contact is a foreseeable and, at times, elemental aspect of games such as rugby and football. Unnecessarily aggressive or violent play is usually, and quite rightly, dealt with 'in-house' by way of on-field penalties or subsequent fines or suspensions imposed respectively by referees and disciplinary tribunals. Moreover, civil liability may follow whereby damages may be awarded, usually in negligence.[28] The question of immediate legal import is: at what point and when is it appropriate for criminal proceedings to be instituted after an injury is caused by a player to an opponent in the course of a sporting event? In

---

[26] *DPP v MacCartan* Unreported, Dublin District Court 1 November 2004. See generally J Anderson, 'Ignorance of the Law is no Defence' *Irish Times* (Dublin 18 December 2004) Sport, Gaelic Games 3.

[27] See generally J Anderson, 'Law and New Order' *Sunday Tribune* (Dublin 16 November 2008) Sport 10, which also contains more details on all three GAA-related convictions noted in this paragraph.

[28] Discussed separately in the next chapter of this text. For an introduction see S Fafinski, 'Consent and the Rules of the Game: The Interplay of Civil and Criminal Liability for Sporting Injuries' (2005) 69 *Journal of Criminal Law* 414; M James, 'The Trouble with Roy Keane' (2002) 1 (3) *Entertainment and Sports Law Journal* published online at www2.warwick.ac.uk/fac/soc/law/elj/eslj/issues/volume1/number3/james.pdf.; and B Livings, 'A Different Ball Game—Why the Nature of Consent in Contact Sports Undermines a Unitary Approach' (2007) 71 *Journal of Criminal Law* 534.

general, the rationale underlying the encroachment of the criminal law into sport is that no particular segment of society should be permitted to commit crime with impunity. It follows in England and Wales that when criminal proceedings are seen to be justified then, depending upon its gravity, a prosecution can be for assault occasioning actual bodily harm contrary to section 47 of the Offences Against the Person Act 1861; or unlawfully and maliciously wounding or inflicting grievous bodily harm contrary to section 20 of the 1861 Act; or wounding or causing grievous bodily harm with intent contrary to section 18 of the 1861 Act. If death results from the assault, the charge could be one of manslaughter or possibly murder, depending on the defendant's intent.[29]

[**5.09**]   The application of the 1861 offences is predicated on criminal proceedings being appropriate in the first place. In the context of on-field violence in sport, a recognisable demarcation line between violence that is part of the rules and spirit of a game and that which is illegitimate is not an easy one to draw. At present, it appears that the leading common law jurisdictions favour the following approach: if the injuring player's conduct is seen to have been within the bounds of what one might reasonably foresee as a physical hazard of the game, the violent act is not unauthorised and will not expose that perpetrator to criminal liability. The doctrinal root of that approach is located in contact sports' long-standing exemption from the normal threshold of consent in the criminal law of assault, that is, the principle of implied sporting consent.[30] The origins of that principle can be traced to a trilogy of late nineteenth century case law; namely *R v Bradshaw*,[31] *R v Moore*[32] and *R v Coney*.[33] In *Bradshaw*, the defendant struck

---

[29] The principal focus here is on assault charges. Homicide charges arising out of sports-related violence are extremely rare though see *R v Hardy*, The Independent (London 27 July 1994) Home News 7 (defendant was cleared of the manslaughter of an opponent during a rugby match in what was reported as the first prosecution for manslaughter in relation to a death on the field in the game's 171-year history); *R v Southby*, Police Review (London 7 February 1969) vol 77, 110 (amateur footballer pleaded guilty on manslaughter plea after initially being charged with the murder of an opponent). See also the manslaughter charges arising out of an amateur Sunday league game in November 2008 when a player died as a result of brain injuries suffered from a single punch to the head: *R v Forwood*, Unreported, Central Criminal Court (Old Bailey) 6 July 2009 (defendant admitted that he had thrown the fatal punch; pleaded guilty to manslaughter; and was sentenced to 28 months' jail); *R v Thompson* Unreported, Central Criminal Court (Old Bailey) 18 August 2009 (defendant sat astride dying player and shouted abuse at him in response to provocative comments but cleared of manslaughter given that he had not delivered the fatal punch). Note also the tragic circumstances in the Canadian case of *R v CC* [2009] ONCJ 249 (CanLII) where the defendant was found guilty of manslaughter. The incident in question involved the defendant, a high school rugby player, throwing the opponent-victim to the ground causing him serious spinal cord injuries from which he died soon after. The judgment of Duncan J of the Ontario Court of Justice gives a succinct and accurate assessment of many of the problematical issues of law and fact encountered in this chapter.

[30] For an introduction to the parameters of this debate see S Gardiner, 'Sports Participation and Criminal Liability' (2007) 15(1) *Sport and the Law Journal* 19; B Livings, '"Legitimate Sport" or Criminal Assault? What are the Roles of the Rules and the Rule-makers in Determining Criminal Liability for Violence on the Sports Field?' (2006) 70 *Journal of Criminal Law* 495.

[31] *R v Bradshaw* (1878) 14 Cox's CC 83.

[32] *R v Moore* (1898) 14 TLR 229.

[33] *R v Coney* (1882) 8 QBD 534.

an opponent with his knee during a football game, resulting in the eventual death of the opponent. Bamwell B's direction to the jury is well established as the historical source of the criminal law's approach to violence in sport:

> If a man is playing according to the rules and practice of the game and not going beyond it, it may be reasonable to infer that he is not actuated by any malicious motive or intention, and that he is not acting in a manner which he knows will be likely to be productive of death or injury. But, independent of the rules, if the prisoner intended to cause serious injury and was indifferent and reckless as to whether he would produce serious injury or not, then the act would not be unlawful. In either case he would be guilty of a criminal act and you must find him guilt; if you are of a contrary opinion you will acquit him.[34]

[**5.10**]   The *Bradshaw* jury, taking into account evidence from an umpire that no unfair play had occurred, acquitted the defendant on the manslaughter charge. In *Moore*, the defendant had jumped knees first into the back of an opponent. He had done so with such force that he threw the victim against an on-rushing goalkeeper. The victim suffered serious internal injuries and died a few days later. In summing up for the jury, who returned a guilty verdict, Hawkins J took an approach similar to that of *Bradshaw*, noting succinctly: 'Football is a lawful game, but a rough one, and persons who play it must be careful to restrain themselves so as not to do bodily harm to any other person'.[35] In *Coney*, the principle that, independent of the rules of the game in question, criminal liability could attach to deliberately or recklessly dangerous play causing serious injury was extended to include non-fatal violence. In the stated case, the participants, organisers and spectators at a prize fight faced various criminal assault and abetting charges. The Court for Crown Cases Reserved held that, because prize fighting was unlawful (primarily because it was inherently injurious to both the participants and standards of public order generally) the consent of the participants was irrelevant.[36] Nevertheless, where the activity could be considered lawful, a number of dicta in *Coney* observed that the question as to whether consent affected the illegal character of the force inflicted was one of reconciling the social utility of the defendant's conduct with the level of injury inflicted.[37]

[**5.11**]   Over half a century later, the English Court of Appeal in *R v Donovan* would reaffirm the 'general rule' that the consent of the victim is immaterial where the defendant has beaten him or her to such a degree of violence that the infliction of bodily harm is a probable consequence. Swift J went on to remark however that the rule was one to which there were a number of 'well-established exceptions', including rough and undisciplined sport or play.[38] In *Attorney General's Reference*

---

[34] *Bradshaw* (1878) 14 Cox's CC 83, 85. Note also the commentary by JH Beale, 'Consent and the Criminal Law' (1895) 8 *Harvard Law Review* 317, 323–25.

[35] *Moore* (1898) 14 TLR 229, 229.

[36] See generally J Anderson, 'The Legal Response to Prize Fighting in Nineteenth Century England and America' (2006) 57 *Northern Ireland Legal Quarterly* 265, 277–78.

[37] See, for instance, *Coney* (1882) 8 QBD 534, 549, Stephen J.

[38] *R v Donovan* [1934] 2 KB 498, 507 and 508–09.

(No 6 of 1980),[39] the Court of Appeal delivered the modern expression of the rule. Lord Lane CJ observed that it was not in the public interest that people should try to cause, or should cause, each other actual bodily 'for no good reason', though, and again in the public interest, that approach was 'not intended to cast doubt on the accepted legality of properly conducted games and sports'.[40] In both cases, the Court of Appeal reiterated that the underlying public interest in the sporting exception to the usual threshold of criminal consent to bodily harm had a long and established history based on Foster's 'manly diversion' view of contact sports that 'intend to give strength, skill and activity, and may fit people for defence, public as well as personal, in time of need'.[41] As noted by the House of Lords in *R v Brown*,[42] the public interest in, and accompanying legality of, contact sports is now slightly more refined than national military preparedness. In *Brown* (where the appellants had participated enthusiastically in consensual, sadomasochistic, homosexual and private encounters for which they were convicted variously for assaults contrary to sections 47 and 20 of the Offences Against the Person Act 1861), the House of Lords affirmed the Court of Appeal's view that the satisfying of the sadomasochistic libido did not (unlike properly conducted sport and games) come within a category of 'good reason' for which departure from the usual threshold of consent in criminal law—that of bodily harm—might be justified.[43] More generally, the House of Lords in *Brown* reiterated the policy justifications for the criminal law of assault's benevolent view of contact sports as one based largely on the societal and health benefits of participation in sport and underpinned by responsible methods of self-regulation through which it is made clear that unsafe behaviour will face meaningful internal sanction.[44]

[**5.12**]   The exemption granted to lawfully conducted sports and games by the House of Lords, which has been adopted in almost all of the leading common law jurisdictions,[45] is not however a 'licence for thuggery' and clearly where the inflicted injury is in deliberate or reckless disregard of the safety of another, and is outside the level of physicality that is incidental to the norms of a properly conducted game, the criminal law's threshold of consent-based toleration

---

[39] *Attorney General's Reference (No 6 of 1980)* [1981] QB 715.

[40] Ibid 719.

[41] M Foster, *Crown Law* (Oxford, Clarendon Press, 1762) 260. See also E East, *Pleas of the Crown* (London, Butterworth, 1803) 268–70 and more generally G Williams, 'Consent and Public Policy' [1962] *Crim LR* 74 and 154.

[42] *R v Brown* [1994] 1 AC 212.

[43] See, in review, M Allen, 'Consent and Assault' (1994) 58 *Journal of Criminal Law* 183 and B Bix, 'Assault, Sado-masochism and Consent' (1993) 109 *LQR* 540.

[44] Lord Mustill's judgment is the most helpful (and succinct) in this regard. See *Brown* [1994] 1 AC 212, 256–75. See also Law Commission, 'Consent and Offences Against the Person' (Law Com CP No 134, 1994) [10.1]–[10.18] and Law Commission, 'Consent in the Criminal Law' (Law Com CP 139, 1995) [12.1]–[12.31].

[45] For an excellent and exhaustive review of the limits of consent in the criminal law of Australia, Canada, the UK and the US, note the judgment of the NZ Court of Appeal in *The Queen v Lee* [2006] NZCA 60, [2006] 3 NZLR 42 [154]–[344], Gazebrook J.

will be exhausted.[46] The sports of rugby union (in England) and ice hockey (in Canada) have, regrettably, provided the criminal courts with occasional instances of egregious violence not ordinarily incidental to those games, and which have demanded prosecution and resulted in convictions. What follows are case studies of both sports and their experience in their respective jurisdictions of the 'reach' of the criminal law. Three general points are noteworthy. First, deliberate, unprovoked assaults, especially of an 'off-the-ball' nature, can end with the culprit serving a custodial sentence. Second, the English Court of Appeal has consistently commended trial courts for their intolerance of unacceptable levels of violence on the playing field—a commendation that should be heeded by all contact sports governing bodies in the jurisdiction. Third, the Canadian case law is of interest for a number of reasons: its technical, legalistic understanding of what the intentional or reckless infliction of injury during sport might be; the extent to which that harmful conduct goes beyond the 'playing culture' of the sport in question; and the manner in which it has informed the English Court of Appeal's most recent decision on the parameters of 'sporting consent'—*R v Barnes*.[47]

No Licence for Thuggery: Rugby Union and the Criminal Law

[**5.13**]   It appears that the first conviction for a sports-related assault arising out of an incident on the rugby field occurred in 1978. In *R v Billinghurst*,[48] the defendant, in an 'off-the-ball' incident during the course of a club game in Wales, punched the opposing scrum-half in the face fracturing his jaw in two places. The victim was a prison officer whose principals were not, apparently, happy to lose their employee's services in such a manner without an attempt to let similar offenders realise the potential consequences of their actions. The defendant was charged with inflicting grievous bodily harm contrary to section 20 of the Offences Against the Person Act 1861. At trial, the only issue was consent. It was argued by the defence that in the modern game of rugby players consent to the

---

[46] Outside the specific issue of contact sports and consent in the criminal law, there has been some criticism of the lack of theoretical consistency and legal certainty underpinning the application of the 'well-established' exceptions rule to the usual bodily harm threshold of consent. The argument, which has usually taken place in the context of sexual offences but still informs the sport-related debate, is that 'in offences against the person the boundaries of capacity and consent have become blurred' such that it cannot be 'stated with confidence how much harm people are able in law to permit against themselves or even to solicit, before the criminal law steps in.' See C Elliot and C de Than, 'The Case for a Rational Reconstruction of Consent in Criminal Law' (2007) 70 *MLR* 225, 248. For an American perspective on this issue, which is returned to in this chapter's postscript on the legality of boxing, see generally V Bergelson, 'The Right to be Hurt: Testing the Boundaries of Consent' (2007) 75 *George Washington Law Review* 165.
[47] *R v Barnes* [2004] EWCA Crim 3246; [2005] 1 Cr App Rep 507.
[48] *R v Billinghurst* [1978] Crim LR 553.

risk of bodily injury and thus the prosecution would have to prove that the blow struck by the defendant was one which was outside the normal expectation of a participant in a game of rugby. Evidence was given by the victim that on previous occasions he had been punched and had himself punched opponents on the rugby field. Moreover, a defence witness—a former Wales international rugby player—gave evidence that in the modern game of rugby punching was the rule rather than the exception. The prosecution argued that public policy imposed limits on the level of violence to which a participant in a contact sport could consent and that whereas a rugby player can consent to vigorous or even overly vigorous physical contact 'on-the-ball', he cannot be licensed to consent to serious injury resulting from any deliberate or reckless physical 'off the ball' contact.

[5.14]   Rutter J directed the jury that rugby was a game of physical contact necessarily involving the use of force and that players are deemed to consent to force 'of a kind which could reasonably be expected to happen during a game'.[49] The trial judge went on to observe that rugby players do not have an unlimited licence to use force and that cases will arise where players will cross the line of accompanying consent. Ultimately, where that line (of consent) has to be drawn was, according to the trial judge, a matter for the jury. That approach—of leaving the threshold of consent to the jury—can now be criticised as somewhat lax on the part of the trial judge, though it might be forgiven given the novelty of the situation. To be fair, the accompanying case commentary in the *Criminal Law Review* was equally vague: 'Those who play games commonly agree that they consent to the infliction of some degree of harm which is outside the rules because they know it is commonly practised. The direction of the learned judge would seem to allow for this. It is unlikely that anyone consents to the deliberate infliction on himself of serious bodily harm'.[50] More usefully, the trial judge reminded the jury of a distinction that they might regard as decisive—between force used in the course of play and force used outside the course of play. The accompanying commentary on the case also highlighted the off-the ball nature of the stated incident and applied the following cricket analogy: 'If, in a cricket match, a fast bowler bowls and hits his opponent on the head and causes serious bodily harm it may well be held that the batsman validly consented to run the risk of that kind of harm; but the position is entirely different if, when the ball is "dead", the bowler throws it at the batsman's head'.[51] With the trial judge's final observation—that by their verdict they could set a standard for the future—in mind, the jury found Billinghurst guilty. He was sentenced to nine months' imprisonment suspended for two years.

[5.15]   In the 30-year period subsequent to *Billinghurst*, a significant number of prosecutions arising out of offences involving unacceptable violence on the

---

[49] Citing Williams (n 41) 81.
[50] [1978] *Crim LR* 553, 554.
[51] Ibid.

rugby field were recorded. In *R v Doble*,[52] the defendant allegedly gouged the eye of an opponent, causing him to lose that eye. Although the jury at Stafford Crown Court acquitted the defendant on the grounds of mistaken identity, the judge recommended that the victim approach the (then) Criminal Injuries Compensation Board.[53] In *R v Gingell*,[54] the defendant faced a charge of inflicting grievous bodily harm contrary to section 20 of the Offences Against the Person Act 1861. During the course of the game in question, the defendant had repeatedly punched an opponent in the face. The victim was pinned to the floor during the punch-up and suffered fractures to his nose, cheekbone and jaw. The defendant pleaded guilty. The court stressed that provocation—in this instance, obstruction and shirt pulling—could not be deemed a mitigating factor and was no excuse for the subsequent blows. The defendant was sentenced to six months' imprisonment, later reduced on appeal to two. Similarly, in *R v Bishop*,[55] the defendant—a Wales international—punched an opponent who lay on the ground during an 'off-the-ball' incident in a club rugby match. Given the intensity of the violence, the personalities involved and the novelty of the prosecution, the case attracted considerable publicity. Bishop pleaded guilty to common assault. He was sentenced to one month's imprisonment, later varied by the Court of Appeal to 12 months' suspended. In mitigation of sentence, Neill LJ took into account the 'charged atmosphere' of the game as well as the 'punishment' Bishop had already received in not being selected thereafter for the Wales rugby team. The Court of Appeal was however careful to reiterate: 'It is not for players, by their own action, to punish other players who they think have being acting unfairly'.[56]

[**5.16**]   In *R v Johnson*,[57] the victim legitimately tackled the defendant. In an ensuing tussle for the ball, the defendant bit the victim's ear lobe and tore it away. The defence argued that the action was committed 'in the heat of the moment' and they pointed to the defendant's previous good character. Lord Lane CJ was unimpressed and stated bluntly: 'unlawful violence … on the football field needs discouraging as much as violence on the terraces or indeed anywhere else'.[58] The defendant was found guilty under section 18 of the Offences Against the Person Act 1861 and was sentenced to six months' imprisonment. In *R v Lloyd*,[59] the victim was tackled and while lying on the ground was kicked in the face with such force as to sustain a fractured cheekbone. The victim subsequently spent four days in hospital. The English Court of Appeal acknowledged that forceful contact was

---

[52] *R v Doble* Unreported, Stafford Crown Court 8–10 September 1980.

[53] Note the award made to a rugby player under that scheme in (1991) 141 NLJ 1725, and the subsequent correspondence at (1992) 142 NLJ 80. Prior to the 1980s, applications of a sports-related nature to the (now) Criminal Injuries Compensation Authority resulted mainly from injuries sustained by spectators consequent to hooligan-related violence at football matches.

[54] *R v Gingell* (1980) 2 Cr App R (S) 198; [1980] Crim LR 661.

[55] *The Times* 18 September and 12 October 1986.

[56] Ibid.

[57] *R v Johnson* (1986) 8 Cr App R (S) 343.

[58] Ibid 345.

[59] *R v Lloyd* (1989) 11 Cr App R (S) 36; [1989] Crim LR 513.

allowed by the rules of Rugby Union (and *semble* the law) but the game was not as Pill LJ put it a 'licence for thuggery'. The plea against a sentence of 18 months' imprisonment for causing grievous bodily harm contrary to section 18 of the Offences Against the Person Act 1861 was dismissed. Similarly, in *R v Devereux*,[60] the defendant, on approaching an opponent from behind and breaking his jaw, was charged with intent to cause grievous bodily harm. He was convicted and sentenced to nine months' imprisonment.

[**5.17**]   In the more recent cases involving rugby violence, the common thread on appeal has been a plea of mitigation against the perceived harshness of the sentence at trial.[61] For instance, in *R v Moss*,[62] the defendant was said to have punched an opponent in the face, fracturing his eye socket. The defendant was convicted of inflicting grievous bodily harm contrary to section 20 of the Offences Against the Person Act 1861 and was sentenced to eight months' imprisonment. On appeal against the severity of the sentence, the appellant asked the Court of Appeal to take into account the following factors: that he had no previous convictions; he had offered to pay compensation; the risk of re-offending was acknowledged by all as being extremely low; a number of 'glowing' character references had been presented to the court; and the appellant was a married man with dependant children who had a small, family business to maintain. The appeal was dismissed. The Court of Appeal noted that the Assistant Recorder had indicated that in sentencing he *had* taken into account the various matters advanced in mitigation. Furthermore, the trial judge had acknowledged that rugby was a contact sport and could result in players receiving injuries but rugby 'was not a licence for thuggery and was a game covered by strict rules; the offence involved an assault off the ball and after play had moved on; serious injury had been inflicted; the offence was so serious that only a custodial sentence could be justified'.[63] In short, the sentence passed in *Moss* was deemed neither 'inappropriate nor excessive'.[64]

[**5.18**]   In the remarkably similar circumstances of *R v Bowyer*,[65] the English Court of Appeal upheld another eight months' imprisonment sentence resulting from a section 20 conviction. In that case, the victim, while retreating to defend his team's line, suffered a severe blow to his face. The victim, who did not see his assailant, was felled to the ground by the impact of the blow, and subsequently discovered that his jaw had been broken in two places. The Court of Appeal's decision was influenced not only by the appellant's lack of remorse but also by the need to emphasise 'that this kind of gratuitous [off-the-ball] violence on the field of play is not to be tolerated. The learned Recorder was obviously concerned about the level of violence that had been generated in the course of this particular

---

[60]   See D Llewellyn, 'Forward Jailed for On-field Punch' *The Independent* (London 23 February 1996) Sport 26.

[61]   See, eg, *R v Calton* [1999] 2 Cr App R (S) 64.

[62]   *R v Moss* [1999] EWCA Crim 1883; [2000] 1 Cr App R (S) 307.

[63]   Ibid [1999] EWCA Crim 1883 [11], Potts J.

[64]   Ibid [12].

[65]   *R v Bowyer* [2001] EWCA Crim 1853; [2002] 1 Cr App R (S) 448.

game. We are told that a number of other players had been sent off during the course of the game for uncovenanted violence which the referee was not prepared to tolerate'.[66] In contrast, in *R v Pepper*,[67] an initial 12-month sentence for an offence contrary to section 20 of the 1861 Act was reduced on appeal to four months. The Court of Appeal took into account the context in which the offence took place—in the 'heat' of a local derby game—and that the appellant had made 'considerable progress' in his life since the offence had been committed. The underlying factual circumstances of the stated case were also taken into account namely that the injury had been sustained by a third party who had sought to intervene in a row between the appellant and an opponent. From the evidence it appeared that the appellant had been hit first by his immediate opponent and was generally lashing out when he caught the victim unawares.

[**5.19**]   It is evident from the stated case law that deliberate, unprovoked assaults, particularly of an 'off-the-ball' nature, can result in relatively lengthy custodial sentences. In *Pepper* for example, although the plea of mitigation was partly successful, the culprit still faced a term of imprisonment and those who play rugby—and who most likely have experienced similar melees on the field of play—should now realise the potential of attaching criminal liability. In addition, the English Court of Appeal has consistently commended trial courts for the strict line with which they have viewed unacceptable levels of violence on the playing field—a trend that should be heeded by all contact sports (amateur or professional) that operate in England such as rugby league[68] and football.[69] In fact, a final, recent and stark illustration of the Court of Appeal's view on criminal violence in sport is provided by the dismissal of the appeal in *R v Garfield*.[70]

[**5.20**]   In the stated case it was alleged that the culprit had stamped on an opponent's head during the course of a rugby game, resulting in a deep 10cm-long laceration to victim's head. The injury occurred during a ruck in which the victim had fallen to the ground. The culprit contended that the stamp with

---

[66] Ibid [2001] EWCA Crim 1853 [16], Wright J.

[67] *R v Pepper* [2002] EWCA Crim 3141.

[68] Note *R v Best* [2004] EWCA Crim 483 where the Court of Appeal upheld that appropriateness of a fine and compensation order arising from a conviction for an assault occasioning actual bodily harm during the course of an amateur rugby league game.

[69] Central to the Court of Appeal's decision in *Moss* was Pill LJ's acknowledgment, [1999] EWCA Crim 1883 [9], of a number of previous, football-related decisions of the Court of Appeal, and his observation that 'nothing in those authorities suggests that the sentence of imprisonment passed in the present case ... was wrong in principle.' See, eg, *R v Birkin* (1988) 10 Cr App R (S) 303; *R v Chapman* (1989) 11 Cr App R (S) 93, [1989] Crim LR 60; *R v Chapman* Unreported, Warwick Crown Court 4 March 2010, Orme J; *R v Cotterill* [2007] EWCA Crim 526, [2007] 2 Cr App R (S) 391; *R v Davies* (1990) 12 Cr App R (S) 308; *R v Goodwin* (1995) 16 Cr App R (S) 885; *R v Kamara The Times* 15 April 1988; *R v Lincoln* (1990) 12 Cr App R (S) 250; *R v Rogers* (1993) 15 Cr App R (S) 393; *R v Shervill* (1989) 11 Cr App R (S) 284; *R v Tasker* [2001] EWCA Crim 2213; [2002] 1 Cr App R (S) 515; *R v Thelwell* [2004] EWCA Crim 208; *R v Ward* Unreported, Teeside Crown Court, 19 May 2009, Fox J QC; and *R v Wilkinson* [2007] EWCA Crim 2456. See also the Scottish cases of *Butcher v Jessop* 1989 SCCR 119 and *Ferguson v Normand* 1995 SCCR 770.

[70] *R v Garfield* [2008] EWCA Crim 130; [2008] 2 Cr App R (S) 62.

his studs was accidental and an unfortunate consequence of 'hard rucking'. The culprit was charged with unlawful wounding pursuant to section 20 of the Offences Against the Person Act 1861. He was found guilty and a sentence of 15 months' imprisonment was imposed. The defendant appealed against the severity of the sentence on two grounds. First, he submitted that the trial judge had taken insufficient account of the excessive delay (of two years) between the offence and the prosecution. Second, he argued that the sentence was difficult to reconcile both with the pre-sentencing report and a series of character references that 'went well beyond the merely positive'. On noting that there was a low risk of the defendant re-offending and that he had expressed genuine remorse (both to the author of the pre-sentencing report and during the course of the game itself), the pre-sentencing report had recommended a suspended sentence order with requirements of supervision and unpaid work. Moreover, a series of seven character references referred generally to the defendant's previous good character, with a particular feature of the references being that the defendant (who had continued to help his local club by coaching players) had subsequently, while saving a work colleague from harm, sustained an injury that would prevent him from ever playing rugby again. The Court of Appeal agreed that the delay in proceedings 'was in itself a substantial punishment' and that the references and pre-sentencing report were all 'substantial mitigating factors' but that the incident involved a stamp to the head of man who was defenceless and thus the trial judge (who had the benefit of hearing and seeing the defendant give evidence) appeared correct in his view that the defendant's conduct had been wholly unacceptable and inexcusable; that the injuries had been inflicted recklessly; and that the offence was so grave that only a custodial sentence could be justified.

[5.21]   The above case law notwithstanding, the central question remains when, as a matter of policy and legal certainty, and on what basis, is it appropriate to consider criminal liability for incidents of sports violence? Problematically, the boundary of implied sporting consent is blurred or, to paraphrase Lord Mustill in *Brown*, it is difficult to identify the 'critical level' at which the purported implied consent attaching to contact sport ordinarily ceases to be an answer to a prosecution for inflicting harm during the course of a game.[71] Recently, the Court of Appeal in England has remarked that criminal proceedings arising from violence in sport 'should be reserved for those situations where the conduct is sufficiently grave to be properly categorised as criminal'.[72] The (somewhat tautological) rationale underlying that judgment—criminal conduct on the field of play is recognisable by its criminality—will be assessed shortly. For now, and in order to have a better understanding of the issues at hand, it is necessary to leave the rugby fields of England for the ice hockey rinks of Canada.

---

[71] *Brown* [1994] 1 AC 212, 258–59.
[72] *Barnes* [2004] EWCA Crim 3246; [2005] 1 Cr App Rep 507 [5] Lord Woolf CJ.

The *Cey* Test: Ice Hockey and the Criminal Law

[**5.22**]   The Supreme Court of Canada has held that participation in contact sports is a 'good reason' in the public interest for granting such activities an exemption from the law of criminal assault's normal threshold of consent—that of actual bodily harm.[73] To a much greater depth than the applicable English jurisprudence, the Canadian courts have attempted, mainly through the frequency of prosecutions taken on foot of injuries sustained during ice hockey games, to identify the circumstances when a defendant might be held to have exceeded the scope of that exceptive (and implied) sporting consent. This has led to the identification of a number of objective factors, whose presence indicate that criminality should attach to the on-field actions of the defendant. The seminal Canadian authority is from 1969 when, during a National Hockey League (NHL) exhibition game in Ottawa, a player with the St. Louis Blues, Wayne Maki, crashed into and fought Ted Green of the Boston Bruins. After the players collided in the corner of the rink while trying to obtain control of the puck, Green pushed and punched Maki in the face with his glove. The two players separated, but then met again in front of the Boston net, this time both swinging their sticks. Green swung at Maki first, striking him on the neck and shoulder. In response, Maki made a vertical swing at Green and his stick first hit Green's raised stick and then Green's head, causing severe injuries. As a result, Maki was charged with assault causing bodily harm, and Green was charged with common assault. In *R v Maki*,[74] a provincial court in Ontario found Maki's claim of self-defence to be a valid one or, at least, the court could not say that Maki was not under a reasonable apprehension of harm to his person. Moreover, the court held that there was reasonable doubt as to the (excessive) nature of the force used. In *R v Green*,[75] the court relied on the doctrine of implied consent to find that no assault was committed and acquitted Green. In both cases the courts appeared influenced by the 'ordinariness'—in the context of professional ice hockey—of the fight and that, in effect, the players' actions had been instinctive and unintentional in nature. Nevertheless, in both *Green* and *Maki* the court stated that, although all players assume certain risks and hazards inherent in the sport, no participant should be taken to consent to malicious, unprovoked or overly violent attacks. The *Maki* court reminded the NHL that 'No sports league, no matter how well organized or self-policed it may be, should thereby render the players in that league immune from criminal prosecution'.[76]

---

[73] *R v Jobidon* [1991] 2 SCR 714; (1991) 66 CCC (3d) 454. See generally J Barnes, *Sports and the Law in Canada* 3rd edn (Toronto, Butterworths, 1996) 251–69 and, more recently, *R v K (S)* [2009] ONCJ 452 (CanLII).

[74] *R v Maki* (1970) 1 CCC (2d) 333, 14 DLR (3d) 164.

[75] *R v Green* (1970) 14 DLR (3d) 137.

[76] *Maki* (1970) 1 CCC (2d) 333, 336, Carter J. See generally G Letourneau and A Monganas, 'Violence in Sports: Evidentiary Problems in Criminal Prosecution' (1978) 16 *Osgoode Hall Law Journal* 577.

[**5.23**]   During the period 1970–1985 more than 100 criminal convictions were secured for offences involving unacceptable violence between ice hockey players during the course of a game.[77] Cases such as *R v Watson*,[78] *R v Moloney*,[79] *R v Henderson*,[80] *R v Gray*,[81] and *R v Coté*[82] demonstrate that since the 1970s applicable Canadian authority has tended towards the view that, by participating in a contact sport such as ice hockey, participants impliedly consent to some bodily contact necessarily incidental to the game but not to overly violent attacks.[83] Crucially, the case law suggests that the line (of criminality) between that which is within the norms of the game in question and that which is beyond its spirit or 'playing culture', should be determined by a number of objective criteria, first discussed in detail by the Saskatchewan Court of Appeal in *R v Cey*.[84] The *Cey* principles demand specific attention because they have informed the debate in a number of other jurisdictions, such as England and Wales, as to when acts of violence on the field of play might attract criminal liability.[85]

[**5.24**]   In *Cey*, a participant in an amateur ice hockey game crosschecked an opponent into the boards surrounding the ice rink. The victim suffered injuries to the face and mouth. At trial, the defendant was acquitted on a charge of assault causing bodily harm. On appeal, the acquittal was overturned and a retrial ordered, principally on the ground that the trial judge did not properly address the issue of implied sporting consent. The Court of Appeal held that the proper approach in instances of alleged criminal assault resulting from a contact sport was to consider first whether there was an express or implied consent to the type of contact involved and second whether that contact was of such a nature that in any event no true consent could be given. In a sports setting, *consent* will almost always be of an assumed or implied nature. According to the court, the nature of the *contact* for which that implied consent is assumed must not be of 'such a high risk of injury and such a distinct probability of serious harm as to be beyond what, in fact, the players commonly consent to, or what, in law, they are capable of consenting to'.[86] Therefore, in application to the facts at hand, the first matter that the trial judge should have sought to have had determined was whether there was an express or implied consent

---

[77] See generally D White, 'Sports Violence as Criminal Assaults: Development of Doctrine by Canadian Courts' (1986) 6 *Duke Law Journal* 1030.

[78] *R v Watson* (1975) 26 CCC (2d) 150.

[79] *R v Maloney* (1976) 28 CCC (2d) 323.

[80] *R v Henderson* (1976) 5 WWR 119.

[81] *R v Gray* (1981) 6 WWR 654.

[82] *Rv Coté* (1981) 22 CR (3d) 97.

[83] For more recent authority see, eg, *R v Bounassisi* [2003] BCPC 408 (CanLII); *R v Chu* [2006] BCPC 587 (CanLII); *R v GT* (1996) 18 Ontario Trial Cases 73; and *R v X* [2009] QCCQ 8477 (CanLII).

[84] *R v Cey* (1989) 48 CCC (3d) 480.

[85] *Barnes* [2004] EWCA Crim 3246; [2005] 1 Cr App Rep 507 [12], Lord Woolf CJ.

[86] *Cey* (1989) 48 CCC (3d) 480 [31] Gerwing JA (Cameron JA concurring).

and second, whether crosschecking the victim exceeded the applicable implied sporting consent.[87]

[**5.25**]   The usefulness of the *Cey* judgment is that the court attempted to provide an objective framework within which the scope and boundaries of implied sporting consent could be assessed. Prior to *Cey*, Canadian case law had suggested that players in a contact sport were presumed to consent to physical conduct that was reasonably incidental and instinctive to the sport, though it was admitted that the type of conduct that a court of law might consider reasonably incidental was 'hard to predict'.[88] In *Cey*, the court sought to delineate the scope of a participant's 'sporting' consent by way of objective criteria, namely: the nature or conditions under which the game in question is played; the nature of the act and surrounding circumstances; the extent of force employed; the degree of risk of injury including the probability of serious harm; and the state of mind of the defendant.[89] The court went on to say that these criteria were 'all matters of fact to be determined with reference to the whole of the circumstances. In large part, they form the ingredients which ought to be looked to in determining whether *in all of the circumstances* the ambit of consent at issue in any given case was exceeded'.[90]

[**5.26**]   The *Cey* principles were utilised in *R v Ciccarelli*,[91] where the defendant was charged with assault for his part in a 'bench-clearing' brawl, which took place after the whistle had blown on a National Hockey League game. Although the victim suffered no bodily harm, the defendant was convicted after striking the opposing player three times on the head with a hockey stick. The trial judge, referring to the objective criteria outlined in *Cey*, found that the defendant's conduct was not of a nature impliedly consented to by the other players. The defendant was sentenced to one day in jail and a $1,000 fine. On appeal, the conviction and accompanying sentence were upheld. The *Cicarelli* judgment has three outstanding points of interest. First, the appellate court held that the objective standard used by the trial judge was preferable to the 'playing culture' standard proposed by counsel for the appellant—that players are deemed to consent to anything that may be expected to happen during a game.[92] Corbett J was of the view that the latter was overly permissive and might pander 'to a public appetite for violence as entertainment'.[93] Second, in applying the *Cey* criteria, the trial judge demonstrated a comprehensive and sensitive understanding of the game in question, and was quite rightly influenced by the fact that 'high sticking' an opponent in the head was unusual even in a game as

---

[87] Ibid [35].
[88] *R v Leyte* (1973) 13 CCC (2d) 458, 459 (school handball game).
[89] *Cey* (1989) 48 CCC (3d) 480 [31], Gerwing JA.
[90] Ibid, italics inserted.
[91] *R v Ciccarelli* (1989) 54 CCC (3d) 121.
[92] Ibid [18]. See also, and subsequently, a similar view taken by Duncan J in *R v CC* [2009] ONCJ 249 (CanLII) [65]–[67].
[93] Ibid [19]–[21].

fast, vigorous and competitive as national league hockey.[94] Third, the appellant submitted that the trial judge had erred in failing to grant a conditional or absolute discharge having regard to the lack of injuries sustained by the victim and to the 'instinctive' nature of the incident. Corbett J dismissed this aspect of the appeal remarking that, although a discharge might have been in the best interests of the defendant, the sentence in question remained appropriate given the overriding public interest in deterring the amount of violence in professional hockey.[95]

[**5.27**]   Since *Cicarelli*, and in line with its principles, there have been a number of high-profile prosecutions of professional ice hockey players, including those of Marty McSorley in 2000[96] and Todd Bertuzzi in 2004.[97] The debate in Canada as to whether the criminal law is, in the first place, an appropriate means of combating violence in sport continues to be deliberated upon, as does the view that when in the rare instance a conviction for a sports assault is obtained, the tender approach to sentencing dilutes the deterrent and denunciation value of such convictions.[98] At this point, it suffices to state that the Canadian approach to implied sporting consent, as underpinned by the objective *Cey* criteria, is a considered and attractive one. An illustration of that approach can be found in *R v LeClerc*,[99] where the defendant was charged with aggravated assault alleged to have occurring during the course of a recreational hockey game. The game was part of a play-off series in an organised recreational league under whose rules no bodily contact was permitted. The defendant and the victim collided in a tussle over the puck during which the defendant hit the victim in the back with his hockey stick. Applying the rules, the referee immediately stopped play, penalising the defendant for 'a deliberate attempt to injure'. The victim suffered a dislocation of a portion of the cervical spine and was permanently paralysed from the neck down. The trial judge, noting that the culprit's conduct was instinctive, reflexive and defensive in nature, acquitted the defendant. The Crown appealed.

[**5.28**]   The appeal, which was dismissed, again raises a number of points of interest. First, the Ontario Court of Appeal agreed with the trial judge that the

---

[94] Ibid [22].

[95] Ibid [38]–[40].

[96] *R v McSorley* [2000] BCPC 117 and 118 (CanLII).

[97] *R v Bertuzzi* [2000] BCPC 472 (CanLII).

[98] In both *McSorley* and *Bertuzzi*, the defendants received inter alia conditional discharges for assault based charges. The sentences included what can only be called a 'sports restraining order' ie, for the duration of their probation the defendants were not permitted to take part in any sporting activity, professional or otherwise, involving the victim. See generally D Feldman, 'Pandora's Box is Open: Criminal Prosecution Implemented; Violent Play in the National Hockey League Eliminated' (2003) 2 *Virginia Sports and Entertainment Law Journal* 310; A Husa and S Thiele, 'In the Name of the Game: Hockey Violence and the Criminal Justice System' (2002) 45 *Criminal Law Quarterly* 509; J Jones and K Stewart, 'Hit Somebody: Hockey Violence, Economics, the Law and the McSorley Decisions' (2002) 12 *Seton Hall Journal of Sports Law* 165; B Ruskin and L Goldsmith, 'The Role of the Criminal Courts in Sport' (2004) 11 *Sports Law Administration & Practice* 8; and J Timmer, 'Crossing the (Blue) Line: Is the Criminal Justice System the Best Institution to Deal with Violence in Hockey?' (2002) 4 *Vanderbilt Journal of Entertainment Law & Practice* 205.

[99] *R v Le Clerc* (1991) 67 CCC (3d) 563.

fundamental question at issue was whether the culprit's conduct—stick hitting the victim on the back near the surrounding boards of the ice-rink—was, in the context of the *Cey* criteria and the game conditions as a whole, so inherently dangerous as to breach the implied consent of the victim.[100] Second, the Crown argued that the scope of the implied sporting consent ought to be narrowed in the stated circumstances because the alleged assault had occurred during the course of a recreational game in which bodily contact was not permitted by the governing rules. The trial judge had found that the 'ideal' of a 'no contact' rule was frequently breached in games of this nature 'where bumps and other contacts resulted in many penalties.' The Ontario Court of Appeal held that the trial judge was quite right to state that, although the no contact rule was relevant in determining the scope of implied consent, it was not by itself determinative of the issue.[101] Third, the Crown argued that the degree of force of the blow to the victim's neck was sufficient of itself to establish criminal conduct. The trial judge had found, and the Court of Appeal agreed, that the blow, though tragic in consequence, resulted from an 'instinctive reflex reaction' done at high speed by the defendant in an attempt to minimise the risk of bodily harm in close proximity to the boards surrounding the ice rink.[102]

[**5.29**]   The *LeClerc* approach is a good one with an inherent and welcome flexibility to its application. It reiterates that the *Cey* principles can act as a guideline for a court in distinguishing what has been called the 'grey area' between conduct that is intrinsically within the spirit of a game and thus impliedly consented to, and that which is extrinsic to its norms thus attracting criminal liability. The *LeClerc* court did however go on to state—and quite rightly—that the *Cey* principles are guidelines only and that the conditions and circumstances of the game *as a whole* should be taken into account before ultimately deciding upon the issue of implied sporting consent. In this, the *LeClerc* decision can be read as being sensitive to criticism that the sober atmosphere of a courtroom objectively applying the rule of law might be ill-suited to assessing the spontaneous and occasionally heated behaviour or 'playing culture' of the game, sport or arena in question.[103] Arguably quite the opposite is the case with, for instance, the trial judge in *LeClerc* demonstrating a clear understanding of, and sensitivity towards, the playing ethos and spirit of the recreational ice hockey game in question. It is of particular note that notwithstanding the fact that the referee had described the foul in question as 'deliberate and vicious'; the fact that the injuries suffered were extremely grave in consequence; and the 'intemperate zeal' of the injuring blow, the trial judge *still* found that the conduct in question was not, taking into account the conditions and circumstances of the game as whole, criminal in nature. Finally, in Canada the *Cey* principles/

---

[100] Ibid [19] and [25], Lacourciere JA.
[101] Ibid [26].
[102] Ibid [28].
[103] See generally S Gardiner, 'The Law and the Sports Field' [1994] *Crim LR* 513 and M James and S Gardiner, 'Touchlines and Guidelines' [1997] *Crim LR* 41.

LeClerc application to implied sporting consent has been usefully applied beyond the ice rink.[104] Moreover, the *Cey/Le Clerc* authority has recently been considered, and largely approved, by the criminal division of English Court of Appeal.

R v Barnes

[**5.30**]   The stated case arose from an incident that occurred in an amateur football match, during which the victim sustained a serious leg injury as a result of a tackle involving the defendant. The defendant was subsequently convicted of unlawfully and maliciously inflicting grievous bodily harm contrary to section 20 of the Offences Against the Person Act 1861. He received a 240-hour community punishment order and had to pay compensation in the sum of £2,609 to the victim. In the defendant's subsequent appeal, he highlighted the fact that the trial judge, in his summing up and in response to a question asked by the jury after they had retired, had made it clear that the appellant should be found guilty only if the prosecution had proved that what had happened was so reckless that it could not have been done 'in legitimate sport' and thus was tantamount to an aggravated assault. The appellant's contention was that the trial judge had not adequately explained to the jury the concept of 'legitimate sport' in the context of the circumstances at hand to the extent that it must have been difficult for the jury to determine what they had to decide in order to find the defendant guilty. The Court of Appeal allowed the appeal, holding the conviction unsafe on the grounds outlined by the appellant.

[**5.31**]   Lord Woolf CJ, delivering the judgment of the court, took as his starting point the fact that most organised sports have their own (relatively sophisticated) disciplinary mechanisms. Those internal procedures, allied to the fact that there was also the possibility for an injured player to obtain damages in a civil action, led Lord Woolf CJ to conclude that 'a criminal prosecution should be reserved for those situations where the conduct is sufficiently grave to be properly categorised as criminal'.[105] On reviewing and recognising the historical public policy basis of the defence of implied consent for contact sports, Lord Woolf acknowledged that a critical aspect of the 'criminality' of such incidents lay in identifying whether the stated conduct breached the limits of that defence, such that, in the case of sections 18 and 20 of the 1861 Act, it might be deemed 'unlawful'.[106] Citing *Cey*

---

[104] See, eg, *R v TNB* (2009) BCPC 117 where the defendant was acquitted on an assault charge arising out of an incident during a high school rugby game. The judgment of Frame J provides an excellent summary of the case law and principles outlined in [5.22]–[5.29] of this text. Of particular note is the brevity with which Frame J summarises this topic when at [93] of his judgment he observes, 'The amalgam of written rules, unwritten code of conduct and guidelines set by a referee in a particular game determine the conduct and contact in the game of rugby to which there is implied consent for the contact and injuries which would ordinarily amount to an assault if they were to occur off the field.'

[105] *Barnes* [2004] EWCA Crim 3246; [2005] 1 Cr App Rep 507 [5].

[106] Ibid [17].

with approval, Lord Woolf noted, 'If what occurs goes beyond what a player can reasonably be regarded as having accepted by taking part in the sport, this indicates that the court will not be covered by the defence'.[107] It followed, according to Lord Woolf, that a player does not (and cannot) reasonably be expected to consent to the intentional infliction of injury.[108] With respect to a test governing the reckless causing of injury, Lord Woolf was of the opinion that where it is claimed that the defendant has shown reckless disregard for the safety of an opponent, a judgment as to whether the defendant's conduct is criminal or not should be viewed objectively using criteria similar to those employed in *Cey*.[109] Similar to *LeClerc*, the English Court of Appeal in *Barnes* noted that even with the *Cey* principles as a guideline, tribunals of fact might still be faced with 'grey areas' blurring the lines between conduct intrinsic to the spirit of a game, and that which is extrinsic to its norms and thus vulnerable to criminal liability.[110]

[5.32] Fundamental to the *Barnes* judgment is Lord Woolf's observation that the *Cey* guidelines would have better enabled the jury to ask whether the injuring tackle in question was, in the context of the game and its rules and its conditions, so violent 'that it could not be regarded as an instinctive reaction, error or misjudgement in the heat of the game'.[111] In contrast, the trial judge had directed the jury along the rather vague grounds of whether the tackle was done 'by way of legitimate sport'. Although, as the Court of Appeal noted, the concept of legitimate sport was not of itself unhelpful, the failure of the trial judge to provide clarification as to its nature, meant that the trial judge's summing up was inadequate, as aggravated by the omission to make 'clear to the jury that there could lawfully be breaches, even serious breaches, of the rules of sport without there necessarily being the commission of a criminal offence'.[112]

[5.33] *Barnes* has attracted some criticism from academic commentators, principally on the grounds that it does not adequately accommodate the 'playing culture' of sport.[113] The debate centres on an extract from paragraph 15 of the *Barnes* judgment (italics inserted):

> In making a judgment as to whether conduct is criminal or not, it has to be borne in mind that, in highly competitive sports, conduct outside the rules can be expected to occur in the heat of the moment, and even if the conduct justifies not only being penalised but also a warning or even a sending off, it still may not reach the threshold level required for it to be criminal. *That level is an objective one and does not depend upon the views of individual players.*

---

[107] Ibid [12] citing *Cey* (1989) 48 CCC (3d) 480 [31], Gerwing JA.
[108] Ibid [13] citing the Law Commission, 'Consent and Offences Against the Person' (n 44) [10.18].
[109] Ibid [15]. The *Cey* guidelines are outlined fully at [5.25] of this text.
[110] Ibid.
[111] Ibid [16].
[112] Ibid [25] and [28]–[29].
[113] See, eg, Livings (n 30) 500–01 and Pendlebury (n 24) [8]–[15]. See also James and Gardiner (n 103) 44 who describe the concept of any sport's 'playing culture' as 'amorphous and dynamic'.

The criticism of the (above) *Barnes* approach is founded on the contention that the criminal law's perspective on violence in sport should be of a more subjective nature; otherwise the physicality (and pleasure) of participating in contact sport might be emasculated. That contention can be rejected on two grounds. First, the playing culture of sport *is* taken into account: the ethos (nature and conditions) of a sport is one of the objective *Cey* criteria approved of by the Court of Appeal in *Barnes*. Second, doubtless it is preferable that sports governing bodies ensure, through the enforcement and updating of their rules and internal disciplinary mechanisms, that unnecessarily violent practices are eliminated; equally however, no organisation or sport is beyond the reach of the criminal law. Unfortunately, an overly subjective approach based on the prevalent playing culture of sport might be used to excuse behaviour that should ordinarily be deemed criminal in nature.

[**5.34**]   The playing fraternity of many sports often find it difficult to accept that their pastime might be subject to the criminal law. The reaction of rugby player, Simon Devereux, convicted for grievous bodily harm with intent after breaking an opponent's jaw during a game, is illustrative of this attitude.[114] On his early release from a sentence of nine months' imprisonment Devereux described the 'flare-up' that led to his prosecution as being 'no different to countless others on rugby pitches the length and breadth of Britain every Saturday of the season'.[115] Later, the trial judge in the case would write of his surprise at the intensity of criticism emanating from the rugby fraternity and sporting press following the Devereux sentence.[116] In short, the mantra of 'what happens of the field; stays on the field', which one former Scottish rugby international acting as a witness in a criminal trial abridged to the expectation of 'punch and be punched', is ingrained in the ethos of many contact sports.[117] That mantra is not necessarily nor always an odious one, but it should never be permitted to excuse overly violent (and often cowardly and cynical) play.[118]

---

[114] See further this text at [5.16].

[115] Quotation taken from C Hewett, 'Rugby Union: Inside Story, Simon Devereux' *The Guardian* (London, 30 August 1996) Sport 8.

[116] J Baker, 'Two High Profile Sports Cases: A View from the Bench' (2001) 9(1) *Sport and the Law Journal* 95, 102–03.

[117] A Dalton and W Chisholm, 'Violence Part of Rugby says Sole as Player Fined for Punch' *The Scotsman* (Edinburgh 14 February 1997) News 1. Subsequently, Mr Sole was publicly rebuked by the Procurator Fiscal and the Scottish Rugby Union, D Douglas, 'SRU Frown on Sole Court Plea' *The Glasgow Herald* (Glasgow 15 February 1997) News 34.

[118] For an interesting application of the balance that must be struck in this regard see the case from Ontario, Canada of *R v TNB* (2009) BCPC 117 and especially the conclusion to Frame J's judgment at [93]–[101]. In that case, (also noted at n 104 of this text) the defendant threw a punch wildly and blindly into a scrum during a game of rugby leading to injury to the victim. Frame J accepted the defendant's evidence that he had thrown the punch without intending to connect with a particular person and with no intent to cause injury. Moreover, Frame J noted that, although the conduct was discouraged by the rules, it was encouraged by the unwritten code of conduct of the game and was recognised as a common part thereof and might even be said, in the context of the game in question, to be a 'legitimate strategy of intimidation'. Frame J acquitted the defendant of the assault charges on the grounds that the Crown had not proven that the defendant had intended to cause serious bodily harm nor that the victim's (implied sporting) consent was vitiated by the extent or force of the blow delivered.

Current Status of the Law of 'Sporting' Assault

[**5.35**]   To reiterate, in addressing the uncertainly as to the attachment of criminal liability for egregiously violent play on the sports field, it is argued that the underlying thrust and sentiment of the *Barnes* judgment should be welcomed, albeit with a residual need to clarify the extent to which the law of sporting assault in England and Wales now relies upon the *Cey* criteria. It is submitted that a summary of the law of sporting assault, as predicated on a breach of an athlete's implied sporting consent to injury during the course of a contact sport, might now read as follows. Contact sports carry the risk of physically invasive collisions. Player-on-player contact is a foreseeable and, at times, elemental hazard of such games. A participant's consent to bodily contact during contact sport encompasses that which is ordinarily and reasonably incidental to the playing of the game in question. It does not extend to conduct that is overtly violent. There is no immunity from the ordinary law of assault for the intentional infliction of injury during a sport or game. A decision by a tribunal of fact as to whether the reckless infliction of injury during a game or sport is criminal in nature should be assessed in light of the following objective criteria:

— The type of sport in question;
— The safety rules, level and conditions under which the game in question was played;
— The 'playing culture' or 'spirit' of the game, recognising that in highly competitive contact sport conduct outside the rules should be expected to occur 'in the heat of the moment' but might not reach the required level of criminality;
— The nature of the injuring act and its surrounding circumstances, recognising that injury inflicted 'off the ball' is more likely to breach the boundaries of implied sporting consent;
— The extent of force employed;
— The degree of risk of injury including the probability of serious harm;
— The state of mind of the defendant.

Again, it must be reiterated that the stated criteria act collectively as a guidelines only and that there may well remain a 'grey area' between conduct that is intrinsic to the spirit of a game and thus within the boundaries of implied sporting consent, and that which is extrinsic to a sport's norms and thus vulnerable to criminal liability. Ultimately, it remains a matter for a tribunal of fact will have to make its determination based on the conditions and circumstances of the game *as a whole*.

Conclusion

[**5.36**]   In the vast majority of cases excessively violent or aggressive play on the sports field will be dealt adequately by on-field penalties or playing suspensions. Moreover, it is preferable that the lead on eliminating inherently excessive violence in a sport comes from within the expertise of the sport itself and that such matters do not end in the criminal courts or indeed, as the next chapter highlights, the civil courts. The experience of sports organisations in Australia, Canada and the US, who have had members prosecuted, convicted and even jailed for sports-related assaults, is that the best way to avoid subsequent proceedings (or at least to confine the reach of the criminal law to only the most exceptional of circumstances involving egregious, gratuitous violence) is to implement schemes based on a combination of the following: better player education; better coaching and refereeing standards; closer monitoring of the effectiveness of safety and playing rules; consistent sanctioning; and the continued empowerment of the authority of internal sports disciplinary mechanisms.[119] In this light, it is instructive that since the game went 'open' in 1995 rugby at all levels has arguably benefited from the above improvements and this is reflected in the fact that the number of prosecutions for rugby-related violence has faded significantly since professionalization in the mid-1990s.[120]

[5.37]   More generally, it must be admitted that the criminal law can be a rather blunt instrument in such circumstances in that it can, for instance, lead to an individual athlete becoming the 'scapegoat' for the unsafe practices of their chosen sport. Moreover, the evidential practicalities of instigating sports-related prosecutions and the unpopularity of such proceedings should not be underestimated. It can be difficult to reconcile the robust, spontaneous, 'agony of the moment' reflexes of the athlete with the appropriate *mens rea* of the stated offence under the law of assault. Nevertheless, no particular segment of society, even one adjudged to have a high social utility such as sport, should be permitted to commit crime with impunity. Contact sport is not a 'licence for thuggery' or as one Canadian judge has put it: 'The playing field is not a criminal law free zone. The laws of the land apply in the same way as they do elsewhere. The legal analysis of whether a crime has been committed on the playing field is the same at it is on the street, though contact sport presents a unique factual context of that analysis'.[121] This chapter suggests that, thanks to the Court of Appeal in *Barnes* and the concomitant Canadian authority, the criminal law is now better prepared as to how to deal with the 'unique factual context' of sport and that the demarcation line between physicality that can be considered reasonable in light of the rules and spirit of the game in question and that which is clearly criminal in nature, is more readily identifiable. At the

---

[119] See generally I Dobinson and D Thorpe, 'What's Wrong with the Commissioner? Some Lessons from Down Under' (2009) 19 *Seton Hall Journal of Sports and Entertainment Law* 105 and W Hicks, 'Preventing and Punishing Player-to-Player Violence in Professional Sports; the Court System versus Self-Regulation' (2001) 11 *Journal of the Legal Aspects of Sport* 209.

[120] The recent lengthy bans against players for the so-called 'eye gouging' offences are a case in point. See M Souster, 'Eye Gouging: War is Declared on the "Ultimate Sin"' *The Times* (London 11 January 2010) Sport 62 and M Souster, 'Attoub Gouge Earns 70-week Ban' *The Times* (London 20 January 2010) 72.

[121] *R v CC* [2009] ONCJ 249 (CanLII) [6], Duncan J.

very least, the increased awareness of the threat of the criminal law 'beyond the touchline' may avert its actuality, and all contact sport will be better served as a result.

Postscript: The Legality of Boxing

[**5.38**]   Fundamental to an understanding of this chapter has been the contention that the criminal law of assault's benevolent view of contact sports is located in the fact that such sports have (and principally due to their long recognised social utility and authoritative self-regulatory nature) justified their inclusion as one of the 'well established' exceptions to the usual 'bodily harm' threshold of consent in the criminal law of assault. In short, when it comes to the legality of contact sports *vis a vis* the norms of the criminal law it appears that there is a 'good reason' in the public interest for extending the usual threshold of criminal consent to one of a implied sports-specific nature. This postscript focuses on one particular and problematical 'contact' sport and asks: how the rationale underpinning the extension of that threshold can be reconciled—indeed, how the criminal law of assault *itself* can be reconciled—with the sport of boxing, where the deliberate infliction of injury, principally to the head and softer areas of the body, is rewarded with points.[122]

[**5.39**]   Very generally, there are two possible approaches that might be taken in replying to the above stated question. First, one could adopt Ashworth's view that the *sui generis* nature of the legality of boxing means that both the debate on the sport's legality is moot or at least should be 'approached with circumspection' and that it certainly would be wrong to use it as a 'benchmark' against which a level of assault-based criminality in contact sports might be set.[123] The alternative is to take a broader approach and to view the sport's legality in its historical and social context, which is that under English law the legality of professional boxing has its origins in an historical anomaly rooted in the sport's coerced evolution from prize fighting to the gloved bout and that in reward for that 'progression' (including the fact that it is a regulated activity entered into by mature consenting adults whose intentions while physically invasive remain essentially sporting in nature) boxing can justifiably take its place under the contact sports-related exception to the usual bodily harm threshold of consent applicable to the ordinary law of criminal assault.

---

[122]   The focus of this postscript is on boxing only though analogies can be drawn to all fist fighting sports in their various styles and to kick boxing or any sport or martial art or sparring activity in which a contestant in that sport or art or activity is required to strike, kick, hit, grapple with, throw or punch an opponent. See generally H Hartley, *Sport, Physical Recreation and the Law* (London, Routledge, 2009) ch 9.

[123]   A Ashworth, *Principles of Criminal Law*, 6th edn (Oxford, Oxford University Press, 2009) 311.

[**5.40**]   The remaining sections of this chapter take this second, broader path.[124] There are two points of note along this path. First, the manner in which the criminal law, in what can be deemed a series of 'pugilistic prosecutions', coerced the prize fighting fraternity in England and America into adopting rules as regularised and as sanitised as the Queensberry Rules of 1865, has been dealt with elsewhere.[125] Broadly, it is suggested that by the late nineteenth century a number of socio-legal factors had combined to conceive both the modern sport *of* boxing and the modern law *on* boxing. In strictly legal terms, the legitimising equation that emerged then, and which remains seminal to the contemporary understanding of the legality of the sport, is that boxing, as regulated by the Queensberry Rules, was not prize fighting: it did not incite social disturbance nor act as a threat to general public morality; it no longer required participants to fight to a standstill; nor could it be considered unacceptably dangerous.[126] The second point of note is that the remaining sections of this chapter briefly expose that 'legitimising equation' to contemporary legal norms both in a specific application to the ordinary criminal law on personal violence and in a broader jurisprudential analysis. In so doing, this postscript asks whether professional boxing's current legal status might be seen to wilt under the glare of that examination and whether, on pain of possible outright proscription, the sport is in desperate need of comprehensive regulatory reform.

Medical Considerations

[**5.41**]   In discussing the legality of boxing one fundamental, preliminary issue needs to be addressed: how dangerous is the sport of boxing both in absolute terms and relative to comparable contact sports? In reviewing the voluminous medical literature on the topic one point quickly becomes clear and that is the need to distinguish between amateur and professional boxing. For a myriad of reasons—shorter bouts, mandatory use of headgear, stringent medical supervision of individual participants and a centralised world governing body through which such matters can be coordinated—amateur boxing has generally tended to be viewed as a relatively 'safe' sport.[127] Accordingly (and despite the merit of Kemp's view that 'the brain simply cannot tell the difference between a punch

---

[124] This approach is also the underlying thesis of J Anderson, *The Legality of Boxing: A Punch Drunk Love?* (London, Birkbeck Press, 2007). See also, and in summary, J Anderson, 'The Business of Hurting People: A Historical, Social and Legal Analysis of Professional Boxing' (2007) 7 *Oxford University Commonwealth Law Journal* 35.

[125] See generally J Anderson, 'The Legal Response to Prize Fighting in England and America' (2006) 57 *Northern Ireland Legal Quarterly* 265.

[126] For an even broader socio-historical perspective on boxing see K Boddy, *Boxing: A Cultural History* (London, Reakiton, 2008) chs 2–5.

[127] For a detailed review of the medical literature see generally Anderson, *The Legality of Boxing* (n 124) ch 5.

that has been paid for and one that is thrown gratuitously')[128] the emphasis in this brief review is on the questionable safety and legality of professional boxing. Here, the medical profession's research on, and view of, the safety of pro-boxing is generally negative in outcome and emphasis.[129]

[**5.42**]   In some ways, the medical profession's negativity is easily understood: during the course of a bout boxers inevitably receive a number of variably weighted blows to the body and head with the peak force of a heavyweight's punch likened to being hit by a 13lb (6kg) padded wooden mallet travelling at 20 mph (32km/h).[130] In the case of body punches, the covering provided by skin, fat and muscle (well toned in the case of boxers) may help dissipate the force of the punch. In the case of a direct punch to the head however the risk of serious injury increases to potentially fatal proportions. This is due not only to the force of the punch itself but also to the unique anatomy of the head and brain: heavy blows can produce violent movements to the head on a variety of rotational planes revolving on the axle of the spinal cord and neck, possibly resulting in concussion. These movements, allied to the fact that the bulk of the brain rests loosely inside the sharp inward projections of the skull, can give rise to an acute subdural haematoma (a blood clot on the surface of the brain). Subsequent brain haemorrhages can result in death. One collection suggests that there have been nearly 1,500 boxing-related deaths worldwide since 1890s.[131]

[**5.43**]   The tragedy of ring fatalities aside, the immediate acute effect of a head punch on a boxer can include grogginess, weakening of the limbs (the characteristic wobble) or concussion.[132] There can also be long term or chronic effects for the 'punch-drunk' fighter, which may only be detected cumulatively towards the end of a boxer's career. The symptoms of this syndrome ('dementia pugilistica') include slurred speech, memory and motor loss, tremors and lack of balance, and possibly personality change.[133] In addition, severed nerve fibres and damaged cells within the brain area do not replenish. Cerebral atrophy is sometimes characterised by enlarged ventricles, which are cavities within the brain that provide a circuit for the protective fluid of the brain that expand to fill the space left by decayed brain tissue. These spaces or holes are known as 'cavum septi pellucidi', and are a

---

[128]   P Kemp, 'A Critique of Published Studies into the Effects of Amateur Boxing: Why is there a Lack of Consensus?' (1995) 81 *Journal of the Royal Naval Medical Service* 182, 189.

[129]   See Anderson, *The Legality of Boxing* (n 124) ch 5 and more recently R Beran and J Beran, 'The Law(s) of the Rings: Boxing and the Law' (2009) 16 *Journal of Law and Medicine* 684.

[130]   J Atha, 'The Damaging Punch' (1985) 291 *British Medical Journal* 1756, 1757.

[131]   See further the Manuel Velazquez Boxing Fatality Collection maintained by J Svnith of the *Journal of Combative Sport* and available online through www.ejmas.com/jcs/jcsart_svinth_a_0700. htm.

[132]   See recently D Coletta, 'Non-neurologic Emergencies in Boxing' (2009) 28 *Clinics in Sports Medicine* 579.

[133]   This was first documented by H Martland, 'Punch Drunk' (1928) 91 *Journal of the American Medical Association* 1103. For more recent research see the findings in J Bazarian *et al*, 'Long-term Neurologic Outcomes after Traumatic Brain Injury' (2009) 24 *Journal of Head Trauma and Rehabilitation* 439.

characteristic of a professional boxer's brain. As a consequence, it has been further suggested that former boxers are generally more likely to sustain natural ageing diseases of the brain, and thus are particularly susceptible to Alzheimer's disease and, possibly, Parkinson's disease.[134]

[5.44] Overall, and translating the results of various studies carried out on this topic, it is estimated that anything between two-thirds and three-quarters of professional boxers will suffer some measurable brain damage as a result of their career, usually the early punch drunk stage of traumatic encephalopathy. In approximately one-fifth of these cases, the disease will progress from the minor stage of slight slurring of the speech and lack of balance, through an intermediate stage typified by effects similar to that of Parkinson's disease, and finally into the severest stage characterised by major loss of cognitive function.[135] This evidence has led implacable critics of professional boxing, such as the British Medical Association (BMA), to argue that even the most stringent of medical safeguards cannot render the sport 'safe' to the (tipping) point that the frequency and severity of injury associated with boxing is of such an inherently dangerous level that the sport should be banned.[136]

Legal Considerations

[5.45] The medical evidence outlined in the above sections leads legal commentators such as Gunn and Ormerod to suggest that in the vast majority of boxing matches serious bodily harm eventuates.[137] Nevertheless, these commentators then go on to observe that 'it is possible that grievous bodily harm will not occur in every fight, especially if two defensive boxers are involved. If so, the legality of boxing generally cannot be challenged on the basis that all bouts necessarily involve the commission of an offence contrary to s.20 or s.18 [of the Offences against the Person Act 1861]'.[138] This comment is, in practical terms, not substantiated by attendance at, or better, participation in, a boxing match. The nature of the sport and the range and degree of injuries sustained underpin the contention that really serious harm—which need not be 'life threatening, dangerous or permanent'[139]—occurs in all boxing matches.

[5.46] Moreover, it might be argued that the nature of a professional boxing match is that grievous bodily harm *must* occur in order to satisfy a key constituent

---

[134] See R Aviv *et al*, 'Cavum Septi Pellucidi in Boxers' (2010) 61 *Canadian Association of Radiologists Journal* 29 and P McCrory, 'Cavum Septi Pellucidi—A Reason to Ban Boxers?' (2002) 36 *British Journal of Sports Medicine* 157.

[135] These are, broadly, the findings of a report by the Health Council of the Netherlands, *Brain Damage in Boxers and Soccer Players* (The Hague, Health Council of the Netherlands, 2003) ch 2.

[136] See generally the British Medical Association, *The Boxing Debate* (London, BMA, 1993). For a summary of the BMA's current position see www.bma.org.uk/health_promotion_ethics/sports_exercise/BoxingPU.jsp.

[137] M Gunn and D Ormerod, 'The Legality of Boxing' (1995) 15 *Legal Studies* 181, 186–87.

[138] Ibid 187.

[139] *R v Bollom* [2003] EWCA Crim 2846; [2004] 2 Cr App R 50 [53] Fulford J.

element of the sport. The rules of the sport encourage blows to the head and discourage 'defensive' boxing. Although aficionados might appreciate the skilful, counterpunching fighter, the general public (including TV executives) is attracted to aggressive, attacking, knockout 'merchants'. The clean strike to the head, in contrast to body punches, is always a scoring punch and boxers endeavour to land as many of these as possible. Moreover, the regulation of the sport is such that it precludes Gunn and Ormerod's exclusively defensive boxers because such boxers would risk disqualification as 'non-triers'. As Lord Mustill observed succinctly in *R v Brown*: 'each boxer tries to hurt the opponent more than he is hurt himself, and aims to end the contest prematurely by inflicting a brain injury serious enough to make the opponent unconscious, or temporarily by impairing his central nervous system through a blow to the midriff, or cutting his skin to a degree which would ordinarily be *well within* the scope of section 20'.[140]

[**5.47**]   More controversially, it must be asked whether boxers foresee and appreciate that serious bodily harm is a consequence that is intrinsic to their participation in a bout and thus might entitle a court to convict pursuant to section 18 of the Offences against the Person Act 1861. Put simply, does every professional boxing match necessarily involve an offence under section 18 of the Offences against the Person Act 1861? If these inter-related questions are answered in the affirmative the repercussions are significant to the point that they undermine the very 'immunity' that has permitted the sport to operate beyond the ordinary law of personal violence for more than a century. Section 18 provides for two offences of aggravated assault, that of wounding or causing grievous bodily harm to another with intent. The word 'wound'—an injury that pierces the continuity of the whole skin—and the term 'grievous bodily harm'—really serious bodily harm—attract the same meaning as that given under section 20 of the 1861 Act. Within the terms of the second offence, the really serious harm has to be 'caused'. In *R v Burstow and Ireland*,[141] the House of Lords held that there was no 'radical divergence' of meaning in section 18's use of the term 'causing' and section 20's use of the term 'inflicting'. There is, however, a critical distinction in the respective fault elements of sections 18 and 20. Section 20's requirement of recklessness is not enough; a section 18 defendant must intend to cause grievous bodily harm. It follows that the elemental question is whether it is an intrinsic and conditional element of a boxing match that the defendant-boxer wounds or causes grievous bodily harm to another with intent?

[**5.48**]   The nature and regulation of the sport make it difficult to see how the answer to the above stated question can be anything other than a positive one. To suggest that a boxer's motivation or desire or purpose is anything other than the physical degradation of their opponent, or to entertain the idea that boxers do not expect the consequence of serious harm is to fundamentally misunderstand, even

---

[140] *Brown* [1994] 1 AC 212, 265, italics inserted.
[141] *R v Burstow and Ireland* [1998] AC 147.

patronise, the sport and its participants. Put simply, a boxer's fists are weapons; they are trained to land with considerable force; they cause serious bodily harm with intent and they contribute to making out the section 18 offence.[142] The clarity and honesty of this approach—that grievous bodily harm occurs in all boxing matches—is attractive. It gives a much more faithful appraisal of the nature of the sport (and the motivations of its participants) and it crystallises much of the debate as to the true and informed nature of a boxer's consent.

[**5.49**] The threshold of consent in English criminal law falls between assault at common law and the offence of assault occasioning actual bodily harm created by section 47 of the 1861 Act. It follows that the consent of the victim is no answer to anyone charged with the latter offence or those above it in the ladder of assault-based offences, unless the circumstance falls within one of the well established exceptions—of which organised sporting contests and games is one such exception.[143] Boxing has been held as coming within that sports-related exemption (and thus has availed itself of the benefits of implied sporting consent) ever since the decision of the Court of Crown Cases Reserved in *R v Coney*.[144] That extension of implied sporting consent to boxing was premised principally on two grounds (a) that it was not prize fighting and, as an organised sport, compared well to the coarseness and disorder of bare fisted fighting; and (b) on balance, it did not, according to the medical opinion of the day, endanger life or health.[145] Nevertheless, and as Glanville Williams observed, the anti-prize fighting cases of the nineteenth century reserved impliedly that fighting of any kind and form might still be declared unlawful 'where the circumstances make it likely that injury or (at least) some kind of serious injury will be caused'.[146] Contemporary medical research, which reflects badly on the sport, now appears sufficient to engage the Williams' reservation in the sense that if the physical exploitation inherent in the sport is as flagrant as is suggested, it must then follow that the sport also exploits the boundaries of modern English criminal law.

[**5.50**] More immediately, the most celebrated attempt to rationalise the legality of boxing can be located in the judgment of Lord Mustill in *R v Brown*.[147] Even there his Lordship, somewhat disappointingly, ended the discussion rather tersely describing the sport as 'another special situation which for the time being stands outside the ordinary law of violence because society chooses to tolerate it'.[148] At best it can be argued that Lord Mustill approached the legality of boxing

---

[142] Compare to the position taken by Gunn and Ormerod (n 137) 188.

[143] See [5.11]–[5.12] of this text.

[144] *R v Coney* (1882) 8 QBD 534.

[145] See also on this point N Parpworth, 'Boxing and Prize Fighting: The Indistinguishable Distinguished' (1994) 2 *Sport and the Law Journal* 4.

[146] G Williams, *Textbook of Criminal Law*, 2nd edn (London, Stevens & Sons, 1978) 583.

[147] *Brown* [1994] 1 AC 212, 262–65.

[148] Ibid 265. See also the exasperation in P Roberts, 'Philosophy, Feinberg, Codification and Consent: A Progress Report on English Experiences of Criminal Law Reform' (2001) 5 *Buffalo Criminal Law Review* 173, 211.

in terms of 'social disutility', which as a model holds that 'unless the prosecution is able to provide persuasive reasons for prohibiting certain conduct, consent will be effective generally up to the level of grievous bodily harm'.[149] The social disutility model is attractive in that it avoids the vagaries of the courts' manipulation of both what is in 'the public interest' and where the threshold of consent to bodily harm lies, epitomised by the majority's attempts in *Brown* to justify exceptions, such as daredevil stunts, in terms of a socially valuable activity or 'rough horse-play', in terms of what 'must be expected' of the schoolyard or barrack room.[150] In sum, it appears more satisfactory that the burden of condemnation should lie on those who wish to criminalise consensual conduct, not on those who wish it to be lawful.

[**5.51**] The social disutility model was, in all but name, availed of by Lord Mustill in his dissent in *Brown*: 'As I have ventured to formulate the crucial question, it asks whether there is good reason to impress upon section 47 an interpretation which penalises the relevant level of harm irrespective of consent, i.e., to recognise sado-masochistic activities as falling into a special category of acts, such as duelling and prize-fighting, which the law says shall not be done'.[151] As arguments against the dangers presented by the conduct in question, such as the possibility of proselytisation and corruption of young men, were not, in his Lordship's opinion, sufficient to justify criminalisation, Lord Mustill would have allowed appeals. It would have been interesting to see his Lordship apply a similar premise to boxing rather than, as noted, ending so abruptly. Nonetheless, where does this leave the legality of the sport? At first instance, even under the more sympathetic social disutility model, professional boxing fails to find solace there because there remain persuasive, cogent reasons related to its health and safety record as to why it might be prohibited. Moreover, and in exacerbation, the nature of the sport is such that serious harm *must and does* occur in all competitive boxing matches. Beyond that there is confusion and no little despair with many writers resignedly taking the view that any attempt to rationalise or accommodate the legality of boxing in the context of an exception to the threshold of consent in assault, or indeed in any context, is futile, and that the sport's status should be deemed *sui generis*.[152] Other suggestions from legal commentators throughout the common law world range from: a reticence to intervene at all until such time as a full public debate on the medical evidence takes place;[153] to the granting of an ad hoc exemption;[154] to calls for the proscription of an activity that can only 'perversely'

---

[149] D Kell, 'Social Disutility and the Law of Consent' (1994) 14 *Oxford Journal of Legal Studies* 121, 127.

[150] Ibid 128.

[151] *Brown* [1994] 1 AC 212, 273.

[152] D McArdle, 'A Few Hard Cases? Sport, Sadomasochism and Public Policy in the English Courts' (1995) 10 *Canadian Journal of Law and Society* 109.

[153] Law Reform Commission of Ireland, 'Report on Non-Fatal Offences Against the Person' (LRC 45, 1994) [9.157].

[154] Law Reform Commission of Canada, 'Assault' (LRCC Working Paper 38, 1984) 32.

be treated as a sport.[155] More helpfully, it is submitted that there is much to learn from the Australian decision in *Pallante v Stadiums Pty Ltd (No 1)*.[156]

[**5.52**]   That case was an action in negligence in which the claimant sought to recover damages in respect of injuries received by him in a professional boxing contest governed by the rules of the Australian Boxing Alliance. Interestingly, the claimant sought to recover damages not from his opponent, but from those who organised and promoted the bout on the ground that the stated parties had a duty of care to prevent the injuries sustained. The defendants sought to strike out the proceedings inter alia as an abuse of legal process, arguing that boxing contests, notwithstanding their evolution from bare fisted fights through the Queensberry Rules and into the modern era, must be considered and declared illegal. As Osborough notes, that 'remarkable contention' was, in effect, an invocation of the *ex turpi causa* principle (or defence of illegality) and demanded that the court consider generally whether boxing was a criminal activity or not.[157] The conclusion to McInerney J's judgment is of interest and worth citing at length:

> ... boxing is not an unlawful and criminal activity so long as, whether for reward or not, it is engaged in by a contestant as a boxing sport or contest, not from motive of personal animosity, or at all events not predominately from that motive, but predominately as an exercise of boxing skill and physical condition in accordance with rules and in conditions the object of which is to ensure that the infliction of bodily injury is kept within reasonable bounds, so as to preclude or reduce, as far as practicable, the risk of either contestant incurring serious bodily injury, and to ensure that victory shall be achieved in accordance with the rules by the person demonstrating the greater skill as a boxer.[158]

[**5.53**]   Although the thrust of McInerney J's approach is praiseworthy; its substantive content is less so. Elements of the judgment as to consensual and 'fair' fights are somewhat imprecise, particularly with regard to the importance placed on the absence or presence of 'hostility'.[159] Moreover, it is of interest that in *R v Brown*, Lord Mustill damned his Australian colleague with faint praise: 'I intend no disrespect to the valuable judgment of McInerney J when I say that the heroic efforts of that learned judge to arrive at an intellectual satisfying account of the apparent immunity of professional boxing from the criminal process have convinced me that the task is impossible'.[160] Lord Mustill was correct and it remains a difficult task to identify to any satisfactory degree the current location of boxing within the norms of the criminal law of personal violence.

[**5.54**]   Self-evidently, one way to achieve clarity would be to ban it but therein lies what can be deemed the 'paradox of proscription'. In a theoretical sense,

---

[155] Farugia (n 11) 500.

[156] *Pallante v Stadiums Pty Ltd (No 1)* [1976] VR 331.

[157] WN Osborough, 'Sport, Freedom and the Criminal Law' in A Whelan (ed), *Law and Liberty in Ireland* (Dublin, Oak Tree Press, 1993) 53.

[158] *Pallante* [1976] VR 331, 343.

[159] See, eg, the criticism made by the Law Reform Commission of Ireland (n 153) [9.160].

[160] *Brown* [1994] 1 AC 212, 265.

Bronitt and McSherry encapsulate that paradox neatly: 'To criminalise conduct places the subject and conduct practically and symbolically beyond the boundaries of legality and civil society. The criminal is literally and legally rendered *out*law … The process of criminalisation, while potently symbolic, weakens the instrumental capacity of law to regulate the prohibited conduct'.[161] Although boxing could, as it is currently operates, be criminalised through an application of the Offences Against the Person Act 1861, the reality of that process would be that proscription would ultimately prove unsatisfactory because it would, in all probability, see the emergence of an unlicensed and even more dangerous fighting sport.[162] Although a recent report by the Dutch Health Council rejected this perspective (noting that it was not supported by the practical experience of countries such as Sweden, Iceland and Norway where professional boxing has been banned for some time);[163] it is clear that the history, culture and popularity of boxing in the UK is of such depth and complexity that a ban on the sport would lead to an underground version of the sport.[164]

[5.55]   In short, a culture of unlicensed events already exists and an outright ban on the extant, licensed version of the sport would achieve little other than a return to the prize fighting days of the mid-nineteenth century when crudely prepared fighters and their backers sought secluded venues in which to fight. That state of affairs would expose boxers to increased levels of harm, lead to secondary criminality such as illegal gambling, and be a waste of policing resources. In brief, it is an accepted and fundamental criminological principle that if the 'evil of criminalisation' would be greater than the evil sought to be eradicated, then the state should consider deploying some of the other techniques available to it, such as education, persuasion or taxation, and avoid resort to the criminal law. The 'education and persuasion' of boxing's governing authorities of the need for stringent medical and regulatory safeguards is, in its adaptive scheme, far more preferable than the consequences that might flow from the sport's abolition. It is argued that, in the short term at least, the professional boxing industry should be given an opportunity to reform itself up to the contemporary norms of a well-regulated and safe sport—a standard that it has singularly failed to maintain. The substance of these reforms form the basis of this postscript's elongated conclusion.

Jurisprudential Considerations

[5.56]   In a jurisprudential sense, it is contended that the following reforms are consistent with a necessarily 'soft' paternalistic approach to the harm caused by the

---

[161] Bronitt and McSherry (n 14) 12.
[162] See the concerns expressed by Gunn and Ormerod (n 137) 188 and N Warburton, 'Freedom to Box' (1998) 24 *Journal of Medical Ethics* 56, 60. See generally R Jones, 'A Deviant Sports Career: Towards a Sociology of Unlicensed Boxing' (1997) 21 *Journal of Sport and Social Issues* 37.
[163] Health Council of the Netherlands (n 135) 49.
[164] See, eg, J Hotten, *Unlicensed: Random Notes for Boxing's Underbelly* (London, Mainstream, 1998).

sport of boxing. It follows that the opportunity to reform should be extended to the sport because if implemented, boxing, as a recognised sport and valid leisure activity, may be reconciled with the wildly competing perspectives of liberalism (favourable; inter alia on the ground of the individual autonomy of boxers) and paternalism (disapproving; inter alia on the ground of the need to protect boxers from themselves). More generally, and as demonstrated by the World Medical Association's declaration against boxing—passed at its Thirty-Fifth Assembly held in Venice in October 1983—the core condemnation of the sport of boxing can be made succinctly and powerfully: 'unlike other sports, the basic intent of boxing is to produce bodily harm in the opponent. Boxing can result in death and produces an alarming incidence of chronic brain injury'.[165] Accordingly, although a number of other sporting activities involve physical risks, boxing is deemed a special case justifying the strictest attention because the nature of the sport 'implies that extra points are given for brain damage'.[166] The remainder of this postscript examines the basic intent of boxing from two perspectives. First, it is posited that to view the infliction of violence as the sole aim of the sport is to misunderstand and dismiss boxing's nuanced levels of discipline, skill and courage. Second, this section will investigate whether there is a good moral reason and a sound philosophical basis to justify the criminalisation of boxing.[167]

[**5.57**] In brief, abolitionists argue that to inflict violence in the manner promoted by boxing goes beyond the norms of contact sport.[168] It is contended that the intentionally violent purpose of boxing means that a boxer must view his opponent simply as an object that must be overcome in as vicious and primitive a manner as possible—by knocking him out.[169] In the language of the sports scientist, the direct and invasive nature of boxing means that the physical intrinsic characteristic of contact sports is wholly replaced by a violent intrinsic. Similarly, and in the language of the sports sociologist, boxing necessitates a disrespectful attitude towards a dehumanised opponent, which is contrary to any reasonable definition of sporting values.[170] Crucially, this perspective permits many in the medical profession to conclude that, although other sports such as mountaineering carry higher risks of injury and death, those statistics can be disregarded as 'an overriding point is that damage to the brain in sporting activities is incidental; in boxing such injury is deliberate'.[171]

---

[165] The World Medical Association's 'Statement on Boxing' is available online at www.wma.net/en/30publications/10policies/b6/index.html.

[166] BMA, *The Boxing Debate* (n 136) 10.

[167] Note generally the approach taken by K Sheard, 'Aspects of Boxing in the Western Civilising Process' (1997) 32 *International Review for the Sociology of Sport* 31.

[168] See typically G Lundberg, 'Boxing Should be Banned in Civilized Countries—Round 3' (1986) 255 *Journal of the American Medical Association* 2483.

[169] Health Council of the Netherlands (n 135) 24–25.

[170] See generally P Davis, 'Ethical Issues in Boxing' (1993–4) 20–21 *Journal of the Philosophy of Sport* 48.

[171] BMA, *The Boxing Debate* (n 136) 68. See also the contributions of Lord Ackner, Hansard HL vol 563 col 289 (5 April 1995) and Baroness Jeger, Hansard HL vol 567 col 1032-3 (6 December 1995) to a debate on a bill purporting to prohibit boxing for profit.

[**5.58**]   In response to the medical profession's general antipathy towards boxing, phenomenological research demonstrates that those who practise the sport see it primarily in terms of skill, courage and discipline.[172] The contention that the sport does not wholly revolve around the infliction of force is, it is claimed, evidenced by the fact that the technical nature of the sport can result in the stronger, more aggressive fighter being defeated by the controlled and skilful pugilist.[173] Moreover, some proponents of the sport argue that, for the sake of consistency, the intent of boxing should reasonably be compared to that of other contact sports such as rugby in the sense that it is unclear how an aggressive rugby tackle to prevent a try is significantly different in intention from a boxer punching an opponent in order to score points.[174] In a specific sense, that approach fails to mention the single, fundamental item that distinguishes contact sports such as rugby from boxing—the ball. The physical relationship between rugby opponents on the pitch is, in effect, an indirect one defined by possession of the ball. One cannot charge without the ball; nor should a player tackle an opponent who does not have possession of the ball. To do so is foul play. In contrast, the physical relationship between boxers in the ring is a direct one defined by the fist. When rugby players speak of 'skill', they are invariably referring to the use of the ball; when boxing commentators speak of 'skill', they are invariably referring to the use of the fist. It follows that in making a try-saving tackle, the rugby player's intention is primarily to prevent the ball crossing the try line. In contrast, in boxing the objective is to hurt your opponent to such an extent that initially he is unable to defend himself, enabling you to score at will and, if possible, to then inflict such hurt as to physically disable him by way of knockout.

[**5.59**]   In a general sense, it is submitted that to deny that the basic intent of boxing is to inflict bodily harm on the opponent is to betray a fundamental lack of understanding of the sport and thus do it a disservice. The basic intent and nature of boxing effectively means that the infliction of harm is unavoidable. As Gunn and Ormerod remark pithily, 'boxing matches cannot be won without punching the other combatant. The nature of a punch must inflict the necessary bodily harm, even if the boxer in question does not have a particularly hard punch'.[175] Boxers accept that the central maxim of their sport is 'hurt and be hurt', and that it is a fundamental attraction of the sport that the participant can exercise advanced

---

[172]   Note the three-year ethnographic study of professional boxing on the south side of Chicago carried out by L Wacquant, 'The Pugilistic Point of View: How Boxers Think and Feel about their Trade' (1995) 24 *Theory and Society* 489 and L Wacquant, 'A Fleshpeddler at Work: Power, Pain and Profit in the Prize Fighting Economy' (1998) 27 *Theory and Society* 1. See also M Burke, 'Is Boxing Violent? Let's Ask Some Boxers' in D Hemphill (ed), *All Part of the Game: Violence and Australian Sport* (Melbourne, Walla Walla Press, 1998).

[173]   P Donnelly, 'Sport as a Site for Popular Resistance' in R Gruneau (ed), *Popular Cultures and Political Practices* (Toronto, Garamond Press, 1988) 77.

[174]   See typically K Jones, 'A Key Moral Issue: Should Boxing be Banned?' (2001) 4 *Culture, Sport, Society* 63, 67. See also Warburton (n 162) 58.

[175]   Gunn and Ormerod (n 137) 186.

levels of physical aggression within the controlled environment of the ring.[176] In sum, because it cannot reasonably or satisfactorily be denied that the objective of professional boxing is anything other than the infliction of bodily harm, the primary focus of the debate on boxing should be on whether that bodily harm can be kept within acceptable limits. Those 'acceptable limits' are not just physical in nature; they are also philosophical in outcome.

[5.60] The philosophical inquiry into the ethical boundaries of the law's attitude to boxing poses fundamental questions for the libertarian and the paternalist.[177] In the classic expression of liberalism found from Mill to Feinberg, it is held that the process of criminalisation should be confined to serious harms to the exclusion of those that fall foul of the maxim *de minimis no curat lex*.[178] The sport of boxing—in particular the professional code where boxers risk serious injury for substantial, if rarely attained, wealth—provides an interesting counterexample for that core element of liberalism. As noted by Irving Kristol, extreme liberalism, with its emphasis on the sanctity of individual autonomy, would clearly not support a ban on boxing and might, *in reductio ad absurdum*, permit a revival of the gladiatorial fights of the Roman arena.[179]

[5.61] In direct response to Kristol's provocation, Feinberg outlines the liberal's case for boxing, which is threefold in nature.[180] First, Feinberg argues that the prohibition of a sport such as boxing would clearly violate a central tenet of liberalism—that of personal autonomy. In this, there is a clear recognition that liberalism supports boxers' freedom to act on their own decisions, 'even if those decisions will probably end up hurting them'.[181] Second, in the scenario of licensed professional boxing, nobody is harmed who does not voluntarily consent in advance to bear the risks involved. This includes those who participate in and attend a boxing match as well as those who do not but might be offended at the knowledge that such a sport occurs. Third, Feinberg, and liberalism in general, has little problem in supporting the existence of professional boxing largely because

---

[176] See B Bredemeier and D Shields, 'Athletic Aggression: An Issue of Contextual Morality' (1986) 3 *Sociology of Sport Journal* 15, who note that this is equally true of combat sports such as the various martial arts.

[177] It also poses interesting questions for so-called 'ringside' physicians who monitor and treat boxers during a bout at the behest of the relevant sanctioning or licensing body. See, eg, M Scwartz, 'Medical Safety in Boxing: Administrative, Ethical, Legislative and Legal Considerations' (2009) 28 *Clinics in Sports Medicine* 505. See also H Brayne, L Sargeant and C Braynes, 'Could Boxing be Banned? A Legal and Epidemiological Perspective' (1998) 316 *British Medical Journal* 1813 who note that since medical cover is a legal licensing requirement at all boxing promotions, the withdrawal of medical cover would immediately place boxing in a difficult position and as such the medical profession could reconsider, in light of its own ethical standards, participation by its members in boxing promotions.

[178] Note the review by F McAuley and P McCutcheon, *Criminal Liability* (Dublin, Round Hall, 2000) 72ff and the discussion of the libertarian/paternalist dichotomy at [4.63]ff of this text.

[179] I Kristol, 'Pornography, Obscenity, and the Case for Censorship' *New York Times* (New York, 28 March 1971) Sunday Magazine 112–13.

[180] J Feinberg, *The Moral Limits of the Criminal Law: Harmless Wrongdoing* (New York, Oxford University Press, 1988) 128–33 and 328–31.

[181] N Dixon, 'Boxing, Paternalism and Legal Moralism' (2001) 27 *Social Theory & Practice* 323, 325.

of the presence of a licensing and regulatory procedure, the purpose of which is to ensure that all parties to the combat genuinely, substantially and voluntarily consent to the fight.[182]

[5.62]   In contrast, the basic premise of what can be termed 'legal paternalism' is that criminalisation of an activity can proceed where it is necessary to prevent harm (physical, psychological or economic) to the party in question and consequently, the legal paternalist advocates just what the liberal denies: the state may be justified in using coercive powers, such as the criminal law, to force a person to act (or not to act) against his will in order to protect his well-being.[183] Accordingly, in setting the boundaries of the criminal law, how would the legal paternalist justify the promotion of a boxer's welfare over and above that boxer's personal autonomy? Dixon succinctly outlines the paternalistic case against the sport: 'the risks of brain damage are so severe that we have a duty to protect fighters from the harm they are likely to suffer'.[184] For the paternalist, exposure to such well-documented, grievous harm is neither a rational decision nor one that should be encouraged for fear of 'coarsening' society as a whole. It follows that if the libertarian's contention is that boxers should be free to act on their own decisions, irrespective of the medical consequences, might that perspective be seen as 'lofty, detached or even callous'?[185]

[5.63]   More fundamentally, paternalism questions whether a fighter's decision to pursue boxing is, in fact and in context, an informed, autonomous selection. Unsurprisingly, it answers this in the negative employing a rationale comparable to that which underpinned the legal demise of duelling, approximately two centuries ago. Outlawing duelling eventually came to be seen as being in the interest of the health and welfare of the privileged elite who felt it necessary to abide by and practise such a 'code of honour'. In short, the prohibition of duelling released that elite from the 'tyranny of custom'.[186] Similarly, the paternalistic case against boxing holds that professional boxers might be seen to be coerced into the ring, exposing themselves to potentially lethal blows to the head, only because they feel that it is the sole accessible means available to release them from the 'tyranny of poverty'. In this light, there is little argument that boxers emerge predominately from socially disadvantaged backgrounds.[187] As Colin Radford, a supporter of the sport, has observed, 'whether a country has a lot of good boxers, or few, is a pretty good indicator of the state of its economy, or of the economic opportunities available to some community within that

---

[182] Feinberg (n 180) 330.

[183] J Feinberg, *The Moral Limits of the Criminal Law: Harm to Others* (New York, Oxford University Press, 1984) 26–27.

[184] Dixon (n 181) 324.

[185] Law Commission, 'Consent in the Criminal Law' (n 44) C.61.

[186] Williams (n 41) 77–78. See generally J Horder, 'The Duel and the English Law of Homicide' (1992) 12 *Oxford Journal of Legal Studies* 12.

[187] See generally J Lae, 'Boxing, Racism and the Socioeconomic Factor' (1989) 45 *Temps Modernes* 126.

country'.[188] Yet, should boxing be dismissed simply as the exploitation of the disadvantaged?[189] Certainly, professional boxers are well aware of their trade's potential cruelty. Wacquant notes the reluctance of even the most passionate of fighters to see their children take up the sport.[190] The primary motivation of professional boxers is, to an exaggerated degree, to make money; it is not the 'taking part' that counts. If fighters were motivated by the intrinsic enjoyment of participation it would be expected that they would be evenly distributed throughout all socioeconomic classes. They are not.[191]

[**5.64**]　Burke best captures this ambivalence towards the sport:

> The boxer understands it as a coerced affection, a poor man's love ... There are no rich, white boxers ... Boxers leave part of themselves in the ring. The body, which has been trained and disciplined to perform the 'sweet craft', does not survive intact. The contradiction in this ruination of the cherished masculine body creates a further ambivalence toward boxing ... Therefore; the boxer's passion is a skewed and malicious one. It is tainted by the idea that boxing, for all its benefits, exacts too high a price.[192]

The juxtaposition of the phrases 'coerced affection' and 'too high a price' neatly encapsulates the paternalistic case against boxing.

[**5.65**]　In short, the paternalist abhors the laissez-faire nature of the liberal view on boxing. Legal paternalism justifies calls for the sport's prohibition in order to protect boxers from themselves; that is, as a consequence of their 'poverty of circumstance', boxers are effectively coerced into a career choice that is neither deliberate nor rational. Nevertheless, paternalism's view of boxing is vulnerable to the charge that it is itself coercive in nature, for the reality is that many of us make lifestyle choices that do not promote or safeguard our immediate or long term well-being: *ergo* smoking, fatty foods, extreme sports, possibly all contact sports, even driving a car, should be targets for criminalisation. It follows that the liberal rejoinder, that paternalism is much less attractive when its implications are made apparent, holds true with regard to the proscription of boxing as much as it does elsewhere.[193] Moreover, the tolerant, liberal view of boxing and, indeed, criminalisation theory in general, is at its strongest when it acknowledges that there is a price to pay for respecting individual autonomy and personal liberty.[194] Even though a boxing career might thus expose that boxer to harm, and serious harm at that, the liberal must accept that choice, as there is no justification for telling

---

[188] C Radford, 'Utilitarianism and the Noble Art' (1988) 63 *Philosophy* 63, 70.

[189] That question is the underlying premise of J Sugden, *Boxing and Society: An International Analysis* (Manchester, Manchester University Press, 1996) 56–88, a superb case study of the boxing subculture that exists in an urban ghetto of Hartford, USA.

[190] See generally L Wacquant, 'The Pugilistic Point of View' (n 172).

[191] Dixon (n 181) 328.

[192] Burke (n 172) 118–19.

[193] R Simon, *Fair Play: Sports, Values and Society* (Boulder, Westview Press, 1991) 58.

[194] J Feinberg, *The Moral Limits of the Criminal Law: Harm to Self* (New York, Oxford University Press, 1986) 77.

an autonomous adult that 'he may not do what he wishes to do now on the sole grounds that he will be sorry later'.[195]

[**5.66**]   Given that the classically defined paternalistic and liberal approaches to the criminalisation of the sport appear at odds, where lies the legality of boxing? A theoretical approach based on the concept of 'soft' or 'moralistic legal' paternalism might offer a workable compromise, satisfying the demands of these competing perspectives and securing boxing's future. In terms of criminalisation, soft paternalism equates to the right of the state to prevent self regarding harmful conduct when, but only when, that conduct is substantially non-voluntary, or when temporary intervention is necessary to establish whether it is voluntary or not.[196] Liberalism has long accepted that 'soft' paternalistic interventions are, in certain circumstances, a regulatory fact of societal life. Hart, for instance, expressly (and pointedly so far as the debate on boxing is concerned) qualified the liberal position by accepting that it is permissible to legislate in order to protect the vulnerable from exploitation and justify the criminalisation of consensual injury.[197] Logically, so long as boxing is adequately regulated and participants are sufficiently informed and educated as to the inherent dangers, the basic tenets of liberalism *must* support the sport because, notwithstanding any reasonable concerns as to the level of violence inflicted during the course of a bout, restrictions upon it remain precluded because boxers *must* be taken to be mature, competent agents invoking a voluntary, autonomous and rational choice of career.[198] Nevertheless, only in as much as liberals are confident that the health and dignity of boxers is paramount in the regulation and administration of the sport should they be satisfied with the sport's current legality. If that balance is skewed, and the necessary medical and welfare precautions are not being enforced, dissatisfaction should rise to the level of proscription.

[**5.67**]   Finally, and to reiterate, the libertarian's view that there is no justification for the proscription or limitation of boxing is a strong one and has protected modern boxing since its inception. Boxers *are* autonomous beings who freely consent to participate in a sport where no harm is caused to others. Nevertheless, paternalism's argument that the degree and seriousness of injuries inflicted is sufficient to justify the legislative limitation of such autonomy is equally well put. In fact, in the case of professional boxing, the paternalist can now rely on significant and compelling medical research as to the incidence of brain injury in the sport. Nevertheless, if those medical concerns are addressed and negated through extensive reforms—based mainly on the 'best practice' operation and administration of modern amateur boxing—then the social utility of the professional sport and the respect for the personal autonomy of its participants (deeply ingrained in the jurisdictions where professional boxing enjoys its highest profile) should be

---

[195] Ibid.
[196] Ibid 12.
[197] HLA Hart, *Law, Liberty and Morality* (Oxford, Oxford University Press, 1963) 51.
[198] 'Small' or 'soft' departures from the classic liberal position are discussed generally by A Fuchs, 'Autonomy, Slavery and Mill's Critique of Paternalism' (2001) 4 *Ethical Theory and Moral Practice* 231.

sufficient to deter any effort to criminalise the 'noble art of self-defence'. Furthermore, and in historical context, it must also be remembered that a century or so ago, prize fighting evaded extinction through fundamental and sometimes painful reform. It assuaged the concerns of the general public, the medical profession and the criminal law through a more effective and safer regulatory regime. Modern boxing should, and must, undergo a similar transformation. The parameters of such a transformation, and the practical steps that must be taken, are now outlined.[199]

What to do With Pro-Boxing?

[**5.68**]   Should modern western societies, where professional boxing is at its most commercial, continue to support the existence of an activity tainted by poor levels of financial and contractual transparency, regulatory incompetence, an anomalous legal status, an ethically dubious participative autonomy and significant neurological dangers, which cumulatively can, on occasion, have fatal consequences? It is argued that the answer is a qualified 'no' where that qualification is based on professional boxing being given an opportunity to implement extensive regulatory reforms. That approach is preferable to proscription, which may only give way to an underground and even more dangerous version of the sport. Taking into account recent legislative-based attempts to regulate boxing in the US[200] and in Australia,[201] it is submitted that any regulatory reform of professional boxing in the UK should include the following 10 points: the establishment of an independent, statutory body for the regulation of boxing for profit; the adoption of strict medical controls based on the model provided by amateur boxing; the introduction of fight 'passports' for individual boxers wherein their fight, medical and licensing history would be recorded; the promotion of mandatory educational courses for professional boxers including financial planning and personal health advice; the requirement that boxers must, prior to receiving a licence to fight, sign a certificate of informed consent similar to that given to patients prior to major brain surgery; that consideration be given to a series of rule changes, including the reduction of championship title fights from 12 to 10 rounds and a ban on blows to

---

[199] Sections [5.68]–[5.73] of this text are informed by the approach taken in J Anderson, 'Time for a Mandatory Count: Regulating for the Reform of the Professional Boxing Industry in the UK' (2005) 13(1) *Sport and the Law Journal* 40.

[200] In the US Congress, there have been repeated attempts by, amongst others, Senator John McCain, to establish a federal US Boxing Commission to administer the Professional Boxing Safety Act 1996. See generally Senator J McCain and K Nahigian, 'A Fighting Chance for Professional Boxing' (2004) 15 *Stanford Law & Policy Review* 7. In May 2009, the US Senate Committee on Commerce, Science and Transportation recommended that Senator McCain's latest bill be considered by the Senate as a whole. For a full text of the Professional Boxing Amendments Bill see www.govtrack.us/congress/billtext.xpd?bill=s111-38.

[201] See, eg, the approach taken in New South Wales through its Combat Sports Act 2008 and in Victoria through the Professional Boxing and Combat Sports Act 1985 (as amended). For an interesting consideration of the effectiveness of the latter scheme see T Zazryn, P McCrory and P Cameron, 'Injury Rates and Risk Factors in Competitive Professional Boxing' (20090 19 *Clinical Journal of Sports Medicine* 20.

the head; the formation of a single world sanctioning body, which would publish a unified, independent and global ranking of boxers; the propagation of a bill of rights for professional boxers, including union formation and membership rights; the codification of all standard contractual arrangements in professional boxing; and mandatory provisions requiring promoters to provide adequate insurance and pension rights for contracted boxers.

[**5.69**]   To be fair to the British Boxing Board of Control (BBBC), in the wake of the tragic events and costly litigation surrounding the injuries sustained by Michael Watson in 1991, there have been significant improvements in the safety standards in British boxing.[202] Moreover, it could be argued that a private regulatory body such as the BBBC, which has a long established history of self-regulation, should not be judged punitively on isolated incidents of malpractice and should simply be encouraged and persuaded to deal internally with professional boxing's problems, albeit in a more aggressive fashion. Unfortunately, the relatively good practice of the BBBC is at odds with the general administrative farrago that is world professional boxing with its 'alphabet soup' of sanctioning authorities, weight divisions and 'world' champions. The darkest side of this administrative farrago is that in most jurisdictions a boxing promotion, and all those associated with its operation—boxers, judges, referees and the facility in which the bout is to be held—must be registered and licensed by the governing state or national boxing authority or appropriate private boxing commission. At first instance, this would suggest that some element of state control and uniformity is present in the holding of boxing events. Certainly, individual state regulatory agencies such as the New York State Athletic Commission and private national entities such as the BBBC have made some admirable efforts to regulate bouts held within their respective jurisdictions. Nonetheless, boxing's major regulatory problem is that if the promoters of a fight are of the opinion that the medical safeguards or licence fees of one state or national commission are too onerous, they simply move to a more 'accommodating' jurisdiction. Focussing on the American experience but in comments that are applicable to the sport worldwide, Laufer neatly encapsulates the dangers of such 'forum shopping':

> Economic motives and the fragmented system of state regulation also induce many boxers and managers to evade the law. A boxer, temporarily deprived of his livelihood by safety regulations in one state, may cross the border into another state and box there

---

[202] On 21 September 1991, a world championship fight between Michael Watson and Chris Eubank was stopped in the final round as Watson appeared unable to defend himself. Watson lost consciousness in the ring and there was a series of delays in treating him ringside and further delays in reaching a neurological trauma hospital. In *Watson v British Boxing Board of Control* [2001] QB 1134, the Court of Appeal held that the BBBC owed a duty of care to ensure an adequate standard of ringside medical treatment for an injured boxer, including the adoption of rules and policies that would protect the health and safety of boxers. The duty was breached by the inadequacy of the BBBC's existing medical guidelines, and this caused foreseeable harm by exacerbating a serious brain injury incurred by Watson during the course of a bout. The case resulted in a £1 million award and the BBBC facing into administration but it also led to a significant overhauling of the BBBC's medical safeguards and regulations surrounding the holding of professional bouts.

using a different name, in reckless disregard of his health. There exists an incomplete and fragmentary exchange of information between many state boxing commissions regarding the routine identification and medical condition of injured boxers. The commission's difficulty in obtaining the accurate medical history of boxers is an international problem as well.[203]

[**5.70**]   In sum, because professional boxing's global administrative structures are based on a weak (and practically non-existent) self-regulatory model—put into stark contrast recently by the difficulties the World Anti-doping Agency has had in implementing its policy and testing regimes within the sport—its vulnerability to legal challenge, even proscription, is heightened.[204] Conspicuously, the gross recklessness in permitting fighters with an unknown medical history to box contrasts with the fact that the medical dangers of the sport are well documented. On a global scale it can be said therefore that the sport has in effect surrendered the self-regulatory competence which it has held since the late 1800s. Ideally, the resulting 'governance vacuum' should be filled by a centralised independent governing body—an international federation for professional boxing—made up of representatives from various national boxing commissions and representative of all elements of the contemporary professional boxing fraternity, including administrators, promoters, media representatives, and former boxers. It must be admitted, however, that an international federation for pro-boxing (sitting atop a governance pyramid *qua* FIFA in football; FINA in swimming, etc) is unlikely in the near future given the vested interests involved currently in the sport.

[**5.73**]   Finally, and returning to the UK, it must also be acknowledged that, although the 10 'soft-paternalistic' reforms mentioned above have the welfare, development and input of the boxing fraternity in mind, even the most advanced statutory regulation will not prevent all boxing-related injuries and deaths. Nonetheless, it is not unreasonable to conclude that strict health and safety standards underpinned by potential criminal liability would mitigate the occurrence of unnecessary loss of life or serious injury. It might even transpire that a safer, more financially transparent sport, led by authoritative governing organisations in the US and UK, would attract a wider (and badly needed) global participative and sponsorship base for the sport. But again that is for the future—or utopia—for now, it suffices to reiterate that although the introductory part of this postscript enquired as to the legality of boxing; the conclusion focuses more on the sport's credibility. In the late 1800s, boxing in Britain received an exemption from the accepted boundaries of the criminal law because it was seen as an acceptably safe, in terms of physicality and morality, alternative to prize fighting. Boxing's veil of credibility and legitimacy has since frayed in the face of its regulatory and medical

---

[203] L Laufer, 'Uniform Health and Safety Standards for Professional Boxing: A Problem in Search of a Federal Solution' (1984) 15 *Columbia Human Rights Law Review* 259, 279–80.

[204] M Costello and N Hassan, 'Boxing's Dirty Secret: Victor Conte Slams Professional Boxing's Drug Testing' BBC News Online 28 January 2010 available online at http://news.bbc.co.uk/sport1/hi/boxing/8485892.stm.

deficiencies. Moreover, the *Brown* litigation has revealed that in the contemporary legal context, the sport's exemption from the English criminal law of assault rests more on an unquestioned assumption than a clear legal principle or authority. Whether these vulnerabilities (which will inevitably come to the fore the next time there is a tragic and possibly televised incident in a boxing ring) will culminate in calls for the sport's proscription remains open to debate. What is known is that the law's response to boxing, or, more precisely, professional boxing's current attitude to the law's definition of a legitimate sporting pursuit, is not up to scratch.

Further Points of Interest and Discussion

1. Violence, sport and the criminal law have been discussed largely in the context of the participants' consent. What role might the defences of accident, self-defence, mistaken identity and even automatism play in any prosecution for 'sporting assault'?
2. Do you think that the so-called *Cey* criteria adequately take into account the 'playing culture' of sports in assessing whether or not violent conduct on the field of play is sufficiently grave to be properly categorised as criminal in nature?
3. The British Medical Association has recently called for a complete ban on a number of combat or mixed martial arts such as ultimate fighting and cage fighting, which they have described as 'human cockfighting'. Having considered the legality of the sport of boxing, what do you think of the legal status of other combat or mixed martial arts sports?
4. In *R v Marsh* [1994] Crim L Rev 52, a rugby league player was charged with inflicting grievous bodily harm on an opponent in an 'off-the-ball' incident. The Court of Appeal held that the defendant could have been cross-examined at trial about his past disciplinary record for violent play on the rugby field. The Court of Appeal noted that such disciplinary findings were in no sense 'convictions' but nonetheless could be properly raised in cross-examination as to the character of the defendant, had the defendant so elected to put his good character to the court.

In light of that ruling, and this chapter as a whole, how would you advise a player who has seriously injured another on the field of play?

6

Civil Liability In Sport

Introduction

[**6.01**]   This chapter considers both personal injury liability for injuries inflicted by a participant upon an opponent during a sporting pursuit and whether tortious liability is an effective means of deterring violent conduct among sports participants.[1] The principal sporting emphasis is (again) on competitive body contact games. The legal emphasis is on the torts of trespass to the person and negligence. The steady flow of cases on participant liability for sports injuries illustrates that the latter is the most likely cause of action, to which the most likely defence is that of *volenti non fit injuria*. Analogous to the law of criminal assault, breach of 'implied sporting consent' or the volenti of the claimant is central in application, as assessed through a number of objective criteria, including the skill level of the injuring party and whether that defendant was acting whithout care of the claimant's safety. These criteria or evidential guidelines, which emerge from a careful doctrinal analysis of the relevant case law, are crucial to the examination of the appropriate degree of care in negligence within the prevailing circumstances of sport. The case law, mainly from the England and Wales jurisdiction but with frequent reference to Australian and North American jurisprudence, also reveals the emergence of a unique evidential standard of care sensitive to the circumstances of sport—that of 'reckless disregard'. The chapter also searches (briefly) for some theoretical coherency within the case law; premising it on Fletcher's idea of reciprocal risk-taking. In addition, the underlying policy-related issue of sport's social utility is discussed, as are practical matters relating to vicarious liability, insurance and the measure of damages for 'lost sporting opportunity'. On the last point, an emerging and complex aspect of participant liability for sporting injury is the quantum of damages appropriate for a player, who through injury, is denied a highly lucrative professional career in elite sport. Moreover, it will be shown how personal injury claims relating

---

[1] Unlike other chapters in this text, the word 'participant' is favoured over the generic use of the term 'athlete'. The chapter draws heavily from the author's previous work in the area and especially J Anderson, 'Personal Injury Liability in Sport: Emerging Trends' (2008) 16 *Tort Law Review* 95. See also N Cox, 'Civil Liability for Foul Play in Sport' (2003) 54 *Northern Ireland Legal Quarterly* 351.

to sports participant liability now extend to a consideration of the duties of coaches, referees, sports governing bodies and schools. Finally, this chapter is set against the backdrop of an apparently spiralling 'compensation culture' and the concomitant threat that that 'blame culture' poses for the future promotion, operation and administration of sport.

Torts and Sports Generally

[**6.02**]   Jahn has argued that the law of torts should be seen as 'the best way to deter violent conduct among athletes and provide them with an adequate remedy for their injuries. Tort law imposes financial liability on the athlete ... and this will hit him where it hurts the most—in his pocket'.[2] Jahn's contention is an inverse of the standard assumption that the admonitory nature of money compensation arising from civil liability is, in comparison to the custodial punishment of the criminal law, the less effective in terms of deterrence.[3] Nevertheless, in the context of deterring violent play in sport, Jahn appears correct, and for two reasons. First, the criminal law is a rather blunt instrument in such circumstances, and can lead to an individual participant becoming the 'scapegoat' for the unsafe practices of their chosen sport.[4] Second, there is no doubt that large damages awards, affecting a delimited part of society, 'get attention'.[5] Accordingly, a compensation award that includes an element of exemplary damages will not only attract significant media attention, it can also have a significant 'trickledown' effect; acting as a reminder for all those involved in that particular sporting community—participants and administrators—that the law's grasp is extensive.[6]

[**6.03**]   High profile examples of large scale, injury-related damages in sports history include: the $3.25 million awarded by a federal district court in 1979 to Houston Rockets professional basketball player, Rudy Tomjanovich for injuries suffered as a result of a blow to the face by the Los Angeles Lakers' Kermit Washington, which led to the stiffest punishment ever imposed on a player by the National

---

[2] G Jahn, 'Civil Liability: An Alternative to Violence in Sporting Events' (1988) 15 *Ohio Northern University Law Review* 243, 253.

[3] For an introduction to the idea of deterrence as an underlying function of the law of torts see S Deakin, A Johnston and B Markesinis, *Markesinis and Deakin's Tort Law* 6th edn (Oxford, Oxford University Press, 2007) 50–52.

[4] See generally the previous chapter of this text and S Fafinski, 'Consent and the Rules of the Game: The Interplay of Civil and Criminal Liability for Sporting Injuries" (2005) 69 *Journal of Criminal Law* 414.

[5] C Sharkey, 'Punitive Damages as Societal Damages' (2003) 113 *Yale Law Review* 347, 349.

[6] For the argument that exemplary damages in the law of torts are driven as much by deterrence as it is by the vindication of the claimant's right see R Stevens, *Torts and Rights* (Oxford, Oxford University Press, 2007) 87.

Basketball Association;[7] two decisions from the mid-1990s by the British Colombia Court of Appeal to uphold total sums in excess of Can$7 million in damages resulting from findings of negligence against hockey players who had body-checked opponents rendering them quadriplegic;[8] the concerns in British professional football arising out of the £900,000 in compensation paid to Bradford FC's Gordon Watson in 1997 as a result of 'the most expensive tackle in British legal history';[9] and the reaction in Australia in 2005 to a professional rugby league player's success in suing two opponents, and their employing club, for career-ending neck injuries sustained in a 'spear tackle'.[10] These proceedings notwithstanding, the (little) empirical evidence that exists suggests that injured sports participants are generally reluctant to commence legal proceedings.[11] A positive reading of these findings might suggest that injured players prefer, on seeing the injuring party sanctioned by the sport's internal disciplinary mechanisms, to seek recompense through their sport's applicable insurance scheme. Evidently, the cost of instigating and sustaining litigation is also a factor, as is, in a slightly more negative vein, the fact that an ethos of 'what happens on the field; stays on the field' is prevalent in many contact sports, discouraging any recourse to the ordinary courts.[12] The import this has for sports governing bodies in ensuring that their internal insurance and disciplinary provisions are satisfactorily drawn will be returned to in the conclusion. For now, the concern is not *why* a sports participant might be motivated to resort to a civil action against an injuring opponent rather *how* they might proceed, in terms of an appropriate cause of action and likely defences.

Sporting Batteries

[**6.04**]   The relevant causes of action for the recovery of damages for sports injuries lie in trespass to the person (battery) and negligence. The most likely defence

---

[7] The blow fractured Tomjanovich's face and skull and led to leakage of cerebral fluid. See *Tomjanovich v California Sports Inc* Unreported, Trial Docket Number H-78-243, Southern District of Texas 10 October 1979; Appeal Docket Number 79-3889, 5th Circuit Court of Appeals 3 December 1979 and, in background, N Tucker, 'Assumption of Risk and Vicarious Liability in Personal Injury Actions brought by Professional Athletes' [1980] *Duke Law Journal* 472.

[8] *Unruh v Webber* (1994) 112 DLR (4th) 83 and *Zapf v Muckalt* (1996) 142 DLR (4th) 438. See generally, B Svoranos, "Fighting? It's All in a Day's Work on the Ice: Determining the Appropriate Standard of a Hockey Player's Liability to Another? (1997) 7 *Seton Hall Journal of Sports Law* 487, 501–02.

[9] *Watson and Bradford City Football Club v Gray and Huddersfield Town Football Club*, Unreported, Queen's Bench Division 29 October 1998, *The Times* 26 November 1998, Hooper J; leave to appeal refused [1999] EWHC Admin 321.

[10] *McCracken v Melbourne Storm Rugby League Football Club & Ors* [2005] NSWSC 107 (holding of liability); [2006] NSWSC 1250 (assessment of damages, Aus$97,500). Both decisions affirmed on appeal, [2007] NSWCA 353, [2007] Aust Torts Reports 81–925.

[11] See above [5.06]–[5.07] of this text.

[12] The 'misplaced machismo' of this ethos also appears to exist in other jurisdictions, including the litigant-friendly environment of the US. See E Rosenthal 'Inside the Lines: Basing Negligence Liability in Sports for Safety Based Rule Violations on the Level of Play' (2004) 72 *Fordham Law Review* 2631, 2632.

to a 'sporting trespass' is consent;[13] and volenti in the case of 'sporting negligence'.[14] Paraphrasing Lord Denning MR in *Letang v Cooper*, trespass to the person can be characterised by its concern for direct intentional acts; negligence by its concern for careless or indirect acts.[15] That distinction prompts three points of relevance. First, sports claimants do not generally seek to pursue cases of trespass to the person. Principally, this is because modern trespass actions are determined by an intentional act on the part of the defendant and thus, in the circumstances of sport, the defendant's mental state would have to be considered in light of the necessarily robust (but well regulated) environment that is sport where players frequently act and react in 'the heat of the moment'.[16] In short, and to borrow the term used in *Wilson v Pringle*, it would appear difficult for a claimant to show that, in the context of a recognisable contact sport, the defendant had acted with the requisite 'hostility'.[17]

[**6.05**]   Second, participation in sport provides a lawful excuse to battery as based on the implied consent of the parties.[18] The degree or level of injury to which a player can consent—that is, the limits of 'implied sporting consent' to a battery— can be determined with reference to the bounds of physical contact generally acceptable in the ordinary conduct of the game in question.[19] The prescient late nineteenth century Scottish case of *Reid v Mitchell* encapsulates the matter succinctly:

> When people engage in a game involving risk, or in a game generally safe, but in which accidents may happen, every player taking part in it takes on himself the risks incident to being a player, and he will have no remedy for any injury he may receive in the course

---

[13]   A likely factual scenario for a battery case is a fracas between opposing players during the course of a collision sport such as rugby. In that instance, self defence might apply where the defendant would have to prove that in the circumstances it was his honest and reasonable belief that he was in imminent danger of being attacked, and that the force used by him was reasonable. See *Ashley & Anor v Chief Constable of Sussex Police* [2008] UKHL 25 [16]-[20], Lord Scott. Similarly, consideration might even be given to a defendant justifying a battery as being 'in defence of a teammate' pursuant to the old common law rule of 'defence of another' operating outside of s 3 of the Criminal Law Act 1967. Provocation by the claimant may be a ground for reducing damages, *Lane v Holloway* [1968] 1 QB 379, 387, Lord Denning MR.

[14]   Note also the potential application of contributory negligence based on a failure to follow safety guidelines as in *Craven v Riches* [2001] EWCA Civ 375. Presumably, it could apply where an injured party failed to wear mandatory protective equipment analogous to *O'Connell v Jackson* [1972] 1 QB 270 (moped driver not wearing a crash helmet) and *Froom v Butcher* [1976] QB 286 (a passenger in a car not wearing a seat belt).

[15]   *Letang v Cooper* [1965] 1 QB 232, 239–40.

[16]   See also S Gardiner *et al*, *Sports Law* 3rd edn (London, Cavendish, 2006) 630 where it is noted that the rarity of sporting battery cases in professional sport might also be explained by the fact that the standard approach in applicable insurance policies is to specifically exclude cover for deliberately inflicted injuries. Accordingly, if an action for battery were successful, the defendant would be personally liable and unable to rely on his or his employing club's insurance. It follows logically that a claimant would not wish to restrict the pool of defendants in this manner.

[17]   *Wilson v Pringle* [1987] QB 237 where the term 'hostility' is not equated with ill-will on the part of the defendant, rather an objectionable and unlawful intrusion on the claimant's rights to physical integrity in light of the circumstances at hand. See J Murphy, *Street on Torts* 12th edn (Oxford, Oxford University Press, 2007) 237.

[18]   *Blake v Galloway* [2004] EWCA Civ 814 [20]–[24], Dyson LJ.

[19]   Paraphrasing the celebrated phrase from *Collins v Wilcock* [1984] 1 WLR 1172, 1177, Goff LJ.

of it, unless, there has been some undue violence or unfair play on the part of some of the others. He takes the risks incident to the game, and the result of these risks must lie where they fall.[20]

This is broadly analogous to the situation that now appears to apply in the law of criminal assault, where conduct beyond that which is ordinarily incidental to the playing of a game and thus not covered by the scope of implied sporting consent, is assessed in light of a number of objective criteria such as its rules and 'playing culture', the nature of the injuring act, the extent of force employed, the degree of risk of injury and the state of mind of the accused.[21]

[**6.06**] Overall, having to surmount the hurdles of intent and implied consent, within the context of the speed and frequency of collisions in contact sport, means that civil actions for sporting batteries are rare in England and Wales, as they are, on similar grounds, in the various jurisdictions of the US[22] and Canada.[23] That is not to say that a sporting battery is a completely implausible cause of action to the point that sports participants can be said to have an effective immunity from civil assault and battery.[24] In Australia, for instance, there have been a number of cases with the seminal authority located in Fox J's judgment in *McNamara v Duncan*.[25] In the stated case, the claimant, who had suffered a fractured skull as a result of being elbowed by an opponent during a game of Australian Rules football, sought damages in battery. The defence was twofold (and typical of sporting battery cases). First, the defendant argued that the elbow was an accidental part of a (late) tackle. Second, even if intentional, the injuring blow was an accepted part of the game to which, impliedly, the claimant had consented. In delivering judgment, Fox J was in no doubt that the defendant had 'meant to do it'[26] and that the defendant's actions went beyond the intention of the rules of the game in question and thus he should be held liable.[27] Fox J reiterated the view held in

---

[20] *Reid v Mitchell* (1885) 12 R 1129, 1132, Lord Young. Note the similar phraseology used in the *Restatement of Torts, Second* 2nd edn (Philadelphia, American Law Institute, 1965) comment b, s 50, 86.

[21] See previously the summary at [5.35].

[22] See the cases noted by D Richardson 'Player Violence: An Essay on Torts and Sports' (2004) 15 *Stanford Law & Policy Review* 133, 139. In the US, the seminal authority is usually taken to be *Averill v Luttrell* (1857) 311 SW (2d) 812 (Tennessee Court of Appeal).

[23] See the cases noted by J Citron and M Abelman, 'Civil Liability in the Arena of Professional Sports' (2003) 36 *University of British Columbia Law Review* 193,198–200. The seminal Canadian authority involving an intentional 'sporting' tort is *Agar v Canning* (1966) 55 WWR 384 (Manitoba Court of Appeal). See recently *Leighton v Best* (2009) CanLII 25972 (Ontario Superior Court of Justice).

[24] Note *Lewis v Brookshaw* (1970) 120 NLJ 413 and the liability at trial of the first named defendant in *Gravil v Carroll and Redruth Rugby Football Club* [2008] EWCA Civ 689.

[25] *McNamara v Duncan* (1971) 26 ALR 584. See generally D Thorpe *et al, Sports Law* (Melbourne, Oxford University Press, 2009) 108–12. For a note on New Zealand see J Francis, 'Manly Diversions' [1997] *New Zealand Law Journal* 158.

[26] Ibid *McNamara v Duncan* (1971) 26 ALR 584, 587 noting: 'I do not suggest that he meant to incapacitate the plaintiff or indeed cause him any serious injury.'

[27] Ibid 589, noting: 'There is but a vague suggestion that hits similar to that made by the defendant do sometimes occur, but nothing more definite, and no evidence that such acts, or similar acts, are common.'

comparable jurisdictions that players in contact sports consent to such violence as is ordinarily and reasonably incidental to, and contemplated by, the playing of the sport in question: 'In the game of Australian Rules football, deliberate injury, in the sense of something done solely and principally with a view to causing sensible hurt, in not justified by the rules and usages of the game. Sensible hurt, produced as a result of intentional acts, is on the other hand an inevitable concomitant of ordinary play'.[28] This 'rules and usages' approach, has not only been adopted in numerous state jurisdictions in Australia, it also provides a useful illustrative summary of the test applied in comparable jurisdictions to consent in intentional sports-related torts.[29]

Sporting Negligence

[**6.07**]   There is little need to resort to the tripartite *Caparo* test to ascertain that sports participants owe each other a duty of care on the sports field.[30] As observed in *Sandhar v Department of Transport*, 'Personal or physical injury directly inflicted is the first building block of negligence. Unless such injury is excused it will almost always be a component part of a breach of a duty of care owed by the party inflicting the injury to the person … injured'.[31] Breach of duty is assessed objectively with reference to the ordinary, prudent person taking reasonable care in the circumstances at hand. In the circumstances of sport, the leading English case on the applicable standard of care appears to be that of *Wooldridge v Sumner & Anor*.[32] In the stated case, the claimant, a professional photographer, who was filming the action within an arena, was knocked down and severely injured during an eventing competition by a horse owned by the first-named defendant and ridden by the second-named defendant. In the course of a judgment, wherein the English Court of Appeal held that negligence on the part of the defendants was not established, Sellers LJ framed the standard of care in the circumstances of sport in the following terms:

> Provided the competition or game is being performed within the rules and the requirement of the sport and by a person of adequate skill and competence, the spectator does not expect his safety to be regarded by the participant. If the conduct is deliberately

---

[28] Ibid. The phrase 'sensible hurt' is somewhat awkward though it appears that is used in its archaic sense of hurt that is 'readily perceived; appreciable'.

[29] Note *Pallante v Stadiums Pty Ltd* [1976] VR 331 (Victoria, boxing); *Giumelli v Johnson* [1991] Aust Torts Reports 81-085 (South Australia, Australian Rules); *Smith v Emerson* [1986] Aust Torts Reports 80-022 (ACT, Australian Rules); *Hilton v Wallace* [1989] Aust Torts Reports 80-231 (Queensland, rugby league); *Silbey v Milutinovic* [1990] Aust Torts Reports 81-013 (ACT, soccer); *Canterbury Bankstown Rugby League Football Club Ltd v Rogers* [1993] Aust Torts Reports 81-246 (NSW, rugby league); and *Re Lenfield* (1993) 114 FLR 195, (1993) Aust Torts Reports 81-222 (ACT, informal rugby).

[30] The necessary ingredients giving rise to a duty of care—foreseeability, proximity and fairness—clearly being present. See *Caparo v Dickman* [1990] 2 AC 605, 617–18, Lord Bridge.

[31] *Sandhar v Department of Transport* [2004] EWCA Civ 1440 [38], May LJ.

[32] *Wooldridge v Sumner* [1963] 2 QB 43.

intended to injure someone whose presence is known or is reckless and in disregard to all safety of others so that it is a departure from the standard which might reasonably be expected in anyone pursuing the competition or game, then the performer might well be liable for any injury his act caused.[33]

[**6.08**]   The above extract prompts four points of interest relating to: a sports participant's duty to spectators; that participant's liability to fellow competitors; the appropriate degree of care for a participant; and the defence of *volenti non fit injuria*. First, the possible liability of a sports participant to a spectator is a matter that has appeared infrequently before the English courts, presumably because *Wooldridge* has established that the competitor would have to have 'very blatantly disregarded'[34] the safety of spectators before he could be held to have failed to exercise reasonable care in the circumstances.[35] Second, it appears logical to suggest that the *Wooldridge* approach to breach of duty in the circumstances of sport applies not only to a participant's regard for the safety of spectators but also to all others proximate to his actions, notably the participant's fellow competitors.[36] Third, there are two elements to the *Wooldridge* approach: momentary lapses of skill and judgement by the participant in the 'agony of the moment' will not amount to negligence provided that (a) the participant can be said to have a reasonable level of skill, judgment and experience, and (b) the participant did not act in a manner that can be adjudged to have been recklessly in disregard of the safety of others immediately involved in that activity.[37] The latter, with its emphasis on breach of safety rules (as opposed to mere lapses in skill), is by far the more important (and problematical) in shaping the courts' approach to incidents of sporting negligence, and will be discussed in detail shortly.[38]

[**6.09**]   It is argued that in the circumstances of sport the reference to a participant's level of skill should not distract from the principal matter (the disregard of safety).[39] As Diplock LJ (as he then was) observed in *Wooldridge*, the duty

---

[33]   Ibid 56–57.

[34]   *Smoldon v Whitworth and Nolan* [1997] PIQR P133, P139, Bingham LCJ. See also *Hall v Brooklands Auto-Racing Club* [1933] 1 KB 205, 214, Scrutton LJ and *Murray v Harringay Arena* [1951] 2 KB 529, 535, Singleton LJ. For an American perspective see B Celedonia, 'Flying Objects: Arena Liability for Fan Injuries in Hockey and Other Sports' (2008) 15 *Sports Lawyers Journal* 115. Note the convictions of two professional footballers who in temper lashed a ball into the stand during the course of a game injuring a spectator: *R v Kirk*, *The Daily Telegraph* 17 October 1995 and *R v Lavin*, *The Times* 26 September 2000.

[35]   Liability to passers-by is well known through the discussion in *Bolton v Stone* [1951] AC 850. For an excellent review of the historical, legal and sporting context surrounding that decision see M Lunney, 'Six and out? *Bolton v Stone* after 50 years' (2003) 24 *Journal of Legal History* 1.

[36]   Note *Harrison v Vincent* [1982] RTR 8, 13, Sir John Arnold P.

[37]   *Wooldridge* [1963] 2 QB 43, 67–68, Diplock LJ.

[38]   See S Yeo, 'Determining Consent in Body Contact Sports' (1998) 6 *Tort Law Review* 199, 209 where he remarks that the underlying explanation of the case law on sporting negligence is the correlation between breach of duty and breach of a safety rule of the game in question.

[39]   There is little reference to this aspect of the test in the more recent case law on the topic. See generally D McArdle and M James, 'Are You Experienced? "Playing Cultures", Sporting Rules and Personal Injury Litigation after *Caldwell v Maguire*' (2005) 13 *Tort Law Review* 193.

owed is a duty of care not a duty of skill.[40] In application to participant liability for sporting injuries, it must be highlighted that the very nature of organised modern sport, particularly games involving invasive physical collisions, results in participants (be it individually or in teams) competing against opponents of a similar skills-set. In regulated competitive sports, mixed ability groupings are rare because in order to maintain a safe and competitive balance (and a sense of enjoyment) most governing bodies operate on a multi-level system of leagues with promotion and relegation ensuring that participants usually compete at the appropriate level.[41]

[**6.10**]   In sum, Diplock LJ's point as to a participant's skill should be interpreted simply as a means of reiterating the fundamental point, which is that in the circumstances of sport where a competitor is going 'all out' to win and thus may 'in the agony of the moment' have little time to think or react, a mere error of judgement or lapse in skill should not necessarily equate to negligence—the defendant/participant's conduct must be such as to evince a reckless disregard of the safety of the claimant.[42] The one residual point of note regarding a participant having 'some modicum of skill' relates to Diplock LJ's caveat that, 'It may well be that a participant in a game or competition would be guilty of negligence … if he took part in it when he knew or ought to have known that his lack of skill was such that, even if he exerted it to the utmost, he was likely to cause injury'.[43] In a largely self-regulated, recreational pursuit such as club golf, Diplock LJ's remarks have some relevance. By way of illustration, Sellers LJ in *Wooldridge* gave an account of an unreported decision in which he had tried where he had found negligence against a golfer who, due to poor skill, had fallen behind his fellow players but on discovering his 'lost' ball, and despite previously assuring otherwise, had proceeded to replace and hit it, resulting in a serious eye injury to the claimant.[44] A more modern example, with a similar reasoning and result, came before the English Court of Appeal in *Pearson v Lightning*,[45] while claims resulting from 'reckless duffers' have occurred with some frequency in Australia,[46] the US[47] and Scotland.[48]

---

[40]   *Wooldridge* [1963] 2 QB 43, 68, Diplock LJ.

[41]   Note *Craven v Riches* [2001] EWCA Civ 375 where an award of damages was made against the organisers of a mixed ability motorcycling event in light of the quadriplegia suffered by the claimant who crashed after being hindered by slower, more inexperienced competitors. According to the Court of Appeal, the organisers' duty of care extended to ensuring that the mixed ability groupings competed separately.

[42]   Echoed by Lord Denning MR in *Wilks v Cheltenham Car Club* [1971] 2 All ER 369, 371.

[43]   *Wooldridge* [1963] 2 QB 43, 68.

[44]   *Wooldridge* [1963] 2 QB 43, 55–56, Sellers LJ citing *Cleghorn v Oldham* (1927) 43 TLR 465, and observing disapprovingly that the defendant was so unskilled that he had 'hit his tee shot no further than the ladies' tee.'

[45]   *Pearson v Lightning* [1998] EWCA Civ 591.

[46]   Eg, *Ollier v Magnetic Island Country Club* [2004] QCA 137, [2004] Aust Torts Reports 81–743.

[47]   See generally D Lazaroff, 'Golfers' Tort Liability: A Critique of an Emerging Standard' (2002) 24 *Hastings Communications and Entertainment Law Journal* 317.

[48]   Eg, *Feeney v Lyall* [1991] SLT 156 and *Lewis v Buckpool Golf Club* [1993] SLT (Sh Ct) 43.

[**6.11**]   The fourth point of interest emanating from *Wooldridge* concerns volenti. *Wooldridge* is a good example of the English courts viewing the principle of assumption of risk in terms of breach of duty rather than as an absolute defence to an admitted negligent act.[49] The general principle, followed in a number of sporting negligence cases, is that by taking part in the game, the injured participant assumed and appreciated the accepted inherent risks of injury associated with the sport.[50] In short, and to paraphrase Diplock LJ in *Wooldridge*, the volenti that is relevant is not volenti to the risk of an injurious tortious act but volenti to the lack of reasonable care that may produce that risk.[51] In this light, it is argued that, similar to the assessment of consent in intentional torts; the courts should, in assessing fault in negligence, utilise a number of objective criteria based around play that is ordinarily incidental to the rules, usages and spirit of the sporting activity in question. In this, the evidential guideline of 'reckless disregard' will be seen to be most useful in determining want of reasonable care by an injuring sports participant.

The 'Sportsman's' Charter

[**6.12**]   The *Wooldridge* approach was quickly, and somewhat sceptically (and old-fashionedly), labelled as 'The "Sportsman's" Charter'.[52] Critics such as Goodhart had little difficulty with the principle that a sporting competitor was not necessarily in breach of his duty to another, and would not be held liable in negligence, for injuries caused by a lapse of skill or judgment in the heat of competition. Nevertheless, the rationale used by the Court of Appeal to support that contention—that elemental to a finding of liability in sporting negligence was a finding of recklessness—was, according to that distinguished commentator, highly questionable.[53] In brief, Goodhart argued that by holding a competitor liable only in those cases in which he had acted in reckless disregard of the safety of another, the Court of Appeal was moving away from the thrust of *Donoghue v Stevenson*.[54] Goodhart's preference, and one which he reiterated would be more in accord with the general principles of negligence, was for a competitor's liability for an injury caused by an error of judgement to be assessed with reference to what a reasonable competitor, being 'a reasonable man of the sporting world', would or would not have done.[55]

---

[49] See, eg, the discussion of *Wooldridge* in Murphy (n 17) 184 and in WVH Rogers *Winfield & Jolowicz on Tort* 17th edn (London, Thomson Sweet & Maxwell, 2006) 1066.

[50] See, eg, *Rootes v Shelton* [1967] 116 CLR 383, 384–86, Barwick CJ.

[51] *Wooldridge* [1963] 2 QB 43, 69.

[52] AL Goodhart, 'The Sportsman's Charter' (1962) 78 LQR 490.

[53] Ibid 492 and somewhat damning the Court of Appeal's judgment with faint praise by remarking, 'It is on this point regarding the reckless disregard for the safety of others that the present case seems to introduce a novel element into the law [of negligence].'

[54] [1932] AC 562.

[55] Goodhart (n 52) 496.

[**6.13**]   Post-*Wooldridge*, the issue of 'the reasonable man of the sporting world versus the reckless disregard of the competitor' has somewhat dominated commentary on participant liability for sporting injuries in England and Wales,[56] and in comparable jurisdictions such as the US[57] and Canada.[58] Taking its lead from Goodhart, the debate is usually approached as if it were one of 'either/or'.[59] It is submitted however that analysis of the subsequent Court of Appeal case law reveals that the matter is more one of 'and/both'. In this, the case synthesis brings to light three points of interest. First, and fundamentally, in using the terminology of 'reckless disregard' the Court of Appeal in *Wooldridge* was not in any way promoting a novel duty of care based on a vague policy-led view of the sporting rules, usages and circumstances of the case.[60] As the literature surrounding *Nettleship v Weston*[61] demonstrates, individualised duties of care are not popular in the orthodox English analysis of the tort of negligence.[62] Neither, as Gearty has pointed out, could a 'spectrum of declining duties' be applied with any consistency to the number of highly-varied pursuits that come under the term 'sport'.[63] Gearty is also correct in his remarks that sport should however 'be treated differently' and to have any conceptual usefulness the duty upon 'the reasonable man of the sporting world' should be modified, evidentially at least, 'to take account of its consensual context'.[64] It is suggested therefore that a 'duty' not to show reckless disregard for an opponent is a useful benchmark in sports negligence cases.

[**6.14**]   Second, it is contended that what McBride has deemed the idealised 'duty to be careful' remains the fulcrum of the application of negligence-based

---

[56] For instance, M Beloff, T Kerr and M Demetriou, *Sports Law* (Oxford, Hart Publishing, 1999) 111–17.

[57] Evidence of reckless conduct has been central to the sports negligence debate in the US since *Hackbart v Cincinnati Bengals Inc* (1979) 601 F (2d) 516 (10th Circuit Court of Appeals). For a general review of the approach of individual states, see M Cole, 'No Blood, No Foul: The Standard of Care in Texas Owed by Participants to one another in Athletic Contests' (2007) 59 *Baylor Law Review* 435, 443–56.

[58] Most Canadian provinces appear to avail themselves of a quasi-recklessness evidential standard of conduct in assessing sports negligence, especially in instances of contact sport. See G Moore, 'Has Hockey been Checked from Behind North of the Border? *Unruh, Zapf* and Canada's Participant Liability Standard' (1998) 5 *Sports Lawyers Journal* 1, 20 and, more generally, T Fenton, 'Actionable Violence or "Just Part of the Game"? Applying Standard Trespass and Negligence Principles to Sports Violence in Canada' (2005) 13 *Tort Law Review* 122.

[59] See, eg, V Pickford, 'Playing Dangerous Games' (1998) 6 *Tort Law Review* 221.

[60] The case law concerning sporting negligence also supports the argument that proximity-based rather than policy-based reasons provide a more consistent rationale for duty of care determinations in negligence. See generally C Witting, 'Duty of Care: An Analytical Approach' (2005) 25 *Oxford Journal of Legal Studies* 33.

[61] *Nettleship v Weston* [1971] 2 QB 691.

[62] Note D Howarth, 'Many Duties of Care—Or a Duty of Care? Notes from the Underground' (2006) 26 *Oxford Journal of Legal Studies* 449.

[63] C Gearty, 'Liability for Injuries Incurred During Sport and Pastimes' [1985] *CLJ* 371, 372: 'At one extreme, the regular duty of care; at the other, no duty at all, as where, for example, the activity partook of the nature of war or of something else in which all was notoriously fair.'

[64] Ibid.

claims to sport.[65] In that light, all that proponents of reckless disregard are advocating is a modified 'sporting' standard of care that is higher than that which normally applies in the law of negligence.[66] The underlying policy aspect of this approach is threefold: the promotion of participation in the healthy, community-based activity that is sport; the avoidance of a flood of litigation arising from sports-related accidents; and a commonsense distinction between excessively harmful conduct and the more routine 'rough and tumble' of sport that should occur freely on the playing field and should not be second-guessed in the courtrooms.[67] It must be stressed that the recklessness-related sporting standard of care is not in any way definitional to a finding of breach of duty in the tort of negligence; it is merely evidential, with the phrase 'reckless disregard for the safety of another' doing no more than providing a useful rationale or guideline or threshold for adjudicating upon the (mis)behaviour of 'the reasonable man of the sporting world'.[68]

[**6.15**]   The third and final point of note, prior to addressing the case law directly, is to admit that the phrase 'reckless disregard' has to its detriment as a criterion in assessing sports participant negligence, been used cumbersomely and imprecisely.[69] Moreover, it is acknowledged that the debate as a whole is vulnerable to criticism that it is of academic concern only, in the sense that as a matter of practice, liability will attach notwithstanding 'if it is found by the tribunal of fact that the defendant failed to exercise that degree of care which was appropriate in all the circumstances [reasonable care], or that he acted in a way to which the plaintiff cannot be expected to have consented [reckless disregard]'.[70] In this light, it is suggested that in order to secure optimal benefit from the phrase, as a rationale for assessing participant liability, the evidential test of reckless disregard should be embedded in a number of objective criteria, such as the rules and playing culture of the game in question. Together these criteria would assist in indicating to a tribunal of fact when a defendant's error of judgement might truly be considered negligent in nature.

---

[65] N McBride, 'Duties of Care—Do They Really Exist?' (2004) 24 *Oxford Journal of Legal Studies* 417.

[66] For theoretical coherency on the variable standard of care in negligence generally see R Kidner, 'The Variable Standard of Care, Contributory Negligence and *Volenti*' (1991) 11 *Legal Studies* 1.

[67] Summarised succinctly by the Supreme Court of New Jersey to mean that the heightened standard of reckless disregard limits liability to clearly unreasonable behaviour and insulates conduct that is inherent to sports and part of the game, *Schick v Ferolito* (2001) 767 A (2d) 962, 965, LaVecchia J.

[68] See similarly D McArdle, 'The Enduring Legacy of Reckless Disregard' (2005) 34 *Common Law World Review* 316.

[69] The Australian courts tend not to allude to the term 'recklessness' even as a factual, evidential guide to liability in sporting negligence. See generally the view of the High Court of Australia in *Rootes v Shelton* [1967] 116 CLR 383 and the comments of Priestly J in *Johnson v Frazer* (1990) 21 NSWLR 89, 94. This 'sensitivity' has been criticised by G Kelly, 'Negligence Actions between Sports Participants: The Measure of Liability' (1992) *Australian Law Journal* 329.

[70] *Condon v Basi* [1985] 1 WLR 866, 868, Sir John Donaldson MR.

Reasonable Care or Reckless Disregard?

[**6.16**]   Less than a decade after *Wooldridge*, the English Court of Appeal was presented with a similar set of facts in *Wilks v Cheltenham Car Club*.[71] In that case, the claimants were spectators at a motor cycle scramble when the participating defendant veered off the course through a set of ropes injuring the claimant. There was no mechanical explanation for how the accident occurred, and the trial court's view that the rope-barriers erected by the organisers of race were adequate was not challenged on appeal. The appeal concerned the finding that, owing to excessive speed, the defendant had lost control of his bike and thus had shown a reckless disregard of the safety of the spectators, and should be held liable in negligence. In the course of his judgment, Lord Denning MR considered *Wooldridge* and the accompanying criticism by Goodhart, and agreed that within *Wooldridge's* factual context, which was not an 'all out' race but a controlled demonstration of skill, Goodhart's commentary as to the appropriate degree of care had some merit.[72] Nevertheless, Lord Denning MR added that in the heat of a competitive race, the test of reckless disregard remained a useful one, though one he clearly viewed in evidential terms only:

> Let me first try to state the duty which lies on a competitor in a race. He must, of course, use reasonable care. But that means reasonable care having regard to the fact that he is a competitor in a race in which he is expected to go 'all out' to win … In a race a reasonable man would do everything he could do to win … [t]hat, I think, is the standard of care expected of him … [but the competitor will be liable] … if his conduct is such as to evince reckless disregard … in other words if his conduct is foolhardy.[73]

[**6.17**]   Phillimore LJ, adopting a similar approach, summarised the position neatly by observing that the test remained simply that of negligence, and that any finding of negligence must be viewed against all the circumstances and thus the guidelines (of a modicum of skill and reckless disregard) mentioned in *Wooldridge* were only to be applied 'if the circumstances warrant them'.[74] The core of this chapter is the submission that the reckless disregard test elucidated in *Wooldridge* is warranted in the circumstances of participant liability for injury during a competitive, contact sport. Further, this warranty is fundamental to an understanding of what many consider the seminal case in participant liability—the Court of Appeal's decision in *Condon v Basi*.[75] In that case, the claimant

---

[71] *Wilks* [1971] 2 All ER 369.
[72] See also Edmund Davies LJ, ibid 374. In ruling, at 375, that the doctrine of *res ipsa loquitur* was not applicable because the accident did not speak for itself, Edmund Davies LJ concluded, 'All happened in a split second, and (assuming the worst against [the second named defendant]) even a slip or misjudgement too slight to be regarded as amounting to negligence could well account for this accident.'
[73] Ibid 370–71.
[74] Ibid 376.
[75] [1985] 1 WLR 866.

instigated proceedings in negligence arising out of an incident during a local foot-ball league game during the course of which the defendant broke the claimant's leg. The county court awarded the claimant £4,900 damages for the injuries he received. The Court of Appeal upheld the decision.

[**6.18**]   The (concise) judgment of the then Master of the Rolls in *Condon v Basi* has attracted some criticism.[76] It must be admitted that a number of indi-vidual facets of the judgment are vulnerable to disapproval. For instance, in light of dicta in *Wooldridge* and *Wilks*, the judgment's opening as to the lack of guidance on the standard of care in competitive sport, is somewhat inauspicious.[77] Moreover, the court's opinion that a higher degree of care is required of a player in a First Division football match [now the Premier League] than of a player is a local league football match was ill-considered.[78] Gearty dismissed it in colourful terms:

> This gives a new dimension to knock-out competitions. Imagine Melchester Rovers, the league leaders, away to non-league Thugs United in the third round of the F.A. Cup. Must Roy continue to play his immaculate game under threat of personal injuries actions whilst all about him the manicured and expensive legs of his teammates are hacked to the ground by the legitimately incompetent?[79]

[**6.19**]   Most importantly, however, is the view that the judgment provides very little (and oft contradictory) guidance to practitioners and players as to breach of duty in instances where parties are engaged together in a sport or pastime, entailing physical contact or otherwise. Donaldson MR relied upon the decision of the High Court of Australia in *Rootes v Shelton*.[80] In that case, the claimant was an experienced water skier who was attempting various 'crossover' manoeu-vres on a wide and apparently clear stretch of river. The usual practice was for drivers to warn skiers of any potential, peripheral dangers because spray from the boat could occasionally blind the water-skier. Temporarily blinded by spray, the skier took a wider arc than normal, and collided with a boat. The skier was severely injured in the incident, and sued the driver of the towing boat for neg-ligence (failure to take due care in control of the boat and failure to warn). The jury found for the claimant. The Supreme Court of New South Wales set aside the verdict on the grounds that the driver of the towing vehicle owed no duty of care to the skier, both being participants in a sport who had, by engaging in the sport, accepted the inherent risks of injury. The injured party appealed suc-cessfully to the High Court where the New South Wales Supreme Court's order was discharged.

---

[76] See, eg, A Felix, 'The Standard of Care in Sport' (1996) 4 *Sport and the Law Journal* 32.

[77] *Condon v Basi* [1985] 1 WLR 866, 867, Sir John Donaldson MR.

[78] Ibid 868.

[79] Gearty (n 63) 373. Gearty suggests that his Lordship clearly cannot have been a football sup-porter and was probably distracted by the defendant's 'wonderful argument that he was such a bad player he owed no duty not to break his opponents' legs with awful tackles.' Note also the rejection by Drake J in *Elliot v Saunders* Unreported, Queen's Bench Division 10 June 1994.

[80] [1967] 116 CLR 383.

[**6.20**]   On appeal, the then Chief Justice of Australia approached the matter in terms similar to Diplock LJ in *Wooldridge* by focussing on the principle of
'assumption of inherent accepted risks', albeit viewing that apparent volenti in
terms of breach of duty rather than as an absolute defence to an admitted negligent act. Noting that the burden rests on the party who makes the claim of volenti,
Barwick CJ concluded that the skier could not be said to have voluntarily assumed
the risk of being towed dangerously close to an observable obstruction while temporarily blinded by spray.[81] In contrast, Kitto J preferred a generalised standard
of care compliant with both *Donoghue v Stevenson* and Goodhart's analysis: 'the
conclusion to be reached must necessarily depend upon the reasonableness, in
relation to the special [sporting] circumstances, of the conduct which caused the
plaintiff's injury'.[82] Donaldson MR cited both approaches, preferring the latter,
but acknowledging, with a hint of impatience, that in either event liability would
attach notwithstanding whether the conduct evidenced a failure to exercise care
reasonable to the circumstances or led to an unacceptable measure of volenti.[83]

[**6.21**]   To some extent, one can empathise with the expeditious and practical
approach taken by the then Master of the Rolls. At first glance, a good example of
liability in sporting circumstances attaching either way, and within a generalised
negligence framework, is the Irish Supreme Court's decision in *McComiskey v
McDermott*.[84] In that case, the claimant and the defendant were travelling as
navigator and driver in the defendant's car while taking part, as a team, in a
rally. Having driven round a corner on a muddy laneway in the dark, the driver
was unexpectedly confronted with an obstacle on the road and in taking evasive action; he skidded into a ditch overturning the car. The navigator suffered
injury, and sued in negligence. At first instance, the defendant was found not
to have been negligent. The Irish Supreme Court agreed, holding that the duty
of care owed by the defendant to the claimant was to drive the car as carefully
as a reasonably prudent competitive rally driver would be expected to drive in
the prevailing circumstances. The difficulty with the approach is that it goes
toward an overly individualised duty of care—that is, the reasonable rally driver.
Individualised duties of care are problematical and can in practice lead to 'absurd'
results.[85] In terms of participant liability, it is better to avoid any 'spectrum of
differing duties' and concentrate on assessing when, as an evidential burden, the
conduct of the reasonable person of the sporting world might attract liability

---

[81] Ibid 386. In point of illustration, Barwick CJ went on to observe, 'The risk of a skier running into
an obstruction which, because submerged or partially submerged or for some other reason, is unlikely
to be seen by the driver … may well be regarded as inherent in the pastime.'

[82] Ibid 389.

[83] *Condon v Basi* [1985] 1 WLR 866, 868.

[84] *McComiskey v McDermott* [1974] IR 75.

[85] Ibid 81–82, Walsh J (dissenting) where he noted that *McComiskey v McDermott* must be viewed
in light of the fact that the highway in question was open to, and was being used, by members of the
public. On the unsuitability of individualised duties of care and the circumstance of sport see [6.13]
of this text.

in negligence. In *Condon v Basi*, the Master of the Rolls, citing directly from the trial judge's conclusion, stated clearly that that evidential boundary should be set against conduct that is in reckless disregard of the safety of others:

> [H]ere was such an obvious breach of the defendant's duty of care towards the plaintiff. He was clearly guilty, as I find the facts, of serious and dangerous foul play which showed a reckless disregard of the plaintiff's safety and which fell far below the standards which might reasonably be expected in anyone pursuing a game.[86]

The Reasonable Person of the Sporting World

[**6.22**]   In review, breach of duty in the circumstance of sport appears premised on whether the defendant was or was not acting as the reasonable person of the sporting world. On the one hand, it can be argued that the yardstick of the reasonable sports participant is somewhat unreal because the 'one thing that makes sports a special and unique form of human experience [may be that] participants are free to be unreasonable'.[87] On the other hand, that freedom to be 'unreasonable' on the sports field cannot be assessed overly subjectively to the point that it equates to immunity from suit. It is submitted that the best way to reconcile the established framework of negligence with the regulated robustness of competitive sports is to set the evidential barometer of the reasonable person of the sporting world between the following parameters: a mere error of judgement or lapse in skill is unlikely to equate to negligence; in contrast, evidence of reckless disregard of the safety of the claimant will most likely go towards a finding of negligence. The key indicative factor between these two points on the scale should be whether the injuring party was acting outside the rules and 'playing culture' of the game. In other words, conduct not ordinarily incidental to the playing of the game is a useful evidential indicator of breach of duty, and, as a matter of practice, is usually supported through evidence supplied by the immediate parties and witnessing players, spectators, officials and experts.

[**6.23**]   Ultimately, it is, of course, a matter for the tribunal of fact to make its determination in light of the circumstances as a whole. The rules or general established practice of a game are indicative only as to the defendant's possible breach of duty.[88] Nevertheless, in the specific context of participant liability in a contact sport, the above approach premised between mere lapses of skill and reckless

---

[86] *Condon v Basi* [1985] 1 WLR 866, 868. In relying on evidential recklessness, Sir John Donaldson MR inconsistently moved away from his previous reliance on Australian case law.

[87] R Yasser, *Torts and Sports: Legal Liability in Professional and Amateur Athletics* (Westport CT, Quorum, 1985) 28.

[88] Note the approach in *Woodroffe-Hedley v Cuthbertson* Unreported, Queen's Bench Division 20 June 1997, *The Times* 21 June 1997 and 7 October 1997, Dyson J where, despite acting within the code of conduct set down by British Mountain Guides standards committee, the defendant was found liable in negligence for the death of a fellow climber. *Cf Day v High Performance Sports Ltd* [2003] EWHC 197.

disregard of player safety, with the rules and playing culture of the game acting as key indicative factor, appears to have found favour in the post-*Condon v Basi* case law. For instance, in *Elliot v Saunders*, where an elite professional footballer unsuccessfully sued another in negligence as a result of a career-ending tackle, Drake J reminded the English High Court that football is a game 'necessarily involving strong physical contact between opposing players, that it is a game sometimes played at very fast speed … [and] … in the heat of the game, the player has no more than literally a fraction of one second in which to make a decision … Therefore an error of judgment or mistake will certainly not always mean that the player has failed to exercise due care'.[89]

[**6.24**]   The claimant's injuries resulted from what is called a 'fifty/fifty' challenge for the ball wherein both players approached and lunged for the ball almost simultaneously and at speed. In assessing negligence, Drake J was satisfied that the defendant had not engaged in 'dangerous and reckless play', noting that the officials at the game had in fact penalised the claimant for the collision in question.[90] Drake J's approach—that an error of judgement in the agony of the game will not always mean that a player has failed to exercise the duty of care appropriate to the circumstances—was followed in *McCord v Swansea Football Club*[91] and in *Watson and Bradford City Football Club v Gray and Huddersfield Town Football Club*.[92] In *McCord* and *Watson v Gray* it was, however, found that the defendant-player had breached the appropriate duty as evidenced by conduct that was so significantly misjudged as to equate to negligence.[93]

[**6.25**]   Arguably, *Caldwell v Maguire*[94] represents the most concerted effort to provide a rationale for approaching liability for sporting injuries, and it is an approach that is broadly consistent with, and gives a synopsis of, the principles originating in *Wooldridge* and crystallising in *Condon v Basi*. In the present case, the claimant was a jockey who was seriously injured during the course of a race. A stewards' inquiry into the incident found that two fellow-jockeys, the first and second named defendants, were guilty of 'careless riding' pursuant to rule 153(iii) of the then Jockey Club Rules.[95] The claimant sued his fellow jockeys in

---

[89]   *Elliot v Saunders* Unreported, Queen's Bench Division 10 June 1994, 9 (of official transcript). See generally E Grayson, 'Drake's Drum-beat for Sporting Remedies/Injuries' (1994) 144 *NLJ* 1094.

[90]   See similarly, in rationale and outcome, *Parry v McGuckin* Unreported, Queen's Bench Division 22 March 1990, Ward J and *Pitcher v Huddersfield Town Football Club* Unreported, Queen's Bench Division 17 July 2001, [2001] All ER (D) 223, Hallet J.

[91]   *McCord v Swansea Football Club* Unreported, Queen's Bench Division 19 December 1996, *The Times* 11 February 1997, Kennedy J.

[92]   *Watson v Gray* Unreported, Queen's Bench Division 29 October 1998, *The Times* 26 November 1998, Hooper J.

[93]   For examples in sports other than football see *Riddle v Thaler* (1998) 1(1) *Sports Law Bulletin* 3 (rugby league); *Leatherland v Edwards* (1999) 2(1) *Sports Law Bulletin* 5 (uni-hockey); and *Elshafey v Clay*, *The Times* 8 August 2001 (schools rugby).

[94]   *Caldwell v Maguire* [2001] EWCA Civ 1054.

[95]   So-called 'jockeying for position' cases have also contributed to this debate in other jurisdictions. See, for instance, in Australia, *Johnson v Frazer* (1990) 21 NSWLR 89 and in the US, *Ordway v Superior Court of Orange County* (1988) 198 Cal App (3d) 98.

negligence. On taking guidance for the extant Court of Appeal case law, the trial judge extracted five principles that could be applied in assessing breach of duty in situations of competitive sport.

1. Each contestant in a lawful sporting contest (and in particular a race) owes a duty of care to each and all other contestants.
2. That duty is to exercise in the course of the contest all care that is objectively reasonable in the prevailing circumstances for the avoidance of infliction of injury to such fellow contestants.
3. The prevailing circumstances are all such properly attendant upon the contest and include its object, the demands inevitably made upon its contestants, its inherent dangers (if any), its rules, conventions and customs, and the standards, skills and judgment reasonably to be expected of a contestant.
4. Given the nature of such prevailing circumstances the threshold for liability is in practice inevitably high; the proof of breach of duty will not flow from proof of no more than an error of judgement or from mere proof of momentary lapse in skill (and thus care) respectively when subject to the stresses of a race. Such are no more than incidents inherent in the nature of the sport.
5. In practice it may therefore be difficult to prove any such breach of duty absent proof of conduct that in point of fact amounts to reckless disregard for the fellow contestant's safety.[96]

[6.26]   In applying these guidelines to the general circumstances at hand, the trial judge remarked that in the particular case of a horse race the prevailing circumstances included an individual contestant's obligations not only to compete for the best possible placing but to ride within the Rules of Racing and the standards, skills and judgement of a professional jockey, which are 'all as excepted by fellow contestants'.[97] In application to the specific incident, and having taken into account the evidence of various experts such as leading ex-jockeys as well as statistics on the incidences of 'careless riding', the trial judge concluded that the defendants were guilty of 'lapses of errors that must be an inevitable concomitant of adrenalin fuelled high speed racing with victory still a prospect'[98] but that the incident in question 'reflected the cut and thrust of serious horse racing; in theory avoidable but in daily practice something that is bound to occur from time to time, no matter how generally careful is the standard of riding'.[99]

[6.27]   The claimant appealed, arguing, inter alia that the fourth and fifth elements of the trial judge's guidelines obliged the claimant to prove recklessness rather than negligence. In the leading judgment, Tuckey LJ dismissed the appeal by highlighting that the trial judge had clearly noted that the fifth proposition's allusion to 'reckless disregard' was to be read in the context of 'the distinction

---

[96] *Caldwell v Maguire* [2001] EWCA Civ 1054 [11], Tuckey LJ.
[97] Ibid.
[98] Ibid [12].
[99] Ibid.

between the expression of legal principle and the practicalities of the evidential burden'.[100] Accordingly, the Court of Appeal held that the trial judge was merely explaining that 'in practice' the prevailing circumstances of competitive sport means that the threshold of liability is high.[101] In this, Tuckcy LJ referred to the fact that in *Smoldon v Whitworth*, where an injured player successfully sued a rugby referee for catastrophic injuries sustained in a collapsed scrum, the Court of Appeal had been invited by the defendant to hold that nothing short of reckless-ness would suffice in breach of duty but that that approach, save as an evidential threshold to liability, was rejected in favour of the more generalised one empha-sising the degree of (reasonable) care appropriate in all the circumstances.[102] It is respectfully submitted that the five *Caldwell* criteria have brought much needed clarity to the issue of the degree of care required by the law of negligence of play-ers in a competitive, contact sport. Before reflecting on some practical aspects of litigation concerning participant liability in sport, five brief points need to be made with respect to the *Caldwell v Maguire* criteria, in particular the role of the rules of the game or sport; the subsequent interpretation and application of the criteria; the use of the concept of recklessness; the possible 'chilling' effect that the criteria might have on sports-related litigation; and the theoretical setting in which the criteria might be placed.

[**6.28**]   First, the *Caldwell v Maguire* criteria are guidelines only, operating within the generalised negligence framework of reasonable care but recognis-ing that in practice 'in an action for damages by one participant in a sporting contest against another participant in the same game or event, the issue of negligence cannot be resolved in a vacuum. It is fact specific'.[103] In underlying this aspect of the litigation, it is of interest to note that in *Caldwell v Maguire*, the Court of Appeal expressly, and rightly, reiterated that it was clear from the authorities that breach of the rules of the sport in question is not determinative of the issue of liability in negligence, and neither, presumably, will adherence to those rules carry an automatic exemption.[104] As highlighted by Gearty, there is a very practical element to this approach relating to problems of proof.[105] For instance, in a football match where the injuring party has been sanctioned by the referee for the misconduct that caused the claimant's injury, and that punish-ment has led to a suspension upheld by the internal disciplinary mechanisms of the governing body, it could be argued that the defendant's factual assessment

---

[100] Ibid [23].

[101] Ibid.

[102] *Smoldon v Whitworth* [1997] PIQR 133, 138–39, Bingham LCJ.

[103] *Caldwell v Maguire* [2001] EWCA Civ 1054 [30], Judge LJ.

[104] Ibid [28], Tuckey LJ and at [34] and [35], Judge LJ, citing from Kitto J's judgment in *Rootes v Shelton* [1967] 116 CLR 383, 389: 'Non-compliance with such rules, conventions or customs (where they exist) is necessarily one consideration to be attended to upon the question of reasonableness; but it is only one, and it may be of much or little or even no weight in the circumstances.'

[105] Gearty (n 63) 373.

is controverted.[106] Accordingly, the potentially serious impact that the shadow of potential litigation might have for internal disciplinary processes in sport, in terms of the fear of prejudice and the unwillingness of parties generally to comply with them is tempered somewhat by the view that breach of the rules of a sport is not determinative of liability.

[**6.29**]	Second, the *Caldwell* criteria are working well, as evidenced by their application in *Gaynor v Blackpool Football Club*[107] and *Richardson v Davies*.[108] In *Gaynor*, the claimant, an aspiring professional footballer, was injured in a 'fifty-fifty' tackle by one of the defendant's players/employees. A determination of liability was sought in pursuit of a claim to recover damages. The *Caldwell v Maguire* criteria were applied to the benefit of the claimant with the trial judge noting that the tackle was extremely 'late'; warranted a red card from the referee; and was executed with such force as to break the claimant's leg even though he was wearing protective shin pads. In *Richardson*, the claimant was an amateur 'Sunday league' player who suffered a multiple leg break as a result of a sliding tackle by the defendant. The claimant sued in negligence with the trial judge observing expressly that the defendant's conduct amounted to 'a reckless disregard' of the claimant's safety.

[**6.30**]	Third, any discomfort with the juxtaposition of recklessness and a generalised negligence framework should be assuaged by the Court of Appeal's careful terminology. Reckless disregard of the safety of another is simply of practical, evidential import as to the defendant's misconduct. Availing themselves of Lord Denning MR's description of the defendant's actions in *Lane v Holloway*, a number of commentators have stated that at the higher end of the threshold of liability, recklessness is used simply to indicate whether the defendant's conduct was 'out of all proportion to the occasion'.[109] More broadly, Gearty has noted that the use of recklessness in *Condon v Basi*, as an evidential guide to the objective assessment of the appropriate degree of care in the prevailing sporting circumstances is 'pure' *R v Caldwell*[110] recklessness, which is 'better housed here than in its current sad lodgings in the criminal law'.[111] There is considerable merit in this approach because *R v Caldwell* recklessness does require an objective and particularised assessment of

---

[106] See *R v Marsh* [1994] Crim LR 52 where a rugby player, charged with inflicting grievous bodily harm on an opponent, was held liable to cross-examination under s 1 of the Criminal Evidence Act 1898 as to his disciplinary record on violent play. The Court of Appeal noted that such disciplinary findings were in no sense convictions but nonetheless could be properly raised in cross-examination as to the character of the accused had the accused so elected to put his good character to the court. See also *R v Wright* [2000] Crim LR 851.

[107] *Gaynor v Blackpool Football Club* [2002] CLY 3280.

[108] *Richardson v Davies* [2006] 1 CLY 405.

[109] *Lane v Holloway* [1968] 1 QB 379, 386. Note D Griffith-Jones, *Law and the Business of Sport* (London, Butterworths, 1997) 12 and T Kevan, 'Sports Personal Injury' [2005] *International Sports Law Review* 61, 65.

[110] *R v Caldwell* [1982] AC 341, a House of Lords decision concerning the meaning of recklessness as the critical fault element in the Criminal Damage Act 1971.

[111] Gearty (n 63) 373.

permissible risk in a disputed factual situation. Moreover, in point of practice, trial judges in sports negligence cases are asking questions similar to Lord Diplock's model direction in *R v Caldwell*, particularly in light of the second element of that test and thus in regard to the sports-defendant, who has failed to give any thought (possibly because they were acting impulsively or in the heat of the moment), thus jury directions are focussing on the possibility of a risk (of serious injury) that might be described as significant and obvious.[112] It follows that the application of *R v Caldwell* recklessness to competitive sport highlights some of the 'blameworthiness' gaps in the present preference in criminal law for a subjective analysis of recklessness,[113] especially as relating to the inadvertent risk taker.[114] That debate is beyond the brief of this text, and returning to point, Geraty's observation, as to a sports participant's duty 'not to be reckless', gives a succinct insight into the underlying rationale used by the courts in cases of sports negligence.[115]

[**6.31**]   Fourth, in the US, a majority of states have held that participants in contact sports breach their duty of care only if they act in reckless disregard of the safety of the injured party through conduct beyond that which is ordinarily incidental to the sport in question.[116] A minority of states hold to the simple negligence standard noting that the same result can be achieved without violating any fundamental tenet of the law of negligence, and without having to consider a spectrum of duties relevant to the particulars of individual sports be they competitive, recreational, contact or non contact.[117] Without rehearsing the merits of the 'reasonable care vs. reckless disregard' debate in an American context, it is of interest to note that in the US generally individual states, regardless of their approach, are conscious of avoiding a 'chilling' effect on participation in sporting pursuits, which are seen as vital to levels of social capital.[118] It follows that the consistent 'tenderness' of state jurisdictions in the US towards sport, irrespective of its reasonable or reckless legal premise, is both an attempt to protect sport from the extremes of the litigious nature of that society and a sensitivity towards the fact that not every misjudgement or foul by a participant in a sports event should expose that party to suit, even if it leads to catastrophic injury to another.[119]

---

[112]   Compare Lord Diplock's direction in *Caldwell* [1982] AC 341, 354 to Hooper J's key question in *Watson v Gray* Unreported, Queen's Bench Division 29 October 1998; *The Times* 26 November 1998, Hooper J: 'Had it been shown, on the balance of probabilities, that a player would have known there was a significant risk that if he tackled in the way he did the other player would be seriously injured?'

[113]   *R v G* [2003] 1 AC 1034, largely restoring *R v Cunningham* [1957] 2 QB 396.

[114]   For an introduction to the criticisms of the purely subjective approach see K Amirthalingam, '*Caldwell* Recklessness is Dead, Long Live Mens Rea's Fecklessness" (2004) 67 *MLR* 491.

[115]   Gearty (n 63) 373.

[116]   See, eg, the Supreme Court of California's decision in *Knight v Jewett* (1992) 834 P (2d) 696 and the case law noted by Cole (n 57).

[117]   See, eg, the Supreme Court of Wisconsin's decision in *Lestina v W Bend Mutual Insurance Company* (1993) 501 NW (2d) 28.

[118]   See generally the review by T Pivateau Griffin, 'Tackling the Competitive Sports Doctrine: A New Proposal for Sports Injuries in Texas' (2007) 9 *Texas Review of Entertainment & Sports Law* 85.

[119]   See the case commentary on *Shin v Ahn* (2007) 165 P (3d) 581 in 'Californian Supreme Court Extends Assumption of Risk to Non-contact Sports' (2008) 12 *Harvard Law Review* 1253.

[**6.32**]   In terms of policy, this is a recognition of what would be understood in England and Wales as sport's social utility, namely the public interest benefits, such as physical well-being and civic participation, accruing from active involvement in sport. In *Smoldon v Whitworth*, for instance, although Bingham LCJ was not impressed by the defendant's contention that if the Court of Appeal did not integrate an element of recklessness into sports negligence cases sports such as rugby would face a flood of litigation and a dearth of referees, the Lord Chief Justice was anxious that those involved in sport appreciated that under ordinary negligence principles it remained extremely difficult for any claimant to establish that a referee had failed to exercise such care and skill as could be reasonably expected in the circumstances of a 'hotly-contested game of rugby football'.[120] In this light, there is little doubt that within the statutory recognition of social utility, contained in section 1 of the Compensation Act 2006, the phrase 'desirable activity' should be taken to include the promotion and protection of games and sporting pursuits.[121]

[**6.33**]   Finally, in terms of theoretical coherency, the jurisprudence in the US, and equally in England and Wales, on sports participant liability can be said to be underpinned by a recognition that 'sporting ventures' are an example of what Fletcher has called 'reciprocal risk taking'.[122] In other words, in a competitive sport 'each participant contributes as much to the community of risk as he suffers from exposure to other participants' and thus liability should attach only to harms resulting from activity 'that unduly exceeds the bounds of reciprocity'.[123] It is suggested that in this analysis any given sporting community, such as the 22 players on a football pitch, can be seen in their entirety as a community of risk, with adherence to the principle of reciprocal risk-taking ensuring that the burdens and benefits of all reasonable risks licensed by the sport are fairly apportioned to the freedom and security of all who participate.

The Practice of Sports Participant Liability

[**6.34**]   Prior to a concluding synopsis on future developments in sports-related liability for personal injury, four matters remain outstanding. The assessment of damages, vicarious liability and the role of the tort of unlawful interference with economic relations will be alluded to briefly while the extension of tortious 'sporting' liability will be dealt with more generally. Common to all these matters are

---

[120]   *Smoldon v Whitworth* [1997] PIQR P133, P147.

[121]   The societal role of sport appeared frequently in the Act's preparatory and consultative process. See generally the documents archived at www.dca.gov.uk/legist/compensation.htm.

[122]   G Fletcher, 'Fairness and Utility in Tort Theory' (1972) 85 *Harvard Law Review* 537, 543–56.

[123]   Ibid 548–49. Sport would also provide an example of the 'reciprocal norms of conduct' mentioned by A Ripstein, 'Philosophy of Tort Law' in J Coleman and S Shapiro (eds), *The Oxford Handbook of Jurisprudence and the Philosophy of Law* (Oxford, Oxford University Press, 2002) 661.

practical issues relating to a claimant's concerns, especially in a high value claim based on a career ending injury, as to the injuring party's lack of insurance and/or inability to satisfy any judgment given in the claimant's favour.[124]

Measure of Damage

[**6.35**]   The levels of player remuneration at the elite level of professional sport are significant, and this is markedly so in the Premier League in England. It follows that for an aspiring young professional footballer (who, for example, is in the process of establishing a reputation at a lower league club) a career-ending tackle or one entailing chronic debilitating injury might entail losses (such as the opportunity to play in the Premier League) which could not be adequately compensated even by the most generous of insurance schemes.[125] Accordingly, in sports-related personal injury cases the quantum of special damages for losses related to prospective earnings may be considerable.[126] The necessarily flexible and individualised approach to damages notwithstanding, a 'loss of chance' trend may be emerging in the measure of compensation for a sports career interrupted or ended by injury to which liability attaches.[127] Specifically, it appears that the baseline 'career model' approach to damages of this kind must be modified somewhat when it comes to assessing the possibility of the claimant realising fully their sporting ambitions and thus significantly enhancing their earnings.[128] In this, a 'percentage loss of chance' approach is taken, as best illustrated by the English Court of Appeal's decision in *Langford v Hebran*.[129]

[**6.36**]   In the stated case, the claimant, a trainee bricklayer, was awarded damages of £423,133 for personal injuries sustained in a road traffic accident. That award included £326,368 for future loss of earnings. The defendant appealed, arguing inter alia that the trial judge had over-valued the claimant's loss attributable to his prospective career as a professional kick-boxer. The claimant had a very successful career as an amateur kick-boxer. Six months prior to the accident he had become the world light middleweight champion, after which he turned

---

[124] These issues are dealt with in greater detail by T Kevan, D Adamson and S Cottrell, *Sports Personal Injury: Law and Practice* (London, Sweet & Maxwell, 2002).

[125] As was the scenario in *Gaynor v Blackpool FC* [2002] CLY 3280.

[126] And, separately, there is also the possibility of consideration for loss of (future) earning capacity pursuant to principles established in *Smith v Manchester Corporation* (1974) 17 KIR 1, discussed recently in *Morgan v UPS Ltd* [2008] EWCA Civ 375.

[127] As based on the principles established in *Chaplin v Hicks* [1911] 2 KB 786. See also *Gregg v Scott* [2005] 2 AC 176, [2005] UKHL 2 [119], Lord Hope.

[128] Note the comments of Moore-Bick LJ in *Brown v Ministry of Defence* [2006] EWCA Civ 546 [24], citing the example of *Doyle v Wallace* [1998] PIQR Q146.

[129] *Langford v Hebran* [2001] EWCA Civ 361. Note the slightly circumspect comments on 'loss of sporting chance' in *Raitt v Lunn* [2003] EWCA Civ 1449 [23], Potter LJ where the Court of Appeal agreed with the trial judge's conclusion that there was no significant adverse effect upon the claimant's long term performance as a professional golfer consequent to hand injuries sustained from a dog bite.

professional. He also subsidised his income by giving weekly classes in kick boxing. At trial, the undisputed medical evidence stated that the effect of his injuries was such that he should not return to labouring but could return to kick boxing, albeit at a lower level than before the accident. The medical evidence also noted that the interruption of the claimant's kick boxing training following the accident had interfered with his nascent career at the sport's highest level.

[**6.37**]   The claim for pre-trial and future loss of earnings had two elements: a basic 'career model' claim plus a percentage of four alternative scenarios based upon escalating success in the claimant's kick boxing career, and reflecting the lost chance of earning from those scenarios. The claimant cited *Doyle v Wallace*[130] in approval of this approach, and stated that having identified the four opportunities lost to the claimant as a result of the accident, the court could then go on to making the necessary mathematical calculations of (a) the percentage chance of each opportunity being realised, and (b) the likely benefit to the claimant of having realised each given opportunity. The basic claim assumed that the claimant's fighting career would last until he was 36, after which he would return full time to being a bricklayer, supplementing his income by holding regular classes in the sport. Of the four alternative scenarios, the first was that he would win one national or European title; the second assumed that after gaining such a title he would move to the US where he would win various state and other titles; the third assumed that he would become world champion for one year; and the fourth assumed that after remaining world champion, the claimant would remain in the US for a period working as a highly sought after professional instructor.[131]

[**6.38**]   In effect, the trial judge accepted the claimant's approach noting that the four alternative scenarios were 'fair and reasonable and in accordance with the evidence' and that in the language of *Doyle v Wallace* there was a 'significant chance' that each of them would occur.[132] Although the Court of Appeal had serious concerns regarding the 'illogicality'[133] and the 'generosity'[134] of aspects of the trial judge's application and arithmetic, it did not question the methodology used, and ultimately dismissed the appeal. Moreover, in rejecting the appellant's contention that the trial judge should have taken a 'broad brush' approach to quantifying future loss and that *Doyle v Wallace* was appropriate only where a court had to consider a single lost opportunity, the Court of Appeal held that the claimant's

   [130] [1998] PIQR Q146 where the trial judge in question accepted that but for the accident the claimant had a 50 per cent chance of becoming a drama teacher rather than a clerk. The claimant was awarded past and future loss of earnings assessed on the basis of taking a middle figure between earnings as a teacher and earnings as a clerk. See also *Anderson v Davies* [1993] PIQR Q187.

   [131] *Langford v Hehran* [2001] EWCA Civ 361 [7], Ward LJ.

   [132] Ibid [10].

   [133] Ibid [18] and [22]. The Court of Appeal evaluated the claimant's chances at 80 per cent for scenario 1; 66 per cent for scenario 2; 40 per cent for scenario 3; and 20 per cent for scenario 4.

   [134] Ibid [31]–[33]. According to the Court of Appeal, some discount had to be factored into the assessment to reflect the fact that none of the scenarios might happen, given that the claimant, although promising, had only ever fought once professionally.

approach was fairer and did not 'involve the same amount of "guesstimating" on the part of the Judge as a board brush approach'.[135]

[**6.39**]   A second sports-related example illustrates that the suggested modified career model approach entails a sophisticated review and interpretation of the evidence. In *Appelton v El Safty*,[136] a professional footballer in his mid-twenties suffered a knee injury in training. The injury should have been treated conservatively, which would have allowed the claimant to resume playing in a matter of months. The claimant was in fact negligently advised by the defendant, an orthopaedic surgeon, to have full reconstructive surgery, which the defendant subsequently carried out in a negligent manner, ultimately resulting in the claimant having to retire from professional football. On admission of negligence, the claimant brought a claim for damages of nearly £7 million.[137] In an exhaustive assessment of the measure of damages (at a figure less than that claimed), the High Court determined that central to the claim were three scenarios based on the claimant having being treated conservatively and returning within six months of the injury, namely: for how long would the claimant then have been able to continue playing professional football; at what level and for which club or type of club would he have played; and, on completion of his playing career, would the claimant but for the defendant's negligence have succeeded in a career as a manager of a club?[138]

[**6.40**]   The first scenario demanded a detailed review of the medical evidence; the second, expert witness evidence as to the claimant's prospects predicated on whether he remained at his employing club or moved to a Premier League team, including all his related remunerations and associated bonuses. The court's review of the third scenario, deemed the most remote, necessitated an analysis of the employment prospects and security of football managers in England.[139] This thoroughness notwithstanding, although the modified career model approach has some merit and application in cases of participant liability for personal injury, there is no doubt that the evaluation of 'lost sporting chance' remains necessarily subjective, and a matter of 'indefinable feel' for the court.[140]

---

[135]   Ibid [15].

[136]   *Appelton v El Safty* [2007] EWHC 631 (QB).

[137]   The claimant's club also attempted to sue the defendant for financial loss but it was unsuccessful in both contract and tort; *West Bromwich Albion FC Ltd v El Safty* [2007] PIQR P7. Although the club recommended the defendant to the player, and arranged a booking over the phone, the Court of Appeal held that the dominant relationship was between the defendant-doctor and the player-patient such that there was no reason to find either the proximity necessary to the creation of a duty of care or the implication of a contract. See further J O'Sullivan, 'Negligent Medical Advice and Financial Loss: Sick as a Parrot?' (2007) 66 *CLJ* 14.

[138]   *Appelton v El Safty* [2007] EWHC 631 (QB) [2], Clarke J.

[139]   Ibid [167] citing in evidence Sir Alex Ferguson's observation that in 2006 'about 62% of managers in the whole country had been sacked'.

[140]   *Langford v Hebran* [2001] EWCA Civ 361 [35], Ward LJ. For an example of that 'indefinable feel', note *McCracken v Melbourne Storm* [2006] NSWSC 1250; [2007] NSWCA 353; [2007] Aust Torts Reports 81-925. In that case, the measure of damages (Aus\$97,500) was influenced by the fact that by not being able to take up another playing contract, the claimant could, and did, devote more time to the development of his property portfolio.

[**6.41**]   The most recent sports-related example of the law relating to loss of chance, and one that cites both *Langford* and *Appelton* occurred in the English High Court on 3 October 2008 and concerned an assessment of the damages to which the claimant, Ben Collett, was entitled following a sporting injury which had occurred during a professional football match in May 2003, for which liability had been admitted.[141] At the time of the injury, the 18-year-old Collett was playing (for the first time) in the 'reserves' team for Manchester United against Middlesbrough's reserve team. As the result of an 'over the ball' high tackle, Collett suffered fractures of the right tibia and fibula. He had been 'spotted' by one of Manchester United's scouts at the age of nine and was recruited for the club's youth academy. As a junior player, he had enjoyed considerable success and, at the age of 18, was apparently on the verge of moving into the adult game or at least Collett hoped and expected to enjoy a successful career as a professional footballer at a high level. Although Collett made a good recovery from the fractures, he never regained his former ability in the game and, two or three years after the accident, he gave up professional football and embarked on another career.

[**6.42**]   In his claim for damages against Middlesbrough, Collett alleged that he had been deprived of his chance of a lucrative career as a professional footballer. It was a large and complex claim and in the event the judge awarded him £4,577,323. At trial, damages for pain, suffering and loss of amenity were agreed, as were the past losses. Unsurprisingly, the main issue was the loss of future earnings for which the judge awarded £3,854,328. An appeal was made inter alia against that part of the award both in terms of its measure and the methodology used in arriving at it. The methodology used was, in effect, the loss of sporting chance approach outlined above. Despite some concern about 'an unrealistically optimistic view' of the claimant's prospective earnings, the Court of Appeal held that the final figure was 'supportable on the very special facts of the case' and the appeal against the loss of sporting chance methodology/approach taken by the trial judge was dismissed in its entirety.[142]

Vicarious Liability

[**6.43**]   A brief review of the case law in England and Wales,[143] the US[144] and Australia[145] illustrates that where the player-employee of a club has inflicted an injury upon the claimant, the vicarious liability of the employing club becomes

---

[141] *Collett v Smith and Middlesbrough FC* [2008] EWHC 1962 (QB). On the law relating to (sporting) loss of chance see especially [93]–[96] of Swift J's lengthy judgment.

[142] *Smith and Middlesbrough FC v Collett* [2009] EWCA Civ 583 [51] Carnwath LJ.

[143] See, eg, *McCord v Swansea* Unreported, Queen's Bench Division 19 December 1996, *The Times* 11 February 1997, Kennedy J and *Watson v Gray* Unreported, Queen's Bench Division 29 October 1998, *The Times* 26 November 1998, Hooper J.

[144] See generally S Rubin, 'The Vicarious Liability of Professional Sports Teams for On-the-field Assaults Committed by their Players' (1999) 1 *Virginia Journal of Sports Law* 266.

[145] See, for instance, *McCracken v Melbourne Storm* [2005] NSWSC 107.

a feature of the litigation. The usefulness of vicarious liability from a claimant's perspective is that it enables that claimant, in seeking satisfaction of any award, to access the employing club's liability insurance.[146] As noted by James and McArdle, in England and Wales the vicarious liability of football clubs for the negligent actions of their employees on the field of play has almost reached a presumptive, uncontested status.[147] Consequently, the apparent expansion of the scope of employers' liability post-*Lister v Hesley Hall Ltd*,[148] premised on a close connection between the employee's tort and the employment, is unlikely to have much impact on professional sports-related cases.[149] Nevertheless, *Lister* can be used to reiterate the employing club's responsibility and potential liability for its players for torts arising from the 'inherent risks of the employment'; as well the employing club's need to insure against the possible misconduct of its players on the field of play.[150]

[**6.44**]   A recent and straightforward sports-related example of vicarious liability can be found in the Court of Appeal's decision in *Gravil v Carroll and Redruth Rugby Football Club*.[151] In that case, the first defendant had punched the claimant during a game of rugby union and was held liable in battery. The claim against the second defendant in vicarious liability failed. The denial of vicarious liability at trial and on first appeal was essentially threefold in nature. First, account was taken of the fact that the claimant and the first defendant were semi-professional players and both had other full time employment. In this, the suggestion was that the participants were playing primarily for the 'love of the game' and loyalty to the club and that contracts of employment were signed simply to prevent the poaching of players by other clubs, thus providing the club with some stability in its player roster. Second, account was taken of the 'off-the-ball' nature of the incident in the sense that it was argued that an employer ought not be held liable

---

[146] For an interesting Canadian example of sports-related vicarious liability see *Henderson v Canadian Hockey Association & Ors* (2010) MBQB 20 (CanLII). In that case, the claimant was injured while refereeing a tournament ice hockey game between players of 12–13 years of age. The claimant suffered spinal injuries when he was suddenly and without warning knocked to the ice by an unidentified player who had left the substitute's bench to enter the playing surface for an 'on the fly' substitution. The claimant's essential complaint was that the line change was not completed with proper care for his safety. He sought damages against the injuring player's coach for negligent performance of the line change. He also sought damages against the manager of the injuring player's team on the basis that the manager was vicariously liable for the negligence of any team member and against various hockey associations based on the claim that they were vicariously liable for the actions of participants in tournaments under their control. On reviewing the applicable Canadian case law on vicarious liability, Simonesen J of the Court of Queen's Bench Manitoba allowed motions dismissing the action from the manager and hockey associations but held the claim against the coach should remain.

[147] M James and D McArdle, 'Player Violence, or Violent Players? Vicarious Liability for Sports Participants' (2004) 12 *Tort Law Review* 131, 135.

[148] *Lister v Hesley Hall* [2001] 2 WLR 1311.

[149] See the straightforward application of vicarious liability in *Vowles v Evans and Welsh Rugby Union* [2003] 1 WLR 1607, where the second-named defendant was held to be vicariously liable for the negligent application of certain safety rules by the first named defendant, a WRU-appointed referee.

[150] For a recent analysis of vicarious liability through the paradigm of 'inherent risks of employment', see generally Po Yen Yap, 'Enlisting Close Connections: A Matter of Course for Vicarious Liability' (2008) 28 *Legal Studies* 197.

[151] [2008] EWCA Civ 689.

for a tort (such as an actionable trespass) which cannot fairly be regarded as a reasonably incidental to the business at hand.[152] Third, and in summary, it was contended that it would not be 'fair and just' to hold an employer liable where the wrongful conduct cannot fairly and properly be regarded as done while acting in the ordinary course of the employee's job.

[6.45]   The Court of Appeal held that the semi-professional nature of the first-named defendant's employment was irrelevant because the player had a con-tract of employment with the second-named defendant under which he was paid a fee and through which he was subject to certain express contractual obligations, including provisions relating to discipline.[153] On reviewing *Lister* and subsequent authorities, the Court of Appeal held that the fundamental question was whether the tort was so closely connected with what was authorised or expected of the employee that it would be fair and just to hold the employer vicariously respon-sible. The Court of Appeal held that there was a very close connection between the punch and the first defendant's employment noting that, although off-the-ball incidents by nature occur when the play is elsewhere and even after the whistle has gone, such incidents remain part of the game and are not in any way independent of it and thus 'they can fairly be regarded as an ordinary (though undesirable) incident of a rugby match'.[154]

[6.46]   The judgment met some media-led alarm as to the potential costs and liabilities, in terms of insurance, that might now be faced by semi-professional clubs, many of whom remain community-based, non-for profit organisations (such as the second-named defendant).[155] It is argued, however, that the policy underpinning the Court of Appeal's approach will operate to the overall benefit of sport. In short, the court argued that there was a clear deterrent element to the attachment of vicarious liability in this instance so as to prevent or minimise the risk of foul play in the future and thus, on pain of vicarious liability, clubs will be motivated to materially decrease the risk of their employee-players misbehaving on the field of play.[156] On a related point, there is no doubt that an employing club should not be able to deny vicarious liability for an intentional tort if that employer is shown to have materially increased the likelihood of occurrence of injury. For instance, in the Australian case of *Canterbury Bankstown Rugby League Football*

---

[152] Ibid [2], Clarke MR, 'the suggested liability for "off-the-ball" assaults committed during games is of sufficient potential importance for professional sporting clubs to provide a compelling reason for this court to entertain an appeal.'

[153] *Gravil v Carroll* [2008] EWCA Civ 689 [9], [10] and [24], Clarke MR. In the absence of such a contract of employment, vicarious liability could not have attached at [10] and [29], Clarke J.

[154] Ibid [23]. See also [37]–[39] where the court, discussing *Deaton Pty Ltd v Flew* (1949) 79 CLR 370, also appeared to doubt the previous position that an act in private retaliation or personal spite should not lead to vicarious liability.

[155] Eg, S Howard, 'Club Must Pay Damages after Player Punched Opponent' *The Independent* (London 18 June 2008) only available online at www.independent.co.uk/news/uk/home-news/club-must-pay-damages-after-player-punched-opponent-849621.html.

[156] *Gravil v Carroll* [2008] EWCA Civ 689 [28], Clarke MR citing *Bazley v Curry* (1999) 174 DLR (4th) 45 [41], McClachlin J.

Club Ltd v Rogers,[157] the claimant argued that the defendant club should be vicariously liable for the injury inflicted intentionally by one of their employees because (a) the defendant club's coach had 'overly' motivated his players to the point where the injuring player could not control his aggression and (b) that coach had also asked his players to 'target' specifically a number of players on the opposition, including the claimant. The New South Wales Court of Appeal accepted the first claim in part but found no evidence of a targeted 'hit list' to underpin the second.

Unlawful Interference with Economic Relations

[**6.47**]   Some analogy to the *Canterbury Bankstown* scenario might be found in an application of the economic tort of conspiracy.[158] Similarly, it is of interest to note the manner in which the claimant's club attempted to raise the tort of unlawful interference with contractual relations in *Watson v Gray*.[159] The 'gist' of the tort is the wrongful interference with the actions of a third party in which the claimant has an economic interest, such that in a sports injury scenario there is a direct intervention by the defendant, the substantially certain consequence of which is to affect adversely the injured player's contract with the claimant club.[160] In *Watson v Gray*, the trial court noted quite rightly that a negligent interference with a contract will not suffice. Given the basis of the claim at hand (negligence), this should have ended the matter—however, Hooper J stated (and the parties accepted) that a finding of recklessness would suffice to make out the tort. As the House of Lords has noted recently, the tort of unlawful interference with economic relations has long been underpinned by the *intentional* infliction of the harm complained of;[161] in any event, by proceeding (incorrectly) on the basis of recklessness the trial judge encountered a number of terminological problems. In short, it was difficult for Hooper J to reconcile his rejection of Bradford FC's claim with the evidence that the injuring tackle was clearly 'dangerous and reckless play' under the rules of the game and in the opinion of the expert witnesses. The awkward nature of this part of Hooper J's judgment was noted subsequently on application for leave to appeal.[162] Overall, the possibility of a trespass-based case of unlawful interference remains open to a club who suffers the loss of an employee-player consequent to

---

[157] [1993] Aust Torts Reports 81–246.

[158] See generally J Jones and K Stewart, 'Hit Somebody: Hockey Violence, Economics, the Law and the McSorley Decisions' (2002) 12 *Seton Hall Journal of Sports Law* 165 who argue that until Canadian civil law uses the potential of vicarious liability, and even the economic tort of conspiracy, to impose financial constraints on professional teams and leagues, using the criminal or civil law to constrain hockey violence will continue to be largely ineffectual.

[159] Unreported, Queen's Bench Division 29 October 1998; *The Times* 26 November 1998, Hooper J.

[160] See generally *Thomson (DC) & Co Ltd v Deakin* [1952] Ch 646 and Murphy (n 17) 378. It follows that, although the injury is done to a third party, the damage suffered by the claimant is not too remote to be compensated.

[161] *OBG Ltd v Allan* [2008] 1 AC 1, 31, Lord Hoffmann.

[162] *Watson v Gray* [1999] EWHC Admin 321 [13], Roch LJ. See also N Cox and A Schuster, *Sport and the Law* (Dublin, Firstlaw, 2004) 210 and 213.

an injury on the field of play. In practice, by utilising this tort, the claimant club is seeking compensation to pay for a replacement player. How comfortable clubs will be in using a tort that effectively results in their penalising each other for the acts of employees, and one that is likely to increase their employer liability costs, is open to debate.

Extending Tortious Liability

[**6.48**]   Personal injury cases emanating from participation in sport now encompasses the liability of referees; coaches; sports governing bodies; organisers of sports events and school authorities. The tortious liability of referees was considered by the Court of Appeal in *Smoldon v Whitworth and Nolan*[163] and in *Vowles v Evans and Wales Rugby Union.*[164] In both cases, the claimant suffered serious neck and spinal injuries as a result of a collapsed scrum during a game of rugby union, and in both instances, a finding of liability against the referee was upheld. The duty of care of referees, and the context in which it occurs, was summarised by Lord Phillips MR in *Vowles*:

> Rugby football is an inherently dangerous sport. Some of the rules are specifically designed to minimise the inherent dangers. Players are dependant for their safety on the due enforcement of the rules. The role of the referee is to enforce rules. Where a referee undertakes to perform that role, it seems to us manifestly fair, just and reasonable that players should be entitled to rely upon the referee to exercise reasonable care in doing so. Rarely if ever does the law absolve from any obligation of care a person whose acts or omissions are manifestly capable of causing physical harm to others in a structured relationship into which they have entered.[165]

[**6.49**]   In *Smoldon v Whitworth*, the assessment of breach of duty took into account that the game in question was an under-19 game for which the safety rules applying to scrums had been specifically reviewed by the world governing authority. The referee in question had received direct communication from his local association on the need to implement strictly the revised rules. Moreover, the evidence was clear that prior to the ill-fated scrum, the referee had failed to enforce the revised rules on a number of occasions despite a warning from an assisting official. Similarly, in *Vowles*, the referee failed to follow a safety regulation, which stated that where no suitably trained replacement was available the game should continue with non-contestable scrums.

[**6.50**]   With respect to the liability of coaches, it appears that the appropriate degree of care is premised on exercising reasonable care in imparting

---

[163] *Smoldon v Whitworth* [1997] PIQR P133.

[164] *Vowles v Evans* [2003] 1 WLR 1607.

[165] Ibid 1617–18. For a comparable American perspective see M Mayer, 'Stepping in to Step out of Liability: The Proper Standard of Liability for Referees in Foreseeable Judgment-call Situations' (2005) 3 *De Paul Journal of Sports Law & Contemporary Problems* 54.

knowledge and skills to those under instruction. Citing dicta from *Van Oppen v Bedford Charity Trustees*,[166] Griffith-Jones argues cogently that a coach may be liable both in misfeasance and nonfeasance for failure to give appropriate instruction or the giving of incorrect advice.[167] *Mountford v Newlands School*[168] is a more recent example of the degree of care required of a person charged with the preparation or selection of participants in a game. In that case, the Court of Appeal was asked to consider whether a teacher (and vicariously the employing school) had breached his duty of care when he allowed a boy, who was well over the age of 15, and who was visually bigger and stronger than many of the other players, to participate in an inter-school under-15 game. During the course of the game, the bigger boy lawfully tackled the smaller claimant, injuring him. The applicable rule within the England Rugby Football Schools' Union's regulations stated that players should not 'normally' be allowed to play other than in their own junior age grouping. Acknowledging that the governing rules were drafted more in guideline than in regulation, the Court of Appeal found that in this case there were no special reasons why the older boy should have been allowed to participate in the game. By permitting the older boy to play, without special circumstance, the teacher had breached his duty towards the other players.[169]

[**6.51**]   The specific duties of sports/physical education teachers and schools (including duties in respect of coaching, supervision, equipment and facilities) will, as Cox and Schuster note, 'depend on a number of factors, most pressingly the vulnerability of the pupils—usually though not always dictated by their age— and the nature of the sport in question'.[170] A recent and instructive Canadian (Supreme Court of British Columbia) case of interest in *Hussack v School District No 33 (Chilliwack)*[171] where the claimant, a 13-year-old boy, sought damages for brain injuries suffered as a result of a physical education class during which he was struck on the face by another boy's hockey stick. The claimant alleged success-fully that the teacher had negligently failed to ensure that that injuring boy had been properly and progressively instructed in the use of a hockey stick and thus the teacher had breached the requisite standard of care expected of a Grade 7 PE teacher trained in British Columbia in the 1990s. The analysis taken by Boyd J of the Supreme Court of British Columbia to the issue of the standard of care to be exercised by school authorities in this regard, as based around that of the careful or prudent teacher, is of interest beyond that province.[172]

---

[166] *Van Oppen v Bedford Charity Trustees* [1990] 1 WLR 235 where a schoolboy, claiming that he had not been properly instructed on how to effect a tackle, unsuccessfully sought damages from his school for injuries sustained during a game of rugby.

[167] Griffith-Jones (n 109) 21.

[168] *Mountford v Newlands School* [2007] EWCA Civ 21.

[169] See generally P Charlish, 'Schoolmaster Tackled Hard over Rugby Incident' (2007) 15 *Tort Law Review* 1.

[170] For an authoritative introduction to the law in Britain and Ireland on this topic see Cox and Schuster (n 162) 235–48.

[171] *Hussack v School District No 33 (Chilliwack)* (2009) BCSC 852.

[172] Ibid [60]–[62].

[**6.52**]   The seminal case in British Columbia is that of *Thornton v Board of School Trustees of School District No 57 (Prince George)*, which established a four-part test, namely (a) whether the activity was suitable to the age and mental and physical condition of the student; (b) whether the student was progressively trained and coached to do the activity properly and to avoid the danger; (c) whether the equipment was adequate and suitably arranged; and (d) whether the performance, having regard to its inherently dangerous nature, was properly supervised.[173] This test must however, as Boyd J noted, be placed in its context and the standard of care expected of teachers and school authorities is very much 'case specific' and relying on precedent from the Supreme Court of Canada, Boyd J noted that it will 'depend upon the number of students being supervised at any given time, the nature of the exercise or activity in progress, the age and degree of skill and training which the student may have received in connection with such activity, the nature and condition of the equipment in use at the time, the competency and capacity of the students involved, and a host of other matters which may be widely varied but which, in a given case, may affect the application of the prudent parent standard to the conduct of the school authorities in the circumstances'.[174]

[**6.53**]   Returning to the broader issues of the duties of coaches, but in light of the above, it is submitted that, although the appropriate degree of care will vary enormously with the circumstances (for instance, the age/experience of the participants and the nature of the sport) the necessary care of a 'coach' (loosely defined) encompasses a general principle that properly instructed and prepared participants will be inculcated with the necessary knowledge and skills on how to enjoy their sport safely, reasonably avoiding injury both to themselves and, where relevant, opponents.[175] A straightforward example is *Gannon v Rotherham MBC* where a 14-year-old schoolboy broke his neck when diving at a steep angle into the shallow end of a swimming pool. A claim for negligence succeeded to the extent of 75 per cent liability against the county council which employed the physical education teacher, who was held not to have prepared the boy with sufficient care on how to effect such a dive safely. Interestingly, the association governing body, the Amateur Swimming Association, was held liable to an extent of 25 per cent because it had not given sufficient warning to teachers and coaches in its notice of the event in question of the potential dangers of entry into a pool by persons unused to the then accepted method.

[**6.54**]   *Gannon v Rotherham MBC* appears to be the first occasion in the UK that a sports governing body had been held liable in negligence for damages

---

[173] *Thornton v Board of School Trustees of School District No 57 (Prince George)* [1976] 5 WWR 240, (1976) 73 DLR (3d) 35 (BCCA).

[174] *Myers v Peel (County) Board of Education* (1981) 123 DLR (3d) 1; [1981] 2 SCR 21, 32, McIntyre J.

[175] Cox and Schuster (n 162) 230–35 on the liability of coaches with regard to general supervision; intensity of training; selection of injured players; proper use of safety and playing equipment; 'standard practice' obligations; and even the provision of emergency medical care. See also A MacCaskey and K Biedzynski, 'A Guide to the Legal Liability of Coaches for a Sport's Participant's Injuries' (1996) 6 *Seton Hall Journal of Sports Law* 7.

comprising personal injury during an event under its control.[176] Subsequently, the issue of the liability of governing bodies was discussed at length by the Court of Appeal in *Watson v British Boxing Board of Control*,[177] where the private organisation formed for the regulation of boxing in Britain was held to have breached its duty of care to ensure an adequate standard of ringside treatment for an injured boxer who suffered serious neurological trauma during the course of a professional bout. The duty of care established by *Watson v British Boxing Board of Control* has been interpreted broadly to encompass a sports governing body's duty to take appropriate care in exercising all regulatory functions concerning the extant and ongoing health and safety of participants.[178]

[**6.55**]   Overall, the potential liabilities of referees, coaches and governing bodies would appear to have clear (and costly) insurance implications for sport, in terms of indemnification, public liability and third party liability. Moreover, with respect to the future promotion of sport, the stated jurisprudence begs the question as to why an individual or parent would volunteer to referee a game, to assist or become a coach, or to get involved in the administration of a sport.[179] In short, is Britain's sporting culture, particularly in its schools, being swamped by its compensation culture?[180] In the US and Australia, a number of states have enacted so-called 'sports volunteer statutes' essentially providing the volunteer with a qualified immunity from tort liability whilst acting as volunteers for recognised organisations.[181] In Britain, a Conservative Party MP unsuccessfully introduced a Private Members' Bill entitled the 'Promotion of Volunteering Bill' to the House of Commons in 2004, which sought to mandate a 'statement of inherent risk' to be presented to people undertaking activities managed by volunteers and voluntary organisations.[182] There is little need to resort to such radical solutions. It is submitted that the stated case law reveals the existence of three 'embankments' preventing a flood of sports-related litigation—the 'fact-specific' nature of the

---

[176]   *Gannon v Rotherham MBC* Unreported, 6 February 1991 Nottingham Crown Court, Rougier J, Halsbury's Laws of England Annual Abridgment 1991 [1767]. The claimant was held 25 per cent contributorily negligent because it was adjudged that he was of a sufficient age and of sufficient experience not to require to be told that one should not enter the shallow end at a steep angle.

[177]   *Watson v British Boxing Board of Control* [2001] QB 1134.

[178]   See generally J George, '*Watson v British Boxing Board of Control*: Negligent Rule-making in the Court of Appeal' (2002) 65 *MLR* 106 and K Lines, 'Thinking Outside the Boxing Ring: The Implications for Sports Governing Bodies following *Watson*' [2007] *International Sports Law Review* 67.

[179]   This debate has been given added emphasis recently with developments surrounding the so-called 'Vetting and Barring Scheme' pursuant to the Safeguarding Vulnerable Peoples Act 2006, noted at point 3 of the 'Further Points of Interest and Discussion' section of this chapter.

[180]   This fear has been augmented by a recent study—L Abernethy and D MacAuley, 'Impact of School Sports Injuries' (2003) 37 *British Journal of Sports Medicine* 354—which concluded that school sports injuries account for just over half of all injuries in secondary school students.

[181]   For the US, see generally K Biedzynski, 'The Federal Volunteers Protection Act: Does Congress Want to Play Ball? (1999) 23 *Seton Hall Legislative Journal* 319. For Australia, see Thorpe *et al* (n 25) 163–64.

[182]   See The House of Commons Library, 'Promotion of Volunteering Bill [Bill 18 of 2003–4], Research Paper 04/21, 3 March 2004' available online at www.parliament.uk/commons/lib/research/rp2004/rp04-021.pdf. For a copy of the Bill see www.publications.parliament.uk/pa/cm200304/cmbills/018/04018.1-i.html.

case law; the tort of negligence's inherent 'control devices'; and policy issues premised on the 'social utility' of sport.

Fact-Specific

[**6.56**]   First, the courts are at pains to point out that sports-related case law is often very much, and expressly, fact-specific. For instance, in the negligent referee cases of *Smoldon v Whitworth* and *Vowles v Evans*, the Court of Appeal stressed that the threshold of liability remains high with a mere error of judgement or oversight in refereeing not being sufficient to establish breach of duty.[183] Subsequently, a clear illustration of that approach can be seen in *Allport v Wilbraham*,[184] where the claimant failed in his claim against the referee of a rugby match during which the participant had suffered catastrophic spinal injuries as a result of an uncontrolled scrum.

Control Devices

[**6.57**]   Second, sports-related negligence is predicated generally on parties acting with reasonable carefulness, as filtered through the tort's traditional 'control devices' of duty, breach, causation and damage. This can mean that even a 'robust' attitude by the duty-owing defendant, such as a coach[185] or a supervising teacher,[186] towards the claimant will not necessarily result in a finding of fault. It also prompts the reminder that central to the governing authority's liability in *Watson v British Boxing Board of Control* was the finding on causative effect; that is, but for the poor quality of the immediate emergency care at ringside, for which the Board took ultimate and direct regulatory responsibility, the claimant's recovery would have been materially enhanced.[187] This can be compared with *Stratton v Hughes*,[188] where, notwithstanding criticism regarding a failure to follow accepted safety standards, the organisers of a motor rally avoided liability because that carelessness had no causative effect on the crash in which the claimant sustained injury.[189] Similarly, remoteness was an underlying issue in the

---

[183]   *Vowles v Evans* [2003] 1 WLR 1607, 1625, Lord Phillips MR.

[184]   *Allport v Wilbraham* [2004] EWCA Civ 1668.

[185]   *Brady v Sunderland Association Football Club Ltd* Unreported, Court of Appeal 17 November 1998, Stuart-Smith, Thorpe, Mummery LLJ. The defendant-club's coach made it clear during training that he had a rather circumspect view of the extent of the claimant's leg complaints. The complaints were in fact related to a rare type of injury, which eventually led to the claimant's retirement for the sport, but not to a finding of liability against the club.

[186]   *Chittock v Woodbridge School* [2002] EWCA Civ 915, where it was noted that the supervision of students on a school skiing trip must be seen within a range of 'reasonable responses'.

[187]   *Watson v British Boxing Board of Control* [2001] QB 1134, 1170–73, Lord Phillips MR.

[188]   *Stratton v Hughes* [1998] EWCA Civ 477.

[189]   Note the careful consideration of causation in *Mountford v Newlands School* [2007] EWCA Civ 21 [18]–[27], Waller LJ, agreeing with the trial judge that the increased risk that the rule was meant to guard against (smaller boys being tackled by bigger boys) eventuated and contributed materially to the

failure of a number of Australian litigants in claims against sports governing bodies for negligence in regulating for, and warning about, the dangers of particularly invasive aspects of the game of rugby, which led to the claimants suffering serious neck and spinal injuries.[190]

[**6.58**]   One of the better sports-related examples of a carefully calibrated analysis of negligence in all its constituent parts is *Wattleworth v Goodwood Road Racing Co Ltd*.[191] In that case the widow of motor racing driver, fatally injured at a local motor racing event, sought inter alia to recover damages from the national and international regulatory bodies of the sport. The claimant argued that the authorities in question had owed her husband a duty of care which they had breached by failing to exercise proper skill and care in their inspection and licensing of the track, manifested in the negligent advice given to the organisers of the event on the construction of a safety barrier, into which the driver crashed and died. Applying *Watson v British Boxing Board of Control*, the court held that the national regulatory body had a duty of care to the participant but had discharged that duty by meeting a reasonable standard of safety with respect to the design and construction of the safety barrier. The court held that the international body did not owe the driver a duty of care on the grounds that the event was not licensed as an international meeting and thus the international body's involvement in the activities at the track was peripheral. In any event, the court noted that the claimant had not, on the facts of the accident, proved a causal link: the driver's death was most likely to have resulted from a violent impact with the modified interior design of the car. Moreover, the court noted obiter that the driver had, in reliance on reasonable safety measures, consented to the risks involved in motor racing and that not only did volenti apply but, on the evidence, the driver would have been contributorily negligent to 20 per cent had one or more of the defendants been found negligent regarding the design of the safety barrier.[192]

Social Utility

[**6.59**]   Third, and in summary, in sports-related cases of the type mentioned, the courts recognised that the occasional 'melancholy accident' will occur but that it is not always necessarily fair, just or reasonable in the circumstances of a

---

injury suffered by the claimant. See also the comprehesive analysis of caustion (in law and in fact) in *Hussack v School District No 33 (Chilliwack)* (2009) BCSC 852 [116]–[191], Boyd J.

[190] See *Agar v Hyde; Agar v Worsley* (2000) 201 CLR 552 (claim against the international rugby football authorities and others for failure to update rules relating to scrimmaging); and *Green v Country Rugby Football League of NSW* [2008] NSWSC 26 (failure to regulate to prevent players of slight physique from playing in certain positions). See also *Malo v South Sydney Junior Rugby Football League* [2008] NSWSC 552 (failure to regulate for the safety of fatigued players).

[191] *Wattleworth v Goodwood Road Racing Co Ltd* [2004] PIQR P25.

[192] See also *Harrison v Vincent* [1982] RTR 8.

regulated, if risky, activity such as sport, that liability should follow.[193] A close analogy to this underlying policy approach, related to sport's social utility, can be derived from occupiers' liability where the thrust of the House of Lords' decision in *Tomlinson v Congleton Borough Council*[194] and the rationale of cases from *Simms v Leigh Rugby Football Club*[195] to *Wattleworth v Goodwood Road Racing Co Ltd*[196] to *Portsmouth Youth Activities Committee v Poppleton*[197] demonstrate that, in this respect, tort law neither encompasses a concept of absolute liability nor does it entail any concomitant duty of compensation for pure accident.[198] In sum, could it be that one of the defining features of sports injuries-related, civil compensation law and policy is the (welcome) imposition of both a higher level of personal responsibility on the individual and attendant personal care for one's safety, thus heralding a move away from the previous communitarian attitude of the ultimate insurer being held liable for the injuries suffered by the individual?[199]

[**6.60**]   Finally, the above 'embankments' are an effective illustration of Murphy's contention that the account for 'desirable activities' in section 1 of

---

[193] See, eg, *Cope v Cassells* [1990] CLY 3296 where the parties were engaged in a demonstration of Aikido, a martial art. D struck C with his knee in an attacking move which, though rare, was not unknown. C suffered a split pancreas but failed to show that D had not exercised the appropriate degree of care.

[194] *Tomlinson v Congleton Borough Council* [2004] 1 AC 46. See also *Tedstone v Bourne Leisure Ltd* [2008] EWCA Civ 654.

[195] *Sims v Leigh Rugby Football Club* [1969] 2 All ER 923. A rugby player, injured when a tackle threw him into collision with a concrete wall surrounding the pitch, attempted to sue the defendant club as occupier of the football ground. Lack of causative effect and the improbability of injury were noted by the court as was the defence of 'risks willingly accepted' pursuant to s 2(5) of the Occupiers Liability Act 1957.

[196] [2004] PIQR P25. In that case, s 2(4)(b) of the Occupiers Liability Act 1957 provided a defence for the organisers.

[197] *Portsmouth Youth Activities Committee v Poppleton* [2008] EWCA Civ 646. The case gives an excellent introduction to the issues, and particularly the boundaries of the duty of care and assumption of responsibility that occupiers and owners of property on which sports events are being organised must bear in mind. The policy approach taken by the court in the stated case was made clear from the first paragraph of May LJ's judgment: 'Adults who choose to engage in physical activities which obviously give rise to a degree of unavoidable risk may find that they have no means of recompense if the risk materialises so that they are injured.' In his review of the case (an unsuccessful claim arising out of an accident at an indoor climbing facility) Norris notes that the case 'should be seen as a clear expression of the courts continuing resolve to emphasise the importance of personal responsibility and of the appellate judges' disinclination to extend the boundaries which define when a duty of care is imposed on one party for the benefit of another.' See W Norris, 'Duty of Care and Personal Responsibility: Occupiers, Owners, Organisers and Individuals' [2008] *Journal of Personal Injuries Law* 187, 195.

[198] *Cf* B Gardiner, 'Liability for Sporting Injuries' [2008] *Journal of Personal Injuries Law* 16 citing *Slack v Glenie & Ors* [2000] All ER (D) 52.

[199] See *Uren v Corporate Leisure (UK) Ltd & Ors* [2010] EWHC 46 (QB) where Field J dismissed the claimant's claim for damages for personal injury and loss sustained in an accident that occurred during a health and fun day at an RAF base. The claimant had dived head first into an inflatable pool as part of a relay game, and was rendered tetraplegic. In determining whether the pool game was reasonably safe and whether the defendants were in breach of their common law duty of care in failing to neuter the game by prohibiting head first entry, Field J held that a balance had to be struck between the risk of injury (very small) and the benefits of sporting activity (physical challenges). In the stated case, the benefits outweighed the risks and thus the defendants were not in breach of their duty of care.

the Compensation Act 2006's, viz the setting of the required standard of care in negligence, which was drafted against the backdrop of an apparently spiralling compensation culture, is, in actuality, unlikely to have a material effect on the approach of the courts because it does no more than 'reflect the existing law'.[200] Moreover, these 'embankments' can be aligned with Steele's remarks that careful analysis of the case law (and statistics) surrounding tort and compensation reveals that what is occurring is more a debate about the existence of a blame culture rather than the actuality of a compensation culture.[201] In sum, the combination of judicial tenderness towards participation in sport, and the nebulous nature of the compensation culture, means that those charged with the promotion of healthy risk-taking activities, such as sports bodies and schools, should not act too defensively to the point where society generally might be deprived of sport's many amenities and opportunities.[202]

Conclusion

[**6.61**]   Litigation arising from participant liability for sports-related personal injury is likely to remain infrequent. Professional sports participants are usually adequately insured against personal accident; thus career-ending injury apart (as in *Elliot v Saunders*) these participants are unlikely to instigate costly legal proceedings.[203] In contrast, cases such as *Condon v Basi* and *Van Oppen v Bedford Charity Trustees* clearly illustrate that an uninsured defendant is fundamental to an understanding of the motivation of 'amateur' claimants. Similarly, inadequate insurance for catastrophic injury was a factor in the claims against the 'collapsing scrum' referees in *Smolden v Whitworth* and *Vowles v Evans*. At all levels of sports participation a stigma operates against recourse to the ordinary courts and thus,

---

[200] Murphy (n 17) 102, where he compares the reaction to s 1 of the 2006 Act with the underwhelming response thus far to s 5B(2)(d) Civil Liability Act 2002 (NSW). For an interesting Australian perspective on this see L Griggs, 'Dangerous Recreational Activities—Stay at Home and Be Safe' [2010] *International Sports Law Review* 9, 20 who argues that sports-related civil liability reforms in Australia have now gone too far to the point that 'the law for sport and dangerous recreational activities now starts at a base of *scienti no fit injuria* (no wrong is committed towards one who has knowledge).'

[201] J Steele, *Tort Law: Text, Cases and Materials* (Oxford, Oxford University Press, 2007) 15.

[202] Ibid 560 referring to J Fulbrook, *Outdoor Activities, Negligence and the Law* (Dartmouth, Ashgate, 2005) 261 on the need for adequate, preventative risk assessment and health and safety management schemes in sport. See also H Hartley, *Sport, Physical Recreation and the Law* (London, Routledge, 2009) ch 6 and the weight given to the expert evidence of a risk assessor in *Uren v Corporate Leisure (UK) Ltd* [2010] EWHC 46 [48]–[57] by Field J.

[203] For an insight into the insurance surrounding an elite professional footballer for personal accident see *Blackburn Rovers Football and Athletic Club Plc v Avon Insurance Plc & Ors* [2006] EWHC 840 (QB). In the US, professional athletes now tend to take out additional private disability insurance. See generally D Cortes, 'Same Injury; Different Coverage: How Privatized Insurance Policies Affect Injured Elite and Non-elite Professional Athletes' (2006) 13 *Villanova Sports and Entertainment Law Journal* 133.

provided adequate insurance-based recompense is available, participants appear to prefer that the matter is left to the sanctioning authority of the relevant internal disciplinary mechanism.[204] It follows that sports organisations, particularly those administering a body contact sport, should not underestimate the value of a basic, mandatory level of insurance cover for all participants, complemented by a thorough, arbitral-based internal disciplinary process.[205]

[**6.62**] If a case based on participant liability for sporting injury goes to trial, it is clear that it will usually proceed on the basis of negligence and take place in the context of the following (five) factors. First, a duty of care is owed by a participant to their fellow participants. Second, the appropriate degree of care to be exercised by the 'reasonable man of the sporting world' is assessed objectively. Third, in that objective analysis it is suggested that momentary lapses of skill or errors in judgement by the defendant should not be sufficient to indicate breach of duty; though reckless disregard for the safety of the claimant should goes towards proof of breach. Between these parameters, breach of or adherence to the rules and conventions of the game in question will be of import to the court's assessment of liability. Fourth, these objective criteria, though useful as an evidential guideline, are in no way determinative of liability. Ultimately, it is a matter for the tribunal of fact to assess whether reasonable care was exercised in the prevailing sporting circumstances *as a whole*.

[**6.63**] Overall, this review of sports-related personal injury liability reflects well on the 'individualist values' of the law of torts more generally, as it attempts a balance between risk on the one hand and individual autonomy on the other.[206] For instance, there is a strong practical aspect to the courts' assessment of whether the injuring participant was acting 'out of all proportion' to the occasion. Equally, there is the clever use of vicarious liability as both an adequate and just remedy and a deterrent against further violent play in sport. There is, arguably, some theoretical coherence in the view that in any given sports environment the participants can be seen as a community of reciprocal risk-takers.

In addition, the civil courts' approach to sports-related injury is underpinned by a forceful policy-based view that the social utility of sport must, as a desirable activity, be protected in the face of continuous exposure to contemporary society's blame culture. Finally, although there is some merit in Gearty's maxim of 'a duty not to be reckless when engaged in sports and pastimes',[207] it is contended that with respect to liability for sporting injuries, it is the 'duty' of sports governing bodies to be reasonably careful in regard to the health and safety of participants, that is of greater importance. The incidents of injury and associated risks in body

---

[204] See Gearty (n 63) 373, 'Negligent sportsmen should be dropped, not sued; the careful player is a bore—and rarely wins.'

[205] In analogy, these provisions could be said to be in line with the thrust of the Pre Action Protocol for Personal Injury Claims available at www.justice.gov.uk/civil/procrules_fin/contents/protocols/prot_pic.htm.

[206] Paraphrasing Lord Hoffmann in *Tomlinson v Congleton Borough Council* [2004] 1 AC 46, 85.

[207] See Gearty (n 63) 373.

contact sports will always be elevated. These risks necessitate the continuing enhancement and implementation of best practice in terms of coaching, refereeing and risk assessment generally.[208] With these regulatory measures, allied to effective insurance and disciplinary codes, the threat of litigation should abate, and the fear of legal proceedings can be controlled. In sum, and as the courts have implied on numerous occasions, reasonable management of sports-related risk means that that risk should normally lie were it falls, be it *on* the pitch, *in* the arena or *beyond* the touchline.

Further Points of Interest and Discussion

1. In *Kerr v Willis* [2009] EWCA Civ 1248, the claimant had suffered a catastrophic spinal injury during an indoor 'friendly' football match. The claimant alleged that the defendant had tackled him from behind after he had played the ball, which had propelled him forward into the wall at the end of the pitch. The claimant argued that the tackle amounted to a foul and that therefore the defendant had breached his duty of care towards the claimant. The defendant denied liability on the basis that his movements were within the rules of the game and what happened was a 'pure' accident. Both limbs of the claimant's arguments were rejected at trial and a subsequent appeal dismissed.

   On reading this case, and in light of the general principles outlined in this chapter, is it now fair to say that, in the context of the law of negligence, the duty of care of a sports participant towards an opponent during the course of a game equates to a 'duty not to be reckless'?
2. Assess the potential of vicarious liability and the economic torts of conspiracy and unlawful interference with economic relations as a means of deterring violent play in team sports.
3. Consider a class discussion on the following issue relating to the promotion of sports volunteering and child protection issues in sport.
   In the autumn of 2009, the Independent Safeguarding Authority (ISA) operating pursuant to the Safeguarding Vulnerable Peoples Act 2006 announced the commencement of a 'Vetting and Barring Scheme' whereby when someone new is recruited to work or volunteer with children or vulnerable people, their status first has to be checked with the Criminal Records Bureau and

---

[208] Note the discussion on the benefits of new safety rules, good coaching and preventative strategies in S Gianotti *et al*, 'Interim Evaluation of the Effect of a New Scrum Law on Neck and Back Injuries in Rugby Union' (2008) 43 *British Journal of Sports Medicine* 427; L Abernethy and C Bleakley, 'Strategies to Prevent Injury in Adolescent Sport: a Systematic Review' (2007) 41 *British Journal of Sports Medicine* 627 and D Chalmers *et al*, 'Tackling Rugby Injuries: Lessons Learned from the Implementation of a Five-year Sports Injury Prevention Programme' (2004) 7 *Journal of Science & Medicine in Sport* 74.

then registered with ISA in order to be permitted to undertake so-called 'regulated activity'. Instructing children or vulnerable adults in sport is viewed as a regulated activity and thus ISA requirements are set to become a key determinative factor in whether or not a sports organisation can allow a new entrant to become a coach, instructor or volunteer. The scope of the ISA scheme has met with significant media alarm as to the effect it will have on the rates of volunteerism in sport.

Taking into account the societal balance that needs to be struck between, on the one hand, safeguarding children, and, on the other hand, promoting volunteerism and participation in 'grassroots' sport, do you think that the ISA scheme will have an overly intrusive effect on sport in the UK? In researching your answer, make use of the resources available online at the National Society for Prevention of Cruelty to Children's Protection in Sport Unit (www.thecpsu. org.uk) and ISA's website (www.isa-gov.org.uk); and see also H Hartley, *Sport, Physical Recreation and the Law* (London, Routledge, 2009) ch 5; A Lewis and J Taylor (eds) *Sport: Law and Practice* 2nd edn (London, Tottel Publishing, 2008) ch D7 and Y Williams, 'Human Rights v Human Responsibilities: Striking a Balance between the Rights of Child Athletes and the Resulting Responsibilities of Volunteers in Sport' (2009) 40 *Cambrian Law Review* 76.

7

Sports-Related Contracts
of Employment

Introduction

[**7.01**] This chapter reviews the legal interests of individual sports participants under club employment contracts. There are four points of note. First, the contractual and quasi-contractual binds and the employment and quasi-employment nature of the 'web' of relationships surrounding professional athletes can be quite nuanced.[1] This chapter opens by explaining why its principal focus is on the contractual arrangements binding a professional footballer as an employee of a club, while paying due regard to an increasingly influential party within the contractual web surrounding modern professional players, namely the role and regulation of player agents. Second, the chapter then moves to a discussion of the formation of, and capacity to, contract in a sporting context. In this, some emphasis is placed on the capacity of minors to contract in light of recent FIFA-led initiatives seeking to protect young talented footballers from potential exploitation by leading football clubs in Europe. Third, the chapter assesses the content and performance of a hypothetical 'standard' sports contract with a focus on some of the terms that are characteristic of such contracts and what occurs on breach of said terms, and including the possibility of termination of contract. It is of particular note that the issue of players terminating contracts prematurely has become a contentious one in football and this overlaps into the text's concluding chapter, which not only continues the debate on 'change of employment' in the context of sport, that is, the legal and sporting regulation of player transfers in European football, but also seeks to locate that debate within the wider context of the (EU-driven) future of sports law in the UK.

---

[1] The 'web of relationships' that surround modern professional players is dealt with succinctly by A Lewis and J Taylor (eds), *Sport: Law and Practice* 2nd edn (London, Tottel Publishing, 2008) ch D1. This chapter has also benefitted from S Gardiner *et al*, *Sports Law* 3rd edn (London, Cavendish, 2006) chs 12–14. For an American perspective see M Cozzillo *et al* (eds), *Sports Law: Cases and Materials* 2nd edn (Durham NC, Carolina Academic Press, 2007) chs 4–6.

A Contractual Web

[**7.02**]   At the nascent stage of professional sport there was a view (on this side of the Atlantic, at least) that those involved in sport, irrespective of whether they were being paid or not, could not truly be described as 'workers'. Almost a century ago, that view was rejected out of hand by the English Court of Appeal in *Walker v Crystal Palace FC*.[2] In the stated case, the Court of Appeal permitted the claimant, a professional footballer, to avail of compensation under the Workmen's Compensation Act 1906 for an accident sustained during a football game. Farwell LJ dismissed the club's appeal succinctly by observing: 'It may be sport to the amateur, but to the man who is paid for it and makes his living thereby it is his work'.[3] For the sake of clarity and brevity, the focus of this chapter remains on the contractual relationship between a 'worker-footballer' and the 'employer-club'. This is because the typical contractual relationship involved in this scenario, and the disputes that typically arise from this relationship are, arguably, more instructive when compared to the multi-layered contractual arrangements that often surround individual sports professionals such as athletes, golfers, tennis players, snooker players and even Formula 1 drivers.[4] Individual sports participants of this kind are effectively self-employed and thus are free to contract directly with either event/tournament organisations and/or international federations/tour organisers.[5] This 'freedom' means that the contractual web surrounding such athletes can be quite dense and difficult to describe with any brevity or clarity. Nevertheless, one of the more interesting and informative contractual 'webs' in sport is that which surrounds professional boxers, and it bears some attention.

Boxers: Trainers; Managers; Promoters; and Conflicts of Interest

[**7.03**]   In the early part of the twentieth century, professional boxers arranged bouts with each other through contractual arrangements negotiated principally by their manager, who in contemporary terms, effectively acted as the boxer's

---

[2] *Walker v Crystal Palace FC* [1910] 1 KB 87.

[3] Ibid 93.

[4] Note, eg, the unusual contractual arrangements and employment status that Formula 1 drivers have with their teams, as evidenced by *Walkinson & Ors v Diniz* [2002] EWCA Civ 180. The two-year contract that Diniz had with the Arrows FI team contained a condition precedent by which he had to provide sponsorship of not less than US$19 million in order to be given the drive for Arrows in the 1997 and 1998 F1 World Championships. For further insight into the contractual issues surrounding the financial sponsorship of a Formula One team see *Force India Formula One Team Ltd v Etihad Airways PJSC & Anor* [2009] EWHC 2768 (QB).

[5] So, eg, a tennis player may have certain contractual obligations with the organisers of individual tournaments (eg, Wimbledon and All England Tennis Club); the Association of Tennis Professionals (the organisers of ATP Tour events); and the International Tennis Federation (the world governing body for the sport). This issue was also of importance in the *Modahl* litigation discussed at [2.23]–[2.24] of this text.

agent. The 'purse' or payment given to each boxer—from which the boxer had to pay a percentage to his trainer, manager, the licensing authority, etc—was largely dependent on gate receipts.[6] The process and bout itself was then sanctioned (in the loosest sense of the word) by the relevant governing body of which, historically, the British Boxing Board of Control (BBBC, a private regulatory body for the sport in the UK) and the New York State Athletic Commission (a statutory body) were of greatest influence. Since then, the sanctioning process in boxing has, to say the least, become a complicated affair with an 'alphabet soup' of world sanctioning bodies and multiple 'world champions'.[7] In the 1920s, a third party began to get involved in the traditional contractual arrangement and so-called fight promoters (often associated with a well known boxing venue) began to arrange fights.[8] Later, in the 1970s, a series of 'independent' promoters, notably Don King and Bob Arum in the US and Barry Hearn, Frank Maloney and Frank Warren in the UK began to emerge and have since played a dominant role in the sport.

[**7.04**]   These promoters have ensured that the financial remuneration of boxers has now moved well beyond a dependency on gate receipts, principally by tapping into the lucrative pay-per-view TV market. In fact, despite the current fragmentation and marginalisation of the sport, these promoters have ensured that major boxing title fights remain the most lucrative individual events in world sport.[9] Individual boxers and their backers remain attracted to these riches and the typical arrangement now is that an ambitious manager will attempt to sign with a successful promoter in the hope of arranging a series of televised bouts for his fighter, with the ultimate objective of eventually engineering a title fight.[10] From a strictly contractual perspective, the interesting point is that it has been

---

[6] On paying all interested parties, it is often the case that the professional boxer is, despite having taken all the physical risk, left with a meagre percentage of the original purse. In this light, although the debate on the legality of boxing usually concentrates on the physical exploitation of boxers in the ring, it is argued the equal concern should be given to the financial exploitation of boxers outside the ring. On a related point see also R Tenorio, 'The Economics of Professional Boxing Contracts' (2000) 1 *Journal of Sports Economics* 363 where it is argued that, unlike most other sports, boxers are guaranteed their purse in advance—irrespective of whether they win, lose or draw; consequently, there is the danger, especially for so-called 'journeymen' boxers, that they will have little incentive to train property and thus the likelihood of a poor showing leading to injury increases.

[7] For a brief review of the administrative farrago that is the global regulation of professional boxing see J Anderson, *The Legality of Boxing* (London, Birkbeck Press, 2007) ch 3.

[8] In the US, the leading promoters such as Tex Rickard (in the 1920s) and Mike Jacobs (in the 1930s and 1940s) were associated with Madison Square Garden in New York. These old style boxing impresarios were replaced in the 1950s by wholesale, mafia-related corruption. See generally K Mitchell, *Jacob's Beach* (London, Yellow Jersey, 2009). In the UK, the post-war era was dominated by promoters such as Jack Solomons who used various London facilities such as the White City Stadium in West London and later still Harry Levene, who promoted fights at London's Albert Hall.

[9] See M Syed, 'A Clash of Two Greats can Define Our Age' *The Times* (London 18 November 2009) Sport 81.

[10] For an insight into the roles of and relationship between managers and promoters see, eg, the discussion in *George Foreman Associates Ltd v Foreman* 389 F Supp 1308 (US District Court, ND Cal, 1974) and in *Hearn and Matchroom Boxing Limited v Collins* [1998] IEHC 187.

common for promoters to have a dual and ostensibly conflicting role as both manager and promoter of the boxer. The conflict lies in the fact that a boxer's manager has a fiduciary duty to organise a programme of contests and events on the boxer's behalf. In contrast, a promoter has a personal and financial interest in all the fights he promotes. This conflict of interest has been a feature of litigation in the English courts, as has the unconscionable even coercive nature of these sports-related forms of personal employment services contracts.[11] The question of whether the balance in the BBBC's current 'approved boxer/manager agreement' remains unfairly or even unconscionably tilted against boxers remains open to debate.[12] Finally, in terms of the general application of principles of contract law, and particularly contracts of service, to sport; boxing undoubtedly provides the richest and most colourful seam of case law: from the enforcement of negative covenants; to the status of future option clauses; to inducing or actual breach of a contract; and the wide gamut of disputes that have arisen between the various characters who populate what the celebrated American sportswriter Jimmy Cannon once called sport's 'red light district'.[13]

Footballers: Sponsors; International Duties; Third Party Owners; and Agents

[**7.05**]   The episodic and often turbulent nature of the contractual relationships associated with a career in professional boxing makes most other sports-related contractual scenarios seem quite prosaic. From this point onwards, the 'default' sport in the analysis of the various contract of employment matters that might

---

[11] See, eg, *Warren v Mendy* [1989] 3 All ER 103 and *Watson v Praeger* [1991] 3 All ER 487 as discussed in S Greenfield and G Osborn, 'A Gauntlet for the Glove: The Challenge to English Boxing Contracts' (1995) 6 *Marquette Sports Law Review* 153 and Anderson (n 7) 157–60.

[12] Clause 6 of that agreement, available online at www.bbbofc.com/documentation.php, deals with 'possible conflicts of interest'. Arguably, the clause is inherently weak because, in a situation where the manager also intends to act as the boxer's promoter, it obliges that manager to inform only the boxer of that intention, and not the independent regulatory body. Therefore, although clause 6 obliges the manager/promoter to, in effect, erect a 'chinese wall' between his roles, the building and maintenance of that wall remains the responsibility of that self same manager/promoter.

[13] A brief (chronological) perusal of the litigation involving, either directly or indirectly, the UK-based promoter, Frank Warren, gives a sense of the range of contractual and related disputes prompted by professional boxing: *Warren v Mendy* [1993] 3 All ER 103 (injunction to compel an employment contract of service); *Warren v Mirror Group Newspapers* Unreported, Court of Appeal (Civil Division) 13 November 1991, Lloyd, Mann LLJ, Sir George Waller (libel arising out of the reportage of the shooting of Mr Warren); *Don King Productions v Warren and Others* [2000] Ch 291 (dissolution of a commercial partnership); *R v Roberts* [2001] EWCA Crim 2282 (prosecution of alleged fraudulent evasion of VAT; acquittal of Mr Warren); *Dalton v Warren t/a Sports Network Europe* [2002] EWHC 746 (QB) (tort of unlawful interference with business); *Rape Crisis Centre v Secretary of State for the Home Department* (2000) SC 527 (application for judicial review surrounding entry of a convicted rapist, Mike Tyson, into the UK); *Warren t/a Sports Network Europe v Revenue and Customs Commissioners* [2005] STI 2038 (VAT and Duties Tribunal, London); *Warren v Hide* [2008] EWHC 3049 (QB) (consideration of a contract); *Warren v Random House* [2009] QB 600 (defamation); *Sports Network v Calzaghe* [2009] EWHC 480 (QB) (oral contracts). A similar exercise with the US-based promoter Don King would be equally colourful.

arise in the context of the professional sport industry is football. In this, and in addition to the general principles of employment[14] and contract law,[15] the following assessment is informed by reference to FIFA's Regulations on the Status and Transfer of Players (October 2009).[16] References to this important document—and its attempts to regulate a number of contentious issues in football such as the status and registration of players, the maintenance of contractual stability between professionals and clubs and compensation payments—are interwoven into the general narrative of this chapter.

[**7.06**]   In this light, although there are, admittedly, various complex aspects to the nature of the contractual arrangements between a professional footballer and a club, the necessarily narrow focus of this chapter means that some issues can only be dealt with briefly, or in some cases not at all. For instance, there is no further mention of the litigation that might arise from separate contracts entered into by football players through sponsorship, endorsement or promotional agreements.[17] The lucrative and influential nature of these contracts was revealed in late 2009/ early 2010 when, ostensibly on the grounds of privacy, the then England football captain, John Terry, sought injunctive relief in order to prevent a newspaper from publishing allegations that he had had an extra-martial affair with the partner of his former Chelsea teammate Wayne Bridge.[18] In overturning the initial interim relief, Tugendhat J noted that the 'real concern' of the applicant was the effect it might have on his various sponsorship and endorsement deals—estimated to be worth up to £4 million annually to Terry[19]—and the sensitivity of his sponsors towards the public image of a person whom they were paying handsomely to promote their products.[20] The John Terry affair also echoed Tiger Woods' spectacular

---

[14]   This chapter is generally informed by N Selwyn, *Selwyn's Law of Employment* 15th edn (Oxford, Oxford University Press, 2008).

[15]   This chapter is generally informed by E McKendrick, *Contract Law: Text, Cases and Materials* 3rd edn (Oxford, Oxford University Press, 2008).

[16]   Available online at www.fifa.com/aboutfifa/documentlibrary/index.html. From here on they will be cited as article 1 FIFA etc. The Regulations are accompanied by a separate explanatory memorandum entitled 'Commentary on the Regulations on the Status and Transfer of Players'. The explanations in the commentary are, inter alia, based on the jurisprudence of FIFA's Dispute Resolution Chamber (DRC) and the Court of Arbitration for Sport (CAS).

[17]   See, for instance, the dispute that arose between a leading female tennis player and her personal sponsors relating to the payment of bonuses predicated on her position in the world rankings in *Martinez v Ellesse International* [1999] EWCA Civ 1133.

[18]   The relief sought was in the form of a so-called 'super injunction'. Whereas ordinarily in such circumstance the applicant would seek an order preventing media organisations from reporting certain facts; a super-injunction seeks to prohibit even mentioning that an order has been obtained. See D Sanderson, 'England Captain Fails to Keep Claims of Affair with Teammates Girlfriend Quiet' *The Times* (London 30 January 2010) News 15.

[19]   See the figures cited by A Hill, 'Shamed Terry Stands to Lose Millions over Affair's Revelation' *The Observer* (London 30 January 2010) Home 9.

[20]   *Terry v Persons Unknown (Rev 1)* [2010] EWHC 119 (QB) and especially [95], [131] and [149], Tugendhat J. On balance, Tugehdat J held, at [149], that an interim order of the kind sought was not 'necessary or proportionate having regard to the level of gravity of the interference with the private life of the applicant that would occur in the event that there is a publication of the fact of an [extra marital] relationship.'

fall from grace at the end of 2009 when he lost a range of sponsorship deals after it was revealed that he had had multiple extra-marital affairs.[21]

[**7.07**]   Another topic that can also only be alluded to briefly is the recent phenomenon of the third party 'ownership' of players. This issue has moved from relatively straightforward breach of contract claims for damages based on innocent misrepresentation and mistake as to the identity of a selling club,[22] and onto the slightly more complex issue of the 'ownership' of a player's economic rights, as discussed previously with regard to the saga surrounding the signing by West Ham United FC of the Argentinean international Carlos Tevez, whose economic rights were apparently owned by a third party.[23] In short, the football authorities in England[24] and globally have sought to prevent clubs from entering into contracts which enable 'any other party to that contract or any third party to acquire the ability to influence in employment and transfer-related matters its independence, its policies or the performance of its teams'.[25] These third-party concerns are a relatively recent phenomenon and the commercial complexity and conflicts of interests that might arise from them have yet to be worked out fully.[26] Two further aspects of the contractual web that surround the footballer-club employment relationship do, however, merit greater analysis: the repercussions that might arise on the selection of a club footballer for a national team; and the matter of player agents in football.

International Duties

[**7.08**]   As is typical of international sport's governance pyramid, an individual footballer will not only have direct contractual relationship with their employing club but also, if selected for the national team, with the relevant national football federation and through that with the relevant regional body (for example,

---

[21]   One study by the University of California, Davis estimated that in the immediate wake of the Woods scandal key sponsors' shareholders lost nearly £7.5billion in stock market returns. See M Hunter, 'Famous Friends are not Always Helpful' *The Times* (London 3 February 2010) Business 48.

[22]   See *Sunderland Association Football Club v Uruguay Montevideo FC* [2001] 2 All ER (Comm) 828.

[23]   See [3.27]–[3.28] of this text.

[24]   See FA Rule C1(b)(iii) and the FA's Third Party Investment in Players Regulations. The latter came into effect on 4 July 2009. The key regulation (reg A1) states that 'No Club may enter into an agreement with a Third Party whereby that Club makes or receives payment to or from, assigns any rights to or incurs any liability in relation to, that Third Party as a result of, or in connection with, the proposed or actual registration (whether permanent or temporary), transfer of registration or employment by it of a Player, unless prior approval has been obtained from the FA.'

[25]   Article 18 bis FIFA.

[26]   Note also the problems posed by the Hero Global Football Fund which aims to generate a profit for its investors by selling player registrations and economic rights to clubs and also loaning money to clubs. See further P Kelso, 'FA and clubs face Tevez II over new third party plans' *The Daily Telegraph* (London 22 July 2009) Sport 10. For a succinct review of the issues see D Geey, 'Third Party Player Ownership: The Regulations for Premier League and Football League Clubs for the 2009/10 Season' (2009) 7 *Entertainment and Sports Law Journal* available online at www2.warwick.ac.uk/fac/soc/law/elj/eslj/issues/volume7/number2/geey.

UEFA) and/or the international governing body (FIFA) as an event or tournament organiser. An interesting application of this issue arose out of the efforts of
a club in Belgium, Charleroi FC, to seek compensation for the injuries sustained
by one of their players while playing for his national team. The player in question, Abdelmajid Oulmers, was selected by Morocco for a friendly international
against Burkina Faso in November 2004. Despite the club's claim that the player
was injured and needed rest, FIFA, referring to its regulations on the obligations of clubs to release players for international duty, ordered that he should
play as selected.[27] Oulmers played and exacerbated his injuries to such an extent
he was unable to play for the remainder of the 2004/2005 season. The club's
insurance policy did not cover the player whilst on international duty. Charleroi
sought compensation from FIFA for this loss and also for the fact that the loss of
Oulmers, one of their key players, was a material cause in their failure to qualify
for the lucrative UEFA Champions League tournament.

[**7.09**]   To recap, the key contractual nexus for the stated litigation was said to
be found in FIFA's regulations governing the release of players for international
duty. As expressed in the stated regulations, FIFA's view was that clubs, and not
national associations, were ultimately responsible (and should be insured against)
such injuries. In 2006, Charleroi FC, as joined by the so-called G-14 Group (of
leading football clubs in Europe) succeeded in obtaining leave from a regional
court in Belgium to obtain a reference for a preliminary ruling from the ECJ on
the following question:

> Do the obligations on clubs and football players having employment contracts with
> those clubs imposed by the provisions of FIFA statutes and regulations providing for
> the obligatory release of players to national federations without compensation, and the
> unilateral and binding determination of the coordinated international match calendar,
> constitute unlawful restrictions of competition or abuses of a dominant position or
> obstacles to the exercise of the fundamental freedoms conferred by the EC Treaty and are
> they therefore contrary to Article 81 and 82 of the Treaty [competition law provisions]
> or to any other provision of Community law, particularly Articles 39 [free movement of
> workers] and 49 [freedom of establishment] of the Treaty.[28]

[**7.10**]   The reaction to the possibility that Charleroi FC's proceedings might
be looked upon favourably by the European Court of Justice (ECJ), ranged
from the measured (that it would simply mean national federations having to
ensure that a player's insurance provision were 'topped-up' in order to cover
international duties); to the hysterical (that the insurance and compensation
obligations on national and international sports governing bodies would be

---

[27] See generally art 2, annexe 1 'Release of players to association teams' to FIFA Regulations on the
Status and Transfer of Players (2009) available online at www.fifa.com/aboutfifa/documentlibrary/
index.html.
[28] Case C-243/06, *Reference for a preliminary ruling from the Tribunal de commerce de Charleroi
lodged on 30 May 2006—SA Sporting du Pays Charleroi and G14 v FIFA* (OJ 2006/C 212/18, 2
September 2006).

such that international representative sport might no longer be feasible).[29] The hyperbole surrounding the latter was related to the fact that the G-14 clubs ensured that Charleroi FC were represented by Jean-Louis Dupont, who had represented Jean-Marc Bosman in his landmark case on player transfers. In the end a deal was reached between the leading European clubs, UEFA and FIFA and the litigation was withdrawn.[30] The deal in question was part of a broader set of negotiations which lead to the disbandment of the G-14 organisation; the creation of the European Club Association—an independent body representing 144 clubs across Europe but recognised by UEFA and FIFA; and the agreement by the football authorities to make 'financial contributions' for players' participation in European Championships and World Cups.[31] In the run up to the World Cup in 2010, FIFA announced that it had siphoned US$40 million of the tournament's revenues into a fund dedicated to clubs whose players were representing their countries at the event in South Africa.[32]

[7.11]   The above payments/deal notwithstanding, managers' complaints regarding the problem of key players coming back injured or 'exhausted' from international commitments (especially friendly matches) or the mid-season scheduling of a tournaments such as the African Nations Cup, has now become a regular feature of the football season in the Premier League in England. The relevant FA regulations (FA Rule D, international and other representative matches and call-ups) which are typical of the rules adopted by other national FAs in Europe, are that a player selected for an international team is obliged to 'attend at the time and place notified to the Player and comply with the arrangements of The Association in every respect, save where there is good and sufficient cause not to do so'.[33] Furthermore, the player's club is obliged to 'do all things necessary to ensure' that the player in question complies with the stated arrangements.[34] The issue of illness or injury constituting 'good and sufficient cause' has occasionally given rise to controversy given that, although receipt of medical evidence from the club's doctors can satisfy the FA, 'the Player shall, in any event, submit to assessment by a medical adviser appointed by The Association'.[35] An interesting negligence-based case might be said to surround the circumstances alleged to have arisen in November 2009 when the Arsenal manager accused the Dutch national team's medical team of minimising the

---

[29] See also S Hollis, 'Players: Sporting Bodies and Clubs fight for Control' (2006) 4 *World Sport Law Report* 6 and P Limbert, 'Compensating Clubs for Players Injured during International Play' (2007) 5 *World Sport Law Report* 5.

[30] See the order of the President of the ECJ of 25 November 2008 removing the case from the ECJ register (OJ 2009/ C 69/56, 21 March 2009).

[31] See P Kelso, 'G14 to Disband as Deal is Struck' *The Guardian* (London 16 January 2008) Sport 4. For further information on the European Clubs' Association see online at www.ecaeurope.com.

[32] See K Eason, 'Biggest Prize Money in History Only Increases the Pain for Irish' *The Times* (London 4 December 2009) Sport 11.

[33] FA Rule D1.

[34] FA Rule D2.

[35] FA Rule D3.

injuries sustained by Robin Van Persie, then Arsenal's principal striker, during a friendly match against Italy.[36]

Agents

[**7.12**]   In December 2009, the FA Premier League (FAPL) in England pub-lished figures regarding payments to agents for the period 1 October 2008 to 30 September 2009. The headline figure was that approximately £71 million was paid to such intermediaries during that period. This was the first time that the FAPL revealed such information, following a change in FA rules in 2007, which was fully supported by the Premier League clubs. The underlying idea of the initiative is to bring greater transparency to the domestic transfer market, amid concerns among supporters and managers that large sums were being wasted on agents' fees.[37] It followed the lead taken by the Football League, which has published a similar set of figures annually since 2004. In the last set of figures, published in August 2009, the total paid in agents' fees in that League was £8.8 million, a £2.3 million reduction from the previous year, and the hope is that the movement to greater transparency in the Premier League will have a similar effect.[38]

[**7.13**]   That hope aside, it must be noted that the above Premier League figures on agents' fees were said to be inclusive of fees paid to agents by clubs in respect of acquiring and/or renegotiating player registrations; fees paid to agents by clubs on behalf of players in respect of acquiring and/or renegotiating player registra-tions; and fees paid to agents by clubs in order to facilitate the outward transfer of player registrations. In this light, a feature of the governance of football agents in England, as regulated by the FA, is the issue of 'dual representation' whereby an authorised agent might have an agency relationship with more than one party in the transaction at hand, that is, with both the player and one of the clubs in the transaction. The recently revised FA Football Regulations permit dual representa-tion but, with the avoidance of conflicts of interest in mind, make it subject to the player's prior consent.[39] In contrast, FIFA's Players' Agents Regulations is strictly limited to the regulation of 'players' agents who introduce players to clubs with a view to negotiating or renegotiating an employment contract or introduce two

---

[36] See G Cox, 'Wenger Fury as Van Persie is out for Season' *The Sunday Telegraph* (London 29 November 2009) Sport 1.

[37] See, eg, M Dart, 'O'Neill Unconvinced by Value of Expensive Middlemen' *The Times* (London 2 December 2009) Sport 97.

[38] See generally M Hughes, 'Big-spending Manchester City Top List by Handing Over £13m in Agents' Fees' *The Times* (London 1 December 2009) Sport 84.

[39] FA Football Agents Regulations (4 July 2009) Regs C1-C11 available online through www.thefa. com/TheFA/RulesandRegulations/Agents.aspx.This is in line with the common law's view of an agent acting for both parties in a transaction (eg, a solicitor acting for both the buyer and seller of a house) that, although such an agent runs a high risk of breaching his duty towards one or other of the parties, especially with regard to sensitive information that might come into his possession, this can be avoided where the principal has given their informed consent to the transaction. For an interesting example of the dual nature of some football agents see *Newcastle United v The Commissioner of Her Majesty's Revenue & Customs* [2007] EWHC 612 (Ch).

clubs to one another with a view to concluding a transfer agreement within one association or from one association to another'.[40] The first part of this definition is preferred in this text.

What do Football Agents do?

[7.14]   The figures on agents' fees also prompt three further questions. What do football agents do to justify such fees? Are they worth it? And, given the huge sums involved, how closely are they regulated? The second question is very much a matter of broader debate and will not be dealt with herein.[41] The first (in terms of the ordinary law of agency in the UK) and third (in terms of internal, FIFA-led regulation of agents) questions are however of interest. Addressing the initial question, it can be said that the role of football player agents is, in essence, twofold in nature: brokering a player's employment contract with a club or transfer to another club by way of giving advice and representation in connection with any contract or renewal of a contract which that player might wish to enter into; and using all reasonable endeavours to promote the player and act in his best interests by inter alia seeking to augment the player's income through personal sponsorship and endorsement deals and the provision of legal, financial planning and tax advice.[42]

[7.15]   In this, the role of a football player agent can be easily reconciled with, and even epitomises, a standard definition of agency at common law. In short, an agency relationship, which is fiduciary in nature, exists where an express or implied agreement between the principal (the player) and agent permits that agent to act on the principal's behalf such that the legal effect of such acts is that the principal is bound by them and through them may incur legal obligations to third parties who have dealt with the agent.[43] In the UK, the main duties and responsibilities of agents at common law (which can be modified somewhat by contract; are subject to some indirect statute-based regulation; and must be judged in their own circumstances)[44] are sixfold.

---

[40]   See art 1(1) FIFA Players' Agents Regulations (1 January 2008). Available online at www.fifa.com/aboutfifa/documentlibrary/index.html.

[41]   Compare P Barclay, 'Clubs must Tackle Curse of Agents and their Inflated Fees' *The Times* (London 7 December 2009) The Game, Sport 8 with J Smith, 'If Agents are Waste of Money, Why Do Clubs Still Happily Pay Us Millions?' *The Times* (London 2 December 2009) Sport 97.

[42]   Lewis and Taylor (n 1) 657 where mention is also made of the occasional 'hand holding' activities 'related to a move to a new club or country, such as assisting with house moves and advising on where to send children to school.' See also M Stein, *How to be a Sports Agent* new edn (Harpenden, High Stakes, 2008). Note also that leading Premier League players are now surrounded by a coterie of advisers including agents, lawyers and PR advisers. See, eg, the 'team' that advises Chelsea's John Terry as named in P Kelso, 'Trouble Grows for Terry and Advisers' *The Daily Telegraph* (London 3 February 2010) Sport 4.

[43]   This chapter is generally informed by R Munday, *Agency: Law and Principles* (Oxford, Oxford University Press, 2010).

[44]   See Lewis and Taylor (n 1) 661–64 who note that the Employment Agencies Act 1973 and the Conduct of Employment Agencies and Employment Business Regulations 2003 may cover certain activities carried out by players' agents.

[**7.16**]   First, and principally, the agent should carry out, and generally in person and with reasonable dispatch, the business they have agreed to undertake with reference to their terms of appointment and the instructions of the principal. Where no definite instructions have been given to the agent or where the agent has discretion, the general rule is that the professional sports agent should 'follow the ordinary, normal course or customs of such a business'.[45] Second, every agent has a duty to exercise proper care, skill or diligence in the carrying out of their undertaking.[46] Third, it is the duty of an agent to keep accurate accounts of all of their transactions and to avoid both the improper mixing of the principal's property with their own and payments made to the agent on the principal's behalf. Failure to keep proper accounts and the failure to be prepared to produce them to the principal at any time can give rise, in the case of a dispute, to a presumption in favour of the principal's grievance.[47] Fourth, and in the light of recent concerns among leading 'celebrity' footballers concerning privacy, it is of interest to note that a long established duty of an agent at common law is to use the materials and information obtained through their capacity as an agent solely for the purposes of the agency and not to use that information in any manner inconsistent with good faith towards the principal such as, for instance, by divulging it to third parties.[48] Where an agent is found to have breached any of these common law duties, the principal's remedy is in effect to claim in damages for breach of contract for the loss (and no more) that is the natural and probable consequence of the breach of duty.[49]

[**7.17**]   Fifth, an agent should not enter into any transaction likely to risk putting their duty towards their principal in conflict with their own interests. This is subject to a situation where the agent has first made the 'fullest' disclosure of the exact nature of their interest known to the principal.[50] Where non-disclosure occurs, the integrity of any 'non-disclosed' transaction is immaterial, and is voidable at the principal's option.[51] Finally, an agent must not acquire any secret profit or benefit from his agency other than that in the principal's reasonable contemplation at the creation of the agency relationship. Put simply, any profit or benefit

---

[45] See generally *World Transport Agency Ltd v Royte (England) Ltd* [1957] 1 Lloyd's Rep 381 (shipping agents).

[46] The question of breach of such as duty is very much one of fact see *Faruk v Wyse* [1988] 2 EGLR 26 (estate agents).

[47] See *Yasuda Fire and Marine Insurance of Europe Ltd v Orion Marine Insurance Underwriting Agency Ltd* [1995] QB 174 (underwriting agents).

[48] It can be argued that the duty pertains irrespective of whether the agency has come to an end. See generally *Lamb v Evans* [1893] 1 Ch 218.

[49] See generally *Salvense & Co v Rederi Aktiebolaget Nordstjernan* [1905] AC 302 (shipbrokers).

[50] Note the analogy to the duty of disclosure of promoters of a company in *Gluckstein v Barnes* [1900] AC 240.

[51] In effect, in this situation the transaction has been induced by misrepresentation and thus a contract-based remedy such as rescission may be available even if the transaction has been completely executed. See *Armstrong v Jackson* [1917] 2 KB 822 (breach of duty by a stockbroker). If the misrepresentation is fraudulent in nature and relates to a serious and abusive failure to disclose relevant information, then ss 2–4 of the Fraud Act 2006 might apply.

accruing to the agent over and above that contemplated by the agreement between the agent and principal should be revealed to the principal.[52] Again, the integrity of any 'secret profit' transaction is immaterial and breach of the rule can result in all related profits and the value of all related benefits being paid over to the principal.[53] The definition of a secret profit or benefit includes any bribe or secret commission—known in football parlance as a 'bung'—received by the agent from a third party with whom the agent is dealing on their principal's behalf and without the knowledge or consent of the principal (or otherwise not in the principal's reasonable contemplation at the creation of the agency).[54]

[7.18] Given the fiduciary nature of the agency relationship, as built on the high level of trust and confidence between the parties, the common law has taken a direct and strict line on the receipt of a secret commissions, whether by gift or consideration, by agents. The common law approach is assessed shortly. Indirectly, some statutory provisions might also be of relevance. For instance, where what occurs is in effect bribery then section 1 of the Prevention of Corruption Act 1906 might apply, as might the conspiracy to defraud offences of section 1 of the Criminal Law Act 1977 and section 12 of the Criminal Justice Act 1987. A recent interesting review of both the law on bribery (including the Bribery Bill currently making its way through the Westminster parliament) and a set of factual circumstances that might be of some analogy to sport (where a club pays an agent a bung in order to secure a player's services) occurred in *Nayar v Denton Wilde Sapte & Advani*.[55] In that case, the claimants alleged that they had paid nearly £400,000 to the second named defendant, a solicitor employed by the first named defendants, in order to secure a contract with a third party. The contract did not materialise owing, the claimants argued, to the negligence of the solicitor and thus the claimants took an action for recovery of their 'deposit'.[56] The court rejected the claim on the ground that the deposit equated to a bribe paid in order to secure an introduction with the third party and consequently the claim should be defeated on *ex turpi causa* grounds.[57]

---

[52] See generally *Boardman v Phipps* [1967] 2 AC 46 (agents acting for a trust seeking to acquire a shareholding in a company).

[53] See generally *Brown v IRC* [1965] AC 244 (interest on clients' money which a solicitor deposited in his own name in a bank deposit account belonged to the claimant and so was not the solicitor's income and could not support a claim by him for earned income relief).

[54] See generally *Reading v Attorney-General* [1951] AC 507 (a soldier in the British army on active duty abroad consented on several occasions to accompany civilian lorries transporting illicit spirits. He always wore his uniform in order to avoid police inspection and he received payment in return. The military authorities subsequently took possession on that money, and the solider was court martialed and jailed. After his release he claimed unsuccessfully for the return of the amount seized.)

[55] *Nayar v Denton Wilde Sapte* [2009] EWHC 3218 (QB) and especially [83]–[96], Hamblen J.

[56] The High Court held that the first named defendants were not vicariously liable for the actions of their employee as her acts were both outside her actual and ostensible authority and role and for personal reward.

[57] The High Court held, however, but for the illegality defence, the solicitor would have been personally liable to the claimants for breach of duty, subject to contributory negligence.

[**7.19**]   At common law, the strictness with which this misconduct is viewed is reflected in the fact that a court does not have to inquire whether the agent, on account of the bribe, acted in a way prejudicial to the principal's interest and neither is it material that the principal's interest might not even have been involved nor that the motivation of the donor was not necessarily in bad faith. In short, there is an irrebuttable presumption at common law that the bung was paid with the intention that the agent should be influenced by it.[58] On discovery of the receipt of the secret commission/bribe/side deal, the general position at common law is that the principal may immediately dismiss the agent and the principal is entitled to treat the transaction entered into as void *ab initio*. Moreover, the effect of the receipt of the bribe is that the agent forfeits any commission in respect of the transaction and becomes liable to the principal for the amount of the bribe. This appears to be the case whether or not the principal decides subsequently to affirm the transaction. Where the principal elects to rescind the transaction, the principal must make *restitutio in integrum* to the other party and return all related benefits under the tainted contract, save the money given to the agent as a bribe, which is generally not treated as a benefit.[59]

[**7.20**]   Helpfully, there is a recent case of interest which addresses specifically the issue of what happens if a football agent in negotiating for his client makes a secret deal with the club for himself on the side. In *Imageview Management Ltd v Kelvin Jack*,[60] the Court of Appeal reviewed the law on this aspect of an agent's duty of fidelity towards the principal,[61] and considered some issues relating to the effect, in terms of unpaid agency fees, of the secret side-deal.[62] The facts of the cases are of interest in what they reveal about the work and operation of player agents in football.[63] Briefly, in July 2004 the defendant, Trinidad and Tobago's international goalkeeper, sought to conclude a deal with Dundee United in order to play professional football. Jack entered into a two-year contract with the claimants (and specifically with a Mr Mike Berry who conducted a sports agency business through Imageview Ltd) in which he agreed to pay them 10 per cent of his monthly salary if Imageview successfully made arrangements for him to sign with a British club. Berry negotiated a two-year contract for Jack with Dundee United.

---

[58]   See generally *Boston Deep Sea Fishing & Ice Co v Ansell* (1888) 39 Ch D 339; *Andrews v Ramsey & Co* [1903] 2 KB 635; and *Rhodes v Macalister* (1923) 29 Com Cas 19, applied and reviewed in detail by Jacob LJ in *Imageview Management Ltd v Jack* [2009] EWCA Civ 63; [2009] 1 Lloyds Rep 436; [2009] Bus LR 1034 [9]–[27].

[59]   The principal also has the right to avoid any contract or transaction entered into by the agent in consequence of, or in connection with, the bribe. See generally *Logicrose v Southend United FC* [1988] 1 WLR 1256.

[60]   *Imageview Management Ltd v Jack* [2009] EWCA Civ 63; [2009] 1 Lloyds Rep 436; [2009] Bus LR 1034.

[61]   On this aspect of the judgment see generally L Macgregor, 'An Agent's Fiduciary Duties: Modern Law Placed in Historical Context' (2010) 14 *Edinburgh Law Review* 121.

[62]   On this aspect of the judgment see generally P Watts, 'Restitution and Conflicted Agents' (2009) 125 *LQR* 369.

[63]   *Imageview* [2009] EWCA Civ 63 [2] Jacob LJ.

At the same time, Berry agreed that Dundee United would pay Imageview Ltd a fee of £3,000 for getting Mr Jack, a non-EU citizen, a work permit. Imageview duly obtained a work permit for Jack and the football club paid the £3,000 fee, though it was uncontested that the actual value of the work done in terms of obtaining the period was no more than £750.

[**7.21**]   Problematically, Berry did not tell Jack about the work permit arrange-ment. A year or so into the deal Jack found out about the side deal and stopped paying his agency fees to Imageview. The proceedings in question related to Imageview's claims for unpaid agency fees and counterclaims by Jack arguing that the monies relating to the secret side deal should be paid to him and that he was entitled to claim back any agency fees already paid to Imageview. At the heart of the substantive issue—an agent's duty of fidelity where there is a realistic pos-sibility of a conflict of interest—was Imageview's contention that the undisclosed side deal was not a conflict of interest in the sense that the side deal was, bluntly, 'none of Mr Jack's business' and moreover that that it was a private and separate arrangement and as such was 'collateral' to the fiduciary duty to the principal. Jacob LJ held that Imageview's negotiation of a side deal had given rise to a clear conflict of interest:

> Put shortly, it is possible that the more it got itself, the less there would or could be for Mr Jack. Moreover, it gave Imageview an interest in Mr Jack signing for Dundee as opposed to some other club where no side deal for Imageview was possible ... The law imposes on agents high standards ... Footballers' agents are not exempt from these. An agent's own personal interests come entirely second to the interests of his client ... An undisclosed but realistic possibility of a conflict of interest is a breach of your duty of good faith to your client.[64]

[**7.22**]   Moreover, Jacob LJ noted that this duty should not cause an agent a problem because all that agent had to do to avoid being in breach of duty was to make a full disclosure. In this, Jacob LJ approved of defence counsel's use of for-mer US Supreme Court Justice Louis Brandeis' celebrated maxim that 'sunlight, is after all, the best of disinfectants'.[65] In application to the facts at hand, Jacob LJ noted that if Berry had told his client that when he was going to negotiate with Dundee United, he was also going to make a deal with the club for himself, then, if Jack had had no objection, there would have been no problem but instead of doing that Mr Berry made a secret deal and breached his duty of fidelity towards his client.[66] The depth and reality of this conflict of interest meant that, although 'there can be cases of harmless collaterality and cases where there is just an hon-est breach of contract' that was not the case here:[67] the secret profit was not only

---

[64] Ibid [6]–[7].

[65] Ibid [7] where with a colourful turn of phrase, Jacob LJ also observed, 'Any agent who is doubtful about his position would do well to do just that—the mere fact that he has doubts will generally be a message for his conscience.'

[66] Ibid [1].

[67] Ibid [29]–[46] for an analysis of the 'collateral' issue.

greater than the work done, it related to, and conflicted with, the very contract that was being negotiated for the principal and thus the agent must forfeit any right to remuneration.[68]

[**7.23**] In light of the above, Jacob LJ held that Jack need pay no more fees to Imageview; was entitled to repayment of the fees paid by him; and could recover all of the £3,000 'work permit fee' received by Imageview. The last point is of some interest in that Imageview claimed that a deduction should be made from the work permit fee to reflect the value (£750) of the work done, which, they claimed, resulted in a benefit to the principal/defendant. In this, Imageview argued that without the deduction the remedy in question might be seen as 'a vehicle for the unjust enrichment' of Mr Jack. Jacob LJ rejected this contention on two grounds. First, and specifically, that work done on the permit 'was never anything Mr Jack was expecting to pay for. It was something he surely knew had to be done before he could play. But it was not a benefit which accrued to him financially'.[69] Second, and more broadly, Jacob LJ pointed out, quite rightly, the underlying policy reason for the strictness of the approach:

> We are here concerned not with merely damages such as those for a tort or breach of contract but with what the remedy should be when the agent has betrayed the trust reposed in him—notions of equity and conscience are brought into play. Necessarily such a betrayal may not come to light. If all the agent has to pay if and when he is found out are damages the temptation to betray the trust reposed in him is all the greater. So the strict rule is there as a real deterrent to betrayal.[70]

[**7.24**] In sum, Jacob LJ concluded that what had occurred in the instant case was 'surreptitious dealing' driven by a secret commission rather than the player's interest. More broadly, at the beginning of his judgment Jacob LJ regretted that, despite the fact that it was well and long established, the courts have found in necessary on occasion to restate the law on an agent's duty of fidelity and disclosure.[71] In a brief concurring judgment Mummery LJ agreed also regretting that it was still necessary in the twenty first century to remind agents about conflicts of duty and interest and the necessity for transparency in the dealings of agents if confidence in them is to continue. The final line of Mummery LJ's remarks is also of particular note as it has clear echoes of what should be expected of football's internal regulation of agents: 'In our age it is more important than it ever was for the courts to hold the precise and firm line drawn between payments openly, and therefore honestly, received by agents, and undeclared payments received by agents secretly, and therefore justly liable to *all* the legal consequences flowing from breaches of an agent's fiduciary obligations'.[72]

---

[68] Ibid [44].
[69] Ibid [59].
[70] Ibid [50].
[71] Ibid [8].
[72] Ibid [65].

How does Football Regulate Agents?

[**7.25**] In the US, and in at least five EU member states, the 'necessity for transparency in the dealings of agents' has found legislative form. In the US, some distinction must be made between agents who operate in college 'amateur' sport and in the four major league sports. In college sport, the primary regulatory body is the National Collegiate Athletic Association, which supports the Uniform Athletes Agents Act 2000 and its implementation in every state. That provision is a model law, which provides a uniform system for regulating college athlete agents and has thus far been adopted in 38 states.[73] In the major league sports, the regulation of agents is carried out through the various players' associations of the NFL, NBA, NHL and MLB, as certified by that sport's commissioner. The certified agent can then represent the player in the negotiation of contracts with clubs, as part of the general collective bargaining agreement (between the clubs and the players' association) governing that particular major league sport.[74] A similar certification process is in place in major league soccer in the US where 'a player, if he so desires, may designate and agent to conduct on his behalf, or to assist him in, the negotiation of an individual salary and/or additional benefits'.[75]

[**7.26**] The five EU jurisdictions where dedicated legislation on sports agents exists are Bulgaria, France, Greece, Hungary and Portugal. In England, however, the regulation of agents has been left largely to the private competency of the FA. The FA's Football Regulations, which have recently (2009) been updated, have a colourful past and have on occasion been challenged in the courts.[76] That colourful past is related to allegations in 2006 suggesting that offers of illegal payments or bungs were not uncommon in football transfers. The source of those allegations, which expressly criticised the role of agents were twofold—claims made by the then Luton Town FC manager Mike Newell and a special investigation by the BBC current affairs television programme *Panorama* broadcast on 19 September 2006. Those allegations resulted in the so-called Stevens or Quest inquiry into the payment of bungs, wherein Lord Stevens, the former Metropolitan Police Commissioner, led a team of forensic

---

[73] Details of the provision can be found in the 'legislation and governance' section of www.ncaa. org. See generally R Ruxin, *An Athlete's Guide to Agents* 5th edn (Sudbury MA, Jones and Bartlett, 2009), K Shropshire and T Davis, *The Business of Sports Agents* 2nd edn (Philadelphia, University of Pennsylvania Press, 2008).

[74] For Major League Baseball see, eg, art IV of the Collective Bargaining Agreement 2007–2011, available online at http://mlbplayers.mlb.com/pa/pdf/cba_english.pdf. See generally P Carfagna, *Representing the Professional Athlete* (Eagan MN, West, 2009).

[75] See s 18.3(i) of the Collective Bargaining Agreement between Major League Soccer and Major League Soccer Players Union, 1 December 2004–31 January 2010, available online at http://www. mlsplayers.org/files/collective_bargaining_agreement__final.pdf.

[76] The regulations and accompanying documentation are available online through www.thefa. com/TheFA/RulesandRegulations/Agents.aspx. The most significant challenge has been the *Stretford* litigation, *Stretford v The FA* [2007] EWCA Civ 238, discussed at point 9 of section [3.35] of this text.

accountants in their examination of 362 transfers, which took place in the Premier League between January 2004 and January 2006. The Lord Stevens' inquiry, which issued its final, extended report in June 2007, prompted a probe—called Operation Apprentice—into corruption in football by the City of London Police's Economic Crime Department and Her Majesty's Revenue and Customs (HMRC). This investigation in turn led to a number of leading figures in football being arrested on suspicion of conspiracy to defraud and false accounting. All of the parties denied any wrongdoing and no convictions were secured, though in January 2010 charges, which again were strenuously denied, were brought against the Tottenham Hotspur manager, Harry Redknapp, relating to the common law offence of tax evasion, arising out Redknapp's time as manager of Portsmouth.[77] More relevantly, the Stevens' inquiry recommended a series of regulatory and compliance-based reforms designed to promote greater transparency in, and more thorough auditing of, player transfers, including the operation and role of agents in such transactions.[78]

[**7.27**]   Given this background, there are three general points of note to the FA Football Agents Regulations, which are a comprehensive set of rules governing all aspects of the football agency business in England.[79] These are the promotion of standard representation contracts; compliance with FIFA's Players' Agents Regulations; and the implementation of a robust and durable licensing regime in order to promote transparency and equality of bargaining power both within the agency relationship and externally in terms of the sporting public's interest and confidence in the dealings of agents. The first point is that a central aspect of the operation of this regulatory scheme is the requirement that a player, acting on independent legal advice, or a club, must have entered into a validly executed written 'representation contract' prior to that agent carrying out any agency activity on his or its behalf.[80] Standard player-agent/club-agent representation contracts, which contain certain 'obligatory' terms, are provide by the FA.[81]

[**7.28**]   The second point of note is that the FA's regulations on agents are made in accordance, and can largely be reconciled, with FIFA's Players' Agents Regulations.[82] The evolution of FIFA's scheme is similar to the FA's in that the

---

[77] See P Kelso, Inquiry's Last Chapter will Leave Business of Football Clear for All to See' *The Daily Telegraph* (London 15 January 2010) Sport 8.

[78] These recommendations have fed into many aspects of the operation of elite professional football in the UK. See, eg, the ban on inducements for agents in order to facilitate the signing of a contract in the FA Premier League's rule K9. The FAPL's rules are available to download in the Official Premier League Handbook 2009/10 at www.premierleague.com/page/Handbook.

[79] All 39 pages of the FA's Football Agents Regulations are available online through www.thefa. com/TheFA/RulesandRegulations/Agents.aspx.

[80] Ibid FA Football Agents Regulations (4 July 2009) Regs B1–B7.

[81] Available online and in word doc form through www.thefa.com/TheFA/RulesandRegulations/ Agents.aspx.

[82] See art 1(5) FIFA Players' Agents Regulations (1 January 2008). Three other international sports federations have developed specific regulations: FIBA (basketball); IAAF (athletics); and the IRB (rugby).

current regulations emerged both from a corruption-concerned past[83] and have defeated legal challenge.[84] More importantly, and this is the third point of note, the FA's scheme, FIFA's scheme and indeed the statute-based of other EU jurisdictions all have a certain commonality in that they are at heart licensing regimes underpinned by codes of conduct and based principally on entry examinations; rights and obligations surrounding the carrying out of the profession (and in particular remuneration-related obligations) and provisions concerning disputes and sanctions for breach of individual aspects of the regime.[85] Apart from the aforementioned issues of conflicts of interest and the payment of secret commissions in connection with transfer deals, further comprehensive analysis of the various aspects of a typical sports agent licensing scheme would take some time and it is not done in this text.[86] Nevertheless, the issue of the regulation of agents will merit further mention in this chapter in regard to individual issues such as the potential economic exploitation of young footballers from countries outside the EU;[87] the unregulated recruitment of young football players from, and the payment of compensation to, so-called training clubs;[88] and the need for greater transparency in the recording and monitoring of football transfers.[89]

[**7.29**]   For now, two final points need to be noted on football agents, and these relate to the future of FIFA's current scheme of regulation and the possible need for a European regulatory framework for the activities of sports agents. The most recent comments emerging from FIFA are somewhat downbeat in tone with regard to the efficacy of its current agent licensing regime: FIFA's Legal Director, Macro Villiger, recently admitting that, 'At the present time, we estimated that

---

[83]   In the context of a UK Presidency of the EU, the sports ministers of France, Germany, Italy, Spain and the UK decided to launch an independent review of the specific nature of sport in EU law generally (and using football as a case study). The Independent European Sport Review, which is often called the Arnaut Report, was published in 2006, and reflected on many aspects of the regulation of sport and football in the EU. It expressed a number of concerns about the lack of regulation of agents. See, eg, ss [3.60]–[3.65] and [5.51]–[5.54] of the Arnaut Report, which is available online through www.independentfootballreview.com.

[84]   In Case T-193/02 *Laurent Piau v Commission of the European Communities and FIFA* [2005] ECR II-209 the Court of First Instance (CFI) rejected the argument made by a French players' agent that FIFA's then agency regulations were inter alia anti-competitive on the ground that they restricted access to the players' agent industry. The CFI recognised that the objectives of FIFA's regulations, based on raising professional standards for players' agent in the general absence of national law and self-regulation, could be justified under the competition law provisions of the EC Treaty as being reasonable, non-discriminatory and proportional. A subsequent appeal to the ECJ was rejected as being both partly inadmissible and unfounded, Cases C-171/05 *Piau* [2006] ECR I-37.

[85]   For an example of a dispute surrounding remuneration of agency fees see *Lichtenstein v Clube Atletica Mineiro* [2005] EWHC 1300 (QB). Art 20 FIFA Players' Agents Regulations (1 January 2008) states that in the absence of an agreement between the parties, the players' agent is entitled to payment of compensation amounting to 3 per cent of the player's annual basic gross income.

[86]   See generally R Siekmann *et al, Players' Agents Worldwide: Legal Aspects* (The Hague, Asser Press, 2007).

[87]   See [7.59]–[7.62] of this text.

[88]   See [7.52]–[7.58] of this text.

[89]   See [7.47] of this text.

only 25% to 30% of all international transfers are conducted via licensed agents'.[90] In effect, this means that over two-thirds of international transfers operate undetected outside both FIFA's supervisory and sanctioning competency. A new set of FIFA Players' Agents Regulation is due to the presented to the FIFA Executive Committee for approval in March 2010. It is speculated that some consideration is to be given to lifting the current requirement that football clubs should only conduct player transfers with licensed players' agents and that a wider and lighter regulatory view of such intermediaries should be tolerated with the underlying idea being that this might encourage clubs and the football industry in general to be more open as to the activities of all agents, licensed or not.[91]

[**7.30**]   The difficulties that FIFA is having in regulating the dealings of agents, and the general lack of harmonisation of regulation in Europe, the busiest football market in the world, prompts the question as to whether there is a need for deeper EU involvement. There has been some discussion of this issue at European level; for instance in March 2007 the European Parliament invited the European Commission to assist football bodies and organisations in ways of enhancing the regulatory and governance schemes surrounding the dealings of agents.[92] Moreover, in July 2007, the European Commission indicated in its White Paper on Sport that it would 'carry out an impact assessment to provide a clear overview of the activities of players' agent in the EU and an evaluation of whether action at EU level is necessary, which will also analyse the different possible option'.[93] This study was completed in November 2009.[94] On the whole that summary is disappointing in that the principal recommendations are 'soft' in nature and revolve mainly around the promotion of further structured and social dialogue between the Commission and the various stakeholders in European football, as operating under the EU's soft competency on sport now contained in Article 165 TFEU.[95]

[**7.31**]   Moreover, although the study contains a wealth of primary material on the operation of the sports agency industry in Europe, its recommendations (contained in Part 4, Chapter 2 of the study) are somewhat slight and flatter to deceive. For example, the study recommends that a binding code of conduct drawn up jointly by sports agents, federations, clubs and players in accordance with Article 37 of Directive 2006/123/EC on Services, which promotes the development of codes of conduct by European professional associations. At first instance, this sounds impressive; but on reflection it is difficult to see how

---

[90] As cited in 'FIFA Considers Dropping Agent Licence Requirement' (2009) 7 (9) *World Sports Law Report* 1.

[91] For a recent review of some of the issues raised herein see M Smienk, 'Regulation in the Market of Sports Agents. Or no Regulation at all?' (2009) 3/4 *International Sports Law Journal* 70.

[92] Point 44 of the European Parliament's Resolution of 29 March 2007 on the future of professional football in Europe (2006/2130(INI)).

[93] European Commission's White Paper on Sport, 11 July 2007, COM(2007) 391 final [4.4].

[94] It is available to download in the 'sports agents' section of http://ec.europa.eu/sport/.

[95] On the specific nature of structured and social dialogue see s5 of the White Paper on Sport (n 93).

this code of conduct would add to the code of conduct formulated by FIFA and its stakeholders in Annexe 1 of FIFA's Players' Agents Regulations. The regret surrounding this study is that there is no doubt the EU regulatory action would have the benefit of increasing legal certainty in the area and that a case for harmonisation, as based on a sports-specific version of Directive 86/653EEC on Self-Employed Commercial Agents,[96] could have been made more forcefully. For now, the matter remains open to debate: on the one hand, there is the contention that a radical and (literal) directive approach is needed from the EU, principally on the ground that what little regulation exists in Europe is either ignored or largely circumvented both to the detriment of the financial credibility of football's transfer system and vulnerable young footballers; on the other hand the latest study for the Commission suggests that for the time being the EU should use its considerable resources to ensure that a sustainable solution for the proper regulation of sports agents comes from within sport itself.[97]

Formation of and Capacity to Contract

[**7.32**]   The two basic elements of this section (formation and capacity to contract) are further broken down in two parts. The formation of sports contract, again with a football focus, is discussed initially by reference to the infrequency of oral, sports-related contracts. This is followed by a brief examination of the emergence of standard and even central contracts in UK sport. The issue of capacity to contract begins with the technicalities of obtaining a work permit for a footballer who comes from outside the EU and associated EEA countries. That discussion then moves to an examination of the capacity of minors to contract and the concerns at all levels of football about the potential exploitation of vulnerable young footballers (and their families) in this regard.

Oral Contracts

[**7.33**]   The combination of the influential role that agents have in the negotiation of contemporary professional sports contracts and the inherent ambiguity that can surround their interpretation, means that oral contracts are virtually non-existent in contemporary professional sport. In short, the uncertain nature of oral contracts means that disputes can often arise surrounding their interpretation. One of the more celebrated disputes in world sport regarding an oral

---

[96] See the suggestion made in the Arnaut Report (n 83) ss[6.85]–[6.86].

[97] For an insightful summary of many of the issues raised herein see RB Martins, 'Players' Agents: Past, Present ... Future? (2009) 3/4 *International Sports Law Journal* (Special Addendum: Players' Agents) 1.

contract resulted in litigation involving the boxer Mike Tyson in *Rooney v Tyson*.[98] The background to the case is that at an early point is his career Tyson promised Rooney that he would retain him as a trainer for as long as he was to fight professionally. Further, under the terms of the oral agreement between the pair, Rooney was to receive 10 per cent of Tyson's boxing earnings as compensation for his personal training services. After the inevitabe falling out between the pair (apparently in connection with Rooney's alleged comments in the media regarding Tyson's divorce proceedings with the actress Robin Givens in 1988) Tyson soon after terminated his boxer-trainer relationship with Rooney. In a federal lawsuit for an alleged breach of an oral personal services agreement, a jury at Federal District Court trial rendered a US$4.5 million verdict for Rooney. Tyson's legal team successfully countered after the trial, arguing that the agreement was for an indefinite duration and was therefore unenforceable under New York state labour law or otherwise gave rise to a presumption that it was terminable at will by either of the parties. Rooney appealed to the Federal Circuit Court of Appeals, who on instruction for the New York State Court of Appeal, were advised (somewhat questionably) that the oral arrangement in question could be seen to have created an agreement of definitive, legally cognisable duration, as based on the 'objectively definable' benchmarks of the commencement and conclusion of Tyson's professional boxing career.[99]

[**7.34**]   On this side of the Atlantic, an example of the problems of construction that can accompany disputed oral agreements in a team sport is provided by *White v Bristol Rugby*.[100] In that case, involving a professional rugby player, Julian White signed a three-year contract to move to Bristol for the start of the 2001/2002 season and received a £15,000 signing-on fee in advance. White subsequently wavered in his enthusiasm for Bristol and became attracted to a move to their great rivals, Bath. White asserted that he had been told during pre-contract negotiations that he could opt out of the contract on repayment of the advance and he attempted to do this. Bristol refused to accept the repayment and White sought a declaration in the High Court that he was not bound by the contract and should not be 'required' to play for Bristol. The three-year contract did however contain an express term stipulating that it was subject to an 'entire agreement' clause and that no oral representation made in the course of negotiations applied in respect of its express terms and conditions. White's application was duly refused by the Bristol Mercantile Court, which held that the 'entire agreement' clause prevented him from relying on an opt-out term.

---

[98] *Rooney v Tyson* 91 NY 2d 685; 697 NE 2d 571; 674 NYS 2d 616 (1998).
[99] See also the dispute that arose over a number of oral contracts between boxing promoter Frank Warren and former world champion Joe Calzaghe in *Sports Network v Calzaghe* [2009] EWHC 480 (QB), resulting in the promoter having to pay the boxer nearly £2 million in damages. A subsequent application for permission to appeal was refused [2009] EWCA Civ 1028.
[100] *White v Bristol Rugby* [2002] IRLR 204.

[**7.35**]   Additionally, White had, rather cheekily, contented that Bristol should pay his salary even though he had not attended for training and had obtained an injunction to prevent Bristol from registering him as a player. Bristol argued, and the High Court agreed, that under the contract White's salary was earned in return for the work that was specified therein and that White's non-performance of said work meant that he was not entitled to be paid, in the absence of an express term that Bristol would pay him even if he did not perform the specified work. The underlying thrust of White's argument in this regard was twofold. First, he argued that Bristol's conduct in failing to pay him his salary was an indication of their acceptance of White's repudiatory breach of the stated contract in refusing to make himself available to train and play for the club. As stated, the court did not accept this argument, noting simply that White was not entitled to any salary from the club because he did not do any work for them, and that there was nothing else in the club's conduct—that they had, for example, entered into negotiations with another player—to suggest that the club had accepted White's repudiation.[101] At common law, the case is important in that it suggests that a contract of employment is not automatically brought to an end where an employee refuses to serve the employee and logically, if White's argument had otherwise been accepted, it would have been tantamount to acknowledging that an employee can, by unilaterally refusing to serve his employer, bring about a termination of contract.[102] The dangers of a White-type argument in football are self-evident where, for instance, a player is not playing regular first team football and feels 'undervalued' by his manager and has an agent whispering in his ear about rumours of interest from other clubs.

[**7.36**]   The second point is that, by highlighting the non-payment of salary, White hoped to draw the court's attention to the fact that the relationship of mutual trust and confidence on which the 'master and servant relationship' is based had been irrevocably destroyed and thus there was little purpose in keeping the contract alive. The High Court noted that in this instance the relationship between the key parties had not irretrievably broken down and that the innocent party, the club, had elected and desired to keep the contract open. The issue of mutual trust and confidence in a personal employment services contract—the category into which, arguably, most sports employment contracts fall—is however of note where a club seeks equitable relief in either seeking an order for the specific performance of a contract or injunctive relief restraining a breach or threatened breach of contract by an employee. In the latter instance, it is open to the court to argue that where there is a clear absence of the high degree of mutual fiduciary trust characteristic of a sports contract, this should be taken into account as a factor militating against the granting of any injunctive relief compelling an

---

[101]   Ibid 212, Havelock-Allen J echoing Asquith J's maxim in *Howard v Pickford Toll Co Ltd* [1951] 1 KB 417, 421 that 'an unaccepted repudiation is a thing writ in water'.
[102]   See generally *Thomas Marshall Ltd v Guinle* [1978] IRLR 174.

employee to work for the stated employer.[103] In this, the courts in their equitable jurisdiction argue pragmatically that it would be impossible and largely futile to attempt to supervise or compel the performance of such a contract.[104] That was the case in *Warren v Mendy*[105] where the Court of Appeal agreed that there was little value in attempting to compel a boxer to hold to an agreement entered into with a manager/promoter.[106] That case is also of interest because, not only did it highlight the mutually fiduciary nature of sports contracts, it also appeared sympathetic to the sports professional on the ground that their 'trade' is a 'very specialised one, requiring dedication, extensive training and expertise and that [as a] professional life [it is] comparatively short'.[107] Overall, and in light of the above case law, it is well to note that in the forthcoming discussion of issues such as the unilateral or procured breach of contract and the sports-specific concerns relating to contractual stability, pragmatic concerns surrounding both the management of the 'unhappy' player and the understandable desire of that player to maximise their potential in the face of an abridged, precarious career, can often result in a club acceding to and even facilitating the transfer of that player, irrespective of their strict contractual rights to the player's services.

Standard and Central Playing Contracts

[**7.37**]   As it transpired, White played with Bristol for two seasons until the single most effective catalyst for player transfer—relegation—facilitated his move to another club. White subsequently admitted to a certain 'naivety' at the time of the Bristol transfer.[108] To be fair, professionalism in rugby union was at that point still at a fairly developmental stage and its complexities and ramifications in contract and employment law were not fully bedded down.[109] Subsequently, the various

---

[103] Similarly, an order of specific performance would not be available to the employer-club and the club would have to confine itself to taking an action in damages for breach of contract against the player.

[104] See also s236 of the Trade Union and Labour Relations (Consolidation) Act 1992 which provides that no court may, whether by way of an order for specific performance of contract or an injunction restraining a breach or threatened breach of such a contract, compel an employee to do any work or attend at any place for the doing of any work.

[105] *Warren v Mendy* [1989] 3 All ER 103.

[106] See also *Mortimer v Beckett* [1920] 1 Ch 571, 581, Russell J where an injunction attempting to restrain a boxer from boxing for another manager was refused on the grounds that if granted the order would force the defendant to employ a particular person as his agent and this was tantamount to granting specific performance of a contract for personal services.

[107] *Warren v Mendy* [1989] 3 All ER 103, 115. Note the approval of the approach taken in *Warren v Mendy* by Strauss J in *Subaru v Burns* Unreported, High Court 12 December 2001. See similarly *Nichols Advanced Vehicle Systems v De Angelis* Unreported, High Court 21 December 1979, Oliver J.

[108] See M Souster, 'White's Move to Pastures New Proves Productive in the Extreme' *The Times* (London 10 October 2009) Sport 18.

[109] Subsequently, Bristol Ruby Club were sued for repudiatory breach of contract and had to pay nearly £150,000 in damages to a claimant on foot of an oral agreement regarding the employment of a coach. See *Stransky v Bristol Rugby Ltd* [2002] All ER (D) 144 (Dec).

stakeholders in professional rugby have, thanks to litigation such as *White*, brought themselves up to speed with such matters. Nevertheless, it took over a decade for the leading professional clubs in England and the Rugby Football Union (RFU) to reach an agreement regarding the availability of players for international duty.[110] For a period the RFU flirted with the idea of centrally contracting England players, as is the policy in cricket and in a number of other rugby jurisdictions (for example, the Irish Rugby Football Union). Central contracts mean that players are employed directly by the sports governing body and are, in effect, leased back to clubs; with the idea being that the sports governing body has ultimate control over the fitness and welfare (and commercial interests) of the players in question in order to ensure optimal performance and availability for the national team.[111] Eventually, in 2007, the RFU announced that it had reached an agreement with clubs on the issue, which was to be based on the compromise idea of elite players' squads whereby clubs would be obliged to facilitate the early release of members of that squad prior to international matches.[112]

[**7.38**]   Returning to individual players, a *White*-like situation could not arise now given that since 2006, and thanks to the input of the Rugby Players' Association, a standard playing contract has been introduced for all Premiership club players.[113] As regards football, it has long been the case that at virtually all levels of professional football in the UK, players enter into a written contract of employment with a club. In this, the player negotiates with the club personally or more usually delegates authority to their authorised agent and/or relies on the player management services made available to them by their union, the Professional Footballers' Association.[114] Before a player enters into contractual negotiations, a preliminary issue is that of the player's capacity to contract. This is of the utmost importance when the player is a minor, though it must also be noted—and taking a very broad view of a player's capacity to contract—that when a UK-based football club seeks to sign a player from outside the EU and

---

[110]   See typically the action taken in *Premier Rugby Ltd v Rugby Football Union* [2006] EWHC 2068 (Comm).

[111]   Central contracting has coincided with one of the most successful periods in Irish rugby union history. The central contracting system used by the England and Wales Cricket Board has discouraged a number of leading English players from signing up to the lucrative Indian Premier League and there have been calls for its review, see J Jackson, 'Future of Central Contracts thrown into Doubt' *The Observer* (London 3 May 2009) News and Features 11.

[112]   The overall arrangement is known as the Long Form Agreement (LFA) signed between the RFU and Premier Rugby Ltd (representing the clubs). See generally S Jones, 'English Games Gets a Clean Bill of Health' *The Sunday Times* (London 18 November 2007) Sport 21. The subsequent departure of a number of leading English international to French clubs (thus placing them outside the LFA) initially presented a problem as regards the selection of these players for the English team. See further S Jones, 'The French Collection' *The Sunday Times* (London 10 May 2009) Sport 18.

[113]   The Professional Rugby Players' Association was founded in 1998. It is a registered not-for-profit trade union and was renamed the Rugby Players' Association in October 2009 'to reflect our expansion and increase in membership to include semi-professional and retired players as well as full-time professionals.' For further information on the services provided by the RPA at www.therpa.co.uk.

[114]   See generally the PFA's website at www.givemefootball.com.

associated EEA, that player must apply for and obtain an appropriate work permit pursuant to the criteria regulated by the UK Border Agency.

Work Permits

[**7.39**]   As regards work permits, the UK Border Agency operates a points based system for football players based on a number of criteria (language skills and maintenance) of which the most important is for the applicant to obtain an endorsement or certificate of sponsorship for the relevant governing body, that is, the FA, the Scottish, Welsh or Irish FAs.[115] In order to obtain a governing body endorsement for the 2009/2010 season, the sponsoring club (which evidently had to be a member of the FA Premier League, the Football League or the Scottish, Welsh and Irish equivalents) had to demonstrate that the player fulfilled the following three criteria: (a) that the player must have played for his country in at least 75 per cent of its competitive 'A' team matches for which he was available for selection, during the two years preceding the date of application; (b) the player's country must be at or above 70th place in the official FIFA World Rankings, when averaged over the two years preceding the date of application; (c) the player must be set to play for a sponsoring club. Although at first instance the criteria appear quite rigid, the first criterion has not always been interpreted in a mechanical way and matters such as the fact that the player in question was unavailable due to injury for international duty has been used successfully on appeal.[116] The second criterion is more difficult to circumvent (given that it is based on the quality of the player's national team, and not the player's ability), and it has led to a number of talented players being refused permits.[117] For instance, in 2008 the attempt by Manchester City to sign Iraq's leading player Nashat Akram was thwarted by a refusal to grant the player a work permit, notwithstanding the fact the Iraq's poor standing in the FIFA world rankings could have been placed in the context of that country's ongoing strife.[118]

---

[115] For the UK Border Agency's requirements, see generally www.ind.homeoffice.gov.uk/employers/points/sponsoringmigrants/eligibility/tier2sports. The other criteria relate to language skills and maintenance capacity. The latter is hardly likely to be of much burden to the modern football professional. An initial application under the so-called 'tier 2' system can be for a length of contract up to three years' maximum.

[116] See, for example, the successful appeal in *R v Secretary of State for Education and Employment ex parte Portsmouth FC*, Unreported, Queen's Bench Division 30 October 1997, McCullough J.

[117] In this light, and in light of suggestions that the criteria are being interpreted more strictly, some commentators have highlighted faults in the current system, notably its failure to allow for the 'Commonwealth dimension' and the disparity of opportunity created by current UK rules, particularly for black African players. See S Pentol, 'Immigration: Football's Rules on non-EEA Players' (2008) 6 *World Sport Law Report* 3.

[118] Work permits are, of course, required for professionals in sports other than football and in the summer of 2009 the UK Border Agency announced that six Australian players with the rugby league club, the Crusaders, were to be deported for visa irregularities. See 'Deportations will Cap Misery for Crusaders' *The Times* (London 19 August 2009) Sport 61.

[**7.40**]   There are three final points to make on work permits. First, and in a general sense, EU immigration law and policy requires that the treatment accorded by each member state to workers of other member states legally employed in their territory should be free from any discrimination based on nationality, as regards working conditions, remuneration and dismissal, relative to its own nationals.[119] Moreover, and on two occasions, the ECJ has noted that this principle of equal treatment extends to workers (and specifically, on the facts, to sportspersons) having an Association or Partnership Agreements with the EU[120] and it also applies to members of certain African, Caribbean and Pacific States who have entered into a partnership agreement with the EU known as the Contonou Agreement (2000).[121] It must however be noted that the extension of this right of non-discrimination to nationals of Association/Contonou member states concerns employment terms and condition only, that is, it extends only to those who are lawfully employed and can be considered as workers, and is not generally seen to extend to laws and rules concerning *access* to employment.[122] Second, there is some debate as to whether work permit requirements necessarily apply where the non-EU/EEA player holds 'dual nationality' with an EU country and even where that is not relevant there is a suggestion, applicable for younger players at least, that the UK work permit requirements can be circumvented by a UK club facilitating the transfer of that player to a club in an EU country with less strict entry requirements, for example, Belgium or the Netherlands, and that after a set period of time, typically three years, players' entry requirements into the EU are sufficiently 'laundered' to enable them to apply safely for a work permit in the UK.

[**7.41**]   It must be stressed that this last point is speculative only and of more direct application is the fact that under FIFA's relevant regulations, namely article 18(4) FIFA, 'the validity of a contract *may not be made subject to* a successful medical examination and/or the grant of a work permit.' The provision holds that conditions precedent of this nature should not be recognised and that the contract remains valid without such clauses. It follows that a club's failure to respect the contract in question represents an 'unconditional breach of contract without just cause'.[123] Although FIFA acknowledge the obligations on players to assist their prospective club in any way they can by providing all necessary information and documentation in order to facilitate the relevant permits, the primary responsibility is with the club to carry out the necessary due diligence before concluding the contract. In addition, violations of this provision are, according to FIFA, linked

---

[119]   See generally European Commission, *Communication from the Commission Policy Plan on Legal Migration* (SEC (2005) 1680), 21 December 2005, COM(2005) 669.

[120]   Case C-483/00 *Deutscher Handballbund v Marios Kolpak* [2003] ECR I-4135 and Case C-265/03 *Simutenkov v Minsterio de Educación y Cultura* [2005] ECR I-2579.

[121]   Article 13(3) of the Contonou Agreement.

[122]   See the discussion in CAS 2008/1485 *FC Midtylland AS v FIFA* [7.4].

[123]   Commentary on the Regulations on the Status and Transfer of Players (n 16) 55. See also art 17 FIFA on the consequences of terminating a contract without just cause, which include provision for the payment of compensation and other sporting sanctions.

to the 'negligence by the new club that has not exercised the usual care expected from it in business life'.[124] In sum, and taking into account the underlying principle of this provision—namely, the potential by a leading football club to abuse the 'inequality of bargaining power' that can exist between it and an individual player—article 18(4) FIFA means that clubs are effectively estopped from reneging on contracts on the ground that the player has either failed to pass a medical or obtain a work permit.

Protection of Minors

[**7.42**]   The general rule at common law is that a minor's contract is voidable at the minor's option: it is not binding on the minor; but is binding on the other party. The underlying policy is not to restrict a minor's freedom of contract, but to protect the minor from exploitation of their inexperience in such matters, such that their naivety might result in their being manipulated into an unnecessarily lengthy or otherwise objectively 'unfair' contract. Nevertheless, it has long been established that contracts for 'necessaries' (typically, goods and services supplied to them for their maintenance) are binding on minors. The word 'necessaries' has been interpreted to extend to contracts made for the minor's benefit such as contracts of apprenticeship, education and service. In *Roberts v Gray*,[125] for example, a minor had attempted to escape his contractual obligations to go on tour as a professional billiard player. The Court of Appeal held that the contract was one for necessaries and for his benefit in terms of teaching, instruction and employment opportunity; and thus was binding on the minor as a whole. An even broader perspective on contracts of service, apprenticeship and education made to the binding benefit of minors can be found in *Doyle v White City Stadium*.[126]

[**7.43**]   In that case, the claimant-minor applied to the British Boxing Board of Control (BBBC) for a licence to fight as a professional boxer in 1932. Under the terms of the licence agreement, the claimant, Jack Doyle, agreed, as was standard practice, to adhere strictly to the governing rules and regulations of the BBBC. The fundamental regulation at issue was the then provision that, where during the course of a fight a boxer was disqualified for misconduct in the ring, that boxer had to forfeit their fee or purse and would only receive 'bare travelling expenses'. In the summer of 1933, Doyle agreed to fight Jack Petersen for the British heavyweight title in a deal that was to see Doyle paid £3,000 win, lose or draw. At the fight, held in White City Stadium on 12 July 1933, Doyle was disqualified in the second round of the bout for repeatedly punching his opponent below the belt and the organisers of the event withheld his purse. Doyle argued that, for lack of capacity, he should not be bound by governing BBBC regulations. The Court of Appeal held

---

[124]   Ibid.
[125]   *Roberts v Gray* [1913] 1 KB 520.
[126]   *Doyle v White City Stadium* [1935] 1 KB 110.

that, by looking at the contract as a whole, Doyle should be held bound by it, with the Court of Appeal noting in particular that the disqualification/forfeiture clause was designed principally to encourage 'clean' fighting and was therefore as much in the interests of the claimant himself (a young, inexperienced fighter) as any other contestant that there should be rules to safeguard him 'as a contestant from any improper conduct on the part of those with whom he may engage in fighting'.[127]

[**7.44**]   It must be remembered that, notwithstanding *Doyle*, there is no general principle to the effect that any contract of employment, apprenticeship or education which might be considered beneficial to a minor, is automatically binding on that minor. The courts have stressed that the contract must be read as a whole, as in *Shears v Mendeloff*,[128] where a minor who was a professional boxer had appointed the claimant as his sole manager on commission and agreed not to take any engagements under any other management without the claimant's consent for three years. In that instance, the court held that the contract was unenforceable against the minor, on the grounds that it was fundamentally a 'trading' contract, and contained oppressive terms and thus could not be construed as being of benefit to the minor. A more modern expression of that principle can be found in *Proform Sports Management Ltd v Proactive Sports Management Ltd and Another*.[129] That litigation surrounded the signing in December 2000 of a player representation agreement between a then 15-year-old Wayne Rooney and the claimants. Under the terms of the agreement, which Rooney and his father signed without any independent legal advice, the claimants were appointed to act as Rooney's 'executive agents' and to carry out all the functions in respect of personal representation on behalf of Rooney's work as a professional footballer for a period of two years.[130] The claimants alleged that, during the course of the stated agency agreement, the defendants and notably the second defendant, Paul Stretford, a director of the defendant company, also entered into a player representation agreement with Rooney. In that light, the claimants brought an action for damages for the tort of unlawful interference with and/or procuring a breach of contract against Proactive Sports Management and Stretford.

[**7.45**]   In the proceedings at hand, the defendants applied for a summary dismissal of the claim on the grounds that no liability for breach could be made out in circumstances where said contract was voidable. In other words, where the person who is alleged to have been induced to breach a contract in any event enjoys the right to rescind that contract, it follows logically that there could no cause of action in tort for procuring breach of that contract. Further, the defendants

---

[127]   Ibid 126, Lord Hanworth MR. See also *Chaplin v Leslie Frewin (Publishers) Ltd* [1966] Ch 71 and *Denmark Productions Ltd v Boscobel Productions Ltd* (1967) 111 *Solicitors' Journal* 715. The latter case concerned a contract between the band, 'The Kinks', and the binding nature of an agency/management agreement that they had, as minors, entered into with the claimant.

[128]   *Shears v Mendeloff* (1914) 30 TLR 342.

[129]   *Proform Sports Management Ltd v Proactive Sports Management Ltd and Another* [2006] EWHC 2903 (Ch), [2007] 1 All ER 542.

[130]   The key clauses in the agreement are noted at [2006] EWHC 2903 (Ch) [5], Judge Hodge QC.

argued, it would not matter in such circumstances whether the contract had already been avoided; because if the contract was one that the minor was entitled to avoid, then liability for the tort of wrongfully interference with, or of inducing the breach of, the contract could not arise. Reviewing the principles and case law surrounding the capacity of minors to contract, the High Court noted that if the agreement with Proform Sports Management could be deemed analogous to a beneficial contract of apprenticeship, education or service it would be enforceable against Rooney and therefore the tortious-based action could follow. Nevertheless, on reading the contract as a whole, and taking into account the fact that Rooney was already with a football club (Everton) and was prevented by FA rules from becoming a professional footballer until he reached 17, the agreement could not be seen as one that enabled Rooney to earn a living or to advance his skills. Consequently, the general rule that a minor's contract was voidable at his option applied to the stated agreement. In sum, the High Court granted the defendant's application for dismissal of the claim, holding that the Proform Sports Management agreement was more analogous to the relatively oppressive 'trading' contract consider in *Shears v Mendeloff*, and could not be reconciled with the binding, enforceable class of contract consider by the Court of Appeal in *Doyle v White City Stadium*.[131]

[**7.46**]   Apart from reminding the reader of Rooney's precocious talent, the stated case also sheds some light on the murky world of the signing, registration and potential exploitation of young players by leading agents and clubs. In a domestic setting, the FA, as noted by the High Court in the above litigation, is sensitive to the dangers in question. FA Rule C1(a)(i) holds that a player under 18 years of age and in receipt of full time education may not enter into a written contract of employment with an FA-affiliated club,[132] while FA Rule C1(a)(ii) holds that a player under 17 years of age may not enter into a written contract of employment with an FA-affiliated club, except under a so-called 'Scholarship' scheme.[133] In an international setting, and pursuant to articles 18 and 19 FIFA respectively, players under the age of 18 may not sign a professional contract for

---

[131] Surprisingly, the High Court did not refer to the previous case of *Alyesbury FC (1997) Ltd v Watford AFC Ltd* Unreported, Queen's Bench Division 12 June 2000, Poole J, where, in similar circumstances, a contract involving a minor-footballer was held unenforceable.

[132] Under the FA's Rules and Regulations, 'full-time' education refers to a child who is of compulsory school age within the meaning of the Education Acts applying in England or who is over the school leaving age but is for the time being attending a school or in full time education in an establishment of further education. It is of note that under the Education and Skills Act 2008 there is a duty on all 'young people' in England to participate in education or training until the age of 18. This 'duty' will be imposed incrementally and it is envisaged that by 2013 it will be compulsory for young people to participate in education or training until the age of 17, and by 2015 up to the age of 18.

[133] See further FA Rule C3(a). The thrust of the scholarship scheme is that players on or after their 14th birthday may be offered a scholarship to commence no earlier than the last Friday in June in the academic year in which they will reach the age of 16—the old school leaving age—provided they are not receiving full time education. The terms of the scholarship must be signed by the player and by a parent or guardian and is subject to approval by the FA. The idea is that on or after the scholarship player's 17th birthday, the player may sign a written contract with the club, subject to this contract being registered by the FA. See also and generally FAPL rule N.

a term longer than three years;[134] and international transfers of players are permitted, and the necessary international transfer certificate is granted, only by FIFA if the player is over the age of 18.[135] Three exceptions apply to the latter rule: where the player's parents move to the country in which the new club is located for reasons not linked to football;[136] or the transfer takes place within the territory of the EU and the EEA and the player is aged between 16 and 18;[137] or the players lives no further than 50km from a national border, and the club for which the player wishes to be registered in the neighbouring country is also within 50km of that border.[138]

[7.47]   The implementation of FIFA's policies on the protection of minors contained in article 19 FIFA, which also apply to any player who has never previously been registered with a club and is not the national of the country in which he wishes to be registered for the first time, is now overseen by a sub-committee of FIFA's Players' Status Committee.[139] In order to achieve its objectives—of giving prior approval for all international transfers involving minors and resolving any related disputes—that Committee utilises a dedicated section of FIFA's web-base Transfer Matching System, which is designed to promote the better monitoring and facilitation of international transfers of all professional players.[140] More

---

[134] Art 18(2) FIFA.

[135] Art 19(1) FIFA.

[136] The term 'parents' and the phrase 'for reasons not linked to football' are supposed to be interpreted in a strict way. See, for instance, the strict interpretation given by CAS in CAS 2005/955/956 *Cadiz CFSAD/Acuna Cabellero v FIFA and Association Paraguaya de Futbol*. In the stated case—involving the transfer of a 16-year-old from Paraguay to Cadiz, and the subsequent 'employment' of his mother in a local restaurant—the Panel upheld FIFA's decision to refuse an international transfer certificate. The Panel also rejected the contention that the applicable FIFA regulations were in conflict with the domestic immigration and employment laws of Spain and Switzerland and held that the regulations were both in pursuance of legitimate objectives and proportionate to the achievement of those objectives. There remains a suspicion that clubs are, in effect, 'buying parents' in order to comply with art 19 FIFA. See M Scott, 'FIFA addresses concerned over Federico Macheda's move' *The Guardian* (London 8 April 2009) Sport 2.

[137] This exception is granted on condition that the player's sporting, training and academic education is guaranteed by the new club. The registration and reporting of minors at club 'academies' is dealt with by article 19bis FIFA: clubs that operate an academy with legal, financial or defacto links to the club are obliged to report and register all attending minors with the relevant national association. FIFA has recently had to consider the problem of private football academies operating outside the normal club/association structure. On this issue see generally C Platts and A Smith, 'The Education and Welfare of Young People in Football Academies in England' (2009) 1 *International Journal of Sports Policy* 329.

[138] The exception is designed to deal with towns and cities whose hinterland or catchment area spans a border. In these cross-border transfers, the player must continue to live at 'home' and the two national associations concerned must give their explicit consent to the player's registration.

[139] See generally arts 19(4), 23 and 25 FIFA.

[140] Put simply, this system (which FIFA hope will be fully operational across all its 208 member associations by October 2010) requires that all data relevant to a transfer must be entered into a web-based tool which acts as a clearance system for the details of the transfer and only then will the electronic issuing of an international transfer certificate be granted. Apart from bringing general transparency to the football transfer system and its specific use for minors, there is a strong anti-money laundering element to this FIFA initiative. See generally P Kelso, 'Transfer System to Clear the Jungle' *The Daily Telegraph* (London 24 February 2010) Sport 15.

broadly, and according to the accompanying commentary to article 19 FIFA, the underlying idea of the regulation is both 'to provide a stable environment for the training and education of [minors]' and to prevent the abuse to which minor have been exposed in the past'. On the latter point, the President of UEFA, Michel Platini, has used the provocative phrase 'child slavery' to describe some of the practices that surround the international transfers of minors, and particularly the alleged behaviour of some agents who seek to bring very young African and Latin American players to Europe.

[**7.48**]   Platini's comments were made in the context of FIFA's announcement in September 2009 that its Dispute Resolution Chamber (DRC) had found that a then 16-year-old Gael Kakuta had breached his contract with the French club Lens in 2007, after being induced to do so by Chelsea. The player was fined and suspended and Chelsea FC was banned from signing players for two consecutive transfer windows.[141] Chelsea FC appealed the decision to CAS receiving a stay on their sanction pending a full CAS hearing. In February 2010, CAS announced that it had ratified a settlement reached by the parties, putting an end to the arbitration procedure. In its announcement, CAS noted that in the settlement both clubs and the player recognised that, consistent with article 19 FIFA, the so-called 'pre-contract' between the then minor, Kakuta, and Lens was not valid. Accordingly, the player could not have terminated that contract prematurely nor with just cause and neither could Chelsea be held liable for inducing a breach of that contract. Consequently, the sanctions imposed on Chelsea (and the player) were lifted.[142] Before returning to the broader issue on the protection of minors, two digressions on the Kakuta affair are worthy of mention: the tort of inducing a breach of contract and the payment of training compensation.

Inducing or Procuring a Breach of Contract

[**7.49**]   Taking the Kakuta affair as a model, Chelsea would have committed the tort of inducing a breach of contract in relation to Lens if: Lens had a contract with Kakuta; Chelsea had induced Kakuta to breach that contract; and when Chelsea induced Kakuta to breach that contract they knew, not just that they were procuring an act, which as a matter of law or construction of the contract was a breach, but that they also actually realised and intended that that procurement would have the effect of inducing a breach of contract.[143] This tort, which has already been discussed indirectly in this chapter, is of a secondary liability nature in the sense that in order to have triggered Chelsea's liability, it would first have

---

[141] The authority for the sporting sanctions imposed on the player can be found in art 17(3) FIFA and on Chelsea in art 17(4) FIFA.

[142] The actual terms of the settlement are, at the request of the parties, to remain confidential. The basic terms of the settlement were given by a press release issued by CAS on 4 February 2010 and available online through www.tas-cas.org/press-release.

[143] See generally the discussion of the tort in N McBride and R Bagshaw, *Tort Law* 3rd edn (Harlow, Pearson Longman, 2008) ch 20, as informed by *OGB Ltd v Allan* [2007] UKHL 21.

to be shown that Kakuta was liable for an actionable breach of contract towards Lens.[144] With that in mind, the tort would have been clearly made out where it could have been demonstrated that Chelsea had persuaded, through the enticement of a better offer, Kakuta into a deliberate breach of his contract with Lens.

[**7.50**]   As it happens, the Kakuta settlement at CAS suggests that no lawful contract existed in the first place between Kakuta and Lens, or at least that Kakuta could have lawfully avoided any contractual relationship with Lens. This Kakuta affair brings to light the whole area of clubs approaching or 'tapping up' players under contract to another club, which in adherence to the principle of contractual stability in football, is strictly policed by football's various authorities. That is not to say that a club may never approach a player contracted with another club. As guided generally by article 18(3) FIFA, a club intending to conclude a contract with a professional player can do so but must inform the player's current club in writing before entering into negotiation with him. Equally, article 18(3) FIFA lays down that a professional player shall only conclude a contract with another club if his contract with his present club has expired or is due to expire within six months. In a domestic, Premier League setting, numerous sections in the FAPL's Rule K are devoted to the issue of approaching contracted players.[145] In some senses, the FAPL's regulations are stricter than article 18(3) FIFA; for example, although rule K1 reiterates the thrust of article 18(3) FIFA on the need to acquire the prior written consent of the player's club, FAPL rule K2 goes on to state that a club can only approach players under contract after the third Saturday in the May of the year of contract expiry.[146]

[**7.51**]   The key regulation in the FAPL's scheme is rule K3, which holds that 'any club which by itself, by any of its officials, by any of its players, by its agent, by any other person on its behalf or by any other means whatsoever makes an approach either directly or indirectly to a contract player except as permitted [otherwise by rule K] shall be in breach of [FAPL Rules]'.[147] Included in this regulatory framework is a regulation (FAPL rule K8) which holds that a statement made publicly by or on behalf of a club expressing interest in acquiring a contract player shall be treated as an indirect approach and thus contrary to rule K3. A similar view, based on FAPL rule K6, is taken of approaches by contracted players, or persons on their behalf. In the infamous tapping up of the then Arsenal player, Ashley Cole, by Chelsea in early 2005, Chelsea were fined £300,000 with

---

[144] It follows that there is no liability where the contract in question could (due to lack of capacity) have been lawfully avoided by the party who was induced to breach it. See the discussion at [7.44]–[7.45] of this text. See also the general application of the tort in *Grieg v Insole* [1978] 1 WLR 302 discussed at [2.61] of this text and *Warren v Mendy* [1989] 3 All ER 103, discussed at [7.36] of this text.

[145] See also and more specifically FAPL rules K1–K9. For the purposes of rule K, the term 'contract player' includes not just Premier League players but a player who has entered into a written contract of employment with a Football League club.

[146] See similarly FAPL rule K7 with regard to approach by players.

[147] The sanctions are contained in FAPL rule R. For an account of an interpretation of an earlier version of rule K see *Middlesbrough Football & Athletic Co (1986) Ltd v Liverpool Football & Athletic Grounds Plc* [2002] EWCA Civ 1929.

a suspended three point deduction for breach of FAPL rule K3 and Cole fined £100,000 for breach of FAPL rule K5.[148]

Training Compensation

[**7.52**]　At the request of the parties, the actual terms of the CAS settlement between Chelsea/Kakuta and Lens are to remain confidential. Consequently, it can only be speculated upon as to whether Chelsea, in order to achieve that settlement, paid Lens a sum analogous to the training compensation and solidarity mechanism mandated under articles 20 and 21 FIFA. According to that provision, training compensation should be paid to a player's training club or clubs when a player signs his first contract as a professional and thereafter each time he is transferred until the end of the season of his 23rd birthday. The provisions concerning the calculation and payment of training compensation are set out in detail in annex 4 of the FIFA Regulations on the Status and Transfer of Players (2009). The thrust of annex 4 is twofold. First, it promotes the principle that between the ages of 12 and 23, a player is in his 'sporting education' and that during that timeframe a club that has invested in the training of such a player is entitled to a financial reward for educating that player up to the age of 21 or, before that, to the point where it is clear that the player's training has effectively terminated.[149] The second principle is that training compensation should benefit all clubs that have contributed to the training of a young player and thus on first registration as a professional, the club with which that player is registered pays training compensation to every club that has contributed to his training, and does so on a pro-rata basis according to the period spent with each club. For every subsequent transfer of the professional player until the end of the season of the player's 23rd birthday, only the last club for which the player was registered is entitled to training compensation for the period that the player was effectively trained by that club.

[**7.53**]　These two principles prompt four further points of interest. First, in order to calculate the compensation due for training and education costs, and in accordance with articles 4 and 5 of annex 4 of the FIFA Regulations on the Status and Transfer of Players (2009), national football associations have been instructed to divide clubs into a maximum of four categories according to the clubs' financial investment in training players. The training costs set for each category correspond to the amount needed to train one player for one year multiplied by an average 'player factor'—the ratio of players who need to be trained to produce one

---

[148] An edited version of the FA commission that investigated this matter is available as 'Greed and Deceit at the Heart of Football' *The Sunday Times* (London 5 June 2006) Sport 12. The then Chelsea manager, Jose Mourinho, was fined £200,000 for breach of the FAPL rule Q on the conduct of managers. Subsequently, Cole's agent was also sanctioned for misconduct contrary to breach of FA rule E and including breach of the FIFA Players' Agents Regulations. For a report on that FA investigation see www.thefa.com/TheFA/Disciplinary/NewsAndFeatures/2006/BarnettDecision.aspx.

[149] See generally CAS 2003/O/527 *Hamburger Sport-Verein eV v Odense Boldklub* (effective termination of training period at 18) and CAS 2004/A/594 *Hapoel Bee-Sheva v Real Racing Club de Santander* (effective termination of training period at 17).

professional player—and that calculation further takes into account the costs that would have been incurred by the new club if it had trained the player itself. In general, the first time a player registers as a professional, compensation is calculated by taking the training costs of the new club multiplied by the number of years of training. For subsequent transfers, the calculation is based on the training costs of the new club multiplied by the number of years of training with the former club.[150] FIFA's (DRC) has the express authority to review the amount of training compensation payable[151] and most importantly—and the matter that is the most contentious in this regard—the DRC has the discretion to adjust the amount of compensation if it is clearly 'disproportionate' to the case under review. CAS has upheld the DRC's view that a club which claims that training compensation is disproportionate bears the burden of proof and that in discharging that burden the evidence provided must be of a 'concrete' financial nature such as invoices, costs of training centres and budgets.[152]

[7.54] Another contentious issue surrounding training compensation has been the status of young players in the sense that the training compensation scheme is triggered only on the first 'professionalisation' of the player. According to article 2(2) FIFA, a professional player is one 'who has a written contract with a club and is paid more for his footballing activity than the expenses he effectively incurs'.[153] Some debate arose as to scholarship-type arrangements for young players prevalent in France and England in particular, whereby players benefiting from additional remuneration under such 'apprenticeships' nonetheless remained registered as amateur by the national federation. The DRC and CAS have held that however a national federation might label or describe such an arrangement is irrelevant and that the investigating authority should look to its substance in ascertaining whether the benefiting player is receiving remuneration beyond those expenses effectively incurred for his footballing activity.[154]

[7.55] The third point of interest is that associated with this training compensation scheme is a so-called 'solidarity' mechanism governed by article 21 FIFA and annex 5 FIFA. The essence of this scheme is that if a professional is transferred before the expiry of his contract, any club that has contributed to his education and training between his 12th and 23rd birthdays receives a proportion of the compensation paid to his former club. It amounts in all to a maximum of 5

---

[150] Note the summary given in the opinion of Advocate General Sharpston delivered on 16 July 2009 in Case C-325/08, Reference for a preliminary ruling under Article 234EC from the Cour de cassation (France), made by decision of 9 July 2008 in the proceedings *Olympique Lyonnais SASP v Olivier Bernard & Newcastle United FC* [10]–[15].

[151] Decisions of the DRC in this regard are available to download at www.fifa.com/aboutfifa/federation/administration/decision.html.

[152] CAS 2004/A/560 *AC Venezia v Club Atlético Mineiro & AS Roma*. See generally M Bakker, 'The Training Compensation System' (2008) 1/2 *International Sports Law Journal* 29.

[153] For a discussion and interesting application of this point within the context of a training compensation payment see CAS 2006/A/1027 *Blackpool FC v Club Topp Oss*.

[154] See further CAS 2003/A/383 *FC Girondins de Bordeaux v Lyngby Boldklub & Lundtofte Boldklub* and CAS 2006/A/1177 *Aston Villa FC v B.93 Copenhagen*.

per cent of the total compensation, spread over the seasons and among the clubs concerned. The fourth point of interest is a twofold jurisdictional one. Pursuant to article 6 of annex 4 of the FIFA Regulations on the Status and Transfer of Players (2009), special training compensation calculation provisions apply for players moving from one national football association to another inside the territory of the EU or associated European Economic Area.[155] Moreover, training compensation in accordance with these regulations applies only in the event of an international transfer. For 'domestic' transfers, the system enforced by the relevant association must be in accordance with article 1(2) FIFA, which mandates inter alia that such domestic regulation should 'provide for a system to reward clubs investing in the training and education of young players.'

[7.56]   Finally, the compatibility of FIFA's training compensation scheme with aspects of EU law was considered recently, albeit indirectly, by the ECJ in *Olympique Lyonnais SASP v Olivier Bernard & Newcastle United FC*.[156] The background to this case was that at the material time of the proceedings (the 1997–1998 season) employment of football players in France was regulated by a Professional Football Charter (PFC), which had the status of a collective agreement for the industry and was incorporated into that country's employment code. The relevant provision in the PFC concerned a category of player know as 'joueurs espoir', namely players between the ages of 16 and 22 employed as trainees by a professional club under a fixed-term contract. At the end of his training with a club, the PFC obliged a 'joueur espoir' to sign his first professional contract with that club, if the club required him to do so. The PFC did not allow for any compensation for the club which provided the training in the event that the player, at the end of his training, refused to sign a professional contract with that club. Nevertheless, where such a scenario arose the club could bring an action for damages against the player for breach of contractual and employment obligations.

[7.57]   Bernard was a 'joueur espoir' with Olympique Lyonais but did not sign a contract with them at the end of his training, signing instead for Newcastle United FC. An employment tribunal ordered Bernard and Newcastle jointly to pay damages for infringement of the PFC and related employment law provisions. On eventual appeal to the Cour de Cassation, that court asked the ECJ whether the scheme constituted a restriction of the principle of freedom of movement for workers laid down in Article 39 EC (now Article 45 TFEU) and if so whether that restriction was justified by the need to encourage the recruitment and training of young players. The ECJ held that Article 45 TFEU does not preclude a scheme which, in order to attain the objective of encouraging the recruitment and training of young players, guarantees compensation to the club which provided the training if, at the end of his training period, a young player signs a professional contract with a club in

---

[155] See, eg, CAS 2006/A/1152 *ADO Den Haag v Newcastle United FC*.

[156] Judgment of the Grand Chamber delivered on 16 March 2010 in Case C-325/08, Reference for a preliminary ruling under Article 234EC from the Cour de cassation (France), made by decision of 9 July 2008 in the proceedings *Olympique Lyonnais SASP v Olivier Bernard & Newcastle United FC*.

another member state, provided that the scheme is suitable to ensure the attainment of that objective and does not go beyond what is necessary to attain it. In the ECJ's opinion, the 'joueur espoir' scheme went beyond what was necessary to achieve that aim principally because the compensation it allowed for went beyond that which could be considered appropriate and proportionate, that is, it went beyond, and was unrelated to, the actual costs of training incurred by the club.[157]

[**7.58**]   The case is of interest because, although no specific approval was given to the current FIFA regulations on training compensation,[158] its principles appear to illustrate FIFA's current scheme in a good light. Indeed, in their observations to the court, the French and UK governments and the EC Commission argued expressly (and in a manner which succinctly encapsulated the FIFA-mandated scheme) that the current provisions comply with the principle of proportionality given that under the regulations: the club, not the player, pays compensation; the compensation is calculated, indeed predicated, on the cost of training the player, adjusted by the ratio of trainees needed to produce one professional player; the scheme has various safeguards and limits inbuilt in order to render the compensation proportionate to the aim sought; and it is supplemented by a solidarity mechanism apportioning compensation between clubs when several have contributed to the training of the player.[159] In short, although FIFA's regulations on training compensation cannot be said to have obtained the blessing of the ECJ on this occasion, they have definitely received a firm nod of approval.

Child Trafficking?

[**7.59**]   Returning to the broader issue, Platini's child trafficking comments relating generally to the Kakuta affair have attracted criticism on account of their perceived inaccuracy and unhelpful hyperbole. For instance, the Arsenal manager, Arsene Wenger, pointed out both that, although of Congolese extraction, Kakuta was born in France and that by prohibiting the international transfer of minors outright, the practice might simply go underground and unregulated to the aggravated detriment of young players.[160] Wenger has a valid point but the manner in which young players are treated at the well resourced clubs such as Arsenal is not the central point of concern: rather it is the manner in which young talented players from developing countries are treated both while on trial at a European club and, most importantly, when, as the majority of these children do, they fail

---

[157] Ibid [38]–[50].

[158] The relevant FIFA regulations were not in force at the material time. Nevertheless, as acknowledged in the opinion of the Advocate General (n 150) [59]–[62] the reasoning in her opinion may well be relevant if and when it may become necessary to examine the compatible of FIFA's regulations with EU Law. It must also be noted that the French scheme has subsequently been amended and now contains domestic rules comparable to FIFA's regulatory scheme for training compensation arising from international transfers.

[159] See opinion of the Advocate General (n 150) [60] and the judgment of the ECJ (n 156) [25].

[160] See D Jones, 'Wenger Dismisses Platini Transfer Plan' *The Independent* (London 11 September 2009) Sport 48.

to convince on trial and are quickly discarded even 'abandoned'. It is this issue, the lack of 'support' for young players, that has exercised the EU and which has in turn highlighted the need for EU member states to apply protective measures for such minors in national legislation and in line with the requirements of the UN Convention on the Rights of the Child (1989).[161] For example, in the European Council's Nice Declaration on Sport (2000) concern was expressed about 'commercial transactions targeting minors in sport, including those from third countries, inasmuch as they do not comply with existing labour legislation or endanger the health and welfare of young sportsmen and -women'.[162] The Council called on sports organisations and member states to investigate and monitor such practices, as has the European Parliament.[163] The European Commission is currently studying how Directive 94/33/EC of 22 June 1994 on the protection of young people at work might apply in this situation.[164]

[**7.60**] At a member state level an interesting approach has been taken in Ireland, which has a long history of 'exporting' young footballers to the UK in particular. The Football Association of Ireland (FAI) has recognised that the protection of minors in sport requires the enhanced regulation of the activities of football 'scouts' or talent identifiers and the better awareness of parents and 'schoolboy' clubs of the implications of their child/player going on trial to a professional club outside the jurisdiction.[165] Moreover, the FAI has recognised that 'support' in this context should include assisting 'returnees' with their reintegration into home society, sport and family.[166] The FAI's approach, which is one

---

[161] See generally the accompanying Commission Staff Working Document to the European Commission, European Commission's White Paper on Sport, 11 July 2007, COM(2007) 391 final [4.5] which notes that the international transfer of young footballers to Europe 'does not fall into the legal definition of trafficking in human beings, which is a very serious crime and implies the transfer of the child for the specific purpose of forced labour, sexual exploitation or other forms of severe exploitation such as begging. However, the situation of young players take abroad for sport training and then abandoned without any support is absolutely unacceptable given the fundamental values recognised by the EU and its Member States. It is also contrary to the values of sport.'

[162] Nice Declaration on the Specific Characteristics of Sports and its Social Function in Europe (Annex IV of the Presidency Conclusions for the Nice European Council, 7–8 December 2000) [13].

[163] European Parliament Resolution of 29 March 2007 on the future of professional football in Europe (2006/2130(INI)) [37].

[164] [1994] OJ L216/12. Commission staff have acknowledged (n 161) that there are 'indications that the practical enforcement of the Directive is only partial with regard to minors in sport'.

[165] In November 2009, the FAI introduced a series of new regulations including: a Scouting Registration Form; Request for Trial Form; Rules relating to Scouts and Players Visiting Senior Clubs and going on Trials; and FAI Advice for Parents & Guardians about Trial Requests & Scouts. The regulations can be viewed and downloaded from the Football Service & Education section of the FAI website, www.fai.ie.

[166] The experience of many young Irish players who have had unsuccessful trials or periods of apprenticeship in England is that they return with few educational qualifications and low self-esteem and thus often have difficulty in getting employment and re-entering football. The FAI, which has a full-time player welfare office employed in England, has assisted such players by providing them with access to education and training. In a football sense, these young players have been encouraged to take up semi-professional opportunities within the domestic League of Ireland, to the undoubted benefit of playing standards in that league.

that might be adopted elsewhere, also illustrates that the protection of minors must be seen in broader terms and particularly in the context of the more effective regulation of player agents and the licensing system for clubs. To be fair, it must be acknowledged that authorities such as UEFA and FIFA are taking their responsibilities seriously in this regard, and their efforts have attracted CAS approval.

[**7.61**]   In *FC Midtylland AS v FIFA*,[167] a Danish Premier League Club came to an arrangement with a Nigerian club, which gave the Danish club an exclusive purchase option on the Nigerian club's most talented players, and included an option permitting Midtylland to enrol younger players in their football academy. The Nigerian club in question was based in that country's largest city, Lagos, which, with a population of over 15 million, had significant potential in terms of identifying talented footballers. In 2006 and 2007, the Danish club registered a number of Nigerian minors with the Danish Football Association (DFA). The players were registered as amateurs, which, in accordance with DFA regulations, entitled the players to receive a total amount of approximately €3,000 subsistence for food and lodging. For residence and work permit purposes, the Danish Immigration Service classified the players as students and the players were given access, on a part time basis, to secondary schooling. In February 2007, FIFPro the worldwide representative body for professional footballers alerted FIFA to the fact that Mitylland's conduct, and that of the DFA, was in violation of article 19(1) FIFA. In October 2007, FIFA's Player Status Committee issued a decision against Mitylland and DFA, severely warning them for their infringement of article 19(1) FIFA.

[**7.62**]   The club subsequently exercised their right to appeal the decision before CAS pursuant to article 60(2) FIFA Statutes. The CAS Panel dismissed the appeal on all (five) points raised by Mittylland. First, the award clarified that article 19 FIFA applies to professional and amateur minor players.[168] Second, the Panel held that none of the exceptions to the general principle contained in article 19(1) FIFA were applicable to the present case.[169] Third, the CAS Panel held that the application of article 19 FIFA to the present case did not contradict any mandatory provision of EU law,[170] and in particular it did not violate the

---

[167] CAS 2008/A/1485 *FC Midtylland AS v FIFA*.

[168] Ibid [7.2].

[169] Ibid [7.3].

[170] Ibid [7.4.2]–[7.4.4]. Of further interest here is the Panel's view that *in any event* the appellant's assumption that EU law would be binding upon CAS, with regard to disputes connect with FIFA Regulations, was incorrect. The Panel observed, [7.4.2]–[7.4.3], 'Article R 58 of the [CAS] Code provides that the Panel shall decide the dispute according to the applicable regulations and the rules of law chosen by the parties. In the present case, it is not disputed that the parties have accepted [article 60(2)FIFA Statutes], which provided for the application of the various regulation of FIFA, and, additionally, Swiss law … .[consequently] … in order to claim that a specific provision of EC Law is to be applied in cases involving [and submitted under FIFA Regulations and Statutes], one has to establish that the relevant EC provisions are of a mandatory nature according to Swiss law, which is the law of the seat of the arbitration.'

prohibition in Contonou Agreement (to which Nigeria and Denmark are parties) of any discrimination based on nationality as regards working conditions. This was because, the Panel found, the players in question could not be considered as legally employed in Denmark, that is, they were not 'workers' but 'students' and thus had to be considered as coming outside the scope of application of article 13(3) of the Contonou Agreement.[171] Fourth, and echoing the comments of an earlier CAS award,[172] the *Mitylland* Panel noted that 'certain rules [of which FIFA's rules limiting the international transfer of minor players are an example] may constitute a restriction to fundamental rights, when such rules pursue a legitimate objective and are proportionate to the objective sought'.[173] Fifth, when the Danish club claimed, in the context of a breach of the non-discrimination principle, that FIFA had been turning a 'blind eye' to the fact that larger clubs—Bayern Munich was mentioned—were in the practice of registering players from South America and elsewhere; the Panel noted forcefully that there was no evidence or support whatsoever to suggest that 'the constant practice of FIFA is to accept the registration of players from outside the EC'.[174] In sum, the CAS Panel in *Mitylland* fully endorsed FIFA's regulatory approach to the international transfer of minors.

Content and Termination of Contract

[**7.63**]   Although the concept of a standard form written contract for a professional footballer is a somewhat nebulous in nature given that the terms of such a contract can vary greatly depending on the age, talent and even the playing position of a player, Form 13A of the FAPL Rules does in effect provide a good working model of a standard contract for a Premier League footballer, and it is the model on which the following sections of this chapter are based.[175] Form 13A has three essential dimensions, reflecting the international, national and specific

---

[171] CAS 2008/A/1485 *Midtylland* [7.4.9]–[7.4.10]. The appellant also claimed that art 19 FIFA contradicted Art 12 ECHR on the freedom of assembly and of association. Again, the Panel took that view that the binding and enforceable effect of the ECHR on FIFA in the present factual circumstances was not something that could be assumed and, furthermore, neither did the Panel, [7.4.17]–[7.4.18], consider that a player's registration with a football club was something protected by Art 12 ECHR because 'it is clear that article 19FIFA does not prevent players from playing football or from joining other people in order to play football.'

[172] CAS 2005/955/956 *Cadiz CFSAD/Acuna Cabellero v FIFA and Association Paraguaya de Futbol* [7.2].

[173] CAS 2008/1485 *Midtylland* [7.4.19].

[174] Ibid [7.5.5]. See generally [7.5] of the *Mitdylland* award where this element of the appellant's case was also dismissed on the ground of an application of the general legal principle of *nemini dolus alienus prodesse debet*: one cannot claim to benefit from the same treatment as another when the treatment granted to the third party would be illegal save where there is evidence that the constant practice of the authorities is to benefit third parties with treatments that are illegal.

[175] The FAPL's rules are available to download as the Official Premier League Handbook 2009/10 at www.premierleague.com/page/Handbook.

contract of employment dimensions to such contracts. First, and with reference to clause 18 of Form 13A (the respect for the 'specificity of football' clause) the document seeks to ensure that such contracts (and all parties to it) have due regard to the 'special relationship and characteristics involved in the employment of football players'. In practical, albeit implied terms, this means that the contract is integrated or incorporated firmly within the governance structure of world football and ultimately to FIFA's Regulations on the Status and Transfer of Players. In parallel, it means that, where grievances arise under such contracts, all parties are bound both to submit all matters of dispute, including those relating to breach or termination of contract, to football-specific tribunals, and to accept the ultimate jurisdiction of CAS.[176]

[**7.64**]   Second, the terms and conditions of Form 13A form part of a number of collective agreements between the parties—on the one hand, the club and FAPL; on the other hand, the player and his union, the PFA—and thus must be seen as part of an overall scheme aimed at regulating gainful employment and working conditions in the Premier League. This point overlaps with the third and final dimension, which is Form 13A's attempt to provide a transparent and standardised basis for the key clauses in such contracts in a manner that respects the norms and values of domestic (and EU) contract of employment law.[177] This three dimensional view of Form 13A aside, the substantial nature of a standard Premier League contract is now characterised by three fundamental, express terms: the duties and obligations of the players; the duties and obligations of clubs; and breach and termination of contract by the club or by the player.[178]

Duties and Obligations of Players

[**7.65**]   Under clause 3 of Form 13A a Premier League player typically agrees, when directed by an authorised office of his employing club, to a dozen duties and obligations:[179] to attend matches in which the club is engaged; to participate in any

---

[176] Internal club disciplinary and grievance procedures are provided in clauses 9 and 10, as supplemented by sch 1 of Form 13A. Outside of those provisions, clause 17 of Form 3A provides the link between the contractual parties (the FAPL, the Premier League club, player) to CAS through its requirement that certain disputes be referred to arbitration in accordance with FA rule K.

[177] See, eg, sch 2 of Form 13A fulfilling the supplementary statement of the initial particulars of employment required by Part 1 of the Employment Rights Act 1996.

[178] A Form 13A contract does of course contain a number of other terms on the technicalities surrounding injury or illness of the player (clause 7); permanent or prolonged incapacity (clause 8); holidays (clause 14); and the confidentially of the contract (clause 16). Pursuant to clause 21, the contract is governed and construed in accordance with English law and the jurisdiction of the English courts. These express terms, which can be varied by agreement between the parties, are paramount to the interpretation of the contract unless overridden by the general law.

[179] Under clause 4 of Form 13A, players also have promotional, community and public relations activities and 'shall attend at and participate in such events as may reasonably be required' by their club or the FAPL or any sponsors or commercial partners thereof. These events usually consist of interviews, appearances and photo opportunities and clause 4 further requires the player, on reasonable notice by the club, to make himself available for at least three hours per week for such activities.

matches in which he is selected to play for the club; to attend at any reasonable place for the purposes of training and match preparation; to play to the best of his skill and ability at all times; except to the extent prevented by injury or illness to maintain a high standard of physical fitness at all times and not to indulge in any activity which might both endanger such fitness or inhibit his mental or physical ability to play, practise or train and might invoke any exclusion of the player's injury cover pursuant to any policy of insurance maintained for the benefit of the club on the player; to submit properly to such medical examinations the club may reasonably require and undergo any subsequent treatment recommended by said medical advisers; to comply with and act in accordance with all lawful instructions of any authorised official of the club; to play football solely for the employing club or as otherwise authorised by that club; to observe the laws of the game when playing football and to play the sport safely by not wearing anything (such a jewellery) which could be dangerous to the player or any other person; to observe the FAPL Rules and internal club rules but in the case of the latter to the extent only that they do not conflict or seek to vary the express terms of the player's contract; on termination of contract for any cause to return to the club in a reasonable condition any property (for example, a car) which has been provided by the club to the player in connection with that player's employment; except as agreed otherwise between the parties to use as his regular place of residence a place that can be deemed reasonably suitably (that is, nearby) for the performance by the player of his duties and particularly his training duties;[180] not to knowingly or recklessly do, write or say anything or omit to do anything which is likely to bring the club or the game of football 'into disrepute' by causing the player or club to be in breach of FAPL rules.

[**7.66**] At first instance, the final duty mentioned in the preceding paragraph, which is clause 3.2.5 of Form 13A, appears to be directed towards preventing players from making ill-considered comments to the media which may reflect badly on the club or league, and to this effect the clause obliges a player to 'give to the club reasonable notice of his intention to make any contributions to the public media in order to allow representation to be made to him on behalf of the club if it so desires'.[181] Although 'bringing the game into disrepute' clauses are used widely throughout world sport, this does not necessarily mean that their use

---

[180] For an interpretation of such contractual residence clauses, albeit in relation to a claim of wrongful dismissal surrounding a contract between a club and its manager see *Macari v Celtic Football & Athletic Co* (1999) SC 628, (2000) SLT 80 (even though Macari established a breach of the term of trust and confidence by Celtic, he had chosen to continue to work and draw his salary, as opposed to rescinding the contract and seeking damages; therefore he was obliged to do that work in accordance with the terms of his contract which included a residence clause obliging him to attend the football ground more regularly and thus the failure to comply with the clause meant that Macari had been in material breach of contract and was not wrongfully dismissed because such repudiatory breach by him justified Celtic's dismissal of him under the general law of contract).

[181] This caveat also extends to clause 4.8 of Form 13A which permits a player 'to make a responsible and reasonable reply or response to any media comment or published statements likely to adversely affect [their] standing or reputation.'

should go unchallenged. For example, Form 13A's use of 'bringing the game of football into disrepute' could be described politely as an attempt to keep players 'on message' about the glories of the Premier League or, in contrast, it could be seen as a means of stifling dissent and diversity of opinion.[182] Moreover, and more broadly, such terms can be described as 'moral' clauses whereby if, for instance, an athlete engages in off-field misbehaviour, such disrepute clauses can be used, at the discretion of the relevant sports governing authority, as the trigger for sports-specific sanction. In 2008, for example, CAS was presented with two cases relating to off-field misbehaviour (excessive alcohol leading to drunken driving charges[183] and excessive alcohol leading to assault charges)[184] by Australian athletes, which resulted in their not being selected for the Australian team for the Beijing Olympics. In both awards, the CAS Panel did not in any way question the breadth of the discretionary disrepute clause at issue and held that, contrary to the claims made by the individual athletes, the accompanying sanction was not disproportionate or manifestly excessive so as to give rise to a finding of irrationality. In sum, the CAS jurisprudence appears to demonstrate that, to borrow the language of administrative law, a claimant in such circumstance would have to demonstrate that in exercising their discretion the relevant decision-maker had acted perversely or in bad faith or so aberrantly that the decision could not be classed as rational.[185]

[**7.67**]   In both of the CAS awards just mentioned, the athlete in question had been charged with a criminal offence (and the nature of the act had attracted significant media attention). In major league sport in the US, the 'off-court' misbehaviour of athletes, some of which involves serious criminal offences, has led to league commissioners invoking 'in the best interest of the sport' clauses of their relevant league's constitution in order to severely sanction the athletes in question.[186] Although in no way can such conduct be condoned, the use of catch-all, ill-defined, 'disrepute' provisions and the motivation for their use (that is, the view that athletes are leaders within the sport itself and role models beyond it and that this justifies restrictions on their personal behaviour) does pose some important questions as to the use of such clauses.[187] As Kim and Parlow have written recently the problem associated with disrepute/best interest clauses are that the (accompanying) 'punishment by professional sports leagues cannot be cleanly defined as either purely private or public in nature ... [and] ... such uncertainty raises serious concerns

---

[182] See generally M Kosla, 'Disciplined for Bringing a Sport into Disrepute: A Framework for Judicial Review' (2001) 25 *Melbourne University Law Review* 654.

[183] CAS 2008/A/1605 *Jongewaard v Australian Olympic Committee*.

[184] CAS 2008/A/1574 *D'Arcy v Australian Olympic Committee*.

[185] Ibid [52].

[186] These charges have related to homicide, rapes, sexual assault, domestic violence and other assault based charges. See generally K Otto, 'Criminal Athletes: An Analysis of Charges, Reduced Charges and Sentences' (2009) 19 *Journal of the Legal Aspects of Sport* 67.

[187] Note the (American) review of the use of such clauses by F Pinguelo and T Cedrone, 'Morals? Who Cares about Morals? An Examination of Morals Clauses in Talent Contract and What Talent Needs to Know!' (2009) 19 *Seton Hall Journal of Sports and Entertainment Law* 347.

about the appropriateness of league punishment, not just in terms of consistency and proportionality, but also in its social function and justification'.[188]

[**7.68**]   In the UK, a disrepute clause was used by the England Rugby Football Union (RFU) against four Bath players who were asked in July 2009 to appear before an RFU disciplinary panel where they were to be charged with 'conduct prejudicial to the interest of the game' under rule 5.12(f) of the RFU's Membership rules, following allegations that they had taken prohibited substances at the club's end of season party. The players eventually received eight-month bans.[189] The argument here is that the sanctioning of players arising from drug testing in the workplace under club employment contracts, which of itself raises important issues regarding health and safety law, data protection and even privacy-related Article 8 ECHR concerns, should not just be 'hooked' or predicated on an abbreviated 'disrepute' charge and should more properly be based on separate, express contractual provisions, which carefully calibrate and factor in the consent and privacy of employees, and, ideally, would be incorporated into a broader, collective illicit drugs policy involving all stakeholders in the sport in question.[190]

Duties and Obligations of Clubs

[**7.69**]   The primary duty of the club is to pay the player the remuneration agreed throughout the duration of the contractual engagement between the parties. Clause 5 of Form 13 of the FAPL Rules deals with the issue of player remuneration and will be returned to shortly. Outside of that fundamental obligation, clause 6 of Form 13A of the FAPL Rules outlines seven standard contractual obligations of a Premier League club towards one of its player-employees:[191] observe all FAPL rules and its own club rules; provide the player each year with copies of said rules

---

[188] J Kim and M Parlow, 'Off-Court Misbehaviour: Sports Leagues and Private Punishment' (2009) 99 *Journal of Criminal Law & Criminology* 573, 597. See also P Coenen, 'Rulings from the Ivory Tower: Player Discipline under the NFL Personal Conduct Policy (2009) 40 *Cambrian Law Review* 9.

[189] See D Hands, 'Bans for Bath Pair Stand as RFU Opts for Instant Justice' *The Times* (London 8 September 2009) Sport 76.

[190] See generally S Farrow, 'Drug Testing under Club Employment Contracts' (2009) 7(8) *World Sports Law Report* 8. To be fair, the RFU have acknowledged this and is introducing an illicit drugs policy in 2010. See G Mairs, 'Harrison backs Drugs Crackdown' *The Daily Telegraph* (London 1 January 2010) Sport 20.

[191] Again, these express terms, which can be varied by agreement between the parties, are paramount to the interpretation of the contract unless overridden by the general law. In this, clubs should be aware that player employees, as with any employee, can avail themselves, where appropriate, of the equal treatment protections of the various anti-discrimination in the workplace legislative provisions of English law such as the Sex Discrimination Act 1975; the Race Relations Act 1976; the Disability Discrimination Act 1995 and the various secondary regulations on employment equality in relation to religious belief, sexual orientation and age. For an introduction to the impact of discrimination law on both amateur and professional sport see Lewis and Taylor (n 1) ch D3. This area is constantly evolving and one of the most recent debates is the scope of application of the sports-related exception contained in s 19 of the Gender Recognition Act, as analysed by D McArdle, 'Swallows and Amazons, or the Sporting Exception to the Gender Recognition Act' (2008) 17 *Social and Legal Studies* 39.

especially those which affect the terms and conditions of the player's employment and with which he is expected to comply; promptly arrange appropriate medical examination and treatment at the club's expense for the player in respect of any injury or illness suffered by the player in the course of employment and not to use or reveal the contents of any medical reports arising there from for any purpose other than the assessment of the player's health and fitness;[192] comply with all relevant statutory provisions relating to industrial injury and health and safety in the workplace, including the adoption of polices for the security, safety and physical well being of the player when carrying out his contractual duties;[193] in any case where the club would otherwise be liable as the employer for any acts or omission of the player in the lawful and proper performance of his playing or training duties, the club is contractually obliged to defend the player against any proceedings brought against him and to indemnify the player from any damages awarded;[194] give the player every opportunity to follow any course of further education or vocational training; release the player as required for representative international duty pursuant to FIFA regulations.[195]

Remuneration

[**7.70**] A player's remuneration beyond their basic wage can include all reasonable hotel and other expenses wholly and exclusively incurred by the player in the perform of his contractual duties (clause 5.2 of Form 13A) and, more importantly, any related bonuses and incentives (as related to, for example, goals scored, appearances made; league point accumulated, etc).[196] Self-evidently, the remuneration received by a contract player under the terms of a written contract of service is taxable as employment income. The tax treatment of footballers by HMRC[197] gives a good insight into the types of payment typically made to footballers as earnings.[198] Apart from basic wages paid as a salary or a certain amount

---

[192] Activity outside the course of employment, as defined in normal industry terms, may not necessarily be covered by the club's policy of insurance for the benefit of players and thus may render the player personally liable. See further clauses 6.1.3, 6.1.5 and 3.2.1 of Form 13A.

[193] See further Farrow (n 190) 8 who notes, in the context of the legal obligations surrounding drug testing of players under club employment contracts, that 'employers have a duty of care (both at common law and under section 2 of the Health and Safety at Work Act 1974) to ensure the health, safety and welfare at work of their employees. In addition, employers are required to assess the risk to health and safety under the Management of Health and Safety at Work Regulations 1992. Accordingly, if an employer allows an employee under the influence of drugs to continue working, the employer could be in breach of this duty by putting that individual, or others with whom they come into contact, at risk.'

[194] For a general discussion on the 'vicarious liability' nature of this clause see [6.43]–[6.46] of this text.

[195] For a general discussion of this topic see [7.08]–[7.11] of this text.

[196] See further the requirements and particulars under paras 8 and 10 of sch 1 to Form 13A.

[197] For further information see www.hmrc.gov.uk/MANUALS/eimanual/EIM64100.htm.

[198] Tax law may not be the most stimulating of subjects but recent rigorous application of national tax codes in the UK (taxability of endorsement income by foreign sports stars who occasionally compete in Britain) and Spain (amendment of the so-called 'Beckham law', which permitted elite foreign footballers to pay lower levels of income tax than Spanish citizens) have, it is claimed, the potential to leave foreign sports stars vulnerable to significantly higher tax liabilities when competing in Britain or Spain. For

per match and associated travelling expenses, payments to footballers that are normally chargeable to tax as employment income include signing-on fees; share of a transfer fee; net monies from any benefit or testimonial matches; loyalty bonuses and termination payments.[199]

[**7.71**]   Reviewing the key employment income sources for footballers, it must be noted that at first, and generally speaking, signing-on fees are payable to the player at the discretion of his new club and will normally have been agreed between the player and the new club during transfer negotiations. In fact, the signing-on fee is often stated in the contract and is normally payable by instalments (taxable on receipt) over the terms of the contract, which may sometimes include the period over which there is an option to extend the contract. Where the player is subsequently transferred at the request of his club, any unpaid instalments for the earlier signing-on fee are payable immediately but where the player requests a transfer, he usually forfeits any such unpaid instalments. The latter can contribute to a player, even one frustrated by lack of playing opportunities, being reluctant to go through the formalities of an official transfer request.[200] In similar terms to a signing-on fee, a player can receive a share of the transfer fee paid for him and it is of note that the tax case law observes (in the context of whether such payments are chargeable to tax) that, although such payments are not obligatory, they are 'expected, are generally asked for, and are usually accorded'.[201]

[**7.72**]   With regard to the net profits of benefit matches and testimonials, the general principle appears to be that where the right to a benefit match is written into the contract or where the player's club always grants a testimonial after a set qualifying period of service (for example, 10 years) the proceeds are taxable. Where there is no entitlement and no custom, the proceeds are not taxable. This is usually the case where the benefit match is organised by a testimonial committee independent of the club and motivated by an effort to demonstrate affection and regard for the 'personal qualities' of the player.[202] The scenario where a highly

---

Britain, see P Shackleton, 'Taxation of Sportspeople in the UK' (2010) 1017 *Tax Journal* 14 and R Watts and K Dowling, 'Taxman Scares off Top Sports Stars' *The Sunday Times* (London 17 January 2010) News 3, citing *Agassi v Her Majesty's Inspector of Taxes* [2006] UKHL 23; [2006] 1 WLR 1380. For Spain, see B Sanchez, 'Changes to Taxation: Impact on Professional Sport' (2010) 8(2) *World Sports Law Report* 8.

[199]   Note also that a footballer who represents England, Scotland, Wales or Northern Ireland may be entitled to a match fee. Payment of said fee is made to the player's club, which subject the fee to PAYE in the normal way.

[200]   On the taxability of signing on fees in football see generally *Shilton v Wilmshurst (Inspector of Taxes)* [1991] 1 AC 684. In that case, the then England goalkeeper Peter Shilton was employed by Nottingham Forest under the terms of a contract due to expire in the summer of 1983. In the summer of 1982, Forest, under some financial pressure, accepted an offer from Southampton for Shilton, subject to his agreement. Under the terms of the transfer deal, worth £325,000, Shilton effectively received a signing-on fee from both clubs and notably £75,000 from Forest as an inducement/thanks for agreeing to the transfer. The House of Lords held that both signing-on fees represented earnings or an emolument from the player's employment with Southampton.

[201]   *Corbett v Duff* [1941] 1 KB 730, 740, Lawrence J.

[202]   See generally *Seymour v Reed* [1927] AC 554 (proceeds from benefit game not treated as earnings and not sourced in employment and seen more by way of a gift).

paid elite footballer who, after a certain length of service, enjoys tax free the net benefits of a testimonial are of course questionable but, to be fair, the recent trend is for footballers to make a large donation from the profits to charity. Three final points—one general and two specific—need to be made on testimonials. First, the frequency of testimonials has decreased substantially in recent years, this is directly related to the fundamental changes in the regulations surrounding the transfer of players that has occurred since the mid-1990s, allowing players greater employment mobility and concomitantly resulting both in a rise in wage levels and shorter term contracts. In short, it is rare for a player to remain with a single club for a period of time long enough to merit a testimonial and, in any event, the wages currently available to players at the elite level hardly need supplementing by accrued benefits from testimonials.[203] Second, it must be noted that benefit matches may also be connected with the termination of employment and may be taxable in full as earnings under section 62 of the Income Tax (Earnings and Pensions) Act 2003. Third, outside of such benefits, clubs might also seek to reward players by way of loyalty bonuses, that is, discretionary lump sum payments to mark the completion of a specified number of years' service. Again, such payments might constitute emoluments that are taxable as employment income.[204]

Image Rights

[**7.73**]   Apart from the above, other kinds of payments may also be taxable and recently HMRC has begun investigating a number of professional football (and cricket and rugby) clubs in an apparent attempt to assess the manner in which such clubs might be using payments for image rights in lieu of salary and thus avoiding avoid income and other taxes, including national insurance contributions.[205] The legal and commercial issues surrounding the image rights of athletes (that is the athlete's right to prevent unauthorised use of their name, likeness or particular characteristics or even idiosyncrasies, such as a nickname, associated with their personality) and the merchandising and promotional activities associated with the exploitation of such rights (by the individual themselves and/or by their club) is a huge area in itself and well documented elsewhere.[206] The specific concern here is with a current HMRC investigation into a practice whereby sports image rights are used to disguise the true (taxable) character of payments made

---

[203] For a wry look at this see G Smith, 'Writhing from a Kick to the Testimonials' *The Times* (London 12 July 2008) Sport 98.

[204] See generally *Weston v Hearn* [1943] 2 All ER 421.

[205] This concern about image rights-related payments being used to evade tax in not a specifically UK matter and has been raised in a recent report by the Financial Action Task Force (FAFT), an intergovernmental body whose purpose is to monitor money laundering and terrorist financing at a global level. See FAFT Report, *Money Laundering through the Football Sector* (FAFT, Paris, July 2009) 26–29 available to download through www.fatf-gafi.org.

[206] For UK perspectives on this see Lewis and Taylor (n 1) ch G3 and for a wider pan-European perspective see I Blackshaw and R Siekmann (eds), *Sports Image Rights in Europe* (The Hague, TMC Asser, 2005). Blackshaw and Siekmann's book also contains a chapter (ch 19 by J Wolohan) on sports image rights in the US.

by a club to a player with the underlying idea being to reduce the tax burden on a player and thus make it more attractive for non-UK nationals, who might be put off by UK tax rates, to sign for Premier League clubs.[207]

[**7.74**]   A brief background to this area of concern is that when a footballer (and the focus here is on a Premier League player) signs for a club he traditionally has two options regarding image rights: either he seeks to profit from selling his own reserved image rights; or he permits the club to use his image (on merchandising for photographic and promotional purposes, etc) for an annual payment.[208] A practice has developed however where the player, in advance of his contract of employment and presumably on the advice of his agent or advisors, forms a company registered and located offshore or in a known tax haven jurisdiction. The player effectively transfers the rights to exploit his image exclusively (and on a worldwide basis) to that company in return for shares in the company and also agrees to undertake any promotional activities as may be directed by that company. The company then contracts on behalf of the player with third parties and notably the player's employing club, in regard to the exploitation of the player's image rights. Any consideration made in respect of such contracts (and some estimates are that such payments can equate to anything from 10 to 20 per cent of the player's salary) are directed towards that offshore company and thus both reduce the tax burden on the player and attract neither deductions for PAYE nor national insurance contributions for the club.

[**7.75**]   In *Sports Club, Evelyn and Jocelyn v Inspector of Taxes*,[209] it was held that there was nothing necessarily illegitimate about a tax avoidance scheme that detaches the payments structure of the player's image rights-related services away from that player's core playing services such that any monies received from the former cannot be regarded as income from that player's employment. Nevertheless, the judgment in that case contained the general caveat that such image rights arrangements would not be vulnerable to the usual rates of tax, and would not be seen as a 'smokescreen' for additional remuneration, only where they could they could be viewed as having a genuine, independent commercial value to third parties over and above the standard playing services provided by such players for such clubs.[210] Bluntly, the HMRC's recent, revised interest in such arrangements is that while in exceptional cases (for example, David Beckham) the image rights of a player may be worth more to a club than his contribution on the field, for the vast majority of players, even at the elite level, their individual

---

[207] See generally P Rees, 'Clubs Fear Impact of Tax Probe' *The Observer* (London 27 September 2009) Sport 8.

[208] This is the thrust of clause 4 (and especially sub clauses 4.4–4.6) of Form 13A of the FAPL Rules, which, except to the extent specifically agreed otherwise by the parties, obliges the player not to exploit their image in a club context in any manner and/or in any media nor grant the right to do so to any third party.

[209] *Sports Club, Evelyn and Jocelyn v Inspector of Taxes* [2000] STC (SCD) 443. The case concerned image rights payments to Dennis Bergkamp and David Platt by Arsenal.

[210] Ibid [70]–[101] reasons for the decision.

image rights and associated promotional services may be of little commercially exploitable value.[211] Nonetheless, in some cases clubs are continuing to pay for image rights to levels that appear incongruously high—so, for instance, in June 2009, it was reported that Newcastle United were paying £675,000 a year for Joey Barton's image rights;[212] while as part of the fall out accompanying Portsmouth FC's financial difficulties in 2009/2010 was a claim by former player Sol Campbell for over £1.5 million owed in unpaid image rights earnings.[213] Although the Barton and Campbell payments appear to reflect little more that poor judgement by the then executives of the stated football clubs, the HMRC's curiosity with similar arrangements in the Premier League is not just with the level of such payments and their (offshore) destination but whether what is truly happening is that clubs are paying salaries under the cover of the smokescreen created by sham image rights companies set up by players to the extent that all parties are really engaged in tax evasion rather that *Sports Club*-type tax avoidance.[214]

Breach and Termination of Contract by Club or Player

[7.76] The following sections consider briefly a scenario where a club or player attempt to end contractual relations with the other party prematurely, that is, before the natural expiry period of the contract. In the Premier League, and pursuant to clause 10 of Form 13A of the FAPL Rules, a club is entitled to terminate the employment of a player by 14 days' written notice to the player if the player 'shall be' guilty of gross misconduct or fails to heed any final written warning given under standard, internal disciplinary procedures or is convicted of any criminal offences where the punishment consists of a sentence of imprisonment of three months or more (which is not suspended).[215] In reality, these three express, material breach contractual scenarios should be viewed more in terms of common law repudiatory breaches whereby given the serious, fundamental nature of such breaches, going to the root of the contract, the innocent party (the club) is, on the ground that it has been denied all intended core benefit under the

---

[211] Interest in footballers' image rights really came to the fore in 2003 when the £24 million paid by Real Madrid to Manchester United for David Beckham was predicated as much on Real Madrid's interest in exploiting Beckham-related merchandising revenue, as it was on playing talent. On the intricacies of that transfer see generally J Carlin, *White Angels: Beckham, Real Madrid and the New Football* (London, Bloomsbury, 2004).

[212] See D White, 'Barton paid £675,000 for Image Rights' *The Sunday Telegraph* (London 14 June 2009) Sport, Soccer 1.

[213] See M Scott, 'Digger: Campbell Case Alerted Taxman' *The Guardian* (London 23 February 2010) Sport 2.

[214] The HMRC's investigation has caused concern for both individual Premier League clubs and the FAPL: see S James, 'West Ham Image Rights on Hold' *The Guardian* (London 18 March 2010) Sport 2 and O Gibson, League Faces New Tax Battle Ground over Image Rights' *The Guardian* (London 17 February 2010) Sport 6.

[215] Clause 10 then goes on to sketch the due notice, rights of appeal and, pending such an appeal hearing, any provisional suspensions that might surround the termination procedure.

contact, entitled to end the contractual relationship by accepting the repudiation, and thus can sue for damages on foot of that breach.[216] In this light, any overview of this area must take into account that in practice, and for three overlapping reasons, club-led terminations are rare and it is often the case that clubs seek to avoid the implication of a material breach and, in effect, affirm the player's repudiatory breach.

[**7.77**]   The first reason for this 'affirmation' approach by clubs to misconduct that otherwise might prompt the termination of its contractual relations with the player is that players are expensively acquired commodities, at best held to relatively short term contracts, and thus because it is a costly exercise to purchase and hold on to players, it is unsurprising that clubs are most reluctant to end contractual relations prematurely. Equally therefore, it is unsurprising that termination under clause 10 applies only in the most egregious of circumstances—'gross' misconduct;[217] convictions resulting in a custodial sentence;[218] or at the very end of a lengthy internal disciplinary procedure.[219] Consequently, it can be argued that the subliminal message to clause 10 is that where a dispute can be resolved short of termination, it should be so resolved, and done so through the relatively sophisticated grievance and disciplinary procedures provided under contract.[220]

[**7.78**]   Second, as in the context of any employment scenario, where an employer dismisses an employee that employer subjects themselves to the requirement and vagaries of the relevant provisions of employment law, and notably to the case law and principles surrounding unfair dismissal.[221] An illustration of the 'vagaries' of this process is provided by *Wise v Filbert Realisations*[222] which was an appeal by Dennis Wise to the Employment Appeal Tribunal (EAT) concerning his complaint of unfair dismissal by Leicester FC. The background to the appeal was that on a pre-season training tour of Finland, Wise was involved in an incident with a team mate, Callum Davidson, which resulted in Davidson sustaining a fractured cheekbone and facial swelling. Initially, Wise was fined two weeks' wages (£50,000) by the then manager of the club and sent home. The club then

---

[216] For the distinction between 'material breach' and 'repudiatory' breach in contract law see generally *Dalkia Utilities Services Plc v Cletech International Ltd* [2006] EWHC 63 (Comm).

[217] See, eg, CAS 2008/A/1644 *Mutu v Chelsea FC* discussed at [7.80] of this text.

[218] See, eg, the termination by Wigan of Marlon King's contract after he was jailed in 2009 for 18 months for assaulting a woman and the termination by West Brom of Lee Hughes's contract after he was given a six-year prison sentence for causing death by dangerous driving in 2004. See generally N Britten, 'Football Star Jailed for Drunken Crash that ended his Career and a Father's Life' *The Daily Telegraph* (London 10 August 2004) News 3 and C Smyth, 'Footballer with Violent History Jailed for Punching a Girl at a Club' *The Times* (London 30 October 2009) News 16. The issue of whether such players should be permitted to return to professional football (as Lee Hughes has) has sparked some debate. See A Campbell, 'Where will Players' Misdemeanours End? With Murder? *The Times* (Scotland edition 10 November 2009) Sport 81.

[219] See clause 9 and sch 1 of Form 13A for the disciplinary procedures surrounding breaches short of termination.

[220] Ibid.

[221] And thus, eg, to the application and requirements of s 98(4) of the Employment Rights Act 1998.

[222] *Wise v Filbert Realisations* [2004] UKEAT 0600 03 0902 (9 February 2004).

suspended Wise pending an investigation into the incident and a subsequent disciplinary hearing took place before the club chairman, which resulted in Wise being dismissed on 14 days' notice on the ground of gross misconduct. The nature of that initial hearing was problematical and it was uncontested that it was procedurally unfair in a number of respects (there seemed to be some suggestion that, given that the club had just been relegated from the Premiership and was in serious financial trouble, the chairman was more anxious than the procedures allowed in letting go a well paid, if troublesome, player). Wise subsequently exercised his right of appeal to a Football League Disciplinary Committee and to the Football League Appeal Committee. Ultimately, the EAT decided that, although Wise most likely committed an assault equivalent to the criminal office of occasioning actual bodily harm, and even though the subsequent two-step appeals process thoroughly reviewed the incident, the original hearing by the club chairman was so defective, and had infected all subsequent dealings with the incident to such an extent, that Wise's appeal should be allowed and a finding of unfair dismissal substituted.

[7.79]   The EAT's decision in the *Wise* case was a very rare instance of that tribunal hearing an elite-level, sports-related dispute. Given the maximum compensatory award for unfair dismissal is, as of February 2010, around £65,000; it is likely that an elite footballer (who could earn that amount in a week) would bring any unfair dismissal claim to the High Court. The costs, delay, adversarial nature and adverse publicity associated with the litigation process is yet another reason for employing clubs to avoid the 'nuclear' option of termination. In short, although it may be somewhat cynical in attitude, on a cost/benefit analysis a club may think it wiser to tolerate a level of on and off-field misconduct that otherwise might justify termination of contractual relations. For many, the most egregious example of this was Newcastle United's decision(s) not to sack Joey Barton (who at the time of writing was still employed on a lucrative contract by that club signed in June 2007, a month after Barton had attacked a team mate on the training pitch at Manchester City) despite being presented with a number of opportunities/excuses to do so including a custodial sentence for a conviction on assault and affray charges in 2008, arising out of an incident outside a Liverpool nightclub and, on his return to playing action, a dispute with the then manager Alan Shearer relating to a tackle made against Liverpool's Xabi Alonso in May 2009.[223] To be fair, a more positive perspective on the approach by Newcastle to Barton is that where a player's misconduct is related to alcohol, drugs, gambling or even anger management problems, it could be argued that under a general duty of care towards one of its employees, a club should support that player in seeking all relevant rehabilitative assistance rather than setting the player adrift.[224]

---

[223] See the interview with Barton by M Dickson, 'Ten Pints, Some Angry Words, a Huge Punch-up' *The Times* (London 10 October 2009) Sport 8.

[224] Note the work of the Sporting Chance Clinic established in 1996 by former England and Arsenal captain and self-confessed alcoholic, Tony Adams, www.sportingchanceclinic.com.

[7.80] In sum, club-instigated terminations are rare but not unknown. The most recent high profile example is the decision in 2004 by Chelsea to terminate Adrian Mutu's contract after he tested positive for cocaine, which led to an elongated series of arbitral proceedings in which Chelsea sought to recover compensation from Mutu for unjustified, unilateral breach of contract. In July 2009, CAS finally announced that an appeal by Mutu against a compensation claim of more than €17 million had been dismissed.[225] The Mutu award contains a number of points of interest relating to unilateral breach of contract 'without just or sporting cause' under FIFA regulations[226] and the manner in which the accompanying compensation might be calculated—in this case, the compensation was based on adding Mutu's unamortised transfer fee (Chelsea had paid Parma €22.5 million for the player in 2003) to the unamortised portion of Mutu's signing-on fee and agent's fees. Moreover, it must be noted that the CAS Panel's award may not be the final word on these proceedings and the case prompts a series of at least four overlapping questions, for example: how much can be made in Mutu's appeal to the Swiss Federal Courts against the CAS award (begun in October 2009) regarding the irrationality and disproportionality of sanction given that the bulk of the award against him is based on the value of his transfer from Parma to Chelsea, a transaction in which he had no input? There are questions as to the enforceability of the award against Mutu, and the jurisdiction of FIFA more generally, if Mutu, as he may have to, decides to declare himself bankrupt or retires? What is the impact of article 17(2) FIFA, which hold that that where a player terminates a contract without just cause and is thus required to pay compensation (as in Mutu's case) the player 'and his new club shall be jointly and severally liable' for its payment? And what will be the contractual repercussions for Mutu with regard to his current club Fiorentina in light of the announcement in January 2010 by the Italian Olympic Committee that the player had tested positive for a banned substance?[227]

[7.81] One final 'lesson' from the Mutu affair may be of interest and it is whether it might encourage other clubs to pursue similar claims against misbehaving players. As Evans observes, professional footballers as employees are not immune from the general principle of English contract of employment law which holds an employee potentially and personally liable in damages for their employer's loss flowing naturally and foreseeably from breach of the employment contract.[228] Although it remains rare for an employer to sue and pursue an employee in such circumstances

---

[225] CAS 2008/A/1644 *Mutu v Chelsea FC*.

[226] Discussed further at [7.82]–[7.100] of this text.

[227] On the art 17(2) FIFA point, even the definition of Mutu's 'new' club is in dispute because although Juventus were interested in the player, they were hindered by a quota set by the Italian football authorities on the signing of non-EU players. Juventus circumvented this quota by agreeing a deal with another Italian club, Livorno, who registered the player with them, and then transferred Mutu to Juventus. On the Muto saga generally see B Caldow, 'The Case of Adrian Mutu: The Final Chapter?' (2009) 16 (6) *Sports Law Administration & Practice* 1 and J de Preter, 'Mutu: Contract Breaches for Misconduct & Compensation' (2009) 7(9) *World Sports Law Report* 3.

[228] C Evans, 'United Kingdom: Not to be Sniffed at; Lessons from the Mutu Affair' *Mondaq Business Briefing* 15 March 2010, available at www.mondaq.com/article.asp?articleid=95568.

(given the effect it can have on employee relations and, more practically, the limited resources of most employees), where the employee is an expensively acquired, lucratively remunerated professional footballer, the context is very different. In that light, Chelsea's pursuit of Mutu might inspire other clubs to consider attempting to recover sums from employees who breach their contract in a material way, and in a warning to all well paid athletes, Evans concludes that the core repercussion of *Mutu* might well be that 'athletes found guilty of doping offences, and other serious indiscretions, may not only lose their employment and face a ban from their sport, but may also face a huge compensation claim from their former employers'.[229]

The 'Cause' of a Player's Premature Termination of Contract

[**7.82**]   Under clause 11 of Form 13A of the FAPL rules, a player is entitled to terminate his contract by 14 days' notice in writing to the club if the club can be shown to have been guilty of serious or persistent breaches of the terms and conditions of contract or has failed to pay any remuneration or other payments or bonuses or benefits due to the player as they fall due or within 14 days thereafter. The latter issue is likely to become more prominent where, as is increasingly the case, clubs at all levels of the professional code in England, struggle financially to avoid administration or worse. The issue of what constitutes a 'serious or persistent' breach of contract by a club towards a player will very much depend on the facts of the case and the specifics of the contract, though it must also be placed in its overall context. That context has two elements to it: one narrow and specific to players' interests; and one broader and applicable to many sports outside football.

Player-Led Causes of Termination

[**7.83**]   At it narrowest, a player's view of a material breach of contract by their employing club is, in reality, often motivated by a number of aggravating personal factors (seldom assuaged by their agent). These include: the unhappy player who is not, for instance, getting regular first team football; or the opportunistic player who after a good run of form with his club or a series of high profile international appearances feels that he is now undervalued by his club; or with due regard to the regulations prohibiting approaches to contracted players, the player who becomes aware that better offers await from other clubs.[230] In practical commercial terms and with respect to the relevant legal and regulatory framework in which player transactions occur in football, there are a number of ways in which the parties can mutually agree to deal with these problems: the unhappy player can be sent

---

[229] Ibid.

[230] The last point is discussed at [7.49]–[7.51] of this text. Note also that as per art 17(5) FIFA, any person such as the player's agent or an official or a player at another club who acts in a manner designed to induce a breach of contract between a player and their current club in order to facilitate the transfer of the player can be sanctioned in a financial and sports-specific manner pursuant to the terms of art 17 FIFA more generally.

out on loan to another club; contracts can be renegotiated to reflect the player's good form; or the parties may simply agree that at the next available window the player can transfer to another club and may, if he wishes, sign a pre-contract arrangement with another club of his choice. Moreover, clubs' and players' legal representatives are aware that, in terms of ordinary contract of employment law on personal services, where an employee seeks, on foot of a breakdown in the necessary level of fidelity that should exist between such parties, to move to another employer, attempting to maintain or enforce existing contractual relations, by way of injunctive relief, will likely be refused by the courts on the grounds that it would be futile to compel the parties to do so and, in any event, impossible to supervise.[231]

[**7.84**]   More broadly, the context surrounding a player seeking to bring a premature end to their contract in order to move to another club reveals issues that go to the very heart of the operation and administration of modern football namely: the tension that arises between players' demands for rights of employment mobility similar to those generally available to all paid workers in Europe (for example, the right to take up paid employment with another club at any time on serving due notice) as against the efforts of clubs and governing bodies to ensure that the specific sporting nature of the professional football industry is not undermined by contractual instability (for example, such that the specific seasonal, financial and league structure of football can be preserved). In legal terms, the epicentre of this tension can, of course, be located in the ECJ's decision in *Bosman*.[232] The concluding chapter explains that decision more fully not only with regard to the free movement of workers and the impact it has had on the transfer and registration of football players but also, and more broadly, by arguing that the aftershocks of *Bosman*, which continue to be felt to this day at all levels of European sport, are slowly forming the future landscape and boundaries of sports law. For now however, the key repercussion from *Bosman* is that, in consultation with the EU Commission and player representative bodies, it led to football's world governing authority FIFA, producing its Regulations on the Status and Transfer of Players. Part IV thereof (articles 13–18 FIFA) concerns the general regulatory guidelines on the termination of a professional player's contract of employment with a club.

FIFA-Mandated Causes of Termination

[**7.85**]   In establishing its position on the maintenance of contractual stability between professional players and clubs, article 13 FIFA sets out FIFA's absolutist, and somewhat utopian, *pacta sunt servanda* position: a contract between a professional and a club may only be terminated upon expiry of the term of the

---

[231] See the discussion at [7.36] of this text.
[232] Case C 415/93 *Union Royal Belge des Société de Football Association ASBL v Bosman* v [1995] ECR I-4921.

contract or by mutual agreement.[233] The remaining provisions on contractual stability are however more rooted in the commercial and contractual reality of the professional football industry and, although a contract cannot be unilaterally terminated during the course of a season (article 16 FIFA), a contract may be terminated by either party where there is 'just cause' (article 14 FIFA). Moreover, an established player who has, in the course of the season, appeared in fewer than 10 per cent of the official matches in which his club has been involved may terminate his contract prematurely on the ground of 'sporting just cause' in the 15 days following the last official match of the season of the club with which he is registered (article 15 FIFA). An article 14 FIFA termination is without consequences of any kind—either payment of compensation or imposition of sporting sanction. An article 15 FIFA termination, which is established on a case by case base with due reference to the player's individual circumstances, will not attract the imposition of sporting sanctions though compensation may be payable to the affected club.

[**7.86**]   At first instance, the basic framework surrounding these provisions, as informed by interpretations given by FIFA's DRC, appears quite straightforward.[234] In general terms, article 15 FIFA can be said to equate to the old common law and implied duty on an employer to provide work for a skilled employee or, more properly, not to unreasonably withhold work from the employee to the detriment of that employee's specialised skills.[235] Self-evidently this is not to say that player has a 'right to play' or a 'right to be selected' for the first team, more that if the player, and particularly a more experienced player whose career may be drawing to a close, is, in effect, surplus to requirements at a club (and is losing fitness and sharpness as a result of not playing at the highest level), that player may have sporting just cause to move on (and thus the opportunity to obtain one final lucrative transfer move). Accordingly, under some circumstances, it could be argued that article 15 FIFA covers a situation where the player argues that they have, to all intents and purposes, been constructively dismissed by their employer but rather than contest that 'dismissal' (and the word is used advisedly), the player seeks to settle the matter with his employing club through article 15 FIFA, and move on.

[**7.87**]   Although the criteria surrounding 'sporting just cause' are relatively vague and remain to be evaluated on a case by case basis, at least article 15 FIFA provides some reference points (for example, the less than 10 per cent game rule) as to when such a situation might arise. Article 14 FIFA is shorn of any guidance as to what the meaning and scope of the phrase 'just cause' might entail and thus the provision might be seen to be vulnerable to being used as a basis for

---

[233] Keep in mind that for players over the age of 18, art 18(2) FIFA mandates that the minimum length of a contract shall be from its effective date until the end of the season; while the maximum length of a contract shall be for five years. Moreover, as per art 18(5) FIFA a player can enter into only one playing contract for the same period. See generally CAS 2008/A/ *Bayal Sall and Saint Etienne v IK Start FC and FIFA*.

[234] See also the explanations and examples provided by the Commentary on the Regulations on the Status and Transfer of Players (n 16) 38–44.

[235] For an excellent review of the law on the right to work see *SG & R Valuations Services v Boudrais* [2008] EWHC 1340 (QB), [2008] IRLR 770 [18]–[26], Cranston J.

vexatious, disruptive challenges by opportunistic claimants. The more positive perspective, and the one favoured here, is that the phrase is necessarily and deliberately broadly drawn and, moreover, that its inherent ambiguity allows authorities to adopt a flexible and creative approach to individual cases and thus aids the principle of contractual stability. In this, a working definition of the phrase, as drawn from a series of CAS awards, might be that a 'just cause' equating to a valid reason for prematurely terminating a contract can based on a contention that the party (employee[236] or employer)[237] could not reasonably have been expected in the circumstances to have continued with the extant contract given that the necessary level of trust, confidence and fidelity between the contracting parties has been shown to have broken down irretrievably. The definition of just cause becomes important when considering the application of article 17 FIFA, which sets out the monetary and sports-specific consequences for players and clubs who, it is alleged, have terminated a contract *without* just cause.

[**7.88**]   There are three fundamental elements to article 17 FIFA. First, in all cases the party in breach without just cause must pay compensation.[238] Pursuant to article 17(1) FIFA, compensation in this regard is calculated with respect to a number of objective sports-specific criteria including: the remuneration and other benefits due to the player under the existing contract up to a maximum of five years; the fees and expenses paid or incurred by the former club (amortised over the term of the contract); and whether the contractual breach fell within the protected period.[239] The 'protected period' refers to a period of three entire

---

[236] From a player's point of view, the non-payment or late payment of remuneration by the employer does in principle—and particularly if repeated—constitute just cause. See CAS 2006/A/1180 *Galatasary SK v Ribéry and Olympique Marseilles* [26], where it was also noted that the amount paid late by the employer must not be 'insubstantial' or 'completely secondary' and, moreover, a prerequisite for terminating the contract for just cause on late payment is that the employee must have a given a warning to the employer to the effect that he has drawn the employer's attention to the fact that the club's conduct is not in accordance with the terms of the contract. See also CAS 2008/A/1568 *Mica & FC Wil 1900 v FIFA & Club PFC Naftex AC Bourgas* where the player claimed unsuccessfully that he had just cause to terminate his contract due to outstanding salary payments.

[237] From a club's point of view, where a player fails to provide his playing services at all or not in time for the beginning of the season or on prompt return from leave, this may justify a termination of contract for just cause. See CAS 2006/A/1141 *MP v FIFA & PFC Krilja* where a Brazilian player abused the rights given to him by his Russian club to return to Brazil on a regular basis to the extent that this 'unrestricted' right of leave justified the termination of contract. See also CAS 2008/A/1448 *Razek & Zamalek SC v PAOK FC & FIFA* where a player sought unsuccessfully to claim that he had just cause to terminate his contract with a Greek club due to having to undergo military service in Egypt, which prevented him from returning to Greece after holidaying at home.

[238] Generally CAS Panels do, however, recognise that, on pain of a reduction of the amount of compensation, the injured party (be it club or player) has some obligation to try and mitigate the damages they are suffering. So, for instance, a player has a duty to at least try to make reasonable efforts to seek other employment possibilities and a club has a duty to at least try to take reasonable measures to find a replacement player. See, in chronological order, CAS 2003/0/535 *Apoel FC v FIFA & Zahari Sirakov*; CAS 2003/0/540 *Karlen v China Chongqing Lifan FC*; CAS 2005/A/866 *FC Hapoel v Siston*; and CAS 2006/A/1062 *De Nghe FC v Etoga*.

[239] Art 17(1) FIFA and thus central to Chelsea FC's pursuit of compensation from Adrian Mutu, culminating in CAS 2008/A/1644 *Mutu v Chelsea FC*, and discussed at [7.80]–[7.81] of this text.

seasons or three years following the entry into force of a contract where such a contract in concluded prior to the player's 28th birthday or two years/seasons where such a contract is concluded after the player's 28th birthday. It must also be noted however that these calculations are subject to both the injured party bearing the burden of proof as to their assertions and, more technically, any training compensation provisions under article 20 FIFA; any express provisions in the contract; and the (labour) laws of the country concerned, usually the law of the country in which the club is located.[240] These technicalities aside, it has been established in CAS jurisprudence that the criteria contained in article 17(1) FIFA are not in the form of an exhaustive checklist and that the relevant arbitral authority has a considerable scope of discretion (short of course of an unreasoned, arbitrary and capricious award) in the application of the criteria. In this, the underlying principle is what common lawyers would recognise as *restitutio in integrum* (the injured party should as far as in practicable be returned to the original state they would have been in if no breach had occurred); and what the civilian law tradition sees as the principle of positive or expectation interest (where the objective is to determine an amount putting the injured party in the position they would have been in if the contract had been performed properly and without violation).[241]

[**7.89**]   Second, in addition to the obligation to pay compensation, sporting sanctions (amounting to a four-month suspension or six months in the case of aggravating circumstances) will be imposed, pursuant to the requirements of article 17(3) FIFA, on any player found to be in unilateral breach of contract without just cause or sporting just cause during the protected period. Outside the protected period, no sporting sanctions attach, though disciplinary measures may be imposed for failure to give due notice of termination within 15 days following the last match of the season. Third, and again in addition to any obligation to pay compensation, sporting sanctions (amounting to the club being banned from registering any new players, either nationally or internationally, for two consecutive transfer window periods) will be imposed, pursuant to the requirements of article 17(5) FIFA, on any club found to be in breach of contract or found to be inducing a breach of contract during the protected period.[242]

Webster v Matuzalem

[**7.90**]   Unsurprisingly, the manner in which the amount of compensation due is calculated pursuant to article 17(1) FIFA compensation has prompted most

---

[240] Otherwise and pursuant to art 60(2) FIFA Statutes, the 'default' jurisdiction is that of Switzerland. For an application of Swiss law in this regard see CAS 2005/A/902 & 903 *Mexes & AS Roma v Auxerre*. See also CAS 2005/A/893 *Metsu v Al-Ain Sports Club*.

[241] See generally, and chronologically, CAS 2006/A/1061 *Filho v Ittihad FC*; CAS 2006/A/110 *Eltaib v Gaziantepsport*; and CAS 2008/A/1453-1469 *Jaramillo & FSV Mainz 05 v CD Once Clada & FIFA*.

[242] Art 17(4) FIFA where it is also presumed that any club signing a player who has terminated his contract without just cause, has induced that player to commit a breach. This provision was central to the Gael Kakuta/Lens/Chelsea FC saga discussed at [7.48]–[7.50] of this text.

debate both at FIFA's DRC and CAS. The recent CAS award involving *FC Shakhtar Donetsk (Ukraine) v Matuzalem Fancelion da Silva (Brazil) and Real Zaragoza SAD (Spain) v FC Shakhtar Donetsk (Ukraine) & FIFA*[243] summarises most of the contentious issues in this regard and it also provides an good, concluding insight into the international transfer of modern elite footballer and the contractual machinations that can surround such transactions. In June 2004, the then 24-year-old Matuzalem (the player) signed an employment contract with Shakhtar Donetsk (the club). It was of a fixed term (and relatively standard) nature for five years, effective from 1 July 2004 until 1 July 2009. Under the terms of the agreement, the player could be transferred to another club only with the consent of the club and payment of compensation to the club (relative to all the associated costs of the transaction such as the cost of the player's rights and search for a substitute, etc). Where, however, a club received a transfer offer in amount of €25 million or above, the club agreed to release the player. On 2 July 2007 (on completion of the protected period) the player notified the club of the fact that he was unilaterally terminating their contractual relationship with immediate effect. On 19 July 2007, the player signed a new contract with Real Zaragoza and was then loaned to Lazio in Italy. In July 2007, the club reacted in three ways: it wrote to the player reminding him that he could transfer within the duration of his contract only with the prior agreement of the club and given that that was not forthcoming only on payment of the €25 million; it wrote to Real Zaragoza informing them that they were jointly and severally liable for the payment of the buyout pursuant to article 17(2) FIFA; and finally it initiated proceedings with the DRC.

[**7.91**]   The DRC held that the €25 million 'buy-out' clause should not to be interpreted as a penal or liquidated damages clause applicable in case of a breach of contract by the player.[244] Nevertheless, there was no doubt that given the unilateral and premature termination of the contract of employment by the player, the player had committed a breach of contract and was therefore liable to pay compensation to the club and, moreover, the DRC found, Real Zaragoza should be held jointly and severally responsible for the payment of such compensation. The DRC calculated the amount of compensation at €6.8 million as based on the remuneration-related, residual value of the player's employment contract with the club; the unamortised fees and expenses paid by the club for the acquisition of the player; and a certain amount of aggravated damages linked to the bad faith of the player who had accepted an increase in his financial entitlements shortly before leaving the club. The club were unhappy with the amount of compensation

---

[243] CAS 2008/A/1519-1520 *FC Shakhtar Donetsk (Ukraine) v Matuzalem Fancelion da Silva (Brazil) and Real Zaragoza SAD (Spain) v FC Shakhtar Donetsk (Ukraine) & FIFA*.

[244] It must be noted that the labour laws of some countries permit, and sometimes oblige, liquidated damages clauses in employment contracts, the rationale of which is to allow the parties to establish in advance and expressly in the contract the amount to be paid by either party in the event of unilateral, premature termination without just cause. See CAS 2007/A/1358 *FC Pyunik Yerevan v Lombe, AFC Rapid Burcharet & FIFA* and CAS 2007/A/1359 *FC Pyunik Yerevan v Edmima Bete, AFC Rapid Burcharet & FIFA*.

awarded by the DRC and appealed the decision to CAS inter alia on the grounds that the DRC did not properly or fully apply all the objective criteria contained in article 17(1) FIFA.

[**7.92**]   At CAS, and throughout the proceedings, it was uncontested by the player that he had unilaterally and prematurely terminated the contract without just cause or sporting just cause. However, relying on a previous CAS award—the so-called *Webster* award[245]—the player argued that once *outside* the protected period a player should be entitled to move to another club simply on the paying off of the residual value of their contract and that there is no economic, moral, regulatory or legal justification for a club to be able to claim the 'market value' of the player as a lost profit. In short, the player acknowledged that the termination of his contract before its expiry was contrary to FIFA regulations and he further acknowledged that he would have to compensate his club for his move to Zaragoa, but what he contested vehemently was the manner in which that compensation was calculated under article 17 FIFA. He argued, *qua Webster*, that the payable compensation should take into account the fact that he had moved after the protected period and thus damages should be limited to the residual, remuneration-related monies left on the (now dead) contract. In contrast, the club argued that the compensation should be based more generally on all the losses associated with the commercial value of the contract rather than its basic employment value and that this approach was consistent with the 'mischief' (unilateral termination or breach of contract without cause before expiry) which the regulations were intended and designed to deal with.[246]

[**7.93**]   Much to the dismay of player representative bodies such as FIFPro (in favour of a *Webster*-inspired enhanced employment mobility principle for its members) and much to the delight of FIFA (in favour of any reiteration of the need for respect for the contractual stability rationale of its regulations) the CAS Panel in *Matuzalem* found for Shakhtar Donetsk and ordered that they be paid nearly €12 million in compensation plus interest at 5 per cent pa from July 2007. A review of the *Matuzalem* award prompts four points of interest. Two of these points are specific to the award itself; and the remaining two are of wider significance. The first is that both *Webster* and *Matuzalem* must be distinguished a little to their facts in that both awards featured players who had admitted that they had unilaterally and prematurely breached their contract, albeit outside the protected period. For breaches within the protected period, the usual and strict interpretation of article 17 FIFA continues as determined by its role as a punitive measure for breaches of the core principle of contractual stability. A practical repercussion of this may well

---

[245]   CAS 2007/A/1298, 1299 & 1300 *Wigan Athletic FC v Heart of Midlothian; Heart of Midlothian v Webster & Wigan Athletic FC; and Webster v Heart of Midlothian.*

[246]   The essence of *Webster* was that Andy Webster, a Scotland international, terminated his contract unilaterally with Hearts for Wigan in May 2006, having spent three years of a four-year contract with the Edinburgh club. The Scottish club sought what they considered to be the player's market value at the time of his premature departure (about £4.6 million). CAS awarded compensation of about £150,000 equating to the residual remuneration value in the remaining one year of the contract.

be that the effective maximum length of contract given to modern footballers will from now on be aligned closely with the protected period and thus be either of a two- or three-year length as appropriate to the age of the player concerned.

[**7.94**]   The second point of note that can be gleaned from *Webster* and *Matuzalem* is that in both instances the player admitted liability and thus what was in contention was the amount of compensation payable to the affected club. The amount of compensation can lie anywhere on the spectrum between, on the one hand, an effective buy out by the player of the remainder of his contract; to, on the other hand, damages for the full commercial value loss of player including losses sustained in acquiring the player, the loss of chance to exploit the player's market-ability and even some aggravating damages for any bad 'sporting' faith shown by the player. At the moment, the DRC and CAS are tending towards the latter end of the spectrum to the point that the damages awarded by CAS to Shakhtar Donetsk were somewhat exemplary in nature. In this, however, the devil is very much in the detail in the sense that the amount of compensation remains dependant on the manner in which a CAS Panel applies, at its discretion, the various compensation criteria outlined in article 17 FIFA to the individual circumstances at hand. The *Matuzalem* Panel was extremely thorough in this regard and the heads of damages through which it addressed article 17 FIFA-related compensation looks set, rightly or wrongly, to provide a template for future awards.

[**7.95**]   The *Matuzalem* Panel assessed the calculation of the compensation owed to Shakhtar Donetsk (the employer-club) by the unjustified termination of contract by Matuzalem (the employee-player) under five headings: *the value of lost services* of Matuzalem for Shakhtar Donetsk, with the amount of salary expenses that the club did not have to pay the player being deducted;[247] *any fees and expenses paid by Shakhtar Donetsk in securing the player's services* such as unamortised transfer fee for the player, agents' fees relating to that transfer, or article 21 FIFA solidarity contributions relating to that transfer;[248] *any fees and expenses incurred by the former club in losing the player's services* including extra replacement costs, training compensation under article 20 FIFA or any additional claim such as one relating to the possible failure to fulfil an obligation towards a third party (a sponsor or event organiser) to whom the presence of the player was contractually warranted;[249] due consideration of the *law of the country concerned*;[250] and a *sporting bad faith*-related indemnity payment.[251]

[**7.96**]   In *Matuzalem*, the first and fifth criteria formed the bulk of the compensation, for which Real Zaragoza were jointly and severally liable; the other heads of damages being dismissed on their facts.[252] As regards the fifth factor,

[247] CAS 2008/A/1519-1520 *Matuzalem* [91]–[125].
[248] Ibid [126]–[132].
[249] Ibid [133]–[143] and [149]–[151].
[250] Ibid [144]–[148].
[251] Ibid [152]–[174].
[252] Ibid [175]–[190].

the bad faith shown by the player was evidenced, according to the CAS Panel, by the fact that the player left the club just a few weeks before the start of the qualification rounds of the UEFA Champions League, after the season in which he had been made captain of the club and a few months after he had accepted an enhancement of his contractual terms. Accordingly, an additional indemnity amounting to six months' salary paid by Shakhtar Donestk was set by the CAS Panel as aggravating damages in this regard. In its initial press release reaction to the award of 21 May 2009, FIFPro criticised the CAS Panel on this special indemnity for taking an overly subjective view of the article 17 FIFA criteria. On this particular issue (the subjectivity or objectivity of the *Matuzalem* Panel's approach to sporting bad faith) the matter is debatable either way; of greater importance is FIFPro's questioning of the manner of calculation under the first head of damages, that is, the value of the loss of services.

[**7.97**]   FIFPro, unsurprisingly, have the narrow 'Websterian' view of football contracts namely that such labour contracts are worth no more that what the parties agreed upon—the salary that a player receives for his efforts to play football to the best of his ability. It follows that where outside the protected period and on due notice a player unilaterally and prematurely breaches his contract, the affected club should at best be compensated for the remuneration-related amount left on that contract and no more. The wider 'Matzualemian' approach is that the value of the services of a player is only partially reflected in the remuneration due to him, since such a club would also have had to make certain expenditures to obtain such services.[253] This is not of itself a contentious perspective (or at odds with *Webster)* but what is problematical is the *Matuzalem* Panel's view that in order to calculate the full amount of the value of the services lost one cannot simply take into consideration the amount of outstanding remuneration but also what a club would—under normal circumstances—have to spend on the transfer market to contract the services of the player in question.[254]

[**7.98**]   In this the *Matuzalem* Panel reiterated that it was only acknowledging the 'economic reality' of world football namely that 'services provided by a player are traded and sought after on the market and are—according to article 17FIFA—worthy of legal protection'.[255] In order to justify this head of damage the *Matuzalem* Panel went to state that there must be a necessary logical nexus between the player's breach or the unjustified termination of contract and the lost opportunity to realise a certain transfer fee-related profit by the club. In the stated circumstances, the Panel held that such a nexus existed and that the best guide to the value of the loss of services could be based on the loan transfer fee for Matuzalem between Real Zaragoza and Lazio, plus the average annual salary paid by the two clubs as capitalised on the remaining two years of the original contract, which came to a little over €11.2 million. The criticism made by FIFPro and

---

[253] Ibid [102].
[254] Ibid.
[255] Ibid [103].

others, to which there is some merit, is twofold. First, it asks whether a loss of chance claim by the former club for the lost opportunity to achieve a transfer fee can in the first place be considered as a recognised head of damages.[256] Second, and crucially, a core criticism of the *Matuzalem* Panel is that the manner in which that lost chance was realised in damages (by application of and reference to a transfer fee) appears to be irreconcilable with the thrust of the ECJ's decision in *Bosman* and may in fact be an attempt to row back on that judgment, the principles of which FIFA and the EU Commission agreed in 2000 would be fundamental to any future regulations on the status and transfer of players. The latter point, which is alluded to in a wider *Bosman*-related context in the concluding chapter of this text, is an interesting one, and one that is, in a specific sense, likely to need addressing by CAS in the near future.[257]

[**7.99**]   The third and fourth points to be taken from *Webster* and *Matuzalem* are of a broader concern. The disparity between the awards illustrates a criticism made earlier in this text relating to the arbitrariness and unpredictability of CAS awards and CAS Panels.[258] A careful analysis of these two awards demonstrates that that criticism may be a little harsh in the sense that article 17 FIFA must be seen to be both equitable in nature and allowing for a certain organic flexibility to reflect the individual sporting and economic circumstances of a player. Sometimes, infusing a legal provision with 'certainty' can result in a process that crystallises into interpretative rigidity, thus rendering that provision ineffective. Moreover, as it is said in succession law that 'no will has a twin', equally no two professional footballers' contracts are exactly the same in individual detail and thus where such contracts are breached prematurely the best that a CAS Panel can do is to assess individualised nature of the arrangements at hand at the time of breach and with reference to the guidance provided by article 17 FIFA. Accordingly, some disparity both of outcome and emphasis will continue to be inevitable in such awards.

[**7.100**]   Finally, the *Matuzalem* scenario is of interest because to a large part it was acknowledged that the player's motivation for moving was driven more for personal reasons than economic gain. The player's wife had not settled in Ukraine and the player's contract with Real Zaragoza was, initially at least, broadly similar to what he had been paid by his previous club. Whether that motivation is credible or not, the general point is that where the very fabric or fidelity of the relationship in a contract of employment for personal services has, for whatever reason, been torn, there is rarely any point in trying to compel the parties to repair it. As stated earlier, in many instances, clubs accept this reality and facilitate a transfer;

---

[256] Ibid [117] where the Panel acknowledged that the merits of this loss of chance approach is 'debateable'.

[257] At the time of writing CAS was still considering a case involving the Egyptian international goalkeeper Essam El-Hadray who prematurely breached a playing contract with the Egyptian club Al-Ahly in order to sign for the Swiss club FC Sion.

[258] See [3.19]–[3.22] of this text.

in others, the matter is brought to a tribunal and even to CAS. Arguably, the core lesson to be learnt from *Webster* and *Matuzalem* is that short of any arbitral and adversarial means of resolving a labour dispute more use should be made of independent mediation and conciliation-based dispute resolution services. Although CAS has a general mediation service (of which, it is argued, parties should make more use), it is also submitted that in a football-specific context, FIFA (or bodies such as UEFA or even individual football associations) should consider, in conjunction with tribunals such as the DRC, the establishment of specialised labour mediation panels, towards which such contentious disputes could be directed and in which the principled objective of contractual stability could be protected in a proportionate and consistent manner.

Conclusion

[**7.101**]   At its simplest this chapter concerns the application of the ordinary law of contract of employment (for personal services) to a scenario where a player enters into an agreement with a club whereby that (player) employee agrees to play football in receipt of regular remuneration from that (club) employer. The application of this part of ordinary contract law to professional football throws up a number of matters unique to the industry at hand. A better understanding of these matters, and the disputes that surround them, can often be located in the fact that, although at the elite level professional footballers are paid handsomely, it should also be borne in mind they have chosen an abridged, precarious and at times unpredictable career path. In addition, it should not be forgotten, and a significant point of note arising from this chapter, that few players reach the elite level and thus in their desperate desire to do so many young players in particular may need to be protected from certain elements within the football industry, seeking to exploit their vulnerability by way of oppressive, unconscionable contractual arrangements.

[**7.102**]   By the time players establish themselves at the elite level, it is likely that their relationship with their employing club will be just one strand in a complex web of contractual agreements involving agents, advisors, sponsors and, indirectly, the administrative demands of national, regional and international federations. As such, this chapter has attempted to illustrate that that web comprises not just of the various obligations of their contract of employment but that it also: incorporates league and FIFA-mandated regulations including exhaustive grievance and disciplinary procedures extending ultimately to CAS; is informed and supplemented by relevant domestic and EU employment law; and thus is subject to the jurisdiction of national tribunals, courts and the ECJ.

[**7.103**]   In essence then, this chapter has attempted to portray the various legal and arbitral dramas that can be played out within the dry, technical clauses of a professional footballer's contract of employment. The next and concluding chapter of this text reveals that all of these contract-related, micro-dramas are in fact taking place again the backcloth of a legal drama that at a macro level is of much greater import to football and indeed to many other sports. That drama, which revolves around the tension between player-led demands for greater employment mobility on the one hand; and a football officialdom-led desire to protect contractual stability on the other, is of itself part of a larger canvas still, upon which the future of sports law in Europe is currently and incrementally being sketched. In sum, the signpost upon which the direction of this chapter, and indeed of this text as a whole, has been heading contains one word—*Bosman*.

Further Points of Interest and Discussion

1. The football authorities in England and elsewhere have overreacted to the potential threat posed by the third party ownership of players' economic interests. Discuss.
2. FIFA's recent announcement that it is, in effect, to abandon its efforts to regulate the activities of agents is defeatist in nature and will lead to the further exploitation of young players in particular. Discuss.
3. Footballers are role models and thus where a footballer has had his playing contract terminated for behaviour that has led to a criminal conviction attracting a custodial sentence, that player should never again be contracted to played football on a professional basis. Discuss.
4. FIFA's regulatory scheme on the payment of training compensation and its so-called solidarity mechanism is both overly complex in nature and possibly an unjustified restriction of the free movement of workers within and throughout the EU. Discuss.
5. FIFA's regulatory scheme on the termination of a contract with just cause lacks certainty and this has led both to an inconsistency in its interpretation at CAS and an overall undermining of the principle of contractual stability in professional football.

8

Conclusion: Brussels or Boston? The Future of Sports Law

Introduction

[**8.01**] This chapter has two inter-linked ambitions: to present a brief legal history of the EU's relationship with sport and through that account to try and signpost the future direction of sports law.[1] In realising these ambitions, and in a manner similar to the previous chapter, the central focus is on professional football, though by the end it is hoped that it will be evident that law-related developments within that industry have had a significant legal impact on and import for all sports. The chapter is presented in three parts further reflecting the national, European and international aspects of the 'story' of modern sports law in the UK.[2] As a prologue to that story, it is necessary to pick up on a point flagged by the previous chapter, which is that when it comes to assessing the contractual relations between a professional footballer and a club, that relationship needs to be located in its wider context namely how disputes relating to the contract are often manifestations of the tensions that exist industry-wide between the

---

[1] Please note that the references made to Community law and the Treaty provisions have been updated to reflect the state of European integration following the entry into effect of the Treaty of Lisbon amending the Treaty on European Union and the Treaty establishing the European Community, [2007] OJ C306/1, 1. In short, individual provisions are referred to by way of the Treaty on the Functioning of the European Union (TFEU); the word 'Union' is preferred over 'Community'; and the term 'EU or Union law' is preferred to 'EC or Community law'.

[2] This chapter has benefitted hugely from the following works: R Blanpain, *The Legal Status of Sportsmen and Sportswomen under International, European and Belgian National and Regional Law* (The Hague Kluwer Law International, 2003); R Blanpain and R Inston, *The Bosman Case: The End of the Transfer System?* (London, Sweet & Maxwell, 1996); R Blanpain, M Colucci, F Hendrickx (eds), *The Future of Sports Law in the European Union* (London, Kluwer, 2008); S Van den Bogaert, *Practical Regulation of the Mobility of Sportsmen in the EU Post Bosman* (The Hague, Kluwer Law International, 2005); B Bogusz, A Cygan and E Szyszczak (eds), *The Regulation of Sport in the European Union* (London, Edward Elgar, 2007); A Caiger and S Gardiner (eds), *Professional Sport in the EU: Regulation and Re-regulation* (The Hague, TMC Asser, 2005); S Gardiner, R Parrish and R Siekmann (eds), *EU, Sport, Law and Policy: Regulation, Re-regulation and Representation* (The Hague, TMC Asser, 2009); R Parrish, *Sports Law and Policy in the European Union* (Manchester, Manchester University Press, 2003); R Parrish and S Miettinen, *The Sporting Exception in European Union Law* (The Hague, TMC Asser, 2008); R Siekmann and J Soek, *The European Union and Sport: Legal and Policy Developments* (The Hague, TMC Asser, 2005); and W Tokarski *et al*, *Two Players—One Goal? Sport in the European Union* (Oxford, Meyer & Meyer, 2004) Especial insight has been gleaned from the work of Professor Stephen Weatherill as collated in *European Sports Law: Collected Papers* (The Hague, TMC Asser Press, 2007).

competing principles of contractual stability (as promoted by football officialdom and 'selling' clubs) and employment mobility (as promoted by individual players and 'buying' clubs'). As noted in the previous chapter, the catalyst for any heightened tension between these principles is usually the desire of a player to transfer to another club against the wishes of the employing club. In pursuing their objectives, elite professional footballers in England traditionally resorted to resolutely common law doctrines such as restraint of trade, while clubs and the football authorities opposed such actions by asserting the reasonableness of their existing player transfer and registration regimes, as predicated on arguments made for the greater good and future stability of the game of football. While a number of individual players had some success in this regard (and the legal success of George Eastham in the 1960s has already been recounted);[3] in actuality the fundamentally restrictive nature of the player transfer system in English football, and throughout Europe, remained largely intact for another three decades.[4] In other words, the dial on the spectrum between contractual stability or rigidity at one end and employment mobility on the other, remained firmly point towards the former. In the mid-1990s, radical change occurred. It came from an unlikely source: the contract-related frustrations of a Belgian footballer called Jean-Marc Bosman,[5] and it follows that the core of this chapter is the contention that throughout the web of 'EU Sports Law' (such as it exists) *Bosman* is the one 'golden thread' that is always seen. The case is therefore, and unsurprisingly, central to the threefold nature of the layout and substance of this chapter: how *Bosman* exposed sport to a legal glare that it had hitherto largely evaded ('addressing the past'); how *Bosman* continues to play a seminal role in determining current sports law policy in the EU ('directing the present'); and how prospectively it is moulding our understanding and use of law in sport ('shaping the future').[6]

Bosman: Addressing the Past

[**8.02**]   The first part of this chapter briefly reviews the European Court of Justice's (ECJ's) judgment in *Bosman*, and outlines its principal repercussions

---

³ *Eastham v Newcastle United FC Ltd & Ors* [1964] Ch 413. See generally [2.56]–[2.61] of this text. For a more recent non-football related example of the application of restraint of trade see *Leeds Rugby Team v Harris* [2005] EWHC 1591 (QB).

⁴ The most well-worn path across the landscape of sports law in the UK is, arguably, that which traces the various legal challenges to the old 'retain and transfer' system of player registration in football. That path, which includes cases such as *Radford v Campbell* (1890) 6 TLR 488; *Kingaby v Aston Villa FC, The Times* 27 and 28 March 1912; and *Eastham* [1964] Ch 413 is best trod in the company of D McArdle, *From Boot Money to Bosman: Football, Society and the Law* (London, Cavendish, 2000) ch 2.

⁵ Case C 415/93 *Union Royal Belge des Société de Football Association ASBL v Bosman* [1995] ECR I-4921.

⁶ See similarly the review of *Bosman* in Part XII of M Poiares Maduro *et al*, *The Past and Future of EU Law: The Classics of EU Law Revisited on the 50th Anniversary of the Rome Treaty* (Oxford, Hart Publishing, 2010).

for professional football in Europe, which, a decade and a half later, can be seen to have been at least threefold in nature. First and in a regulatory sense, *Bosman* led to greater dialogue between the EU Commission and the various football (UEFA/FIFA) authorities, as manifested in FIFA's Regulations on the Status and Transfer of Players.[7] Second and in a strictly legal sense, the case inspired more thorough analysis of possible sports-related applications of various internal market freedoms to sport notably Articles 45–48 TFEU (free movement of workers) and Articles 56–62 TFEU (free movement of services). With regard to the former, note must also be made of the related issues of the prohibition in Article 18 TFEU of any discrimination on the grounds of nationality. The third repercussion is that aspects of the Advocate General's opinion in *Bosman* effectively acted as the catalyst for the greater application of Articles 101 and 102 TFEU (competition law) to sports-related economic activities and that since then the rapier-like thrust of antitrust investigation into sporting activity has had the most profound effect not just on the legal and administrative autonomy of sport but increasingly on what is called the 'specificity' of sport.

Bosman: Legal Background

[**8.03**] On 12 December 1974, the ECJ published its ruling in *Walrave and Koch v Association Union Cycliste Internationale* (UCI)[8] where it had been asked by a court in the Netherlands whether a provision in the rules of the UCI relating to medium distance world cycling championships behind pacemaker-motorcycles, according to which the pacemaker had to be of the same nationality as the cyclist, was incompatible with the fundamental freedoms on movement of workers and the provision of services. The action was brought against the UCI and the Dutch and Spanish cycling federations by two Dutch nationals who normally took part as pacemakers in such races. Aspects of the ECJ's reply to the preliminary reference continue to appear in sports-related litigation before the ECJ, most notably the Court's view that 'having regard to the objectives of the [Union], the practice of sports is subject to [EU] law only in so far as it constitutes an economic activity within the meaning of [Article 3 TFEU] and when such activity has the character of gainful employment or remunerated service it comes more particularly with the scope ... of [Articles 45–48 or 56–62 TFEU]'.[9]

[**8.04**] *Walrave and Koch* also marks the beginning of the ECJ's view that for free movement of athletes to have any real effect, two principles must be respected: there must be no regulatory obstacles to free movement of workers, pursuant to Article 45 TFEU, and there must be no discrimination on grounds

---

[7] The multi-faceted impact of this document on player contracts in football was alluded to throughout ch 7 of this text.

[8] Case 36/74 *Walrave and Koch v Association Union Cycliste Internationale* [1974] ECR 1405.

[9] Ibid [4] and [5].

of nationality in the performance of such sports activities, pursuant to Article 45(2) TFEU.[10] The ECJ further clarified the prohibition of discrimination point in three ways. First, it held that the geographical application of the provision is binding on all legal relationships entered into or having taken effect in the territory of the Union.[11] Second, it held that the prohibition of discrimination on the basis of nationality should not be restricted to acts of public authorities because if so constrained the application of the non-discrimination principle could be compromised and undermined, to the detriment of access to gainful employment throughout the Union, by collective decisions or rules adopted by private parties such as sports bodies.[12] Third, the ECJ in *Walrave and Koch* held that a limited and proportionate restriction to the prohibition on discrimination, and thus an exception to the principle of free movement, would be recognised in matters such as 'the composition of sports teams, in particular national teams, the formation of which is a question of purely sporting interest and as such has nothing to do with economic activity'.[13]

[**8.05**]   The ECJ built upon the above in *Donà v Mantero*.[14] In that case, a preliminary reference was made to the ECJ requesting clarification as to the compatibility of free movement rules with regard to a rule of the Italian Football Federation under which only players who were affiliated to that Federation could take part in matches as professionals or semi-professionals wherein 'affiliation' in that capacity was in principle and actuality open only to players of Italian nationality. In the stated case, the ECJ reiterated its view that regulations based on nationality which limited the mobility of athletes could not be held to be in conformity with the principle of free movement of workers and thus prima facie the Italian regulations were incompatible with said principle.[15] Nevertheless, the ECJ also reiterated and recognised that an exception to the principle would be recognised if such regulations were for (limited and proportionate) reasons of a non-economic nature.[16] Consequently, the adoption of rules excluding foreign players from participating in certain matches for reasons which relate to the particular nature and context of such matches (for example, matches between national teams of different countries) and are thus of sporting interest only, would not be prohibited.[17]

[**8.06**]   As a result of the *Donà v Mantero*, UEFA, in consultation with the Commission, agreed both to abolish the restrictions on the number of foreign

---

[10] And in line with the general prohibition of discrimination on the grounds on nationality laid down in Art 18 TFEU.

[11] Ibid [28].

[12] Ibid [17] and [18].

[13] Ibid [8] and [9]. See also [10] where the ECJ held it would then be a matter for the national court to determine the nature of the activity in question and thus in the context of the stated case it was for the national court to determine whether in the sport in question the pacemaker and the cyclist constituted a team.

[14] Case 13/76 *Donà v Mantero* [1976] ECR 133.

[15] Ibid [11].

[16] Ibid [14].

[17] Ibid [19].

players that a club could have under contract, insofar as they are nationals of member states; and to fix at two the number of such players who were allowed to take part in a match, with the restriction not applying to players who had been resident for five years in the territory of the relevant association. After further discussion with the Commission—which in some ways were the first example of what is now called 'structured or social dialogue' between the Commission on football's key stakeholders—UEFA adopted the so-called '3+2' rule, under which from 1 July 1992 the number of foreign players whose name could be included on a team sheet could be to no less than three per team, plus two 'assimilated' players who had played in that country for five years without interruption. The rule applied to club matches organised by UEFA itself (the European Cup, UEFA Cup and Cup Winners' Cup) and as a minimum applied to member states' first division leagues, though it was open, as in England (where players from Wales, Scotland and both parts of Ireland were not held as foreign despite being from different football associations) to allow more foreign players. The 3+2 rules would, of course, later form part of the *Bosman* proceedings.[18]

Bosman: The Ruling

[**8.07**] Keeping in mind the above legal background,[19] the abridged synopsis of the *Bosman* ruling might read as follows: in *Bosman* the ECJ reiterated that, having regard to the objectives of the Union, sport is subject to EU law (and notably the fundamental freedoms facilitating the creation of an internal market) only insofar as it constitutes an economic activity within the meaning of the objectives of the Union found in Article 3 TFEU and that the activities of professional or semi-professional footballers, where they are in gainful employment or provide a remunerated service, are of the necessary 'economic' nature.[20] With specific regard to the free movement of worker-athletes, the ECJ in *Bosman* applied the two-step approach of *Walrave and Koch* and *Donà v Mantero* and held that

---

[18] Case C 415/93 *Bosman* [1995] ECR I-4921 [38]–[39], Opinion of Advocate General Lenz. See also [25]–[27] of the ECJ's decision in *Bosman*.

[19] Note also, the somewhat forgotten, Case 222/86 *UNECTEF v Heylens* [1987] ECR 4097. In that case, the defendant was a Belgian national and the holder of a Belgian football trainer's diploma. He was engaged by Lille Olympic as the club's professional football trainer. An application to the French sports authorities for recognition of the equivalence of his Belgian diploma was rejected. Heylens continued to serve as Lille's coach but was then pursued for violation of both French sports law and the French criminal code with regard to wrongful assumption of title. A criminal court in Lille had doubts about the compatibility of the French legislation with the rules of the free movement of workers including a concern that at a key point in the internal sports proceedings the defendant had not been furnished with reasons for the refusal to recognise his qualification. The French court asked for clarification from the ECJ. The Court replied that where in a member state access to an professional occupation is dependent upon the possession of a national diploma or foreign equivalent, the principle of free movement of workers entitles that person to effective judicial review of any decision to refuse recognition of his qualification and through which both the legality of the decision under community law can be reviewed and, for the person concerned, to ascertain the reasons for the decision.

[20] Case C 415/93 *Bosman* [1995] ECR I-4921 [73].

for that freedom to have any real legal effect, two principles had to be respected: there must be no regulatory obstacles to free movement (such as restrictions on the free movement or transfer of footballers after the expiry of contract)[21] and there must be no discrimination on grounds of nationality in the performance of such sports activities (such as nationality quotas in sports clubs).[22] The *Bosman* Court also reiterated, as it had done in *Walrave and Koch* and *Donà v Mantero*, that a (limited and proportionate) exception to the principle of free movement of athletes for non-economic reasons could be recognised, and particularly where the factual matter at hand concerned a sports federation's right to select national athletes for national competitions.[23] This summary does not, by definition, tell the full story of *Bosman* and two to three further points need to be made briefly: the factual background to the case and how it provided the basis of *Bosman*'s claim; and the reasoning used by the ECJ in upholding his claim; and crucially how the ECJ dismissed the justifications raised by the football authorities in defence of European football's then transfer and regulatory scheme, as informed by Advocate General Lenz's influential opinion. Thereafter, a review of some of the case law that followed in the immediate impact of *Bosman* is carried out, including how the legal repercussions of the case eventually manifested themselves in terms of the material changes in the regulation of football worldwide.

The Basis of Bosman's Claim

[**8.08**]   The facts of Bosman are probably best understood with reference to what would usually occur in a 'normal' industry where a worker is employed on a fixed term contract, that is, on expiry of the contract, the worker generally becomes a free agent and is entitled to move without burden to another employer if they so desire or remain with the current employer by way of a renewal option or as a matter of choice. The transfer rules in operation in football in the 1990s were far from 'normal' however;[24] free agency on expiry of contract was not permitted and the rules in place revolved around a transfer system which demanded that in the event of a change in club by a player whose contract had expired, a transfer fee had to paid and until the fee was paid the player's registration certificate could be withheld and thus the transfer would not have the necessary clearance. The free movement of a player was further hampered by the fact that clubs operating in the transfer market also had to take into account that system's football-specific nationality quotas, namely the 3+2 rule.

---

[21] Ibid [92]–[114].

[22] Ibid [115]–[137].

[23] Ibid [76]. See also [82] and [83] where the ECJ in *Bosman* yet again dismissed any claim that the principles of free movement applied only to the actions of public authorities.

[24] The then transfer rules in place in Belgium, in a number of other EU jurisdictions and under UEFA/FIFA were exhaustively reviewed in Opinion of Advocate General Lenz, Case C 415/93 *Bosman* [1995] ECR I-4921 [6]-[41]. See also [3]–[24] of the ECJ's decision.

[**8.09**]   All of these matters came to a head in the summer of 1990 when Belgian national Jean-Marc Bosman sought, on expiry of his contract with a Belgian club, to transfer to the French club US Dunkerque. Owing to doubts as to the latter club's ability to pay, the player's registration certificate was withheld by the Belgian football authorities. Given the workings of the system, this meant that Bosman's extant playing status, future career and general earning capacity was dependent on the whim and mercy of RC Liège. Although Bosman managed, through various interim orders secured in the Belgian courts, to obtain both maintenance from the club and the freedom to make himself available to potential suitors, it became clear that his search for a new employer would be a fruitless one because, it seems, on foot of his challenge to the transfer system, all the major stakeholders in European football had ensured informally that all dealings with the player were to be boycotted.[25] In reaction to that boycott, Bosman stepped up his legal challenge to the validity of the transfer system and rules on foreign player then in place in European football eventually prompting a Belgian court to seek preliminary reference from the ECJ as to the compatibility of such rules and accompanying nationality quotas with the Union's free movement and competition law provisions.

UEFA's Defence and the ECJ's Decision

[**8.10**]   As the Advocate General in *Bosman* stated pithily, 'The importance of the present case is obvious. The answer to the question of the compatibility with [Union] law of the transfer system and rules on foreign players will have decisive influence on the future professional football in the [Union] … and be of interest to a large number of citizens in the [Union] who are football enthusiasts'.[26] How right he was and looking back it is not surprising that the football authorities (as led by UEFA) defended their position stoutly. In fact, prior to addressing the two substantive matters of concern, the ECJ had to deal with and overcome two preliminary matters of concern including the jurisdiction of the court to give a preliminary ruling on the questions submitted (dismissed on the ground that the questions submitted by the Belgian court met the necessarily 'objective need' for the purpose of settling disputes properly brought before it);[27] and arguments that the free movement principle (now contained in Article 45 TFEU) was not applicable at all to the case at hand. The latter preliminary argument was threefold in nature.

The Applicability of the Fundamental Freedom of Movement

[**8.11**]   The Belgian football authorities argued, rather quaintly, that only the major European clubs should be regarded as 'undertakings' whereas clubs such as RC Liège carried on an 'economic activity' only to a 'negligible extent' and

---

25 Ibid Opinion of Advocate General Lenz [47].
26 Ibid [56] and [62].
27 Case C 415/93 *Bosman* [1995] ECR I-4921 [55]–[67].

that, in any event, the transfer rules in question did not concern the *employment* relationships between players and clubs but the *business* relationships between clubs and the consequences of freedom to affiliate to a sporting federation and thus the free movement principle was not applicable to the case at hand.[28] The ECJ dismissed this contention by observing that it was not necessary, for the purpose of the application of the free movement provision, for the employer to be an undertaking; all that was (and is) required is the existence of, or the intention to create, an employment relationship and, in any event, given that employing clubs were obliged to pay fees on recruiting a player from another club, this meant that an employment relationship was created in the sense that a player's opportunity of finding employment (and the terms under which such employment might be offered) was affected directly and materially by this requirement.[29]

[**8.12**]   Second, UEFA argued that the case at hand presented difficulties in distinguishing between the economic and sporting aspect of football and while they acknowledged reluctantly that the former was amenable to EU law review; any investigation of the latter, it claimed, would severely impact on the 'autonomy' of sport. In fact, UEFA contended a decision in favour of Bosman would call into question 'the organisation of football as a whole'.[30] In this, UEFA pleaded, in one of the first manifestations of what is now called the 'specificity of sport' approach, that in the event of the application of free movement principles to professional footballers, 'a degree of flexibility would be essential because of the particular nature of the sport'.[31] UEFA's position was supported by a submission from the German government, which stressed that 'in most cases a sport such as football is not an economic activity' and that some legal analogy could be made to sport's advantage by way of [Article 167 TFEU's] respect for the national and regional diversity of the 'cultures' of the member states.[32]

[**8.13**]   The first part of the German government's submission is a reminder of the response of the celebrated American sportswriter, Jim Murray, when asked, in the context of the sport's enduring antitrust exemption, whether baseball was a business: 'If it isn't, General Motors is a sport.' The German government's submission on the need to respect the cultural diversity of sport was also given short shrift by the ECJ who pointed to the fact that the limited competence under Article 167 TFEU was trumped by the fundamental freedom at issue and which, the ECJ noted, somewhat testily, was what the national court had sought clarity upon. More importantly, the ECJ recognised expressly that the temporal effect of its judgment would have significant consequences for football and that such repercussions had to be 'weighed carefully'; nevertheless, they could not 'go so far

---

[28] Ibid [70].
[29] Ibid [75].
[30] Ibid [71].
[31] Ibid.
[32] Ibid [72].

as to diminish the objective character of the law and compromise' and the ECJ's applications of the law to the facts at hand. In any event, the ECJ reminded the parties that, consistent with *Walrave and Koch* and *Donà v Mantero*, sports rules and practices that could be justified on non-economic grounds did not come within the scope of the provisions at issue provided that such rules were limited in objective and proportionate in outcome.[33]

[**8.14**]   Third, the strongest part of the German government's submission in *Bosman* appeared to be its deduction that by virtue of both the freedom of association enjoyed by sports federations under national law and enshrined in Article 11 ECHR, and the principle of subsidiarity, intervention by public and EU authorities in the area of sport should be confined to what was strictly necessary.[34] The ECJ acknowledged both inter-related points but concluded that if a sports body's rules referred to by a national court result in a restriction of the free movement of professional athletes, they cannot be seen as necessary to ensure the enjoyment of that freedom of association, nor can they be seen as an inevitable result thereof.[35] Overall then, the ECJ confirmed in *Bosman* that private sports associations cannot restrict rights conferred on individuals by EU law, and neither the freedom of association nor the subsidiarity principle can be invoked or balanced against fundamental freedoms to uphold such rules. In sum, the ECJ rejected the various 'preliminary' objections to the very application of the free movement principle to the activities of professional athletes[36] and in a final reiteration before addressing the substantive issues, reminded the parties that the principle extended to actions of both public and private associations where such actions sought to regulated gainful employment of workers in a collective manner.[37]

Transfer Rules, Obstacle to the Free Movement of Workers

[**8.15**]   The first substantive point of contention on the regulation by the Belgian football authorities and UEFA/FIFA of the gainful employment environment of professional footballers, related to the compatibility of the transfer system (rules

---

[33] See also [88]–[91] of the ECJ's decision in *Bosman* where UEFA were also unsuccessful in their argument that the dispute at hand was one which was 'wholly internal' to a member state and thus fell outside the ambit of the free movement principle. UEFA's contention was that the dispute concerned a Belgian player whose transfer fell through because of the conduct of a Belgian club and a Belgian sports federation. The ECJ rejected this argument on the ground that Bosman had clearly entered into a contract of employment with an undertaking in another member state and had further sought to accept that offer of gainful employment in that state and thus within the meaning of the free movement provisions, the proceedings could not be classified as purely internal.

[34] Ibid [72].

[35] Ibid [79]–[80].

[36] See also [126]–[131] of the Opinion of Advocate General Lenz who found that none of the arguments on the inapplicability of the free movement principle were 'convincing'.

[37] Ibid [82]–[97] where the ECJ further reiterated that any public/private divide would lead to a risk of creating inequality in the application of free movement of workers in the EU, and that such a risk was aggravated in the case of professional footballers given that the source and application of transfer rules differed across the EU.

and fees) with the EU's free movement principle.[38] The fundamental matter at
issue was Bosman's claim that football's transfer rules constituted an obstacle to
the fundamental freedom of movement given that they precluded and deterred
him (a national of an EU member state) from leaving his country of origin in
order to exercise his right to free movement to enter the territory of another
member state and reside there in order to pursue an economic activity, and that
this was the case even if such rules applied without regard to his nationality.[39]
The ECJ agreed with Bosman concluding that the transfer rules were an obstacle
to the freedom of movement because, even after the expiry of a player's contract
of employment with a club, a professional footballer could not pursue his professional activity with another club established in another member state unless and
until a transfer fee agreed between both clubs, or otherwise determined in accordance with the regulation of the applicable sports body's rules, had been paid to
the player's former club.[40] It must be noted, however, that the battle on whether
football's transfers rules were prima facie an obstacle to free movement of workers was in many ways a 'phoney war' in the sense that the ultimate outcome was
to be determined with regard to whether it might be possible to hold that the
transfer rules 'pursued a legitimate aim compatible with the Treaty and were justified by pressing reasons of public interest … and that … the application of those
rules … [is] … such as to ensure achievement of the aim in question and not go
beyond what is necessary for that purpose'.[41]

[**8.16**]   The justifications raised were threefold in nature: the need to maintain
a financial and competitive sporting equilibrium in football; that transfer fees
were merely compensation for the costs incurred in the training and development of players and thus were fundamental to the search for talent and the training of young players; and that the transfer rules were necessary to safeguard the
worldwide organisation of football. Moreover, an underlying element of all of
these points was that the transfer fee system was integral to the survival of smaller
(feeder/amateur) clubs. On the first point, the ECJ recognised that the objective
of maintaining a balance between clubs 'by preserving a certain degree of equality
and uncertainty as to results' could be accepted as legitimate but that the transfer
rules then in place were an inadequate means of maintaining such financial and
competitive balance.[42] In effect, the ECJ argued that the transfer rules skewed
the balance between clubs because they neither precluded the richest clubs from

---

[38] Ibid [92]–[114]. See also the exhaustive analysis of this issue in [193]–[252] of the Opinion of
Advocate General Lenz.

[39] Ibid [95]–[96] of the ECJ's decision.

[40] Ibid [99]–[101]. See similarly at [102]–[103] of the ECJ's decision, the rejection of the argument
made by the football authorities based on Joined Cases C-267/91 and C-268/91 *Keck and Mithouard*
[1993] ECR I-6097 (where restrictions or prohibitions on selling arrangements for goods applied
equally and with the same effect to all relevant traders operating within a national territory, such
arrangements might fall outside the ambit of EU law) because of the direct effect football's transfer
rules had to players' access to the employment market in other member states.

[41] Ibid [104].

[42] Ibid [106].

securing the services of the best players nor prevented the availability of financial resources from being a decisive factor in competitive sport.[43]

[**8.17**]　On the second point, the argument that football's transfer rules were necessary for and limited to the compensation of clubs for the expenses which they had to incur in paying fees on recruiting 'their' player was dismissed bluntly by the ECJ on the grounds that 'it seeks to justify the maintenance of obstacles to freedom of movement for workers simply on the ground that such obstacles were able to exist in the past'.[44] The ECJ did, however, accept that the prospect of receiving transfer, development or training fees was likely to encourage football clubs to seek new talent and train young players but that equally (because of the impossibility in predicting with any certainty the sporting future of young players; only a limited number of whom would go on to play the sport professionally) those fees were 'by nature contingent and uncertain and in any event unrelated to the actual cost borne by clubs of training both future professional players and those who will never play professionally'.[45] In sum, the ECJ concluded that the prospect of receiving such fees could not therefore be either a decisive factor in encouraging the recruitment and training of young players or an adequate means of financing such activities, particularly in the case of smaller clubs.[46] As regards both of the above 'justifications', the ECJ was also of the opinion that similar objectives could be realised 'at least as efficiently' by other means not impeding the free movement of workers and in this the Court pointed to the alternative suggested by Advocate General Lenz, which was based on the redistribution of part of the income (gate receipt and TV rights revenue) of leading clubs.[47]

[**8.18**]　On the third point, UEFA was concerned that a change in the transfer rules in what was traditionally football's most lucrative market would adversely affect the stability of the worldwide organisation of football. This 'concern' was dismissed.[48] The ECJ held that the effect of its decision would be that it would no longer be possible within the EU to make the transfer of a professional footballer (whose contract had expired and who is a national of a member state) to a club in another member state dependent on the payment of a transfer fee. Nevertheless, the Court noted that it would, on the other hand, remain open to football associations in non-member states to maintain those rules and thus a club in the EU wishing to engage a player who had previously played for a club in a non-member country would still have to pay a transfer fee even if that player was a national of an EU member state. The distinction in the application of different rules to transfers intra-Union and those between clubs in the EU and those affiliated to national associations outside the EU was, in the ECJ's opinion, 'unlikely to pose

---

[43]　Ibid [107]. See also [218]–[225] of the Opinion of Advocate General Lenz.
[44]　Ibid [113].
[45]　Ibid [109].
[46]　Ibid.
[47]　Ibid [110]. See [226]–[234] of the Opinion of Advocate General Lenz.
[48]　Ibid [112].

any particular difficulties' and particularly so given that the existing transfer rules within the national associations of certain member states of the EU differed from each other, from UEFA's guidelines and international (FIFA-led) norms.[49]

[**8.19**]   The Advocate General had also dismissed these concerns, clearly stating that UEFA was somewhat exaggerating the difficulties that might result for football on a global scale.[50] Moreover, and in a manner that neatly summarises the subsequent approach of the ECJ, and more recently the Commission, on the amenability of the economic aspects of sport to EU law review, Advocate General Lenz concluded on this point that, 'There is thus nothing to prevent the [Union] being treated as a unit within which transfer fees are to be dispensed with, while being maintained for transfers to or from non-member countries. Moreover, that altogether corresponds in my opinion to the logic of the internal market'.[51] Looking back therefore on this part of both the ECJ's decision and the Advocate General's opinion in *Bosman*, there was a clear recognition that sport was special and moreover, given that no comparable system existed in other economic areas, that the transfer system for professional players was both an example of the specificity of sport and had certain legitimate aims regarding the integrity and stability of football in mind. Nevertheless, the ECJ was equally of the opinion that sport was not so special that it should be permitted, by way of placing football transfer rules fully beyond the reach of EU law, to distort the overall logic, and to override one of the key objectives (free movement), of the internal market. In short, in that instance, there could be only one winner.[52]

Foreign Player Quotas and the Free Movement of Workers

[**8.20**]   The second substantive point of contention on the regulation by the Belgian football authorities and UEFA/FIFA of the gainful employment environment of professional footballers, related to the compatibility of nationality-based player quotas in club competitions with the EU's free movement principle.[53] The fundamental matter at issue was Bosman's claim that football's transfer rules violated the abolition of any discrimination based on nationality between workers contained in Article 45(2) TFEU.[54] The ECJ agreed with Bosman that nationality clauses were an obstacle to the freedom of movement and further noted that the fact that, although those clauses might not be said to directly concern the employment of such players (on which there was no restriction), such clauses did restrict the extent to which clubs could field such players in official matches and thus logically because 'participation in such matches is the essential purpose of

---

[49]   Ibid. See also [22]–[23] of the ECJ's judgment.
[50]   See [246]–[247] of the Opinion of Advocate General Lenz, 'no insuperable difficulties should arise'.
[51]   Ibid [246].
[52]   Ibid [114].
[53]   Ibid [115]–[137]. See also the exhaustive analysis of this issue in [151]–[192] of the Opinion of Advocate General Lenz.
[54]   Ibid [117]–[118] of the ECJ's decision.

a professional player's activity' rules restricting that participation also restricted the chances of employment of such players.[55] Again, it must be noted that the battle on whether football's foreign player quotas were prima facie an obstacle to free movement of workers was in many ways a 'phoney war' in the sense that the ultimate outcome was again to be determined with regard to whether it might be possible to justify such quotas.[56]

[8.21] The justifications raised were fourfold in nature. All four were rejected though the arguments contained therein have a lingering importance to this day in terms of what is called the 'home-grown rule' debate.[57] The first justification was that such clauses 'serve to maintain the traditional link between each club and its country, a factor of great importance in enabling the public to identify with its favourite team and ensuring that clubs taking part in [UEFA] competitions effectively represent their countries'.[58] The ECJ dismissed this 'traditional link' by noting that even though national championships are played between clubs from different regions, towns or localities, there are no quotas restricting the right of clubs to field players from other regions, towns or localities in such matches and, moreover, in UEFA competitions participation is limited to 'clubs which have achieved certain results in competition in their respective countries without any particular significance being attached to the nationalities of their players'.[59]

[8.22] The second justification was that nationality quotas were necessary to 'create a sufficient pool of national players to provide the national teams with top players to field in all team positions'.[60] In response, the ECJ noted, whilst national teams must by definition be made up of players having the nationality of the relevant country, those players 'need not necessarily be registered to play for clubs in that country'.[61] Furthermore, although the 'burden' of the free movement of workers was that it opened up the employment market in one member state to nationals in other member states and thus effectively reduced workers' chances of securing employment in their 'own' member state; the 'benefit' of the principle was that it offered such workers the prospect of employment in other member states.[62] The third justification put forward by UEFA and the Belgian football authorities was that nationality quotas helped 'maintain a competitive balance between clubs by preventing the richest clubs from appropriating the services of the best players.' The ECJ dismissed this summarily by noting that such quotas, as based on the 3+2 rule, in strict terms applied only to the field of play during UEFA competitions (it applied only as a minimum for national leagues) and thus

---

[55] Ibid [120].
[56] Ibid [121].
[57] Note the brief discussion of that rule at [8.36]–[8.37] of this text.
[58] Case C 415/93 *Bosman* [1995] ECR I-4921 [123].
[59] Ibid [131]–[132].
[60] Ibid [124].
[61] Ibid [133].
[62] Ibid [134].

outside of that team sheet restriction there was no general bar on clubs recruiting (and hoarding) the best national players.[63]

[8.23]   The fourth justification focused initially on the exception to the free movement principle's abolition of discrimination against workers recognised in *Donà v Mantero*, (and in *Walrave and Koch*) namely that a limited and proportionate exception would be recognised in matters of a non-economic nature such as the composition of sports teams, and in particular national teams, the formation of which was a question of purely sporting interest.[64] Here, the ECJ noted that the clauses in question did not concern specific matches between teams representing their countries but applied to all official matches between clubs and, consequently, to the essence of the economic activity of professional players.[65] UEFA then pointed out that in light of *Donà v Mantero* it had entered into discussions with the Commission on how best to proceed and the ultimate result of that collaboration had been the rule at challenge, that is, the 3+2 rule.[66] In this, the ECJ noted that, except where such powers are expressly conferred upon the Commission, it may not give guarantees concerning the compatibility of specific practices with EU law and that under no circumstances does the Commission have the power to authorise practices (such as those at issue) which are contrary to EU law.[67] In sum, the ECJ concluded that the free movement principle precluded the application of nationality-based player quotas within the jurisdiction of the EU on the grounds that to hold otherwise would mean that not only would the principle be deprived of its practical effect but that the fundamental right of free access to employment which EU law confers individually on each worker in the Union would be rendered 'nugatory'.[68]

Bosman: The Immediate Aftermath

[8.24]   Without overly exaggerating or trivialising the matter, it might be said that the immediate reaction of UEFA and the football authorities worldwide to the *Bosman* litigation displayed the classic four stages of grief—denial; then anger; followed by depression; and finally acceptance. The 'denial' stage is clear from the increasingly desperate attempts, outlined above, by UEFA and others in the course of the proceedings before the ECJ to justify the transfer rules' restriction of free movement. UEFA's 'anger' at the judgment meant that, in some ways, it failed to comprehend that the decision could have been much worse in that the ECJ was

---

[63] The most celebrated example of the effect of the 3+2 rule occurred in the group stages of the previous Champions League tournament (1994/1995) when Barcelona beat Manchester United 4-0 at the Nou Camp with the English club hampered by the fact that the rule led to manager Alex Ferguson dropping Danish international goalkeeper Peter Schmeichal from the first 11.

[64]   Ibid [122].
[65]   Ibid [128].
[66]   Ibid [126].
[67]   Ibid [136].
[68]   Ibid [129].

relatively sympathetic when it came to concluding upon aspects of the temporal effect of its judgment.[69] Although the normal approach where a matter of EU law has been clarified by way of preliminary ruling to the ECJ was that the 'clarified' rule could, in effect, be interpreted retrospectively; the ECJ acknowledged that in the particular circumstances of *Bosman*, the legal uncertainty regarding the compatibility of football's transfer rules with EU law was such that the retrospective effect of the free movement principles could not be relied upon in support of claims relating to transfer fees which had already been paid or were still payable under any obligation arising the date of the judgment.[70] This addressed a key and very practical concern for the football authorities and many clubs, who were fearful that the effect of *Bosman* would be to open a floodgate of backdated claims, the potential quantum of which they even equated to an 'expropriation'.[71]

[8.25]   The 'depression' stage was probably well under way when cases such as *Deutscher Handballbund v Kolpak*[72] and *Simutenkov v Minsiterios de Educación y Cultura*,[73] demonstrated to UEFA that a *Bosman*-inspired, EU law review of the economic aspects of sport was going to be an enduring, rather than isolated, matter of future contention for football worldwide. The stated cases resulted in the jurisdictional and geographical impact of *Bosman* being expanded to virtually all parts of Europe. In the former case, Kolpak was a Slovak national and the holder of a valid residency permit for Germany. He was employed on a fixed-term contract by a German handball team. The sports governing body issued him a player's licence but effectively endorsed that licence with reference to the fact that he was a national of a non-member country. Kolpak challenged this endorsement, arguing that he was entitled to participate in competitions under the same conditions as German and other EU nations by reason of the prohibition of discrimination resulting from the combined provisions of the then EC Treaty and an Association Agreement (AA) with Slovakia. The ECJ, noting that the AA had direct effect, also agreed that it should be interpreted as precluding the application to professional athletes of Slovak nationals, otherwise lawfully employed by a club established in a member state, of a rule drawn up by a sports body in a member state under which a club could only field a limited number of players from non-member countries not party to a European Economic Area agreement. In *Simutenkov,* the claimant was a Russian national and the holder of both a valid residency and work permit for Spain. He was employed on a professional football contract with

---

[69] Ibid [139]–[146]. The 'angry' or, more properly, confused reaction of sports bodies to *Bosman* is recounted expertly by S Weatherill, 'Do Sporting Associations make Law or are they merely Subject to it? (1999) 13 *Journal of the Society of Advanced Legal Studies* 24.

[70] Ibid [144]. *Cf* [146] of the decision: 'With regard to nationality clauses, however, there are no grounds for a temporal limitation of the effects of this judgment. In the light of the *Walrave* and *Donà* judgments, it was not reasonable for those concerned to consider that the discrimination resulting from those clauses was compatible with [the free movement principle].'

[71] See further [247] of the Opinion of Advocate General Lenz.

[72] Case 483/00 *Deutscher Handballbund v Kolpak* [2003] ECR I-4315.

[73] Case 265/03 *Simutenkov v Minsiterios de Educación y Cultura* [2005] ECR I-2579.

Club Deportivo Tenerife and held a Spanish football federation licence as a non-EU player. Simutenkov sought, with Tenerife's support, to apply to replace his non-EU licence with one held by a national of the EU as based on an *Kolpak*-like interpretation of the EU's then Partnership and Co-operation Agreement with Russia. The ECJ, affirming *Kolpak*, held for Simuntenkov.

[**8.26**]   By the time the above had concluded it must be admitted that UEFA and FIFA were coming to terms with the implications of *Bosman* and this 'acceptance' can be seen in the reaction to *Lehtonen v FRBSB*.[74] That case concerned the transfer rules of the Belgian Basketball Federation, which imposed certain restrictions on players previously registered with a federation of another country. The point of contention was that, according to the regulations, the deadline for the transfer of players within Europe was the end of February, after which only players from outside Europe could be transferred. The regulations further specified dates during which transfers were allowed with any transfers outside those windows resulting in the transferred player not being allowed to take part in the game. The claimant was a Finnish national who was employed by a Belgian club but who, according to the sport's international governing body (FIBA), failed to meet the required deadline for transfers. Consequently, the club decided not to field the player for a while, a move that frustrated the player and led to the litigation at hand.

[**8.27**]   The ECJ, in line with previous authorities, reiterated the sport was subject to EU law insofar as it constituted an economic activity, of which the paid employment of a professional basketball player was within the meaning of such an 'activity'.[75] It also noted that the freedom of movement principle did not preclude rules or practices in the field of sport excluding foreign players from certain matches for reasons which are not of an economic nature, so long as (a) the nature and context of such rules were for purely sporting interest only and typically in the case of matches between national teams of different countries and (b) those exclusionary rules were limited to their proper objective and could not be relied upon to exclude all sporting activity from the reach of EU law.[76] The argument made in *Lehtonen* by the defending sports authorities was that, although the transfer windows rule might well constitute an obstacle to the free movement of players who wish to pursue their activity in another member state by preventing Belgian clubs from fielding players from other member states where they have been engaged after a specified period;[77] that restriction could be justified on the grounds that its objective was one of ensuring the equity and regularity of the sporting competition in question. In sum, the argument made, and entertained by the ECJ, in this case was that the proper functioning of the championship in question was intrinsic to the competency of the sports bodies in question and that transfer windows designed to prevent players from joining another club during

---

[74] Case 176/96 *Lehtonen v FRBSB* [2000] ECR I-2681.
[75] Ibid [32]; [43]–[44]; and [46].
[76] Ibid [34].
[77] Ibid [47]–[50].

the season could be seen as a limited and proportionate means of protecting the overall integrity and stability of that championship.[78]

[**8.28**]   *Lehtonen* implied therefore that certain restrictions on the employment mobility of professional athletes could be justified in order to ensure that certain important characteristics relating to the proper functioning of sports competitions were protected and that one of the limited, proportionate ways of realising that objective was the use of transfer windows. Within a year of the *Lehtonen* judgment, FIFA, in agreement with UEFA, and after consultation with the EU Commission, undertook to change its existing regulations on the status and transfer of players.[79] Key aspects of the latest (October 2009) edition of those regulations—notably the provisions on the regulations' jurisdictional scope; the amateur or professional status of players; maintenance of contractual stability between professional players and clubs; international transfers involving minors; training compensation and solidarity mechanisms; and its dispute resolution services—have all been covered in detail in chapter 7 of this text while the impact of both *Bosman* (in terms of the process surrounding a player's registration, passport and international clearance certificate)[80] and *Lehtonen* (in terms of the winter/summer transfers windows)[81] on the regulations is also plainly evident.

[**8.29**]   Finally, Herbert Kingaby scratched at it; George Eastham cracked it; but Jean-Marc Bosman well and truly smashed the glass ceiling that restricted the employment mobility of professional football players. The removal of that ceiling let in the light that was free agency on expiry of contract, but it also revealed a much altered sporting, regulatory and legal landscape for professional football in Europe and, in effect, worldwide. The outstanding feature of this new regulatory landscape is that the tension between, on the one hand, the concerns of employers/clubs/leagues for contractual stability and the demands of employees/players/agents for greater employment mobility on the other; are now played out principally under the agreed parameters of FIFA's Regulations on the Status and Transfer of Players. In short, the *Kinabgy/Eastham* disputes of the past, then argued before the ordinary courts, are now echoed in the *Webster/Matuzalem* disputes of the present, now argued before the Court of Arbitration for Sport (CAS).[82] In terms of an altered sporting landscape, the term 'on a Bosman' has entered the vernacular of professional football, as used most typically (and threateningly) by a player who, nearing the end of his contract, reminds his club that, unless better renewal terms are offered or unless his frustrations at not being permitted to move to another club notwithstanding his existing contract are assuaged, he is soon to become a free agent and thus all of the player's inherent value will be lost to the club.

---

[78] Ibid [51]–[60].

[79] Note the Commission's Press Release 'Outcome of Discussions between the Commission and FIFA/UEFA on FIFA Regulations on International Football Transfers' IP/01/314, Brussels 5 March 2001.

[80] Eg, arts 5, 7 and 9 FIFA.

[81] Art 6 FIFA.

[82] See [7.90]–[7.100] of this text.

[**8.30**]   This point illustrates a fundamental repercussion of the *Bosman* ruling in the sense that for the first century or so of professional football, the power within a contract lay clearly and unequally with club directors and league administrators. In the twenty first century, this has changed utterly. The servitude of the past has been replaced by the liberties of the present where the terms of short, lucrative contracts are negotiated, enhanced and renewed in a contractual environment that its undoubtedly player (and player-agent) friendly. Whether this has or has not 'been good for the game' is more a matter of football punditry than legal analysis.[83] In strict legal terms, *Bosman* was a serious but necessary breach of the administrative autonomy of sport. In defending itself from what it perceives to be a continuing legal attack on their jurisdiction and competencies, sports bodies have now retreated to a line built around the defence of the specificity of sport. Both the widening and deepening nature of this so-called 'attack' on sport and the nature and scope of the so-called 'specificity' of sport are now addressed.

Bosman: Directing the Present

[**8.31**]   Although for over 35 years sport, insofar as it constitutes an economic activity, has been expressly recognised as being subject to EU law pursuant to the objectives set out in Article 3 TFEU, it was not until *Bosman* that serious concerted thought was given at an EU institutional level to sports law and policy, most notably at Commission level[84] but also by the European Parliament[85] and even by the Council of the European Union.[86] What follows is an account of the 'Big-Bang' effect that *Bosman* has had on EU law-related interest in all sport, and not just the contractual machinations of professional football. There are two elements to this account. First, the wider, 'soft' competency interest in sport, as including the recreational, social, cultural and even political aspects of sport, and as epitomised by Article 165 TFEU. Second, the 'hard' legal interest in the economic attributes of the sports industry, which some sports bodies fear has deepened to a point where a stage will soon be reached that the ECJ will uphold arguments made by

---

[83] The irony is that Bosman himself was from many years afterwards embittered by the whole experience. See the interview with him by J Jackson, 'Show me the Money' *The Observer* (London 8 January 2006) Sport 10.

[84] See European Commission, White Paper on Sport, 11 July 2007, COM(2007) 391 and accompanying Commission Staff Working Document, 11 July 2007, SEC(2007) 935. See previously the report from the EC Commission to the European Council, The Helsinki Report on Sport, 10 December 1999, COM(1999) 644. The importance of the Helsinki Report is that it led to the establishment of the Sports Unit of the Commission's Directorate-General on Education and Culture see http://ec.europa.eu/sport/index_en.htm.

[85] See, eg, the European Parliament resolution of 8 May 2008 on the White Paper on Sport (2007/2261(INI)), [2009] OJ C271 E/7, 12 November, 51.

[86] See recently annex 5, European Council Declaration on Sport, Conclusions of the Presidency of the European Council meeting in Brussels, 11–12 December 2008.

individual professional athletes that even ostensibly 'purely sporting' rules have inherently economic attributes and thus should, where unreasonable and disproportionate in effect, be struck down as incompatible with a fundamental freedom or competition law norm guaranteed under EU law.

The 'Widening' of EU Sports Law

[**8.32**]   This 'wider' interest (which can in fact be traced back to the Adonnino reports on 'A People's Europe' in the mid-1980s[87] and on through Declaration 29 of Amsterdam Treaty (1997)[88] and into the 'Nice Declaration' of 2000)[89] identifies the societal contribution that sport can make in promoting certain policies relating to education; public health; volunteering and active citizenship; anti-racism and antidiscrimination; social inclusion and integration; and even external relations and sustainable development.[90] All of these points are mentioned in section 2 of the European Commission's 'White Paper on Sport' (2007), and the realisation of the general objectives therein await the interpretation of the scope of the 'soft' sports competence contained in Article 165 TFEU. With regard to sport, Article 165 TFEU states both that the EU 'shall contribute to the promotion of European sporting issues, while taking account of the specific nature of sport, its structures based on voluntary activity and its social and educational function' and that EU action 'shall be aimed at developing the European dimension in sport, by promoting fairness and openness in sporting competitions and cooperation between bodies responsible for sports, and by protecting the physical and moral integrity of sportsmen and sportswomen, especially the youngest sportsmen and sportswomen.'

[**8.33**]   There is little that can be disagreed with there and much that is laudable in the first express mention of sport in an EU Treaty but from a strictly legal perspective, the competence of the provision is softened somewhat by Article 165(4) TFEU, which holds that the provision's overall objectives can be realised only through the adoption of incentive measures, excluding any harmonisation of the laws and regulations of member states, by the European Parliament or Council;[91] or through the adoption of recommendations by the European

---

[87] See European Commission, A People's Europe: Communication from the Commission to the European Parliament, 7 July 1988, COM(1988) 331.

[88] [1997] OJ C340/3, 136.

[89] See annex 4, Declaration on the Specific Characteristics of Sport and its Social Function in Europe of Which Account should be taken in Implementing Common Policies, Conclusions of the Presidency of the European Council meeting in Nice, 7–10 December 2000 (Nice Declaration).

[90] This broader approach to sport's societal rule is also prominent in the Council of Europe's approach to sport, notably the European Sports Charter (1992), and as recognised in Art 165(3) TFEU. See generally www.coe.int/t/dg4/sport/sportineurope/default_EN.asp. See also JL Chappelet, *Autonomy of Sport* (Strasbourg, Coucnil of Europe Publishing, 2010) and R Siekmann and J Soek (eds), *The Council of Europe and Sport: Basic Documents* (The Hague, TMC Asser Press, 2007).

[91] Such measures are to be adopted after the Parliament and Council have 'acted in accordance with the ordinary legislative procedure, after consulting the Economic and Social Committee and the Committee of the Regions.'

Council.[92] Papers on the interpretation of this provision, which only entered into force in December 2009, are currently being awaited from the Commission[93] and thus no further speculative analysis on the legal impact of Article 165 TFEU is undertaken here.[94] For what is it worth, some guidance as to the influence the provision might have on sports law can be gleaned from the work of Van den Bogaert and Vermeersch who, commenting on the previous incarnation of this provision—Article III-282 of the Treaty establishing a Constitution for Europe—noted that the provision's restrictive and soft nature relegated the EU to a secondary role revolving around supporting, coordinating and complementing sports-related actions that remain primarily (and in accordance with the principle of subsidiarity) matters for member states and sports federations.[95] Accordingly, these commentators acknowledge that in strict legal terms such a provision 'would have no immediate bearing' on the EU's indirect approach to sport and thus 'its importance seems to be of a mere symbolic nature'.[96] Nevertheless, Van den Bogaert and Vermeersch go on to observe, quite rightly, that this symbolic recognition of sport as 'official' EU policy 'could very well constitute the decisive impetus for the [EU's] institutions to firmly subject sporting activities in their economic dimensions to the Treaty's trade law rules and to keep the privileged treatment linked with the special status of sport within appropriate proportions, balancing the special features of sport evenly with the exigencies of free movement and competition law'.[97] It is to the deepening 'exigencies' of free movement and competition law that we now turn.

The 'Deepening' of EU Sports Law

[**8.34**]   There are four points to note with regard to the deepening, *Bosman*-inspired interest that EU law is purported to have on the operation of modern sport. The first reverts back to the core of the *Bosman* decision: the incompatibility of football's transfers rules and practices with both the principles of

---

[92] Such recommendations are to be adopted on foot of proposals made by the Commission.

[93] On 8 April 2010, the Commission launched an online consultation (open until 1 June 2010) on the EU's strategic choices for the implementation of the new EU competence in the field of sport. See further ec.europa.eu/sport/news/news915_en.htm.

[94] Outside of strict legal analysis, there is no doubt that initiatives such as the first formal Council meeting of EU Sports Ministers (scheduled for May 2010) and the possibility of a major EU sports funding programme from 2012 (of a broader reach than the EURATHLON programmes of the mid-1990s), will entail huge benefits for all levels of sport in the EU and that in an overall sense Art 165 TFEU has ensured that the EU 'agenda-setting' role in sport has been greatly enhanced. Previously, EU sports policy, such as it existed, was ad hoc in nature as discussed by B Garcia, 'From Regulation to Governance and Representation: Agenda Setting and the EU's Involvement in Sport' (2007) 5(1) *Entertainment and Sports Law Journal* published online at www2.warwick.ac.uk/fac/soc/law/elj/eslj/issues/volume5/number1/garcia.

[95] S Van den Bogaert and A Vermeersch, 'Sport and the EC Treaty: A Tale of Uneasy Bedfellows' (2006) 31 *European Law Review* 821, 838.

[96] Ibid.

[97] Ibid.

free movement of labour and the related prohibitions on nationality-based discrimination regarding access to employment. Free movement of workers is not the only fundamental freedom that has had an impact on sport and the (somewhat forgotten) freedom on the provision of services in examined in its sports-related context. The third point is that, although, since football's transfer rules for expired contracts and the rules concerning nationality clauses for clubs were found to be contrary to the free movement principle, the ECJ held that it was not necessary to rule on their compatibility with Articles 101 and 102 TFEU;[98] competition law has since become the most frequent (and bluntest, depending on your point of view) means of EU-law related review of the practices and rules of sport. In this, the fourth point of note is that the interpretation and application of competition law to sport will be seen as important not just in its specific legal context but also because it will be shown to give the starkest illustration of the 'specificity of sport' defence, and it is the parameters of that 'defence' which are likely to determine the course of the evolutionary path of sports law in Europe for many years to come.

Free Movement and Nationality Post-Bosman

[**8.35**]   The enduring, direct effect of *Bosman* in this regard can be seen in a number of ways, for example, the application of free movement *simpliciter* in the ECJ's recent decision of *Olympique Lyonnais SASP v Olivier Bernard & Newcastle United FC*[99] and in the reaffirmation by independent international bodies such as CAS that direct discrimination based on nationality clearly violates a fundamental premise of EU law.[100] One of the more interesting matters here is that surrounding the so-called home-grown player rule.[101] The essence of this debate is that UEFA is of the opinion that a number of the justifications raised in *Bosman* regarding the 3+2 rule—the weakening of the traditional link or affiliation between club and locality; the adverse impact on the quality of national teams; the need to maintain a competitive balance in European club football; and the need to encourage the education and training of young players—retain some residual importance.[102] In this, UEFA, although now acknowledging that the 3+2 rule was a disproportionate means of realising the objective of increasing the number of 'local' players in football squads, is nonetheless of the view that there remains some wriggle room to formulate rules requiring clubs to include a certain quota

---

[98] Case C 415/93 *Bosman* [1995] ECR I-4921 [138].

[99] Case C-325/08 *Olympique Lyonnais SASP v Olivier Bernard & Newcastle United FC*, 16 March 2010, as discussed at [7.56]–[7.58] of this text.

[100] See recently CAS 2009 /A/1842 *Ethnikos Asteras FC v Hellenic Football Federation*, as reported by G Ioannidis, 'Greek FA Accepts Nationality Restrictions Violate EU Law' (2009) 7 (8) *World Sports Law Report* 6.

[101] See generally L Freeburn, 'European Football's Home-Grown Players Rules and the Nationality Discrimination under the European Community Treaty' (2009) 20 *Marquette Sports Law Review* 177.

[102] See [8.22]–[8.23] of this text.

of 'locally trained' players[103] and that such quotas 'could be accepted as being compatible with the provisions on the free movement of persons if they do not lead to any direct discriminations based on nationality'.[104]

[**8.36**] The general framework in which objective justification of such quotas might be achieved is neatly summarised by two of the leading writers in the area, Miettinen and Parrish, who note that even though a home-grown player rule might seek 'to achieve similar aims as the *Bosman* 3+2 rule … nonetheless … it is legally distinguishable in that although the objective is an attempt to link attributes of residence and players' club affiliations, the method employed does not constitute direct nationality discrimination but indirect discrimination which arises from requirements which more nationals than non-nationals are likely to fulfil'.[105] Finally, leaving further speculation on the technicalities and compatibility of a home-grown player rule to one side,[106] the overall impact that free movement law, anti-discrimination policies and indeed *Bosman* itself has had on domestic and European professional football was seen clearly in two instances during in 2009/2010 season. The domestic example occurred on 30 December 2009 when the starting line-ups in the Arsenal versus Portsmouth Premier League game were the first in top flight football not to feature an English player;[107] while the European example occurred on 28 April 2010 when the Italian club Inter Milan qualified for the final of Champions League after a game against Barcelona in which Inter's Portuguese coach started with a team that did not feature one Italian. Inter's starting line up—of four Brazilians; four Argentineans; and one player each from the Netherlands, Cameroon and Macedonia—is one on the most visible exhibitions of the influence that *Bosman* has had, and continues to have, on elite professional football at a global level.

---

[103] The idea here is that a locally trained player is a player who, regardless of nationality and age, has been registered with his club for a period of three entire seasons, or for 36 months in total, whilst between the ages of 15 and 21 (a 'club-trained player') and that an association-trained equivalence would also be recognised ie, one who fulfils the club-trained criteria but with another club in the same national football association. See generally S Miettinen and R Parrish, 'Nationality Discrimination in Community Law: An Assessment of UEFA Regulations Governing Player Eligibility for European Club Competitions (The Home-Grown Player Rule)' (2007) 5(2) *Entertainment and Sports Law Journal* available online at www2.warwick.ac.uk/fac/soc/law/elj/eslj/issues/volume5/number2/miettinen_parrish.

[104] See s 2.3 of the European Commission's White Paper on Sport, 11 July 2007, COM(2007) 391.

[105] Miettinen and Parrish (n 103) [17]. See also [27] where the authors contrast UEFA's efforts with the 'ill conceived' efforts of FIFA in promoting a 6+5 system given 'the unequivocal refusal of [the ECJ] to accept this type of agreement in *Bosman*.'

[106] The most recent effort by FIFA to promote its 6+5 rule was the report it commissioned from the Institute of European Affairs based in Dusseldorf, which claimed that the rule could be deemed compatible with EU law. A summary of the report can be downloaded at ineaonline.com/download/regel/gutachten_eng.pdf. The claim was met with much circumspection by the Commission in May 2009. See, eg, M Scott, 'Digger: EC Thumbs-down for FIFA again' *The Guardian* (London 1 May 2009) Sport 2.

[107] The match featured players from 15 countries among the 22 starters: seven French players; two Algerians; and one player each from Bosnia, Ireland, Israel, Iceland, South Africa, Scotland, Germany, Spain, Belgium, Wales, Cameroon, Croatia and Russia. A decade earlier, Chelsea became the first English club to field an entirely foreign starting line-up against Southampton on 26 December 1999.

*Freedom to Provide Services Post-*Bosman

[**8.37**]   In the ratio of *Walrave and Koch, Donà v Mantero* and *Bosman*, the ECJ held that sport is subject to EU law insofar as it constitutes an economic activity within the meaning of Article 3 TFEU, where such activity has the character of gainful employment *or* remunerated service and thus, in this regard, sport comes particularly with the scope of Articles 45 to 48 TFEU (free movement of workers) *or* Articles 56 to 62 TFEU (the fundamental freedom to provide services within the EU) respectively. With respect to the latter, a case of interest is the *Deliège* ruling of 2000 in which the ECJ had to consider by way of a preliminary reference from a Belgian court (and with selection for the Atlanta Olympics imminent) the selection criteria based on a limit or quota on the number of national participants eligible to compete in international judo competitions.[108] The claimant's challenge was based on the contention that as a provider of services within the meaning of the provisions on the freedom to provide services, the systematic requirement of a quota and selection at national level was a barrier to her freedom to pursue an activity of an economic nature.

[**8.38**]   The ECJ held that sporting activities and, in particular, a high ranking athlete's participation in an international competition, are capable of involving the provision of a number of separate, but closely related, services which may fall within the scope of the provisions on the freedom to provide services even if some of those services are not paid for by those for whom they are performed.[109] The example given by the Court in *Deliège*, was where the organiser of an international competition offers athletes an opportunity to engage in their sporting competition with others and, at the same time, the athletes, by participating in the competition, enable the organiser to put on a sports event which the public may attend, which television broadcasters may retransmit and which may be of interest of interest to advertisers and sponsors. Moreover, the ECJ observed, in such a scenario the athletes provide their sponsors with publicity, the basis for which is the sporting activity itself.[110] With the above in mind, one of the most concrete examples of a sports-related application of the freedom to provide services can be found with regard to access to sports-related broadcasting. Directive 89/552/EC (TV Without Frontiers) as updated by Directive 97/36/EC and amended by Directive 2007/65/EC (Audiovisual Media Services) permits a member state of the EU to ensure that broadcasters under its jurisdiction do not broadcast on an exclusive basis events which are regarded by that member state as being of 'major importance for society'—such as sporting events and tournaments—in such a way as to deprive a substantial proportion of that state's public of the possibility of viewing such events by live or deferred coverage. This objective is realised by asking member states to draw up a list of designated, protected events, which it

---

[108] Joined Cases C 51/96 & 191/97 *Deliège v LFJ et Disciplines ASBL* [2000] ECR I-2549.
[109] Ibid [56].
[110] Ibid [57].

considers of such importance that they should be available wholly or partially live or deferred. The list is then verified by the Commission and is subject to mutual recognition by other EU member states.[111]

[**8.39**]   Returning to the *Deliège* ruling itself, the ECJ held that sports rules requiring professional and semi-professional athletes to have been authorised or selected by their national federation in order to be able to participate in a high-level international sports competitions, which does not include national teams competing against each other, does not of itself constitute a restriction on the freedom to provide services, so long as it is derived 'from a need inherent to the organisation of such a competition'.[112] In other words, although such a selection system may prove more favourable to one category of athlete over another, it cannot be inferred from that fact alone that the system constitutes a restriction on the freedom to provide services provided that the system has as its objective the protection of certain important characteristics of sporting competition and pursues the objectives in a limited proportionate manner and from a sporting interest only. In this, *Deliège* is important in that, in combination with other ECJ rulings, it reiterates that limited and proportionate sports-related restrictions on both the principle of free movement and freedom to provide services have been accepted as regards the right to select national athletes for national team competitions (*Walrave and Koch*, *Donà v Mantero* and *Bosman*); the need to limit the number of participants in a competition (*Deliège*); and the setting of deadlines for transfers of players in team sports (*Lehtonen*).

[**8.40**]   Finally, one of the more interesting aspects of the compatibility of economic activities relating to sport and the freedom to provide services is the growing number of gambling-related cases and in particular the provision of internet based or remote gambling services.[113] These are a number of sports-specific aspects to these cases relating inter alia to the fact that taxes raised from gambling-related sources and state lotteries are often used by governments to fund 'grassroots' sport and that online gaming companies are becoming highly prevalent as sponsors of football clubs and leagues throughout Europe. A recent case of

---

[111] In the UK, the Television Act 1954 originally gave the Government the power to draw up a list of protected events. The first list was drawn up in 1956. Now, s 299 of the Communications Act 2002, which modifies Part IV of the Broadcasting Act 1996, gives the Secretary of State for Culture, Media and Sport the power to maintain a list of sporting events of national interest divided into two categories: Group A (full live coverage on free-to-air channels); and Group B (deferred highlights offered to free-to-air broadcasters by pay-TV). The Code on Sports and Other Listed and Designated Events is administered by the communications regulator Ofcom and is available at www.ofcom.org. uk/tv/ifi/codes/code_sprt_lstd_evts. A thorough review of the Code by an Independent Advisory Panel to the Culture Secretary was published in November 2009. It recommended a single list of protected sports events but overall the so-called Davies review met with a mixed response. The report can be downloaded at www.culture.gov.uk/images/publications/independentpanelreport-to-SoS-Free-to-air-Nov2009.pdf. See further B Keane and F Savino, 'The Davies Report on UK Listed Events – A Question of Sport or Television' (2010) 21 *Entertainment Law Review* 69.

[112] Joined Cases C 51/96 & 191/97 *Deliège v LFJ et Disciplines ASBL* [2000] ECR I-2549 [69].

[113] For an introduction see generally D Doukas and J Anderson, 'The Dice is Loaded: Commercial Gambling and the European Court of Justice' (2008) 27 *Oxford Yearbook of International Law* 237.

interest involves a sponsorship deal between one such company (Bwin) and the Portuguese football league.[114] In that case, Portuguese legislation granted the respondents, operating under strict governmental control, the exclusive national rights to operate lotteries, games of chance and sporting bets, including via the internet. The legislation also provided for penalties in the form of fines that could be imposed on those who organise or advertise services in contravention of that exclusive right. Bwin, a private online gaming company established in Gibraltar, entered into a sponsorship agreement with the Portuguese Professional Football League in 2005 and on foot of this agreement the parties were fined for offering and advertising games of chance via the internet. On reference from a criminal court in Oporto, the ECJ held that the Portuguese legislation constituted a restriction on the freedom to provide services but it was justified by overriding factors relating to the public interest notably the objective of combating fraud and financial crime. Interestingly, and in light of the increasing frequency with which online betting companies are sponsoring sports event and clubs, the ECJ also noted that the restrictions on the BWin/LPFP deal were justified because 'the possibility cannot be ruled out that an operator which sponsors some of the sporting competitions on which it accepts bets and some of the teams taking part in those competitions may be in a position to influence their outcome directly or indirectly and thus increase its profits'.[115]

Competition Law and Sport Post-Bosman

[8.41]   The economic activities of sport fall within the scope of the competition law provisions of Article 101 TFEU (where the concern is with forbidding agreements between undertakings and decisions by associations of undertakings that prevent, restrict or distort competition in the internal market, subject to certain narrowly defined exceptions or justifications) and Article 102 TFEU (where the concern is with prohibiting the abuse by one or more undertakings of a dominant position within the internal market).[116] The recent *Motoe* case notwithstanding,[117] EU competition law's application to sport is usually discussed within the context of Article 101(1) TFEU and that provision's narrowly

---

[114] Case C-42/07 *Liga Portuguesa de Futebol Profissional (CA/LPFP) and Bwin International Ltd v Departamento de Jogos da Santa Casa da Misericórdia de Lisboa*, 8 September 2009.

[115] Ibid [71].

[116] This section is guided by E Szyszczak, 'Competition and Sport' (2007) 32 *European Law Review* 95 and A Vermeersch, 'All's Fair in Sport and Competition? The Application of EC Competition Rules to Sport' (2007) 3 *Journal of Contemporary European Research* 238.

[117] Case C-49/07 *Motoe v Elliniko Dimosio* [2008] ECR I-4863 and the case note by A Vermeersch at (2009) 46 *Common Market Law Review* 1327. In that case, the Grand Chamber noted that a system of undistorted competition can be guaranteed only if equality of opportunity is secured between the various economic operators in the relevant market and thus to entrust to an undertaking (which in this case organised and commercially exploited motor cycling competitions in Greece) the administrative task of granting or denying consent to applications for authorisation to organise such sports events is tantamount to defacto conferring on that undertaking powers that clearly and abusively place it at an obvious advantage over its competitors.

defined exceptions or justifications (Article 101(3)). In *Bosman*, the ECJ held that, since football's transfer rules for expired contracts and the rules concerning nationality clauses for clubs were contrary to the free movement principle; it was not necessary for it to rule on the compatibility of those rules with Articles 101 (and 102) TFEU.[118] Advocate General Lenz in his wide-ranging and influential opinion,[119] had, however, considered that the rules limiting the employment of foreign players infringed Article 101(1) TFEU because they restricted 'the possibilities for individual clubs to compete with each other by engaging players'.[120] In this, the Advocate General was in agreement with the Commission, which had observed that the rules in question 'share ... [and thus distort] ... sources of supply' within the meaning of Article 101(1)(c)TFEU.[121] Similarly, with respect to the transfer rules, the Advocate General concluded in his Opinion that the rules in question also violated Article 101 TFEU because they replaced the 'normal system of supply and demand by a uniform machinery which leads to the existing competition situation being preserved ... even after the contract has expired the player remains assigned to his former club for the time being'.[122] In contrast, 'under normal competitive conditions', that is, if the obligation to pay transfer fees did not exist, a player could transfer freely after the expiry of his contract and choose the club which offered him the best terms and, therefore, in the Advocate General's Opinion, the extant rules on transfer restricted competition. Post-*Bosman*, competition law's examination of the economic activities of sport can be divided into two broad categories:[123] its application to certain revenue-generating activities connected with sport—the example chosen here is media rights;[124] and its application to the organisation of sport—the example chosen here is with regard to the rulings of the Court of First Instance (CFI) and the ECJ in the *Meca-Medina* case.[125]

---

[118] Case C415/93 *Bosman* [1995] ECR I-4921 [138].

[119] Ibid [262]–[286] Opinion of Advocate General Lenz.

[120] Ibid [262].

[121] Ibid.

[122] Ibid.

[123] As a starting point on the applicability of competition law to sport, this chapter will make full use of annex 1, Sport and EU Competition Rules, to the EU Commission's Staff Working Document (n 84).

[124] Other examples here include the application of competition law to the package tours/ticketing arrangements of sporting events such as FIFA World Cup tournaments. See further the summary of EU Commission's Decision of 27 October 1992 relating to a proceeding pursuant to Article 85 EEC (Case IV/33.384 and 33.378—1990 Football World Cup) [1992] OJ L326, 12 November, 31 and the summary of the Commission's Decision of 20 July 1999 relating to a proceeding pursuant to Article 82 EC (Case IV/36.888—1998 Football World Cup) [2000] OJ L5, 8 January, 55.

[125] Other examples here include the application of competition law to rules restricting the multiple ownership of sports clubs and the rules concerning ancillary activities such as the regulation and licensing of agents. See respectively the EU Commission's decision of 25 June 2002 relating to a proceeding pursuant to Art 81(1)EC Treaty (Case COMP 37.806—ENIC/UEFA rule on the multiple ownership of football clubs) as noted in the Commission's Press Release 'Commission close Investigation into UEFA Rule on Multiple Ownership of Football Clubs' IP/02/942, Brussels 27 June 2002; and Case T-193/02 *Laurent Piau v Commission of the European Communities and FIFA* [2005] ECR II-209.

Revenue-Generating Activities

[**8.43**]   The value of media rights and TV rights in particular to modern sport
are significant to the point that the operation of many sports is underwritten to a
very large and, arguably very precarious, extent by such monies.[126] Equally, and as
noted in chapter 1 of this text,[127] sport media rights are particularly attractive for
many commercial media operators because sport has been shown to be an important sales driver in attracting consumers into subscribing to other audiovisual
content offered on pay-TV operators' platforms such as premium movie channels,
internet and phone services.[128] The combination of this mutual interest; the fact
that the 'product' in question is both of an 'instant demand' focus (consumers
will only pay premium amounts for access to live sports events; the life span and
value of deferred 'highlights' coverage is much less); and is of a limited nature (TV
rights are usually concentrated in a single organisation such as the FA Premier
League); it is unsurprising that the area of sports media rights is 'particularly
sensitive to antitrust violations'.[129]

[**8.44**]   The issue that has most concerned the EU Commission in this regard
involves the joint or collective selling or bundling of rights to broadcast games
played by football clubs as considered in the Commission's decisions in *UEFA
Champions League*,[130] *German Bundesliga*[131] and *FA Premier League*.[132] These
decisions demonstrate that the collective selling of media rights by a sports league
and associated clubs prima facie constitutes a horizontal restriction of competition under Article 101 TFEU. This is because a collective selling entity, which sells
all sports media rights on an exclusive basis for an extended period of time to one
single operator in one defined market (that is, one particular pay-TV company),
effectively forecloses other operators in the market from accessing that product
to the competitive harm of those other operators. Moreover, as noted by the
Commission, 'operators in neighbouring [media] markets (such the internet)
cannot access the exclusively sold rights … and … this may hamper the development of new services in neighbouring markets'.[133]

---

[126] For a contemporary review of this matter and other sports media rights issues see I Blackshaw, S
Cornelius and R Siekmann, *TV Rights and Sport: Legal Aspects* (The Hague, TMC Asser Press, 2009).

[127] See [1.12]–[1.13] of this text.

[128] The mutual benefits are such that sports organisations and TV companies will go to great
lengths to protect their interests from any potential exploitation by third parties. See, eg, Case
C-403/08 *FA Premier League & Ors v QC Leisure & Ors* [2008] OJ C301, 22 November 2008, 19.

[129] EU Commission's Staff Working Document (n 84) 54.

[130] Commission Decision of 23 July 2003 relating to a proceeding pursuant to Article 81EC Treaty
(Case 37.398—Joint selling of the commercial rights of the UEFA Champions League) [2003] OJ L291,
8 November, 25.

[131] Commission Decision of 19 January 2005 relating to a proceeding pursuant to Article 81EC Treaty
(Case 37.214—Joint selling of the media rights to the German Bundesliga) [2005] OJ L134, 27 May, 46.

[132] Commission decision relating to a proceeding pursuant to Article 81(1)EC Treaty (Case
C(2006)868—Selling of the media rights to the FA Premier League) as noted in the Commission's
Press Release 'Commission makes commitments from FA Premier League Legally Binding' IP/06/356,
Brussels 22 March 2006.

[133] EU Commission's Staff Working Document (n 84) 54.

[**8.45**]   At the same time, the Commission has also acknowledged that collective selling has some benefits that may, depending on the circumstances and conditions, come under the scope of Article 101(3) TFEU and may, therefore, may be deemed a justified restriction.[134] These justifications are related to the fact that collective selling by a league and its clubs (for example, the FA Premier League) can, in association with the fair distribution of the revenues from the sale of media rights and on the basis of the principle of financial solidarity, work to sustain the competitive integrity and long term financial viability of the league in question.[135] In short, the argument is that the financial solidarity and long term financial robustness of a league is undermined by individual selling of sports media rights because without robust financial solidarity mechanisms the gap between the richer and poorer clubs inevitably increases year on year to the detriment of that league's competitive balance or edge. Finally, while the principle of financial solidarity appears to a certain extent to be alive and well in leagues such as the Premier League in England, it will be of interest in future years to see how loyal the owners of successful but indebted clubs such as Manchester United, Liverpool and Chelsea remain to that principle, given the huge revenues that clubs such as Real Madrid and Barcelona are generating from the individual exploitation of domestic broadcasting rights.[136]

Organisation of Sport

[**8.46**]   The *Meca-Medina* rulings of the CFI[137] and the third Chamber of the ECJ[138] are of the utmost important in the sense that it was the first time that the Court directly applied competition law to the 'organisational' rules of sport. Moreover, in doing so the ECJ provided a methodological framework facilitating the future examination of the compatibility sporting rules with Articles 101 (and 102) TFEU. The case concerned a complaint by two professional long-distance swimmers whose samples, after testing at an international competition in Brazil in 1999, were found to have prohibited levels of nandrolone, a proscribed performance enhancing substance. The world governing body for swimming, FINA, consistent with International Olympic Committee-mandated

---

[134] These conditions include those familiar to fans of the Premier League in England such as the selling of rights in individual rights packages (live, deferred and highlights) following an open and transparent tendering process and that the duration of rights contracts should not generally exceed three years. See generally D McAuley, 'Exclusivity for All and Collectively for None: Refereeing Broadcasting Rights between the Premier League, the European Commission and BSkyB' (2004) 25 *European Competition Law Review* 370.

[135]   In the Nice Declaration (n 89) point 15, the European Council noted that moves to encourage mutualisation of part of the revenue from sales of media rights would be beneficial to the principle of solidarity between all levels of sport including its amateur, educational and voluntary aspects of sport. In this, the Nice Declaration echoed the point made at [226]–[234] of the Opinion of Advocate General Lenz in Case C415/93 *Bosman* [1995] ECR I-4921.

[136]   See N Blythe, 'Business of Sport Debate: Why TV is the Key to Real Success' *BBC News Online* 2 March 2010 available at http://news.bbc.co.uk/1/hi/business/8545202.stm.

[137]   Case T-313/02 *Meca Medina and Majcen v Commission* [2004] ECR II-3291.

[138]   Case C-519/04 *Meca Medina and Majcen v Commission* [2006] ECR I-6991.

policy, initially imposed a four-year suspension on the swimmers, which was subsequently reduced by half by CAS. The applicants argued throughout the process that the limit set under the applicable testing criteria was not sensitive enough to allow for the endogenous production of nandrolone in the body (they claimed that its presence could be explained by the eating of boar meat) and that as such the limit could lead to the 'conviction' of innocent or merely negligent athletes. On this basis, the swimmers in question challenged the compatibility of the applicable anti-doping rules in their sport inter alia on the ground that the strict liability-related flaws in the disciplinary system surrounding these rule infringed the rights of professional athletes under Articles 101 and 102 TFEU.

[**8.47**]   In August 2002 the Commission published its decision in which it considered the claim by the swimmers but, after analysing the anti-doping rules at issue against the normal assessment criteria of competition law, concluded that the rules in question did not fall foul of the prohibitions contained in Articles 101 and 102 TFEU. The swimmers then instigated the stated court proceedings. The starting point for a technical legal understanding of those proceedings is a principle first mentioned in *Walrave and Koch*, and refined in *Donà v Mantero*, *Bosman* and *Deliège*: in assessing the compatibility of the economic activities of sport with EU law, rules concerning questions of purely sporting interest remain out of reach of such assessment given their non-economic nature, but that that 'immunity' for purely sporting rules is a qualified exemption and must remain limited to its proper objective and cannot therefore be relied upon to exclude the whole of the sporting activity from the scope of EU law's reach.[139] Crucially, at paragraph 27 of its judgment the ECJ in *Meca-Medina* went on to hold that 'it is apparent that the mere fact that a rule is purely sporting in nature does not have the effect of removing from the scope of the Treaty the person engaged in the activity governed by that rule or the body which has laid it down.' Moreover, the ECJ held that the CFI had erred in law by holding that the fact that purely sporting rules of a non-economic nature falling outside the scope of the free movement principle meant 'straightaway' that those rules could also have nothing to do with the necessary economic relationships that concern competition law.[140] In short, the ECJ held that, unlike the CFI, it would give consideration to whether the rules in question, emanating from an undertaking or association of undertakings, restricted competition or abused a dominant position, and whether that restriction or abuse affected trade between member states.[141]

[**8.48**]   In its review, the ECJ noted that, because they could lead to the exclusion of athletes from sports events, the sanctions under the anti-doping rules at hand were capable of producing restrictive effects on competition.[142]

---

[139] Ibid [25]–[26].
[140] Ibid [31]–[34], as then undertaken at [40]–[56].
[141] Ibid [30].
[142] Case C-519/04 *Meca Medina* [2006] ECR I-6991 [47].

Nevertheless, and guided by its decision in *Wouters*,[143] the ECJ also observed that not every sporting rule based on agreements or decisions of undertakings, which in the abstract imply a violation of Article 101 TFEU, necessarily fall within the prohibition laid down in that provision and that for a 'real time' application of Article 101(1) TFEU account should be taken of (a) the overall context in which the decision was taken or produces it effects and, more specifically, of its objectives; (b) whether the consequential effects restrictive of competition are inherent in the pursuit of those objectives; and (c) are proportionate to them.[144]

[**8.49**]   Applying this approach to the case at hand, the ECJ held that the anti-doping rules in question did not infringe Article 101(1) TFEU because (a) in overall context the objective of said rules was, as none of the parties disputed, to combat doping in order for competitive sport to be conducted fairly and that it included the need to safeguard equal chances for athletes, athletes' health, and the integrity and objectivity of competitive sport and ethical values in sport; (b) the anti-doping rules were, despite limiting the applicants' freedom of action, justified within the meaning of Article 101 TFEU as a legitimate objective inherent in the organisation and proper conduct of competitive sport because their very purpose was to ensure healthy rivalry between athletes; and (c) the accompanying sanctions were (in terms of both the initial threshold for the presence of a banned substance and the ultimate severity of penalty) necessary and limited to ensuring effective enforcement of the doping ban and thus were neither disproportionate nor excessive. The repercussions of this judgment are still being played out almost five years later and, for reasons now explained, the *Meca-Medina* judgment will, it is submitted, remain pivotal in determining the direction of EU sports law for a little while yet.

Bosman: Shaping the Future?

[**8.50**]   The remainder of the chapter—shaping the future (of 'EU sports law')—is predicated on the answer to the following question: to what depth will EU law, as tipped by its provisions on competition law, continue to drill down into the economic, and possibly even the non-economic, dimensions of sport? At present, many leading sports organisations, while acknowledging that total immunity from the application of EU law, allowing fully autonomous internal administration of their affairs, is a non-runner in terms of policy and practice,[145] remain aggrieved at two aspects of the EU Commission's and ECJ's approach to

---

[143] Case C-309/99 *Wouters v Algemene Raad van de Nederlandse Orde van Advocaten* [2002] ECR I-1577.

[144] Case C-519/04 *Meca Medina* [2006] ECR I-6991 [42].

[145] See Van den Bogaert and Vermeersch (n 95) 837 who noted (pre-Lisbon) that such an exemption would most likely have to be formalised in a Treaty amendment or a Protocol and thus subject to the (cumbersome and fraught process of) approval of all EU Member states.

the compatibility of sporting activity with EU law. The first is the extended reach of competition law whereby; notwithstanding the final outcome of *Meca-Medina*, sports organisations such as UEFA contend that the general approach of the ECJ in that ruling implies that the EU-law 'drill' is heading inexorably to such depths that it is threatening to destabilise the core 'specificity of sport' and that logically 'purely' sporting rules and even the 'structural' autonomy of sporting organisations appear vulnerable to legal scrutiny. The second concern that leading sports organisations have is with what they perceive generally to be the unpredictable and inconsistent nature of the legal review of their activities and that this uncertainty is creating problems regarding the economic and administrative operation of sport. Consequently, this third part of the chapter assesses the legitimacy of this two-part 'grievance' and does so with especial regard to the EU Commission's response to it, as contained in section 4.1 of its 'White Paper on Sport' (2007). The crux of that response is as follows:

> The case law of the European courts and decisions of the European Commission show that the specificity of sport has been recognised and taken into account. They also provide guidance on how EU law applies to sport. In line with established case law, the specificity of sport will continue to be recognised, but it cannot be construed so as to justify a general exemption from the application of EU law ... and ... in respect of the regulatory aspects of sport, the assessment whether a certain sporting rule is compatible with [for instance] EU competition law can only be made on a case-by-case basis.

EU Law and the Specificity of Sport

[**8.51**]   When the UK, along with Ireland and Denmark, formally joined the then EEC in 1973, leading sports organisations (such as the FA) and their regional governing bodies in Europe (UEFA), would hardly have expected that that Community's laws and courts would have had such a profound effect on sport. Even when, a year later, the ECJ published its decision in *Walrave and Koch*, the judgment barely dented the confidence that such organisations had in their unique administrative autonomy. They have since been disabused of that notion in a series of ECJ rulings and, in adjusting (slowly and reluctantly) to this new reality, sports organisations have accepted that they are no longer uniquely sovereign in their economic activity-related competencies.[146] Moreover, they have adopted—though they would probably prefer the term 'retreated to'—a position whereby, on recognising the futility in attempting to deny before the Commission or the ECJ the very applicability of EU law to sport, they try instead to work within the EU's legal framework in order to convince it that prima facie

---

[146] In many respects it could be argued that leading sports organisations have not yet fully accepted this new legal reality as can be seen in the IOC's response to the enactment of Art 165 TFEU, which, while largely positive, contained the view that the EU should 'support not regulate' sport. See the IOC Press Release 'Lisbon Treaty Gives a Boost to Sport' 30 November 2009, available through www.olympic.org/en/content/Media.

restrictions on free movement or distortions of competition can be justified. This position is based on what is termed the 'specificity of sport' or 'sporting exception' approach: here, sports governing bodies seek to argue that, given the uniqueness of the European 'model' of sport;[147] its high social utility;[148] and residual distinctive characteristics distinguishing it from other industries and service sectors;[149] it should be afforded a special protected status within the EU's legal framework equating to a partial immunity (at least) from the application of aspect of EU law to which other 'normal' industries are subject.

[8.52] In light of the above, the problem that leading sports organisations have with the *Meca-Medina* ruling (its ultimate outcome notwithstanding) is that even the adjusted line of defence that is the specificity of sport was overrun by the ECJ in the course of the stated judgment and therefore, paraphrasing the arguments made by a number of sports organisations:[150] what is to stop a differently constituted ECJ from holding, in the near future, that a particular aspect of anti-doping policy (for example, its strict liability nature, the whereabouts rules, etc) is an unjustified violation of competition law (or, indeed, a violation of the fundamental freedoms of movement and services) on the grounds that it is disproportionate to the overall objective of proscribing the abuse of performance enhancing substances in sport? Similarly, so the argument goes, who is to say that rules concerning selection criteria for sporting competitions or rules concerning the composition of national teams or even the rules of the game (such as the rules fixing the length of matches, etc) are not now also vulnerable to legal challenge? In short, it is suggested by certain sporting entities that the post-*Meca-Medina* reality is that the reach of EU competition law has become such that there is no longer an area of regulatory authority in sport that can be deemed 'purely' sporting in nature.

[8.53] These claims can be rejected comprehensively on three grounds. First, any fair objective reading of the ECJ's ruling reveals that a sensitivity towards the special nature of sport pervades the judgment as a whole and more specifically still that there was a clear understanding by the Court of the balance that must be struck between attempting to eradicate doping from sport on the one hand

---

[147] Reference here is to European 'model' of sport's with its pyramidal structure of competitions from grassroots to elite level, as bound together by national and European-wide, sport-specific federations.

[148] Reference here is to the positive contribution that sports can make in facilitating important educational, public health, cultural, volunteering and recreational programmes.

[149] Reference here is to the necessary interdependence and mutuality of interest that must exist *between* competitors in order to maintain the long term interest of participants, supporters, consumers and sponsors.

[150] Although written just prior to the publication of the ECJ's decision in *Meca-Medina*, the concerns that many sports organisations have with the reach of EU competition law is summarised in chs 3 and 6 of the Arnaut Report, The Independent European Sport Review, which is available online through www.independentfootballreview.com. See also the paper released by Gianni Infantino, Director of Legal Affairs at UEFA on 2 October 2006 entitled '*Meca Medina*: a Step Backwards for the European Sports Model and the Specificity of Sport?' available to download as supporting documentation at www.uefa.com/uefa/management/legal/index.html.

(and thus the need to use a policy of strict liability) and protecting the rights of individual athletes on the other (who may have valid excuses or reasons why their samples breached permitted thresholds). Moreover, the key element of the methodology used in *Meca-Medina*—namely the *Wouters* criteria—was expressly tailored towards the specific sporting context of the case and thus *Meca-Medina* can be said to have produced the following, entirely reasonable, analysis: that, in assessing the compatibility of sporting rules with Articles 101 and 102 TFEU, account is taken of the regulatory context in which such rules and their objectives were adopted and that the legal provisions in question do not impede sporting rules that pursue legitimate objectives relating to the organisation and proper conduct of sport, which are intrinsic or inherent and proportionate to the achievement of those objectives. As ever in matters of EU sports law, the issue is best encapsulated by Weatherill: '... as *Meca-Medina* itself shows, there remains scope for sport to protect its right to assert internal expertise in taking decisions that have both sporting and economic implications. The ECJ has collapsed the idea that there are purely sporting practices unaffected by [EU] law despite their economic effect, but it has not refused to accept that sport is special. Its message to governing bodies—explain how!'[151]

The Case-by-Case Development of EU Sports Law

[**8.54**] Overlapping with the specificity of sport debate, is a concern that leading sports organisations have with the incremental case-by-case approach favoured by the EU Commission in its White Paper on Sport and the concomitantly 'eccentric' development of EU sports policy and law. Taking a general, summative view of the position of sports bodies such as UEFA and FIFA,[152] they argue that the case-by-case approach is unhelpful in two regards: first, the unpredictability and uncertainty of the current state of the law means that it is difficult for such bodies to plan ahead without fearing a 'Bosman II'; and second, the Commission's approach means that development of EU sport law is more a process of default than design in that it is progressing haphazardly along reactionary lines as a result of 'accidents of litigation'.[153] Leading sports bodies would prefer a more proactive approach and thus would have expected the Commission in its White Paper to have at least formulated general guidelines on the application of EU law to the sports sector. In contrast (and again taking a general, summative view of their position) the Commission argues that the case-by-case approach can be supported by four factors: that it is the most sensitive and flexible means of accommodating the special characteristics of sport within the matrix of EU law; that there is a hidden

---

[151] S Weatherill, 'Anti-doping Revisited: The Demise of the Rule of Purely Sporting Interest' (2006) 27 *European Competition Law Review* 645, 657.

[152] See typically, ss [3.60]–[3.65] and [5.51]–[5.54] of the Arnaut Report (n 150).

[153] S Weatherill, 'The White Paper on Sport as an Exercise in "Better Regulation"' (2008) (1/2) *International Sports Law Journal* 3, 5.

agenda in sports bodies' calls for 'legal certainty' in this regard; that as regards propounding general guidelines the Commission is in a position of 'damned if they do; damned if they don't'; and that sports bodies should place less emphasis on trying to, in effect, self-legislate in the area of sport and greater emphasis on the availing of the White Paper's calls for greater structured and social dialogue between the EU and the various stakeholders in sport. This is because such 'dialogue' can ensure, in a preventative manner, that comprehensive, equitable and durable solutions can be found for the various problems that will continue to arise in reconciling the specificity of the sports industry with inter alia the fundamental freedoms of the EU.

[**8.55**]   In unpacking the first of these four factors, the Commission reiterates that the ECJ, notably in *Meca-Medina*, has taken into account the specificity of sport to the point that as regards EU competition law it has held that restrictive effects on competition are not necessarily in breach of EU competition rules, provided that they are inherent in the organisation and proper conduct of competitive sport and that their effects are proportionate to, and do not go beyond what is necessary for, the legitimate, genuine sporting interest pursued. Crucially, the Commission argues that in order to undertake an assessment that is both comprehensive in nature and fair to the parties, each step (and particularly the second one concerning the necessity for proportionality) must be reviewed with regard to the individual facts and features of the case at hand.[154] Similarly, as regards freedom of movement of workers the ECJ has taken into account the considerable social importance of sport (as an overriding reason in the public interest) to the point that sports-related rules that inhibit free movement nonetheless might escape prohibition where they are applied in a non-discriminatory manner and their effects are proportionate to, and do not go beyond what is necessary for, the legitimate, genuine sporting interest pursued. Again, the argument can be made here that in order to undertake an assessment that is both comprehensive in nature and fair to the parties, each step (the non-discriminatory application and the proportionate effect) can only be reviewed properly with regard to the individual facts and features of the case at hand, that is, on a case-by-case basis.[155]

[**8.56**]   What is meant by the second factor is that there are two ways of looking at sports bodies' calls for certainty and consistency in EU law's application to sport. The first, and the more positive, way of looking at it is that sports bodies are attempting, for understandable reasons, to halt the drill down of EU law into the sports sphere in order to protect sport from external, legally-driven influences that do not necessarily understand the delicate, interdependent complexities of modern European sport. In this light, the doomsday scenario for sports organisations is, as noted earlier, a situation where an overly rigorous application of the rules of free movement of workers and nationality lead to the demise of

---

[154] EU Commission's Staff Working Document (n 84) 69.
[155] Ibid 104.

national representative teams and an equally zealous application of competition law leaves even the 'rules of the game' vulnerable to review by the Commission and ECJ. The second, and more negative, view of sports bodies calls for legal certainly and general guidelines is that sports bodies are deliberately exaggerating the extant threat posed by EU law in the sense that the Commission and ECJ have repeatedly stated that they have no intention of destabilising the core historical, social and cultural aspects of sport and have taken, and will continue to take, into account the special characteristics of sport and thus all that the EU wants to do is to avoid a return to a situation where sports self regulatory authority is such that certain organisations feel that they can use it to cloak discriminatory and monopolistic practices.[156] Put another way, and somewhat simplistically, while the various football governing bodies would ideally like to row back on *Bosman*, because, for instance, of the fact that its free agency principles have allowed too much wealth and power to become concentrated on leading players and clubs; the Commission counters that in the round professional football has thrived financially since the mid-1990s. In short, the EU Commission can argue that as a consequence of being exposed to the various fundamental freedoms of the internal market, the resulting unleashing of market forces have actually served European football very well.

[8.57]   The third and fourth factors can be taken together. The idea here is that if the Commission had gone ahead and given recommendations or general guidelines on the application of EU law to sport, it is likely the sports bodies would have accused it of being overly *dirigiste* in its attitude towards sport. The underlying theme to the Commission's White Paper on Sport appears to be that, in attempting to reconcile the regulatory operation of sport with the fundamental legal freedoms of EU, greater use should be made of the various means of structured and social dialogue outlined in section 5 of that Paper. This 'better regulation' approach, which essentially entails a general EU strategy designed to promote the selection of smarter, sustainable regulatory techniques, means that in terms of sport, the Commission would prefer if policy initiatives came from within sport itself or at national level and that as that policy evolved into regulatory form the Commission would play a limited, consultative role based on the provision of legal advice as to the compatibility of that sporting policy/practice/regulation with EU law.[157] This soft approach should not be underestimated and, as the (re)drafting of FIFA's Regulations on the Status and Transfer of Players in the decade or so after *Bosman* exemplified, it can equate to policy of 'targeted harmonisation', as strengthened by the fact that this 'harmonisation' is not to be imposed from the top (by the EU) but is bottom up in nature (from within sport). There is no doubt that the Commission hopes that this subsidiarity-led

---

[156] See, eg, the comments in Case C 415/93 *Bosman* [1995] ECR I-4921 [215], Opinion of Advocate General Lenz.

[157] See generally http://ec.europa.eu/governance/better_regulation/index_en.htm and S Weatherill (ed), *Better Regulation* (Oxford, Hart Publishing, 2007).

quest for better regulation/targeted harmonisation in sport will be given added 'momentum' by the White Paper.[158] In this, and similar to a situation where mediation is used to resolve a legal dispute, there is again no doubt that where all the relevant stakeholders in a process buy or opt into such 'dialogue', the resulting solution, regulatory or otherwise, attracts a high level of compliance and durability because all parties feel that they have 'ownership' of that solution.

Conclusion

[**8.58**]   This chapter has been underpinned by a view that the future of sports law in the UK lies eastwards in Brussels and in Luxembourg, as determined by proposals and decisions of the EU Commission and the ECJ. This chapter, and indeed this text, concludes by observing that sports law on this side of the Atlantic could benefit from the occasional glance westwards toward the US because there are some interesting comparisons to be made between the so-called American and European 'models' of sport, and particularly with regard to the legal and financial structures of elite professional sport.[159] At first instance, there are, as noted in this text's preface, significant differences between these models with many features of major league sport in the US—team franchising, salary caps, powerful union, player drafts, the absence of relegation and promotion—appearing anathema to European sports administrators, clubs and supporters.[160] Looking at the broader picture however, and with especial regard to the key legal debate (contractual stability versus employment mobility) in the key European sport (football), there is much to inform EU law from manner in which US federal law has had to deal with similar debates in sports such as baseball and American football.

[**8.59**]   In the US, the pattern of restrictive transfer-related litigation between players and their unions on the one hand, and clubs and leagues on the other, has evolved in three steps; first, these disputes were played out exclusively within the contract/private law arena; second, they resulted in proceedings involving the application of antitrust law and principle and particularly section 1 of the Sherman Act 1890 on interstate commerce; and finally they have evolved into

---

[158] Weatherill (n 153) 3.

[159] Unfortunately, this is not something that has attracted much review or analysis apart from L Halgreen, *European Sports Law: A Comparative Analysis of the European and American Models of Sport* (Copenhagen, Forlaget Thomson, 2004) and S Weatherill, 'Resisting the Pressures of "Americanization": The Influence of European Community Law on the "European Sports Model"' in S Greenfield and G Osborn (eds), *Law and Sport in Contemporary Society* (London, Frank Cass, 2000) 155–81.

[160] The American model is followed in other jurisdictions and in other sports, eg, the National Rugby League (NRL) in Australia. In April 2010, a NRL investigation revealed systematic salary cap breaches by the Melbourne Storm franchise—shadow contracts resulted in players being paid over the maximum allowed under NRL rules—and the club was stripped of its 2007 and 2009 Premiership titles. See A Davies and M Knox, 'As Tempest Rages, Questions Cloud Air; League's Dirty Deals' *The Sydney Morning Herald* (Sydney 24 April 2010) News and Features 7.

applications of federal labour law.[161] On the last point, in the late 1960s, the various institutional stakeholders (league officials, club owners and players' unions) in a number of the major league sports in the US decided that rather than allow *Bosman*-type 'accidents of litigation' to determine the future of their sport, they would take the initiative by embracing federal labour law and using antitrust exemptions thereunder to negotiate and implement collective bargaining agreements (CBAs).[162] The important point here is that EU sports law appears to be following a pattern similar to that of the US or, at least, that European sports law has completed two out of the three steps mentioned, and rather than see their careers constrained by the restrictive legal structures of their industry, individual players have sought through contract and competition and free movement law to influence and change the legal nature of their industry to their benefit.[163]

[**8.60**] Thanks to the better regulation/targeted harmonisation approach, facilitated by the structured dialogue paradigm outlined in section 5 of the White Paper, European sports law has taken another half step forward in its evolutionary progress. All the stakeholders therein appear relatively happy with this but in the near future could it happen that a major European sport—football being the obvious example—decides to take the full and final step forward and embrace fully labour law and industry-wide collective bargaining agreements?[164] And so,

---

[161] For a comprehensive review of this process see R Berry and W Gould, 'A Long Deep Drive to Collective Bargaining: Of Players, Owners, Brawls and Strikes' (1981) 31 *Case Western Reserve Law Review* 685. See also P Weiler and G Roberts, *Sports and the Law: Text, Cases and Problems* 3rd edn (Westport Conn, Thomson West, 2004) chs 2–4.

[162] Generally, the US courts have looked favourably upon the 'sanctity' of collectively-bargained terms between professional sports leagues and players' unions. See M McCann, 'Justice Sonya Sotomayor and the Relationship between Leagues and Players: Insights and Implications' (2010) 42 *Connecticut Law Review* 901. For a modern insight into the workings of a collective bargaining agreement in a major league sport in the US, and particularly the manner in which such CBAs seek to negate the impact of competition/antitrust law, see S Alford, 'Dusting off the AK-47: An Examination of NFL Players' Most Powerful Weapon in An Antitrust Lawsuit against the NFL' (2009) 88 *North Carolina Law Review* 212.

[163] The obvious example here is the litigation taken by Curt Flood in the 1970s (*Flood v Kuhn* 407 US 258 (1972)) challenging both the reserve clause in baseball (which operated in manner similar to football's old retain and transfer system) and that sport's exemption from federal antitrust law, as established in *Federal Baseball Club v National League* 259 US 200 (1922). Although Flood failed to convince the court that his sport should be held amenable to antitrust investigation, as others had—*US v International Boxing Club* 348 US 236 (1955); *Radovitch v National Football League* 352 US 445 (1957); and *Haywood v National Basketball Association* 401 US 1204 (1971)— his actions set off a train of events (a *Floodgate*) the changed the face of baseball (Curt Flood Act 1997, 15 USC s26(b)) and American sports more generally. See generally A Belth, *Stepping Up: The Story of Curt Flood and His Fight for Baseball Players' Rights* (New York, Persea, 2006); R Goldman, *One Man Out: Curt Flood versus Baseball* (Kansas, Lawrence University Press, 2008); B Synder, *A Well-Paid Slave: Curt Flood's Fight for Free Agency in Professional Sports* (New York, Plume, 2006); P Weiler, *Leveling the Playing Field: How the Law Can Make Sports Better for Fans* (Cambridge; Mass, Harvard University Press, 2000) ch 9; and S Weiss, *The Curt Flood Story: The Man Behind the Myth* (Columbia; MO, University of Missouri Press, 2007).

[164] Traces of this approach were purportedly raised by UEFA at some point as a defence in the *Bosman* litigation. See Case C 415/93 *Bosman* [1995] ECR I-4921 [271]–[272], Opinion of Advocate General Lenz.

for example, were UEFA to suggest that the Champions' League should evolve into a 32-club European 'super' league (ESL); would not the obvious financial and legal model for such a league be a Euro-centric version of the National Football League in the US, as supported by a collective bargaining agreement between all parties?[165] Admittedly, it remains unlikely at present that leading European clubs (through the European Clubs Association), player representative bodies (such as FIFPro Europe), and UEFA/FIFA could ever reach a consensus of how such an ESL might operate but drawing on the American experience it should be reiterated that there could nonetheless be advantages for all parties in the collective bargaining approach.[166]

[**8.61**]   From the players' point of view they would have unprecedented parity of representation with the other parties in negotiating the future contractual and commercial landscape of their sport, and including progress on issues such as greater employment mobility. From the clubs' point of view, the collective strength of a CBA would lead to the accrual of significant benefits in negotiating broadcasting contracts and exclusive sponsorship deals. Moreover, a CBA might bring enhanced employment autonomy for clubs because if the structure of a CBA can be taken to equate to a joint venture where all the stakeholders therein are 'directors' of that venture, then the parties could benefit from what is called 'single economic entity' recognition. The possible advantage here is that because a single economic entity or undertaking cannot conspire with itself, clubs might, through the CBA, obtain the partial immunity or targeted exemptions that they crave from the reach of Articles 101 and 102 TFEU. The contention is that, while the concerted actions of several competing undertakings would likely be unlawful under Article 101 TFEU; where a joint venture exists, a defence of single economic entity could be made out based on the absence of the plurality of actors required for a violation of Article 101 TFEU.[167] Would this joint venture, the idea of which is that undertakings, who would otherwise be rivals, pool their capital and share the risk of loss (as well as the opportunity for profit) fall foul of Article 102 TFEU and particularly that provision's concerns regarding abuses of a dominant position in a marketplace? The argument could be made that this football-specific venture could be reconciled with Article 102 TFEU because it is designed simply to enable the venture to compete more efficiently against other

---

[165] Examples of the 'Euro-centric' nature of such a league would not mean that the league would be run on a franchising model featuring franchises such as the Arsenal Gunners, the Manchester Reds, the Chelsea Pensioners, etc but that the league would based on the 32 leading European clubs, selected through UEFA's rankings, as divided into two divisions of 16 clubs with promotion and relegation between each and play-offs for entry into division B among national league champions. Moreover, instead of a player draft system as in the US, one could tailor the existing transfer widow system.

[166] It is further unlikely, eg, that the Association of European Professional Football Leagues would agree to such a 'super' league. For further information on this body see www.epfl-europeanleagues.com.

[167] On the single entity argument in EU law see generally Cases T 68/89, T 77/89 and T 78/89 *SIV v the Commission* [1992] ECR II-1403 [357] and Case C 73/95P *Viho v the Commission* [1996] ECR I-5457 [16].

'sellers' of sports-related entertainment in the general professional sports and entertainment market of the EU.[168]

[**8.62**]   Interestingly, this single entity argument, which has had, according to some commentators, a 'puzzling persistence',[169] is being considered at present by the US Supreme Court in *American Needle v NFL*.[170] The case is based on a challenge by a sportswear manufacturer against an exclusive sports apparel deal between the NFL, its independently owned franchises (clubs) and Reebok. The case is being defended on the ground that a single entity cannot collude against itself and that the exclusive Reebok deal was simply the product of a horizontal agreement among the directors of a joint venture acting unilaterally as a single entity.[171] That defence, which was successfully (and surprisingly)[172] mounted at the US Court of Appeals in August 2008, could, if approved by the US Supreme Court, largely shield professional sports leagues and their clubs for any significant vulnerability to section 1 of the Sherman Act's prohibition of concerted action in interstate commerce that leads to unreasonable restraint of trade and thus such leagues 'could become uniquely sovereign and commanding' in the operation of their internal markets.[173] On these grounds, it is not surprising that both amicus

---

[168] And thus satisfying the interpretation of Art 102 TFEU established seminally in Case 85/76 *Hoffmann-La Roche v the Commission* [1979] ECR 461 [4] and [91].

[169] G Feldman, 'The Puzzling Persistence of the Single Entity Arguments for Sports Leagues: American Needle and the Supreme Court's Opportunity to Reject a Flawed Defence' [2009] *Wisconsin Law Review* 835. See also M Edelman, 'Why the "Single Entity" Defence can Never Apply to NFL Clubs: A Primer on Property-rights Theory in Professional Sports' (2008) 18 *Fordham Intellectual Property, Media & Entertainment Law Journal* 891; J McKeown, '2008 Antitrust Developments in Professional Sports: To the Single Entity and Beyond (2009) 19 *Marquette Sports Law Review* 363; R Paolino, 'Upon Further Review: How NFL Network in Violating the Sherman Act' (2009) 16 *Sports Law Journal* 1; and S Semeraro, 'Is the National Football League a "Single Entity" Incapable of Conspiring under the Sherman Act? The Supreme Court will Decide' (2009) 32 *Thomas Jefferson Law Review* 1.

[170] Two decisions of the US District Court for the Northern District of Illinois, reported at 496 F Supp 2d 941 (2007) and F Supp 2d 7901(2007) held, on grant of summary judgment, that in regard to the deal in question the NFL and its member teams constituted a single entity exempted from s 1 of the Sherman Act 1890. The decisions were affirmed by the US Court of Appeals for the Seventh Circuit, as reported at *American Needle Inc v National Football League et al* 538 F 3d 736 (2008). In June 2009, the US Supreme Court announced that it had granted review as petitioned by American Needle, as noted at 129 S Ct 2859 (2009). Oral arguments were heard in January 2010.

[171] The defence relies both on Rehnquist J's dissenting judgment in *North American Soccer League v NFL* 459 US 1074, 1075–77 where the subsequent Chief Justice spoke of a 'covenant of joint venturers' and more generally on the rationale of the Supreme Court's decision in *Copperweld Corporation v Independence Tube Corporation* 467 US 752 (1984).

[172] The surprise lies in the fact that more than half a century ago the US Supreme Court in *Radovitch v National Football League* 352 US 445 (1957) held that the NFL and other professional sports leagues (baseball apart) were subject to s 1 of the Sherman Act 1890. Moreover, and as noted by counsel for American Needle in his petition for a writ of certiorari on 17 November 2008 and again in the merit brief to the Supreme Court on 18 September 2009, every federal appellate decision since, and some of the lower courts as well, have applied *Radovitch* strictly. The merit briefs for petitioner and respondent in this case and the accompanying amicus briefs are available to view under *American Needle v National Football League*, Docket No 08-661, www.abanet.org/publiced/preview/briefs/jan2010.shtml.

[173] See generally M McCann, 'American Needle v NFL: An Opportunity to Reshape Sports Law' (2010) 119 *Yale Law Journal* 726, 728.

briefs from a number of major sports in the US have been filed in support of the NFL and that the *Yale Law Journal* has described *American Needle* as the 'most meaningful sports law controversy of recent memory'.[174]

[**8.63**]   From UEFA's perspective, a CBA negotiated with its 32 leading clubs would present an ideal means of promoting 'good governance' in the sport as a whole in the sense that such a CBA would probably mandate that in order to participate in the ESL clubs would have to respect the same basic rules on financial management and transparency including limits on squad sizes; and quasi-salary caps by way of limits on clubs' expenditure on salaries and transfers as set against a percentage of clubs' turnover from gate receipts, merchandising and TV monies; and punishments for unmanageable debts such as transfer embargos, points deductions or even relegation. In other words, a CBA for any ESL would likely give UEFA the opportunity to promote its current 'Financial Fair Play' concept, the main purpose of which is to improve the economic viability and long term stability of those clubs who regularly participate in UEFA competitions across Europe by encouraging long term investments in clubs (such as in facilities and youth development) over short term speculative spending (so-called 'financial doping').[175] At present, UEFA is pursuing its financial fair play or 'balancing the books' concept through its licensing system for clubs—in order to obtain a licence to participate in UEFA competitions clubs are required to meet certain financial and infrastructural criteria.[176] A CBA would, however, provides an enhanced means of enforcing such a programme and could also include related licensing provisions regarding discrimination, violence, protection of minors and training standards, and thus also provide a template for similar licensing requirements at a national level.

[**8.64**]   Arguably, the forgotten beneficiaries of an American-style collective bargaining agreement attaching to a European super league might be football supporters. In the American model of major league sport, the view is that the long term commercial robustness of a league can only be sustained—in terms of maintaining spectator/consumer interest and thus adding to gate receipts, merchandising and TV subscriptions—if all the stakeholders in that league cooperate

---

[174] Ibid.

[175] For further information on this programme, which UEFA hopes will be implemented on a phased basis for the 2012/2013 season, see www.uefa.com/uefa/footballfirst/protectingthegame/financialfairplay. UEFA's revelation in 2008 that 18 Premier League clubs owed almost £3.5 billion more than the other 714 top European clubs put together was, apparently, a key motivation in the establishment of this programme. See D Conn, 'Inside Sport: Football; Vast Wages at Heart of Premier League Debt Mountain' *The Guardian* (London 24 February 2010) Sport 6. Given the levels of indebtedness among Premier League clubs (from Portsmouth to Manchester United) including an overreliance on owner investment to underwrite player wages and transfer fees (Chelsea and Manchester City) UEFA's proposals have caused some alarm as to leading clubs' participation in UEFA competitions. See M Dickinson, 'Hey, Big Spender: Here is the New Reality' *The Times* (London 27 March 2010) Sport 4–5.

[176] See further www.uefa.com/uefa/footballfirst/protectingthegame/clublicensing.

off field to create a fair and balance match up *on the field*.[177] Consequently, the American model of major league sport is very much interventionist in nature, such that, and principally through CBAs, the internal labour market or economy of a sport is strictly regulated and centrally planned and based on what Europeans would identify as a principle of financial solidarity.[178] This is to ensure that not only is any generated revenue shared and distributed equally among all the clubs but it is also meant 'to design team line ups and league schedules in a manner that leaves fans never knowing for sure who is going to win the immediate game or the season championship'[179] but—and this is crucial—at the same time providing a '*Moneyball* reassurance' that through both the right coaching/talent identification programmes and legitimate manipulation of the player draft/budgetary cap systems, at some point a fan's club should go on a winning run and might even win a championship.[180]

[8.65] In contrast, the criticism of the European model of sport, and particularly at the elite level of football, is that it operates on an overly free market and light-touch regulation basis such that the game's money and talent has become concentrated more and more in a handful of clubs, as epitomised by Chelsea/Manchester United's recent domination of the Premier League (which, it appears, can only be broken by increased 'fit and proper' foreign ownership of English clubs) and Barcelona/Madrid's long standing domination of *La Liga* (as aggravated by these clubs' capacity to negotiate their own domestic broadcasting deals). In contrast, the view in France and in the *Bundesliga* in Germany is that there is some merit in the 'financial solidarity' of the American model in order to prevent the consumer and commercial base of these national leagues becoming overly narrow and dependent on certain clubs.[181] Borrowing from the language of EU competition law, the trend in France and Germany appears to be that some proportionate restrictions on competition in football can be justified and be seen to be necessary where they have a positive economic effect on all parties, including consumers, in that common (football) market.[182]

---

[177] Weiler, *Levelling the Playing Field* (n 163) 2.

[178] Note in this light the comments in Case C 415/93 *Bosman* [1995] ECR I-4921 [227], Opinion of Advocate General Lenz.

[179] Weiler, *Levelling the Playing Field* (n 163) 3.

[180] The 'Moneyball reassurance' refers to the influential book by Michael Lewis that followed the low-budget major league baseball franchise—the Oakland A's—and the manner in which that franchise, thanks mainly to its innovative general manager Billy Beane, transformed itself into a successful, competitive franchise belying its budget and revenue capacity. See M Lewis, *Moneyball: The Art of Winning an Unfair Game* (New York, Norton, 2003).

[181] See J Jackson, 'Football: State of the Nation; A Fit and Proper League. With Fans Coming First, Cheap Ticket Prices, and Sound Financial Management, the Bundesliga is the Antithesis of the Premier League' *The Observer* (London 11 April 2010) Sport 12 and A Lawrence, 'Football: State of the Nation; France. New Wave of Coaches brings New Wave of French Optimism' *The Observer* (London 21 March 2010) Sport 10.

[182] See, eg, the attitude of the ECJ in Case C234/89 *Delimitis v Henninger Brau AG* [1991] ECR I-935.

[**8.66**] So does collective bargaining, permitting certain sports as joint ventures/single economic entities to establish exclusively internal labour market, present a picture of the future landscape of sport in Europe? No appears to be the answer and in all likelihood the single entity will not survive scrutiny at the US Supreme Court, not just because to permit it would belie more that 50 years of legal precedent, but because it would also mistakenly characterise the operations of the league in question, which similar to other major league sports operate substantively on a partnership basis between the league and the independently owned and operated franchises/clubs. In short, the US Supreme Court applying what is called the fact-intensive, 'rule of reason' approach in antitrust law investigation is likely to reject the NFL's single entity/effective merger defence and see through this attempt to circumvent competition law.[183] Similarly, stakeholders in any collective agreement surrounding an ESL would also be likely to be viewed as parties to a concerted practice by an 'association of undertakings' within the proscribed meaning of Article 101 TFEU.[184]

[**8.67**] In sum, it is all too easy to dismiss the American 'sports' model as a rootless, overly consumerist one based on silly-sounding franchises with shallow histories and loyalty only to the municipal administration most willing to build a stadium;[185] and to forget that the US has the oldest established professional sports market in the world and, as a result, the most vibrant and complex sports law state and federal jurisdictions. There is a lot to learn from the common experience and (mistakes) made in the US—notably the top heavy revenue dependency on both sides of the Atlantic on TV monies; and thus deeper comparative legal analysis would doubtless prove productive and informative.[186] The above, which gives only a flavour of what might be achieved in comparative analysis, nevertheless demonstrates two important points. First, and specific to antitrust/competition law, the American experience suggests that the better approach for sports organisations is not to seek sweeping single entity/specificity of sport exemptions, which are likely to be rejected by the Supreme Court/ECJ; but more to pursue 'targeted exemptions' by way of Congressional (in the form of federal acts)/Commission (through the consultative, structured dialogue process) approval.[187]

---

[183] See generally McCann (n 173) 777–81. The rule of reason in terms of EU competition law was discussed in Case C 415/93 *Bosman* [1995] ECR I-4921 [265] –[270], Opinion of Advocate General Lenz.

[184] See, eg, the view taken of FIFA/UEFA as an association of undertakings in Case T-193/02 *Laurent Piau v Commission of the European Communities and FIFA* [2005] ECR II-209 [68] –[75] and Case T46/92 *Scottish Football Association v the Commission* [1994] ECR II-1039.

[185] See, for instance, T Humphries, 'Cautionary Tales for the Land of the Free (Market)' *The Irish Times* (Dublin 19 April 2010) Sport 12.

[186] In many ways, what sports law needs in this regard is the equivalent of S Szymanski, *Playbooks and Checkbooks: An Introduction to the Economics of Modern Sports* (Princeton; NJ, Princeton University Press, 2009) which is informed inter alia by a comparative approach between the US and European models of sport, of which the most relevant in the immediate context is ch 3, 'Sports and Antitrust'. See also, and altogether more light-heartedly, S Kuper and S Szymanski, *Why England Lose: and Other Curious Phenomena Explained* (London, HarperSport, 2009).

[187] S Szymanski, *Playbooks and Checkbooks: An Introduction to the Economics of Modern Sports* (Princeton; NJ, Princeton University Press, 2009) ch 5, 'Sports and Broadcasting' on the manner in

[**8.68**]   In a more general sense, the European sports model undoubtedly differs significantly from the American model in historical development and contemporary structure and thus any crossover between the two will remain limited, but aspects of the financial stability, equality and the sustained success of 'major league' model are surely attractive for certain European-focused sports investors.[188] Moreover, although there is no doubt that the free marketing ways of the Premier League in England has given it huge success since in foundation in 1992, and that football has much more global appeal and potential than its American counterpart, the eye-watering amount of debt and subsequent administration of Portsmouth in 2010 is a warning as to that League's unregulated excesses, as is the fact that the American owners of Britain's most successful football clubs, Liverpool and Manchester United, have acted in a manner which has both burdened those clubs with significant long term debt and which those owners know, (given their experience as franchise owners in the US) is behaviour that would not be tolerated in the American model.[189]

[**8.69**]   Finally, it would, I believe, be beneficial for all those involved in the development of EU sports law, on occasion, to glance westwards towards, say, Boston for guidance, rather than continually looking inwards towards Brussels for direction. That is not to criticise the lead taken by the Commission on sports law matters but merely to suggest that greater comparative analysis would enrich the EU approach, particularly at this critical time when much symbolic momentum has been provided for EU sports policy and law by Article 165 TFEU. EU sports law is still at a nascent or adolescent stage, and could do with guidance from the mature adult that is American sports law—even if that adult is somewhat insular and set in his ways! Whether or not this suggestion is taken on board awaits to be seen but what is clear for now is that the law and lawyers will, for good or ill, continue to play an influential role in sport's future. Returning to a point made in this text's preface, the best that can be hoped for is that in fulfilling its role, the law will conduct itself as the best referees do: with unfussy consistency or what, in the context of this chapter's focus, competition law might call a de minimis approach to the application of regulations designed ultimately to protect the true essence of sport (and of law)—fair play.

---

which the NFL lobbied the US Congress to exempt the collective selling of broadcasting rights (to free-to-air networks) leading to the Sports Broadcasting Act 1961, 15 USC s1291; and how, when the value of such rights escalated in Europe, nearly 40 years later, similar legal issues had to be considered by the EU Commission. The outcome of the Commission's deliberations is reviewed at [8.43]–[8.45] of this text.

[188] In 2010, *Forbes Magazine*, reporting on 'The Most Valuable Teams in Sports' observed that 'fuelled by ever-increasing television contract and by a wave of new, revenue producing stadiums, today's NFL is worth US$33.3billion, up from US$11.6billion a decade ago.' That report can be accessed at www.forbes.com/business/sportsmoney.

[189] For a useful resource on the evolving story on the financial challenges facing Premier League Clubs see the permanent Business of Sport website maintained by the BBC's Business and Economics Unit, www.bbc.co.uk/businessofsport.

Further Points of Interest and Discussion

1. By adhering to a 'case-by-case' approach and refusing to countenance a 'general guidelines' approach to the application of EU law to sport, the Commission is not just abdicating its responsibility as an EU institution but it is also exposing sports organisations, events, clubs, players and even supporters to the whims and vagaries of EU law, and notably Articles 101 and 102 TFEU.

   Is this a fair and reasonable assessment of the EU Commission's attitude to sports? Give reasons for your answer with primary reference to the 'White Paper on Sport' (2007).

2. Article 165 TFEU expressly precludes the EU from taking any harmonising measures in the area of sport. If this preclusion was removed, is there an area of sports law that you have come across in this text or elsewhere (for example, the regulation of doping; the regulation of the transfers of minors in football; child protection more generally; cross-border security for major sporting events in the EU; sports-relating broadcasting and TV rights; sports-related money laundering and financial crime; sports-related gambling; or the regulation of agents) that you would consider amenable to, and which might benefit from, harmonisation at a supranational EU level?

3. In summary, this text as a whole has attempted to address seven key issues in sports law: to provide a taxonomy of sports law as a valid, engaging and discrete field of legal inquiry; to illustrate that sports disputes are better arbitrated than litigated; to challenge the current orthodoxy on the regulation of doping in sport; to demonstrate that where a party recklessly endangers the safety of another during the course of a sporting event the reach of civil, and sometimes criminal, law, extends beyond the touchline; to explain the detail of a standard player contract in football and place that contractual relationship in its wider regulatory context; to provide a narrative on the development of EU sports law through recounting the story of Jean-Marc Bosman; and to propose that in their social and structured 'dialogue' on sport, the various European stakeholders might in respect of legal initiatives find it productive to give the occasional glance westwards toward the US.

   What did you think of the manner in which this text addressed these issues? Is there any area or areas that could have been dealt with better and/or more comprehensively? Is there anything within a broad definition of sports law not covered by this text that you would like to see included in the future?

   I would like to hear from you and you can email me directly at jack.anderson@qub.ac.uk

   I look forward to your comments.

INDEX